Game Development Concepts in C++

Elevate Your Skills with Unreal Engine

Sheikh Sohel Moon

Apress®

Game Development Concepts in C++: Elevate Your Skills with Unreal Engine

Sheikh Sohel Moon
Khulna, Bangladesh

ISBN-13 (pbk): 979-8-8688-1398-6   ISBN-13 (electronic): 979-8-8688-1399-3
https://doi.org/10.1007/979-8-8688-1399-3

Copyright © 2025 by Sheikh Sohel Moon

This work is subject to copyright. All rights are reserved by the Publisher, whether the whole or part of the material is concerned, specifically the rights of translation, reprinting, reuse of illustrations, recitation, broadcasting, reproduction on microfilms or in any other physical way, and transmission or information storage and retrieval, electronic adaptation, computer software, or by similar or dissimilar methodology now known or hereafter developed.

Trademarked names, logos, and images may appear in this book. Rather than use a trademark symbol with every occurrence of a trademarked name, logo, or image we use the names, logos, and images only in an editorial fashion and to the benefit of the trademark owner, with no intention of infringement of the trademark.

The use in this publication of trade names, trademarks, service marks, and similar terms, even if they are not identified as such, is not to be taken as an expression of opinion as to whether or not they are subject to proprietary rights.

While the advice and information in this book are believed to be true and accurate at the date of publication, neither the authors nor the editors nor the publisher can accept any legal responsibility for any errors or omissions that may be made. The publisher makes no warranty, express or implied, with respect to the material contained herein.

    Managing Director, Apress Media LLC: Welmoed Spahr
    Acquisitions Editor: Spandana Chatterjee
    Editorial Project Manager: Gryffin Winkler

Cover designed by eStudioCalamar

Cover image designed by Freepik on freepik.com

Distributed to the book trade worldwide by Springer Science+Business Media New York, 1 New York Plaza, New York, NY 10004. Phone 1-800-SPRINGER, fax (201) 348-4505, e-mail orders-ny@springer-sbm.com, or visit www.springeronline.com. Apress Media, LLC is a Delaware LLC and the sole member (owner) is Springer Science + Business Media Finance Inc (SSBM Finance Inc). SSBM Finance Inc is a **Delaware** corporation.

For information on translations, please e-mail booktranslations@springernature.com; for reprint, paperback, or audio rights, please e-mail bookpermissions@springernature.com.

Apress titles may be purchased in bulk for academic, corporate, or promotional use. eBook versions and licenses are also available for most titles. For more information, reference our Print and eBook Bulk Sales web page at http://www.apress.com/bulk-sales.

Any source code or other supplementary material referenced by the author in this book is available to readers on GitHub. For more detailed information, please visit https://www.apress.com/gp/services/source-code.

If disposing of this product, please recycle the paper

Table of Contents

About the Author xxxiii

About the Technical Reviewer xxxv

Acknowledgments xxxvii

Introduction xxxix

Chapter 1: Core Collision Mechanics 1

   Blocking Movement 2
      Basic Usage 2
      Advanced Techniques 3
      Practical Applications 3
      Algorithm Overview 3
      Reviewing the Code 4
      Setting Up the Maze and Player 4
      Implementing Movement Restrictions 11

   Triggering Events 15
      Basic Usage 15
      Advanced Techniques 16
      Practical Applications 16
      Algorithm Overview 17
      Reviewing the Code 17
      Handling Interactive Elements 22
      Implementing Dynamic Events 26

TABLE OF CONTENTS

- Interaction Detection 30
    - Basic Usage 31
    - Advanced Techniques 31
    - Practical Applications 31
    - Algorithm Overview 32
    - Reviewing the Code 32
    - Handling Player Interactions 36
    - Implementing Interaction Responses 40
    - Use Cases 41
    - InteractionType Demonstration 42
- Physics Reactions 44
    - Basic Usage 45
    - Advanced Techniques 45
    - Practical Applications 45
    - Algorithm Overview 46
    - Reviewing the Code 46
    - Applying Forces 49
    - Handling Collisions 50
    - Advanced Physics Reactions 52
- Environmental Effects 54
    - Basic Usage 54
    - Advanced Techniques 55
    - Practical Applications 55
    - Algorithm Overview 55
    - Reviewing the Code 56
    - Applying Environmental Effects 59
    - Handling Interactions 60
    - Advanced Environmental Effects 61

TABLE OF CONTENTS

Hit Detection 63
    Basic Usage 63
    Advanced Techniques 64
    Practical Applications 64
    Algorithm Overview 64
    Reviewing the Code 65
    Setting Up Hit Detection 65
    Implementing Hit Processing 69
    Advanced Hit Detection Techniques 69

Item Collection 72
    Basic Usage 72
    Advanced Techniques 72
    Practical Applications 73
    Algorithm Overview 73
    Reviewing the Code 74
    Implementing Item Effects 78
    Advanced Item Collection Techniques 80

Summary 83

Chapter 2: Advanced Collision Mechanics 85
    Damage Calculation 86
        Basic Usage 87
        Advanced Techniques 87
        Practical Applications 87
        Algorithm Overview 88
        Reviewing the Code 88
        Implementing Damage Calculation 90
        Advanced Damage Calculation Techniques 92

TABLE OF CONTENTS

Projectile Deflection 94
- Basic Usage 95
- Advanced Techniques 95
- Practical Applications 95
- Algorithm Overview 96
- Reviewing the Code 96
- Implementing Deflection Logic 99
- Advanced Projectile Deflection Techniques 100

Platforming Mechanic 102
- Basic Usage 102
- Advanced Techniques 103
- Practical Applications 103
- Algorithm Overview 104
- Reviewing the Code 105
- Implementing Basic Platforming Mechanics 110
- Advanced Platforming Techniques 112

Area-of-Effect (AoE) Damage 114
- Basic Usage 114
- Advanced Techniques 115
- Practical Applications 115
- Algorithm Overview 116
- Reviewing the Code 116
- Advanced AoE Techniques 121

Character Knockback 125
- Basic Usage 125
- Advanced Techniques 126
- Practical Applications 126

TABLE OF CONTENTS

    Algorithm Overview 127
    Reviewing the Code 128
    Advanced Knockback Techniques 132

Character Pushback 136
    Basic Usage 136
    Advanced Techniques 137
    Practical Applications 137
    Algorithm Overview 138
    Reviewing the Code 139
    Advanced Pushback Techniques 142

Object Destruction 146
    Basic Usage 146
    Advanced Techniques 147
    Practical Applications 147
    Algorithm Overview 148
    Reviewing the Code 149
    Advanced Destruction Techniques 152

Object Pickup 155
    Basic Usage 156
    Advanced Techniques 156
    Practical Applications 157
    Algorithm Overview 158
    Reviewing the Code 158
    Advanced Pickup Techniques 162

Character Respawn Handling 167
    Basic Usage 167
    Advanced Techniques 168
    Practical Applications 168

TABLE OF CONTENTS

- Algorithm Overview 169
- Reviewing the Code 170
- Advanced Respawn Techniques 173
- Terrain Deformation 177
  - Basic Usage 178
  - Advanced Techniques 179
  - Practical Applications 180
  - Algorithm Overview 180
  - Reviewing the Code 181
  - Advanced Terrain Deformation Techniques 184
- Object Scaling on Collision 187
  - Basic Usage 188
  - Advanced Techniques 188
  - Practical Applications 189
  - Algorithm Overview 190
  - Reviewing the Code 191
  - Advanced Scaling Techniques 194
- Object Rotation on Collision 197
  - Basic Usage 197
  - Advanced Techniques 198
  - Practical Applications 199
  - Algorithm Overview 200
  - Reviewing the Code 201
  - Advanced Rotation Techniques 204
- Particle Effects on Collision 207
  - Basic Usage 207
  - Advanced Techniques 208
  - Practical Applications 209

TABLE OF CONTENTS

    Algorithm Overview 209

    Reviewing the Code 210

    Advanced Particle Techniques 213

Summary 216

Chapter 3: Interaction Mechanics 217

Opening Doors 218

    Basic Usage 218

    Advanced Techniques 218

    Practical Applications 219

    Algorithm Overview 219

    Reviewing the Code 220

    Advanced Techniques 223

Activating Traps 227

    Basic Usage 227

    Advanced Techniques 228

    Practical Applications 228

    Algorithm Overview 228

    Reviewing the Code 229

    Advanced Techniques 232

Starting Cutscenes 237

    Basic Usage 237

    Advanced Techniques 237

    Practical Applications 238

    Algorithm Overview 238

    Reviewing the Code 239

    Advanced Techniques 243

TABLE OF CONTENTS

- Dialogue Systems 247
  - Basic Usage 247
  - Advanced Techniques 248
  - Practical Applications 248
  - Algorithm Overview 248
  - Reviewing the Code 249
  - Advanced Techniques 253
- NPC Interactions 257
  - Basic Usage 258
  - Advanced Techniques 258
  - Practical Applications 258
  - Algorithm Overview 259
  - Reviewing the Code 259
  - Advanced Techniques 266
- Inventory System 273
  - Basic Usage 273
  - Advanced Techniques 273
  - Practical Applications 274
  - Algorithm Overview 274
  - Reviewing the Code 275
  - Advanced Techniques 279
- Quest Activation 283
  - Basic Usage 284
  - Advanced Techniques 284
  - Practical Applications 284
  - Algorithm Overview 285
  - Reviewing the Code 285
  - Advanced Techniques 290

TABLE OF CONTENTS

Mini-Game Initiation 293
    Basic Usage 293
    Advanced Techniques 294
    Practical Applications 294
    Algorithm Overview 294
    Reviewing the Code 295
    Advanced Techniques 300

Puzzle-Solving Mechanics 304
    Basic Usage 304
    Advanced Techniques 304
    Practical Applications 305
    Algorithm Overview 305
    Reviewing the Code 305
    Implementing Puzzle Interaction 309
    Advanced Mechanics Code Example 313

Trading Systems 317
    Basic Usage 317
    Advanced Techniques 317
    Practical Applications 318
    Algorithm Overview 318
    Reviewing the Code 318
    Implementing the Trading System 321
    Advanced Mechanics Code Example 324

Summary 328

Chapter 4: Environmental Mechanics 329

Dynamic Weather Systems 330
    Basic Usage 330
    Advanced Techniques 331

TABLE OF CONTENTS

- Practical Applications 331
- Algorithm Overview 332
- Reviewing the Code 332
- Day-Night Cycles 340
  - Basic Usage 341
  - Advanced Techniques 341
  - Practical Applications 342
  - Algorithm Overview 343
  - Reviewing the Code 343
- Environment Hazards 349
  - Basic Usage 350
  - Advanced Techniques 350
  - Practical Applications 351
  - Algorithm Overview 351
  - Reviewing the Code 352
- Dynamic Lighting Changes 357
  - Basic Usage 357
  - Advanced Techniques 358
  - Practical Applications 359
  - Algorithm Overview 359
  - Reviewing the Code 360
- Terrain Generation 366
  - Basic Usage 367
  - Advanced Techniques 367
  - Practical Applications 368
  - Algorithm Overview 368
  - Reviewing the Code 369

TABLE OF CONTENTS

Water and Fluid Dynamics 372
    Basic Usage 372
    Advanced Techniques 373
    Practical Applications 373
    Algorithm Overview 374
    Reviewing the Code 374
Environmental Sound Effects 377
    Basic Usage 377
    Advanced Techniques 378
    Practical Applications 378
    Algorithm Overview 379
    Reviewing the Code 379
Dynamic Lighting Changes 382
    Basic Usage 382
    Advanced Techniques 383
    Practical Applications 384
    Algorithm Overview 384
    Reviewing the Code 384
Terrain Texturing 388
    Basic Usage 388
    Advanced Techniques 388
    Practical Applications 389
    Algorithm Overview 389
    Reviewing the Code 390
Interactive Foliage 392
    Basic Usage 393
    Advanced Techniques 393
    Practical Applications 394

TABLE OF CONTENTS

    Algorithm Overview 394

    Reviewing the Code 395

Summary 397

Chapter 5: Character Mechanics 399

  Character Movement 400

    Basic Usage of Character Movement 401

    Advanced Techniques 401

    Practical Applications 402

    Algorithm Overview 402

    Reviewing the Code 403

  Jumping Mechanics 408

    Basic Usage 408

    Advanced Techniques 409

    Practical Applications 409

    Algorithm Overview 410

    Reviewing the Code 410

  Crouching and Prone Mechanics 414

    Key Differences Between Crouching and Prone 415

    Practical Applications 415

    Basic Structure 416

    Crouching Code Implementation 416

    Prone Mechanic Extension 420

  Swimming Mechanics 423

    Basic Implementation 423

    Advanced Techniques 424

    Practical Applications 425

    Algorithm Overview 425

    Reviewing the Code 426

Climbing Mechanics 430
Basic Implementation 431
Advanced Techniques 431
Practical Applications 432
Algorithm Overview 432
Reviewing the Code 433
Stealth Mechanics 437
Key Elements of Stealth Mechanics 437
Basic Implementation 438
Advanced Techniques 438
Practical Applications 439
Algorithm Overview 439
Reviewing the Code 440
Combat Mechanics 444
Basic Combat Mechanics 444
Advanced Combat Techniques 445
Practical Applications 446
Algorithm Overview 446
Reviewing the Code 447
Health and Stamina System 451
Basic Usage of Health and Stamina Systems 452
Advanced Techniques 452
Practical Applications 453
Algorithm Overview 454
Reviewing the Code 454
Skill Trees and Abilities 459
Basic Structure of Skill Trees 459
Types of Abilities and Skills 460

TABLE OF CONTENTS

    Advanced Skill Tree Techniques 461
    Practical Applications 462
    Algorithm Overview 463
    Reviewing the Code 463
  Character Customization 467
    Basic Usage 467
    Advanced Customization 468
    Practical Applications 469
    Algorithm Overview 470
    Reviewing the Code 470
  Summary 474

Chapter 6: Combat Mechanics 475
  Melee Combat 477
    Basic Usage of Melee Combat 477
    Advanced Techniques 478
    Practical Applications 479
    Algorithm Overview 479
    Reviewing the Code 480
  Ranged Combat 485
    Basic Usage 486
    Advanced Techniques 487
    Practical Applications 488
    Algorithm Overview 488
    Reviewing the Code 489
  Magic and Spells 494
    Basic Magic System Mechanics 494
    Advanced Magic System Features 495
    Practical Applications in Different Genres 496

TABLE OF CONTENTS

- Algorithm Overview for Magic System 497
- Reviewing the Code 497

Combat AI 501
- Core Components of Combat AI 502
- Decision-Making in Combat AI 503
- Pathfinding and Movement 503
- Combat AI and Adaptation 504
- Reviewing the Code 504
- Alternative Approach Using Behavior Trees 509

Hit Detection and Response 512
- Understanding Hit Detection 512
- Raycasting Techniques in Unreal Engine 513
- Implementing Hit Detection 514
- Hit Response and Feedback 515
- Advanced Hit Detection: Parrying and Blocking 515
- Reviewing the Code 516

Combo Systems 518
- Key Elements of a Combo System 519
- Designing a Combo System 520
- Reviewing the Code 521
- Balancing Combo Systems 523

Special Moves and Finishing Moves 524
- What Is Special Moves? 525
- Key Characteristics of Special Moves 525
- What Is Finishing Move? 526
- Key Characteristics of Finishing Moves 527
- Designing Special and Finishing Moves 528
- Reviewing the Code 529

TABLE OF CONTENTS

    Damage Types and Resistances 531
        What Are Damage Types? 532
        Applying Damage Types in Combat 533
        What Are Resistances? 534
        Balancing Damage Types and Resistances 535
        Reviewing the Code 537
    Enemy Spawning 539
        Types of Enemy Spawning 540
        Factors Influencing Enemy Spawning 542
        Balancing Enemy Spawns 543
        Reviewing the Code 544
    Boss Fights 549
        Types of Boss Fights 549
        Key Elements of an Engaging Boss Fight 551
        Reviewing the Code 552
    Summary 557

Chapter 7: Physics and Dynamics 559
    Practical Applications of Physics Systems 560
    Key Applications 560
    Rigid Body Dynamics 561
        Basic Usage of Rigid Body Dynamics 562
        Advanced Techniques 563
        Practical Applications 564
        Algorithm Overview 564
        Reviewing the Code 565

Soft Body Dynamics 568
- Basic Usage of Soft Body Dynamics 568
- Advanced Techniques 569
- Practical Applications 569
- Algorithm Overview 570
- Reviewing the Code 571

Particle Systems 576
- Basic Usage of Particle Systems 577
- Advanced Techniques 577
- Practical Applications 578
- Algorithm Overview 579
- Reviewing the Code 579

Cloth Simulation 584
- Basic Usage of Cloth Simulation 584
- Advanced Techniques 585
- Practical Applications 586
- Algorithm Overview 586
- Reviewing the Code 587

Vehicle Physics 590
- Basic Usage of Vehicle Physics 590
- Advanced Techniques 591
- Practical Applications 592
- Algorithm Overview 592
- Reviewing the Code 593

Rope and Chain Physics 596
- Importance of Rope and Chain Physics 596
- Core Components of Rope and Chain Physics 597
- Reviewing the Code 597

TABLE OF CONTENTS

- Destructive Environments 602
  - Importance of Destructible Environments 602
  - Core Components of Destructible Environments 603
  - Reviewing the Code 603
- Fluid Dynamics 609
  - Importance of Fluid Dynamics 609
  - Core Components of Fluid Dynamics 609
  - Reviewing the Code 610
- Gravity Manipulation 614
  - Core Components of Gravity Manipulation 615
  - Reviewing the Code 615
- Force Fields 619
  - Importance of Force Fields 619
  - Core Components of Force Fields 620
  - Reviewing the Code 620
- Summary 624

Chapter 8: Audio and Visual Effects 625

- Sound Triggering on Events 626
  - Importance of Sound Triggering on Events 626
  - Core Components of Sound Triggering 627
  - Reviewing the Code 627
- Dynamic Music Systems 631
  - Importance of Dynamic Music Systems 631
  - Core Components of Dynamic Music Systems 632
  - Reviewing the Code 633

TABLE OF CONTENTS

Visual Feedback on Actions 637
    Importance of Visual Feedback on Actions... 637
    Core Components of Visual Feedback 638
    Reviewing the Code.. 638
Screen Shakes and Camera Effects.. 642
    Importance of Screen Shakes and Camera Effects 642
    Core Components of Screen Shakes and Camera Effects.......................... 643
    Reviewing the Code.. 643
Post-Processing Effects.. 646
    Core Components of Post-Processing Effects 646
    Reviewing the Code.. 647
UI Animations 650
    Importance of UI Animations 650
    Core Components of UI Animations 651
    Reviewing the Code.. 651
HUD Design 654
    Importance of HUD Design 654
    Core Components of HUD Design 655
    Reviewing the Code.. 655
Dialogue Sound Effects... 658
    Importance of Dialogue Sound Effects 658
    Reviewing the Code.. 659
Environmental Ambience 662
    Importance of Environmental Ambience.. 663
    Core Components of Environmental Ambience 663
    Advanced Audio Settings and Features 664
    Reviewing the Code.. 664

TABLE OF CONTENTS

Particle Effects on Interactions 668
    Importance of Particle Effects on Interactions 668
    Core Components of Particle Effects on Interactions 668
    Reviewing the Code 669
Summary 671

Chapter 9: AI and Pathfinding 673

Basic AI Movement 674
    Importance of Basic AI Movement 674
    Core Components of Basic AI Movement 674
    Reviewing the Code 675
Advanced Pathfinding 678
    Importance of Advanced Pathfinding 679
    Core Components of Advanced Pathfinding 679
    Reviewing the Code 680
    Usage Example 684
Enemy Patrols and Combat 684
    Importance of Enemy Patrols and Combat 685
    Core Components of Enemy Patrols and Combat 685
    Reviewing the Code 686
Companion and Stealth AI 692
    Importance of Companion and Stealth AI 693
    Core Components of Companion and Stealth AI 693
    Reviewing the Code 694
Dynamic AI Response 703
    Importance of Dynamic AI Response 704
    Core Components of Dynamic AI Response 704
    Reviewing the Code 705

AI Decision Trees 709
    Importance of AI Decision Trees 710
    Core Components of AI Decision Trees 710
    Reviewing the Code 711
Pathfinding Optimization 714
    Importance of Pathfinding Optimization 714
    Core Components of Pathfinding Optimization 715
    Reviewing the Code 716
AI State Machines 719
    Importance of AI State Machines 720
    Core Components of AI State Machines 720
    Reviewing the Code 721
Summary 724

Chapter 10: Networking and Multiplayer 727

Basic Networking Concepts 728
    Importance of Basic Networking Concepts 728
    Core Components of Basic Networking Concepts 729
    Reviewing the code 729
Player Synchronization 732
    Importance of Player Synchronization 732
    Core Components of Player Synchronization 732
    Reviewing the Code 733
Networked Player Interactions 737
    Importance of Networked Player Interactions 737
    Core Components of Networked Player Interactions 738
    Remote Procedure Calls (RPCs) and Network Proxies 738
    Reviewing the Code 739

TABLE OF CONTENTS

Multiplayer Game Modes 743
    Importance of Multiplayer Game Modes 743
    Common Types of Multiplayer Game Modes 743
    Key Elements of Multiplayer Game Modes 744
    Reviewing the Code 744

Lobby Systems 748
    Importance of Lobby Systems 748
    Key Features of a Lobby System 749
    Reviewing the Code 749

Networked AI 754
    Importance of Networked AI 754
    Key Features of Networked AI 754
    Reviewing the Code 755

Lag Compensation 758
    Importance of Lag Compensation 759
    Key Features of Lag Compensation 759
    Reviewing the Code 759

Server Authority 764
    Importance of Server Authority 764
    Key Features of Server Authority 765
    Reviewing the Code 765

Matchmaking Systems 768
    Importance of Matchmaking Systems 768
    Core Features of Matchmaking Systems 769
    Reviewing the Code 769

Voice and Text Chat 773
    Importance of Voice and Text Chat 773
    Core Features of Voice and Text Chat 774

Options for Voice Chat 774
Reviewing the Code 775
Summary 778

Chapter 11: Advanced Mechanics 779

Procedural Generation 780
    Importance of Procedural Generation in Games 780
    Core Components of Procedural Generation 780
    Reviewing the Code 781
    Example Usage 784
Save and Load Systems 785
    Importance of Save and Load Systems 785
    Core Components of Save and Load Systems 786
    Reviewing the Code 786
Modding Support 790
    Importance of Modding Support 790
    Reviewing the Code 791
VR Mechanics 794
    Importance of VR Mechanics 795
    Core Components of VR Mechanics 795
    Reviewing the Code 796
AR Mechanics 800
    Importance of AR Mechanics 800
    Core Components of AR Mechanics 801
    Reviewing the Code 801
Performance Optimization 806
    Importance of Performance Optimization 806
    Core Components of Performance Optimization 806
    Reviewing the Code 807

TABLE OF CONTENTS

- Cross-Platform Development 811
  - Importance of Cross-Platform Development 811
  - Core Components of Cross-Platform Development 812
  - Reviewing the Code 812
- Advanced Scripting Techniques 816
  - Importance of Advanced Scripting Techniques 816
  - Core Components of Advanced Scripting 816
  - Reviewing the Code 817
- Plugin and Middleware Integration 820
  - Importance of Plugin and Middleware Integration 820
  - Core Components of Plugin and Middleware Integration 821
  - Reviewing the Code 821
- Future Trends in Game Development 824
  - Importance of Understanding Future Trends 824
  - Core Trends in Game Development 825
  - Reviewing the Code 825
- Summary 828

Chapter 12: Case Studies 831

- Implementing a Complete Level 832
  - Importance of a Complete Level 832
  - Core Components of Level Design 832
  - Reviewing the Code 833
- Creating a Boss Fight 835
  - Importance of Boss Fights 836
  - Core Components of a Boss Fight 836
  - Reviewing the Code 837

TABLE OF CONTENTS

Multiplayer Arena 842
    Importance of a Multiplayer Arena 843
    Core Components of a Multiplayer Arena 843
    Reviewing the Code 844

Developing a Quest System 848
    Importance of a Quest System 848
    Core Components of a Quest System 849
    Reviewing the Code 849

Building a Dynamic Weather System 853
    Importance of a Dynamic Weather System 853
    Core Components of a Dynamic Weather System 854
    Reviewing the Code 854

Summary 859

Chapter 13: Appendix 861

Unreal Engine Cheat Sheet 862
    Editor Hotkeys 862

Common Errors and Fixes 866
    1. Compiler Errors in C++ 866
    2. Blueprint Compilation Issues 867
    3. Runtime Errors 868
    4. Network and Replication Issues 869
    5. Asset Loading and Path Issues 869
    6. Miscellaneous Errors 870

Additional Resources 871
    1. Official Unreal Engine Documentation 871
    2. Unreal Engine Forums 871
    3. Unreal Engine YouTube Channel 872

TABLE OF CONTENTS

    4. UE4 AnswerHub 872
    5. Online Learning Platforms 872
    6. Unreal Slackers (Discord Community) 873
    7. GitHub Repositories and Sample Projects 873
    8. Community Tutorials and Blogs 873
    9. Online Communities and Social Media 874
Glossary of Terms 875
    A 875
    B 875
    C 876
    D 876
    E 876
    F 877
    G 877
    H 877
    I 878
    J 878
    K 878
    L 878
    M 879
    N 879
    O 879
    P 880
    Q 880
    R 880
    S 880
    T 881

TABLE OF CONTENTS

U 881
V 881
W 882

Index **883**

About the Author

Sheikh Sohel Moon is a passionate game and VR developer dedicated to creating immersive experiences. He has over five years of experience in Unreal Engine and VR, including game design, programming, and optimization. He likes to stay up to date with the latest technologies and trends in the gaming industry, and under his leadership projects have earned recognition, such as being featured in Epic Mega Grant submissions and the Netflix series *The Future Of*.

He is extremely committed to the constructive power of games and virtual reality in creating meaningful experiences. His work has been acknowledged in prestigious competitions, including the Hult Prize and the Khulna University CSE FEST, highlighting his contributions to the field. Sohel holds a degree in Computer Science and Engineering from Khulna University and continues to push the boundaries of interactive digital experiences through his freelance work and self-driven projects.

About the Technical Reviewer

Rahul Sharma is an Unreal developer with two years of hands-on experience in Unreal Engine, backed by a degree in Computer Science and Engineering. With a strong foundation in software development and programming, he brings both technical expertise and a deep passion for game development. Beyond just skills, his true drive comes from a lifelong love for games and the creativity that fuels their creation.

Acknowledgments

I extend my heartfelt gratitude to Tahsin Ar Rahman (Aan), who has been more than just a friend—he has been a lifelong brother and mentor. His unwavering support and guidance have played a crucial role in shaping my journey.

A special thank-you to Marufa Jahan (Mitu), the friend who has always been there to listen. Your patience, understanding, and ability to help me navigate through life's challenges mean more to me than words can express.

This book would not have been possible without the presence of these incredible people in my life.

Introduction

This book is uniquely designed for intermediate to advanced game developers, offering a comprehensive guide to creating complex, engaging, and performance-driven games using Unreal Engine and C++. Whether you are an indie developer, a student, or a professional, this book will equip you with the tools and knowledge to take your skills to the next level.

Why This Book?

In the rapidly evolving world of game development, staying ahead requires creativity and a deep understanding of the technical aspects of game mechanics. This book bridges the gap between basic knowledge and advanced application, offering a comprehensive guide to implementing sophisticated game mechanics. With a hands-on approach, detailed explanations, and practical examples, you will learn how to bring your game ideas to life efficiently and effectively.

Structure of the Book

The book is divided into several chapters, each focusing on a different aspect of game development:

- **Chapter 1: Core Collision Mechanics**—An overview of the fundamental principles of collision systems
- **Chapter 2: Advanced Collision Mechanics**—In-depth collision detection and response systems coverage

INTRODUCTION

- **Chapter 3: Interaction Mechanics**—Exploring various player interactions within the game environment
- **Chapter 4: Environmental Mechanics**—Implementing dynamic environments and effects
- **Chapter 5: Character Mechanics**—A comprehensive look at character control and behavior
- **Chapter 6: Combat Mechanics**—Detailed examination of combat systems and strategies
- **Chapter 7: Physics and Dynamics**—Understanding and applying physics-based simulations
- **Chapter 8: Audio and Visual Effects**—Enhancing games with sound and visual feedback
- **Chapter 9: AI and Pathfinding**—Developing intelligent and responsive AI systems
- **Chapter 10: Networking and Multiplayer**—Creating robust multiplayer experiences
- **Chapter 11: Advanced Mechanics**—Advanced techniques and future trends in game development
- **Chapter 12: Case Studies**—Real-world examples of game development projects
- **Chapter 13: Appendix**—Supplementary materials, cheat sheets, and additional resources

Each chapter has code snippets, ensuring a hands-on, practical understanding of the concepts discussed.

Continuous Learning

Game development is an ever-evolving field. Stay updated with the latest trends, tools, and techniques by engaging with the broader game development community. Participate in forums, attend conferences, and follow industry news to keep your skills sharp and your knowledge current.

This book is your guide to mastering advanced game mechanics in Unreal Engine using C++. By the time you finish, you will have the skills and confidence to tackle complex game development challenges and create immersive, high-performance games. Let us begin this exciting journey into the world of advanced game development!

CHAPTER 1

Core Collision Mechanics

Collisions, in game development, are the first point at which differing game objects interact with each other. A collision event occurs when two or more objects touch or overlap positions in a game. Such a simple concept, yet it forms a fundamental basis for most of the gameplay mechanics—and for good reason.

Collisions are fundamental to how a player interacts with the game world. By implementing a simple collision system, we demonstrate implementation details for game interactivity. When you know this simple system, you can come up with a ton of interesting mechanics—avoiding things in the environment, interacting with objects, or even moving through a level. Imagine your player character running through a maze, avoiding walls, and picking up items. This is where our journey begins, and by the end of this chapter, you'll be able to implement these mechanics yourself.

Collisions can also be used for more advanced functionality. Advanced collision techniques are very important for high-end physics-based interactions, environmental destruction, and complex combat mechanics. Using collisions in a very clever way, we will improve gameplay incredibly, making it even more enjoyable and real. Think of games where the environment is destructible or where something bounces in a very lifelike way because of the application of advanced collision techniques. Let's take a closer look at them, and you will reach the point where you can build much more realistic and interactive games.

In this chapter, we delve into collision mechanics; we first start with the basics, then hit more complex applications. By the end, you should have a good idea of how collisions are detected and resolved and how they can be used to implement all sorts of gameplay mechanics. You will be set up to create better, more realistic games.

Blocking Movement

Blocking Movement is the mechanics that inflict limitations and restrictions on object movement. Any game simulation concerning spatial navigation must impose the laws of physics through these mechanics. Imagine you are making a maze; you wouldn't want the player to just walk through walls. Blocking movement assures that navigation of a player is realistic and fits with the physics of the in-game world.

Basic Usage

Blocking movement is when some object or player character can be denied free movement due to blocking obstacles. Such obstacles are talking with the moving object with areas they own. If an object or a player character enters these areas, their movement can be blocked or redirected.

This general use case will let us visualize and build the game environment by specifying positions and sizes for non-movable blockades or obstructions.

Advanced Techniques

These are techniques where interactive obstacles that the player can destroy or move are added, for example, a door that opens and closes after a player's action or switches to trigger environmental changes. This kind of simulation with physics could also give real collision responses as in pushing and knocking objects back.

Think of the simple addition of a door in your maze that will open and close only when a lever is pulled. It adds an interactive element, hence increasing the player's experience.

Practical Applications

Blocking movement plays a crucial role in game development, influencing how characters and objects interact within the game world. Below are some key applications of blocking movement:

- Creating realistic obstacles in the environment
- Designing collision-based puzzles or challenges
- Simulating how characters and objects interact with each other in a game
- Reinforcing rules of the game world, like gravity and friction

Algorithm Overview

Let's imagine the algorithm for blocking movement:

1. **Initialization**: Place the player and the obstacles in the game scene.

CHAPTER 1   CORE COLLISION MECHANICS

2. **Collision Detection**: Check repeatedly whether there is a collision between the player and the obstacles.

3. **Collision Resolution**: Detect and resolve collisions with good physics responses, including blocking and deflection of movement.

4. **Interaction Handling**: Implement interactivity within the obstacles (like doors or triggers), which modify obstacle behavior based on player actions.

This serves as the core algorithm for blocking movement mechanics implementation within Unreal Engine.

Reviewing the Code

Now that we've explored the general concepts and applications of blocking movement, let's dive into the specifics of how to implement these mechanics in Unreal Engine. This section will walk you through the process of setting up your game environment, starting with the foundational elements required to create a maze and configure player movement.

Setting Up the Maze and Player

Having discussed general concepts and the way blocking movement is being used, now let's get into the details of actual block implementation within Unreal Engine and setting your game environment from basic components that create a maze to player movement.

Configuring Maze

Listing 1-1 declares class AMazeWall, intended to be a wall in the maze of Unreal Engine. The following is an explanation of the principal elements that perform their functions:

- **MazeWall Class**: This class inherits from AActor. This means it will become one entity that can then exist in a game world. It represents a static mesh wall inside the maze.

- **BeginPlay Function**: This is a function that gets called when the game starts or when an actor is spawned. It was used to initialize any parameters or states that needed setup before the start of gameplay.

- **Tick Function**: It calls every frame of gameplay. This function is used to keep updating the state of an actor continuously but doesn't change behavior directly in this case.

- **MazeWall Property**: This UStaticMeshComponent will be responsible for defining the visual appearance of the wall. It is visible, and it will react to the game's physics and collision system.

Listing 1-1. MazeWall.h

```
#pragma once

class UStaticMeshComponent;

#include "CoreMinimal.h"
#include "GameFramework/Actor.h"
#include "MazeWall.generated.h"
```

CHAPTER 1 CORE COLLISION MECHANICS

```
UCLASS()
class MYGAME_API AMazeWall : public AActor
{
    GENERATED_BODY()
public:
    AMazeWall();

protected:
    virtual void BeginPlay() override;

public:
    virtual void Tick(float DeltaTime) override;

private:
    UPROPERTY(VisibleAnywhere)
    UStaticMeshComponent* MazeWall;
};
```

Listing 1-2 sets up the behavior of the class AMazeWall, through which it is defined how it will interact with other elements in the game world.

- **CreateDefaultSubobject**: A function that creates an instance of the class UStaticMeshComponent named MazeWall. This component renders the wall in the game environment and handles collision interactions.

- **SetCollisionEnabled**: This method belongs to the MazeWall component and is called to activate collision detection and physics responses. This means that, when active, the wall will be able to interact with other objects and characters according to the collision system implemented in the game.

- **SetCollisionResponseToAllChannels**: The ECR_Block sets the collision response, which ensures that the wall blocks all collision channels. This simply means that the wall prevents the penetration of any player character or other objects across it, rendering it a physical barrier inside the maze.

- **BeginPlay**: This is a function that gets called when the game starts or, if it's a wall actor, when the actor is spawned. It is a place to initialize any extra settings or properties; here, it just inherits the default behavior from its parent class.

- **Tick**: It is called once every frame while in play. Here, this function is overridden to probably update the state of the wall or change its behavior; however, it inherits the default behavior from its parent class.

Listing 1-2. MazeWall.cpp

```
#include "MazeWall.h"
#include "Components/StaticMeshComponent.h"

AMazeWall::AMazeWall()
{
    PrimaryActorTick.bCanEverTick = true;

    MazeWall = CreateDefaultSubobject<UStaticMeshComponent>
    (TEXT("MazeWall"));
    RootComponent = MazeWall;

    MazeWall->SetCollisionEnabled(ECollisionEnabled::QueryAnd
    Physics);
```

```
    MazeWall->SetCollisionResponseToAllChannels(ECollision
    Response::ECR_Block);
}
void AMazeWall::BeginPlay()
{
    Super::BeginPlay();
}
void AMazeWall::Tick(float DeltaTime)
{
    Super::Tick(DeltaTime);
}
```

Configuring Player Collision

Now it's time to set up collision settings for the player character to collide with maze walls.

Listing 1-3 defines the player character in Unreal Engine. Here's a breakdown of its components and functions:

- **PlayerCharacter Class**: This class defines an actor that represents the player character in the game. It inherits from ACharacter, which provides basic functionality for a player-controlled character.

- **BeginPlay Function**: This function is called when the game starts or when the player character is spawned. It is used for initialization tasks that need to occur when the actor begins play.

- **Tick Function**: The Tick function is called every frame during gameplay. It is used to update the actor's state, though, in this example, it inherits default behavior from its parent class.

- **PlayerCapsule**: This private member is a pointer to a UCapsuleComponent, which is used to define the collision shape of the player character. The capsule shape is commonly used for player characters to handle collisions with the environment.

Listing 1-3. PlayerCharacter.h

```
#pragma once

class UCapsuleComponent;

#include "CoreMinimal.h"
#include "GameFramework/Character.h"
#include "PlayerCharacter.generated.h"

UCLASS()
class MYGAME_API APlayerCharacter : public ACharacter
{
    GENERATED_BODY()

public:
    APlayerCharacter();

protected:
    virtual void BeginPlay() override;

public:
    virtual void Tick(float DeltaTime) override;

private:
    UPROPERTY(VisibleAnywhere)
    UCapsuleComponent* PlayerCapsule;
};
```

CHAPTER 1   CORE COLLISION MECHANICS

The implementation details for the APlayerCharacter class in Listing 1-4 are as follows:

- **CreateDefaultSubobject**: This function creates an instance of UCapsuleComponent named PlayerCapsule. It is used to define the player's collision shape and is set as the root component of the player character.

- **SetCollisionEnabled**: This method enables collision detection and physics responses for the PlayerCapsule component. It allows the player character to interact with the game world based on physics simulations.

- **SetCollisionResponseToAllChannels**: By setting the collision response to ECR_Block, the player character will block all collision channels. This ensures that the player character cannot pass through obstacles, such as maze walls.

Listing 1-4. PlayerCharacter.cpp

```
#include "PlayerCharacter.h"
#include "Components/CapsuleComponent.h"

APlayerCharacter::APlayerCharacter()
{
    PrimaryActorTick.bCanEverTick = true;

    PlayerCapsule = CreateDefaultSubobject<UCapsuleComponent>
    (TEXT("PlayerCapsule"));
    RootComponent = PlayerCapsule;

    PlayerCapsule->SetCollisionEnabled(ECollisionEnabled::
    QueryAndPhysics);
```

```
    PlayerCapsule->SetCollisionResponseToAllChannels(ECollision
    Response::ECR_Block);
}
void APlayerCharacter::BeginPlay()
{
    Super::BeginPlay();
}
void APlayerCharacter::Tick(float DeltaTime)
{
    Super::Tick(DeltaTime);
}
```

Implementing Movement Restrictions

Unreal Engine handles collision responses automatically, restricting player movement when they collide with maze walls. This ensures realistic navigation through the game environment.

Advanced Blocking Movement

For more interactive experiences, such as doors and switches, we can add trigger volumes (Listings 1-5 and 1-6). The ADoorTrigger class is designed to handle interactions with a trigger volume that can activate or deactivate a door or similar mechanism. Here's a breakdown of its components and functions:

- **DoorTrigger Class**: This class represents an actor that utilizes a trigger volume to detect when other actors enter or exit its defined area. This is typically used to create interactive elements, like doors, that respond to player actions.

CHAPTER 1 CORE COLLISION MECHANICS

- **BeginPlay Function**: This function is called when the game starts or when the ADoorTrigger actor is spawned. It's used to set up any necessary initial states or configurations for the actor.

- **Tick Function**: This function is called every frame during gameplay. It's used to update the actor's state if needed, although, in this case, it may inherit default behavior or be left unimplemented.

- **DoorTrigger**: This private member is a pointer to an ATriggerVolume that defines the area where interactions occur. This trigger volume detects when other actors enter or exit its bounds.

- **OnOverlapBegin Function**: This function is a callback that is triggered when another actor begins to overlap with the trigger volume. It can be used to implement logic for opening the door or activating other interactive elements.

- **OnOverlapEnd Function**: This function is called when an actor stops overlapping with the trigger volume. It can be used to implement logic for closing the door or deactivating the interactive elements.

Listing 1-5. DoorTrigger.h

```
#pragma once

class ATriggerVolume;

#include "CoreMinimal.h"
#include "GameFramework/Actor.h"
#include "DoorTrigger.generated.h"
```

```cpp
UCLASS()
class MYGAME_API ADoorTrigger : public AActor
{
    GENERATED_BODY()

public:
    ADoorTrigger();

protected:
    virtual void BeginPlay() override;

public:
    virtual void Tick(float DeltaTime) override;

private:
    UPROPERTY(VisibleAnywhere)
    ATriggerVolume* DoorTrigger;

    UFUNCTION()
    void OnBeginOverlap(UPrimitiveComponent* Overlapped
    Component, AActor* OtherActor, UPrimitiveComponent*
    OtherComp, int32 OtherBodyIndex, bool bFromSweep, const
    FHitResult & SweepResult);

    UFUNCTION()
    void OnEndOverlap(UPrimitiveComponent* OverlappedComponent,
    AActor* OtherActor, UPrimitiveComponent* OtherComp, int32
    OtherBodyIndex);
};
```

CHAPTER 1   CORE COLLISION MECHANICS

The following methods and functions are crucial for setting up and managing the ADoorTrigger class's behavior in Unreal Engine:

- **CreateDefaultSubobject**: This function initializes a new ATriggerVolume component named DoorTrigger, which acts as the trigger area for detecting overlaps. This component is set as the root of the actor, ensuring it is the primary element interacting with the game world.

- **AddDynamic**: AddDynamic is a function used in Unreal Engine to bind a delegate to an event. It allows you to associate an event (like overlap events) with a specific function that will be called when that event is triggered.

Listing 1-6. DoorTrigger.cpp

```cpp
#include "DoorTrigger.h"
#include "Engine/TriggerVolume.h"
#include "Components/BoxComponent.h"

ADoorTrigger::ADoorTrigger()
{
    PrimaryActorTick.bCanEverTick = true;

    DoorTrigger = CreateDefaultSubobject<ATriggerVolume>
    (TEXT("DoorTrigger"));
    RootComponent = DoorTrigger;

    DoorTrigger->OnActorBeginOverlap.AddDynamic(this, &ADoorTrigger::OnOverlapBegin);
    DoorTrigger->OnActorEndOverlap.AddDynamic(this, &ADoorTrigger::OnOverlapEnd);
}
```

```cpp
void ADoorTrigger::OnOverlapBegin(AActor* OverlappedActor,
AActor* OtherActor)
{
    // Implement door opening logic here
}

void ADoorTrigger::OnOverlapEnd(AActor* OverlappedActor,
AActor* OtherActor)
{
    // Implement door closing logic here
}
```

This section explored the fundamentals of blocking movement mechanics in game development. From understanding basic collision concepts to implementing advanced techniques like interactive obstacles, you've gained insights into how collisions drive realistic interactions within game environments.

In the next section, we'll delve deeper into triggering events, exploring how interactions between game objects can dynamically influence gameplay.

Triggering Events

Triggering events involve mechanisms that respond to specific conditions or actions within a game. These events can range from opening doors to activating traps, adding dynamic elements to gameplay.

Basic Usage

Triggering events occur when a player character or object interacts with designated trigger volumes or objects in the game world. These interactions typically initiate changes in the game environment or trigger predefined actions.

CHAPTER 1   CORE COLLISION MECHANICS

Advanced Techniques

These techniques focus on adding interactive obstacles and dynamic events that react to player actions. For example, you could implement a wall-run detection system, where the player triggers a wall-running animation and movement sequence upon reaching a specific wall. Additionally, combat hit events can be used to trigger damage effects or visual cues when a punch lands or when a character is hit by an attack. Wall climbing triggers can also be used to initiate specific climbing animations or behaviors when the player character touches certain surfaces.

Practical Applications

Triggering events are a cornerstone of interactive game design, adding depth and engagement to gameplay. They allow game developers to create dynamic and responsive environments that react to player actions and decisions. By integrating trigger mechanisms, you can enhance the gaming experience in several ways:

- Creating interactive elements like doors, switches, and traps
- Designing puzzles and challenges that require player interaction to progress
- Implementing dynamic game events based on player decisions or game state changes
- Enhancing immersion by simulating cause-and-effect relationships within the game world

CHAPTER 1   CORE COLLISION MECHANICS

Algorithm Overview

Understanding how to effectively implement triggers involves a systematic approach:

1. **Event Initialization**: Begin by setting up trigger volumes or objects within the game scene. These components are essential for detecting when a player interacts with specific areas or objects.

2. **Event Detection**: Continuously monitor for interactions between players and trigger objects. This involves checking for overlap or collision events that indicate a player has interacted with a trigger.

3. **Event Resolution**: Execute predefined actions or changes in response to triggered events. This could include opening doors, changing game states, or other actions that affect gameplay.

4. **Sequence Handling**: Manage event sequences and dependencies to ensure coherent gameplay progression. Proper sequencing ensures that events unfold logically and that game state changes are handled smoothly.

Reviewing the Code

The ATriggerVolume class defines an area in the game world that triggers events when a player or another actor interacts with it. It handles the initialization of the trigger volume and manages the events that occur when actors overlap with it.

CHAPTER 1 CORE COLLISION MECHANICS

The following is a detailed breakdown of the code and its functionality in Listing 1-7:

- **TriggerVolume Class**: This class represents a trigger volume in the game world. It is derived from AActor, allowing it to be placed in the level and interact with other actors.

- **BeginPlay Function**: This function is called when the game starts or when the actor is spawned. It is used for any initialization specific to the trigger volume, ensuring that all necessary setup occurs at the start of the game.

- **Tick Function**: The Tick function is called every frame. While it does not perform any operations in this implementation, it is available for future updates or continuous checks related to the trigger volume.

- **TriggerBox Property**: This is a UBoxComponent that defines the physical boundary of the trigger volume. It is used to detect overlaps with other actors.

- **OnOverlapBegin and OnOverlapEnd Functions**: These are callback functions that handle events when actors begin or end their overlap with the trigger volume. They can be used to trigger specific actions, such as opening a door or activating a trap.

Listing 1-7. TriggerVolume.h

```
#pragma once

class ATriggerVolume

#include "CoreMinimal.h"
```

```cpp
#include "GameFramework/Actor.h"
#include "TriggerVolume.generated.h"

UCLASS()
class MYGAME_API ATriggerVolume : public AActor
{
    GENERATED_BODY()

public:
    ATriggerVolume();

protected:
    virtual void BeginPlay() override;

public:
    virtual void Tick(float DeltaTime) override;

private:
    UPROPERTY(VisibleAnywhere)
    UBoxComponent* TriggerBox;

    UFUNCTION()
    void OnOverlapBegin(UPrimitiveComponent* Overlapped
    Component, AActor* OtherActor, UPrimitiveComponent*
    OtherComp, int32 OtherBodyIndex, bool bFromSweep,
    const FHitResult& SweepResult);

    UFUNCTION()
    void OnOverlapEnd(UPrimitiveComponent* OverlappedComponent,
    AActor* OtherActor, UPrimitiveComponent* OtherComp,
    int32 OtherBodyIndex, bool bFromSweep, const FHitResult&
    SweepResult);
};
```

CHAPTER 1   CORE COLLISION MECHANICS

Listing 1-8 highlights the most important parts of this code, including CreateDefaultSubobject, SetCollisionEnabled, OnComponentBeginOverlap, OnComponentEndOverlap, OnOverlapBegin, and OnOverlapEnd.

- **Constructor Initialization**: The CreateDefaultSubobject function creates a UBoxComponent named TriggerBox. This component acts as the collision boundary for the trigger volume. The PrimaryActorTick.bCanEverTick property is set to true to ensure the Tick function is called every frame.

- **Collision Settings**: The SetCollisionEnabled method is set to ECollisionEnabled::QueryOnly, which means the component will detect overlaps but not participate in physical collisions. SetCollisionResponseToAllChannels is set to ECollisionResponse::ECR_Overlap, meaning the trigger box will generate overlap events with all channels.

- **Event Bindings**: The OnComponentBeginOverlap and OnComponentEndOverlap methods are bound to the OnOverlapBegin and OnOverlapEnd functions, respectively. This binding allows the trigger volume to respond to overlap events by executing the specified logic.

- **Overlap Handlers**: OnOverlapBegin and OnOverlapEnd are placeholder functions where you can implement specific logic for when an actor enters or exits the trigger volume. This might include actions like opening a door, activating a trap, or other game-specific events.

Listing 1-8. TriggerVolume.cpp

```cpp
#include "TriggerVolume.h"
#include "Components/BoxComponent.h"

ATriggerVolume::ATriggerVolume()
{
    PrimaryActorTick.bCanEverTick = true;

    TriggerBox = CreateDefaultSubobject<UBoxComponent>
    (TEXT("TriggerBox"));
    RootComponent = TriggerBox;

    TriggerBox->SetCollisionEnabled(ECollisionEnabled::Query
    Only);
    TriggerBox->SetCollisionResponseToAllChannels(ECollision
    Response::ECR_Overlap);

    TriggerBox->OnComponentBeginOverlap.AddDynamic(this,
    &ThisClass::OnOverlapBegin);
    TriggerBox->OnComponentEndOverlap.AddDynamic(this,
    & ThisClass::OnOverlapEnd);
}

void ATriggerVolume::BeginPlay()
{
    Super::BeginPlay();
}

void ATriggerVolume::Tick(float DeltaTime)
{
    Super::Tick(DeltaTime);
}
```

CHAPTER 1   CORE COLLISION MECHANICS

```
void ATriggerVolume::OnOverlapBegin(AActor* OverlappedActor,
AActor* OtherActor)
{
    // Implement event logic here (e.g., door opening, trap
        activation)
}
void ATriggerVolume::OnOverlapEnd(AActor* OverlappedActor,
AActor* OtherActor)
{
    // Implement event reset logic here (if needed)
}
```

Handling Interactive Elements

Interactive elements in a game provide a way for players to engage with various objects and mechanisms. These objects can include switches, levers, or any elements that respond to player actions. Here's a detailed look at the AInteractiveObject class and its implementation.

The AInteractiveObject class is designed to represent interactive elements in the game world. Here's a detailed breakdown of its components and functionality:

- **InteractiveObject Class**: This class inherits from AActor and represents an object that players can interact with. It forms the basis for objects like switches and levers that can be activated or deactivated.
- **ObjectMesh Property**: This property is a UStaticMeshComponent that provides the visual representation of the interactive object. It is the root component, meaning it forms the base of the actor in the game world.

- **bIsActive Property**: This boolean flag indicates whether the object is currently active. It helps manage the state of the object and determines whether it should perform specific actions.

- **Interact Function**: This function handles interactions with the object. It toggles the object's state between active and inactive and executes the corresponding logic based on the current state.

Listing 1-9. InteractiveObject.h

```cpp
#pragma once

class UStaticMeshComponent;

#include "CoreMinimal.h"
#include "GameFramework/Actor.h"
#include "InteractiveObject.generated.h"

UCLASS()
class MYGAME_API AInteractiveObject : public AActor
{
    GENERATED_BODY()

public:
    AInteractiveObject();

protected:
    virtual void BeginPlay() override;

public:
    virtual void Tick(float DeltaTime) override;
```

CHAPTER 1　CORE COLLISION MECHANICS

```
private:
    UPROPERTY(VisibleAnywhere, EditDefaultsOnly, Category =
    "Interactive Object")
    UStaticMeshComponent* ObjectMesh;

    bool bIsActive;

    UFUNCTION()
    void Interact();
};
```

The provided code outlines the implementation of interactive objects in the game. Here's a closer look at the key components:

- **Constructor Initialization**: The CreateDefaultSubobject function creates the visual component of the interactive object, and PrimaryActorTick.bCanEverTick ensures that the Tick function is called every frame.

- **State Management**: The bIsActive flag tracks the object's state, determining whether it is currently active or not. This flag is essential for toggling the object's behavior.

- **Interaction Logic**: The Interact function defines how the object responds to player interactions. It toggles the object's state and executes specific logic based on whether the object is being activated or deactivated.

Listing 1-10. InteractiveObject.cpp

```
#include "InteractiveObject.h"
#include "Components/StaticMeshComponent.h"

AInteractiveObject::AInteractiveObject()
```

CHAPTER 1   CORE COLLISION MECHANICS

```
{
    PrimaryActorTick.bCanEverTick = true;

    ObjectMesh = CreateDefaultSubobject<UStaticMeshComponent>
    (TEXT("ObjectMesh"));
    RootComponent = ObjectMesh;
    bIsActive = false;
}

void AInteractiveObject::BeginPlay()
{
    Super::BeginPlay();
}

void AInteractiveObject::Tick(float DeltaTime)
{
    Super::Tick(DeltaTime);
}

void AInteractiveObject::Interact()
{
    // If the object is already active, deactivate it and exit
       the function

    if (bIsActive)
    {
        bIsActive = false;  // Deactivate object (e.g., close
                               door, disable trap)
        return;  // Exit as no further actions are needed
    }
```

```
    // If the object is not active, activate it
    bIsActive = true;  // Activate object (e.g., open door,
                                       trigger trap)
    // Implement activation logic here
}
```

Implementing Dynamic Events

Unreal Engine's ability to manage dynamic events enables the creation of complex and engaging gameplay scenarios. By using event sequences, you can orchestrate actions and responses that evolve based on specific triggers and conditions, enhancing the interactivity and immersion of the game. The UEventChain class provides a robust mechanism for managing such dynamic events.

Advanced Event Sequences

The UEventChain class facilitates the creation and management of sequences of events that depend on specific conditions or triggers. This class is essential for orchestrating complex event chains, allowing for advanced gameplay scenarios.

The UEventChain class is designed to manage sequences of events, each of which can be triggered with a specific delay. Here's a detailed breakdown of its components:

- **EventChain Class**: This class extends UObject and manages a sequence of events. It allows for the orchestration of complex event chains by using timers and delegates.

- **StartEventChain Function**: This function initiates the event sequence, starting with the first event in the EventSequence array. It ensures that the sequence begins when called.

- **AddEvent Function**: This function adds a new event to the sequence. Each event is associated with a time delay and a delegate function, which is executed when the event is triggered.

- **EventTimerHandle**: A FTimerHandle is used to manage and track the timing of events. It ensures that events are executed at the appropriate times.

- **EventSequence Array**: This array holds the delegates for each event in the sequence. It allows for the dynamic scheduling and execution of events.

- **ExecuteEvent Function**: This function executes the current event and schedules the next one based on the specified delay. It uses the timer manager to handle the timing and sequencing of events.

Listing 1-11. EventChain.h

```
#pragma once

#include "CoreMinimal.h"
#include "UObject/NoExportTypes.h"
#include "EventChain.generated.h"

/**
 *
 */
UCLASS()
```

CHAPTER 1   CORE COLLISION MECHANICS

```
class MYGAME_API UEventChain : public UObject
{
    GENERATED_BODY()
public:
    UEventChain();

    void StartEventChain();
    void AddEvent(float TimeDelay, FTimerDelegate Timer
    Delegate);
private:
    FTimerHandle EventTimerHandle;
    TArray<TTuple<float, FTimerDelegate>> EventSequence;

    void ExecuteEvent(int32 EventIndex);
};
```

The code implementation for the UEventChain class showcases the management of event sequences with delays. Here's a breakdown of how the code works:

- **Constructor Initialization**: The default constructor initializes the UEventChain instance, but no specific initialization is required in this case.
- **ExecuteEvent Function**: This function executes the event at the given index and schedules the next event based on a delay. The lambda function is used to capture the current event index and ensure that events are executed in sequence.

Listing 1-12. EventChain.cpp

```cpp
#include "EventChain.h"
#include "Engine/World.h"

UEventChain::UEventChain()
{
}

void UEventChain::StartEventChain()
{
    if (EventSequence.Num() > 0)
    {
        ExecuteEvent(0);
    }
}
void UEventChain::AddEvent(float TimeDelay, FTimerDelegate
TimerDelegate)
{
    // Adding a tuple with TimeDelay and TimerDelegate to the
       EventSequence
    EventSequence.Add({ TimeDelay, TimerDelegate });
}

void UEventChain::ExecuteEvent(int32 EventIndex)
{
    if (EventIndex < EventSequence.Num())
    {
        // Execute the event delegate
        EventSequence[EventIndex].Value.ExecuteIfBound();

        // Increment event index
        EventIndex++;
```

CHAPTER 1   CORE COLLISION MECHANICS

```
            // If there are more events, set a timer for the
               next one
            if (EventIndex < EventSequence.Num())
            {
                float NextDelay = EventSequence[EventIndex].Key;
                GetWorld()->GetTimerManager().SetTimer
                (EventTimerHandle, [this, EventIndex]()
                {
                    ExecuteEvent(EventIndex);
                }, NextDelay, false);
            }
        }
    }
}
```

This section explored the mechanics of triggering events in game development, from basic event detection to advanced event sequences. You've gained insights into how these mechanisms create interactive and dynamic gameplay experiences within game environments.

In the next section, we will delve into interaction detection. This topic will cover how to effectively detect and manage player interactions with various game elements.

Interaction Detection

Interaction detection in game development refers to identifying when and how players interact with objects within the game world. This mechanism enables dynamic responses to player actions, such as picking up items, opening doors, or triggering conversations.

Imagine your character approaches a treasure chest. Interaction detection allows the game to recognize this proximity and trigger an event where the chest opens, revealing its contents.

Basic Usage

Interaction detection occurs when a player performs an action, like pressing a button, near an interactive object. The system checks if the player is within a specified range or meets certain conditions to trigger the interaction.

This basic application helps in defining how the game responds to player actions, ensuring interactive objects react appropriately.

Advanced Techniques

Advanced techniques involve complex interaction systems where multiple conditions must be met for interactions to occur. These systems can include context-sensitive interactions, where the player's action varies based on the situation or object.

For example, a single button press might open a door if the player is nearby or pick up an item if the player is looking at it.

Practical Applications

Interaction detection is crucial for the following:

- Enabling player-object interactions
- Facilitating dialogue systems and NPC interactions
- Managing inventory systems and item pickups
- Enhancing environmental storytelling through interactive elements

CHAPTER 1   CORE COLLISION MECHANICS

Algorithm Overview

Let's visualize the algorithm used for interaction detection:

1. **Initialization**: Set up interactive objects and define their properties within the game scene.

2. **Condition Monitoring**: Continuously monitor player actions and proximity to interactive objects.

3. **Interaction Detection**: Check if interaction conditions are met (e.g., player is close and presses a button).

4. **Event Activation**: Execute predefined actions or changes in response to successful interaction detection.

This algorithm forms the basis for implementing interaction detection mechanics in Unreal Engine.

Reviewing the Code

The InteractiveObject class in Unreal Engine defines an object that players can interact with in the game world. This includes managing initialization, condition checking, and handling interactions. The following sections break down the InteractiveObject class, providing a comprehensive look at its components and functions.

This header file defines the AInteractiveObject class, which inherits from AActor, making it a part of the game world and allowing it to be interacted with.

- **InteractiveObject Class**: This class represents an object that can be interacted with within the game. It inherits from AActor, meaning it is a game entity with physical presence and behavior.

- **AInteractiveObject Constructor**: The constructor sets default values and initializes the object's components. It prepares the object to be used in the game by creating a static mesh component and setting the initial state of interaction.

- **OnInteract Function**: This function is intended to handle interactions with the object. The implementation of the interaction logic is placed here, and it will be executed when the player interacts with the object. It checks if the object is interactable before proceeding.

Listing 1-13. InteractiveObject.h

```
class UStaticMeshComponent;

#include "CoreMinimal.h"
#include "GameFramework/Actor.h"
#include "InteractiveObject.generated.h"

UCLASS()
class MYGAME_API AInteractiveObject : public AActor
{
    GENERATED_BODY()

public:
    AInteractiveObject();

protected:
    virtual void BeginPlay() override;

public:
    virtual void Tick(float DeltaTime) override;
```

```
private:
    UPROPERTY(VisibleAnywhere)
    UStaticMeshComponent* ObjectMesh;

    UFUNCTION()
    void OnInteract();

    bool bIsInteractable;
};
```

Listing 1-14 provides the functionality for the AInteractiveObject class, detailing how it behaves during gameplay. Here are the main components:

- **CreateDefaultSubobject**: This function creates an instance of UStaticMeshComponent, which represents the visual component of the interactive object. This component is set as the root, ensuring that it is the primary component for rendering and handling collisions.

- **PrimaryActorTick.bCanEverTick**: This line enables the object to receive updates every frame, allowing it to perform tasks or checks continuously during gameplay.

- **ObjectMesh Initialization**: The ObjectMesh is assigned to the root component, ensuring that it is the main part of the actor and will be visible in the game world.

- **bIsInteractable Initialization**: This boolean flag is set to true by default, indicating that the object is interactable. It allows for dynamic changes to the object's interaction state.

- **Interact Function**: This function defines what happens when the player interacts with the object. It checks if the object is interactable before executing the interaction logic. The specific logic for interactions, such as opening a door or triggering a trap, would be implemented here.

Listing 1-14. InteractiveObject.cpp

```
#include "InteractiveObject.h"
#include "Components/StaticMeshComponent.h"

AInteractiveObject::AInteractiveObject()
{
    PrimaryActorTick.bCanEverTick = true;

    ObjectMesh = CreateDefaultSubobject<UStaticMeshComponent>
    (TEXT("ObjectMesh"));
    RootComponent = ObjectMesh;

    bIsInteractable = true;
}
void AInteractiveObject::OnInteract()
{
    if (bIsInteractable)
    {
        // Implement interaction logic here
    }
}
```

CHAPTER 1   CORE COLLISION MECHANICS

Handling Player Interactions

The PlayerCharacter class is designed to manage player interactions with interactive objects in the game. It includes setting up input bindings, checking for interactable objects, and handling player input for interactions.

In Listing 1-15, the header file outlines the APlayerCharacter class, which extends the ACharacter class. It is responsible for handling player actions, such as interacting with objects in the game world. It consists of the following components:

- **PlayerCharacter Class**: This class represents the player's character in the game. It manages player-specific actions, including interacting with objects and handling input.

- **APlayerCharacter Constructor**: The constructor initializes the player character, enabling it to receive updates every frame by setting PrimaryActorTick.bCanEverTick to true.

- **BeginPlay Function**: This function is called when the game begins or when the player character is spawned. It is used to set up input bindings. Specifically, it binds the "Interact" action to the OnInteract function, allowing the player to perform interactions using a specified input (e.g., a key press).

- **Tick Function**: This function is called every frame, enabling the character to continuously check for interactable objects. It also ensures that the CheckForInteractableObjects function is executed in each frame to detect nearby interactive elements.

CHAPTER 1   CORE COLLISION MECHANICS

- **OnInteract Function**: This function is intended to handle the player's interaction input. When the player triggers the interaction action (e.g., by pressing a key), this function will be called to execute the interaction logic.

- **CheckForInteractableObjects Function**: This function is designed to check for interactive objects in the vicinity of the player. It will be used to determine which objects the player can interact with, potentially involving collision detection or distance checks.

Listing 1-15. PlayerCharacter.h (APlayerCharacter Class)

```
#pragma once

#include "CoreMinimal.h"
#include "GameFramework/Character.h"
#include "PlayerCharacter.generated.h"

UCLASS()
class MYGAME_API APlayerCharacter : public ACharacter
{
    GENERATED_BODY()
public:
    APlayerCharacter();
protected:
    virtual void BeginPlay() override;
    virtual void SetupPlayerInputComponent(class
    UInputComponent* PlayerInputComponent) override;
public:
    virtual void Tick(float DeltaTime) override;
```

```
private:
    UFUNCTION()
    void OnInteract();

    void CheckForInteractableObjects();
};
```

This implementation file provides the actual functionality for the APlayerCharacter class, detailing how it handles player interactions and checks for nearby interactive objects:

- **PrimaryActorTick.bCanEverTick**: This line ensures that the player character is updated every frame, allowing it to perform actions and checks continuously.

- **Timer Setup**: SetTimer(InteractionTimerHandle, this, &APlayerCharacter::CheckForInteractableObjects, 1.0f, true) will call CheckForInteractableObjects every one second. The true parameter makes it a repeating timer.

- **OnInteract Function**: This function is a placeholder for the interaction logic. When the player initiates an interaction, this function will be called to execute any relevant actions (e.g., opening a door, picking up an item).

- **CheckForInteractableObjects Function**: This function is meant to check for nearby interactive objects. The actual implementation will involve logic to detect objects within a certain range or through collision checks, allowing the player to interact with them if they are close enough.

Listing 1-16. PlayerCharacter.cpp (APlayerCharacter Class)

```cpp
#include "PlayerCharacter.h"
#include "InteractiveObject.h"
#include "GameFramework/PlayerController.h"
#include "Components/InputComponent.h"

APlayerCharacter::APlayerCharacter()
{
    PrimaryActorTick.bCanEverTick = true;
}

void APlayerCharacter::BeginPlay()
{
    Super::BeginPlay();

    InputComponent->BindAction("Interact", IE_Pressed, this,
    &APlayerCharacter::OnInteract);
}

void APlayerCharacter::Tick(float DeltaTime)
{
    Super::Tick(DeltaTime);

    CheckForInteractableObjects();
}

void APlayerCharacter::OnInteract()
{
    // Implement interaction logic here
}

void APlayerCharacter::CheckForInteractableObjects()
{
    // Implement logic to check for nearby interactive objects
}
```

```cpp
void APlayerCharacter::SetupPlayerInputComponent(UInput
Component* PlayerInputComponent)
{
    Super::SetupPlayerInputComponent(PlayerInputComponent);

    // Bind the "Interact" action to the OnInteract method

    PlayerInputComponent->BindAction("Interact", IE_Pressed,
    this, &APlayerCharacter::OnInteract);
}
```

Implementing Interaction Responses

In Unreal Engine, interactions can trigger a range of responses, from animations and UI updates to modifications in game state. This section will explore advanced systems for managing complex interactions that respond to multiple conditions and context-sensitive scenarios.

Advanced Interaction Systems

The ComplexInteractionSystem class is designed to manage sophisticated interaction scenarios, handling interactions that are dependent on various conditions and contexts. This class provides a way to set up and manage interactions within the game.

This header file defines the UComplexInteractionSystem class, which extends UObject. It is used for managing complex interactions within the game world.

- **ComplexInteractionSystem Class**: This class is responsible for managing complex interaction systems within the game. It keeps track of interactive objects and their interaction states, facilitating context-sensitive interactions.

- **UComplexInteractionSystem Constructor**: The constructor initializes the interaction system. It sets up the internal data structures to manage interactive objects and their states.

- **AddInteractiveObject Function**: This method allows you to add interactive objects to the interaction system. By maintaining a list of these objects (InteractiveObjects), the system can manage and process interactions for each one.

- **HandleInteraction Function**: This function is designed to handle interactions based on the type of interaction specified. It uses a map (InteractionStates) to manage and check the states associated with different interaction types.

Use Cases

- **Opening a Door**: When the player interacts with a door (triggered by proximity), the interaction could trigger an animation to open the door and play a sound effect.

- **Picking Up an Item**: When the player interacts with an item (e.g., a key or health potion), the item is added to the player's inventory and a message is displayed in the UI to notify the player of the pickup.

- **Starting a Quest**: When the player interacts with a non-playable character (NPC), the interaction could trigger the beginning of a quest, updating the quest log and displaying the relevant dialogue options.

CHAPTER 1   CORE COLLISION MECHANICS

InteractionType Demonstration

- **InteractionType::Activate**: Used when interacting with objects that are meant to be activated, such as buttons, levers, or doors. For example, InteractionType::Activate could trigger the opening of a door or the activation of a trap.
- **InteractionType::PickUp**: Used for items the player can collect or add to their inventory. For example, InteractionType::PickUp could be used when the player collects a health potion or a weapon from the environment.
- **InteractionType::Talk**: Used for dialogues with NPCs. For example, InteractionType::Talk would trigger a dialogue sequence with an NPC, possibly triggering a quest or revealing story elements.

Listing 1-17. ComplexInteractionSystem.h

```
#pragma once

#include "CoreMinimal.h"
#include "UObject/NoExportTypes.h"
#include "ComplexInteractionSystem.generated.h"

UCLASS()
class MYGAME_API UComplexInteractionSystem : public UObject
{
    GENERATED_BODY()

public:
    UComplexInteractionSystem();
```

CHAPTER 1   CORE COLLISION MECHANICS

```
    void AddInteractiveObject(AInteractiveObject*
    InteractiveObject);
    void HandleInteraction(FString InteractionType);
private:
    TArray<AInteractiveObject*> InteractiveObjects;
    TMap<FString, bool> InteractionStates;
};
```

This implementation file provides the functional details for the UComplexInteractionSystem class, defining how it manages interactions and interactive objects:

- **UComplexInteractionSystem Constructor**: The constructor ensures that the interaction system is properly initialized. At this stage, no specific functionality is defined beyond basic setup.

- **AddInteractiveObject Function**: This method adds an AInteractiveObject to the InteractiveObjects array. This allows the interaction system to keep track of all interactive objects in the game, enabling it to process interactions related to these objects.

Listing 1-18. ComplexInteractionSystem.cpp

```
#include "ComplexInteractionSystem.h"
#include "InteractiveObject.h"

UComplexInteractionSystem::UComplexInteractionSystem()
{
}
```

CHAPTER 1   CORE COLLISION MECHANICS

```cpp
void UComplexInteractionSystem::AddInteractiveObject
(AInteractiveObject* InteractiveObject)
{
    InteractiveObjects.Add(InteractiveObject);
}

void UComplexInteractionSystem::HandleInteraction(FString
InteractionType)
{
    // Implement interaction handling logic here
}
```

This section explored the mechanics of interaction detection in game development. From understanding basic interaction concepts to implementing advanced techniques like complex interaction systems, you've gained insights into how interactions create engaging and dynamic gameplay experiences.

In the next section, we will delve into physics reactions. Here, we'll examine how physical interactions and reactions can be simulated within your game, adding realism and depth to gameplay through the application of physical forces and responses.

Physics Reactions

Physics reactions in game development refer to how objects respond to physical interactions and forces within the game world. These mechanics ensure realistic behavior when objects collide, fall, or interact with each other, adhering to the laws of physics.

Imagine a game where a character throws a rock at a stack of crates. Physics reactions handle how the rock impacts the crates, causing them to topple over realistically.

CHAPTER 1   CORE COLLISION MECHANICS

Basic Usage

Basic physics reactions involve setting up objects with physical properties, such as mass, friction, and restitution. These properties determine how objects move and interact when forces are applied. This basic application allows developers to simulate realistic behaviors for game objects, enhancing immersion.

Advanced Techniques

Advanced techniques include simulating complex interactions like ragdoll physics, where characters' bodies react dynamically to collisions, or soft-body physics, where objects deform upon impact.

For example, when a character is knocked down by an explosion, ragdoll physics make the fall look realistic as limbs react naturally to forces.

Practical Applications

Physics reactions are crucial for

- Simulating realistic object behavior and interactions
- Enhancing gameplay with dynamic environmental reactions
- Creating believable character movements and responses
- Implementing destructible environments and objects

CHAPTER 1   CORE COLLISION MECHANICS

Algorithm Overview

Let's visualize the algorithm used for physics reactions:

1. **Initialization:** Set up objects with physical properties within the game scene.
2. **Force Application:** Apply forces to objects based on player actions or environmental factors.
3. **Collision Detection:** Continuously check for collisions between objects.
4. **Physics Calculation:** Calculate the resulting motion and reactions based on physical properties and applied forces.
5. **Visual Update:** Update the visual representation of objects to reflect their physical state.

This algorithm forms the basis for implementing physics reaction mechanics in Unreal Engine.

Reviewing the Code

The PhysicalObject class demonstrates how to define and manage physical objects within a game environment. This involves handling initialization, applying forces, and managing collision responses.

This class represents an object with physical properties and behavior, including physics simulation and collision handling.

- **APhysicalObject Class:** Defines an object with physical properties. It manages initialization and setup related to physics simulation.
- **BeginPlay Function:** Called when the game starts, initializing the physical object.

CHAPTER 1 CORE COLLISION MECHANICS

- **Tick Function**: Updates the object's state every frame.
- **ObjectMesh**: A UStaticMeshComponent representing the visual and physical representation of the object.
- **PhysicsConstraint**: A component used to define and manage physics constraints for the object.

Listing 1-19. PhysicalObject.h

```cpp
#pragma once
class UStaticMeshComponent;

#include "CoreMinimal.h"
#include "GameFramework/Actor.h"
#include "PhysicalObject.generated.h"

UCLASS()
class MYGAME_API APhysicalObject : public AActor
{
    GENERATED_BODY()

public:
    APhysicalObject();

private:
    UPROPERTY(VisibleAnywhere)
    UStaticMeshComponent* ObjectMesh;

    UPROPERTY(VisibleAnywhere)
    UPhysicsConstraintComponent* PhysicsConstraint;
};
```

This setup ensures that the PhysicalObject is fully prepared for interaction with the game world, capable of responding to forces and collisions effectively.

CHAPTER 1 CORE COLLISION MECHANICS

- **APhysicalObject Constructor**: Initializes the object, setting up physics simulation and collision detection
- **SetSimulatePhysics**: Enables physics simulation for the object mesh, allowing it to react to physical forces
- **SetCollisionEnabled**: Enables collision detection and physics responses

Listing 1-20. PhysicalObject.cpp (PhysicalObject Class)

```
#include "PhysicalObject.h"
#include "Components/StaticMeshComponent.h"
#include "PhysicsEngine/PhysicsConstraintComponent.h"

APhysicalObject::APhysicalObject()
{
    PrimaryActorTick.bCanEverTick = true;

    ObjectMesh = CreateDefaultSubobject<UStaticMeshComponent>
    (TEXT("ObjectMesh"));
    RootComponent = ObjectMesh;

    PhysicsConstraint = CreateDefaultSubobject<UPhysics
    ConstraintComponent>(TEXT("PhysicsConstraint"));
    PhysicsConstraint->SetupAttachment(RootComponent);

    ObjectMesh->SetSimulatePhysics(true);
    ObjectMesh->SetCollisionEnabled(ECollisionEnabled::Query
    AndPhysics);
}

void APhysicalObject::BeginPlay()
{
    Super::BeginPlay();
}
```

```
void APhysicalObject::Tick(float DeltaTime)
{
    Super::Tick(DeltaTime);
}
```

Applying Forces

The ApplyForce function allows you to dynamically influence physical objects in the game world by applying forces based on interactions or environmental changes. This function checks if the object is simulating physics before applying the force, ensuring that only appropriate objects respond to such interactions.

Additionally, you can think of the force's direction as being dynamic—often, a force can be applied along the object's forward vector (i.e., its direction) or along its normal. This gives you flexibility in defining how forces affect the object, such as pushing it forward or applying force in response to external stimuli.

This function is crucial for creating responsive and interactive environments, where objects react to player actions or environmental stimuli in a realistic manner.

- **ApplyForce Function**: Applies a specified force to the object if it is simulating physics

Listing 1-21. PhysicalObject.cpp (ApplyForce Function)

```
void APhysicalObject::ApplyForce(FVector Force)
{
    // Ensure that physics simulation is enabled
    if (ObjectMesh && ObjectMesh->IsSimulatingPhysics())
    {
        // Optionally, adjust force based on direction
            (forward, normal, etc.)
```

CHAPTER 1 CORE COLLISION MECHANICS

```
    // Example of applying force based on forward vector:
    FVector ForceDirection = ObjectMesh->GetForward
    Vector();
    // Apply force in the chosen direction, you can scale it
        as needed
    ObjectMesh->AddForce(ForceDirection * Force.Size());
    // Apply scaled force in the direction of the
    forward vector
  }
}
```

Handling Collisions

The NotifyHit function is designed to manage the behavior of objects when they collide with other objects in the game world. By implementing custom logic within this function, you can tailor the reactions to collisions, such as triggering effects or changing the object's state.

This function enables you to define how your objects interact upon impact, contributing to a more immersive and dynamic gameplay experience.

- **NotifyHit Function**: Called when the object collides with another object, allowing for custom collision reaction logic

Listing 1-22. PhysicalObject.cpp (NotifyHit Function)

```
void APhysicalObject::NotifyHit(
    class UPrimitiveComponent* MyComp,
    AActor* Other,
    class UPrimitiveComponent* OtherComp,
```

CHAPTER 1   CORE COLLISION MECHANICS

```cpp
    bool bSelfMoved,
    FVector HitLocation,
    FVector HitNormal,
    FVector NormalImpulse,
    const FHitResult& Hit)
{
    // Check if the object is in a state to react to collisions
    if (bCanReactToCollision)
    {
        // Trigger collision reactions based on custom logic
        // For example, react to specific objects or types of
          collisions

        if (Other && Other->IsA(APlayerCharacter::Static
        Class()))
        {
            // Handle player interaction with the object
            // Example: Apply damage, trigger event, etc.
            HandlePlayerCollision(Other);
        }

        // Optional: Reset the flag after a short delay to
          prevent multiple reactions
        // This can be done using a timer or simple flag
          manipulation
        bCanReactToCollision = false;

        // Example cooldown (5 seconds cooldown, customizable)
        GetWorld()>GetTimerManager().SetTimer(CollisionCooldown
        TimerHandle, this, &APhysicalObject::ResetCollision
        Flag, 5.f, false);
    }
}
```

CHAPTER 1 CORE COLLISION MECHANICS

```cpp
void APhysicalObject::ResetCollisionFlag()
{
    // Enable collision reactions again after cooldown
    bCanReactToCollision = true;
}

void APhysicalObject::HandlePlayerCollision(AActor* OtherActor)
{
    // Implement logic for when the object collides with
        the player
    // This could be damaging the player, triggering a sound
        effect, etc.

    if (OtherActor)
    {
        // Example: Trigger a specific response, like damage

        APlayerCharacter* Player = Cast<APlayerCharacter>
        (OtherActor);
        if (Player)
        {
            // Damage logic or other interaction logic
            Player->ApplyDamage(10);
        }
    }
}
```

Advanced Physics Reactions

In Unreal Engine, ragdoll physics can be directly controlled within the ACharacter class. By setting the character's skeletal mesh to simulate physics and adjusting the collision profile, characters can dynamically

CHAPTER 1 CORE COLLISION MECHANICS

respond to physical impacts. This method enhances realism by allowing the character's body to react naturally to collisions, without needing additional classes or complex setups.

This section explains the components and functionality of the updated player class:

- **SetCollisionProfileName("Ragdoll")**: This sets the collision profile to "Ragdoll", which is typically predefined in Unreal Engine. This profile ensures that the character's mesh behaves like a ragdoll, with appropriate physics and collision handling.

- **SetAllBodiesBelowSimulatePhysics("root", true)**: This enables physics simulation on all bones below the "root" bone in the character's skeleton, simulating full ragdoll behavior.

- **DisableMovement()**: Disables character movement after the ragdoll is activated to prevent player control while the ragdoll physics take over.

Listing 1-23. PlayerCharacter.cpp (Updated)

```
void APlayerCharacter::EnableRagdoll()
{
    // Set the collision profile to 'Ragdoll' for the mesh
    GetMesh()->SetCollisionProfileName("Ragdoll");

    // Enable physics simulation on all bones below the root
    GetMesh()->SetAllBodiesBelowSimulatePhysics("root", true);

    // Optionally, disable character movement once ragdoll is
        activated
    GetCharacterMovement()->DisableMovement();
}
```

CHAPTER 1   CORE COLLISION MECHANICS

This section explored the fundamentals of physics reactions in game development. We covered the essential concepts of physical properties, the application of forces, collision handling, and advanced techniques like ragdoll physics. By integrating these mechanics, you can create a more realistic and immersive game experience.

In the next section, we will delve into **environmental effects**. We will examine how to incorporate dynamic environmental elements to further enhance the gameplay experience and create more engaging and interactive game worlds.

Environmental Effects

Environmental effects in game development refer to the simulation of various natural phenomena and environmental interactions that affect gameplay and enhance the immersive experience. These effects can range from weather conditions and lighting changes to destructible environments and dynamic terrain deformation.

Imagine a game where a character navigates through a forest during a storm. The environmental effects, such as rain, wind, and lightning, create a dynamic and immersive atmosphere.

Basic Usage

Basic environmental effects involve setting up static and dynamic elements that simulate natural phenomena. These elements can include weather conditions like rain and snow, lighting effects like day-night cycles, and interactive environment components like destructible objects.

This basic application allows developers to create realistic and immersive environments that respond to player actions and enhance the overall gameplay experience.

Advanced Techniques

Advanced techniques include the use of particle systems for detailed weather effects, dynamic lighting for real-time changes in the environment, and procedural generation for creating varied and expansive landscapes.

For instance, procedural generation can be applied to create a vast and diverse forest where each playthrough presents a unique exploration experience. Additionally, spawning various visual effects like muzzle flashes, bullet traces, and aura effects can enhance combat and magical encounters, bringing more dynamism and immersion into the game world.

Practical Applications

Environmental effects are crucial for

- Creating immersive and realistic game worlds
- Enhancing gameplay with dynamic and interactive environments
- Simulating natural phenomena and environmental interactions
- Adding depth and complexity to game environments

Algorithm Overview

Let's visualize the algorithm used for environmental effects:

1. **Initialization**: Set up the environment with static and dynamic elements.
2. **Effect Application**: Apply environmental effects based on predefined conditions or player actions.

3. **Interaction Handling**: Implement interactions between the player and environmental elements.

4. **Visual Update**: Continuously update the visual representation of environmental effects.

5. **Dynamic Changes**: Adjust environmental effects in real time based on game events or player actions.

This algorithm forms the basis for implementing environmental effects in Unreal Engine.

Reviewing the Code

The WeatherEffect class is designed to simulate environmental weather effects like rain and snow. This involves initializing the effect, applying it within the game environment, and managing visual updates through the game loop.

Listing 1-24 explains the following components and functionality of the WeatherEffect class:

- **WeatherEffect Class**: Represents an object that simulates weather effects using particle systems
- **UParticleSystemComponent**: Manages the particle system that simulates the weather effect

Listing 1-24. WeatherEffect.h

```
#pragma once

class UParticleSystemComponent;

#include "CoreMinimal.h"
#include "GameFramework/Actor.h"
#include "WeatherEffect.generated.h"
```

```cpp
UCLASS()
class MYGAME_API AWeatherEffect : public AActor
{
    GENERATED_BODY()
public:
    AWeatherEffect();
protected:
    virtual void BeginPlay() override;
public:
    virtual void Tick(float DeltaTime) override;
private:
    // Use EditDefaultsOnly if this property is set in the
       Blueprint and not at runtime
    UPROPERTY(EditDefaultsOnly, BlueprintReadOnly, Category =
    "Weather Effects")

    UParticleSystemComponent* WeatherParticleSystem;};
```

This section explains the implementation details in the WeatherEffect.cpp file:

- **AWeatherEffect Constructor**: Initializes the weather effect, setting up the particle system for simulation
- **BeginPlay Function**: Sets up initial conditions for the weather effect at the start of the game
- **Tick Function**: Continuously updates the weather effect, allowing for dynamic changes throughout the game

CHAPTER 1   CORE COLLISION MECHANICS

Listing 1-25. WeatherEffect.cpp (WeatherEffect Class)

```cpp
#include "WeatherEffect.h"
#include "Particles/ParticleSystemComponent.h"
#include "UObject/ConstructorHelpers.h"

AWeatherEffect::AWeatherEffect()
{
    PrimaryActorTick.bCanEverTick = true;

    // Create a default subobject for the weather
        particle system
    WeatherParticleSystem = CreateDefaultSubobject
    <UParticleSystemComponent>(TEXT("WeatherParticleSystem"));
    RootComponent = WeatherParticleSystem;

    // Binding a static particle system asset (hinted for
        static mesh binding)
    static ConstructorHelpers::FObjectFinder<UParticleSystem>
    ParticleAsset(TEXT("ParticleSystem'/Game/Myfiles/
    P_Explosion.P_Explosion'"));
    if (ParticleAsset.Succeeded())
    {
        WeatherParticleSystem->SetTemplate(ParticleAsset.
        Object);  // setting the particle asset to the
        component
    }
}

void AWeatherEffect::BeginPlay()
{
    Super::BeginPlay();
}
```

```cpp
void AWeatherEffect::Tick(float DeltaTime)
{
    Super::Tick(DeltaTime);
}
```

Applying Environmental Effects

The EffectApplication function is responsible for applying environmental effects based on predefined conditions or player actions.

This section explains the ApplyWeatherEffect function:

- **ApplyWeatherEffect Function**: Sets the appropriate particle system template based on the specified weather effect type (e.g., rain or snow)

Listing 1-26. WeatherEffect.cpp (ApplyWeatherEffect Function)

```cpp
void AWeatherEffect::ApplyWeatherEffect(FString EffectType)
{
    if (EffectType == "Rain")
    {
        // Assigning the rain particle system to the
           WeatherParticleSystem component
        static ConstructorHelpers::FObjectFinder<UParticle
        System> RainParticleAsset(TEXT("ParticleSystem'/Game/
        Myfiles/P_Rain.P_Rain'"));
        if (RainParticleAsset.Succeeded())
        {
            WeatherParticleSystem->SetTemplate(RainParticle
            Asset.Object);
        }
    }
```

```
    else if (EffectType == "Snow")
    {
        // Assigning the snow particle system to the
            WeatherParticleSystem component
        static ConstructorHelpers::FObjectFinder<UParticle
        System> SnowParticleAsset(TEXT("ParticleSystem'/Game/
        Myfiles/P_Snow.P_Snow'"));
        if (SnowParticleAsset.Succeeded())
        {
            WeatherParticleSystem->SetTemplate(SnowParticle
            Asset.Object);
        }
    }
}
```

Handling Interactions

The OnPlayerEnter function is called when the player enters a specific area, triggering the application of a weather effect (e.g., rain). See Listing 1-27.

Listing 1-27. WeatherEffect.cpp (for OnPlayerEnter Function)

```
void AWeatherEffect::OnPlayerEnter(AActor* PlayerActor)
{
    // Implement logic for interacting with the player
    ApplyWeatherEffect("Rain");
}
```

Advanced Environmental Effects

The DynamicLighting class is designed to manage dynamic lighting changes within the game, such as simulating day-night cycles. It includes methods for adjusting lighting in real time based on different conditions.

This section explains the components and functionality of the DynamicLighting header class:

- **DynamicLighting Class**: Manages dynamic lighting changes in the game environment

- **UpdateLighting Function**: Adjusts lighting settings based on the time of day, simulating day-night cycles

Listing 1-28. DynamicLighting.h

```
#pragma once

#include "CoreMinimal.h"
#include "UObject/NoExportTypes.h"
#include "DynamicLighting.generated.h"

UCLASS()
class MYGAME_API UDynamicLighting : public UObject
{
    GENERATED_BODY()
public:
    UDynamicLighting();

    void UpdateLighting(float TimeOfDay);
};
```

CHAPTER 1   CORE COLLISION MECHANICS

This section explains the implementation details in the DynamicLighting.cpp file:

- **DynamicLighting Class**: Manages dynamic lighting changes in the game environment
- **UpdateLighting Function**: Adjusts lighting settings based on the time of day, enabling a realistic day-night cycle within the game

Listing 1-29. DynamicLighting.cpp

```cpp
#include "DynamicLighting.h"
#include "Engine/DirectionalLight.h"

UDynamicLighting::UDynamicLighting()
{
}

void UDynamicLighting::UpdateLighting(float TimeOfDay)
{
    // Implement dynamic lighting changes based on the
       time of day
    if (TimeOfDay < 12.0f)
    {
        // Morning lighting setup
    }
    else
    {
        // Evening lighting setup
    }
}
```

This section explored the fundamentals of environmental effects in game development. From understanding basic weather effects to implementing advanced techniques like dynamic lighting and procedural generation, you've gained insights into how environmental mechanics enhance realism and immersion in games.

In the upcoming section, we will delve into hit detection. This topic covers the essential process of determining interactions between objects, which is crucial for responsive gameplay. We will examine both basic and advanced techniques for hit detection, exploring how they contribute to the accuracy and depth of game mechanics.

Hit Detection

Hit detection in game development refers to the process of determining when and where interactions occur between objects, typically involving combat or collisions. Effective hit detection is crucial for ensuring accurate and responsive gameplay, especially in action-oriented games.

Imagine a scenario where a character swings a sword, and the game needs to determine if the sword hits an enemy. Hit detection ensures that these interactions are detected accurately and in real time.

Basic Usage

Basic hit detection involves checking for collisions or overlaps between objects using bounding volumes such as spheres, boxes, or capsules. This technique is straightforward and efficient, making it suitable for many types of games.

This basic application allows developers to implement core gameplay mechanics, such as detecting hits in combat or interactions with the environment.

Advanced Techniques

Advanced hit detection techniques include raycasting, pixel-perfect collision detection, and skeletal hitboxes. These methods provide more precision and can handle complex scenarios, such as detecting hits on specific body parts or in fast-paced action sequences.

For example, skeletal hitboxes can be used to detect hits on different parts of a character's body, allowing for more nuanced damage calculations.

Additionally, you can make use of custom collision channels to handle specialized interactions. By defining your own collision channels, you can fine-tune what objects or characters can interact with each other, providing more control over hit detection and collision resolution. This is especially useful for creating unique gameplay mechanics, such as different damage types or detecting interactions with non-physical objects like triggers or events.

Practical Applications

Hit detection is essential for

- Implementing combat mechanics
- Detecting collisions and interactions
- Calculating damage and effects
- Enhancing gameplay realism and responsiveness

Algorithm Overview

Let's visualize the algorithm used for hit detection:

1. **Initialization**: Set up the objects involved in hit detection.

2. **Collision Detection**: Continuously check for collisions or overlaps between objects.

3. **Hit Processing**: When a hit is detected, apply appropriate responses (e.g., damage, effects).

4. **Interaction Handling**: Implement additional logic based on the type of hit (e.g., critical hits, environmental interactions).

5. **Visual Update**: Update the visual representation of hits, such as showing damage effects or animations.

This algorithm forms the basis for implementing hit detection in Unreal Engine.

Reviewing the Code

The HitDetection class is designed to manage hit detection logic, including initialization, collision detection, and hit processing. It utilizes a sphere component to detect overlaps and respond accordingly.

Setting Up Hit Detection

The HitDetection class defines an object that manages hit detection within the game. It handles initialization, collision detection, and processing of hit events.

This section explains the components and functionality of the HitDetection class:

- **HitDetection Class**: Represents an object that manages hit detection using a sphere component

CHAPTER 1   CORE COLLISION MECHANICS

- **USphereComponent**: Manages the sphere used for detecting overlaps
- **OnComponentBeginOverlap**: Event triggered when an object overlaps with the sphere component

Listing 1-30. HitDetection.h

```
#pragma once

class USphereComponent;

#include "CoreMinimal.h"
#include "GameFramework/Actor.h"
#include "HitDetection.generated.h"

UCLASS()
class MYGAME_API AHitDetection : public AActor
{
    GENERATED_BODY()

public:
    AHitDetection();

protected:
    virtual void BeginPlay() override;

public:
    virtual void Tick(float DeltaTime) override;

private:
    UPROPERTY(VisibleAnywhere)
    USphereComponent* HitSphere;
```

CHAPTER 1   CORE COLLISION MECHANICS

```
UFUNCTION()
void OnOverlapBegin(class UPrimitiveComponent*
OverlappedComp, class AActor* OtherActor, class
UPrimitiveComponent* OtherComp, int32 OtherBodyIndex, bool
bFromSweep, const FHitResult & SweepResult);
};
```

This section explains the implementation details in the HitDetection.cpp file:

- **AHitDetection Constructor**: Initializes the hit detection component and sets up the sphere for collision detection

- **BeginPlay Function**: Sets up initial conditions for hit detection when the game starts

- **Tick Function**: Continuously updates the hit detection logic every frame

- **OnOverlapBegin Function**: Handles the logic for processing hits when an overlap event is detected by the sphere component

Listing 1-31. HitDetection.cpp

```
#include "HitDetection.h"
#include "Components/SphereComponent.h"

AHitDetection::AHitDetection()
{
    PrimaryActorTick.bCanEverTick = true;

    HitSphere = CreateDefaultSubobject<USphereComponent>(TEXT
    ("HitSphere"));
    RootComponent = HitSphere;
```

CHAPTER 1   CORE COLLISION MECHANICS

```cpp
    HitSphere->OnComponentBeginOverlap.AddDynamic(this,
    &AHitDetection::OnOverlapBegin);
}

void AHitDetection::BeginPlay()
{
    Super::BeginPlay();
}

void AHitDetection::Tick(float DeltaTime)
{
    Super::Tick(DeltaTime);
}

void AHitDetection::OnOverlapBegin(UPrimitiveComponent*
OverlappedComp, AActor* OtherActor, UPrimitiveComponent*
OtherComp, int32 OtherBodyIndex, bool bFromSweep, const
FHitResult & SweepResult)
{
    // If the hit has already been processed, exit the function
    if (bHasHit)
    {
        return;
    }

    // Process the hit
    // Implement hit processing logic here

    // Set the flag to true to prevent reprocessing the
       same hit
    bHasHit = true;
}
```

CHAPTER 1   CORE COLLISION MECHANICS

Implementing Hit Processing

The ProcessHit function is responsible for handling the logic of processing hits and applying effects, such as damage or status effects, to the hit actor.

This section explains the ProcessHit function:

- **ProcessHit Function**: Applies damage or effects to the hit actor when a hit is detected

Listing 1-32. HitDetection.cpp (for the ProcessHit Function)

```cpp
void AHitDetection::ProcessHit(AActor* HitActor)
{
    if (HitActor)
    {
        // Implement logic for applying damage or effects to
           the hit actor
    }
}
```

Advanced Hit Detection Techniques

Raycasting is a technique used for precise hit detection, particularly useful in fast-paced action games where accuracy is critical.

This section explains the PerformRaycast function:

- **PerformRaycast Function**: Performs a raycast from the actor's location forward, detecting any blocking hits along the way.

- **LineTraceSingleByChannel**: Executes the raycast and checks for collisions along the line, allowing precise hit detection.

CHAPTER 1   CORE COLLISION MECHANICS

- **Custom Collision Channels**: Replace ECC_ GameTraceChannel1 with the custom collision channel you defined in your project settings. Custom collision channels provide precise control over how raycasts interact with objects. If a trace hits an object with a channel set to Ignore, it bypasses the object without detecting a hit, ideal for background elements or non-interactive objects. With an Overlap response, the trace detects the object but doesn't block or collide with it, perfect for triggers or non-blocking interactions. A Block response ensures the trace stops when it hits an object in the custom channel, useful for barriers or walls. In the Details Panel of an Actor's component, you can configure the collision presets to your custom channel and specify whether it should Block, Overlap, or Ignore for specific channels, allowing you to fine-tune how different objects interact in the game world. For instance, you could set a character's weapons to block certain objects while ignoring others, ensuring dynamic and customized interactions.

Listing 1-33. HitDetection.cpp (for the PerformRaycast Function)

```
void AHitDetection::PerformRaycast()
{
    FVector Start = GetActorLocation();
    FVector ForwardVector = GetActorForwardVector();
    FVector End = ((ForwardVector * 1000.0f) + Start);
    FHitResult HitResult;

    FCollisionQueryParams CollisionParams;
    CollisionParams.AddIgnoredActor(this);
```

CHAPTER 1   CORE COLLISION MECHANICS

```
    // Use a custom collision channel for more precise hit
        detection
    // Replace ECC_MyCustomChannel with your actual custom
        collision channel
    GetWorld()->LineTraceSingleByChannel(HitResult, Start, End,
    ECC_MyCustomChannel, CollisionParams);
if (HitResult.bBlockingHit)
{
    // Process the hit - Implement your logic for interaction
        with the object
}
    if (HitResult.bBlockingHit)
    {
        // Implement logic for processing the raycast hit
    }
}
```

This section explored the fundamentals of hit detection in game development. From understanding basic collision detection to implementing advanced techniques like raycasting, you've gained insights into how hit detection drives accurate and responsive interactions within games.

In the next section, we will explore item collection, a fundamental game mechanic that enhances player engagement through the collection of various items. We will examine how item collection mechanics can be implemented and how they contribute to a rewarding gameplay experience.

71

CHAPTER 1   CORE COLLISION MECHANICS

Item Collection

Item collection is a fundamental mechanic in many games, enabling players to interact with the game world by picking up items. These items can range from simple collectibles like coins and health packs to more complex objects like weapons and power-ups. Effective item collection mechanics enhance player engagement and reward exploration.

Imagine you're designing a treasure hunt game. Players need to collect items scattered across the game world to progress or gain advantages. Item collection mechanics ensure that these interactions are smooth and rewarding.

Basic Usage

Basic item collection involves detecting when the player character collides with or interacts with an item. Upon collision, the item is collected, and any associated effects (e.g., increasing the player's score or health) are applied.

This basic application allows developers to implement core gameplay mechanics, such as rewarding players for exploration and interaction.

Advanced Techniques

Advanced item collection techniques include inventory systems, item spawning, and conditional collection. These methods provide more depth and complexity, allowing for sophisticated gameplay scenarios.

For example, an inventory system allows players to manage and use collected items strategically, while item spawning can dynamically place items based on game conditions.

Practical Applications

Item collection is essential for

- Implementing collectibles and rewards
- Enhancing player progression and engagement
- Facilitating inventory management and item usage
- Creating dynamic and interactive game environments

Algorithm Overview

Let's visualize the algorithm used for item collection:

1. **Initialization**: Set up the player and items within the game scene.

2. **Collision Detection**: Continuously check for collisions or interactions between the player and items.

3. **Item Collection**: When a collision is detected, collect the item and apply any associated effects (e.g., update inventory, increase score).

4. **Visual and Audio Feedback**: Provide feedback to the player through animations, sounds, or UI updates.

5. **Conditional Collection**: Implement additional logic for conditional collection, such as requiring a specific item or condition to collect another item.

This algorithm forms the basis for implementing item collection mechanics in Unreal Engine.

CHAPTER 1 CORE COLLISION MECHANICS

Reviewing the Code

The CollectibleItem class is designed to represent a collectible item within the game. This includes handling its initialization, managing its visual representation, and detecting collisions with players or other game elements for item collection.

This section provides an overview of the CollectibleItem class and its key components.

- **CollectibleItem Class**: Represents a collectible item using a sphere component for collision detection
- **BeginPlay Function**: Initializes the item when the game starts
- **Tick Function**: Updates the item's state every frame
- **CollisionSphere**: A USphereComponent used to detect overlapping events with other actors, such as the player character
- **OnOverlapBegin Function**: A function that is triggered when another object, like the player, overlaps with the collision sphere, signaling the collection of the item

Listing 1-34. CollectibleItem.h

```
Class USphereComponent;

#include "CoreMinimal.h"
#include "GameFramework/Actor.h"
#include "CollectibleItem.generated.h"

UCLASS()
class MYGAME_API ACollectibleItem : public AActor
{
    GENERATED_BODY()
```

```cpp
public:
    ACollectibleItem();

protected:
    virtual void BeginPlay() override;

public:
    virtual void Tick(float DeltaTime) override;

private:
    UPROPERTY(VisibleAnywhere)
    USphereComponent* CollisionSphere;

    UFUNCTION()
    void OnOverlapBegin(class UPrimitiveComponent* 
    OverlappedComp, class AActor* OtherActor, class 
    UPrimitiveComponent* OtherComp, int32 OtherBodyIndex, bool 
    bFromSweep, const FHitResult & SweepResult);
};

UPROPERTY(EditDefaultsOnly, BlueprintReadOnly, Category = 
"Effects")
USoundBase* CollectSound;   // To assign sound effects from 
                                Blueprint or Editor

UPROPERTY(EditDefaultsOnly, BlueprintReadOnly, Category = 
"Effects")
UParticleSystem* CollectEffect;   // To assign particle effects 
                                     from Blueprint or Editor
```

CHAPTER 1   CORE COLLISION MECHANICS

This section explains the core functions and components used to implement the collectible item functionality.

- **ACollectibleItem Constructor**: Initializes the collectible item, creating a sphere component for collision detection and binding the overlap event to the OnOverlapBegin function.
- **CollisionSphere Initialization**: The USphereComponent is created and assigned as the root component, used to detect overlaps with other actors.
- **OnOverlapBegin Function**: Triggered when another actor overlaps the sphere, indicating the item has been collected, followed by the destruction of the item.

Listing 1-35. CollectibleItem.cpp

```
#include "CollectibleItem.h"
#include "Components/SphereComponent.h"
#include "GameFramework/Actor.h"
#include "Kismet/GameplayStatics.h"

ACollectibleItem::ACollectibleItem()
{
    PrimaryActorTick.bCanEverTick = true;

    CollisionSphere = CreateDefaultSubobject<USphereComponent>
    (TEXT("CollisionSphere"));
    RootComponent = CollisionSphere;

    CollisionSphere->OnComponentBeginOverlap.AddDynamic(this,
    &ACollectibleItem::OnOverlapBegin);
}
```

```cpp
void ACollectibleItem::BeginPlay()
{
    Super::BeginPlay();
}

void ACollectibleItem::Tick(float DeltaTime)
{
    Super::Tick(DeltaTime);
}
// In CollectibleItem.h
private:
    static int32 CollectedItemCount; // Static counter to track
                                    total collected items
// In CollectibleItem.cpp
int32 ACollectibleItem::CollectedItemCount = 0; // Initialize
static variable

void ACollectibleItem::OnOverlapBegin(UPrimitiveCompone
nt* OverlappedComp, AActor* OtherActor, UPrimitiveComponent*
OtherComp, int32 OtherBodyIndex,
bool bFromSweep, const FHitResult & SweepResult)
{
    if (OtherActor && (OtherActor != this))
    {
        // Increase the count when an item is collected
        CollectedItemCount++;

        // Optionally, print the count for debugging
        UE_LOG(LogTemp, Log, TEXT("Items Collected: %d"),
        CollectedItemCount);
```

CHAPTER 1 CORE COLLISION MECHANICS

```
        // Implement item collection logic here
        Destroy();
    }
}
```

Implementing Item Effects

The ApplyItemEffect function is responsible for applying the specific effects of a collectible item (such as increasing the player's score or health) when the item is collected. It also plays an audio cue to provide feedback to the player.

This section explains the ApplyItemEffect function and how it affects the player's interaction with the collectible item:

- **Sound Binding**: ConstructorHelpers::FObjectFinder<U SoundBase> is used to load the CollectSound from the specified location.

- **Particle Effect Binding**: Similar to the sound, Construc torHelpers::FObjectFinder<UParticleSystem> is used to load a particle effect, which is spawned when the item is collected.

- **Sound and Particle Effect Execution**: In the OnOverlapBegin method, if the sound and particle assets are valid, they are played/spawned when the item is collected.

Listing 1-36. ApplyItemEffect Function in CollectibleItem.cpp

```
ACollectibleItem::ACollectibleItem()
{
    PrimaryActorTick.bCanEverTick = true;

    // Initialize collision component
```

CHAPTER 1   CORE COLLISION MECHANICS

```cpp
    CollisionSphere = CreateDefaultSubobject<USphereComponent>(
    TEXT("CollisionSphere"));

    RootComponent = CollisionSphere;

    CollisionSphere->OnComponentBeginOverlap.AddDynamic(this,
    &ACollectibleItem::OnOverlapBegin);

    // Bind sound and particle system assets through
        ConstructorHelpers
    static ConstructorHelpers::FObjectFinder<USoundBase>
    SoundAsset(TEXT("SoundWave'/Game/Audio/CollectSound.
    CollectSound'"));
    if (SoundAsset.Succeeded())
    {
        CollectSound = SoundAsset.Object;
    }

    static ConstructorHelpers::FObjectFinder<UParticleSystem>
    ParticleAsset(TEXT("ParticleSystem'/Game/Particles/
    CollectEffect.CollectEffect'"));
    if (ParticleAsset.Succeeded())
    {
        CollectParticleEffect = ParticleAsset.Object;
    }
}

void ACollectibleItem::OnOverlapBegin(UPrimitiveCompone
nt* OverlappedComp, AActor* OtherActor, UPrimitiveComponent*
OtherComp, int32 OtherBodyIndex,
                                    bool bFromSweep, const
                                    FHitResult & SweepResult)
{
    if (OtherActor && (OtherActor != this))
```

```cpp
    {
        // Increase the count when an item is collected
        CollectedItemCount++;

        // Optionally, print the count for debugging
        UE_LOG(LogTemp, Log, TEXT("Items Collected: %d"),
        CollectedItemCount);

        // Play sound effect on collection
        if (CollectSound)
        {
            UGameplayStatics::PlaySoundAtLocation(this,
            CollectSound, GetActorLocation());
        }

        // Play particle effect on collection
        if (CollectParticleEffect)
        {
            UGameplayStatics::SpawnEmitterAtLocation(GetWor
            ld(), CollectParticleEffect, GetActorLocation());
        }

        // Implement item collection logic here
        Destroy();
    }
}
```

Advanced Item Collection Techniques

An advanced item collection system involves the introduction of an inventory system to track, store, and manage items collected by the player. This allows the player to collect multiple items and use them at appropriate times, rather than items being immediately consumed or applied.

CHAPTER 1   CORE COLLISION MECHANICS

The implementation of an inventory system includes key components for managing item collection and usage effectively:

- **InventoryComponent Class**: Manages the inventory system, storing collected items and their usage

- **AddItem Function**: Adds an item to the inventory and applies its effects or updates the UI

Listing 1-37. InventoryComponent.h

```
#pragma once

class ACollectibleItem;

#include "CoreMinimal.h"
#include "Components/ActorComponent.h"
#include "InventoryComponent.generated.h"

UCLASS(ClassGroup=(Custom), meta=(BlueprintSpawnableComponent))
class MYGAME_API UInventoryComponent : public UActorComponent
{
    GENERATED_BODY()
public:
    UInventoryComponent();

protected:
    virtual void BeginPlay() override;

public:
    void AddItem(ACollectibleItem* Item);

private:
    UPROPERTY(VisibleAnywhere)
    TArray<ACollectibleItem*> Items;
};
```

CHAPTER 1　CORE COLLISION MECHANICS

Listing 1-38. InventoryComponent.cpp

```cpp
#include "InventoryComponent.h"
#include "CollectibleItem.h"

UInventoryComponent::UInventoryComponent()
{
    PrimaryComponentTick.bCanEverTick = false;
}

void UInventoryComponent::BeginPlay()
{
    Super::BeginPlay();
}

void UInventoryComponent::AddItem(ACollectibleItem* Item)
{
    if (Item)
    {
        Items.Add(Item);
        Item->Destroy();
        // Implement logic to update inventory UI or apply
           item effects
    }
}
```

　　This section explored the fundamentals of item collection mechanics in game development. From understanding basic collision detection to implementing advanced techniques like inventory systems, you've gained insights into how item collection enhances gameplay and rewards player interaction.

Summary

As we conclude our exploration of core collision mechanics, we've uncovered the essential building blocks that shape virtual interactions. From blocking movement to triggering events and detecting interactions, these mechanics serve as the invisible framework that governs how objects and characters navigate digital worlds.

Collisions are more than mere technicalities—they define the rules of engagement, setting the stage for meaningful interactions and immersive experiences. Whether it's a door that refuses to open, a platform that carries a player forward, or a simple item pickup that sparks progress, every collision contributes to the flow of gameplay.

In the next chapter, we will dive into advanced collision mechanics, where we move beyond detection and into dynamic reactions. From damage calculation and knockback effects to terrain deformation and visual impact, we'll explore how collisions shape action-packed encounters and bring worlds to life with deeper realism and interactivity.

CHAPTER 2

Advanced Collision Mechanics

Collisions are more than just detecting when two objects touch—they can drive dynamic interactions that shape gameplay. Advanced collision mechanics allow for richer, more immersive experiences by introducing physics-based responses, environmental effects, and combat interactions. By extending collision mechanics beyond simple object detection, we can create gameplay that feels more natural and engaging.

This chapter explores collision mechanics in depth, starting with the basics before diving into more advanced implementations, learning how they enhance interactivity and realism. By the end, you will be able to implement physics-driven collision responses that make gameplay feel more immersive. You will learn how to use collisions for dynamic combat, movement, and environmental effects, creating a richer gaming experience. With a strong understanding of these mechanics, you will be able to design and develop games where collisions are not just about object detection but are integral to storytelling, strategy, and player engagement. Mastering collision mechanics will set you up to create more interactive and lifelike games.

While basic collisions determine when two objects interact, advanced techniques expand their impact. Physics-based reactions play a significant role in making objects behave realistically upon impact, whether bouncing off surfaces or crumbling into fragments. Combat interactions rely

CHAPTER 2   ADVANCED COLLISION MECHANICS

on collision mechanics to implement features like knockback effects, projectile deflection, and area-of-effect damage, ensuring that battles feel dynamic and impactful. Environmental effects further enhance gameplay by altering terrain, breaking objects, and triggering visual effects such as particle explosions or lighting changes. By mastering these mechanics, we can create deeper, more interactive gameplay experiences.

Damage calculation plays a crucial role in combat mechanics, determining how much damage a character or object takes upon impact. Projectile deflection introduces an added layer of strategy, allowing objects to change direction upon hitting surfaces. Platforming mechanics also heavily rely on collisions to enable wall jumps, ledge grabs, and movement adjustments that enhance player mobility. Area-of-effect (AoE) damage allows certain collisions—like explosions or magical attacks—to affect a radius rather than just a single object. Character knockback and pushback mechanics make combat and movement more dynamic by pushing entities away based on impact force. Object destruction enables realistic environmental breakage, where objects shatter or deform upon collision. Object pickup mechanics allow players to collect or interact with items, while character respawn handling resets player positions when they fall or die. Terrain deformation modifies the game world dynamically, such as craters forming upon heavy impacts. Object scaling and rotation upon collision create visual depth, making objects react differently based on the collision force and angle. Finally, particle effects on collision add realism by triggering visual feedback like sparks, dust, or fire when objects interact.

Damage Calculation

Damage calculation is a crucial mechanic in games, determining how much damage a player or enemy takes from attacks or environmental hazards. This mechanic influences gameplay balance, player strategy, and overall game difficulty. Effective damage calculation systems ensure that the game remains challenging and fair.

Imagine you're designing a combat game. When a player attacks an enemy, you need to calculate how much damage the enemy takes based on various factors like the player's attack power, the enemy's defense, and any active buffs or debuffs. Damage calculation mechanics handle these computations, impacting the game's dynamics and player experience.

Basic Usage

Basic damage calculation involves determining the amount of damage dealt to a target based on the attack's power and the target's defense. This calculation typically includes basic arithmetic operations and may incorporate random elements to add variability.

This basic application allows developers to implement core combat mechanics, ensuring that attacks and defenses interact logically and predictably.

Advanced Techniques

Advanced damage calculation techniques include incorporating critical hits, damage types (e.g., physical, magical), resistances, and status effects. These methods provide more depth and complexity, allowing for sophisticated combat scenarios.

For example, a critical hit might deal double damage, while certain enemies might have resistances or vulnerabilities to specific damage types, influencing the player's choice of attacks.

Practical Applications

Damage calculation is essential for

- Implementing balanced combat systems
- Influencing player strategy and decision-making

- Enhancing game difficulty and progression
- Creating dynamic and varied combat encounters

Algorithm Overview

Let's visualize the algorithm used for damage calculation:

1. **Initialization**: Set up the attacker and target with their respective stats (e.g., attack power, defense).
2. **Base Damage Calculation**: Calculate the base damage using the attacker's power and target's defense.
3. **Apply Modifiers**: Incorporate any modifiers (e.g., critical hits, damage type multipliers, status effects).
4. **Random Variance**: Optionally add a random element to vary the damage slightly.
5. **Final Damage Application**: Apply the calculated damage to the target, updating their health or status.

This algorithm forms the basis for implementing damage calculation mechanics in Unreal Engine.

Reviewing the Code

This section defines a struct that encapsulates the character's statistical data, such as health, attack power, and defense. This struct plays a vital role in the gameplay mechanics by managing the initialization and modification of these stats, ensuring that the character's attributes are easily accessible and modifiable throughout the game.

CHAPTER 2 ADVANCED COLLISION MECHANICS

Listings 2-1 and 2-2 set up a struct which is crucial for managing character interactions and combat mechanics, allowing for easy adjustments based on gameplay events:

- **FCharacterStats Struct**: Holds character stats like health, attack power, and defense
- **EditAnywhere and BlueprintReadWrite**: Allow the stats to be edited in the Unreal Engine editor and accessed in Blueprints

Listing 2-1. CharacterStats.h

```cpp
#pragma once

#include "CoreMinimal.h"
#include "CharacterStats.generated.h"

USTRUCT(BlueprintType)
struct MYGAME_API FCharacterStats
{
    GENERATED_BODY()
public:
    UPROPERTY(EditAnywhere, BlueprintReadWrite, Category = "Stats")
    float Health;

    UPROPERTY(EditAnywhere, BlueprintReadWrite, Category = "Stats")
    float AttackPower;

    UPROPERTY(EditAnywhere, BlueprintReadWrite, Category = "Stats")
    float Defense;
};
```

CHAPTER 2　ADVANCED COLLISION MECHANICS

Listing 2-2. CharacterStats.cpp

```
#include "CharacterStats.h"

// This file is intentionally left blank as FCharacterStats is
a data-only struct.
```

Implementing Damage Calculation

This section defines a function responsible for calculating and applying damage during combat interactions between characters. It takes into account both the attacker's and target's stats to determine the final damage dealt.

Listings 2-3 and 2-4 implement the damage calculation, which is critical for ensuring balanced combat mechanics and enhancing the gameplay experience by accurately reflecting the effects of character interactions.

- **CalculateDamage Function**: Calculates the damage based on the attacker's power and the target's defense, applying a random variance to add unpredictability

- **ApplyDamage Function**: Applies the calculated damage to the target, updating their health

Listing 2-3. DamageCalculation.h

```
#pragma once

#include "CoreMinimal.h"
#include "CharacterStats.h"
#include "DamageCalculation.generated.h"

UCLASS()
class MYGAME_API UDamageCalculation : public UObject
```

```cpp
{
    GENERATED_BODY()
public:
    UFUNCTION(BlueprintCallable, Category = "Combat")
    static float CalculateDamage(const FCharacterStats&
    AttackerStats, const FCharacterStats& TargetStats);

    UFUNCTION(BlueprintCallable, Category = "Combat")
    static void ApplyDamage(FCharacterStats& TargetStats, float
    Damage);
};
```

Listing 2-4. DamageCalculation.cpp

```cpp
#include "DamageCalculation.h"
#include "CharacterStats.h"

float UDamageCalculation::CalculateDamage(const
FCharacterStats& AttackerStats, const FCharacterStats&
TargetStats)
{
    // Base damage calculation
    float BaseDamage = AttackerStats.AttackPower - TargetStats.
    Defense;
    if (BaseDamage < 0)
    {
        BaseDamage = 0;
    }

    // Apply random variance (optional)
    float DamageVariance = FMath::RandRange(0.9f, 1.1f);
    float FinalDamage = BaseDamage * DamageVariance;
```

CHAPTER 2 ADVANCED COLLISION MECHANICS

```
    return FinalDamage;
}
void UDamageCalculation::ApplyDamage(FCharacterStats&
TargetStats, float Damage)
{
    TargetStats.Health -= Damage;
    if (TargetStats.Health < 0)
    {
        TargetStats.Health = 0;
    }
}
```

Advanced Damage Calculation Techniques

This section modifies the existing damage calculation to include a chance for critical hits, which deal extra damage. Critical hits add an element of excitement and unpredictability to combat scenarios. Listing 2-5 integrates critical hits, making the combat system more dynamic and rewarding, encouraging players to build characters that maximize their chances for impactful attacks.

- **Critical Hit Chance**: Computes the base damage by subtracting the target's defense from the attacker's attack power. It then applies a critical hit multiplier based on the hit bone (e.g., headshots deal 2.5x damage, chest hits deal 1.5x, and limb shots reduce damage to 75%). Finally, a random variance is applied to introduce slight unpredictability in the final damage output.

CHAPTER 2　ADVANCED COLLISION MECHANICS

Listing 2-5. DamageCalculation.cpp (Critical Hit Chance)

```cpp
float UDamageCalculation::CalculateDamage(const
FCharacterStats& AttackerStats, const FCharacterStats&
TargetStats, EHitBoneType HitBone)
{
    // Base damage calculation
    float BaseDamage = AttackerStats.AttackPower - TargetStats.Defense;
    if (BaseDamage < 0)
    {
        BaseDamage = 0;
    }

    // Critical hit multiplier based on hit bone
    float CriticalMultiplier = 1.0f;

    switch (HitBone)
    {
        case EHitBoneType::Head:
            CriticalMultiplier = 2.5f; // Headshots deal 2.5x damage
            break;
        case EHitBoneType::Chest:
            CriticalMultiplier = 1.5f; // Chest hits deal 1.5x damage
            break;
        case EHitBoneType::Limb:
            CriticalMultiplier = 0.75f; // Limb shots deal 75% damage
            break;
        default:
```

```
                CriticalMultiplier = 1.0f; // Normal damage for
                other areas
                break;
    }
    // Apply the multiplier
    BaseDamage *= CriticalMultiplier;

    // Apply random variance (optional)
    float DamageVariance = FMath::RandRange(0.9f, 1.1f);
    float FinalDamage = BaseDamage * DamageVariance;

    return FinalDamage;
}
```

This section explored the fundamentals of damage calculation mechanics in game development. From understanding basic damage calculations to implementing advanced techniques like critical hits and random variance, you've gained insights into how damage calculation influences combat balance and player experience.

Projectile Deflection

Projectile deflection is a dynamic mechanic where projectiles (like arrows, bullets, or spells) can change direction upon colliding with objects or characters. This mechanic adds depth and realism to gameplay, influencing strategy and interaction in combat scenarios.

Imagine you're designing a game where a player can deflect enemy projectiles using a shield. The projectiles' paths change, potentially hitting other enemies or environmental objects. This mechanic enhances the player's defensive capabilities and adds an additional layer of strategy to combat.

Basic Usage

Basic projectile deflection involves detecting collisions between projectiles and deflecting surfaces, then calculating the new trajectory based on the angle of impact and the properties of the deflecting surface.

This basic application allows developers to implement core projectile mechanics, ensuring that projectiles interact realistically with the environment and characters.

Advanced Techniques

Advanced projectile deflection techniques include incorporating factors like projectile speed, surface material properties, and deflection angles. These methods provide more depth and realism, allowing for sophisticated projectile interactions.

For example, different surfaces may deflect projectiles at different angles or with varying degrees of force. Additionally, some projectiles may be designed to pierce through certain surfaces but deflect off others.

Practical Applications

Projectile deflection is essential for

- Enhancing defensive gameplay mechanics
- Creating dynamic and interactive combat scenarios
- Adding strategic elements to player actions
- Increasing the realism and immersion of the game environment

CHAPTER 2   ADVANCED COLLISION MECHANICS

Algorithm Overview

Let's visualize the algorithm used for projectile deflection:

1. **Initialization**: Set up the projectile and deflecting surfaces within the game scene.

2. **Collision Detection**: Continuously check for collisions between the projectile and deflecting surfaces.

3. **Deflection Calculation**: When a collision is detected, calculate the new trajectory based on the angle of impact and surface properties.

4. **Apply Deflection**: Update the projectile's trajectory and velocity accordingly.

5. **Final Impact Handling**: Determine the final impact effects based on the new trajectory (e.g., damage to enemies or objects).

This algorithm forms the basis for implementing projectile deflection mechanics in Unreal Engine.

Reviewing the Code

This class defines the properties and behavior of a projectile in the game. It manages the initialization, movement, and collision detection necessary for projectiles to interact with the game world effectively.

Listings 2-6 and 2-7 detail the implementation and functionality of the projectile system within the game, focusing on how projectiles behave and interact with the environment.

CHAPTER 2   ADVANCED COLLISION MECHANICS

- **Projectile Class**: Defines the properties and behavior of a projectile, including collision detection
- **OnHit Function**: Handles collision events and triggers deflection logic when the projectile hits a surface

Listing 2-6. Projectile.h

```
#pragma once

#include "CoreMinimal.h"
#include "GameFramework/Actor.h"
#include "Projectile.generated.h"

UCLASS()
class MYGAME_API AProjectile : public AActor
{
    GENERATED_BODY()

public:
    AProjectile();

protected:
    virtual void BeginPlay() override;

public:
    virtual void Tick(float DeltaTime) override;

private:
    UPROPERTY(VisibleAnywhere)
    UStaticMeshComponent* ProjectileMesh;

    UPROPERTY(VisibleAnywhere)
    class UProjectileMovementComponent* ProjectileMovement;
```

CHAPTER 2 ADVANCED COLLISION MECHANICS

```
    UFUNCTION()
    void OnHit(UPrimitiveComponent* HitComponent, AActor*
    OtherActor, UPrimitiveComponent* OtherComponent, FVector
    NormalImpulse, const FHitResult& Hit);
};
```

Listing 2-7. Projectile.cpp

```
#include "Projectile.h"
#include "GameFramework/ProjectileMovementComponent.h"
#include "Components/StaticMeshComponent.h"

AProjectile::AProjectile()
{
    PrimaryActorTick.bCanEverTick = true;

    ProjectileMesh = CreateDefaultSubobject
    <UStaticMeshComponent>(TEXT("ProjectileMesh"));
    RootComponent = ProjectileMesh;

    ProjectileMovement = CreateDefaultSubobject<UProjectile
    MovementComponent>(TEXT("ProjectileMovement"));
    ProjectileMovement->bShouldBounce = true;

    ProjectileMesh->OnComponentHit.AddDynamic(this,
    &AProjectile::OnHit);
}

void AProjectile::BeginPlay()
{
    Super::BeginPlay();
}
```

CHAPTER 2 ADVANCED COLLISION MECHANICS

```
void AProjectile::Tick(float DeltaTime)
{
    Super::Tick(DeltaTime);
}

void AProjectile::OnHit(UPrimitiveComponent* HitComponent,
AActor* OtherActor, UPrimitiveComponent* OtherComponent,
FVector NormalImpulse, const FHitResult& Hit)
{
    // Implement deflection logic here
}
```

Implementing Deflection Logic

In the OnHit function, the deflection logic calculates the new trajectory of the projectile after it collides with a surface. This involves determining the impact normal and reflecting the projectile's incoming velocity to establish a new direction.

Listing 2-8 implements this logic, enhancing the gameplay experience by providing more dynamic projectile interactions within the game world.

- **Impact Normal**: The normal vector of the surface at the point of impact
- **Incoming Velocity**: The velocity of the projectile before impact
- **GetReflectionVector**: Calculates the deflection direction based on the incoming velocity and impact normal
- **Velocity Update**: Updates the projectile's velocity to reflect the new trajectory

CHAPTER 2　ADVANCED COLLISION MECHANICS

Listing 2-8. Projectile.cpp (Add This for the Deflection Function)

```cpp
void AProjectile::OnHit(UPrimitiveComponent* HitComponent,
AActor* OtherActor, UPrimitiveComponent* OtherComponent,
FVector NormalImpulse, const FHitResult& Hit)
{
    FVector ImpactNormal = Hit.Normal;
    FVector IncomingVelocity = ProjectileMovement->Velocity;

    // Calculate deflection direction
    FVector DeflectionDirection = FMath::GetReflectionVector
    (IncomingVelocity, ImpactNormal);
    ProjectileMovement->Velocity = DeflectionDirection *
    ProjectileMovement->InitialSpeed;
}
```

Advanced Projectile Deflection Techniques

To enhance the deflection logic in your projectile class, you can modify the existing code to take into account various surface properties like material type and elasticity. This allows for more realistic interactions when the projectile hits different surfaces.

Listing 2-9 implements this functionality, leading to more realistic interactions between projectiles and the game environment, allowing players to adapt their strategies based on how different surfaces respond to projectiles.

- **OnHit Function**: Handles projectile collision with different surfaces.

- **Penetrable Surface Check**: Uses ComponentHasTag ("Penetrable") to determine if the projectile should pass through an object. If penetrable, the velocity is reduced to simulate penetration.

CHAPTER 2 ADVANCED COLLISION MECHANICS

- **Deflection Calculation**: If the surface is not penetrable, the projectile's direction is reflected using the impact normal, and elasticity is applied to simulate realistic deflection.

Listing 2-9. Projectile.cpp (Updated Code for Deflection Logic)

```cpp
void AProjectile::OnHit(UPrimitiveComponent* HitComponent,
AActor* OtherActor, UPrimitiveComponent* OtherComponent,
FVector NormalImpulse, const FHitResult& Hit)
{
    FVector ImpactNormal = Hit.Normal;
    FVector IncomingVelocity = ProjectileMovement->Velocity;

    // Check if the surface is penetrable
    bool bIsPenetrable = OtherComponent->ComponentHasTag
    ("Penetrable");

    if (bIsPenetrable)
    {
        // Reduce velocity and allow penetration through
           the surface
        ProjectileMovement->Velocity = IncomingVelocity * 0.5f;
        // Example penetration speed reduction
    }
    else
    {
        // Calculate deflection direction
        FVector DeflectionDirection = FMath::GetReflection
        Vector(IncomingVelocity, ImpactNormal);

        // Apply surface properties (e.g., elasticity)
```

```
        float SurfaceElasticity = 0.8f; // Example elasticity
                                                        value
        ProjectileMovement->Velocity = DeflectionDirection *
        ProjectileMovement->InitialSpeed * SurfaceElasticity;
    }
}
```

This section explored the fundamentals of projectile deflection mechanics in game development. From understanding basic deflection calculations to implementing advanced techniques like surface properties and elasticity, you've gained insights into how projectile deflection influences gameplay dynamics and player strategy.

Platforming Mechanic

Platforming mechanics are fundamental in many games, especially in genres like platformers and action-adventure games. These mechanics involve the player character navigating through levels by jumping between platforms, avoiding obstacles, and solving puzzles.

Imagine you're developing a classic platformer game where the player controls a character who can jump, climb, and interact with various platforms. The platforming mechanics determine how the character moves within the game environment, offering challenges and opportunities for exploration.

Basic Usage

Basic platforming mechanics include

- **Jumping**: Allows the player character to leap from one platform to another

CHAPTER 2   ADVANCED COLLISION MECHANICS

- **Climbing**: Enables the character to ascend or descend on vertical surfaces or ladders
- **Gravity and Physics**: Governs how the character interacts with the environment, including falling, jumping heights, and collisions with platforms

These mechanics form the foundation for creating levels that require precise timing, spatial awareness, and skillful maneuvering from players.

Advanced Techniques

Advanced platforming techniques expand on the basic mechanics, including

- **Double Jump**: Allows the character to perform an additional jump in mid-air, increasing mobility and reaching distant platforms
- **Wall Jump**: Enables the character to bounce off walls to reach higher or distant areas
- **Platform Interactions**: Introduces moving platforms, destructible platforms, and platforms affected by environmental factors like wind or gravity

These techniques add complexity and depth to platforming challenges, encouraging players to master advanced movement techniques and explore more dynamic environments.

Practical Applications

Platforming mechanics are essential for

- **Level Design**: Creating challenging and engaging platforming levels

CHAPTER 2   ADVANCED COLLISION MECHANICS

- **Puzzle-Solving**: Incorporating platform-based puzzles that require players to navigate through obstacles and traps
- **Exploration**: Encouraging exploration of hidden areas and secrets within the game world
- **Skill Development**: Allowing players to improve their reflexes, timing, and spatial awareness through platforming challenges

Algorithm Overview

Let's outline the algorithm used for implementing basic platforming mechanics:

1. **Initialization**: Set up the player character and platforms within the game scene.
2. **Input Handling**: Detect player input for movement, jumping, and interacting with platforms.
3. **Gravity and Physics**: Apply gravity to the player character, affecting their movement and interactions with platforms.
4. **Collision Detection**: Continuously check for collisions between the player character and platforms.
5. **Jump Mechanism**: Implement a jump function that allows the character to leap to designated heights or distances.
6. **Platform Interaction**: Define behaviors for interacting with different types of platforms (e.g., stationary, moving, destructible).

CHAPTER 2   ADVANCED COLLISION MECHANICS

7. **Environment Interactions**: Incorporate environmental factors that influence platforming, such as wind, slippery surfaces, or gravity shifts.

This algorithm forms the basis for implementing platforming mechanics in Unreal Engine or similar game development environments.

Reviewing the Code

This section focuses on setting up the player character class in your game, which includes defining its properties and behaviors related to movement and interaction with platforms.

Listings 2-10 and 2-11 set up the PlayerCharacter class, providing a solid foundation for character movement and interaction within the game world.

- **Enhanced Input Implementation**: Uses UEnhancedInputComponent for proper UE standards, replacing the default input binding.

- **Enhanced Input Mapping Context**: The MappingContext is added in BeginPlay() to allow dynamic input bindings.

- **SetupPlayerInputComponent Function**: Binds movement and jump actions using UEnhancedInputComponent.

- **MoveForward and MoveRight Functions**: Use FInputActionValue for handling input magnitude properly.

- **JumpAction Function**: Handles jump input with FInputActionValue for compatibility with enhanced input.

CHAPTER 2　ADVANCED COLLISION MECHANICS

Listing 2-10. PlayerCharacter.h

```cpp
#pragma once

#include "CoreMinimal.h"
#include "GameFramework/Character.h"

class UCapsuleComponent;

#include "PlayerCharacter.generated.h"

UCLASS()
class MYGAME_API APlayerCharacter : public ACharacter
{
    GENERATED_BODY()

public:
    APlayerCharacter();

protected:
    virtual void BeginPlay() override;

public:
    virtual void Tick(float DeltaTime) override;

    void MoveForward(float Value);
    void MoveRight(float Value);
    void JumpAction();

private:
    UPROPERTY(VisibleAnywhere)
    UCapsuleComponent* PlayerCapsule;
};
```

Listing 2-11. PlayerCharacter.cpp

```cpp
#include "PlayerCharacter.h"
#include "Components/CapsuleComponent.h"
#include "GameFramework/CharacterMovementComponent.h"
#include "EnhancedInputComponent.h"
#include "EnhancedInputSubsystems.h"
#include "GameFramework/PlayerController.h"

APlayerCharacter::APlayerCharacter()
{
    PrimaryActorTick.bCanEverTick = true;

    PlayerCapsule = GetCapsuleComponent();
    PlayerCapsule->InitCapsuleSize(42.f, 96.0f);

    GetCharacterMovement()->bOrientRotationToMovement = true;
    // Rotate character to moving direction
    GetCharacterMovement()->JumpZVelocity = 600.f;
}

void APlayerCharacter::BeginPlay()
{
    Super::BeginPlay();

    APlayerController* MyController = Cast<APlayerController>
    (GetController());
    if (MyController)
    {
        UEnhancedInputLocalPlayerSubsystem* Subsystem = ULocal
        Player::GetSubsystem<UEnhancedInputLocalPlayerSub
        system>(MyController->GetLocalPlayer());
        if (Subsystem)
```

CHAPTER 2 ADVANCED COLLISION MECHANICS

```cpp
        {
            Subsystem->AddMappingContext(MappingContext, 0);
        }
    }
}

void APlayerCharacter::Tick(float DeltaTime)
{
    Super::Tick(DeltaTime);
}

void APlayerCharacter::MoveForward(const FInputAction
Value& Value)
{
    if ((Controller != nullptr) && (Value.GetMagnitude()
    != 0.0f))
    {
        const FRotator Rotation = Controller->GetControl
        Rotation();
        const FVector Direction = FRotationMatrix(Rotation).
        GetScaledAxis(EAxis::X);
        AddMovementInput(Direction, Value.GetMagnitude());
    }
}

void APlayerCharacter::MoveRight(const
FInputActionValue& Value)
{
    if ((Controller != nullptr) && (Value.GetMagnitude()
    != 0.0f))
    {
        const FRotator Rotation = Controller->GetControl
        Rotation();
```

CHAPTER 2　ADVANCED COLLISION MECHANICS

```
        const FVector Direction = FRotationMatrix(Rotation).
        GetScaledAxis(EAxis::Y);
        AddMovementInput(Direction, Value.GetMagnitude());
    }
}

void APlayerCharacter::JumpAction(const
FInputActionValue& Value)
{
    if (CanJump())
    {
        bPressedJump = true;
    }
}

void APlayerCharacter::SetupPlayerInputComponent(UInput
Component* PlayerInputComponent)
{
    Super::SetupPlayerInputComponent(PlayerInputComponent);

    UEnhancedInputComponent* MyInputComponent = Cast<UEnhanced
    InputComponent>(PlayerInputComponent);
    if (MyInputComponent)
    {
        MyInputComponent->BindAction(MoveAction, ETrigger
        Event::Triggered, this, &APlayerCharacter::Move
        Forward);
        MyInputComponent->BindAction(LookAction, ETrigger
        Event::Triggered, this, &APlayerCharacter::MoveRight);
        MyInputComponent->BindAction(JumpAction, ETrigger
        Event::Triggered, this, &APlayerCharacter::JumpAction);
    }
}
```

CHAPTER 2 ADVANCED COLLISION MECHANICS

Implementing Basic Platforming Mechanics

This section defines the properties and behaviors of platforms within the game environment. Platforms are typically used for player navigation, challenges, and interactions in the game world.

Listings 2-12 and 2-13 implement the Platform class, serving as a fundamental building block for creating platforms in your game environment. It can be expanded further by adding additional properties and functions, such as moving platforms, platforms that disappear when stepped on, or platforms with special effects.

- **Platform Class**: Represents a platform within the game environment using a static mesh component
- **BeginPlay Function**: Initializes the platform's properties and settings when the game starts
- **Tick Function**: Updates the platform's state every frame

Listing 2-12. Platform.h

```cpp
#pragma once

class UStaticMeshComponent;

#include "CoreMinimal.h"
#include "GameFramework/Actor.h"
#include "Platform.generated.h"

UCLASS()
class MYGAME_API APlatform : public AActor
{
    GENERATED_BODY()
```

CHAPTER 2 ADVANCED COLLISION MECHANICS

```
public:
    APlatform();

protected:
    virtual void BeginPlay() override;

public:
    virtual void Tick(float DeltaTime) override;

private:
    UPROPERTY(VisibleAnywhere)
    UStaticMeshComponent* PlatformMesh;
};
```

Listing 2-13. Platform.cpp

```
#include "Platform.h"
#include "Components/StaticMeshComponent.h"

APlatform::APlatform()
{
    PrimaryActorTick.bCanEverTick = true;

    PlatformMesh = CreateDefaultSubobject<UStaticMeshComponent>
    (TEXT("PlatformMesh"));
    RootComponent = PlatformMesh;

    PlatformMesh->SetMobility(EComponentMobility::Movable);
    PlatformMesh->SetCollisionEnabled(ECollisionEnabled::
    QueryAndPhysics);
    PlatformMesh->SetCollisionResponseToAllChannels(ECollision
    Response::ECR_Block);
}
```

CHAPTER 2   ADVANCED COLLISION MECHANICS

Advanced Platforming Techniques

This enhancement to the jump function allows the player character to perform a second jump in mid-air, significantly increasing mobility and enabling access to higher platforms.

Listing 2-14 implements the double jump mechanism, enhancing gameplay by allowing the player character to leap again while in mid-air, providing additional mobility and enabling access to higher or otherwise unreachable platforms.

- **Double Jump Logic**: Checks if the character is already in mid-air (falling state) and allows them to perform a second jump.

- **LaunchCharacter**: This function is called to apply an upward force to the character. It takes three parameters.

- **FVector(0, 0, GetCharacterMovement()->JumpZ Velocity)**: This vector specifies the velocity for the jump. The Z component is set to the character's jump velocity, allowing for a powerful upward leap.

- **false**: This parameter specifies whether to reset the vertical velocity before applying the jump force. In this case, it is set to false, meaning the current vertical velocity will not be reset.

- **true**: This parameter indicates whether to allow the character to perform additional jumps. Setting this to true permits the double jump.

CHAPTER 2   ADVANCED COLLISION MECHANICS

Listing 2-14. PlayerCharacter.cpp (for Double Jump Function)

```cpp
void APlayerCharacter::JumpAction()
{
    if (CanJump())
    {
        if (GetCharacterMovement()->IsFalling())
        {
            // Implement double jump logic here
            LaunchCharacter(FVector(0, 0, GetCharacter
            Movement()->JumpZVelocity), false, true);
        bCanDoubleJump = false; // Disable double jump after it
        has been used
        }
        else
        {
            bPressedJump = true;
            bCanDoubleJump = true; // Allow double jump after
            landing on the ground
        }
    }
}
```

This section explored the fundamentals of platforming mechanics in game development. From understanding basic movement and jumping mechanics to implementing advanced techniques like double jumps, you've gained insights into how platforming enhances gameplay dynamics and player interaction within the game world.

CHAPTER 2   ADVANCED COLLISION MECHANICS

Area-of-Effect (AoE) Damage

Area-of-effect (AoE) damage mechanics are used in many games to simulate attacks or effects that impact multiple targets within a specified area. This mechanic is crucial for creating strategic gameplay elements such as spells, explosions, or environmental hazards that affect surrounding entities.

Imagine you're developing a fantasy RPG where the player character can cast powerful spells that damage all enemies within a certain radius. Unreal's Radial Damage system can be leveraged to handle and interact with the environment seamlessly, utilizing the already defined mechanics for efficient implementation of AoE (area of effect) spells, ensuring that both enemies and the surroundings are affected appropriately.

Basic Usage

Basic AoE damage mechanics include

- **Effect Radius:** Defines the area around the point of impact where the damage or effect is applied
- **Damage Calculation:** Determines how damage is calculated based on the proximity of entities within the AoE radius
- **Visual and Audio Feedback:** Provides visual and audio cues to indicate the AoE effect, such as explosions, shockwaves, or magical bursts

These mechanics allow developers to create impactful abilities or environmental hazards that challenge players to strategize their movements and actions.

Advanced Techniques

Advanced AoE techniques expand on basic mechanics, including

- **Persistent Effects**: Introduces ongoing effects within the AoE radius, such as lingering damage over time (DoT) or debuffs
- **Dynamic AoE Size**: Allows for variable AoE sizes based on game conditions or character abilities
- **Environmental Interaction**: Enables AoE effects to interact with the game environment, triggering secondary effects like terrain deformation or object destruction

These techniques enhance gameplay depth by introducing strategic considerations and dynamic interactions between characters, environments, and effects.

Practical Applications

AoE damage mechanics are essential for

- **Combat Systems**: Integrating powerful spells or attacks that affect multiple enemies or allies
- **Environmental Hazards**: Creating traps, explosions, or natural disasters that impact gameplay
- **Tactical Gameplay**: Encouraging players to position themselves strategically to maximize AoE damage or avoid being caught in enemy AoE attacks
- **Boss Battles**: Designing challenging encounters where bosses unleash devastating AoE attacks that require quick reflexes and strategic positioning from players

CHAPTER 2   ADVANCED COLLISION MECHANICS

Algorithm Overview

Let's outline the algorithm used for implementing AoE damage mechanics:

1. **Initialization**: Set up AoE abilities or effects within the game scene.

2. **Trigger Detection**: Detect when an AoE ability or effect is triggered, such as when a spell is cast or an explosion occurs.

3. **Area Detection**: Determine the affected area or radius where the AoE damage or effect will be applied.

4. **Entity Detection**: Identify entities (characters, objects) within the AoE radius that will be affected by the damage or effect.

5. **Damage Calculation**: Calculate damage or apply effects to each entity within the AoE radius based on their proximity to the center of the AoE.

6. **Visual and Audio Feedback**: Provide visual and audio cues to indicate the AoE effect, enhancing gameplay immersion and feedback.

This algorithm forms the basis for implementing AoE damage mechanics in Unreal Engine or similar game development environments.

Reviewing the Code

This component can be used in various scenarios, such as explosive effects or spells that affect multiple targets within a certain radius, enhancing gameplay dynamics through tactical decision-making.

CHAPTER 2   ADVANCED COLLISION MECHANICS

Listings 2-15 and 2-16 implement AoE damage, allowing developers to design more engaging combat mechanics and environmental effects, fostering strategic gameplay.

- **AoEDamageComponent Class**: Implements a component that applies AoE damage within a specified radius.

- **BeginPlay Function**: Initializes default values for AoE radius and damage amount and sets up event binding for triggering AoE damage application.

- **TickComponent Function**: Updates the component's state every frame.

- **ApplyAoEDamage Function**: Calculates and applies damage to all characters within the AoE radius based on their proximity to the center of the AoE.

- **Damage Event Implementation**: When damage is applied to a character, the TakeDamage method is triggered. You can customize the TakeDamage method to update the health of the character directly or use an alternative method such as Character->UpdateHealth (DamageAmount); if you have a custom health management system.

Listing 2-15. AoEDamageComponent.h

```
#pragma once

#include "CoreMinimal.h"
#include "Components/ActorComponent.h"
#include "AoEDamageComponent.generated.h"
```

```cpp
UCLASS( ClassGroup=(Custom), meta=(BlueprintSpawnable
Component) )
class MYGAME_API UAoEDamageComponent : public UActorComponent
{
    GENERATED_BODY()

public:
    UAoEDamageComponent();

    UPROPERTY(EditAnywhere, Category = "AoE Damage")
    float AoERadius;

    UPROPERTY(EditAnywhere, Category = "AoE Damage")
    float DamageAmount;

protected:
    virtual void BeginPlay() override;

public:
    virtual void TickComponent(float DeltaTime, ELevelTick
    TickType, FActorComponentTickFunction* ThisTickFunction)
    override;

    UFUNCTION()
    void ApplyAoEDamage();
};
```

Listing 2-16. AoEDamageComponent.cpp

```cpp
#include "AoEDamageComponent.h"
#include "DrawDebugHelpers.h"
#include "Engine/World.h"
#include "GameFramework/Character.h"
#include "Kismet/GameplayStatics.h"
#include "Kismet/KismetSystemLibrary.h"
```

CHAPTER 2   ADVANCED COLLISION MECHANICS

```
UAoEDamageComponent::UAoEDamageComponent()
{
    PrimaryComponentTick.bCanEverTick = true;

    AoERadius = 200.0f;
    DamageAmount = 50.0f;
}

void UAoEDamageComponent::BeginPlay()
{
    Super::BeginPlay();

    // Bind the ApplyAoEDamage function to a trigger event or
        game action
    // Example: UFUNCTION() TriggeredBySpellCast();
    // Bind function: TriggeredBySpellCast.AddDynamic(this,
        &UAoEDamageComponent::ApplyAoEDamage);
}

void UAoEDamageComponent::TickComponent(float DeltaTime,
ELevelTick TickType, FActorComponentTickFunction*
ThisTickFunction)
{
    Super::TickComponent(DeltaTime, TickType,
    ThisTickFunction);
}

void UAoEDamageComponent::ApplyAoEDamage()
{
    FVector Center = GetOwner()->GetActorLocation();

    // Draw debug sphere for visualization
    DrawDebugSphere(GetWorld(), Center, AoERadius, 12,
    FColor::Red, false, 2.0f);
```

CHAPTER 2   ADVANCED COLLISION MECHANICS

```
// Using SphereOverlapActors to efficiently find
   overlapping actors
TArray<AActor*> OverlappingActors;
TArray<TEnumAsByte<EObjectTypeQuery>> ObjectTypes;
ObjectTypes.Add(UEngineTypes::ConvertToObjectType
(ECollisionChannel::ECC_Pawn));   // Check for enemy pawns
(players or AI characters)

UKismetSystemLibrary::SphereOverlapActors(
    GetWorld(),
    Center,
    AoERadius,
    ObjectTypes,
    ACharacter::StaticClass(),
    TArray<AActor*>(),
    OverlappingActors
);

for (AActor* Actor : OverlappingActors)
{
    // Apply damage to the actor within AoE radius
    ACharacter* Character = Cast<ACharacter>(Actor);
    if (Character)
    {
        // Call TakeDamage to handle health reduction
           (this could be a custom function in the
           character class)
        FDamageEvent DamageEvent;
        Character->TakeDamage(DamageAmount, DamageEvent,
        nullptr, nullptr);

        // You can implement your own damage handling or
           health update here for the character, such as:
```

```
            // Character->UpdateHealth(DamageAmount);
        }
    }
}
```

Advanced AoE Techniques

To enhance the AoE damage mechanic, you can extend its functionality to interact with the game environment. This includes triggering explosions that can destroy nearby objects or deform the terrain, adding an extra layer of depth and immersion to your gameplay. Here's how to implement these features.

Listings 2-17 and 2-18 implement the EnvironmentalInteraction Component, enhancing gameplay by allowing dynamic interactions with the environment, such as triggering explosions that can affect nearby objects and terrain.

- **EnvironmentalInteractionComponent Class**: Implements a component that triggers environmental interactions, such as explosions, within the game environment.

- **TriggerExplosion Function**: Simulates an explosion effect at the owner actor's location, affecting surrounding objects or terrain.

- **Radial Force**: A radial force is applied to the area of the explosion to simulate the pushback or impact of the explosion.

- **Chaos Destruction**: Objects with a UChaosDestructible Component are found in the radius, and destruction is triggered using the ApplyDamage function to fracture or break the destructible meshes.

CHAPTER 2 ADVANCED COLLISION MECHANICS

Listing 2-17. EnvironmentalInteractionComponent.h

```cpp
#pragma once

#include "CoreMinimal.h"
#include "Components/ActorComponent.h"
#include "EnvironmentalInteractionComponent.generated.h"

UCLASS( ClassGroup=(Custom), meta=(BlueprintSpawnable Component) )
class MYGAME_API UEnvironmentalInteractionComponent : public UActorComponent
{
    GENERATED_BODY()

public:
    UEnvironmentalInteractionComponent();

protected:
    virtual void BeginPlay() override;

public:
    virtual void TickComponent(float DeltaTime, ELevelTick TickType, FActorComponentTickFunction* ThisTickFunction) override;

    UFUNCTION()
    void TriggerExplosion();
};
```

Listing 2-18. EnvironmentalInteractionComponent.cpp

```cpp
#include "EnvironmentalInteractionComponent.h"
#include "Engine/World.h"
#include "DrawDebugHelpers.h"
```

```
UEnvironmentalInteractionComponent::UEnvironmentalInteraction
Component()
{
    PrimaryComponentTick.bCanEverTick = true;
}

void UEnvironmentalInteractionComponent::BeginPlay()
{
    Super::BeginPlay();

    // Bind the TriggerExplosion function to an event or
        game action
    // Example: UFUNCTION() TriggeredBySpellCast();
    // Bind function: TriggeredBySpellCast.AddDynamic(this,
        &UEnvironmentalInteractionComponent::TriggerExplosion);
}

void UEnvironmentalInteractionComponent::TickComponent(float
DeltaTime, ELevelTick TickType, FActorComponentTickFunction*
ThisTickFunction)
{
    Super::TickComponent(DeltaTime, TickType,
    ThisTickFunction);
}

void UEnvironmentalInteractionComponent::TriggerExplosion()
{
    FVector Center = GetOwner()->GetActorLocation();

    // Apply explosion effects to surrounding objects
        or terrain
    DrawDebugSphere(GetWorld(), Center, 500.0f, 12,
    FColor::Blue, false, 2.0f);
```

CHAPTER 2   ADVANCED COLLISION MECHANICS

```
// Spawn a radial force component to simulate the
   explosion's force
URadialForceComponent* RadialForce = NewObject<URadialForce
Component>(GetOwner());
RadialForce->AttachToComponent(GetOwner()->GetRoot
Component(), FAttachmentTransformRules::KeepWorldTransform);
RadialForce->Radius = 500.0f; // Explosion radius
RadialForce->ForceStrength = 1000.0f; // Explosion force
strength
RadialForce->bImpulseVelChange = true;
RadialForce->FireImpulse();

// Implement destruction logic using Chaos Destruction (for
   destructible objects)
TArray<AActor*> OverlappingActors;
GetOverlappingActors(OverlappingActors);

for (AActor* Actor : OverlappingActors)
{
    // Check if the actor has a Chaos Destructible Mesh
       component
    UChaosDestructibleComponent* DestructibleComponent =
    Cast<UChaosDestructibleComponent>(Actor->GetComponent
    ByClass(UChaosDestructibleComponent::StaticClass()));
    if (DestructibleComponent)
    {
        // Apply destruction effect (e.g., trigger
           fracturing of the mesh)
        DestructibleComponent->ApplyDamage(100.0f, Center,
        FVector(1, 0, 0), 500.0f);
    }
}
}
```

CHAPTER 2   ADVANCED COLLISION MECHANICS

This section explored the fundamentals of area-of-effect (AoE) damage mechanics in game development. From understanding basic AoE radius and damage calculations to implementing advanced techniques like environmental interactions, you've gained insights into how AoE mechanics enhance strategic gameplay and create dynamic effects within the game world.

Character Knockback

Character knockback mechanics are fundamental in games to simulate the impact of powerful attacks or environmental forces on characters. This mechanic is crucial for creating dynamic combat experiences where players and enemies react realistically to forces applied to them.

Imagine you're designing a fighting game where characters can execute strong melee attacks that push opponents backward. The character knockback mechanics determine how these attacks affect the opponent's movement and positioning during combat.

Basic Usage

Basic character knockback mechanics include

- **Force Application**: Applying a force vector to characters when they are hit by an attack or environmental effect
- **Movement Calculation**: Determining how far and in which direction characters are pushed based on the force applied
- **Recovery Time**: Specifying a recovery time or stun duration during which characters cannot perform actions after being knocked back

These mechanics allow developers to create impactful combat interactions where characters must strategize their positioning and timing to avoid being pushed into dangerous situations.

Advanced Techniques

Advanced character knockback techniques expand on basic mechanics, including

- **Directional Influence**: Allowing players to influence their knockback trajectory slightly by inputting directional commands during the knockback animation
- **Combo Integration**: Integrating knockback into combo sequences where consecutive attacks can chain into each other to create continuous knockback effects
- **Environmental Interaction**: Enabling environmental elements or interactive objects to apply knockback forces to characters, adding complexity to gameplay scenarios

These techniques enhance combat depth by introducing nuanced interactions between characters, attacks, and the game environment.

Practical Applications

Character knockback mechanics are essential for

- **Combat Dynamics**: Enhancing melee and ranged combat with realistic reactions to attacks and environmental hazards
- **Positional Strategy**: Encouraging players to use knockback strategically to control the battlefield and gain positional advantage

- **Environmental Hazards**: Creating traps or hazards that push characters into dangerous areas or obstacles, adding challenge and complexity to gameplay
- **Boss Battles**: Designing challenging boss encounters where bosses can execute powerful attacks that knock back players, requiring quick reflexes and strategic positioning

Algorithm Overview

Let's outline the algorithm used for implementing character knockback mechanics:

1. **Force Calculation**: Calculate the force vector applied to characters based on the attack or environmental effect.
2. **Direction Determination**: Determine the direction in which characters are pushed based on the force vector and their current facing direction.
3. **Movement Application**: Apply the calculated force to characters' movement components to simulate knockback.
4. **Stun Duration**: Implement a stun or recovery period during which characters cannot perform actions after being knocked back.
5. **Collision Handling**: Handle collisions with other characters, objects, or terrain during the knockback animation to ensure realistic interactions.

This algorithm forms the basis for implementing character knockback mechanics in Unreal Engine or similar game development environments.

CHAPTER 2 ADVANCED COLLISION MECHANICS

Reviewing the Code

Implementing character knockback adds another dynamic layer to gameplay by allowing characters to be pushed away from an impact source. Below is the breakdown of how to implement a knockback system using a custom KnockbackComponent.

Listings 2-19 and 2-20 implement the KnockbackComponent, creating a versatile system that can easily be integrated into multiple aspects of gameplay, improving the combat and environmental interaction experience.

- **KnockbackComponent Class**: Implements a component that applies knockback to characters within a specified direction and force.

- **ApplyKnockback Function**: Applies a force to push the character in the specified knockback direction, disables character input during stun duration, and schedules the end of stun recovery.

- **Physics Check**: The code checks if the TargetMesh (character's skeletal mesh) is simulating physics.

- **LaunchCharacter Fallback**: If the mesh isn't simulating physics, it falls back to using LaunchCharacter() for the knockback.

- **EndStun Function**: Ends the stun period and re-enables character input after the specified stun duration.

Listing 2-19. KnockbackComponent.h

```cpp
#pragma once

#include "CoreMinimal.h"

class AActor;
class UCapsuleComponent;

#include "KnockbackComponent.generated.h"

UCLASS( ClassGroup=(Custom), meta=(BlueprintSpawnable Component) )
class MYGAME_API UKnockbackComponent : public UActorComponent
{
    GENERATED_BODY()

public:
    UKnockbackComponent();

    UPROPERTY(EditAnywhere, Category = "Knockback")
    float KnockbackForce;

    UPROPERTY(EditAnywhere, Category = "Knockback")
    float StunDuration;

protected:
    virtual void BeginPlay() override;

public:
    virtual void TickComponent(float DeltaTime, ELevelTick TickType, FActorComponentTickFunction* ThisTickFunction) override;

    UFUNCTION()
    void ApplyKnockback(FVector KnockbackDirection);
};
```

CHAPTER 2 ADVANCED COLLISION MECHANICS

Listing 2-20. KnockbackComponent.cpp

```cpp
#include "KnockbackComponent.h"
#include "Components/ActorComponent.h"
#include "GameFramework/Character.h"
#include "GameFramework/Controller.h"
#include "Components/CapsuleComponent.h"

UKnockbackComponent::UKnockbackComponent()
{
    PrimaryComponentTick.bCanEverTick = true;

    KnockbackForce = 1000.0f;
    StunDuration = 1.0f;
}

void UKnockbackComponent::BeginPlay()
{
    Super::BeginPlay();

    // Bind the ApplyKnockback function to a trigger event or
       game action
    // Example: UFUNCTION() TriggeredByStrongAttack();
    // Bind function: TriggeredByStrongAttack.AddDynamic(this,
       &UKnockbackComponent::ApplyKnockback);
}

void UKnockbackComponent::TickComponent(float DeltaTime,
ELevelTick TickType, FActorComponentTickFunction* This
TickFunction)
{
    Super::TickComponent(DeltaTime, TickType, This
    TickFunction);
}
```

CHAPTER 2   ADVANCED COLLISION MECHANICS

```cpp
void UKnockbackComponent::ApplyKnockback(FVector Knock
backDirection)
{
    ACharacter* Character = Cast<ACharacter>(GetOwner());
    if (Character && Character->GetController())
    {
        // Apply force to push character in the specified
            direction
        FVector KnockbackVelocity = KnockbackDirection * Knock-
        backForce;

        // Check if the character's mesh is simulating physics
        USkeletalMeshComponent* TargetMesh = Character->
        GetMesh();
        if (TargetMesh && TargetMesh->IsSimulatingPhysics())
        {
            // If simulating physics, apply impulse instead of
                launching
            TargetMesh->AddImpulse(KnockbackVelocity, NAME_
            None, true);
        }
        else
        {
            // Otherwise, use the LaunchCharacter function to
                apply knockback
            Character->LaunchCharacter(KnockbackVelocity,
            true, true);
        }

        // Stun the character for a specified duration
        Character->DisableInput(Character->GetController());
```

```cpp
        GetWorld()->GetTimerManager().SetTimer(TimerHandle_
        Stun, this, &UKnockbackComponent::EndStun,
        StunDuration, false);
    }
}
void UKnockbackComponent::EndStun()
{
    ACharacter* Character = Cast<ACharacter>(GetOwner());
    if (Character && Character->GetController())
    {
        // Re-enable character input after stun duration
            expires
        Character->EnableInput(Character->GetController());
    }
}
```

Advanced Knockback Techniques

Allowing players to influence their knockback trajectory introduces an additional layer of control during gameplay. This mechanic, often referred to as **directional influence (DI)**, gives players the ability to input movement commands during knockback to adjust their trajectory slightly, offering a chance for better recovery or repositioning.

Listings 2-21 and 2-22 implement the DirectionalInfluenceComponent, allowing players to exert limited control over their character's knockback trajectory by applying directional input. This feature provides players with the ability to adjust their character's movement mid-knockback, adding a layer of skill-based recovery mechanics.

CHAPTER 2   ADVANCED COLLISION MECHANICS

- **DirectionalInfluenceComponent Class**: Implements a component that allows players to influence their knockback trajectory slightly by inputting directional commands during the knockback animation

- **ApplyDirectionalInfluence Function**: Modifies the knockback direction based on player input direction, allowing players to slightly adjust their knockback trajectory

Listing 2-21. DirectionalInfluenceComponent.h

```
#pragma once

#include "CoreMinimal.h"

class AActor;

#include "DirectionalInfluenceComponent.generated.h"

UCLASS( ClassGroup=(Custom), meta=(BlueprintSpawnableComponent) )
class MYGAME_API UDirectionalInfluenceComponent : public UActorComponent
{
    GENERATED_BODY()

public:
    UDirectionalInfluenceComponent();

protected:
    virtual void BeginPlay() override;
```

CHAPTER 2 ADVANCED COLLISION MECHANICS

```cpp
public:
    virtual void TickComponent(float DeltaTime, ELevelTick
    TickType, FActorComponentTickFunction* ThisTickFunction)
    override;

    UFUNCTION()
    void ApplyDirectionalInfluence(FVector Direction);
};
```

Listing 2-22. DirectionalInfluenceComponent.cpp

```cpp
#include "DirectionalInfluenceComponent.h"
#include "Components/ActorComponent.h"
#include "GameFramework/Character.h"

UDirectionalInfluenceComponent::UDirectionalInfluenceComponent()
{
    PrimaryComponentTick.bCanEverTick = true;
}

void UDirectionalInfluenceComponent::BeginPlay()
{
    Super::BeginPlay();

    // Bind the ApplyDirectionalInfluence function to a trigger
       event or game action
    // Example: UFUNCTION() TriggeredByPlayerInput();
    // Bind function: TriggeredByPlayerInput.AddDynamic
       (this, &UDirectionalInfluenceComponent::ApplyDirectional
       Influence);
}

void UDirectionalInfluenceComponent::TickComponent(float
DeltaTime, ELevelTick TickType, FActorComponentTickFunction*
ThisTickFunction)
```

```
{
    Super::TickComponent(DeltaTime, TickType, This
    TickFunction);
}
void UDirectionalInfluenceComponent::ApplyDirectionalInfluence
(FVector Direction)
{
    ACharacter* Character = Cast<ACharacter>(GetOwner());
    if (Character)
    {
        // Modify the knockback direction based on player input
           direction
        // Example: Calculate modified knockback velocity using
           Direction vector
        FVector ModifiedKnockbackVelocity = Direction *
        Character->LaunchCharacterMaxForce;
        Character->LaunchCharacter(ModifiedKnockbackVelocity,
        true, true);
    }
}
```

This section explored the fundamentals of character knockback mechanics in game development. From understanding basic knockback force application to implementing advanced techniques like directional influence, you've gained insights into how knockback mechanics enhance combat dynamics and player interaction within the game world.

CHAPTER 2   ADVANCED COLLISION MECHANICS

Character Pushback

Character pushback mechanics involve the deliberate movement of characters due to various interactions within the game environment. Unlike knockback, which typically involves forceful impacts or attacks, pushback mechanics focus on intentional or environmental interactions that move characters without necessarily stunning them.

Imagine designing a game where characters can be pushed by environmental hazards like strong winds, moving platforms, or even by other characters during cooperative or competitive gameplay.

Basic Usage

Basic character pushback mechanics include

- **Environmental Forces**: Implementing environmental elements that exert forces on characters, such as wind zones, water currents, or conveyor belts
- **Interactive Objects**: Designing objects within the game environment that characters can interact with to cause pushback, such as pushing blocks or movable platforms
- **Collaborative Gameplay**: Enabling cooperative gameplay mechanics where players can push each other to solve puzzles or navigate obstacles

These mechanics add layers of interactivity and challenge by requiring players to adapt to dynamic movement scenarios within the game world.

Advanced Techniques

Advanced character pushback techniques expand on basic mechanics, including

- **Dynamic Force Adjustment**: Adjusting the intensity and direction of pushback forces based on game events or player actions
- **Physics-Based Simulation**: Implementing realistic physics interactions where characters' movement and weight affect pushback dynamics
- **Combination with Other Mechanics**: Integrating pushback mechanics with other gameplay elements like platforming challenges or puzzle-solving sequences

These techniques enhance gameplay depth by introducing complex interactions that require strategic planning and coordination among players.

Practical Applications

Character pushback mechanics are essential for

- **Environmental Challenges**: Creating platforming or puzzle challenges where characters must navigate through moving or dynamic environments
- **Teamwork and Cooperation**: Facilitating cooperative gameplay where players must coordinate pushback actions to achieve objectives or solve puzzles

- **Environmental Hazards**: Designing hazards that push characters into traps or obstacles, adding difficulty and suspense to gameplay sequences
- **Interactive Physics**: Enhancing immersion through realistic physics interactions that simulate how characters react to external forces

Algorithm Overview

Let's outline the algorithm used for implementing character pushback mechanics:

1. **Force Calculation**: Calculate the force vector applied to characters based on environmental factors, interactive objects, or player actions.
2. **Direction Determination**: Determine the direction in which characters are pushed based on the force vector and their current position or facing direction.
3. **Movement Application**: Apply the calculated force to characters' movement components to simulate pushback.
4. **Collision Handling**: Handle collisions with other characters, objects, or terrain during the pushback animation to ensure realistic interactions.
5. **Interactive Object Interaction**: Implement interaction logic for objects that can be pushed by characters, affecting pushback dynamics.

This algorithm serves as a framework for implementing character pushback mechanics in Unreal Engine or similar game development environments.

Reviewing the Code

PushbackComponent introduces a mechanism in which characters experience a force that moves them away from a source, simulating pushback effects that could result from actions like explosions, powerful attacks, or environmental hazards. Below is a breakdown of the PushbackComponent.h code structure.

Listings 2-23 and 2-24 implement the PushbackComponent class, introducing functionality to apply pushback to characters based on a specified direction and force. This component simulates the effect of characters being pushed away, such as from explosions or strong impacts, enhancing the game's realism and responsiveness to environmental interactions.

- **PushbackComponent Class**: Implements a component that applies pushback to characters within a specified direction and force
- **BeginPlay Function**: Initializes default values for pushback force and sets up event binding for triggering pushback application
- **TickComponent Function**: Updates the component's state every frame
- **ApplyPushback Function**: Applies a force to push the character in the specified pushback direction

Listing 2-23. PushbackComponent.h

```
#pragma once

#include "CoreMinimal.h"

class AActor;
class UCapsuleComponent;
```

CHAPTER 2   ADVANCED COLLISION MECHANICS

```cpp
#include "PushbackComponent.generated.h"

UCLASS( ClassGroup=(Custom), meta=(BlueprintSpawnable
Component) )
class MYGAME_API UPushbackComponent : public UActorComponent
{
    GENERATED_BODY()
public:
    UPushbackComponent();

    UPROPERTY(EditAnywhere, Category = "Pushback")
    float PushbackForce;

protected:
    virtual void BeginPlay() override;

public:
    virtual void TickComponent(float DeltaTime, ELevelTick
    TickType, FActorComponentTickFunction* ThisTickFunction)
    override;

    UFUNCTION()
    void ApplyPushback(FVector PushbackDirection);
};
```

Listing 2-24. PushbackComponent.cpp

```cpp
#include "PushbackComponent.h"
#include "Components/ActorComponent.h"
#include "GameFramework/Character.h"
#include "GameFramework/Controller.h"
#include "Components/CapsuleComponent.h"
```

```cpp
UPushbackComponent::UPushbackComponent()
{
    PrimaryComponentTick.bCanEverTick = true;

    PushbackForce = 500.0f;
}

void UPushbackComponent::BeginPlay()
{
    Super::BeginPlay();

    // Bind the ApplyPushback function to a trigger event or
       game action
    // Example: UFUNCTION() TriggeredByEnvironmentalForce();
    // Bind function: TriggeredByEnvironmentalForce.
       AddDynamic(this, &UPushbackComponent::ApplyPushback);
}

void UPushbackComponent::TickComponent(float DeltaTime,
ELevelTick TickType, FActorComponentTickFunction* ThisTick-
Function)
{
    Super::TickComponent(DeltaTime, TickType, ThisTick-
    Function);
}

void UPushbackComponent::ApplyPushback(FVector Pushback-
Direction)
{
    ACharacter* Character = Cast<ACharacter>(GetOwner());
    if (Character && Character->GetController())
    {
        USkeletalMeshComponent* TargetMesh = Character->
        GetMesh();
```

```cpp
    if (!TargetMesh || PushbackDirection.IsZero())
        {return;} // Exit if no mesh is found or
        pushback direction is zero

    // Apply force to push character in the specified
       direction
    FVector PushbackVelocity = PushbackDirection *
    PushbackForce;
    Character->LaunchCharacter(PushbackVelocity,
    true, true);
    }
}
```

Advanced Pushback Techniques

The intensity and direction of pushback forces can be dynamically adjusted based on in-game events, player interactions, or external factors like environmental hazards. This makes the pushback more responsive to the situation, providing more immersive gameplay experiences.

Listings 2-25 and 2-26 implement the DynamicPushbackComponent class, applying dynamic pushback to characters where the force intensity can be adjusted based on game events or interactions, creating more responsive and varied pushback effects.

- **DynamicPushbackComponent Class**: Implements a component that applies dynamic pushback to characters with adjustable force intensity based on game events.

- **ApplyDynamicPushback Function**: Applies a force to push the character in the specified pushback direction with adjusted intensity.

CHAPTER 2 ADVANCED COLLISION MECHANICS

- **Mesh Check**: Before applying the pushback force, it checks if the character has a valid mesh (TargetMesh).
- **Direction Validation**: It ensures that the Pushback-Direction isn't a zero vector (IsZero()), which would prevent unnecessary calculations.

Listing 2-25. DynamicPushbackComponent.h

```
#pragma once

#include "CoreMinimal.h"

class AActor;
class UCapsuleComponent;

#include "DynamicPushbackComponent.generated.h"

UCLASS( ClassGroup=(Custom), meta=(BlueprintSpawnable
Component) )
class MYGAME_API UDynamicPushbackComponent : public
UActorComponent
{
    GENERATED_BODY()

public:
    UDynamicPushbackComponent();

protected:
    virtual void BeginPlay() override;

public:
    virtual void TickComponent(float DeltaTime, ELevelTick
    TickType, FActorComponentTickFunction* ThisTickFunction)
    override;
```

CHAPTER 2 ADVANCED COLLISION MECHANICS

```
    UFUNCTION()
    void ApplyDynamicPushback(FVector PushbackDirection, float
    Intensity);
};
```

Listing 2-26. DynamicPushbackComponent.cpp

```cpp
#include "DynamicPushbackComponent.h"
#include "Components/ActorComponent.h"
#include "GameFramework/Character.h"

UDynamicPushbackComponent::UDynamicPushbackComponent()
{
    PrimaryComponentTick.bCanEverTick = true;
}

void UDynamicPushbackComponent::BeginPlay()
{
    Super::BeginPlay();

    // Bind the ApplyDynamicPushback function to a trigger
       event or game action
    // Example: UFUNCTION() TriggeredByEvent();
    // Bind function: TriggeredByEvent.AddDynamic(this,
       &UDynamicPushbackComponent::ApplyDynamicPushback);
}

void UDynamicPushbackComponent::TickComponent(float DeltaTime,
ELevelTick TickType, FActorComponentTickFunction* This
TickFunction)
{
    Super::TickComponent(DeltaTime, TickType, This
    TickFunction);
}
```

CHAPTER 2 ADVANCED COLLISION MECHANICS

```cpp
void UDynamicPushbackComponent::ApplyDynamicPushback(FVector PushbackDirection, float Intensity)
{
    ACharacter* Character = Cast<ACharacter>(GetOwner());
    if (Character)
    {
        USkeletalMeshComponent* TargetMesh = Character->GetMesh();
        if (!TargetMesh || PushbackDirection.IsZero())
                {return;} // Exit if no mesh is found or
                 pushback direction
        is zero

        // Apply force to push character with adjusted
          intensity and direction
        FVector DynamicPushbackVelocity = PushbackDirection * Intensity;
        Character->LaunchCharacter(DynamicPushbackVelocity, true, true);
    }
}
```

This section explored the fundamentals of character pushback mechanics in game development. From understanding basic pushback force application to implementing advanced techniques like dynamic force adjustment, you've gained insights into how pushback mechanics enhance gameplay dynamics and environmental interactions within the game world.

CHAPTER 2   ADVANCED COLLISION MECHANICS

Object Destruction

Object destruction mechanics involve the process of removing or altering game objects based on various triggers or interactions within the game environment. This mechanic is crucial for creating dynamic and interactive gameplay experiences where objects can be damaged, destroyed, or dismantled during gameplay.

Imagine designing a game where players can destroy obstacles, structures, or even enemies using weapons, explosives, or other interactive elements.

Basic Usage

Basic object destruction mechanics include

- **Destructible Objects**: Implementing game objects that can be destroyed or damaged through player actions or environmental hazards

- **Explosions and Impact**: Using explosives, projectiles, or powerful attacks to inflict damage and destroy objects

- **Environmental Interactions**: Designing interactive elements in the environment that cause objects to break or collapse, such as collapsing bridges or destructible barriers

  - *Hint: The Chaos Destruction plugin in Unreal Engine can be used to simulate realistic object destruction. This plugin allows objects to fracture, break, and collapse dynamically in response to environmental forces, explosions, or player interactions. By using this plugin, you can create immersive and dynamic destruction effects in your game environment.*

CHAPTER 2   ADVANCED COLLISION MECHANICS

These mechanics add realism and immersion to the game world by allowing players to interact with and alter their surroundings.

Advanced Techniques

Advanced object destruction techniques expand on basic mechanics, including

- **Particle Effects**: Creating visual and auditory effects to simulate explosions, crumbling structures, or disintegrating objects
- **Damage Modeling**: Implementing systems that simulate realistic object damage based on impact points, force, and type of attack
- **Chain Reactions**: Designing scenarios where destroying one object triggers a sequence of destruction events, affecting surrounding objects or structures

These techniques enhance gameplay depth by introducing complex interactions and consequences based on player actions and environmental factors.

Practical Applications

Object destruction mechanics are essential for

- **Combat and Strategy**: Allowing players to strategically weaken or eliminate obstacles, enemies, or defensive structures
- **Environmental Puzzles**: Creating puzzles or challenges where object destruction is necessary to progress or reveal hidden pathways

- **Dynamic Environments**: Simulating dynamic and evolving environments where structures can be altered or destroyed, affecting gameplay tactics
- **Interactive Storytelling**: Enhancing narrative elements by allowing players to influence the game world through destructive actions

Algorithm Overview

Let's outline the algorithm used for implementing object destruction mechanics:

1. **Detection**: Detect triggers or interactions that initiate object destruction, such as collisions, attacks, or scripted events.
2. **Damage Calculation**: Calculate the amount and type of damage inflicted on the object based on the triggering event or interaction.
3. **Visual Feedback**: Instantiate particle effects, sound effects, and visual cues to represent object damage or destruction.
4. **Object State Update**: Update the object's state, such as changing its mesh, disabling its collision, or removing it from the game world.
5. **Chain Reactions**: Implement logic for chain reactions if object destruction triggers additional events or affects other objects.

This algorithm provides a framework for integrating object destruction mechanics into Unreal Engine or similar game development environments.

CHAPTER 2   ADVANCED COLLISION MECHANICS

Reviewing the Code

The class encapsulates functionalities such as health management, destruction effects, and any relevant properties that determine the behavior of destructible objects when impacted or interacted with.

Listings 2-27 and 2-28 implement the DestructibleObject class, representing a destructible object in the game world with health properties and destruction functionality that dictate how the object behaves when damaged.

- **DestructibleObject Class**: Represents a destructible object in the game world with health properties and destruction functionality
- **BeginPlay Function**: Initializes default values for object health and sets up initial state
- **Tick Function**: Updates the object's state every frame
- **TakeDamage Function**: Reduces the object's health based on the amount of damage received and triggers destruction if health drops to zero or below
- **DestroyObject Function**: Implements destruction effects and removes the object from the game world when destroyed

Listing 2-27. DestructibleObject.h

```
#pragma once

#include "CoreMinimal.h"
#include "GameFramework/Actor.h"

Class UStaticMeshComponent;
```

CHAPTER 2   ADVANCED COLLISION MECHANICS

```cpp
#include "DestructibleObject.generated.h"

UCLASS()
class MYGAME_API ADestructibleObject : public AActor
{
    GENERATED_BODY()

public:
    ADestructibleObject();

protected:
    virtual void BeginPlay() override;

public:
    virtual void Tick(float DeltaTime) override;

    UPROPERTY(VisibleAnywhere)
    UStaticMeshComponent* DestructibleMesh;

    UPROPERTY(EditDefaultsOnly, Category = "Destruction")
    float MaxHealth;

    UPROPERTY(BlueprintReadOnly, Category = "Destruction")
    float CurrentHealth;

    UFUNCTION()
    void TakeDamage(float DamageAmount);

private:
    void DestroyObject();
};
```

Listing 2-28. DestructibleObject.cpp

```cpp
#include "DestructibleObject.h"
#include "Components/StaticMeshComponent.h"

ADestructibleObject::ADestructibleObject()
{
    PrimaryActorTick.bCanEverTick = true;

    DestructibleMesh = CreateDefaultSubobject<UStaticMesh
    Component>(TEXT("DestructibleMesh"));
    RootComponent = DestructibleMesh;

    MaxHealth = 100.0f;
    CurrentHealth = MaxHealth;
}

void ADestructibleObject::BeginPlay()
{
    Super::BeginPlay();
}

void ADestructibleObject::Tick(float DeltaTime)
{
    Super::Tick(DeltaTime);
}

void ADestructibleObject::TakeDamage(float DamageAmount)
{
    CurrentHealth -= DamageAmount;
    if (CurrentHealth <= 0)
    {
        DestroyObject();
    }
}
```

```cpp
void ADestructibleObject::DestroyObject()
{
    // Implement destruction effects and remove object from
        game world
    Destroy();
}
```

Advanced Destruction Techniques

The chain reaction implementation introduces logic that allows the destruction of one object to initiate destruction events for nearby objects. This mechanic enhances gameplay dynamics by creating opportunities for strategic planning and exciting visual effects.

Listings 2-29 and 2-30 implement the ChainReactionComponent class, which triggers a chain reaction of destruction events for nearby destructible objects. This component adds depth to gameplay by creating a cascading effect when objects are destroyed, encouraging strategic interactions.

- **ChainReactionComponent Class**: Implements a component that triggers a chain reaction of destruction events for nearby destructible objects

- **BeginPlay Function**: Initializes the component and sets up event binding for triggering chain reaction functionality

- **TickComponent Function**: Updates the component's state every frame

- **TriggerChainReaction Function**: Detects nearby destructible objects and applies damage to initiate a chain reaction of destruction events

Listing 2-29. ChainReactionComponent.h

```
#pragma once

#include "CoreMinimal.h"

class AActor;

#include "ChainReactionComponent.generated.h"

UCLASS( ClassGroup=(Custom), meta=(BlueprintSpawnable
Component) )
class MYGAME_API UChainReactionComponent : public
UActorComponent
{
    GENERATED_BODY()

public:
    UChainReactionComponent();

protected:
    virtual void BeginPlay() override;

    UFUNCTION()
    void TriggerChainReaction();
};
```

Listing 2-30. ChainReactionComponent.cpp

```
#include "ChainReactionComponent.h"
#include "Components/ActorComponent.h"
#include "DestructibleObject.h"

void UChainReactionComponent::BeginPlay()
{
    Super::BeginPlay();
```

CHAPTER 2   ADVANCED COLLISION MECHANICS

```
    // Bind the TriggerChainReaction function to a trigger
       event or game action
    // Example: UFUNCTION() TriggeredByExplosion();
    // Bind function: TriggeredByExplosion.AddDynamic(this,
       &UChainReactionComponent::TriggerChainReaction);
}

void UChainReactionComponent::TickComponent(float DeltaTime,
ELevelTick TickType, FActorComponentTickFunction* This
TickFunction)
{
    Super::TickComponent(DeltaTime, TickType, This
TickFunction);
}

void UChainReactionComponent::TriggerChainReaction()
{
    TArray<AActor*> NearbyObjects;
    GetOwner()->GetOverlappingActors(NearbyObjects,
    ADestructibleObject::StaticClass());

    // Check if there are no objects in the array
    if (NearbyObjects.Num() < 1)
    {
        return; // Exit if no nearby destructible objects
    }

    for (AActor* Object : NearbyObjects)
    {
        if (Object) // Ensure that the object is valid
        {
            ADestructibleObject* Destructible = Cast
            <ADestructibleObject>(Object);
```

```
            if (Destructible && Destructible != GetOwner())
            {
                Destructible->TakeDamage(50.0f); // Example
                    damage amount
            }
        }
    }
}
```

This section explored the fundamentals of object destruction mechanics in game development. From understanding basic object health management to implementing advanced techniques like chain reactions and damage modeling, you've gained insights into how object destruction enhances gameplay dynamics and environmental interactions within the game world.

Object Pickup

Object pickup mechanics involve the ability for players to interact with and acquire items, weapons, or power-ups within the game world. This mechanic is fundamental in many genres, including adventure games, RPGs, and shooters, where players collect resources to enhance their abilities, progress through levels, or achieve specific objectives.

Imagine designing a game where players can gather weapons from defeated enemies, collect health packs scattered throughout levels, or acquire key items needed to unlock new areas.

Basic Usage

Basic object pickup mechanics include

- **Interactable Objects**: Designing game objects that players can approach and interact with to pick up or acquire
- **Inventory Management**: Implementing systems to track and manage collected items, displaying them in an inventory menu or HUD
- **Power-Ups and Enhancements**: Introducing temporary or permanent boosts to player abilities, health, or character attributes through picked-up items
- **Story Progression**: Using key items or plot-related objects as triggers to advance the game's storyline or unlock new gameplay areas

These mechanics provide players with incentives to explore game environments, engage with interactive elements, and strategically plan their inventory management.

Advanced Techniques

Advanced object pickup techniques expand on basic mechanics, including

- **Unique Item Effects**: Designing items with special effects or abilities that significantly impact gameplay, such as invisibility cloaks, teleportation devices, or time-slowing artifacts
- **Interactive Collectibles**: Introducing collectible items that contribute to side quests, hidden objectives, or achievement systems, encouraging exploration and rewarding completionists

- **Multiplayer Integration**: Implementing multiplayer-specific pickup mechanics, such as shared loot in cooperative games or competitive power-ups in PvP environments
- **Dynamic Spawning**: Creating systems that dynamically spawn and distribute items based on player progression, difficulty level, or game events, ensuring balanced gameplay and strategic challenges

These techniques enhance gameplay depth by providing diverse and rewarding player interactions with game objects and environments.

Practical Applications

Object pickup mechanics are essential for

- **Game Progression**: Allowing players to acquire essential items, resources, or tools needed to overcome obstacles, defeat enemies, or solve puzzles
- **Character Customization**: Offering players opportunities to enhance their characters' abilities, skills, or attributes through collected items or power-ups
- **Reward Systems**: Implementing rewards for exploration, achievement, or completion of objectives, fostering player engagement and satisfaction
- **Puzzle-Solving**: Introducing items or clues that players must collect and use strategically to progress through complex puzzles or unlock hidden content

CHAPTER 2   ADVANCED COLLISION MECHANICS

Algorithm Overview

Let's outline the algorithm used for implementing object pickup mechanics:

1. **Detection**: Detect player interaction or proximity to pickup objects within the game world.

2. **Interaction Handling**: Define behavior for picking up objects, such as adding them to the player's inventory, applying immediate effects, or triggering event sequences.

3. **Inventory Management**: Track and manage collected items, updating the player's inventory UI or menu to reflect current items and their status.

4. **Effect Application**: Apply effects or modifications to the player's character, abilities, or game environment based on the picked-up object.

5. **Feedback and Notification**: Provide visual, auditory, or HUD feedback to inform the player of successful pickups, changes in inventory status, or activation of acquired items.

This algorithm provides a framework for integrating object pickup mechanics into Unreal Engine or similar game development environments.

Reviewing the Code

Listing 2-31 implements the PickupItem class, encapsulating the properties and behaviors associated with collectible items within the game environment. These items can be picked up by players to enhance gameplay, providing various effects such as health restoration, power-ups, or inventory additions.

Listing 2-31. PickupItem.h

```
#pragma once

class USaticMeshComponent;
class USphereComponent;

#include "CoreMinimal.h"
#include "GameFramework/Actor.h"
#include "PickupItem.generated.h"

UCLASS()
class MYGAME_API APickupItem : public AActor
{
    GENERATED_BODY()

public:
    APickupItem();

protected:
    virtual void BeginPlay() override;

public:
    virtual void Tick(float DeltaTime) override;

    UPROPERTY(VisibleAnywhere)
    UStaticMeshComponent* PickupMesh;

    UPROPERTY(VisibleAnywhere)
    USphereComponent* CollisionSphere;

    UPROPERTY(EditDefaultsOnly, Category = "Pickup")
    FName ItemName;

    UPROPERTY(EditDefaultsOnly, Category = "Pickup")
    float PickupRadius;
```

```
    UFUNCTION()
    void OnPlayerPickup(class APlayerCharacter* Player);
private:
    bool bIsPickupable;
};
```

Listing 2-32 implements the PickupItem class, representing collectible items within the game world and equipping them with essential collision detection and interaction functionalities.

- **PickupItem Class**: Represents a pickup item in the game world with collision detection and interaction functionalities

- **BeginPlay Function**: Initializes default values for pickup item properties and sets up collision detection for player interaction

- **Tick Function**: Updates the pickup item's state every frame

- **OnPlayerPickup Function**: Handles player interaction events when the player character overlaps with the pickup item's collision sphere, triggering pickup effects or modifications

Listing 2-32. PickupItem.cpp

```
#include "PickupItem.h"
#include "Components/StaticMeshComponent.h"
#include "Components/SphereComponent.h"
#include "PlayerCharacter.h"
```

```cpp
APickupItem::APickupItem()
{
    PrimaryActorTick.bCanEverTick = true;

    PickupMesh = CreateDefaultSubobject<UStaticMeshComponent>
    (TEXT("PickupMesh"));
    RootComponent = PickupMesh;

    CollisionSphere = CreateDefaultSubobject<USphereComponent>
    (TEXT("CollisionSphere"));
    CollisionSphere->SetupAttachment(RootComponent);
    CollisionSphere->SetSphereRadius(PickupRadius);
    CollisionSphere->SetCollisionEnabled(ECollisionEnabled::
    QueryOnly);
    CollisionSphere->SetCollisionResponseToAllChannels
    (ECollisionResponse::ECR_Overlap);

    bIsPickupable = true;
}

void APickupItem::BeginPlay()
{
    Super::BeginPlay();
    CollisionSphere->OnComponentBeginOverlap.AddDynamic
    (this, &APickupItem::OnPlayerPickup);
}

void APickupItem::OnPlayerPickup(APlayerCharacter* Player)
{
    if (bIsPickupable)
    {
        // Add logic here to apply effects or modify player
            state upon pickup
        bIsPickupable = false;
```

```
        Destroy();
    }
}
```

Advanced Pickup Techniques

The InventoryManagement class is designed to handle the systems necessary for managing player inventory and tracking collected items effectively. This system not only keeps a record of all items the player has picked up but also manages the associated effects and modifications these items can apply to the player character.

Listings 2-33 and 2-34 implement the InventoryManager class, a crucial component for managing the player's inventory within the game. It handles the process of adding or removing items, as well as applying effects or modifications based on the items collected by the player.

- **Inventory Structure (FInventoryItem)**: A structure is used to hold the item's name and count in the inventory. This is helpful for tracking quantities of each item.

- **AddItemToInventory()**: The function checks if the item already exists in the inventory. If it does, it increments the count; otherwise, it adds a new item.

- **RemoveItemFromInventory()**: This removes an item from the inventory, reducing the count or deleting it if the count reaches zero.

- **ApplyItemEffect()**: This is where the logic for applying effects (such as buffs or healing) would go, using the item name as an identifier.

Listing 2-33. InventoryManager.h

```cpp
#pragma once

#include "CoreMinimal.h"
#include "UObject/NoExportTypes.h"
#include "InventoryManager.generated.h"

// Define a structure to hold item information, including the
// item type and its count in inventory

USTRUCT(BlueprintType)

struct FInventoryItem
{
    GENERATED_BODY()

    UPROPERTY(EditAnywhere, BlueprintReadWrite, Category =
    "Inventory")
    FName ItemName;

    UPROPERTY(EditAnywhere, BlueprintReadWrite, Category =
    "Inventory")
    int32 ItemCount;

    FInventoryItem() : ItemName(NAME_None), ItemCount(0) {}
};

UCLASS()
class MYGAME_API UInventoryManager : public UObject
{
    GENERATED_BODY()

public:
    UInventoryManager();
```

```cpp
    // Add an item to the inventory
    UFUNCTION(BlueprintCallable)
    void AddItemToInventory(FName ItemName);

    // Remove an item from the inventory
    UFUNCTION(BlueprintCallable)
    void RemoveItemFromInventory(FName ItemName);

    // Apply the effect of an item
    UFUNCTION(BlueprintCallable)
    void ApplyItemEffect(FName ItemName);
protected:
    // Inventory array to store the items and their counts
    UPROPERTY(VisibleAnywhere, BlueprintReadOnly, Category = "Inventory")
    TArray<FInventoryItem> Inventory;
};
```

Listing 2-34. InventoryManager.cpp

```cpp
#include "InventoryManager.h"

UInventoryManager::UInventoryManager()
{
    // Initialize any necessary inventory setup here
}

void UInventoryManager::AddItemToInventory(FName ItemName)
{
    // Search if the item is already in the inventory
    for (FInventoryItem& Item : Inventory)
    {
        if (Item.ItemName == ItemName)
```

CHAPTER 2   ADVANCED COLLISION MECHANICS

```
        {
            // If the item already exists, increase the count
            Item.ItemCount++;
            return;
        }
    }

    // If the item is not found, add a new entry with a
        count of 1
    FInventoryItem NewItem;
    NewItem.ItemName = ItemName;
    NewItem.ItemCount = 1;
    Inventory.Add(NewItem);
}

void UInventoryManager::RemoveItemFromInventory(FName ItemName)
{
    // Loop through the inventory to find and remove the item
    for (int32 Index = 0; Index < Inventory.Num(); Index++)
    {
        if (Inventory[Index].ItemName == ItemName)
        {
            // Decrease the item count or remove entirely
            if (Inventory[Index].ItemCount > 1)
            {
                Inventory[Index].ItemCount--;
            }
            else
            {
                Inventory.RemoveAt(Index);
            }
            return;
```

```cpp
        }
    }
}

void UInventoryManager::ApplyItemEffect(FName ItemName)
{
    // Implement logic to apply the effect of the item
        (e.g., healing, buff, etc.)
    for (const FInventoryItem& Item : Inventory)
    {
        if (Item.ItemName == ItemName)
        {
            // Apply the effect based on the item, could
                involve applying buffs, healing, etc.

            // Example:
            UE_LOG(LogTemp, Warning, TEXT("Applied effect of
            item: %s"), *ItemName.ToString());

            return;
        }
    }
}
```

This section explored the fundamentals of object pickup mechanics in game development. From understanding basic interactions and inventory management to implementing advanced techniques like item effects and multiplayer integration, you've gained insights into how object pickup enhances player engagement and gameplay progression within the game world.

Character Respawn Handling

Character respawn handling involves managing the process by which player characters or entities return to the game world after being defeated or eliminated. This mechanic is crucial in multiplayer shooters, action games, and battle royales, where players must re-enter gameplay after being taken out.

Imagine designing a game where defeated players respawn at designated locations, with different respawn rules affecting gameplay strategies and dynamics.

Basic Usage

Basic character respawn handling includes

- **Respawn Points**: Setting up predefined locations where players respawn after being eliminated or defeated
- **Respawn Timers**: Implementing timers that dictate how long players must wait before respawning back into the game
- **Spawn Protection**: Providing temporary invulnerability or safe spawn zones to prevent immediate elimination upon respawning
- **Death Penalties**: Applying penalties or consequences upon respawn, such as losing collected items or progress

These mechanics ensure fair gameplay and balance in competitive or cooperative multiplayer environments.

Advanced Techniques

Advanced respawn handling techniques expand on basic mechanics, including

- **Dynamic Respawn Locations**: Introducing dynamic or strategic respawn point allocation based on game events, player locations, or team strategies
- **Spawn Influence**: Modifying game conditions or objectives based on respawn dynamics, influencing team tactics and gameplay outcomes
- **Respawn Mechanics Customization**: Allowing players to customize respawn preferences or strategies through in-game settings or options
- **Multiple Lives Systems**: Implementing systems where players have multiple lives or respawns before permanent elimination, adding strategic depth and tension to gameplay

These techniques enhance player immersion, strategy, and engagement in respawn-related gameplay scenarios.

Practical Applications

Character respawn handling is essential for

- **Competitive Gameplay**: Facilitating fair and balanced gameplay in competitive multiplayer modes, ensuring eliminated players can rejoin the action without disrupting game flow

- **Strategic Planning**: Allowing players to strategize respawn tactics, such as choosing optimal respawn points or coordinating team respawns for tactical advantages

- **Player Retention**: Minimizing player frustration by providing opportunities for redemption and continued participation in game sessions

- **Game Mode Diversity**: Supporting diverse game modes, such as respawn-based objectives or last-player-standing scenarios, with tailored respawn mechanics

Algorithm Overview

Let's outline the algorithm used for character respawn handling:

1. **Elimination Detection**: Detect when a player character is eliminated or defeated within the game environment.

2. **Respawn Initialization**: Determine the respawn location and conditions based on predefined rules or dynamic factors.

3. **Respawn Timer**: Start a respawn countdown timer, indicating when the player character can re-enter gameplay.

4. **Spawn Protection**: Provide temporary invulnerability or safe zones upon respawn to prevent immediate elimination.

5. **Respawn Confirmation**: Confirm player readiness to respawn and reintroduce the character into the game world.

This algorithm provides a structured approach to implementing character respawn handling mechanics in Unreal Engine or similar game development environments.

Reviewing the Code

This section focuses on defining respawn points within the game world where player characters return after being eliminated. The respawn handling system is crucial for maintaining game flow and player engagement, ensuring that players can quickly re-enter the action without significant downtime.

Listings 2-35 and 2-36 implement the RespawnPoint class, representing a designated location in the game world where player characters can respawn after being eliminated. This class plays a vital role in maintaining the flow of gameplay by ensuring players have a smooth transition back into the action.

- **RespawnPoint Class**: Represents a respawn point in the game world where player characters respawn after elimination
- **BeginPlay Function**: Initializes default values for respawn point properties and sets up overlap detection for player respawn
- **Tick Function**: Updates the respawn point's state every frame
- **RespawnPlayer Function**: Handles player respawn events when a player character overlaps with the respawn zone, triggering respawn at a random location within the zone

Listing 2-35. RespawnPoint.h

```cpp
#pragma once

class UBoxComponent;

#include "CoreMinimal.h"
#include "GameFramework/Actor.h"
#include "RespawnPoint.generated.h"

UCLASS()
class MYGAME_API ARespawnPoint : public AActor
{
    GENERATED_BODY()

public:
    ARespawnPoint();

protected:
    virtual void BeginPlay() override;

public:
    virtual void Tick(float DeltaTime) override;

    UPROPERTY(VisibleAnywhere)
    UBoxComponent* RespawnZone;

    UPROPERTY(EditAnywhere, Category = "Respawn")
    bool bIsActive;

    UFUNCTION()
    void RespawnPlayer(class APlayerCharacter* Player);

private:
    FVector GetRandomRespawnLocation();
};
```

CHAPTER 2   ADVANCED COLLISION MECHANICS

Listing 2-36. RespawnPoint.cpp

```cpp
#include "RespawnPoint.h"
#include "Components/BoxComponent.h"
#include "PlayerCharacter.h"
#include "Components/BoxComponent.h"

ARespawnPoint::ARespawnPoint()
{
    PrimaryActorTick.bCanEverTick = true;

    RespawnZone = CreateDefaultSubobject<UBoxComponent>(TEXT
    ("RespawnZone"));
    RootComponent = RespawnZone;

    bIsActive = true;
}
void ARespawnPoint::BeginPlay()
{
    Super::BeginPlay();
    RespawnZone->OnComponentBeginOverlap.AddDynamic(this, &ARes
    pawnPoint::RespawnPlayer);
}

void ARespawnPoint::RespawnPlayer(APlayerCharacter* Player)
{
    if (bIsActive)
    {
        FVector SpawnLocation = GetRandomRespawnLocation();
        Player->RespawnAtLocation(SpawnLocation);
        bIsActive = false; // Prevent multiple respawns at the
        same point simultaneously
    }
}
```

```
FVector ARespawnPoint::GetRandomRespawnLocation()
{
    if (RespawnZone)
    {
        // Get the center location of the RespawnZone
        FVector ZoneCenter = RespawnZone-
        >GetComponentLocation();

        // Define the radius within which the random point will
            be found
        float Radius = 500.0f;   // Adjust the radius as needed

        // Try to get a random reachable point within the
            radius of the RespawnZone
        FVector RandomPoint = UGameplayStatics::GetRandom
        ReachablePointInRadius(GetWorld(), ZoneCenter, Radius);

        return RandomPoint;
    }

    // Return default location if RespawnZone is not valid
    return FVector::ZeroVector;
}
```

Advanced Respawn Techniques

Dynamic respawn allocation involves creating systems that adjust respawn points in real time based on various game conditions. This technique enhances gameplay by strategically placing respawn points to optimize player experience and game balance.

Listings 2-37 and 2-38 implement the RespawnManager class, overseeing the allocation, activation, and deactivation of respawn points within the game environment. This class plays a critical role in enhancing gameplay dynamics by responding to various game conditions and player actions.

CHAPTER 2   ADVANCED COLLISION MECHANICS

- **RespawnManager Class**: Manages respawn point allocation, activation, and deactivation based on dynamic or strategic game conditions
- **SetRespawnPoint Function**: Sets a specific respawn point location based on game events or player actions
- **ActivateRespawnPoint Function**: Activates a respawn point for player use, allowing respawn events to occur at designated locations
- **DeactivateRespawnPoint Function**: Temporarily or permanently deactivates a respawn point, modifying respawn dynamics and strategic gameplay decisions

Listing 2-37. RespawnManager.h

```
#pragma once

#include "CoreMinimal.h"
#include "UObject/NoExportTypes.h"
#include "RespawnManager.generated.h"

UCLASS()
class MYGAME_API URespawnManager : public UObject
{
GENERATED_BODY()

public:
URespawnManager();

// Function to set a specific respawn point location
UFUNCTION(BlueprintCallable)
void SetRespawnPoint(FVector RespawnLocation);
```

```cpp
// Function to activate a respawn point for player use
UFUNCTION(BlueprintCallable)
void ActivateRespawnPoint();

// Function to deactivate a respawn point temporarily or
permanently
UFUNCTION(BlueprintCallable)
void DeactivateRespawnPoint();

protected:
// Stores the current respawn location
FVector CurrentRespawnLocation;

// Timer handle to manage the reactivation of a respawn point
FTimerHandle RespawnTimerHandle;

// Respawn point's active status
bool bIsRespawnActive;

// Function to reset the respawn point to active after a delay
void ResetRespawnPoint();
};
```

Listing 2-38. RespawnManager.cpp

```cpp
#include "RespawnManager.h"
#include "GameFramework/Actor.h"
#include "Engine/World.h"
#include "TimerManager.h"

URespawnManager::URespawnManager()
{
    // Initialize default values
    bIsRespawnActive = true;
}
```

CHAPTER 2   ADVANCED COLLISION MECHANICS

```cpp
void URespawnManager::SetRespawnPoint(FVector RespawnLocation)
{
    // Set the player's current location as the respawn
       location
    CurrentRespawnLocation = RespawnLocation;

    // Optionally, trigger other logic like updating a UI or
       activating a checkpoint
}

void URespawnManager::ActivateRespawnPoint()
{
    if (!bIsRespawnActive)
    {
        // Logic to activate the respawn point if it was
           previously deactivated
        bIsRespawnActive = true;
        // Optionally, notify other systems about the
           activation
    }
}

void URespawnManager::DeactivateRespawnPoint()
{
    if (bIsRespawnActive)
    {
        // Deactivate the respawn point temporarily
        bIsRespawnActive = false;

        // Optionally, add logic to notify the player or
           gameplay systems
```

```
        // Set a timer to reset the respawn point after a delay
            (e.g., 5 seconds)
        GetWorld()->GetTimerManager().SetTimer(RespawnTimer
        Handle, this, &URespawnManager::ResetRespawnPoint,
        5.0f, false);
    }
}

void URespawnManager::ResetRespawnPoint()
{
    // Reset the respawn point to active after the delay
    bIsRespawnActive = true;

    // Optionally, add logic to notify players about respawn
        point reactivation
}
```

This section explored the fundamentals of character respawn handling mechanics in game development. From understanding basic respawn mechanics and spawn protection to implementing advanced techniques like dynamic respawn allocation and multiplayer integration, you've gained insights into how respawn handling enhances player experience and strategic gameplay in various gaming scenarios.

Terrain Deformation

Terrain deformation involves modifying the shape or structure of the game environment's terrain based on player actions, environmental effects, or dynamic events. This mechanic adds realism, interactivity, and strategic depth to games focused on exploration, combat, or environmental interaction.

CHAPTER 2   ADVANCED COLLISION MECHANICS

Imagine designing a game where players can carve paths, create barriers, or trigger environmental changes through terrain deformation mechanics.

Basic Usage

Basic terrain deformation includes

- **Digging and Excavation**: Allowing players to dig trenches, tunnels, or holes in the terrain using specific tools or actions.

- **Building and Construction**: Enabling players to construct structures, walls, or barriers that alter the landscape and provide strategic advantages.

- **Erosion and Destruction**: Implementing natural erosion or destruction effects that change terrain features over time or due to environmental factors.

- **Dynamic Terrain Modification**: Supporting dynamic changes in terrain shape or topology based on game events, such as explosions or earthquakes.

- **Dynamic Actor Placement**: Large actors (like heavy machinery, buildings, or vehicles) require flat surfaces to be placed. By using terrain deformation, you can dynamically adjust the landscape to accommodate large objects. When placing a large building, the system automatically flattens the area within the footprint of the building. If the ground is uneven, it reshapes the terrain beneath the structure.

These mechanics enhance gameplay immersion and player agency by allowing them to shape the game world according to their strategies or playstyles.

Advanced Techniques

Advanced terrain deformation techniques expand on basic mechanics, including

- **Real-Time Physics Simulation:** Integrating physics-based algorithms to simulate realistic terrain deformation effects, such as soil displacement or material erosion.

- **Persistent Terrain Changes:** Ensuring persistent changes to terrain deformation effects across game sessions or multiplayer interactions, affecting long-term gameplay strategies.

- **Interactive Environmental Effects:** Introducing interactive elements like weather systems, volcanic eruptions, or dynamic water flow that dynamically alter terrain features.

- **Player-Driven Environments:** Allowing players to collaboratively or competitively modify shared game environments, influencing world dynamics and strategic gameplay outcomes.

- **Procedural Terrain Changes:** Use procedural techniques to dynamically alter the landscape at intervals, changing the area a player is currently interacting with. This allows for constant changes to the environment, keeping the gameplay fresh and unpredictable.

These techniques enable complex environmental interactions and emergent gameplay scenarios driven by terrain deformation mechanics.

CHAPTER 2   ADVANCED COLLISION MECHANICS

Practical Applications

Terrain deformation is essential for

- **Exploration and Discovery**: Facilitating exploration-driven gameplay where players uncover hidden paths, resources, or secrets through terrain manipulation

- **Combat and Defense**: Supporting tactical combat strategies where players use terrain features as cover, obstacles, or defensive structures in battle

- **Environmental Puzzle-Solving**: Creating puzzles or challenges that require players to manipulate terrain to progress, solve mysteries, or unlock new areas

- **Dynamic World Events**: Introducing dynamic events or catastrophes like landslides, floods, or avalanches that reshape the game environment and challenge player strategies

Algorithm Overview

Let's outline the algorithm used for terrain deformation:

1. **Terrain Initialization**: Initialize the game environment with predefined terrain features, including heightmaps, textures, and initial topology.

2. **Deformation Input Detection**: Detect player inputs or triggers that initiate terrain deformation actions, such as digging, building, or destruction.

3. **Terrain Modification**: Apply algorithms or methods to modify terrain geometry, textures, or material properties based on deformation actions.

4. **Physics Simulation**: Integrate real-time physics simulations to handle dynamic changes in terrain shape, erosion effects, or structural integrity.

5. **Persistence and Synchronization**: Ensure persistent terrain changes across game sessions or multiplayer interactions, synchronizing terrain deformation effects for all players.

This algorithm provides a structured approach to implementing terrain deformation mechanics in Unreal Engine or similar game development environments.

Reviewing the Code

This section introduces the classes and functions designed to manage terrain deformation mechanics in the game, allowing for interactions such as digging, building structures, and simulating erosion effects.

Listings 2-39 and 2-40 implement the TerrainDeformer class, managing terrain modifications based on player interactions. It offers mechanics such as digging and building that enhance the dynamic nature of gameplay, allowing players to reshape the environment and impact both gameplay and strategy.

- **TerrainDeformer Class**: Represents an actor that deforms terrain based on player actions, including digging and building mechanics
- **DigTerrain Function**: Implements digging mechanics to modify terrain geometry or material properties based on specified location and radius
- **BuildStructure Function**: Implements building mechanics to construct structures or obstacles on the terrain, affecting gameplay dynamics and environmental interactions

Listing 2-39. TerrainDeformer.h

```cpp
#pragma once

class UStaticMeshComponent;

#include "CoreMinimal.h"
#include "GameFramework/Actor.h"
#include "TerrainDeformer.generated.h"

UCLASS()
class MYGAME_API ATerrainDeformer : public AActor
{
    GENERATED_BODY()
public:
    ATerrainDeformer();

protected:
    virtual void BeginPlay() override;

public:
    virtual void Tick(float DeltaTime) override;

    UFUNCTION(BlueprintCallable)
    void DigTerrain(FVector DigLocation, float DigRadius);

    UFUNCTION(BlueprintCallable)
    void BuildStructure(FVector BuildLocation, float StructureSize);

private:
    UPROPERTY(EditDefaultsOnly, Category = "Deformation")
    UStaticMeshComponent* TerrainMesh;

    UPROPERTY(EditDefaultsOnly, Category = "Deformation")
    UMaterialInterface* DeformationMaterial;
```

CHAPTER 2 ADVANCED COLLISION MECHANICS

```cpp
    UPROPERTY(EditDefaultsOnly, Category = "Deformation")
    float DigDepth;

    UPROPERTY(EditDefaultsOnly, Category = "Deformation")
    float BuildHeight;
};
```

Listing 2-40. TerrainDeformer.cpp

```cpp
#include "TerrainDeformer.h"
#include "Components/StaticMeshComponent.h"

ATerrainDeformer::ATerrainDeformer()
{
    PrimaryActorTick.bCanEverTick = true;

    TerrainMesh = CreateDefaultSubobject<UStaticMeshComponent>(
    TEXT("TerrainMesh"));
    RootComponent = TerrainMesh;

    DigDepth = 100.0f;
    BuildHeight = 200.0f;
}
void ATerrainDeformer::BeginPlay()
{
    Super::BeginPlay();

    if (TerrainMesh) // Ensure TerrainMesh is valid before
    accessing it
    {
        TerrainMesh->SetMaterial(0, DeformationMaterial);
    }
}
```

CHAPTER 2   ADVANCED COLLISION MECHANICS

```
void ATerrainDeformer::Tick(float DeltaTime)
{
    Super::Tick(DeltaTime);
}

void ATerrainDeformer::DigTerrain(FVector DigLocation, float
DigRadius)
{
    // Implement logic to dig terrain at DigLocation with
       specified radius and depth
    // Modify terrain geometry or material properties based on
       dig action
}

void ATerrainDeformer::BuildStructure(FVector BuildLocation,
float StructureSize)
{
    // Implement logic to build a structure at BuildLocation
       with specified size and height
    // Modify terrain geometry or material properties to
       incorporate built structure
}
```

Advanced Terrain Deformation Techniques

The real-time physics simulation technique focuses on integrating advanced physics algorithms into the terrain deformation mechanics, enhancing the realism and interactivity of the environment. This approach allows for dynamic responses to player actions, ensuring that the terrain behaves in a physically plausible manner as it is manipulated.

Listings 2-41 and 2-42 integrate physics-based simulations, enhancing the interactive experience within the game world.

CHAPTER 2   ADVANCED COLLISION MECHANICS

- **TerrainPhysics Class**: Manages physics-based algorithms for terrain deformation, including erosion simulation and impact force application
- **SimulateTerrainErosion Function**: Simulates erosion effects on terrain based on specified erosion strength and rate, modifying terrain geometry or material properties accordingly
- **ApplyPhysicsForces Function**: Applies physics forces to simulate impact on terrain, influencing terrain deformation dynamics and environmental interactions

Listing 2-41. TerrainPhysics.h

```
#pragma once

#include "CoreMinimal.h"
#include "UObject/NoExportTypes.h"
#include "TerrainPhysics.generated.h"

UCLASS()
class MYGAME_API UTerrainPhysics : public UObject
{
    GENERATED_BODY()

public:
    UTerrainPhysics();

    UFUNCTION(BlueprintCallable)
    void SimulateTerrainErosion(float ErosionStrength);

    UFUNCTION(BlueprintCallable)
    void ApplyPhysicsForces(FVector ImpactPoint, float ImpactForce);
```

CHAPTER 2　ADVANCED COLLISION MECHANICS

```cpp
private:
    UPROPERTY(EditDefaultsOnly, Category = "Physics")
    float TerrainStrength;

    UPROPERTY(EditDefaultsOnly, Category = "Physics")
    float ErosionRate;

    UPROPERTY(EditDefaultsOnly, Category = "Physics")
    float ImpactForceMultiplier;
};
```

Listing 2-42. TerrainPhysics.cpp

```cpp
#include "TerrainPhysics.h"

UTerrainPhysics::UTerrainPhysics()
{
    TerrainStrength = 1000.0f;
    ErosionRate = 0.5f;
    ImpactForceMultiplier = 500.0f;
}

void UTerrainPhysics::SimulateTerrainErosion(float ErosionStrength)
{
    if (!TerrainMesh) return;

    TArray<FVector> Vertices;
    TerrainMesh->GetVerticesWithinRadius(ErosionPoint, DeformationRadius, Vertices);

    for (FVector& Vertex : Vertices)
    {
        FVector Downward = FVector(0, 0, -1); // Simulating downward erosion effect
```

```
        Vertex += Downward * (ErosionStrength * ErosionRate);
    }

    TerrainMesh->UpdateMesh();
}

void UTerrainPhysics::ApplyPhysicsForces(FVector ImpactPoint,
float ImpactForce)
{
    // Implement physics-based force application to simulate
      impact on terrain
    // Apply forces to terrain vertices or material properties
      based on impact point and force intensity
}
```

This section explored the fundamentals of terrain deformation mechanics in game development. From understanding basic terrain modification techniques to implementing advanced physics simulations and environmental effects, you've gained insights into how terrain deformation enhances realism, interactivity, and strategic depth in gaming experiences.

Object Scaling on Collision

Object scaling on collision involves altering the size or scale of game objects dynamically based on collision events. This mechanic adds visual feedback, gameplay dynamics, and interactive elements to games where object size affects player strategies or environmental interactions.

Imagine designing a game where objects grow, shrink, or transform in response to collisions, enhancing gameplay challenges or puzzle-solving mechanics.

CHAPTER 2 ADVANCED COLLISION MECHANICS

Basic Usage

Basic object scaling on collision includes

- **Collision Detection**: Continuously checking for collisions between game objects and designated trigger volumes or collision zones
- **Scaling Mechanism**: Implementing algorithms or functions that adjust the scale or size of objects based on collision impact, velocity, or specific game rules
- **Visual Feedback**: Providing visual cues or animations to indicate object scaling effects, enhancing player immersion and feedback during gameplay
- **Gameplay Effects**: Introducing gameplay effects or challenges where object size influences navigation, puzzle-solving, combat strategies, or environmental interactions

These mechanics allow developers to create dynamic and responsive game worlds where object scaling on collision affects player decisions and gameplay outcomes.

Advanced Techniques

Advanced object scaling techniques expand on basic mechanics, including

- **Procedural Scaling Algorithms**: Integrating procedural algorithms to dynamically adjust object scale based on complex collision interactions or environmental factors

- **Interactive Transformations**: Allowing players to trigger object scaling through interactive elements, puzzles, or gameplay actions, influencing game progression or narrative outcomes

- **Real-Time Physics Simulation**: Implementing physics-based simulations to calculate object scaling effects, ensuring realistic and dynamic responses to collision events

- **Multiplayer Synchronization**: Synchronizing object scaling effects across multiplayer environments, ensuring consistent gameplay experiences and interactions for all players

These techniques enable developers to create engaging and immersive gameplay scenarios where object scaling on collision enhances strategic depth, player agency, and interactive storytelling.

Practical Applications

Object scaling on collision is used in various game development applications, including

- **Environmental Puzzle-Solving**: Designing puzzles or challenges where players manipulate object size through collisions to navigate obstacles, reach objectives, or unlock new areas

- **Combat Strategy**: Introducing combat mechanics where object scaling affects attack range, damage output, or defensive capabilities, requiring strategic positioning and timing

CHAPTER 2   ADVANCED COLLISION MECHANICS

- **Platforming and Navigation**: Enhancing platforming mechanics where object scaling influences jump heights, obstacle traversal, or pathfinding through dynamic terrain or level designs

- **Interactive Storytelling**: Integrating object scaling as a narrative device where character progression, emotional arcs, or plot twists are influenced by collision-driven transformations

Algorithm Overview

Let's outline the algorithm used for object scaling on collision:

1. **Initialization**: Initialize game objects with default scale, collision settings, and interaction parameters.

2. **Collision Detection**: Continuously monitor collisions between objects and designated collision zones or trigger volumes.

3. **Scaling Calculation**: Calculate new object scale based on collision impact, velocity, or predefined scaling rules.

4. **Visual Feedback**: Update object visuals, animations, or particle effects to reflect scaling changes and provide player feedback.

5. **Gameplay Integration**: Integrate object scaling effects into gameplay mechanics, puzzles, combat scenarios, or narrative events to enhance player engagement and immersion.

This algorithm provides a structured approach to implementing object scaling on collision mechanics in Unreal Engine or similar game development environments.

Reviewing the Code

The ScalingObject class implements mechanics for dynamically scaling objects in response to collision events. This functionality enhances gameplay by providing visual feedback and interaction depth when objects come into contact.

Listings 2-43 and 2-44 implement the ScalingObject class, representing an actor that dynamically adjusts its size in response to collisions with other actors in the game environment. This mechanic enhances gameplay by providing interactive feedback to players.

- **ScalingObject Class**: Represents an actor that scales in response to collisions, adjusting size based on collision impulse magnitude

- **OnObjectCollision Function**: Event handler triggered when the object collides with another actor or collision component, initiating scaling calculations based on collision impulse

- **ScaleObject Function**: Calculates and applies new object scale based on collision impulse magnitude, adjusting object visuals or animations to reflect scaling changes

CHAPTER 2   ADVANCED COLLISION MECHANICS

Listing 2-43. ScalingObject.h

```cpp
#pragma once

class UStaticMeshComponent;
class USphereComponent;

#include "CoreMinimal.h"
#include "GameFramework/Actor.h"
#include "ScalingObject.generated.h"

UCLASS()
class MYGAME_API AScalingObject : public AActor
{
    GENERATED_BODY()

public:
    AScalingObject();

protected:
    virtual void BeginPlay() override;

public:
    virtual void Tick(float DeltaTime) override;

    UFUNCTION()
    void OnObjectCollision(UPrimitiveComponent* HitComponent,
    AActor* OtherActor, UPrimitiveComponent* OtherComp, FVector
    NormalImpulse, const FHitResult& Hit);

private:
    UPROPERTY(VisibleAnywhere)
    UStaticMeshComponent* ObjectMesh;

    UPROPERTY(VisibleAnywhere)
    USphereComponent* CollisionSphere;
```

CHAPTER 2　ADVANCED COLLISION MECHANICS

```
    UPROPERTY(EditDefaultsOnly, Category = "Scaling")
    float MinScale;

    UPROPERTY(EditDefaultsOnly, Category = "Scaling")
    float MaxScale;

    UPROPERTY(EditDefaultsOnly, Category = "Scaling")
    float CollisionThreshold;

    bool bIsScalingEnabled;

    void ScaleObject(float ImpulseMagnitude);
};
```

Listing 2-44. ScalingObject.cpp

```
#include "Components/StaticMeshComponent.h"
#include "Components/SphereComponent.h"
#include "ScalingObject.h"

AScalingObject::AScalingObject()
{
    PrimaryActorTick.bCanEverTick = true;

    ObjectMesh = CreateDefaultSubobject<UStaticMeshComponent>
    (TEXT("ObjectMesh"));
    RootComponent = ObjectMesh;

    CollisionSphere = CreateDefaultSubobject<USphereComponent>
    (TEXT("CollisionSphere"));
    CollisionSphere->SetupAttachment(RootComponent);

    MinScale = 0.5f;
    MaxScale = 2.0f;
    CollisionThreshold = 500.0f;
    bIsScalingEnabled = true;
```

```cpp
    CollisionSphere->OnComponentHit.AddDynamic(this, &AScaling
    Object::OnObjectCollision);
}

void AScalingObject::OnObjectCollision(UPrimitiveComponent*
HitComponent, AActor* OtherActor, UPrimitiveComponent*
OtherComp, FVector NormalImpulse, const FHitResult& Hit)
{
    if (!bIsScalingEnabled)
        return;

    float ImpulseMagnitude = NormalImpulse.Size();
    if (ImpulseMagnitude > CollisionThreshold)
    {
        ScaleObject(ImpulseMagnitude);
    }
}

void AScalingObject::ScaleObject(float ImpulseMagnitude)
{
    float ScaleFactor = FMath::Lerp(MinScale, MaxScale,
    ImpulseMagnitude / CollisionThreshold);
    FVector NewScale = FVector(ScaleFactor);

    ObjectMesh->SetWorldScale3D(NewScale);

    // Add visual feedback or animation here
}
```

Advanced Scaling Techniques

Incorporating procedural scaling algorithms allows for a more nuanced and dynamic response to collisions, enhancing the interactivity and realism of the game environment. These algorithms can take various factors into account to adjust object scale effectively.

CHAPTER 2   ADVANCED COLLISION MECHANICS

Listings 2-45 and 2-46 implement the ProceduralScaling class, managing the algorithms that dynamically adjust the scale of objects in response to various collision factors. This class plays a crucial role in enhancing the realism and interactivity of the game environment.

- **ProceduralScaling Class**: Manages procedural algorithms for adjusting object scale based on collision intensity, velocity, or dynamic factors
- **AdjustObjectScale Function**: Calculates and applies procedural scaling effects to game objects, enhancing gameplay dynamics, visual feedback, and interactive storytelling through collision-driven transformations

Listing 2-45. ProceduralScaling.h

```
#pragma once

#include "CoreMinimal.h"
#include "UObject/NoExportTypes.h"
#include "ProceduralScaling.generated.h"

UCLASS()
class MYGAME_API UProceduralScaling : public UObject
{
    GENERATED_BODY()
public:
    UProceduralScaling();

    UFUNCTION(BlueprintCallable)
    void AdjustObjectScale(float CollisionIntensity, float Velocity);
```

CHAPTER 2   ADVANCED COLLISION MECHANICS

```cpp
private:
    UPROPERTY(EditDefaultsOnly, Category = "Scaling")
    float MinScaleFactor;

    UPROPERTY(EditDefaultsOnly, Category = "Scaling")
    float MaxScaleFactor;

    UPROPERTY(EditDefaultsOnly, Category = "Scaling")
    float CollisionImpactThreshold;

    UPROPERTY(EditDefaultsOnly, Category = "Scaling")
    float MaxVelocityFactor;
};
```

Listing 2-46. ProceduralScaling.cpp

```cpp
#include "ProceduralScaling.h"

UProceduralScaling::UProceduralScaling()
{
    MinScaleFactor = 0.5f;
    MaxScaleFactor = 2.0f;
    CollisionImpactThreshold = 1000.0f;
    MaxVelocityFactor = 5.0f;
}

void UProceduralScaling::AdjustObjectScale(float CollisionIntensity, float Velocity)
{
    float ScaleFactor = FMath::Lerp(MinScaleFactor, MaxScaleFactor, CollisionIntensity / CollisionImpactThreshold);
    float VelocityFactor = FMath::Lerp(1.0f, MaxVelocityFactor, Velocity);
```

```
    float FinalScale = ScaleFactor * VelocityFactor;

    // Apply scaling logic to game objects based on collision
        intensity and velocity factors
    // Modify object scale or visual properties dynamically to
        reflect scaling effects
}
```

This section explored the fundamentals of object scaling on collision mechanics in game development. From understanding basic scaling techniques to implementing advanced procedural algorithms and interactive transformations, you've gained insights into how object scaling enhances gameplay immersion, strategic depth, and player engagement in dynamic gaming experiences.

Object Rotation on Collision

Object rotation on collision involves dynamically altering the orientation or rotation of game objects in response to collision events. This mechanic adds interactive elements, gameplay dynamics, and visual feedback to games where object rotation affects player strategies, environmental interactions, or puzzle-solving mechanics.

Imagine designing a game where objects rotate, spin, or reorient themselves upon collision, influencing gameplay challenges, platformer games, puzzles, navigation strategies, or combat tactics.

Basic Usage

Basic object rotation on collision includes

- **Collision Detection**: Continuously monitoring collisions between game objects and designated trigger volumes or collision zones

CHAPTER 2   ADVANCED COLLISION MECHANICS

- **Rotation Mechanism**: Implementing algorithms or functions that adjust the orientation or rotation of objects based on collision impact, velocity, or specific game rules
- **Visual Feedback**: Providing visual cues or animations to indicate object rotation effects, enhancing player immersion and feedback during gameplay
- **Gameplay Effects**: Introducing gameplay effects or challenges where object orientation influences navigation, puzzle-solving, combat strategies, or environmental interactions

These mechanics allow developers to create dynamic and responsive game worlds where object rotation on collision enhances player decisions, strategic depth, and interactive storytelling.

Advanced Techniques

Advanced object rotation techniques expand on basic mechanics, including

- **Procedural Rotation Algorithms**: Integrating procedural algorithms to dynamically adjust object rotation based on collision intensity, velocity, or environmental factors
- **Interactive Transformations**: Allowing players to trigger object rotation through interactive elements, puzzles, or gameplay actions, influencing game progression or narrative outcomes

- **Real-Time Physics Simulation**: Implementing physics-based simulations to calculate object rotation effects, ensuring realistic and dynamic responses to collision events

- **Multiplayer Synchronization**: Synchronizing object rotation effects across multiplayer environments, ensuring consistent gameplay experiences and interactions for all players

These techniques enable developers to create engaging and immersive gameplay scenarios where object rotation on collision enhances gameplay dynamics, puzzle-solving challenges, and player agency.

Practical Applications

Object rotation on collision is used in various game development applications, including

- **Environmental Puzzle-Solving**: Designing puzzles or challenges where players manipulate object orientation through collisions to navigate obstacles, reach objectives, or unlock new areas

- **Combat Strategy**: Introducing combat mechanics where object rotation affects attack angles, defensive maneuvers, or tactical positioning, requiring strategic planning and spatial awareness

- **Platforming and Navigation**: Enhancing platforming mechanics where object rotation influences jump trajectories, obstacle traversal, or pathfinding through dynamic terrain or level designs

- **Interactive Storytelling**: Integrating object rotation as a narrative device where character progression, emotional arcs, or plot twists are influenced by collision-driven transformations

Algorithm Overview

Let's outline the algorithm used for object rotation on collision:

1. **Initialization**: Initialize game objects with default rotation, collision settings, and interaction parameters.

2. **Collision Detection**: Continuously monitor collisions between objects and designated collision zones or trigger volumes.

3. **Rotation Calculation**: Calculate new object rotation based on collision impact, velocity, or predefined rotation rules.

4. **Visual Feedback**: Update object visuals, animations, or particle effects to reflect rotation changes and provide player feedback.

5. **Gameplay Integration**: Integrate object rotation effects into gameplay mechanics, puzzles, combat scenarios, or narrative events to enhance player engagement and immersion.

This algorithm provides a structured approach to implementing object rotation on collision mechanics in Unreal Engine or similar game development environments.

CHAPTER 2   ADVANCED COLLISION MECHANICS

Reviewing the Code

This section outlines the classes and functions responsible for handling the mechanics of object rotation in response to collisions. The functionality encompasses collision detection, precise rotation calculations, and providing visual feedback to enhance player interaction with the game environment.

Listings 2-47 and 2-48 implement the RotationOnCollision class, managing the rotation of game objects when they collide with other actors or components.

- **RotationObject Class**: Represents an actor that rotates in response to collisions, adjusting orientation based on collision impulse magnitude
- **OnObjectCollision Function**: Event handler triggered when the object collides with another actor or collision component, initiating rotation calculations based on collision impulse
- **RotateObject Function**: Calculates and applies new object rotation based on collision impulse magnitude, adjusting object visuals or animations to reflect rotation changes

Listing 2-47. RotationObject.h

```
#pragma once

class UStaticMeshComponent;
class USphereComponent;

#include "CoreMinimal.h"
#include "GameFramework/Actor.h"
#include "RotationObject.generated.h"
```

CHAPTER 2 ADVANCED COLLISION MECHANICS

```cpp
UCLASS()
class MYGAME_API ARotationObject : public AActor
{
    GENERATED_BODY()
public:
    ARotationObject();

    UFUNCTION()
    void OnObjectCollision(UPrimitiveComponent* HitComponent,
    AActor* OtherActor, UPrimitiveComponent* OtherComp,
                          FVector NormalImpulse, const FHit
                          Result& Hit);
private:
    UPROPERTY(VisibleAnywhere)
    UStaticMeshComponent* ObjectMesh;

    UPROPERTY(VisibleAnywhere)
    USphereComponent* CollisionSphere;

    UPROPERTY(EditDefaultsOnly, Category = "Rotation")
    float MaxRotationAngle;

    UPROPERTY(EditDefaultsOnly, Category = "Rotation")
    float CollisionThreshold;

    bool bIsRotationEnabled;

    void RotateObject(float ImpulseMagnitude);
};
```

CHAPTER 2   ADVANCED COLLISION MECHANICS

Listing 2-48. RotationObject.cpp

```cpp
#include "Components/StaticMeshComponent.h"
#include "Components/SphereComponent.h"
#include "RotationObject.h"

ARotationObject::ARotationObject()
{
    PrimaryActorTick.bCanEverTick = true;

    ObjectMesh = CreateDefaultSubobject<UStaticMeshComponent>
    (TEXT("ObjectMesh"));
    RootComponent = ObjectMesh;

    CollisionSphere = CreateDefaultSubobject<USphereComponent>
    (TEXT("CollisionSphere"));
    CollisionSphere->SetupAttachment(RootComponent);

    MaxRotationAngle = 90.0f;
    CollisionThreshold = 500.0f;
    bIsRotationEnabled = true;

    CollisionSphere->OnComponentHit.AddDynamic(this, &ARotation
    Object::OnObjectCollision);
}

void ARotationObject::OnObjectCollision(UPrimitiveComponent*
HitComponent, AActor* OtherActor, UPrimitiveComponent*
OtherComp, FVector NormalImpulse, const FHitResult& Hit)
{
    if (!bIsRotationEnabled)
        return;

    float ImpulseMagnitude = NormalImpulse.Size();
    if (ImpulseMagnitude > CollisionThreshold)
```

```cpp
    {
        RotateObject(ImpulseMagnitude);
    }
}

void ARotationObject::RotateObject(float ImpulseMagnitude)
{
    float RotationAngle = FMath::Lerp(0.0f, MaxRotationAngle,
    ImpulseMagnitude / CollisionThreshold);

    // Determine dynamic rotation axis
    float Yaw = FMath::RandBool() ? RotationAngle : 0.0f;
    float Pitch = FMath::RandBool() ? RotationAngle : 0.0f;
    float Roll = FMath::RandBool() ? RotationAngle : 0.0f;

    FRotator RotationDelta = FRotator(Pitch, Yaw, Roll);
    ObjectMesh->AddLocalRotation(RotationDelta);

    // Add visual feedback or animation here
}
```

Advanced Rotation Techniques

This section delves into the implementation of advanced procedural algorithms designed to dynamically adjust the rotation of objects based on various factors such as collision intensity, velocity, and environmental influences. These techniques enhance the realism and responsiveness of object interactions within the game.

Listings 2-49 and 2-50 implement the ProceduralRotation class, managing the procedural algorithms responsible for dynamically modifying object rotation based on multiple parameters.

CHAPTER 2　ADVANCED COLLISION MECHANICS

- **ProceduralRotation Class**: Manages procedural algorithms for dynamically adjusting object rotation in response to collision intensity, velocity, and predefined rotation constraints. It ensures that objects rotate in a physically intuitive way based on in-game interactions.

- **AdjustObjectRotation Function**: Calculates and applies procedural rotation effects to game objects, enhancing gameplay dynamics, visual feedback, and interactive storytelling through collision-driven transformations.

Listing 2-49. ProceduralRotation.h

```
#pragma once

#include "CoreMinimal.h"
#include "UObject/NoExportTypes.h"
#include "ProceduralRotation.generated.h"

UCLASS()
class MYGAME_API UProceduralRotation : public UObject
{
    GENERATED_BODY()
public:
    UProceduralRotation();

    UFUNCTION(BlueprintCallable)
    void AdjustObjectRotation(float CollisionIntensity, float Velocity);
private:
    UPROPERTY(EditDefaultsOnly, Category = "Rotation")
    float MaxRotationAngle;
```

CHAPTER 2 ADVANCED COLLISION MECHANICS

```cpp
    UPROPERTY(EditDefaultsOnly, Category = "Rotation")
    float CollisionImpactThreshold;

    UPROPERTY(EditDefaultsOnly, Category = "Rotation")
    float MaxVelocityFactor;
};
```

Listing 2-50. ProceduralRotation.cpp

```cpp
#include "ProceduralRotation.h"

UProceduralRotation::UProceduralRotation()
{
    MaxRotationAngle = 180.0f;
    CollisionImpactThreshold = 1000.0f;
    MaxVelocityFactor = 5.0f;
}

void UProceduralRotation::AdjustObjectRotation(float CollisionIntensity, float Velocity)
{
    float RotationAngle = FMath::Lerp(0.0f, MaxRotationAngle, CollisionIntensity / CollisionImpactThreshold);
    float VelocityFactor = FMath::Lerp(1.0f, MaxVelocityFactor, Velocity);

    // Determine the axis of rotation dynamically based on
       object properties or procedural logic
    float Yaw = ShouldRotateOnYaw ? RotationAngle * VelocityFactor : 0.0f;
    float Pitch = ShouldRotateOnPitch ? RotationAngle * VelocityFactor : 0.0f;
    float Roll = ShouldRotateOnRoll ? RotationAngle * VelocityFactor : 0.0f;
```

```
FRotator RotationDelta = FRotator(Pitch, Yaw, Roll);
// Apply rotation logic to game objects based on collision
    intensity, velocity, and expected rotation behavior
// Ensure the rotation aligns with procedural expectations
    and object-specific rotational constraints
}
```

This section explored the fundamentals of object rotation on collision mechanics in game development. From understanding basic rotation techniques to implementing advanced procedural algorithms and interactive transformations, you've gained insights into how object rotation enhances gameplay immersion, strategic depth, and player engagement in dynamic gaming experiences.

Particle Effects on Collision

Particle effects on collision involve creating visual and interactive effects that trigger when game objects collide. These effects enhance gameplay immersion, provide visual feedback, and signify dynamic interactions within the game environment.

Imagine designing a game where collisions generate bursts of sparks, explosions, or magical effects, intensifying player experiences and highlighting critical gameplay events.

Basic Usage

Basic particle effects on collision include

- **Collision Detection**: Monitoring collisions between game objects, characters, or projectiles to trigger particle effects

- **Particle Systems**: Implementing predefined or custom particle systems that generate visual effects like sparks, smoke, fire, or magical auras upon collision
- **Impact Visualization**: Enhancing gameplay feedback by visualizing collision impacts through particle animations, textures, or dynamic lighting effects
- **Gameplay Feedback**: Providing players with visual cues that signify successful hits, critical strikes, or environmental interactions through particle effect feedbacks like in shooting games

These mechanics enable developers to create dynamic, visually appealing game experiences where particle effects on collision enrich gameplay feedback and narrative storytelling.

Advanced Techniques

Advanced particle effect techniques expand on basic mechanics, including

- **Dynamic Particle Parameters**: Adjusting particle behaviors, emission rates, or visual properties based on collision intensity, object types, or environmental factors
- **Interactive Particle Systems**: Allowing players to interact with particle effects through gameplay actions, triggering chain reactions, or environmental changes
- **Multilayered Effects**: Combining multiple particle systems or effect layers to create complex collision-driven visual narratives, enhancing gameplay depth and immersion
- **Performance Optimization**: Optimizing particle effect rendering, simulation, or spawning processes to maintain game performance across various platforms or multiplayer environments

These techniques empower developers to create immersive, responsive game worlds where particle effects on collision contribute to gameplay dynamics, strategic depth, and narrative coherence.

Practical Applications

Particle effects on collision are used in various game development applications, including

- **Combat Visual Feedback**: Enhancing combat mechanics with particle effects that signify weapon impacts, spell casts, or environmental destruction
- **Environmental Interaction**: Visualizing environmental interactions such as object collisions, terrain deformations, or interactive physics simulations through dynamic particle animations
- **Exploration and Discovery**: Guiding player exploration by highlighting interactive objects, hidden pathways, or narrative clues through distinctive particle effects
- **Emotional and Narrative Expression**: Amplifying emotional storytelling or narrative pacing by integrating particle effects that reflect character interactions, plot developments, or dramatic events

Algorithm Overview

Let's outline the algorithm used for implementing particle effects on collision:

1. **Initialization**: Set up particle systems and collision triggers within the game environment.

CHAPTER 2   ADVANCED COLLISION MECHANICS

2. **Collision Detection**: Continuously monitor collisions between game objects, characters, or projectiles.

3. **Particle Emission**: Trigger predefined or custom particle systems upon collision events.

4. **Visual Feedback:** Update particle system parameters, such as emission rates, colors, or trajectories, to reflect collision impacts.

5. **Performance Optimization**: Optimize particle effect rendering, simulation, or spawning processes to ensure smooth gameplay performance.

This algorithm provides a structured approach to implementing particle effects on collision mechanics in Unreal Engine or similar game development environments.

Reviewing the Code

This section outlines the implementation of particle effects triggered by collision events, focusing on the associated classes and functions that manage collision detection, particle system activation, and visual feedback within the game environment.

Listings 2-51 and 2-52 implement the AParticleCollision class, serving as the central component responsible for managing particle effects that occur upon collisions.

- **AParticleCollision Class:** Represents an actor that triggers particle effects upon collision events, visualizing impacts through dynamic particle system animations

- **BeginPlay Function:** Initializes default values and sets up collision detection for particle effect interactions

CHAPTER 2   ADVANCED COLLISION MECHANICS

- **Tick Function**: Updates object state and properties every frame

- **OnObjectCollision Function**: Event handler triggered when the object collides with another actor or collision component, spawning particle effects at the collision impact point

- **UGameplayStatics::SpawnEmitterAtLocation**: Utility function to spawn particle emitters at specific world locations, triggering collision-driven particle animations or effects

Listing 2-51. ParticleCollision.h

```
#pragma once

#include "CoreMinimal.h"
#include "GameFramework/Actor.h"

class UBoxComponent;
class UParticleSystemComponent;
class UParticleSystem;
class UPrimitiveComponent;

#include "ParticleCollision.generated.h"

UCLASS()
class MYGAME_API AParticleCollision : public AActor
{
    GENERATED_BODY()

public:
    AParticleCollision();
```

```cpp
protected:
    virtual void BeginPlay() override;
public:
    virtual void Tick(float DeltaTime) override;
private:
    UPROPERTY(VisibleAnywhere)
    UBoxComponent* CollisionBox;

    UPROPERTY(VisibleAnywhere)
    UParticleSystemComponent* ParticleSystem;

    UPROPERTY(EditDefaultsOnly, Category = "Particles")
    UParticleSystem* CollisionParticles;

    UFUNCTION()
    void OnObjectCollision(UPrimitiveComponent* HitComponent,
    AActor* OtherActor, UPrimitiveComponent* OtherComp, FVector
    NormalImpulse, const FHitResult& Hit);
};
```

Listing 2-52. ParticleCollision.cpp

```cpp
#include "ParticleCollision.h"
#include "Components/BoxComponent.h"
#include "Particles/ParticleSystemComponent.h"
#include "Particles/ParticleSystem.h"
#include "Components/PrimitiveComponent.h"

AParticleCollision::AParticleCollision()
{
    PrimaryActorTick.bCanEverTick = true;

    CollisionBox = CreateDefaultSubobject<UBoxComponent>(TEXT
    ("CollisionBox"));
```

CHAPTER 2   ADVANCED COLLISION MECHANICS

```
    RootComponent = CollisionBox;

    ParticleSystem = CreateDefaultSubobject<UParticleSystem
    Component>(TEXT("ParticleSystem"));
    ParticleSystem->SetupAttachment(RootComponent);

    CollisionParticles = nullptr; // Set the particle system to
    be assigned in the editor

    CollisionBox->OnComponentHit.AddDynamic(this, &AParticle
    Collision::OnObjectCollision);
}

void AParticleCollision::OnObjectCollision(UPrimitiveComponent*
HitComponent, AActor* OtherActor, UPrimitiveComponent*
OtherComp, FVector NormalImpulse, const FHitResult& Hit)
{
    if (CollisionParticles)
    {
        UGameplayStatics::SpawnEmitterAtLocation(GetWorld(),
        CollisionParticles, Hit.ImpactPoint);
    }
}
```

Advanced Particle Techniques

This section focuses on enhancing particle effects by introducing dynamic parameters that adjust based on various in-game factors. This approach allows for more immersive and responsive visual effects during collisions.

Listings 2-53 and 2-54 implement these techniques, enriching the visual aesthetics of the game while also contributing to the overall gameplay experience by ensuring that particle effects are responsive and contextually appropriate.

CHAPTER 2   ADVANCED COLLISION MECHANICS

- **UDynamicParticles Class**: Manages dynamic particle parameters for adjusting particle behaviors, emission rates, or visual properties based on collision intensity, object types, or environmental factors

- **AdjustParticleEffects Function**: Modifies particle system parameters dynamically to simulate realistic collision effects, enhance gameplay immersion, or provide visual feedback through interactive particle animations

Listing 2-53. DynamicParticles.h

```
#pragma once

class UParticleSystemComponent;
class UParticleSystem;

#include "CoreMinimal.h"
#include "UObject/NoExportTypes.h"
#include "DynamicParticles.generated.h"

UCLASS()
class MYGAME_API UDynamicParticles : public UObject
{
    GENERATED_BODY()

public:
    UDynamicParticles();

    UFUNCTION(BlueprintCallable)
    void AdjustParticleEffects(float CollisionIntensity,
    FVector CollisionDirection);

private:
```

```cpp
    UPROPERTY(EditDefaultsOnly, Category = "Particles")
    UParticleSystem* ImpactParticles;

    UPROPERTY(EditDefaultsOnly, Category = "Particles")
    float MaxEmissionRate;

    UPROPERTY(EditDefaultsOnly, Category = "Particles")
    FVector ParticleDirection;
};
```

Listing 2-54. DynamicParticles.cpp

```cpp
#include "DynamicParticles.h"
#include "Particles/ParticleSystemComponent.h"
#include "Particles/ParticleSystem.h"

UDynamicParticles::UDynamicParticles()
{
    ImpactParticles = nullptr; // Set the particle system to be
                                  assigned in the editor
    MaxEmissionRate = 100.0f;
    ParticleDirection = FVector(1.0f, 0.0f, 0.0f);
}
void UDynamicParticles::AdjustParticleEffects(float
CollisionIntensity, FVector CollisionDirection)
{
    if (ImpactParticles)
    {
        float EmissionRate = FMath::Lerp(0.0f, MaxEmissionRate,
        CollisionIntensity);
        ParticleDirection = CollisionDirection;

        // Modify particle system parameters based on collision
           intensity and direction
```

CHAPTER 2   ADVANCED COLLISION MECHANICS

```
        // Adjust particle emission rates, colors,
            trajectories, or dynamic properties
    }
}
```

This section explored the fundamentals of particle effects on collision mechanics in game development. From understanding basic particle system implementations to integrating advanced techniques such as dynamic parameter adjustments and interactive particle systems, you've gained insights into how particle effects enhance gameplay feedback, visual storytelling, and immersive player experiences in Unreal Engine or similar game development environments.

Summary

With our deep dive into advanced collision mechanics complete, we've seen how collisions extend far beyond simple object detection. They define the weight behind a blow, the arc of a projectile, and the explosive force of an impact. From knockback effects and AoE damage to terrain deformation and dynamic object interactions, collisions are integral to fluid and engaging gameplay.

More than just physics calculations, these mechanics breathe energy into a game's world, making every action feel responsive and consequential. Whether it's a crumbling wall, a rebounding projectile, or a character thrown back from a heavy attack, these effects ensure that every interaction leaves a mark.

Looking ahead, our journey continues into the realm of interaction mechanics. Here, we'll explore how games foster deeper connections through dialogue systems, empower through inventories and quests, and captivate through interactive storytelling. It's a realm where every interaction carries meaning and where the player's choices resonate within the game world.

CHAPTER 3

Interaction Mechanics

In game development, interaction mechanics are the bridge between the player and the game world. They define how players engage with the environment, characters, and objects, creating a dynamic and immersive experience. From simple actions like opening a door to complex systems like NPC interactions and inventory management, interaction mechanics are crucial for building a compelling game.

At their core, interaction mechanics allow players to perform actions that affect the game world. This can range from picking up items and activating traps to initiating dialogues and solving puzzles. The simplicity or complexity of these interactions can significantly impact the player's immersion and enjoyment.

Advanced interaction mechanics involve more intricate systems and responses. For instance, an inventory system that manages player items, a dialogue system with branching storylines, or a quest system that tracks player progress and goals. These advanced mechanics add depth and richness to the gameplay, offering players a more engaging experience.

In this chapter, we will delve into various interaction mechanics, providing detailed explanations and practical code examples. By the end of this chapter, you will have a comprehensive understanding of how to implement interactive elements in your game, enhancing player engagement and immersion.

CHAPTER 3   INTERACTION MECHANICS

Opening Doors

Opening doors is a fundamental mechanic in many games, providing access to new areas and contributing to the sense of exploration and progression. Doors can serve various purposes, from simple barriers to complex puzzles, and can be controlled by different triggers such as player proximity, switches, or key items.

Imagine a game where unlocking a door requires solving a puzzle or finding a hidden key. The satisfaction of opening that door after overcoming a challenge adds to the player's sense of accomplishment and immersion.

Basic Usage

In its simplest form, door opening involves detecting when the player is near the door and then triggering an animation to open it. This can be achieved using collision detection and triggers.

Advanced Techniques

Advanced door mechanics can include various conditions for opening, such as requiring specific items, solving puzzles, or meeting certain criteria. Additionally, doors can have states like locked, unlocked, or jammed, adding layers of complexity and interaction.

Consider a scenario where a door can only be opened by activating a series of switches in a specific order. This adds an element of puzzle-solving and strategy to the game, engaging players more deeply.

Practical Applications

The integration of door mechanics in game design serves various purposes, enhancing gameplay, puzzles, and narrative progression:

- **Progression Control**: Use doors to control player progression and guide them through the game world.

- **Puzzle Elements**: Incorporate doors as part of puzzles, requiring players to think and solve challenges.

- **Narrative Tools**: Use locked or hidden doors to create curiosity and drive the story forward.

Algorithm Overview

The algorithm for implementing door mechanics involves several key steps to ensure smooth interactions and functionality:

1. **Initialization**: Set up the door and player detection components.

2. **Detection**: Check if the player is within the door's activation zone.

3. **Condition Check**: Verify if the conditions to open the door are met (e.g., player has a key).

4. **Activation**: Trigger the door's opening animation.

5. **State Management**: Optionally, manage the door's state (e.g., locked, unlocked).

CHAPTER 3 INTERACTION MECHANICS

Reviewing the Code

In this section, we establish the components necessary for the implementation of doors and player detection mechanisms within Unreal Engine. This setup is crucial for creating interactive environments that respond to player actions effectively.

Listing 3-1 establishes these components and their interactions, creating a robust system for managing door mechanics in Unreal Engine, allowing for dynamic player engagement with the game world.

- **Door Class**: Defines an actor that represents a door in the game
- **TriggerBox**: A box component used to detect player presence
- **bIsLocked**: A boolean variable to check if the door is locked
- **OnOverlapBegin Function**: Callback function called when an actor begins overlapping with the trigger box

Listing 3-1. Door.h

```
#pragma once

#include "CoreMinimal.h"
#include "GameFramework/Actor.h"

class UBoxComponet;
class UPrimitiveComponent;

#include "Door.generated.h"

UCLASS()
class MYGAME_API ADoor : public AActor
```

```cpp
{
    GENERATED_BODY()
public:
    ADoor();

protected:
    virtual void BeginPlay() override;

public:
    virtual void Tick(float DeltaTime) override;

private:
    UPROPERTY(VisibleAnywhere)
    UBoxComponent* TriggerBox;

    UPROPERTY(EditAnywhere)
    bool bIsLocked;

    UFUNCTION()
    void OnBeginOverlap (UPrimitiveComponent*
    OverlappedComponent, AActor* OtherActor,
    UPrimitiveComponent* OtherComp, int32 OtherBodyIndex,
    bool bFromSweep, const FHitResult& SweepResult);
};
```

Listing 3-2 implements the ADoor class, establishing various components and functionalities to manage the door's behavior within the game. The class is designed to detect player interactions and determine whether the door should open or remain locked.

- **CreateDefaultSubobject**: Creates an instance of UBoxComponent for the trigger box
- **SetCollisionEnabled**: Enables collision detection for the trigger box

CHAPTER 3   INTERACTION MECHANICS

- **SetCollisionResponseToAllChannels**: Sets the collision response to overlap all channels, ensuring the trigger box detects overlaps
- **OnComponentBeginOverlap**: Event triggered when an actor overlaps with the trigger box, used to call the OnOverlapBegin function
- **OnOverlapBegin Function**: Checks if the door is locked and implements the logic for opening the door if it is not locked

Listing 3-2. Door.cpp

```
#include "Door.h"
#include "Components/BoxComponent.h"

ADoor::ADoor()
{
    PrimaryActorTick.bCanEverTick = true;

    TriggerBox = CreateDefaultSubobject<UBoxComponent>
    (TEXT("TriggerBox"));
    RootComponent = TriggerBox;

    TriggerBox->SetCollisionEnabled(ECollisionEnabled::
    QueryOnly);
    TriggerBox->SetCollisionResponseToAllChannels
    (ECollisionResponse::ECR_Overlap);
    TriggerBox->OnComponentBeginOverlap.AddDynamic(this,
    &ADoor::OnOverlapBegin);

    bIsLocked = false; // Default to unlocked
}
```

```
void ADoor::BeginPlay()
{
    Super::BeginPlay();
}

void ADoor::Tick(float DeltaTime)
{
    Super::Tick(DeltaTime);
}

void ADoor:: OnBeginOverlap (UPrimitiveComponent*
OverlappedComponent, AActor* OtherActor, UPrimitiveComponent*
OtherComp, int32 OtherBodyIndex, bool bFromSweep, const
FHitResult & SweepResult)
{
    if (!bIsLocked)
    {
        // Implement door opening logic here
    }
}
```

Advanced Techniques

For more interactive doors, we can add conditions and state management.

Listing 3-3 implements the AAdvancedDoor class, building upon the functionality of a standard door by integrating advanced mechanics related to key requirements. This enhances the interaction possibilities for players, adding depth to the gameplay experience.

- **AdvancedDoor Class**: Extends the basic door functionality
- **RequiredKey**: Specifies the key item required to open the door

CHAPTER 3 INTERACTION MECHANICS

Listing 3-3. AdvancedDoor.h

```
#pragma once

#include "CoreMinimal.h"
#include "GameFramework/Actor.h"

class UBoxComponent;

#include "AdvancedDoor.generated.h"
UCLASS()
class MYGAME_API AAdvancedDoor : public AActor
{
    GENERATED_BODY()
public:
    AAdvancedDoor();

protected:
    virtual void BeginPlay() override;

public:
    virtual void Tick(float DeltaTime) override;

private:
    UPROPERTY(VisibleAnywhere)
    UBoxComponent* TriggerBox;

    UPROPERTY(EditAnywhere)
    bool bIsLocked;

    UPROPERTY(EditAnywhere)
    FString RequiredKey;

    UFUNCTION()
```

```
    void OnBeginOverlap (UPrimitiveComponent*
    OverlappedComponent, AActor* OtherActor,
    UPrimitiveComponent* OtherComp, int32 OtherBodyIndex, bool
    bFromSweep, const FHitResult & SweepResult);
};
```

Listing 3-4 implements the AAdvancedDoor class in the AdvancedDoor.cpp file, enhancing door mechanics by integrating key requirements and collision detection.

- **RequiredKey**: Specifies the key item required to open the door.
- **OnComponentBeginOverlap**: Checks if the door is locked and if the player has the required key, then implements the logic for opening the door.
- **HasKey Function**: Placeholder function to check if the player has the required key. This function should be implemented based on the game's inventory system.

Listing 3-4. AdvancedDoor.cpp

```
#include "AdvancedDoor.h"
#include "Components/BoxComponent.h"

AAdvancedDoor::AAdvancedDoor()
{
    PrimaryActorTick.bCanEverTick = true;

    TriggerBox = CreateDefaultSubobject<UBoxComponent>
    (TEXT("TriggerBox"));
    RootComponent = TriggerBox;

    TriggerBox->SetCollisionEnabled(ECollisionEnabled::
    QueryOnly);
```

CHAPTER 3   INTERACTION MECHANICS

```cpp
    TriggerBox->SetCollisionResponseToAllChannels(ECollisionRes
    ponse::ECR_Overlap);
    TriggerBox->OnComponentBeginOverlap.AddDynamic(this,
    &AAdvancedDoor::OnOverlapBegin);

    bIsLocked = true; // Default to locked
}
void AAdvancedDoor::BeginPlay()
{
    Super::BeginPlay();
}

void AAdvancedDoor::Tick(float DeltaTime)
{
    Super::Tick(DeltaTime);
}

void AAdvancedDoor::OnOverlapBegin(UPrimitiveComponent*
OverlappedComponent, AActor* OtherActor, UPrimitiveComponent*
OtherComp, int32 OtherBodyIndex, bool bFromSweep, const
FHitResult & SweepResult)
{
    if (!bIsLocked || HasKey(OtherActor))
    {
        // Implement door opening logic here
    }
}

bool AAdvancedDoor::HasKey(AActor* OtherActor)
{
    // Check if the player has the required key
```

```
// This is a placeholder function and should be implemented
based on the game's inventory system
return true;
}
```

In this section, we explored the fundamentals and advanced techniques of opening doors in game development. From detecting player presence to implementing complex conditions for opening, these mechanics add depth and interaction to your game.

In the next subtopic, we will delve into the intricacies of activating traps, learning how to add danger and strategy to your game environment.

Activating Traps

Activating traps is a crucial mechanic in many games, adding elements of danger and strategy to the gameplay. Traps can serve as obstacles that challenge players, requiring careful navigation and quick reflexes to avoid them. They can be triggered by various conditions, such as player proximity, time-based events, or interactions with other objects.

Imagine a game where players must traverse a dungeon filled with traps that activate when they step on pressure plates. These traps add a layer of difficulty and excitement, requiring players to think and react swiftly.

Basic Usage

In its simplest form, activating traps involves detecting when the player or another game object triggers the trap. This can be achieved using collision detection and triggers. Once triggered, the trap performs its designated action, such as dealing damage, restricting movement, or causing other effects.

Advanced Techniques

Advanced trap mechanics can include various triggering conditions and complex behaviors. Traps can be part of intricate puzzles, require multiple conditions to activate, or reset after a certain period. Additionally, traps can interact with other game mechanics, such as enemies, items, or environmental elements.

Consider a scenario where traps are part of a puzzle that requires players to deactivate them in a specific sequence to proceed. This adds depth and complexity, engaging players in thoughtful gameplay.

Practical Applications

Traps serve as formidable obstacles that players must either navigate around or disable. By strategically placing traps in various locations, developers can create tension and excitement in gameplay. For instance:

- **Obstacle Creation**: Use traps to create challenging obstacles that players must navigate or disable.
- **Puzzle Integration**: Incorporate traps into puzzles, requiring players to solve challenges to avoid or deactivate them.
- **Environmental Interaction**: Use traps to interact with other game elements, creating dynamic and engaging environments.

Algorithm Overview

To implement trap mechanics, the following algorithm can be employed:

1. **Initialization**: Set up the trap and its triggering components.

CHAPTER 3   INTERACTION MECHANICS

2. **Detection**: Continuously check for triggering conditions (e.g., player proximity).

3. **Activation**: Trigger the trap's action when conditions are met.

4. **Reset/Deactivation**: Optionally, reset or deactivate the trap after a certain period or condition.

Reviewing the Code

We start by defining the components for traps and their triggering mechanisms.

Listing 3-5 implements the Trap class, defining an actor that represents a trap in the game. It includes several key components and functions.

- **BeginPlay Function**: Called when the game starts or when spawned, used for initialization

- **Tick Function**: Called every frame, updates the actor's state

- **TriggerBox**: A box component used to detect player or object presence

- **OnOverlapBegin Function**: Callback function called when an actor begins overlapping with the trigger box

Listing 3-5. Trap.h

```
#pragma once

#include "CoreMinimal.h"
#include "GameFramework/Actor.h"

class UBoxComponent;
```

CHAPTER 3 INTERACTION MECHANICS

```cpp
#include "Trap.generated.h"
UCLASS()
class MYGAME_API ATrap : public AActor
{
    GENERATED_BODY()
public:
    ATrap();
protected:
    virtual void BeginPlay() override;
public:
    virtual void Tick(float DeltaTime) override;
private:
    UPROPERTY(VisibleAnywhere)
    UBoxComponent* TriggerBox;

    UFUNCTION()
    void OnOverlapBegin(class UPrimitiveComponent* OverlappedComponent, class AActor* OtherActor, class UPrimitiveComponent* OtherComp, int32 OtherBodyIndex, bool bFromSweep, const FHitResult & SweepResult);
};
```

Listing 3-6 implements the Trap class, serving as a fundamental building block for trap mechanics in the game by providing essential functionality for detecting player interactions.

- **CreateDefaultSubobject**: Creates an instance of UBoxComponent for the trigger box
- **SetCollisionEnabled**: Enables collision detection for the trigger box

CHAPTER 3 INTERACTION MECHANICS

- **SetCollisionResponseToAllChannels**: Sets the collision response to overlap all channels, ensuring the trigger box detects overlaps
- **OnComponentBeginOverlap**: Event triggered when an actor overlaps with the trigger box, used to call the OnOverlapBegin function
- **OnOverlapBegin Function**: Checks for valid overlapping actors and implements the logic for activating the trap

Listing 3-6. Trap.cpp

```
#include "Trap.h"
#include "Components/BoxComponent.h"

ATrap::ATrap()
{
    PrimaryActorTick.bCanEverTick = true;

    TriggerBox = CreateDefaultSubobject<UBoxComponent>
    (TEXT("TriggerBox"));
    RootComponent = TriggerBox;

    TriggerBox->SetCollisionEnabled(ECollisionEnabled::
    QueryOnly);
    TriggerBox->SetCollisionResponseToAllChannels(
    ECollisionResponse::ECR_Overlap);
    TriggerBox->OnComponentBeginOverlap.AddDynamic(this,
    &ATrap::OnOverlapBegin);
}
```

```cpp
void ATrap::BeginPlay()
{
    Super::BeginPlay();
}

void ATrap::Tick(float DeltaTime)
{
    Super::Tick(DeltaTime);
}

void ATrap::OnOverlapBegin(UPrimitiveComponent*
OverlappedComponent, AActor* OtherActor, UPrimitiveComponent*
OtherComp, int32 OtherBodyIndex, bool bFromSweep, const
FHitResult & SweepResult)
{
    if (OtherActor && (OtherActor != this) && OtherComp)
    {
        // Implement trap activation logic here
    }
}
```

Advanced Techniques

For more interactive traps, we can add complex triggering conditions and behaviors.

Listing 3-7 implements the AdvancedTrap class, enhancing the basic trap functionality by providing additional features for trap activation and resetting.

- **AdvancedTrap Class**: Extends the basic trap functionality, enabling more complex behaviors and interactions.

- **bIsArmed**: A boolean variable that indicates whether the trap is currently armed and ready to activate.

- **ActivateTrap Function**: This function contains the logic that executes when the trap is activated, such as triggering damage, effects, or animations.

- **ResetTrap Function**: This function handles the logic required to reset the trap after it has been triggered, allowing it to be rearmed and used again.

Listing 3-7. AdvancedTrap.h

```
#pragma once

#include "CoreMinimal.h"
#include "GameFramework/Actor.h"

class UBoxComponent;

#include "AdvancedTrap.generated.h"
UCLASS()
class MYGAME_API AAdvancedTrap : public AActor
{
    GENERATED_BODY()

public:
    AAdvancedTrap();

protected:
    virtual void BeginPlay() override;

public:
    virtual void Tick(float DeltaTime) override;
```

```cpp
private:
    UPROPERTY(VisibleAnywhere)
    UBoxComponent* TriggerBox;

    UPROPERTY(EditAnywhere)
    bool bIsArmed;

    UFUNCTION()
    void OnOverlapBegin(class UPrimitiveComponent*
    OverlappedComponent, class AActor* OtherActor, class
    UPrimitiveComponent* OtherComp, int32 OtherBodyIndex, bool
    bFromSweep, const FHitResult & SweepResult);

    void ActivateTrap();
    void ResetTrap();
};
```

Listing 3-8 implements the AdvancedTrap class, building upon the base trap functionality by introducing more sophisticated activation and resetting mechanisms.

- **bIsArmed**: Boolean variable to check if the trap is armed
- **OnComponentBeginOverlap**: Checks if the trap is armed and if valid overlapping actors are present, then calls ActivateTrap
- **ActivateTrap Function**: Handles the logic for trap activation and disarms the trap after activation
- **ResetTrap Function**: Handles the logic for resetting and rearming the trap

CHAPTER 3   INTERACTION MECHANICS

Listing 3-8. AdvancedTrap.cpp

```
#include "AdvancedTrap.h"
#include "Components/BoxComponent.h"

AAdvancedTrap::AAdvancedTrap()
{
    PrimaryActorTick.bCanEverTick = true;

    TriggerBox = CreateDefaultSubobject<UBoxComponent>
    (TEXT("TriggerBox"));
    RootComponent = TriggerBox;

    TriggerBox->SetCollisionEnabled(ECollisionEnabled::
    QueryOnly);
    TriggerBox->SetCollisionResponseToAllChannels(
    ECollisionResponse::ECR_Overlap);
    TriggerBox->OnComponentBeginOverlap.AddDynamic(this,
    &AAdvancedTrap::OnOverlapBegin);

    bIsArmed = true; // Default to armed
}
void AAdvancedTrap::BeginPlay()
{
    Super::BeginPlay();
}
void AAdvancedTrap::Tick(float DeltaTime)
{
    Super::Tick(DeltaTime);
}
```

CHAPTER 3 INTERACTION MECHANICS

```cpp
void AAdvancedTrap::OnOverlapBegin(UPrimitiveComponent*
OverlappedComponent, AActor* OtherActor, UPrimitiveComponent*
OtherComp, int32 OtherBodyIndex, bool bFromSweep, const
FHitResult & SweepResult)
{
    if (bIsArmed && OtherActor && (OtherActor != this) &&
    OtherComp)
    {
        ActivateTrap();
    }
}

void AAdvancedTrap::ActivateTrap()
{
    // Implement trap activation logic here
    // For example, deal damage to the player or spawn a
    visual effect

    bIsArmed = false; // Disarm the trap after activation
}

void AAdvancedTrap::ResetTrap()
{
    // Implement trap resetting logic here
    // For example, reset the trap after a certain period

    bIsArmed = true; // Re-arm the trap
}
```

In this section, we explored the fundamentals and advanced techniques of activating traps in game development. From detecting triggers to implementing complex activation conditions, these mechanics add challenge and excitement to your game.

CHAPTER 3   INTERACTION MECHANICS

In the next subtopic, we will delve into the intricacies of starting cutscenes, learning how to add narrative and cinematic elements to enhance your game.

Starting Cutscenes

Cutscenes are scripted events in games that use non-interactive sequences to advance the storyline, provide exposition, or heighten the drama. These sequences often involve cinematic techniques like camera movements, animations, and dialogues to create a movie-like experience for the player.

Imagine a game where, after completing a challenging level, the player is rewarded with a cutscene revealing crucial plot points and character development. These moments can significantly enhance the storytelling aspect of your game, providing players with a deeper understanding of the narrative.

Basic Usage

Starting a cutscene typically involves triggering a sequence of predefined events. This can be achieved through various means, such as reaching a certain point in the game, interacting with specific objects, or completing particular objectives. The key components of a cutscene include camera control, animations, dialogue, and transitions.

Advanced Techniques

Advanced cutscenes can feature branching narratives, player choices, and dynamic content that changes based on player actions. This adds a layer of interactivity and personalization to the storytelling, making each playthrough unique.

Consider a game where cutscenes change based on the player's decisions throughout the game. This not only provides replay value but also makes the player feel more connected to the story.

Practical Applications

Cutscenes can serve multiple purposes in game design, enhancing the overall experience and narrative depth. Here are some key applications:

- **Narrative Progression**: Use cutscenes to advance the storyline and provide context for the player's actions.
- **Character Development**: Reveal backstories, motivations, and relationships through cinematic sequences.
- **Emotional Engagement**: Create memorable and emotionally impactful moments that resonate with players.

Algorithm Overview

The implementation of cutscenes can be broken down into several crucial steps:

1. **Initialization**: Set up the cutscene components and define the sequence of events.
2. **Trigger Detection**: Detect the conditions under which the cutscene should start.
3. **Cutscene Execution**: Play the cutscene, controlling camera, animations, and dialogue.
4. **Conclusion**: Transition back to gameplay after the cutscene ends.

Reviewing the Code

Setting up cutscenes and their triggering mechanisms involves several key steps. This process ensures that cutscenes are seamlessly integrated into the gameplay, enhancing the narrative experience.

Listing 3-9 implements this structured approach, providing a clear understanding of the cutscene's functionalities and establishing a foundation for further development and enhancements. By maintaining organized code, you can easily modify or expand the cutscene elements as needed.

- **Cutscene Class**: This class defines an actor that represents a cutscene in the game. It handles the sequence of events that unfold during the cutscene, including camera movements and character dialogues.

- **StartCutscene Function**: This function is responsible for starting the cutscene sequence. It orchestrates the various components needed to bring the cutscene to life.

- **CameraActor:** This property references the actor that will be used for camera control during the cutscene. It enables dynamic camera movements to enhance the storytelling experience.

- **ActorsInCutscene**: This array contains references to all the actors involved in the cutscene. These could be characters or objects that will interact during the cutscene.

- **Dialogues**: This array holds strings representing the dialogues that will be displayed during the cutscene. It allows for a structured way to present multiple lines of dialogue.

CHAPTER 3   INTERACTION MECHANICS

- **PlayDialogue Function**: This private function is responsible for playing a specific dialogue based on the provided index. It ensures that the correct line of dialogue is displayed at the appropriate time.

- **EndCutscene Function**: This function concludes the cutscene and transitions the game back to normal gameplay. It resets any changes made during the cutscene, such as camera settings, and restores player control.

Listing 3-9. Cutscene.h

```
#pragma once

#include "CoreMinimal.h"
#include "GameFramework/Actor.h"
#include "Cutscene.generated.h"

UCLASS()
class MYGAME_API ACutscene : public AActor
{
    GENERATED_BODY()

public:
    ACutscene();

protected:
    virtual void BeginPlay() override;

public:
    virtual void Tick(float DeltaTime) override;

    void StartCutscene();
```

```cpp
private:
    UPROPERTY(EditAnywhere)
    AActor* CameraActor;

    UPROPERTY(EditAnywhere)
    TArray<AActor*> ActorsInCutscene;

    UPROPERTY(EditAnywhere)
    TArray<FString> Dialogues;

    void PlayDialogue(int32 Index);
    void EndCutscene();
};
```

Listing 3-10 implements this structured flow, ensuring a seamless storytelling experience that draws players deeper into the game's narrative.

- **StartCutscene Function**: Sets the camera view to the CameraActor and starts the cutscene sequence by playing dialogues

- **PlayDialogue Function**: Plays the dialogue based on the given index

- **EndCutscene Function**: Concludes the cutscene and transitions back to gameplay

Listing 3-10. Cutscene.cpp

```cpp
#include "Cutscene.h"
#include "GameFramework/Actor.h"

ACutscene::ACutscene()
{
    PrimaryActorTick.bCanEverTick = true;
}
```

CHAPTER 3   INTERACTION MECHANICS

```cpp
void ACutscene::BeginPlay()
{
    Super::BeginPlay();
}

void ACutscene::Tick(float DeltaTime)
{
    Super::Tick(DeltaTime);
}

void ACutscene::StartCutscene()
{
    if (CameraActor)
    {
        // Set the camera view to CameraActor
        // Implement camera control logic here
    }

    for (int32 i = 0; i < Dialogues.Num(); i++)
    {
        PlayDialogue(i);
    }

    EndCutscene();
}

void ACutscene::PlayDialogue(int32 Index)
{
    if (Index < Dialogues.Num())
    {
        // Implement dialogue playback logic here
        // For example, display the dialogue on screen
    }
}
```

```
void ACutscene::EndCutscene()
{
    // Implement cutscene conclusion logic here
    // For example, switch the camera back to the player
}
```

Advanced Techniques

For more interactive cutscenes, we can add branching narratives and player choices.

The AInteractiveCutscene class builds upon the foundation of traditional cutscenes by incorporating interactive elements that allow players to make choices that influence the narrative:

- **InteractiveCutscene Class**: Extends the basic cutscene functionality
- **DialogueChoices**: Map of dialogue choices and their corresponding outcomes
- **HandlePlayerChoice Function**: Handles the player's choice during the cutscene

Listing 3-11. InteractiveCutscene.h

```
#pragma once

#include "CoreMinimal.h"
#include "GameFramework/Actor.h"
#include "InteractiveCutscene.generated.h"

UCLASS()
class MYGAME_API AInteractiveCutscene : public AActor
```

CHAPTER 3   INTERACTION MECHANICS

```cpp
{
    GENERATED_BODY()
public:
    AInteractiveCutscene();
protected:
    virtual void BeginPlay() override;
public:
    virtual void Tick(float DeltaTime) override;

    void StartCutscene();

private:
    UPROPERTY(EditAnywhere)
    AActor* CameraActor;

    UPROPERTY(EditAnywhere)
    TArray<AActor*> ActorsInCutscene;

    UPROPERTY(EditAnywhere)
    TArray<FString> Dialogues;

    UPROPERTY(EditAnywhere)
    TMap<FString, FString> DialogueChoices;

    void PlayDialogue(int32 Index);
    void EndCutscene();
    void HandlePlayerChoice(FString Choice);
};
```

Listing 3-12 implements a framework for interactive storytelling, encouraging players to make decisions that shape their gameplay experience.

CHAPTER 3   INTERACTION MECHANICS

- **DialogueChoices**: Map that stores dialogue choices and their outcomes
- **HandlePlayerChoice Function**: Handles the player's choice and changes the cutscene outcome accordingly

Listing 3-12. InteractiveCutscene.cpp

```cpp
#include "InteractiveCutscene.h"
#include "GameFramework/Actor.h"

AInteractiveCutscene::AInteractiveCutscene()
{
    PrimaryActorTick.bCanEverTick = true;
}

void AInteractiveCutscene::BeginPlay()
{
    Super::BeginPlay();
}

void AInteractiveCutscene::Tick(float DeltaTime)
{
    Super::Tick(DeltaTime);
}

void AInteractiveCutscene::StartCutscene()
{
    if (CameraActor)
    {
        // Set the camera view to CameraActor
        // Implement camera control logic here
    }
```

CHAPTER 3 INTERACTION MECHANICS

```cpp
    for (int32 i = 0; i < Dialogues.Num(); i++)
    {
        PlayDialogue(i);
    }

    EndCutscene();
}
void AInteractiveCutscene::PlayDialogue(int32 Index)
{
    if (Index < Dialogues.Num())
    {
        // Implement dialogue playback logic here
        // For example, display the dialogue on screen

        // Check for player choices
        if (DialogueChoices.Contains(Dialogues[Index]))
        {
            FString PlayerChoice = DialogueChoices[Dialogues
            [Index]];
            HandlePlayerChoice(PlayerChoice);
        }
    }
}

void AInteractiveCutscene::HandlePlayerChoice(FString Choice)
{
    // Implement logic for handling player choices
    // For example, change the cutscene outcome based on
    the choice
}
```

```
void AInteractiveCutscene::EndCutscene()
{
    // Implement cutscene conclusion logic here
    // For example, switch the camera back to the player
}
```

In this section, we explored the fundamentals and advanced techniques of starting cutscenes in game development. From simple sequences to interactive narratives, cutscenes enhance the storytelling and cinematic experience of your game.

In the next subtopic, we will delve into the intricacies of dialogue systems, learning how to create engaging conversations between characters.

Dialogue Systems

Dialogue systems are a crucial part of many games, providing a means for characters to interact with each other and with the player. These systems can range from simple linear dialogues to complex branching conversations that change based on player choices.

Consider a role-playing game (RPG) where the player's choices in dialogue affect the storyline and character relationships. A robust dialogue system allows for immersive storytelling and player engagement.

Basic Usage

A basic dialogue system typically involves a series of predefined text lines displayed to the player. This can be implemented using simple text boxes or more complex UI elements. The player may advance the dialogue by pressing a button or making a choice.

Advanced Techniques

Advanced dialogue systems can include branching paths, where player choices affect the conversation's direction and outcome. This adds depth and replayability to the game, as players can explore different dialogue options and storylines.

Imagine a game where the player's dialogue choices determine the fate of a character or unlock different missions. This creates a dynamic and engaging experience for the player.

Practical Applications

The practical applications of dialogue systems are significant:

- **Storytelling**: Convey the game's narrative and provide context for the player's actions.
- **Character Development**: Flesh out characters' personalities, backstories, and relationships through dialogue.
- **Player Choice**: Allow players to influence the story and game world through their dialogue choices.

Through these various facets, dialogue systems enhance gameplay by intertwining storytelling, character development, and player agency, ultimately leading to a richer gaming experience.

Algorithm Overview

The algorithm for implementing a dialogue system involves several key stages that ensure smooth and interactive conversations within the game. Here's a breakdown of the main components:

1. **Initialization**: Set up the dialogue system components and load dialogue data.

2. **Trigger Detection**: Detect when the player initiates a dialogue.

3. **Dialogue Execution**: Display dialogue lines and handle player input.

4. **Branching Paths:** Implement logic for branching dialogues based on player choices.

5. **Conclusion**: End the dialogue and transition back to gameplay.

By following these steps, the dialogue system can effectively facilitate engaging interactions that enhance storytelling and player agency within the game.

Reviewing the Code

In this section, we focus on defining the essential components of the dialogue system and establishing the conditions that will trigger dialogues within the game. This setup is crucial for enabling dynamic interactions between characters and the player.

Listing 3-13 establishes a foundational structure for implementing a dialogue system that enhances player interaction and narrative depth within the game.

- **DialogueSystem Class**: Defines an actor that represents a dialogue system in the game
- **StartDialogue Function**: Function to start the dialogue sequence
- **Dialogues**: Array of dialogues to be displayed during the interaction

CHAPTER 3 INTERACTION MECHANICS

- **DialogueChoices**: Map of dialogue choices and their corresponding outcomes

- **CurrentDialogueIndex**: Index to keep track of the current dialogue line

- **DisplayDialogue Function**: Displays a specific dialogue based on the index

- **HandlePlayerChoice Function**: Handles the player's choice during the dialogue

- **EndDialogue Function**: Ends the dialogue and transitions back to gameplay

Listing 3-13. DialogueSystem.h

```
#pragma once

#include "CoreMinimal.h"
#include "GameFramework/Actor.h"
#include "DialogueSystem.generated.h"

UCLASS()
class MYGAME_API ADialogueSystem : public AActor
{
    GENERATED_BODY()

public:
    ADialogueSystem();

protected:
    virtual void BeginPlay() override;

public:
    virtual void Tick(float DeltaTime) override;

    void StartDialogue();
```

```
private:
    UPROPERTY(EditAnywhere)
    TArray<FString> Dialogues;

    UPROPERTY(EditAnywhere)
    TMap<FString, FString> DialogueChoices;

    int32 CurrentDialogueIndex;

    void DisplayDialogue(int32 Index);
    void HandlePlayerChoice(FString Choice);
    void EndDialogue();
};
```

Listing 3-14 outlines the implementation of a dialogue system within the game, providing structure for narrative interactions.

- **StartDialogue Function**: Starts the dialogue sequence by displaying the first dialogue line

- **DisplayDialogue Function**: Displays the dialogue based on the given index and checks for player choices

- **HandlePlayerChoice Function**: Handles the player's choice and changes the dialogue flow accordingly

- **EndDialogue Function**: Concludes the dialogue and transitions back to gameplay

Listing 3-14. DialogueSystem.cpp

```
#include "DialogueSystem.h"
#include "GameFramework/Actor.h"

ADialogueSystem::ADialogueSystem()
{
    PrimaryActorTick.bCanEverTick = true;
```

CHAPTER 3 INTERACTION MECHANICS

```cpp
    CurrentDialogueIndex = 0;
}
void ADialogueSystem::BeginPlay()
{
    Super::BeginPlay();
}

void ADialogueSystem::Tick(float DeltaTime)
{
    Super::Tick(DeltaTime);
}

void ADialogueSystem::StartDialogue()
{
    if (Dialogues.Num() > 0)
    {
        DisplayDialogue(CurrentDialogueIndex);
    }
}

void ADialogueSystem::DisplayDialogue(int32 Index)
{
    if (Index < Dialogues.Num())
    {
        // Implement dialogue display logic here
        // For example, show the dialogue text on screen

        // Check for player choices
        if (DialogueChoices.Contains(Dialogues[Index]))
        {
            FString PlayerChoice = DialogueChoices[Dialogues
            [Index]];
```

```cpp
        HandlePlayerChoice(PlayerChoice);
        }
    }
}

void ADialogueSystem::HandlePlayerChoice(FString Choice)
{
    // Implement logic for handling player choices
    // For example, change the dialogue flow based on
    the choice
}

void ADialogueSystem::EndDialogue()
{
    // Implement dialogue conclusion logic here
    // For example, resume gameplay
}
```

Advanced Techniques

For more interactive dialogues, we can add branching paths and dynamic content that changes based on player choices.

Listing 3-15 defines a branching dialogue system, allowing for more dynamic interactions in gameplay.

- **BranchingDialogueSystem Class**: Extends the basic dialogue functionality
- **BranchingChoices**: Map of branching choices and their corresponding dialogue lines
- **HandleBranchingChoice Function**: Handles the player's branching choices and changes the dialogue flow accordingly

CHAPTER 3   INTERACTION MECHANICS

Listing 3-15. BranchingDialogueSystem.h

```cpp
#pragma once

#include "CoreMinimal.h"
#include "GameFramework/Actor.h"
#include "BranchingDialogueSystem.generated.h"

UCLASS()
class MYGAME_API ABranchingDialogueSystem : public AActor
{
    GENERATED_BODY()
public:
    ABranchingDialogueSystem();

protected:
    virtual void BeginPlay() override;

public:
    virtual void Tick(float DeltaTime) override;

    void StartDialogue();

private:
    UPROPERTY(EditAnywhere)
    TArray<FString> Dialogues;

    UPROPERTY(EditAnywhere)
    TMap<FString, TArray<FString>> BranchingChoices;

    int32 CurrentDialogueIndex;

    void DisplayDialogue(int32 Index);
    void HandleBranchingChoice(FString Choice);
    void EndDialogue();
};
```

Listing 3-16 implements a branching dialogue system, providing a more interactive storytelling experience and enriching gameplay with meaningful choices and outcomes.

- **BranchingChoices**: Map that stores branching choices and their corresponding dialogue lines
- **HandleBranchingChoice Function**: Handles the player's branching choices and changes the dialogue flow accordingly

Listing 3-16. BranchingDialogueSystem.cpp

```cpp
#include "BranchingDialogueSystem.h"
#include "GameFramework/Actor.h"

ABranchingDialogueSystem::ABranchingDialogueSystem()
{
    PrimaryActorTick.bCanEverTick = true;
    CurrentDialogueIndex = 0;
}

void ABranchingDialogueSystem::BeginPlay()
{
    Super::BeginPlay();
}

void ABranchingDialogueSystem::Tick(float DeltaTime)
{
    Super::Tick(DeltaTime);
}
```

CHAPTER 3   INTERACTION MECHANICS

```cpp
void ABranchingDialogueSystem::StartDialogue()
{
    if (Dialogues.Num() > 0)
    {
        DisplayDialogue(CurrentDialogueIndex);
    }
}

void ABranchingDialogueSystem::DisplayDialogue(int32 Index)
{
    if (Index < Dialogues.Num())
    {
        // Implement dialogue display logic here
        // For example, show the dialogue text on screen

        // Check for branching choices
        if (BranchingChoices.Contains(Dialogues[Index]))
        {
            TArray<FString> Choices = BranchingChoices
            [Dialogues[Index]];
            for (const FString& Choice : Choices)
            {
                HandleBranchingChoice(Choice);
            }
        }
    }
}

void ABranchingDialogueSystem::HandleBranchingChoice
(FString Choice)
{
    // Implement logic for handling branching choices
```

```
    // For example, change the dialogue flow based on
    the choice
}

void ABranchingDialogueSystem::EndDialogue()
{
    // Implement dialogue conclusion logic here
    // For example, resume gameplay
}
```

In this section, we explored the fundamentals and advanced techniques of dialogue systems in game development. From simple linear dialogues to complex branching conversations, these systems enhance the storytelling and player engagement in your game.

In the next subtopic, we will delve into NPC interactions, learning how to create meaningful and dynamic interactions between players and non-player characters.

NPC Interactions

Non-player characters (NPCs) are integral to creating an immersive game world. They populate the game environment, provide quests, interact with the player, and contribute to the story and atmosphere. NPC interactions can range from simple exchanges of dialogue to complex behavior patterns and decision-making processes.

Consider a game where NPCs can react to the player's actions, offer assistance, or become adversaries based on the player's choices. Effective NPC interactions enhance the game's depth and player engagement.

CHAPTER 3 INTERACTION MECHANICS

Basic Usage

A basic NPC interaction system involves detecting when the player is near an NPC and initiating an interaction, such as a dialogue or action. This can be implemented using collision detection or proximity triggers.

Advanced Techniques

Advanced NPC interaction systems can include dynamic behaviors, state machines, and AI-driven responses. These systems allow NPCs to exhibit lifelike behaviors, react to the player's actions, and interact with each other.

Imagine a game where NPCs have schedules, react to time of day, and remember past interactions with the player. This creates a living, breathing game world that feels real and responsive.

Practical Applications

These practical applications illustrate how NPCs contribute significantly to gameplay mechanics, enhancing player engagement and the overall depth of the game world:

- **Quests**: NPCs can provide quests, rewards, and storyline progression.
- **Trade**: NPCs can act as merchants, offering items for sale or trade.
- **Combat**: NPCs can be allies or enemies, engaging in combat with the player.
- **Storytelling**: NPC interactions can reveal backstory, lore, and character development.

Algorithm Overview

This algorithm outlines the key steps involved in implementing NPC interactions, enhancing the overall gameplay experience:

1. **Initialization**: Set up the NPC components and behaviors.

2. **Proximity Detection**: Detect when the player is near an NPC.

3. **Interaction Execution**: Trigger the interaction, such as dialogue or action.

4. **Behavioral Responses**: Implement dynamic behaviors based on the player's actions.

5. **Conclusion**: End the interaction and transition back to gameplay.

This structured approach to NPC interactions fosters a more engaging and interactive game environment.

Reviewing the Code

We start by defining the components for NPCs and their proximity detection mechanisms. This involves creating a system that can recognize when the player enters the vicinity of an NPC, allowing for interactions to occur.

Listing 3-17 implements the NPC interaction system, creating immersive and engaging experiences for players by facilitating meaningful interactions with non-player characters (NPCs).

- **NPCSystem Class**: Defines a character that represents an NPC in the game

CHAPTER 3   INTERACTION MECHANICS

- **ENPCInteractionType**: Enum that categorizes NPCs into Dialogue, Quest, Trade, or Combat types
- **Interact Function**: Initiates an interaction with the NPC based on its interaction type
- **Dialogues**: Array of dialogues the NPC can display
- **Quests**: Array of quests the NPC can provide
- **InteractionRadius**: Radius within which the player can interact with the NPC
- **bIsPlayerNearby**: Boolean to check if the player is within the interaction radius
- **CheckProximity Function**: Checks if the player is within the interaction radius
- **ExecuteInteraction Function**: Executes the interaction logic based on the NPC's type (Dialogue, Quest, Trade, Combat)
- **EndInteraction Function**: Ends the interaction and transitions back to gameplay

Listing 3-17. NPCSystem.h

```
#pragma once

#include "CoreMinimal.h"
#include "GameFramework/Character.h"
#include "NPCSystem.generated.h"

// Enum to categorize NPC interactions
UENUM(BlueprintType)
```

```cpp
enum class ENPCInteractionType : uint8
{
    Dialogue UMETA(DisplayName = "Dialogue"),
    // NPCs that offer dialogues
    Quest UMETA(DisplayName = "Quest"),
    // NPCs that give quests
    Trade UMETA(DisplayName = "Trade"),
    // NPCs that allow trading
    Combat UMETA(DisplayName = "Combat")
    // NPCs that engage in combat
};

UCLASS()
class MYGAME_API ANPCSystem : public ACharacter
{
    GENERATED_BODY()

public:
    // Constructor: Initializes default values
    ANPCSystem();

protected:
    // Called when the game starts or when the NPC is spawned
    virtual void BeginPlay() override;

public:
    // Called every frame to check for player proximity
    virtual void Tick(float DeltaTime) override;

    // Function to handle player interactions with the NPC
    void Interact();
```

CHAPTER 3 INTERACTION MECHANICS

```
private:
    // Determines the type of interaction this NPC provides
    UPROPERTY(EditAnywhere, Category = "NPC Interaction")
    ENPCInteractionType InteractionType;

    // Stores possible dialogue options for the NPC
    UPROPERTY(EditAnywhere, Category = "NPC Interaction")
    TArray<FString> Dialogues;

    // Stores available quests that the NPC can assign
    UPROPERTY(EditAnywhere, Category = "NPC Interaction")
    TArray<FString> Quests;

    // Defines the radius in which the player must be to
    trigger interaction
    UPROPERTY(EditAnywhere, Category = "NPC Interaction")
    float InteractionRadius;

    // Boolean flag to check if the player is nearby
    bool bIsPlayerNearby;

    // Checks if the player is within interaction range
    void CheckProximity();

    // Executes the appropriate interaction based on the
    NPC type
    void ExecuteInteraction();

    // Ends the interaction and resets states if necessary
    void EndInteraction();
};
```

Listing 3-18 outlines the key functions and properties of the ANPCSystem class, facilitating various types of interactions between non-player characters (NPCs) and players in the game.

CHAPTER 3 INTERACTION MECHANICS

- **CheckProximity Function**: Checks if the player is within the interaction radius and sets bIsPlayerNearby accordingly

- **Interact Function**: Initiates the interaction if the player is nearby

- **ExecuteInteraction Function**: Determines the interaction type (Dialogue, Quest, Trade, or Combat) and executes the corresponding logic

- **HandleDialogue Function**: Displays the NPC's dialogue if available

- **HandleQuest Function**: Starts a quest if the NPC has one

- **HandleTrade Function**: Placeholder function for future trade mechanics

- **HandleCombat Function**: Placeholder function for NPC combat behavior

- **EndInteraction Function**: Concludes the interaction and transitions back to gameplay

Listing 3-18. NPCSystem.cpp

```
#include "NPCSystem.h"
#include "GameFramework/Character.h"

ANPCSystem::ANPCSystem()
{
    PrimaryActorTick.bCanEverTick = true;
    InteractionRadius = 200.0f;
```

CHAPTER 3 INTERACTION MECHANICS

```cpp
    bIsPlayerNearby = false;
    NPCInteractionType = ENPCInteractionType::Dialogue;
    // Default interaction type
}
void ANPCSystem::BeginPlay()
{
    Super::BeginPlay();
}

void ANPCSystem::Tick(float DeltaTime)
{
    Super::Tick(DeltaTime);
    CheckProximity();
}

void ANPCSystem::CheckProximity()
{
    // Implement proximity detection logic here
    // Example: Check if the player is within the
    InteractionRadius
}

void ANPCSystem::Interact()
{
    if (bIsPlayerNearby)
    {
        ExecuteInteraction();
    }
}
```

CHAPTER 3   INTERACTION MECHANICS

```cpp
void ANPCSystem::ExecuteInteraction()
{
    switch (NPCInteractionType)
    {
        case ENPCInteractionType::Dialogue:
            HandleDialogue();
            break;

        case ENPCInteractionType::Quest:
            HandleQuest();
            break;

        case ENPCInteractionType::Trade:
            HandleTrade();
            break;

        case ENPCInteractionType::Combat:
            HandleCombat();
            break;

        default:
            break;
    }

    EndInteraction();
}

void ANPCSystem::HandleDialogue()
{
    if (Dialogues.Num() > 0)
    {
        FString Dialogue = Dialogues[0];
        // Implement dialogue display logic here
    }
}
```

```cpp
void ANPCSystem::HandleQuest()
{
    if (Quests.Num() > 0)
    {
        FString Quest = Quests[0];
        // Implement quest initiation logic here
    }
}

void ANPCSystem::HandleTrade()
{
    // Implement trade logic here (e.g., open trade UI)
}

void ANPCSystem::HandleCombat()
{
    // Implement combat engagement logic here (e.g., trigger attack behavior)
}

void ANPCSystem::EndInteraction()
{
    // Implement interaction conclusion logic here
    // Example: Resume gameplay
}
```

Advanced Techniques

For more dynamic NPC interactions, we can implement state machines and AI behaviors to allow NPCs to exhibit lifelike behaviors and respond to the player's actions.

CHAPTER 3   INTERACTION MECHANICS

Listing 3-19 implements the AAdvancedNPCSystem class, extending basic NPC functionality by incorporating state management, allowing NPCs to respond dynamically to player actions and game events.

- **ENPCState Enum**: Defines different NPC states, such as Idle and Interacting, ensuring structured state management
- **Dialogues**: Array storing NPC dialogues for interaction
- **Quests**: Array containing quests the NPC can provide
- **InteractionRadius**: Defines the distance within which a player can interact with the NPC
- **bIsPlayerNearby**: Boolean that checks if the player is within the interaction radius
- **CurrentState**: Tracks the NPC's current state, such as Idle or Interacting
- **CheckProximity Function**: Detects if the player is within the interaction radius
- **Interact Function**: Initiates interaction if the player is nearby
- **ExecuteInteraction Function**: Executes interaction logic, such as displaying dialogues or starting quests
- **ChangeState Function**: Changes the NPC's state and updates behaviors accordingly
- **EndInteraction Function**: Ends the interaction and transitions back to the default state

CHAPTER 3   INTERACTION MECHANICS

Listing 3-19. AdvancedNPCSystem.h

```cpp
#pragma once

#include "CoreMinimal.h"
#include "GameFramework/Character.h"
#include "AdvancedNPCSystem.generated.h"

UENUM(BlueprintType)
enum class ENPCState : uint8
{
    Idle       UMETA(DisplayName = "Idle"),
    Interacting UMETA(DisplayName = "Interacting")
};

UCLASS()
class MYGAME_API AAdvancedNPCSystem : public ACharacter
{
    GENERATED_BODY()

public:
    AAdvancedNPCSystem();

protected:
    virtual void BeginPlay() override;

public:
    virtual void Tick(float DeltaTime) override;

    void Interact();

private:
    UPROPERTY(EditAnywhere, Category = "NPC")
    TArray<FString> Dialogues;

    UPROPERTY(EditAnywhere, Category = "NPC")
    TArray<FString> Quests;
```

```
UPROPERTY(EditAnywhere, Category = "NPC")
float InteractionRadius;

UPROPERTY(VisibleAnywhere, Category = "NPC")
ENPCState CurrentState; // NPC state using Enum

bool bIsPlayerNearby;

void CheckProximity();
void ExecuteInteraction();
void ChangeState(ENPCState NewState);
void EndInteraction();
};
```

Listing 3-20 implements this functionality, enabling NPCs to engage in dynamic, state-based interactions with players, improving realism and responsiveness.

- **AAdvancedNPCSystem Constructor**: Initializes NPC properties, such as InteractionRadius, bIsPlayerNearby, and CurrentState

- **BeginPlay Function**: Sets up initial logic when the game starts

- **Tick Function**: Continuously checks player proximity and updates NPC behavior based on the CurrentState

- **CheckProximity Function**: Determines if the player is within the interaction radius

- **Interact Function**: Changes the NPC state to Interacting and triggers interaction logic if the player is nearby

- **ExecuteInteraction Function**: Displays dialogues or initiates quests if available, then calls EndInteraction()

CHAPTER 3　INTERACTION MECHANICS

- **ChangeState Function**: Updates the NPC's current state and modifies behavior accordingly
- **EndInteraction Function**: Resets NPC state to Idle, allowing for new interactions

Listing 3-20. AdvancedNPCSystem.cpp

```cpp
#include "AdvancedNPCSystem.h"
#include "GameFramework/Character.h"

AAdvancedNPCSystem::AAdvancedNPCSystem()
{
    PrimaryActorTick.bCanEverTick = true;
    InteractionRadius = 200.0f;
    bIsPlayerNearby = false;
    CurrentState = ENPCState::Idle; // Default state
}

void AAdvancedNPCSystem::BeginPlay()
{
    Super::BeginPlay();
}

void AAdvancedNPCSystem::Tick(float DeltaTime)
{
    Super::Tick(DeltaTime);
    CheckProximity();

    // Implement state-based behavior
    switch (CurrentState)
    {
    case ENPCState::Idle:
        // Idle behavior: NPC could roam, animate, or wait
        break;
```

```cpp
    case ENPCState::Interacting:
        // Interacting behavior: NPC might perform a gesture or
        play an animation
        break;
    }
}

void AAdvancedNPCSystem::CheckProximity()
{
    // Implement proximity detection logic
    // Example: Check if the player is within InteractionRadius
}

void AAdvancedNPCSystem::Interact()
{
    if (bIsPlayerNearby)
    {
        ChangeState(ENPCState::Interacting);
        ExecuteInteraction();
    }
}

void AAdvancedNPCSystem::ExecuteInteraction()
{
    // Implement interaction logic (e.g., display dialogue or
    start a quest)

    if (Dialogues.Num() > 0)
    {
        FString Dialogue = Dialogues[0];
        // Implement dialogue display logic here
    }
```

```cpp
    if (Quests.Num() > 0)
    {
        FString Quest = Quests[0];
        // Implement quest initiation logic here
    }

    EndInteraction();
}

void AAdvancedNPCSystem::ChangeState(ENPCState NewState)
{
    CurrentState = NewState;

    // Implement state change logic (e.g., play animation,
    update UI)
}

void AAdvancedNPCSystem::EndInteraction()
{
    ChangeState(ENPCState::Idle);
    // Implement logic to conclude the interaction
}
```

In this section, we explored the fundamentals and advanced techniques of NPC interactions in game development. From simple proximity-based interactions to complex state-driven behaviors, these systems enhance the game's depth and player engagement.

In the next subtopic, we will delve into the inventory system, learning how to create and manage player inventories and item interactions.

Inventory System

The inventory system is a crucial component of many games, allowing players to manage items they collect, use, and equip throughout their journey. This system can range from simple item storage to complex management involving crafting, trading, and equipment mechanics.

Consider a role-playing game (RPG) where players collect various items such as weapons, potions, and quest items. A well-designed inventory system enhances the gameplay experience by providing an intuitive interface for item management.

Basic Usage

A basic inventory system involves storing items the player collects and providing functionality to add, remove, and use these items. This can be implemented using a simple data structure such as an array or list.

Advanced Techniques

Advanced inventory systems can include features such as item stacking, categorization, sorting, and equipment management. These systems often integrate with other gameplay mechanics like crafting, trading, and combat.

Imagine a game where players can combine items to create new ones, trade with NPCs, and equip gear that affects their stats and abilities. This adds depth and strategy to the gameplay.

Practical Applications

A well-organized inventory can reduce frustration and improve satisfaction by enabling players to easily locate and utilize their items.

- **Item Collection**: Players can collect items found in the game world.
- **Crafting**: Players can combine items to create new ones.
- **Trading**: Players can trade items with NPCs or other players.
- **Equipment Management**: Players can equip items that affect their abilities and stats.

Algorithm Overview

The following steps outline the core functionality of an inventory system, guiding its implementation and integration within the game:

1. **Initialization**: Set up the inventory components and data structures.
2. **Item Collection**: Add items to the inventory when collected.
3. **Item Management**: Provide functionality to view, use, and remove items.
4. **Equipment Management**: Allow players to equip and unequip items.
5. **Conclusion**: Ensure the inventory system integrates seamlessly with other game mechanics.

CHAPTER 3 INTERACTION MECHANICS

Reviewing the Code

The following foundational setup ensures that players can efficiently manage their items, enhancing gameplay dynamics and strategic planning.

Listing 3-21 defines the core components of the inventory system, managing player items within the game.

- **FInventoryItem Struct**: Defines the structure of an inventory item, including its name and quantity

- **InventorySystem Class**: Manages the player's inventory, including adding, removing, and using items

- **Inventory Array**: Stores the collection of items in the player's inventory

- **FindItem Function**: Finds an item in the inventory by name

Listing 3-21. InventorySystem.h

```
#pragma once

#include "CoreMinimal.h"
#include "GameFramework/Actor.h"
#include "InventorySystem.generated.h"

USTRUCT(BlueprintType)
struct FInventoryItem
{
    GENERATED_BODY()

    UPROPERTY(EditAnywhere, BlueprintReadWrite)
    FString ItemName;
```

```cpp
    UPROPERTY(EditAnywhere, BlueprintReadWrite)
    int32 Quantity;

    FInventoryItem()
    {
        ItemName = "";
        Quantity = 1;
    }
};

UCLASS()
class MYGAME_API AInventorySystem : public AActor
{
    GENERATED_BODY()

public:
    AInventorySystem();

protected:
    virtual void BeginPlay() override;

public:
    virtual void Tick(float DeltaTime) override;

    void AddItem(FString ItemName, int32 Quantity);
    void RemoveItem(FString ItemName, int32 Quantity);
    void UseItem(FString ItemName);

private:
    UPROPERTY(EditAnywhere, BlueprintReadWrite)
    TArray<FInventoryItem> Inventory;

    FInventoryItem* FindItem(FString ItemName);
};
```

Listing 3-22 implements the functionality of the inventory management system defined in the header file. Here's a breakdown of the key components:

- **AddItem Function**: Adds an item to the inventory or increases its quantity if it already exists

- **RemoveItem Function**: Removes an item from the inventory or decreases its quantity

- **UseItem Function**: Uses an item from the inventory, reducing its quantity

- **FindItem Function**: Finds an item in the inventory by name

Listing 3-22. InventorySystem.cpp

```cpp
#include "InventorySystem.h"

AInventorySystem::AInventorySystem()
{
    PrimaryActorTick.bCanEverTick = true;
}

void AInventorySystem::BeginPlay()
{
    Super::BeginPlay();
}

void AInventorySystem::Tick(float DeltaTime)
{
    Super::Tick(DeltaTime);
}
```

CHAPTER 3 INTERACTION MECHANICS

```cpp
void AInventorySystem::AddItem(FString ItemName, int32 Quantity)
{
    FInventoryItem* Item = FindItem(ItemName);
    if (Item)
    {
        Item->Quantity += Quantity;
    }
    else
    {
        FInventoryItem NewItem;
        NewItem.ItemName = ItemName;
        NewItem.Quantity = Quantity;
        Inventory.Add(NewItem);
    }
}

void AInventorySystem::RemoveItem(FString ItemName, int32 Quantity)
{
    FInventoryItem* Item = FindItem(ItemName);
    if (Item && Item->Quantity >= Quantity)
    {
        Item->Quantity -= Quantity;
        if (Item->Quantity == 0)
        {
            Inventory.RemoveSingle(*Item);
        }
    }
}
```

```cpp
void AInventorySystem::UseItem(FString ItemName)
{
    FInventoryItem* Item = FindItem(ItemName);
    if (Item && Item->Quantity > 0)
    {
        // Implement item usage logic here
        Item->Quantity--;
        if (Item->Quantity == 0)
        {
            Inventory.RemoveSingle(*Item);
        }
    }
}

FInventoryItem* AInventorySystem::FindItem(FString ItemName)
{
    for (FInventoryItem& Item : Inventory)
    {
        if (Item.ItemName == ItemName)
        {
            return &Item;
        }
    }
    return nullptr;
}
```

Advanced Techniques

For more advanced inventory systems, we can implement features such as item stacking, sorting, and categorization. We can also integrate the inventory with other game mechanics such as crafting and trading.

CHAPTER 3   INTERACTION MECHANICS

Listing 3-23 extends the functionality of the basic inventory system defined in the Listing 3-21 file. Here's a detailed breakdown of its components:

- **AdvancedInventorySystem Class**: This class inherits from AInventorySystem, enhancing the basic inventory management capabilities. It introduces new functionalities like sorting and categorizing items, making it suitable for more complex inventory requirements in games.

- **SortInventory Function**: This function (not yet implemented in the header file) is intended to allow players to organize their inventory items based on certain criteria, such as item name, type, or rarity. Sorting improves the user experience by making it easier to find items within the inventory.

- **CategorizeItems Function**: This function (also not yet implemented) will categorize items into groups, such as weapons, potions, or crafting materials. This organization facilitates better management and retrieval of items, making it easier for players to navigate their inventory.

- **CategorizedInventory Map**: This private member variable is a TMap that stores items organized by category. Each key in the map represents a category (e.g., "Weapons," "Potions"), and the associated value is an array of FInventoryItem structs. This structure allows for efficient access and management of categorized items, providing an intuitive way for players to view their inventory.

Listing 3-23. AdvancedInventorySystem.h

```
#pragma once

#include "CoreMinimal.h"
#include "InventorySystem.h"
#include "AdvancedInventorySystem.generated.h"

UCLASS()
class MYGAME_API AAdvancedInventorySystem : public AInventorySystem
{
    GENERATED_BODY()
public:
    AAdvancedInventorySystem();

protected:
    virtual void BeginPlay() override;

public:
    virtual void Tick(float DeltaTime) override;

    void SortInventory();
    void CategorizeItems();

private:
    UPROPERTY(EditAnywhere, BlueprintReadWrite)
    TMap<FString, TArray<FInventoryItem>> CategorizedInventory;
};
```

Listing 3-24 implements the functionality defined in the Listing 3-23 file. Here's a detailed breakdown of its components:

- **SortInventory Function**: This function sorts the items in the player's inventory alphabetically by their name. The Sort method uses a lambda function that compares two FInventoryItem objects, returning true if the name of item A is less than that of item B. Sorting improves the organization of items, making it easier for players to find what they need quickly.

- **CategorizeItems Function**: This function organizes the items in the inventory by type and stores them in the CategorizedInventory map. It begins by clearing any existing categories with CategorizedInventory.Empty().

Listing 3-24. AdvancedInventorySystem.cpp

```cpp
#include "AdvancedInventorySystem.h"

AAdvancedInventorySystem::AAdvancedInventorySystem()
{
    PrimaryActorTick.bCanEverTick = true;
}

void AAdvancedInventorySystem::BeginPlay()
{
    Super::BeginPlay();
}

void AAdvancedInventorySystem::Tick(float DeltaTime)
{
    Super::Tick(DeltaTime);
}

void AAdvancedInventorySystem::SortInventory()
{
    Inventory.Sort([](const FInventoryItem& A, const
    FInventoryItem& B) {
        return A.ItemName < B.ItemName;
    });
}
```

```cpp
void AAdvancedInventorySystem::CategorizeItems()
{
    CategorizedInventory.Empty();
    for (const FInventoryItem& Item : Inventory)
    {
        FString Category = "General"; // Determine category
        based on item properties
        if (!CategorizedInventory.Contains(Category))
        {
            CategorizedInventory.Add(Category,
            TArray<FInventoryItem>());
        }
        CategorizedInventory[Category].Add(Item);
    }
}
```

In this section, we explored the fundamentals and advanced techniques of inventory systems in game development. From simple item storage to complex management involving crafting and trading, these systems are essential for enhancing gameplay.

In the next subtopic, we will delve into quest activation, learning how to create and manage quests that drive the game's story and provide players with objectives.

Quest Activation

Quest activation is a key aspect of game design that engages players by providing them with objectives and goals. Quests can range from simple tasks to complex story-driven missions, and they often include rewards for completion. Effective quest activation can enhance the narrative and provide a sense of progression.

CHAPTER 3 INTERACTION MECHANICS

Imagine a role-playing game (RPG) where players receive quests from non-playable characters (NPCs), discover quests through exploration, or trigger them through specific in-game events. These quests guide players through the game's world and storyline.

Basic Usage

A basic quest activation system involves setting up quests, activating them based on certain triggers, and tracking their progress. This can be implemented using a simple state machine to manage quest states such as inactive, active, completed, and failed.

Advanced Techniques

Advanced quest systems can include branching quests, dynamic objectives, and dependencies between quests. These systems often integrate with other gameplay mechanics like dialogue systems, NPC interactions, and inventory systems.

Imagine a game where players' choices affect the outcome of quests, leading to multiple endings or different story paths. This adds depth and replayability to the game.

Practical Applications

Quest activation systems can significantly enhance the overall gaming experience by providing structured objectives and meaningful interactions. Here are some key practical applications:

- **Story Progression**: Guide players through the main story and side quests.

- **Rewards**: Provide incentives such as experience points, items, and currency for completing quests.

CHAPTER 3　INTERACTION MECHANICS

- **World Building**: Enhance the game's lore and world through quest narratives.

- **Player Engagement**: Keep players engaged with varied and challenging objectives.

Algorithm Overview

The algorithm for a quest activation system can be broken down into several key steps to ensure efficient management and execution of quests:

1. **Initialization**: Set up the quest components and data structures.

2. **Quest Activation**: Activate quests based on triggers such as NPC interactions or player actions.

3. **Quest Tracking**: Track the progress of active quests.

4. **Quest Completion**: Handle the completion and rewards of quests.

5. **Conclusion**: Ensure the quest system integrates seamlessly with other game mechanics.

Reviewing the Code

To establish a robust quest system, we begin by defining the necessary components and structures that will manage quests efficiently. This includes creating classes and data structures to represent quests, their states, and associated rewards.

Listing 3-25 implements the quest system, enabling dynamic interaction and progression for players throughout the game.

CHAPTER 3   INTERACTION MECHANICS

- **FQuest Struct**: Defines the structure of a quest, including its name, description, active status, and completion status
- **QuestSystem Class**: Manages the player's quests, including activation, tracking, and completion
- **Quests Array**: Stores the collection of quests
- **FindQuest Function**: Finds a quest in the collection by name

Listing 3-25. QuestSystem.h

```
#pragma once

#include "CoreMinimal.h"
#include "GameFramework/Actor.h"
#include "QuestSystem.generated.h"

USTRUCT(BlueprintType)
struct FQuest
{
    GENERATED_BODY()

    UPROPERTY(EditAnywhere, BlueprintReadWrite)
    FString QuestName;

    UPROPERTY(EditAnywhere, BlueprintReadWrite)
    FString Description;

    UPROPERTY(EditAnywhere, BlueprintReadWrite)
    bool bIsActive;

    UPROPERTY(EditAnywhere, BlueprintReadWrite)
    bool bIsCompleted;
```

```cpp
    FQuest()
    {
        QuestName = "";
        Description = "";
        bIsActive = false;
        bIsCompleted = false;
    }
};

UCLASS()
class MYGAME_API AQuestSystem : public AActor
{
    GENERATED_BODY()

public:
    AQuestSystem();

protected:
    virtual void BeginPlay() override;

public:
    virtual void Tick(float DeltaTime) override;

    void ActivateQuest(FString QuestName);
    void CompleteQuest(FString QuestName);
    void TrackQuestProgress(FString QuestName, int32 Progress);

private:
    UPROPERTY(EditAnywhere, BlueprintReadWrite)
    TArray<FQuest> Quests;

    FQuest* FindQuest(FString QuestName);
};
```

CHAPTER 3 INTERACTION MECHANICS

Listing 3-26 implements the functionalities of the quest system, enabling players to activate, complete, and track quests throughout the game.

- **ActivateQuest Function**: Activates a quest if it is inactive and not completed
- **CompleteQuest Function**: Completes a quest if it is active and not completed
- **TrackQuestProgress Function**: Tracks the progress of an active quest
- **FindQuest Function**: Finds a quest in the collection by name

Listing 3-26. QuestSystem.cpp

```cpp
#include "QuestSystem.h"

AQuestSystem::AQuestSystem()
{
    PrimaryActorTick.bCanEverTick = true;
}

void AQuestSystem::BeginPlay()
{
    Super::BeginPlay();
}

void AQuestSystem::Tick(float DeltaTime)
{
    Super::Tick(DeltaTime);
}
```

```cpp
void AQuestSystem::ActivateQuest(FString QuestName)
{
    FQuest* Quest = FindQuest(QuestName);
    if (Quest && !Quest->bIsActive && !Quest->bIsCompleted)
    {
        Quest->bIsActive = true;
        // Additional logic for activating the quest (e.g.,
        displaying quest log)
    }
}

void AQuestSystem::CompleteQuest(FString QuestName)
{
    FQuest* Quest = FindQuest(QuestName);
    if (Quest && Quest->bIsActive && !Quest->bIsCompleted)
    {
        Quest->bIsCompleted = true;
        Quest->bIsActive = false;
        // Additional logic for completing the quest (e.g.,
        awarding rewards)
    }
}

void AQuestSystem::TrackQuestProgress(FString QuestName, int32 Progress)
{
    FQuest* Quest = FindQuest(QuestName);
    if (Quest && Quest->bIsActive && !Quest->bIsCompleted)
    {
        // Implement progress tracking logic here (e.g.,
        updating objectives)
    }
}
```

CHAPTER 3 INTERACTION MECHANICS

```cpp
FQuest* AQuestSystem::FindQuest(FString QuestName)
{
    for (FQuest& Quest : Quests)
    {
        if (Quest.QuestName == QuestName)
        {
            return &Quest;
        }
    }
    return nullptr;
}
```

Advanced Techniques

For more advanced quest systems, we can implement features such as branching quests, dynamic objectives, and dependencies between quests. We can also integrate the quest system with other game mechanics such as dialogue systems and inventory systems.

Listing 3-27 implements the AAdvancedQuestSystem class, building upon the foundational quest system by incorporating advanced features such as branching quests and dependencies.

- **AdvancedQuestSystem Class**: Extends the basic quest system with branching and dependency features
- **QuestDependencies Map**: Stores dependencies between quests

Listing 3-27. AdvancedQuestSystem.h

```cpp
#pragma once

#include "CoreMinimal.h"
#include "QuestSystem.h"
```

CHAPTER 3   INTERACTION MECHANICS

```cpp
#include "AdvancedQuestSystem.generated.h"

UCLASS()
class MYGAME_API AAdvancedQuestSystem : public AQuestSystem
{
    GENERATED_BODY()

public:
    AAdvancedQuestSystem();

protected:
    virtual void BeginPlay() override;

public:
    virtual void Tick(float DeltaTime) override;

    void BranchQuest(FString QuestName, FString NewQuestName);
    void SetQuestDependency(FString QuestName, FString
    DependentQuestName);

private:
    UPROPERTY(EditAnywhere, BlueprintReadWrite)
    TMap<FString, FString> QuestDependencies;
};
```

Listing 3-28 implements advanced functionalities for managing quests in the AAdvancedQuestSystem.cpp file, enhancing the quest system with branching capabilities and dependencies.

- **BranchQuest Function**: Activates a new quest based on the completion of an existing quest
- **SetQuestDependency Function**: Sets a dependency between two quests, ensuring one quest must be completed before the other can be activated

Listing 3-28. AdvancedQuestSystem.cpp

```cpp
#include "AdvancedQuestSystem.h"

AAdvancedQuestSystem::AAdvancedQuestSystem()
{
    PrimaryActorTick.bCanEverTick = true;
}

void AAdvancedQuestSystem::BeginPlay()
{
    Super::BeginPlay();
}

void AAdvancedQuestSystem::Tick(float DeltaTime)
{
    Super::Tick(DeltaTime);
}

void AAdvancedQuestSystem::BranchQuest(FString QuestName,
FString NewQuestName)
{
    FQuest* Quest = FindQuest(QuestName);
    if (Quest && Quest->bIsCompleted)
    {
        ActivateQuest(NewQuestName);
    }
}

void AAdvancedQuestSystem::SetQuestDependency(FString
QuestName, FString DependentQuestName)
{
    if (FindQuest(QuestName) && FindQuest(DependentQuestName))
    {
```

```
        QuestDependencies.Add(QuestName, DependentQuestName);
    }
}
```

In this section, we explored the fundamentals and advanced techniques of quest activation in game development. From simple quest activation to complex branching and dependencies, these systems are essential for driving the game's narrative and providing players with engaging objectives.

In the next subtopic, we will delve into mini-game initiation, learning how to create and manage mini-games within your main game.

Mini-Game Initiation

Mini-games within larger games provide variety and additional engagement for players. They can range from simple puzzles to full-fledged arcade games and often offer rewards or progress toward larger game objectives. Mini-games can be used to break the monotony of the main gameplay loop and introduce new mechanics or challenges.

Imagine a role-playing game (RPG) where players can play card games, participate in races, or solve riddles to earn rewards or progress the story. Implementing a robust mini-game initiation system can greatly enhance player experience and retention.

Basic Usage

To initiate a mini-game, we need to set up triggers or events that start the mini-game, handle the transition between the main game and the mini-game, and manage the state and outcomes of the mini-game.

CHAPTER 3   INTERACTION MECHANICS

Advanced Techniques

Advanced mini-game systems can include dynamic difficulty adjustments, integration with the main game's narrative and mechanics, and seamless transitions back to the main game. They can also track player performance and offer adaptive rewards based on player skill level.

Imagine a game where mini-games scale in difficulty based on the player's performance in the main game, providing a tailored challenge that keeps players engaged.

Practical Applications

Mini-games serve multiple functions in the gaming experience, enhancing engagement and providing meaningful rewards.

- **Player Engagement**: Keep players entertained with varied gameplay experiences.
- **Rewards**: Offer unique rewards that can be used in the main game.
- **Skill Development**: Provide opportunities for players to develop and test different skills.
- **Narrative Integration**: Use mini-games to enhance the storyline and provide character development opportunities.

Algorithm Overview

The initiation and management of mini-games require a structured approach to ensure they enhance gameplay without disrupting the main game flow. This algorithm outlines the essential steps to create an engaging mini-game system.

1. **Initialization**: Set up the mini-game components and data structures.

2. **Mini-Game Initiation**: Trigger the mini-game based on specific events or player actions.

3. **Mini-Game State Management**: Manage the state of the mini-game, including transitions and outcomes.

4. **Mini-Game Completion**: Handle the completion and rewards of the mini-game.

5. **Conclusion**: Ensure the mini-game integrates seamlessly with the main game.

Reviewing the Code

To create an engaging mini-game system, we begin by defining the essential components that will allow for flexible and dynamic mini-game interactions within the larger game environment. The components include data structures to represent mini-games, triggers for activation, and methods to handle gameplay transitions.

Listing 3-29 implements the MiniGameSystem, facilitating engaging and interactive mini-games within the larger game context, ensuring players have varied experiences that contribute to overall gameplay enjoyment.

- **FMiniGame Struct**: This structure defines the properties of a mini-game, including its name, description, active status, and completion status, allowing for organized data management.

- **MiniGameSystem Class**: This class is responsible for managing the player's mini-games, facilitating their initiation, tracking progress, and marking completion.
- **MiniGames Array**: This array stores a collection of mini-games available within the game, enabling easy access and management.
- **FindMiniGame Function**: This function searches for a mini-game within the collection using its name, making it easy to locate and manipulate specific mini-games as needed.

Listing 3-29. MiniGameSystem.h

```
#pragma once

#include "CoreMinimal.h"
#include "GameFramework/Actor.h"
#include "MiniGameSystem.generated.h"

USTRUCT(BlueprintType)
struct FMiniGame
{
    GENERATED_BODY()

    UPROPERTY(EditAnywhere, BlueprintReadWrite)
    FString MiniGameName;

    UPROPERTY(EditAnywhere, BlueprintReadWrite)
    FString Description;

    UPROPERTY(EditAnywhere, BlueprintReadWrite)
    bool bIsActive;
```

```cpp
    UPROPERTY(EditAnywhere, BlueprintReadWrite)
    bool bIsCompleted;

    FMiniGame()
    {
        MiniGameName = "";
        Description = "";
        bIsActive = false;
        bIsCompleted = false;
    }
};

UCLASS()
class MYGAME_API AMiniGameSystem : public AActor
{
    GENERATED_BODY()

public:
    AMiniGameSystem();

protected:
    virtual void BeginPlay() override;

public:
    virtual void Tick(float DeltaTime) override;

    void StartMiniGame(FString MiniGameName);
    void CompleteMiniGame(FString MiniGameName);
    void TrackMiniGameProgress(FString MiniGameName, int32
    Progress);

private:
    UPROPERTY(EditAnywhere, BlueprintReadWrite)
    TArray<FMiniGame> MiniGames;

    FMiniGame* FindMiniGame(FString MiniGameName);
};
```

CHAPTER 3 INTERACTION MECHANICS

Listing 3-30 implements the MiniGameSystem, allowing for the initiation, tracking, and completion of mini-games, providing a seamless experience for players.

- **StartMiniGame Function**: This function checks if a mini-game is inactive and not completed before initiating it, ensuring that players can only engage in available mini-games.
- **CompleteMiniGame Function**: This function marks a mini-game as completed if it is currently active, allowing for the transition back to the main game and the awarding of rewards.
- **TrackMiniGameProgress Function**: This function is responsible for tracking the player's progress in an active mini-game, allowing for the updating of objectives as players progress.
- **FindMiniGame Function**: This function iterates through the collection of mini-games to locate a specific mini-game by name, providing easy access to modify its state as needed.

Listing 3-30. MiniGameSystem.cpp

```
#include "MiniGameSystem.h"

AMiniGameSystem::AMiniGameSystem()
{
    PrimaryActorTick.bCanEverTick = true;
}
```

CHAPTER 3 INTERACTION MECHANICS

```cpp
void AMiniGameSystem::BeginPlay()
{
    Super::BeginPlay();
}

void AMiniGameSystem::Tick(float DeltaTime)
{
    Super::Tick(DeltaTime);
}

void AMiniGameSystem::StartMiniGame(FString MiniGameName)
{
    FMiniGame* MiniGame = FindMiniGame(MiniGameName);
    if (MiniGame && !MiniGame->bIsActive && !MiniGame->bIsCompleted)
    {
        MiniGame->bIsActive = true;
        // Additional logic for starting the mini-game
        (e.g., transitioning to mini-game mode)
    }
}

void AMiniGameSystem::CompleteMiniGame(FString MiniGameName)
{
    FMiniGame* MiniGame = FindMiniGame(MiniGameName);
    if (MiniGame && MiniGame->bIsActive && !MiniGame->bIsCompleted)
    {
        MiniGame->bIsCompleted = true;
        MiniGame->bIsActive = false;
        // Additional logic for completing the mini-game (e.g.,
        awarding rewards, transitioning back to main game)
    }
}
```

```cpp
void AMiniGameSystem::TrackMiniGameProgress(FString 
MiniGameName, int32 Progress)
{
    FMiniGame* MiniGame = FindMiniGame(MiniGameName);
    if (MiniGame && MiniGame->bIsActive && !MiniGame->
    bIsCompleted)
    {
        // Implement progress tracking logic here (e.g.,
        updating objectives)
    }
}

FMiniGame* AMiniGameSystem::FindMiniGame(FString MiniGameName)
{
    for (FMiniGame& MiniGame : MiniGames)
    {
        if (MiniGame.MiniGameName == MiniGameName)
        {
            return &MiniGame;
        }
    }
    return nullptr;
}
```

Advanced Techniques

For more advanced mini-game systems, we can implement features such as dynamic difficulty adjustments, integration with the main game's narrative and mechanics, and seamless transitions back to the main game. We can also track player performance and offer adaptive rewards based on player skill level.

Listing 3-31 implements the AdvancedMiniGameSystem, enhancing the basic mini-game functionality by introducing difficulty adjustments and reward systems tailored to individual mini-games.

- **AdvancedMiniGameSystem Class**: Extends the basic mini-game system with difficulty adjustment and reward features
- **MiniGameDifficulties Map**: Stores difficulty levels for mini-games
- **MiniGameRewards Map**: Stores rewards for completing mini-games

Listing 3-31. AdvancedMiniGameSystem.h

```
#pragma once

#include "CoreMinimal.h"
#include "MiniGameSystem.h"
#include "AdvancedMiniGameSystem.generated.h"

UCLASS()
class MYGAME_API AAdvancedMiniGameSystem : public AMiniGameSystem
{
    GENERATED_BODY()
public:
    AAdvancedMiniGameSystem();

protected:
    virtual void BeginPlay() override;
```

```cpp
public:
    virtual void Tick(float DeltaTime) override;

    void AdjustDifficulty(FString MiniGameName, int32
    DifficultyLevel);
    void SetMiniGameReward(FString MiniGameName, FString
    Reward);
private:
    UPROPERTY(EditAnywhere, BlueprintReadWrite)
    TMap<FString, int32> MiniGameDifficulties;

    UPROPERTY(EditAnywhere, BlueprintReadWrite)
    TMap<FString, FString> MiniGameRewards;
};
```

Listing 3-32 implements the AdvancedMiniGameSystem class, extending the functionality of the base mini-game system by dynamically adjusting difficulty levels and assigning rewards.

- **AdjustDifficulty Function**: Adjusts the difficulty level of a mini-game
- **SetMiniGameReward Function**: Sets the reward for completing a mini-game

Listing 3-32. AdvancedMiniGameSystem.cpp

```cpp
#include "AdvancedMiniGameSystem.h"

AAdvancedMiniGameSystem::AAdvancedMiniGameSystem()
{
    PrimaryActorTick.bCanEverTick = true;
}
```

```cpp
void AAdvancedMiniGameSystem::BeginPlay()
{
    Super::BeginPlay();
}

void AAdvancedMiniGameSystem::Tick(float DeltaTime)
{
    Super::Tick(DeltaTime);
}

void AAdvancedMiniGameSystem::AdjustDifficulty(FString
MiniGameName, int32 DifficultyLevel)
{
    if (FindMiniGame(MiniGameName))
    {
        MiniGameDifficulties.Add(MiniGameName,
        DifficultyLevel);
        // Additional logic for adjusting the mini-game
        difficulty
    }
}

void AAdvancedMiniGameSystem::SetMiniGameReward(FString
MiniGameName, FString Reward)
{
    if (FindMiniGame(MiniGameName))
    {
        MiniGameRewards.Add(MiniGameName, Reward);
        // Additional logic for setting the mini-game reward
    }
}
```

In this section, we explored the fundamentals and advanced techniques of mini-game initiation in game development. From basic mini-game activation to dynamic difficulty adjustments and reward systems, these techniques enhance the variety and engagement of your game.

In the next subtopic, we will delve into puzzle-solving mechanics, learning how to create and manage puzzles.

Puzzle-Solving Mechanics

Puzzle-solving mechanics are fundamental in game design, challenging players with tasks that require logical thinking and creative problem-solving skills.

Basic Usage

Implementing puzzle-solving mechanics involves creating interactive challenges within the game environment. These challenges can range from unlocking doors to manipulating objects to reveal hidden pathways.

Advanced Techniques

Advanced puzzle mechanics include

- **Dynamic Puzzles**: Puzzles that adapt based on player actions
- **Sequential Puzzles**: Multilayered puzzles requiring step-by-step solutions
- **Narrative Integration**: Puzzles that advance the game's storyline or character development

CHAPTER 3   INTERACTION MECHANICS

Practical Applications

These mechanics are integral in various game genres, including

- Adventure games
- RPGs
- Escape rooms
- Platformers

Algorithm Overview

The puzzle-solving mechanics operate through a structured algorithm to ensure engaging gameplay:

1. **Initialization**: Set up puzzle elements.
2. **Player Interaction**: Allow players to interact with elements.
3. **Condition Checking**: Continuously check for puzzle completion.
4. **Resolution**: Trigger appropriate responses upon completion.
5. **Feedback**: Provide feedback and rewards.

Reviewing the Code

To effectively implement puzzle-solving mechanics within a game, it's essential to set up the various elements that make up the puzzles. This involves defining the structures, properties, and behaviors of the puzzle components.

CHAPTER 3   INTERACTION MECHANICS

Listing 3-33 defines and manages the PuzzleElement class, an actor used to create puzzle pieces in the game with functionality for interacting with players and updating its state over time.

- **APuzzleElement Class**: This class defines an actor in the game world that represents a puzzle element. It provides functionality for responding to player interactions, updating states of each frame, and initializing game objects.

- **BeginPlay Function**: Called when the game begins or when the actor is first spawned. It sets up initial values and any preparatory logic needed before gameplay starts.

- **Tick Function**: This function is called once per frame, allowing for real-time updates to the puzzle element. It's essential for any continuous checks or updates the puzzle element needs during gameplay.

- **OnInteract Function**: A placeholder function where logic is added for what happens when a player interacts with this puzzle piece. This could include changing the state of the puzzle or triggering further game events.

- **PuzzleMesh Component**: A UStaticMeshComponent that visually represents the puzzle element in the game. This component is essential for giving the puzzle element a physical form within the game environment.

Listing 3-33. PuzzleElement.h

```cpp
#pragma once

#include "CoreMinimal.h"
#include "GameFramework/Actor.h"
class UStaticMeshComponent;

#include "PuzzleElement.generated.h"

UCLASS()
class MYGAME_API APuzzleElement : public AActor
{
    GENERATED_BODY()

public:
    APuzzleElement();

protected:
    virtual void BeginPlay() override;

public:
    virtual void Tick(float DeltaTime) override;

    UFUNCTION()
    void OnInteract();

private:
    UPROPERTY(VisibleAnywhere)
    UStaticMeshComponent* PuzzleMesh;
};
```

Listing 3-34 implements the puzzle element actor, focusing on how it interacts with the game world. The following points summarize the key components of this implementation:

- **CreateDefaultSubobject**: This function creates the static mesh component that represents the puzzle element in the game. This component is vital for giving the puzzle a visible, interactive form in the game world.

- **SetCollisionEnabled**: This method enables collision detection and physics for the puzzle element. It allows the game engine to detect when the player or other objects interact with the puzzle element, making it an essential part of the interaction system.

- **SetCollisionResponseToAllChannels**: This method ensures the puzzle element responds to all types of interactions in the game environment by blocking all other objects, making the puzzle piece responsive to the game physics and player inputs.

- **OnInteract Function**: This function will contain the logic for what happens when the player interacts with the puzzle element. This might involve solving the puzzle, updating the element's state, or triggering game events based on the interaction.

Listing 3-34. PuzzleElement.cpp

```
#include "PuzzleElement.h"
#include "Components/StaticMeshComponent.h"

APuzzleElement::APuzzleElement()
{
    PrimaryActorTick.bCanEverTick = true;

    PuzzleMesh = CreateDefaultSubobject<UStaticMeshComponent>
    (TEXT("PuzzleMesh"));
    RootComponent = PuzzleMesh;
```

```cpp
    PuzzleMesh->SetCollisionEnabled(ECollisionEnabled::
    QueryAndPhysics);
    PuzzleMesh->SetCollisionResponseToAllChannels(
    ECollisionResponse::ECR_Block);
}

void APuzzleElement::BeginPlay()
{
    Super::BeginPlay();
}

void APuzzleElement::Tick(float DeltaTime)
{
    Super::Tick(DeltaTime);
}

void APuzzleElement::OnInteract()
{
    // Implement puzzle interaction logic here
}
```

Implementing Puzzle Interaction

In this section, we explore the interaction logic that allows players to engage with and solve puzzles. Puzzle interaction is a key aspect of gameplay in many genres, ensuring that players must think critically and make decisions to progress.

Listing 3-35 implements the PuzzleInteraction class, managing the logic required for players to interact with multiple puzzle elements. It continuously checks the puzzle's status and ensures the correct conditions are met to solve the puzzle.

CHAPTER 3 INTERACTION MECHANICS

- **APuzzleInteraction Class**: This class handles the logic for managing interactions between the player and the puzzle elements. It tracks whether the puzzle is solved and manages the puzzle elements involved.

- **BeginPlay Function**: Initializes the puzzle elements at the start of the game. This function prepares the puzzle for interaction, setting up any necessary references to the puzzle elements.

- **Tick Function**: Called once per frame, this function continuously checks the puzzle's status to determine if all conditions for solving the puzzle have been met.

- **CheckPuzzleCondition Function**: This is a placeholder function where you implement the logic to check whether the puzzle is solved. It evaluates the states of all puzzle elements and sets the bIsPuzzleSolved boolean accordingly.

- **PuzzleElements Array**: This array holds references to all the puzzle elements that need to be checked. It allows for efficient management and interaction with the puzzle pieces during gameplay.

- **bIsPuzzleSolved Boolean**: This boolean tracks whether the puzzle has been solved. It ensures that once the puzzle is completed, the game can trigger the appropriate responses.

Listing 3-35. PuzzleInteraction.h

```
#pragma once

#include "CoreMinimal.h"
#include "GameFramework/Actor.h"
#include "PuzzleInteraction.generated.h"
```

```cpp
UCLASS()
class MYGAME_API APuzzleInteraction : public AActor
{
    GENERATED_BODY()
public:
    APuzzleInteraction();
protected:
    virtual void BeginPlay() override;
public:
    virtual void Tick(float DeltaTime) override;

    UFUNCTION()
    void CheckPuzzleCondition();
private:
    TArray<APuzzleElement*> PuzzleElements;
    bool bIsPuzzleSolved;
};
```

This file provides the actual implementation of the puzzle interaction logic, including how the puzzle elements are initialized and how the puzzle's condition is continuously monitored:

- **Initialize Puzzle Elements**: In the BeginPlay function, puzzle elements can be initialized by populating the PuzzleElements array. This would typically involve locating all puzzle elements in the scene and assigning them to the array for later reference and condition checking.

- **CheckPuzzleCondition Function**: This function implements the logic for determining whether the puzzle is solved. It evaluates the current state of each puzzle element. If all elements are in the correct state, the puzzle is marked as solved by setting bIsPuzzleSolved to true.

- **Tick Function**: The Tick function continuously calls CheckPuzzleCondition every frame to ensure real-time updates on the puzzle's status. This ensures that the game reacts immediately once all conditions are met for solving the puzzle.

Listing 3-36. PuzzleInteraction.cpp

```
#include "PuzzleInteraction.h"
#include "PuzzleElement.h"

APuzzleInteraction::APuzzleInteraction()
{
    PrimaryActorTick.bCanEverTick = true;
    bIsPuzzleSolved = false;
}

void APuzzleInteraction::BeginPlay()
{
    Super::BeginPlay();

    // Initialize puzzle elements
    // Example: Find all puzzle elements in the scene and add
    them to the PuzzleElements array
}
```

```cpp
void APuzzleInteraction::Tick(float DeltaTime)
{
    Super::Tick(DeltaTime);

    CheckPuzzleCondition();
}

void APuzzleInteraction::CheckPuzzleCondition()
{
    // Implement condition checking logic here
    // Example: If all puzzle elements are in the correct
    state, set bIsPuzzleSolved to true
}
```

Advanced Mechanics Code Example

In more complex game designs, puzzles evolve based on player interactions, making the experience dynamic and engaging. Dynamic puzzles adapt to player actions, offering new challenges as they progress.

Listing 3-37 outlines the key elements of this dynamic puzzle implementation.

- **ADynamicPuzzle Class**: Represents a dynamic puzzle that responds to player interactions. This class manages the puzzle's state and behavior throughout gameplay.

- **OnPlayerInteraction Function**: Handles player interactions, which trigger changes in the puzzle's components.

- **PuzzleMeshes Array**: Stores the static mesh components that make up the dynamic puzzle. These are the visual elements players see and interact with.

Chapter 3 Interaction Mechanics

- **bIsPuzzleSolved Boolean**: A boolean variable that tracks whether the puzzle has been solved. This ensures that the game knows when to trigger specific events upon puzzle completion.

Listing 3-37. DynamicPuzzle.h

```cpp
#pragma once

#include "CoreMinimal.h"
#include "GameFramework/Actor.h"
class UStaticMeshComponent;

#include "DynamicPuzzle.generated.h"
UCLASS()
class MYGAME_API ADynamicPuzzle : public AActor
{
    GENERATED_BODY()
public:
    ADynamicPuzzle();

protected:
    virtual void BeginPlay() override;

public:
    virtual void Tick(float DeltaTime) override;

    UFUNCTION()
    void OnPlayerInteraction();
```

```
private:
    UPROPERTY(VisibleAnywhere)
    TArray<UStaticMeshComponent*> PuzzleMeshes;

    bool bIsPuzzleSolved;
};
```

This implementation includes the following key aspects:

- **BeginPlay Function**: Sets up the puzzle by initializing the mesh components in the PuzzleMeshes array. This is where the puzzle elements are gathered and prepared for interaction.

- **Tick Function**: The Tick function runs every frame, constantly checking whether the puzzle has been solved by evaluating the puzzle conditions.

- **OnPlayerInteraction Function**: This function contains the logic for handling player interactions with the puzzle. When a player interacts, the state of the puzzle changes, and the game responds accordingly.

Listing 3-38. DynamicPuzzle.cpp

```
#include "DynamicPuzzle.h"
#include "Components/StaticMeshComponent.h"

ADynamicPuzzle::ADynamicPuzzle()
{
    PrimaryActorTick.bCanEverTick = true;
    bIsPuzzleSolved = false;
}
```

CHAPTER 3   INTERACTION MECHANICS

```cpp
void ADynamicPuzzle::BeginPlay()
{
    Super::BeginPlay();

    // Initialize puzzle meshes
    // Example: Find and add all dynamic puzzle elements to the
    PuzzleMeshes array
}

void ADynamicPuzzle::Tick(float DeltaTime)
{
    Super::Tick(DeltaTime);

    // Continuously check for puzzle completion
    if (!bIsPuzzleSolved)
    {
        // Check condition for puzzle completion
    }
}

void ADynamicPuzzle::OnPlayerInteraction()
{
    // Implement puzzle interaction logic here
}
```

This section explored the fundamentals of puzzle-solving mechanics in game development, covering basic usage, advanced techniques, and providing detailed code examples for implementation. By understanding these concepts, you can create engaging puzzles that challenge and entertain players.

In the next section, we will delve into trading systems, exploring how to implement systems that allow players to buy, sell, and trade items within the game world.

Trading Systems

Trading systems are crucial in many games, allowing players to buy, sell, and trade items with other players or NPCs. These systems enhance player interaction and can add depth to the game economy and overall gameplay experience.

Basic Usage

Implementing a trading system involves creating a user interface for trading, setting up tradeable items, and managing transactions between entities.

Advanced Techniques

Advanced trading systems include

- **Dynamic Pricing**: Prices fluctuate based on supply and demand.
- **Bartering**: Allows players to trade items without using currency.
- **Trade Restrictions**: Certain items can only be traded under specific conditions.
- **Player-to-Player Trading**: Secure and seamless transactions between players.

Practical Applications

These mechanics are integral in

- RPGs
- MMORPGs
- Simulation games
- Strategy games

Algorithm Overview

The following outlines the basic structure of a trading system in a game:

1. **Initialization**: Set up tradeable items and trading entities.
2. **User Interface**: Create a UI for trading interactions.
3. **Transaction Management**: Handle the logic for buying, selling, and trading items.
4. **Inventory Updates**: Update the player's or NPC's inventory post-transaction.
5. **Feedback**: Provide feedback on successful or failed trades.

Reviewing the Code

To implement a tradeable item, we can use a custom class that represents the in-game object, complete with properties such as the item's name and value.

Listing 3-39 implements the ATradeableItem class, serving as a fundamental building block for tradeable items within the game. This class encapsulates the essential properties and methods that define a tradeable item.

- **ATradeableItem Class**: Represents an item that can be traded in the game
- **ItemName**: Stores the name of the item
- **ItemValue**: Stores the value of the item, which can be used for pricing in the trading system

Listing 3-39. TradeableItem.h

```
#pragma once

#include "CoreMinimal.h"
#include "GameFramework/Actor.h"
#include "TradeableItem.generated.h"

UCLASS()
class MYGAME_API ATradeableItem : public AActor
{
    GENERATED_BODY()

public:
    ATradeableItem();

protected:
    virtual void BeginPlay() override;

public:
    virtual void Tick(float DeltaTime) override;

    UPROPERTY(EditAnywhere, BlueprintReadWrite,
    Category="Trading")
```

```
    FString ItemName;

    UPROPERTY(EditAnywhere, BlueprintReadWrite, 
    Category="Trading")
    int32 ItemValue;
};
```

Listing 3-40 defines the constructor and key functions in the implementation file, contributing to the item's functionality within the game.

- **ATradeableItem Constructor**: Initializes the item and sets it to tick every frame
- **BeginPlay Function**: Called when the game starts or when the actor is spawned, used for initialization
- **Tick Function**: Called every frame, allowing updates to the item's state if necessary

Listing 3-40. TradeableItem.cpp

```cpp
#include "TradeableItem.h"

ATradeableItem::ATradeableItem()
{
    PrimaryActorTick.bCanEverTick = true;
}

void ATradeableItem::BeginPlay()
{
    Super::BeginPlay();
}
```

```
void ATradeableItem::Tick(float DeltaTime)
{
    Super::Tick(DeltaTime);
}
```

Implementing the Trading System

In this section, we will implement the trading system mechanics, which will handle interactions between players or NPCs for buying, selling, or trading items. The trading system will also manage inventories and currency exchanges between the trading entities.

Listing 3-41 implements the ATradingSystem class, serving as the core component responsible for managing the trading mechanics between different entities within the game. This class encapsulates the functionality required to facilitate item trades.

- **ATradingSystem Class**: Manages the trading logic between entities
- **TradeItem Function**: Handles the trading logic between the buyer and seller for a specific item
- **UpdateInventory Function**: Updates the inventory of the involved actors, either adding or removing the traded item
- **UpdateCurrency Function**: Updates the currency of the involved actors based on the transaction

Listing 3-41. TradingSystem.h

```
#pragma once

#include "CoreMinimal.h"
#include "GameFramework/Actor.h"
#include "TradingSystem.generated.h"
```

CHAPTER 3   INTERACTION MECHANICS

```cpp
UCLASS()
class MYGAME_API ATradingSystem : public AActor
{
    GENERATED_BODY()
public:
    ATradingSystem();

protected:
    virtual void BeginPlay() override;

public:
    virtual void Tick(float DeltaTime) override;

    UFUNCTION(BlueprintCallable, Category="Trading")
    void TradeItem(AActor* Buyer, AActor* Seller,
    ATradeableItem* Item);

private:
    void UpdateInventory(AActor* Actor, ATradeableItem* Item,
    bool bAddItem);
    void UpdateCurrency(AActor* Actor, int32 Amount);
};
```

Listing 3-42 implements the key functions that drive the trading system's functionality and facilitate interactions between buyers and sellers.

- **TradeItem Function**: Handles the main logic of trading items between a buyer and a seller. It checks for valid actors and the item, then updates inventories and currency values accordingly.

- **UpdateInventory Function**: This function would include logic to add or remove the item from the actor's inventory, depending on whether the item is being bought or sold.

- **UpdateCurrency Function**: This function would include logic to add or subtract the item's value from the actor's currency.

Listing 3-42. TradingSystem.cpp

```
#include "TradingSystem.h"
#include "TradeableItem.h"

ATradingSystem::ATradingSystem()
{
    PrimaryActorTick.bCanEverTick = true;
}
void ATradingSystem::BeginPlay()
{
    Super::BeginPlay();
}
void ATradingSystem::Tick(float DeltaTime)
{
    Super::Tick(DeltaTime);
}
void ATradingSystem::TradeItem(AActor* Buyer, AActor* Seller,
ATradeableItem* Item)
{
    if (Buyer && Seller && Item)
```

```cpp
    {
        // Implement trading logic here
        int32 ItemValue = Item->ItemValue;

        // Update Seller's inventory and currency
        UpdateInventory(Seller, Item, false);
        UpdateCurrency(Seller, ItemValue);

        // Update Buyer's inventory and currency
        UpdateInventory(Buyer, Item, true);
        UpdateCurrency(Buyer, -ItemValue);

        // Provide feedback on trade completion
    }
}

void ATradingSystem::UpdateInventory(AActor* Actor,
ATradeableItem* Item, bool bAddItem)
{
    // Implement inventory update logic here
}

void ATradingSystem::UpdateCurrency(AActor* Actor,
int32 Amount)
{
    // Implement currency update logic here
}
```

Advanced Mechanics Code Example

In this section, we introduce the concept of dynamic pricing, which adjusts the prices of items based on factors like supply and demand. This mechanic adds complexity to the trading system, making it more engaging and realistic.

Listing 3-43 defines the DynamicPricing class and its key functions in the header file.

- **ADynamicPricing Class**: Manages dynamic pricing for tradeable items based on supply and demand
- **AdjustPrices Function**: Adjusts the prices of items dynamically
- **TradeableItems Array**: Stores references to all tradeable items affected by dynamic pricing
- **UpdateItemPrice Function**: Updates the price of a specific item based on predefined logic

Listing 3-43. DynamicPricing.h

```
#pragma once

#include "CoreMinimal.h"
#include "GameFramework/Actor.h"
#include "DynamicPricing.generated.h"
UCLASS()
class MYGAME_API ADynamicPricing : public AActor
{
    GENERATED_BODY()
public:
    ADynamicPricing();

protected:
    virtual void BeginPlay() override;

public:
    virtual void Tick(float DeltaTime) override;
```

CHAPTER 3 INTERACTION MECHANICS

```
    UFUNCTION(BlueprintCallable, Category="Trading")
    void AdjustPrices();

private:
    TArray<ATradeableItem*> TradeableItems;
    void UpdateItemPrice(ATradeableItem* Item);
};
```

Listing 3-44 implements how dynamic pricing is applied to tradeable items in the implementation file.

- **BeginPlay Function**: Initializes the tradeable items by adding relevant items to the TradeableItems array
- **AdjustPrices Function**: Iterates through all tradeable items and updates their prices based on dynamic pricing logic
- **UpdateItemPrice Function**: Adjusts the price of each item based on factors such as supply and demand

Listing 3-44. DynamicPricing.cpp

```
#include "DynamicPricing.h"
#include "TradeableItem.h"

ADynamicPricing::ADynamicPricing()
{
    PrimaryActorTick.bCanEverTick = true;
}

void ADynamicPricing::BeginPlay()
{
    Super::BeginPlay();
```

```cpp
    // Initialize tradeable items
    // Example: Find and add all tradeable items to the
    TradeableItems array
}

void ADynamicPricing::Tick(float DeltaTime)
{
    Super::Tick(DeltaTime);

    AdjustPrices();
}

void ADynamicPricing::AdjustPrices()
{
    for (ATradeableItem* Item : TradeableItems)
    {
        UpdateItemPrice(Item);
    }
}

void ADynamicPricing::UpdateItemPrice(ATradeableItem* Item)
{
    // Implement dynamic pricing logic here
    // Example: Adjust Item->ItemValue based on supply and
    demand factors
}
```

This section covered the fundamentals of trading systems in game development, including basic usage, advanced techniques, and detailed code examples. By mastering these concepts, you can create robust and engaging trading systems that enhance the player's experience.

CHAPTER 3   INTERACTION MECHANICS

Summary

As we conclude our exploration of interaction mechanics, we have examined the essential systems that facilitate dynamic player engagement within the game world. From responsive NPC interactions to trade systems and puzzle-solving, these mechanics create immersive and meaningful experiences. By implementing structured frameworks such as dialogue systems, trading mechanics, and interactive objects, we establish the foundation for seamless and intuitive player interactions. These systems not only enhance gameplay depth but also ensure that every action contributes to a richer and more interactive virtual world. In the next chapter, we will delve into environmental mechanics, exploring dynamic weather systems, day-night cycles, and various environmental interactions that bring your game world to life.

CHAPTER 4

Environmental Mechanics

The actual keys to player immersion and interaction with game worlds are the environmental mechanics. They include everything that would differ, aside from aesthetics alone, in the way the player interacts with and experiences such a world. Everything from dynamic weather to terrain generation, these elements form the backbone of realism in gameplay.

Environmental mechanics constitute, to a certain extent, the underlying basis of what players observe and interact with their surroundings. Day-night cycles, weather effects, and features of terrain all add so much more to an already decently developed atmosphere. For instance, in one of these games, rain would gradually alter the aspect of the environment, restrict visibility, and sometimes even the movements of players.

Understanding these simple things will allow developers to make a living, responding world, adding so much more depth to the gameplay. You will now go through the creation of these basic features and understand how they can change your game in this chapter.

Further beyond that, advanced environmental mechanics have continuously allowed developers to push the bar on just how deep an interaction within games can go. Dynamic weather systems, fluid dynamics, and interactive foliage enable rich and immersive experiences responding in near real-time to the player's actions. Take, for example, creating a

CHAPTER 4   ENVIRONMENTAL MECHANICS

scene of a sudden storm: it visually changes but affects the game as some pathways now become slippery or shrouded in visibility. Mastering such advanced techniques allows you to create vibrant worlds that can surprise and sometimes even frustrate players in new ways, creating far more engaging and realistic gameplay. In this section, we will delve deeper into such advanced systems and explore how to use them effectively.

This chapter will teach the student various environmental mechanics, ranging from very basic to more complex: dynamic weather and day-night cycles and environmental hazards—the works. By the end of this chapter, you'll know how these mechanics are set into action, and most importantly they're so integral in the creation of a believable game world. All of it starts with your first steps toward making your games more realistic and interesting.

Dynamic Weather Systems

One of the most powerful ways to make a virtual game world seem alive and real is by implementing dynamic weather systems that will display emulated natural weather. This boosts the in-game atmosphere and provides additional layers of complexity regarding gameplay. Whether it is a surprise storm that disrupts a mission, fog limiting visibility, or even a bright and sunny day that invites exploration, dynamic weather will be a key factor in shaping what the gamer will be experiencing.

Basic Usage

A dynamic weather system increases the feeling of immersion by emulating natural weather patterns within a game environment. Basic uses of it would be the simple transitions of the weather, like from rain to snow and further to clear skies. In this way, developers can create life in their game world by adding natural changes, such as day turning into night and then into rain or fog.

Advanced Techniques

Advanced dynamic weather systems provide simulated environmental effects like wet surfaces, snow accumulation, and even in-game player or NPC behavior influenced by weather. The following may or may not be included in the system:

1. **Real-Time Weather Transitions**: Seamless transitions between different weather states, such as from rain to snow or from clear skies to thunderstorms

2. **Wind System**: Affects the particle system, trees, and other moving objects in the environment

3. **Localized Weather Zones**: Meaning different regions in the game world will have different weather conditions

4. **Environmental Impact on Gameplay**: Such as weather interference with the player's movement, AI behavior, and visibility

Practical Applications

The weather system can be applied to many game genres:

- **Open-World Games**: Weather affects regions differently, impacting quests or interactions.

- **Survival Games**: Environmental effects influence how players interact with the world, such as cold weather reducing player health.

- **Simulation Games**: The game displays dynamic weather patterns, just like in the real world—be it farming, flying, or driving.

Algorithm Overview

Dynamic weather is achieved using a few different algorithms:

1. **Weather State Management**: The model controls transitions of weather types such as clear, rain, snow, fog, or thunderstorms.

2. **Environmental Effects**: The algorithms calculate environmental looks in weather changes. For example, wet terrain in rain or snow building up in snow.

3. **Weather Impact on Objects**: Weather changes affect NPCs, players, and environmental objects. For example, movement speed may be reduced due to snow.

Reviewing the Code

We are going to walk through constructing a basic dynamic weather system. We will go over the code and explain each section thoroughly, so by the end of the chapter you should have an idea of how to apply dynamic weather in your own game.

Listing 4-1 declares the AMazeWall class, which serves as a wall within the maze in Unreal Engine. The following explanation details the principal elements and their respective functions:

- The class **AWeatherManager** derives from the class AActor; it means it will be placed into the game world and can interact with other game objects. This controls the dynamic weather system from determining the current state to updating environmental effects accordingly.

CHAPTER 4   ENVIRONMENTAL MECHANICS

- Enum **EWeatherState** defines four kinds of weather conditions: Sunny, Rainy, Foggy, and Stormy. The use of UMETA here allows the weather states to appear in Unreal's editor and, by extension, via Blueprints and easily alterable by designers.

- The **CurrentWeatherState** type stores the current weather of a game world. This state will be used to define what weather effects are active and will allow dynamic changes in the weather at runtime.

- Public function **SetWeatherState()** will give the chance to dynamically change the current weather state. This function, invoked with a new weather state, is going to change CurrentWeatherState and invoke the function UpdateWeatherEffects() with respective weather effects.

- The main function of the **UpdateWeatherEffects()** is to change the game world state according to the current weather. It checks which type of weather state is active, such as Sunny or Rainy, and then calls the respective private function to apply the particular weather.

- These private methods—**ChangeWeatherToSunny()**, **ChangeWeatherToRainy()**, etc.—would implement the particular changes in a game world, depending on the type of weather. In this case, each of these functions would alter lighting, particle effects—for instance, rain—and probably a skybox to simulate selected weather.

CHAPTER 4   ENVIRONMENTAL MECHANICS

Listing 4-1. WeatherManager.h

```cpp
#pragma once

#include "CoreMinimal.h"
#include "GameFramework/Actor.h"
#include "WeatherManager.generated.h"

UENUM(BlueprintType)
enum class EWeatherState : uint8
{
    Sunny UMETA(DisplayName = "Sunny"),
    Rainy UMETA(DisplayName = "Rainy"),
    Foggy UMETA(DisplayName = "Foggy"),
    Stormy UMETA(DisplayName = "Stormy"),
};

UCLASS()
class MYGAME_API AWeatherManager : public AActor
{
    GENERATED_BODY()

public:
    AWeatherManager();

protected:
    virtual void BeginPlay() override;

public:
    virtual void Tick(float DeltaTime) override;

    UPROPERTY(EditAnywhere, BlueprintReadWrite, Category = "Weather")
    EWeatherState CurrentWeatherState;
```

```cpp
    UFUNCTION(BlueprintCallable, Category = "Weather")
    void SetWeatherState(EWeatherState NewState);

    UFUNCTION(BlueprintCallable, Category = "Weather")
    void UpdateWeatherEffects();

private:
    void ChangeWeatherToSunny();
    void ChangeWeatherToRainy();
    void ChangeWeatherToFoggy();
    void ChangeWeatherToStormy();
    void ApplyWeatherSettings(float LightIntensity, bool
    bEnableRain, bool bEnableFog);

};
```

Listing 4-2 declares the AWeatherManager class, designed to manage a dynamic weather system in Unreal Engine. The following section explains the main elements and their respective functions.

- **SetWeatherState()**: This primary method changes the weather dynamically. It updates the current weather state and calls UpdateWeatherEffects() to apply appropriate environmental changes.

- **UpdateWeatherEffects()**: Based on the current weather state, this function routes execution to the corresponding weather-specific function such as ChangeWeatherToRainy() or ChangeWeatherToFoggy().

- **ApplyWeatherSettings()**: A refactored helper method that centralizes the adjustment of light intensity and toggling of rain and fog effects. This promotes cleaner, modular code and simplifies the logic across different weather types.

- **ChangeWeatherToSunny()/ChangeWeatherToRainy() /ChangeWeatherToFoggy()/ChangeWeatherToStormy()**: These functions now act as wrappers that call ApplyWeatherSettings() with specific parameters to simulate their respective weather conditions.

- **GetDirectionalLight()**: A utility function that locates the first directional light actor in the scene and returns its light component so it can be modified by the weather system.

- **ToggleRain()** and **ToggleFog()**: Placeholder helper functions meant to enable or disable particle effects (such as rain or fog) based on the weather state. These can later be implemented using UParticleSystemComponent or Niagara systems.

Listing 4-2. WeatherManager.cpp

```
#include "WeatherManager.h"
#include "Engine/World.h"
#include "Kismet/GameplayStatics.h"
#include "Components/DirectionalLightComponent.h"
#include "Particles/ParticleSystemComponent.h"
#include "Engine/DirectionalLight.h"

// Constructor: Sets default values
AWeatherManager::AWeatherManager()
{
    PrimaryActorTick.bCanEverTick = true;
}

// BeginPlay: Called when the game starts
void AWeatherManager::BeginPlay()
```

```cpp
{
    Super::BeginPlay();

    // Initialize with a default weather state
    SetWeatherState(EWeatherState::Sunny);
}
// Tick: Called every frame
void AWeatherManager::Tick(float DeltaTime)
{
    Super::Tick(DeltaTime);

    // Optional: Add logic to dynamically change weather
    over time
}

// SetWeatherState: Change the current weather state and
update effects
void AWeatherManager::SetWeatherState(EWeatherState
NewWeatherState)
{
    CurrentWeatherState = NewWeatherState;
    UpdateWeatherEffects();
}

// UpdateWeatherEffects: Apply the relevant changes based on
the current weather state
void AWeatherManager::UpdateWeatherEffects()
{
    switch (CurrentWeatherState)
    {
        case EWeatherState::Sunny:
            ChangeWeatherToSunny();
            break;
```

```
        case EWeatherState::Rainy:
            ChangeWeatherToRainy();
            break;

        case EWeatherState::Foggy:
            ChangeWeatherToFoggy();
            break;

        case EWeatherState::Stormy:
            ChangeWeatherToStormy();
            break;
    }
}

// Refactored base function to apply weather settings
void AWeatherManager::ApplyWeatherSettings(float
LightIntensity, bool bEnableRain, bool bEnableFog)
{
    UDirectionalLightComponent* DirectionalLight =
    GetDirectionalLight();
    if (DirectionalLight)
    {
        DirectionalLight->SetIntensity(LightIntensity);
    }

    ToggleRain(bEnableRain);
    ToggleFog(bEnableFog);
}

// ChangeWeatherToSunny: Set environment to sunny conditions
void AWeatherManager::ChangeWeatherToSunny()
{
    ApplyWeatherSettings(3.0f, false, false);
}
```

CHAPTER 4   ENVIRONMENTAL MECHANICS

```cpp
// ChangeWeatherToRainy: Set environment to rainy conditions
void AWeatherManager::ChangeWeatherToRainy()
{
    ApplyWeatherSettings(1.5f, true, false);
}

// ChangeWeatherToFoggy: Set environment to foggy conditions
void AWeatherManager::ChangeWeatherToFoggy()
{
    ApplyWeatherSettings(1.0f, false, true);
}

// ChangeWeatherToStormy: Set environment to stormy conditions
void AWeatherManager::ChangeWeatherToStormy()
{
    ApplyWeatherSettings(0.5f, true, false);
}

// GetDirectionalLight: Helper function to find the first
directional light in the scene
UDirectionalLightComponent* AWeatherManager::GetDirectionalLight()
{
    TArray<AActor*> Lights;
    UGameplayStatics::GetAllActorsOfClass(GetWorld(),
    ADirectionalLight::StaticClass(), Lights);

    if (Lights.Num() > 0)
    {
        return Cast<ADirectionalLight>(Lights[0])->
        GetLightComponent();
    }

    return nullptr;
}
```

339

```
// ToggleRain: Placeholder for enabling/disabling rain
particle systems
void AWeatherManager::ToggleRain(bool bEnable)
{
    // TODO: Implement logic to activate/deactivate rain
    particle systems
}

// ToggleFog: Placeholder for enabling/disabling fog
particle systems
void AWeatherManager::ToggleFog(bool bEnable)
{
    // TODO: Implement logic to activate/deactivate fog
    particle systems
}
```

In this section, we learned the very basics for developing dynamic weather systems in games. From basic transitions of weather to the advanced techniques, including environmental impact and localized weather zones, you've learned about how weather systems enhance immersion and affect gameplay.

In the next section, we take a closer look at the day-night cycles. Further building on the previous weather system, we are going to incorporate natural transitions of day and night, often working together with the weather.

Day-Night Cycles

A day-night cycle accommodates a smooth transition of a game between day and night. Transitions can be simple, affecting lighting and even skybox textures, or complex, involving advanced gameplay mechanics. The most basic cycle would simply change the color and intensity of the

CHAPTER 4   ENVIRONMENTAL MECHANICS

lighting, while a more complex one would include temperature effects, different events during the day, and behavior modifications of NPCs or enemies.

Basic Usage

A day-night cycle, in its simplest word definition, is the one that transitions smoothly from day to night states. It typically contains the following:

- **Changes in Lighting**: The brightness and color of the light are changed to represent the rising and setting sun.

- **Skybox**: The color of the sky changes from blue skies to starry night.

- **Time Progression**: A system responsible for maintaining the in-game time and controlling the transition between day and night.

These are normally catered for, in simpler implementations, through interpolations between different lighting values and sky textures during a set period.

Advanced Techniques

Advanced techniques for enhancing day-night cycles would include the following:

- **Realistic Shadows**: Shadows change direction and length depending on the time of day.

- **Celestial Movement**: Simulating the movement of the sun and moon across the sky.

- **NPC and Enemy Behavior**: Enemies may be more aggressive at night, and NPCs might follow a daily routine, such as closing shops at dusk.
- **Dynamic Weather**: The day-night system may interact with the dynamic weather system, where certain weather events are more likely at specific times (e.g., fog in the early morning).
- **Environmental Changes**: Some games can introduce new elements like opening night-specific locations or activating specific events, such as a lunar eclipse or meteor shower.

Practical Applications

Day-night cycles are widely used across various genres, including

- **Open-World Games**: NPC behavior may differ with day-night changes, enemy encounters, and quests.
- **Survival Games**: Some resources or perils may only appear during nighttime; hence, players are often encouraged to base their activity on time.
- **Simulation Games**: Games with farming or city-building simulations utilize the day-and-night cycles in controlling activities and gameplay cycles, such as crop growth or opening hours for businesses.

CHAPTER 4   ENVIRONMENTAL MECHANICS

Algorithm Overview

The following is the interaction of systems involved in the processing cycle of day and night:

- **Time Management System**: Responsible for keeping track of in-game time, assessing what time of day it currently is, and initiating transitions.

- **Lighting Adjustments**: Changes the intensity, color, and position of lights to simulate sunrises and sunsets.

- **Skybox Transitions**: These can switch between any other skybox textures or smoothly interpolate them during day-night transitions.

- **Celestial Body Movement**: Creates an animation in which the sun and moon move across the sky, casting shadows of different shapes as they shift.

Reviewing the Code

This would include some of the basic mechanics of tracking game time and dynamic changes in environmental states according to the flow of time. By the end of this section, you'll be clear on how this integration is to be carried out in your game.

Listing 4-3 primarily defines the ADayNightManager class and its usage in this header file.

- **ADayNightManager**: This class manages the day-night cycle by keeping track of the in-game time and adjusting the environment accordingly.

- **TimeOfDay**: This property represents the current in-game time. It is a float where 0 represents midnight, 6 represents dawn, 12 represents noon, and 18 represents dusk.

- **TimeSpeedMultiplier**: This allows you to control how fast time moves in the game. For example, a value of 1 makes time pass in real time, while higher values speed up the day-night cycle.

- **SunLight**: A reference to the directional light that acts as the sun in the game world. This is crucial for adjusting lighting based on the time of day.

- **UpdateDayNightCycle()**: This function is called every tick to update the state of the day-night cycle, including lighting, sun position, and any other relevant environmental changes.

Listing 4-3. DayNightManager.h

```
#pragma once

#include "CoreMinimal.h"
#include "GameFramework/Actor.h"
#include "DayNightManager.generated.h"

UCLASS()
class MYGAME_API ADayNightManager : public AActor
{
    GENERATED_BODY()

public:
    ADayNightManager();

protected:
    virtual void BeginPlay() override;
```

CHAPTER 4 ENVIRONMENTAL MECHANICS

```
public:
    virtual void Tick(float DeltaTime) override;

    // Directional light actor reference
    UPROPERTY(EditAnywhere, BlueprintReadWrite, Category =
    "Lighting")
    AActor* SunLight;

    // Current time in HHMM format (e.g., 0930 = 9:30 AM)
    UPROPERTY(EditAnywhere, BlueprintReadWrite, Category
    = "Time")
    int32 CurrentTime = 1200;

    // Real seconds that represent one in-game minute
    UPROPERTY(EditAnywhere, BlueprintReadWrite, Category
    = "Time")
    float SecondsPerMinute = 1.0f;

private:
    // Tracks real-time progress toward the next in-game minute
    float TimeAccumulator = 0.0f;

    void UpdateDayNightCycle();
    void UpdateLighting();
    void UpdateSunPosition();
    void IncrementTime();
    float GetTimeAsFloat() const;
};
```

Listing 4-4 presents the implementation of the following functions:

- **UpdateDayNightCycle()**: This method calls two helper functions, UpdateLighting() and UpdateSunPosition(), to adjust the environmental lighting and sun's position based on the current time.

CHAPTER 4   ENVIRONMENTAL MECHANICS

- **UpdateLighting()**: Adjusts the sun's intensity. The cosine function smoothly transitions the light intensity from full brightness at noon to darkness at night.

- **UpdateSunPosition()**: Rotates the sun's position in the sky based on the current time. The sun completes one full rotation (from rising in the east and setting in the west) every 24 in-game hours.

Listing 4-4. DayNightManager.cpp

```cpp
#include "DayNightManager.h"
#include "Engine/World.h"
#include "Kismet/GameplayStatics.h"
#include "Components/DirectionalLightComponent.h"

// Constructor: Sets default values
ADayNightManager::ADayNightManager()
{
    PrimaryActorTick.bCanEverTick = true;
    CurrentTime = 1200; // Start at noon
    SecondsPerMinute = 1.0f;
    TimeAccumulator = 0.0f;
}

// Called when the game starts
void ADayNightManager::BeginPlay()
{
    Super::BeginPlay();
}
```

CHAPTER 4   ENVIRONMENTAL MECHANICS

```cpp
// Called every frame
void ADayNightManager::Tick(float DeltaTime)
{
    Super::Tick(DeltaTime);

    // Accumulate real time
    TimeAccumulator += DeltaTime;

    if (TimeAccumulator >= SecondsPerMinute)
    {
        TimeAccumulator -= SecondsPerMinute;
        IncrementTime();
    }

    UpdateDayNightCycle();
}

// Converts CurrentTime (HHMM) to float (e.g., 9.5 = 9:30 AM)
float ADayNightManager::GetTimeAsFloat() const
{
    int32 Hours = CurrentTime / 100;
    int32 Minutes = CurrentTime % 100;
    return Hours + (Minutes / 60.0f);
}

// Increments the in-game time by one minute
void ADayNightManager::IncrementTime()
{
    int32 Minutes = CurrentTime % 100;
    int32 Hours = CurrentTime / 100;

    Minutes++;
```

```
    if (Minutes >= 60)
    {
        Minutes = 0;
        Hours++;
        if (Hours >= 24)
        {
            Hours = 0;
        }
    }

    CurrentTime = Hours * 100 + Minutes;
}

// Updates lighting and sun position each frame
void ADayNightManager::UpdateDayNightCycle()
{
    UpdateLighting();
    UpdateSunPosition();
}

// Adjust the light intensity based on time of day
void ADayNightManager::UpdateLighting()
{
    if (SunLight)
    {
        float TimeFloat = GetTimeAsFloat();
        float Intensity = FMath::Clamp(FMath::Cos((TimeFloat - 6.0f) / 12.0f * PI), 0.0f, 1.0f);
        SunLight->GetLightComponent()->SetIntensity(Intensity * 3.0f); // Light intensity ranges from 0 to 3
    }
}
```

```cpp
// Rotate the sun to simulate day-night cycle
void ADayNightManager::UpdateSunPosition()
{
    if (SunLight)
    {
        float TimeFloat = GetTimeAsFloat();
        FRotator NewRotation = FRotator((TimeFloat / 24.0f) *
        360.0f - 90.0f, 0.0f, 0.0f);
        SunLight->SetActorRotation(NewRotation);
    }
}
```

This section covered the essentials of building a day-night cycle in a game, from managing in-game time to updating lighting and sun positions dynamically. You've learned the importance of these systems in enhancing immersion and gameplay.

In the next section, we'll explore environmental hazards, their usage, and how to create them.

Environment Hazards

Within game development, environmental hazards are dynamic components within the game world that pose some sort of challenge or threat to a player. Natural disasters, traps, and toxic zones—forcing players to adapt and strategically interact with the environment—are just a few examples. In placing environmental hazards within games, gameplay deepens to allow for more immersive and engaging experiences, since there is always some sort of obstacle that players must get through or survive.

CHAPTER 4   ENVIRONMENTAL MECHANICS

Basic Usage

At the most basic level, environmental hazards function as static or scripted elements that damage the player if they come into contact with them or stay too close for too long. Examples include

- **Lava**: Causes continuous damage when the player touches it
- **Spikes or Traps**: Deal instant damage upon contact
- **Poisonous Zones**: Gradually drain the player's health when they enter

Implementing such basic hazards often involves simple collision detection paired with health reduction mechanics.

Advanced Techniques

More advanced environmental hazards interact dynamically with the world and can affect not only the player but also NPCs and even the environment itself. Examples of advanced hazards include

- **Dynamic Weather Effects**: Rain, snowstorms, or extreme heat can reduce the player's visibility, movement speed, or stamina.
- **Natural Disasters**: Earthquakes, floods, or tornadoes can alter the game environment, damaging structures or triggering new events that force the player to adapt.
- **Time-Limited Hazards**: Hazards like rising tides or lava flows that give the player a limited window of time to escape or find shelter.

CHAPTER 4   ENVIRONMENTAL MECHANICS

- **Interactive Hazards**: Objects or environmental elements that players can manipulate to turn a hazard into an advantage, such as using falling rocks to block enemies or triggering a trap against pursuing foes.

Practical Applications

Environmental hazards are widely used across various game genres and settings, from platformers to open-world exploration games:

- **Survival Games**: Constantly changing environments, such as storms or temperature drops, require players to find shelter, build protection, or manage resources.
- **Action-Adventure Games**: Games like *The Legend of Zelda* or *Uncharted* use environmental hazards to create challenging puzzles or tense escape sequences.
- **Horror Games**: Dangerous environments like collapsing buildings, poisonous gas, or fire create urgency and enhance the fear factor, forcing players to move quickly and cautiously.

Algorithm Overview

Creating an environmental hazard involves a few critical components working together:

- **Trigger Zones**: Detect when the player or other objects enter a hazardous area.
- **Damage System**: Applies damage or other negative effects (e.g., slowing movement or reducing visibility) to the player or NPCs based on proximity to the hazard.

- **Event Handling**: In more complex systems, the hazard may cause events like an environmental collapse, summoning enemies, or changing weather patterns.

- **Timing Mechanism**: Determines how long a hazard is active or when it will appear.

Reviewing the Code

In this section, we'll look at building a simple environmental hazard system using Unreal Engine. We will create a class for a damage-dealing hazard, which can be extended to include more complex behaviors like timed hazards or dynamic interactions.

Listing 4-5 highlights key components in the header file, including AHazardZone, DamagePerSecond, bIsActive, and the functions OnPlayerEnter() and OnPlayerExit(), which collectively define and manage the hazard zone's behavior.

- **AHazardZone**: This class defines the hazard zone, which deals damage to the player if they enter it. The hazard could be anything from a fire pit to a toxic area.

- **DamagePerSecond**: Defines how much damage is dealt to the player each second they remain inside the hazard.

- **bIsActive**: A boolean that lets developers turn the hazard on or off dynamically during gameplay.

- **OnPlayerEnter() and OnPlayerExit()**: These functions handle what happens when the player enters or exits the hazard zone, ensuring the correct application of damage or effects.

CHAPTER 4   ENVIRONMENTAL MECHANICS

Listing 4-5. HazardZone.h

```
#pragma once
#include "CoreMinimal.h"
#include "GameFramework/Actor.h"
#include "HazardZone.generated.h"

// Forward declarations
class UBoxComponent;
class AMyPlayerCharacter;
UCLASS() class MYGAME_API AHazardZone : public AActor {
GENERATED_BODY()
public: AHazardZone();
protected: virtual void BeginPlay() override;
public: virtual void Tick(float DeltaTime) override;

// Damage and activation toggle
UPROPERTY(EditAnywhere, BlueprintReadWrite, Category =
"Hazard") float DamagePerSecond;

UPROPERTY(EditAnywhere, BlueprintReadWrite, Category =
"Hazard") bool bIsActive;

// Collision box for detecting overlaps
UPROPERTY(VisibleAnywhere, BlueprintReadOnly, Category =
"Hazard") UBoxComponent* TriggerZone;

// Overlap handlers
UFUNCTION()
void OnPlayerEnter(UPrimitiveCompone
nt* OverlappedComponent, AActor* OtherActor,
UPrimitiveComponent* OtherComp, int32 OtherBodyIndex,
bool bFromSweep, const FHitResult& SweepResult);
```

CHAPTER 4   ENVIRONMENTAL MECHANICS

```
UFUNCTION()
void OnPlayerExit(UPrimitiveComponent* OverlappedComponent,
AActor* OtherActor,UPrimitiveComponent* OtherComp, int32
OtherBodyIndex);

private:

// Reference to the overlapping player

UPROPERTY() AMyPlayerCharacter* PlayerCharacter; };
```

Listing 4-6 implements hazard event triggers in this .cpp file, managing player interactions within a designated hazardous area. Key functions include OnPlayerEnter(), which detects player entry and applies damage; OnPlayerExit(), which resets the reference to stop damage application; and Tick(), which continuously inflicts damage at the defined DamagePerSecond rate while the player remains in the hazard zone.

- **OnPlayerEnter()**: This function detects when the player enters the hazard zone. When triggered, it references the player character so that damage can be applied.

- **OnPlayerExit()**: This function is triggered when the player leaves the hazard zone. It resets the reference to stop applying damage.

- **Tick()**: While the player is inside the hazard, the Tick() function continuously applies damage at the specified DamagePerSecond rate, giving a constant risk to the player.

Listing 4-6. HazardZone.cpp

```
#include "HazardZone.h"
#include "MyPlayerCharacter.h"
#include "Components/BoxComponent.h"
```

CHAPTER 4 ENVIRONMENTAL MECHANICS

```cpp
// Constructor: Sets default values
AHazardZone::AHazardZone()
{
    PrimaryActorTick.bCanEverTick = true;

    DamagePerSecond = 10.0f;
    bIsActive = true;

    // Create and set up the collision component
    TriggerZone = CreateDefaultSubobject<UBoxComponent>(TEXT("TriggerZone"));
    RootComponent = TriggerZone;

    TriggerZone->SetCollisionEnabled(ECollisionEnabled::QueryOnly);
    TriggerZone->SetCollisionObjectType(ECC_WorldDynamic);
    TriggerZone->SetCollisionResponseToAllChannels(ECR_Ignore);
    TriggerZone->SetCollisionResponseToChannel(ECC_Pawn, ECR_Overlap);
    TriggerZone->SetGenerateOverlapEvents(true);

    // Bind overlap events
    TriggerZone->OnComponentBeginOverlap.AddDynamic(this, &AHazardZone::OnPlayerEnter);
    TriggerZone->OnComponentEndOverlap.AddDynamic(this, &AHazardZone::OnPlayerExit);

    PlayerCharacter = nullptr;
}

// BeginPlay: Called when the game starts
void AHazardZone::BeginPlay()
{
    Super::BeginPlay();
}
```

CHAPTER 4   ENVIRONMENTAL MECHANICS

```cpp
// Tick: Called every frame
void AHazardZone::Tick(float DeltaTime)
{
    Super::Tick(DeltaTime);

    if (bIsActive && PlayerCharacter)
    {
        PlayerCharacter->TakeDamage(DamagePerSecond * DeltaTime);
    }
}

// OnPlayerEnter: Called when a player enters the hazard zone
void AHazardZone::OnPlayerEnter(UPrimitiveComponent*
OverlappedComponent, AActor* OtherActor,UPrimitiveComponent*
OtherComp, int32 OtherBodyIndex,
bool bFromSweep, const FHitResult& SweepResult)
{
    if (OtherActor && OtherActor->IsA(AMyPlayerCharacter::
    StaticClass()))
    {
        PlayerCharacter = Cast<AMyPlayerCharacter>(OtherActor);
    }
}

// OnPlayerExit: Called when a player exits the hazard zone
void AHazardZone::OnPlayerExit(UPrimitiveComponent*
OverlappedComponent, AActor* OtherActor,UPrimitiveComponent*
OtherComp, int32 OtherBodyIndex)
{
    if (OtherActor == PlayerCharacter)
    {
        PlayerCharacter = nullptr;
    }
}
```

This section covered the implementation of environmental hazards, exploring both basic hazards and advanced dynamic systems that challenge the player and create immersive gameplay. By integrating hazards like lava pits, poison zones, and dynamic weather, you can add a layer of complexity and realism to your game environments.

In the next section, we'll shift focus to dynamic lighting changes, exploring how lighting can dramatically influence the mood, visibility, and overall atmosphere of your game world.

Dynamic Lighting Changes

Dynamic lighting is a powerful tool in game development that enhances the visual fidelity and immersive experience of a game world. By implementing real-time lighting changes, developers can create varied atmospheres, adjust visibility, and influence player emotions during gameplay. This section will cover the fundamentals of dynamic lighting, including its basic usage, advanced techniques, practical applications, and algorithms that make it possible.

Basic Usage

Dynamic lighting involves adjusting light sources in real time to reflect changes in the game environment. Basic uses include

- **Day-Night Cycles**: Transitioning between day and night to create a realistic world where lighting changes based on time
- **Environmental Interactions**: Altering lighting based on player actions or environmental events, such as explosions or spellcasting

- **Shadows**: Implementing shadows that change according to the light source and the objects present in the scene, enhancing realism

These basic implementations can dramatically impact the gameplay experience, providing players with visual cues and immersing them in the game's narrative.

Advanced Techniques

Advanced dynamic lighting techniques allow for even more nuanced control over the lighting environment. Some of these techniques include

- **Volumetric Lighting**: Creating beams of light that interact with particles in the air, adding depth and atmosphere to scenes
- **Global Illumination**: Simulating how light bounces off surfaces, affecting the color and intensity of light in the environment
- **Dynamic Shadowing**: Utilizing shadow maps that adapt to moving light sources and objects, ensuring that shadows remain accurate as the game progresses
- **Light Probes**: Using light probes to capture the lighting information at specific points in the game world, allowing for more accurate lighting calculations in dynamic environments

These advanced techniques enhance realism and can significantly impact gameplay by affecting visibility and player perception.

Practical Applications

Dynamic lighting can be applied across various game genres:

- **Horror Games**: Create tension and fear through flickering lights or sudden changes in lighting to catch players off guard.
- **Action Games**: Enhance fast-paced gameplay with dynamic light changes that reflect the intensity of battles or events.
- **Adventure Games**: Use lighting to guide players through environments, highlighting important areas or paths.
- **Simulation Games**: Implement realistic lighting changes that mimic real-world scenarios, such as weather changes or time progression.

By leveraging dynamic lighting effectively, developers can craft engaging experiences that resonate with players.

Algorithm Overview

Dynamic lighting systems can be achieved through various algorithms, including

- **Light Source Management**: Controlling the creation, removal, and updating of light sources in the game world
- **Shadow Mapping**: Calculating shadows based on the position of light sources and the geometry of objects in the scene
- **Lighting Interpolation**: Smoothly transitioning lighting states over time, allowing for seamless day-night cycles or environmental changes

These algorithms work together to create a cohesive and dynamic lighting experience in the game.

Reviewing the Code

In this section, we will construct a basic dynamic lighting system. We will walk through the code and provide detailed explanations, ensuring you understand how to implement dynamic lighting in your own game.

Listing 4-7 defines the ADynamicLightManager class, managing dynamic lighting with customizable day/night cycles, real-time adjustments, and time tracking.

- The ADynamicLightManager class manages the dynamic lighting system within the game.
- The DayLength and NightLength properties allow developers to customize the length of day and night cycles.
- The SetDayLength and SetNightLength functions enable real-time adjustments to these properties during gameplay.
- The CurrentTime variable keeps track of the time of day, while the bIsDay boolean indicates whether it is currently day or night.

Listing 4-7. DynamicLightManager.h

```
#pragma once

#include "CoreMinimal.h"
#include "GameFramework/Actor.h"
#include "DynamicLightManager.generated.h"
```

```cpp
UCLASS()
class MYGAME_API ADynamicLightManager : public AActor
{
    GENERATED_BODY()
public:
    ADynamicLightManager();

protected:
    virtual void BeginPlay() override;

public:
    virtual void Tick(float DeltaTime) override;

    UPROPERTY(EditAnywhere, BlueprintReadWrite, Category = "Lighting")float DayLength;   // Time for a full day cycle in seconds

    UPROPERTY(EditAnywhere, BlueprintReadWrite, Category = "Lighting")float NightLength; // Time for a full night cycle in seconds

    UFUNCTION(BlueprintCallable, Category = "Lighting")
    void SetDayLength(float NewDayLength);

    UFUNCTION(BlueprintCallable, Category = "Lighting")
    void SetNightLength(float NewNightLength);

private:
    void UpdateLighting(float DeltaTime);
    void TransitionToDay();
    void TransitionToNight();

    float CurrentTime; // Track the current time of day
    bool bIsDay; // Track whether it's currently day or night
};
```

Listing 4-8 utilizes the header file to implement dynamic lighting changes. It initializes day/night cycles, updates lighting transitions in `Tick()`, and modifies light intensity with `UpdateLighting()`, ensuring smooth day-night shifts.

- The ADynamicLightManager constructor initializes the day and night lengths, as well as the current time of day.

- In the BeginPlay method, the lighting system initializes to daytime conditions.

- The Tick method updates the current time and checks whether to transition between day and night.

- The UpdateLighting function modifies the intensity of the directional light based on the time of day, providing a smooth transition between day and night.

- The TransitionToDay and TransitionToNight functions handle any additional changes needed when transitioning between day and night, such as modifying the skybox.

- The GetDirectionalLight helper function retrieves the first directional light in the scene for manipulation.

Listing 4-8. DynamicLightManager.cpp

```
#include "DynamicLightManager.h"
#include "Engine/DirectionalLight.h"
#include "Kismet/GameplayStatics.h"

// Constructor: Sets default values
ADynamicLightManager::ADynamicLightManager()
{
```

```cpp
    PrimaryActorTick.bCanEverTick = true;
    DayLength = 120.0f; // Default 2 minutes for day cycle
    NightLength = 60.0f; // Default 1 minute for night cycle
    CurrentTime = 0.0f;
    bIsDay = true;
}

// BeginPlay: Called when the game starts
void ADynamicLightManager::BeginPlay()
{
    Super::BeginPlay();
    TransitionToDay();
}

// Tick: Called every frame
void ADynamicLightManager::Tick(float DeltaTime)
{
    Super::Tick(DeltaTime);
    UpdateLighting(DeltaTime);
}

// SetDayLength: Update the length of the day cycle
void ADynamicLightManager::SetDayLength(float NewDayLength)
{
    DayLength = NewDayLength;
}

// SetNightLength: Update the length of the night cycle
void ADynamicLightManager::SetNightLength(float NewNightLength)
{
    NightLength = NewNightLength;
}
```

CHAPTER 4 ENVIRONMENTAL MECHANICS

```cpp
// UpdateLighting: Update the lighting based on current time
void ADynamicLightManager::UpdateLighting(float DeltaTime)
{
    CurrentTime += DeltaTime;
float TotalDayTime = DayLength + NightLength;
CurrentTime = FMath::Fmod(CurrentTime, TotalDayTime);

float NormalizedTime = CurrentTime / TotalDayTime;
// Ranges from 0 to 1 across full cycle

// Cosine wave to simulate sunrise → midday → sunset
float LightIntensity = 0.0f;

if (CurrentTime < DayLength)
{
    if (!bIsDay)
    {
        TransitionToDay();
    }

    // Day curve: peak at midday
    float DayProgress = CurrentTime / DayLength;
    // 0 at sunrise, 1 at sunset
    LightIntensity = FMath::Clamp(FMath::Cos((DayProgress -
    0.5f) * PI) * 5.0f, 0.0f, 5.0f); // Max intensity = 5
}
else
{
    if (bIsDay)
    {
        TransitionToNight();
    }
```

```
    // Night intensity stays low
    LightIntensity = 0.2f; // Example base intensity for
    moonlight or ambient night light
}

UDirectionalLight* DirectionalLight = GetDirectionalLight();
if (DirectionalLight)
{
    DirectionalLight->SetIntensity(LightIntensity);
}
}

// TransitionToDay: Handle the transition to daytime lighting
void ADynamicLightManager::TransitionToDay()
{
    bIsDay = true;
    // Additional logic for daytime transition (e.g.,
    adjusting skybox)
}

// TransitionToNight: Handle the transition to nighttime lighting
void ADynamicLightManager::TransitionToNight()
{
    bIsDay = false;
    // Additional logic for nighttime transition (e.g.,
    adjusting skybox)
}

// Helper function: Get the directional light in the scene
UDirectionalLight* ADynamicLightManager::GetDirectionalLight()
```

CHAPTER 4   ENVIRONMENTAL MECHANICS

```
{
    TArray<AActor*> Lights;
    UGameplayStatics::GetAllActorsOfClass(GetWorld(),
    ADirectionalLight::StaticClass(), Lights);

    if (Lights.Num() > 0)
    {
        return Cast<UDirectionalLight>(Lights[0]);
    }
    return nullptr;
}
```

In this section, we explored the implementation of dynamic lighting changes, covering its fundamental concepts and various applications in game development. By utilizing dynamic lighting techniques, developers can significantly enhance the player experience, creating engaging and immersive game worlds.

In the next section, we will focus on terrain generation, discussing how procedural methods can be utilized to create diverse and expansive game environments that enhance exploration and gameplay.

Terrain Generation

Terrain generation is a critical aspect of game development, allowing developers to create expansive and diverse landscapes that enhance gameplay and immersion. By leveraging procedural generation techniques, developers can produce varied terrains that keep the gaming experience fresh and engaging. This section will cover the fundamentals of terrain generation, including the methods and algorithms commonly used to create realistic environments.

Basic Usage

Basic terrain generation involves creating landscapes that can range from simple flat surfaces to complex mountainous regions. Developers often start with heightmaps, which are grayscale images where the intensity of each pixel represents elevation. Using heightmaps, game engines can generate 3D terrains by interpreting pixel values as height data, enabling the creation of diverse landscapes with minimal effort.

Advanced Techniques

Advanced terrain generation techniques involve incorporating additional features to enhance realism and variety. These techniques may include

- **Noise Functions**: Algorithms like Perlin noise and Simplex noise are often used to generate natural-looking terrains. They create smooth, continuous variations in elevation, mimicking real-world landscapes.

- **Erosion Simulation**: This technique simulates natural processes like water and wind erosion, resulting in more realistic terrain features such as valleys, rivers, and cliffs.

- **Biomes and Ecosystems:** By implementing biome-specific rules, developers can create different environmental zones, such as deserts, forests, and tundras, each with unique characteristics and flora.

CHAPTER 4 ENVIRONMENTAL MECHANICS

Practical Applications

Terrain generation is widely applied in various game genres, including

- **Open-World Games**: Games like *The Elder Scrolls V: Skyrim* and *Minecraft* utilize procedural terrain generation to create vast worlds for exploration.

- **Simulation Games**: Games such as *Cities: Skylines* and *Planet Coaster* use terrain generation to design landscapes that impact gameplay mechanics and aesthetics.

- **Survival Games**: In games like *Rust* and *The Forest*, terrain generation creates challenging environments that players must navigate and survive in.

Algorithm Overview

The algorithms used for terrain generation can be categorized into two main types:

1. **Heightmap Generation Algorithms**: These algorithms create elevation data that can be visualized as 2D heightmaps.

    - **Perlin Noise**: Produces smooth, continuous noise patterns suitable for generating natural terrains

    - **Diamond-Square Algorithm**: A fractal-based approach that recursively divides a grid to create varied terrains

CHAPTER 4   ENVIRONMENTAL MECHANICS

2. **Procedural Generation Algorithms**: These focus on creating the overall structure and features of the terrain.

   - **Voronoi Diagrams**: Useful for generating regions and features based on distance to a set of points, creating natural-looking land formations.

   - **Marching Cubes Algorithm**: This algorithm is often employed to create 3D meshes from volumetric data, allowing for detailed terrain shapes.

Reviewing the Code

To implement terrain generation in a game, developers typically use a combination of heightmap processing and mesh generation. Below is a code template that outlines the basic structure of a terrain generation system.

Listing 4-9 defines the `TerrainGenerator` class in `TerrainGenerator.h`, including essential methods and properties for terrain generation:

- **Constructor**: Initializes the width and height of the terrain.

- **GenerateTerrain**: This method is responsible for calling the noise application and erosion processes.

- **GetHeightmap**: Returns the generated heightmap for further processing or visualization.

- **ApplyNoise and ErodeTerrain**: Private methods used for modifying the terrain based on noise functions and erosion simulations.

CHAPTER 4   ENVIRONMENTAL MECHANICS

Listing 4-9. TerrainGenerator.h

```cpp
// TerrainGenerator.h
#pragma once
#include <vector>

class TerrainGenerator {
public:
    TerrainGenerator(int width, int height);
    void GenerateTerrain();
    std::vector<std::vector<float>> GetHeightmap() const;

private:
    int m_width;
    int m_height;
    std::vector<std::vector<float>> m_heightmap;

    void ApplyNoise();
    void ErodeTerrain();
};
```

Listing 4-10 implements the terrain generation methods declared in the header file. It initializes terrain dimensions, applies noise for height variation, and includes a placeholder for erosion logic. The GetHeightmap() method provides access to the generated height data for rendering or further processing.

Listing 4-10. TerrainGenerator.cpp

```cpp
// TerrainGenerator.cpp
#include "TerrainGenerator.h"
#include <random>
```

CHAPTER 4   ENVIRONMENTAL MECHANICS

```cpp
TerrainGenerator::TerrainGenerator(int width, int height)
    : m_width(width), m_height(height) {
    m_heightmap.resize(height, std::vector<float>(width, 0.0f));
}

void TerrainGenerator::GenerateTerrain() {
    ApplyNoise();
    ErodeTerrain();
}

void TerrainGenerator::ApplyNoise() {
    std::default_random_engine generator;
    std::uniform_real_distribution<float> distribution(0.0f, 1.0f);

    for (int y = 0; y < m_height; ++y) {
        for (int x = 0; x < m_width; ++x) {
            m_heightmap[y][x] = distribution(generator);
            // Simple noise application
        }
    }
}

void TerrainGenerator::ErodeTerrain() {
    // Implement erosion simulation logic here
}

std::vector<std::vector<float>> TerrainGenerator::GetHeightmap() const {
    return m_heightmap;
}
```

In this section, we explored terrain generation and its significance in creating engaging game environments. From the basic usage of heightmaps to advanced techniques like noise functions and erosion simulations, we uncovered various methods developers use to craft diverse landscapes. Additionally, we examined practical applications across different game genres and provided an algorithm overview to help understand the underlying processes.

In the next section, we will discuss water and fluid dynamics, focusing on how realistic water interactions can enhance gameplay and contribute to immersive environments.

Water and Fluid Dynamics

Water and fluid dynamics are critical components in game development, significantly impacting the realism and immersion of a game's environment. This section covers the fundamental principles of simulating water movement, behaviors, and interactions, including surface tension, wave propagation, and the effects of buoyancy.

Basic Usage

In game development, water can be implemented in various forms, from simple animated textures to complex fluid simulations. Basic usage often involves

- **Water Surfaces**: Represented using shaders and animated textures to create the illusion of movement
- **Collision Detection**: Ensuring that players and objects interact realistically with water surfaces

Advanced Techniques

Advanced water dynamics can enhance realism through methods such as

- **Particle Systems:** Used to simulate splashes, ripples, foam, and surface disturbance during player or object interaction
- **Navier-Stokes Equations:** Applied to simulate complex fluid dynamics, enabling more natural and physically accurate water flow and wave propagation
- **Real-Time Reflection and Refraction:** Techniques that dynamically adjust based on camera angle and lighting, creating visually compelling water surfaces
- **Buoyancy Simulation:** Allows objects and characters to float, sink, or bob based on their mass and volume, adding immersion and gameplay depth
- **Terrain Deformation on Shores:** Simulates the interaction between water and land, such as wet sand impressions, erosion effects, or mud buildup, enhancing environmental responsiveness

Practical Applications

Water and fluid dynamics are essential in various game genres, including

- **Action-Adventure Games:** Enhancing exploration in environments with rivers, lakes, and oceans.
- **Simulation Games:** Realistic fluid behavior is crucial in games focusing on environmental management or physics-based puzzles.
- **Racing Games:** Accurate water dynamics can affect vehicle handling and performance.

CHAPTER 4   ENVIRONMENTAL MECHANICS

Algorithm Overview

The algorithms for simulating water often include

- **Wave Generation**: Techniques for creating and controlling wave patterns

- **Fluid Simulation**: Methods for calculating the movement of water particles, often using grid-based or particle-based approaches

- **Surface Interaction**: Algorithms for handling interactions between objects and the water surface

Reviewing the Code

In this section, we will review the code template for simulating water dynamics, breaking down the relevant functions and classes that will be employed.

Listing 4-11 defines the WaterSimulation class, encapsulating water simulation functionality. It includes methods for initialization, physics-based updates, rendering, wave generation, and fluid dynamics calculations.

- **WaterSimulation Class**: This class encapsulates the functionality for simulating water.

- **Constructor**: Initializes the water grid dimensions.

- **Update Method**: Responsible for updating the water state based on physics calculations.

- **Render Method**: Renders the water surface.

- **GenerateWaves**: A private method for creating wave patterns.

- **ApplyFluidDynamics**: A private method for updating particle positions according to fluid dynamics principles.

Listing 4-11. watersimulation.h

```
#pragma once

#include <vector>
#include "Vector3.h"

class WaterSimulation {
public:
    WaterSimulation(int width, int height);
    void Update(float deltaTime);
    void Render();

private:
    int width;
    int height;
    std::vector<Vector3> waterParticles;

    void GenerateWaves();
    void ApplyFluidDynamics();
};
```

Listing 4-12 implements the `WaterSimulation` class, initializing the grid, updating water dynamics, generating waves, and handling rendering and physics-based fluid movement.

- **Constructor**: Initializes the grid size and generates initial wave patterns
- **Update Method**: Calls the ApplyFluidDynamics method to update water particles based on elapsed time

CHAPTER 4   ENVIRONMENTAL MECHANICS

- **Render Method**: Placeholder for the rendering logic, which would visually represent the water
- **GenerateWaves**: Contains logic to create initial wave conditions
- **ApplyFluidDynamics**: Implements the physics calculations for water particle movement

Listing 4-12. watersimulation.cpp

```cpp
#include "WaterSimulation.h"
#include <cmath>

WaterSimulation::WaterSimulation(int width, int height)
    : width(width), height(height) {
    waterParticles.resize(width * height);
    GenerateWaves();
}

void WaterSimulation::Update(float deltaTime) {
    ApplyFluidDynamics();
}

void WaterSimulation::Render() {
    // Rendering code for the water surface goes here
}

void WaterSimulation::GenerateWaves() {
    // Code to initialize wave patterns in the
    waterParticles vector
}

void WaterSimulation::ApplyFluidDynamics() {
    // Physics calculations to update the positions of water
    particles
}
```

In this section, we examined water and fluid dynamics, focusing on their role in enhancing the realism and immersion of game environments. From basic surface simulations to advanced techniques involving particle systems and fluid dynamics equations, we explored various methods developers utilize to create engaging water interactions.

In the next section, we will discuss environmental sound effects, highlighting how audio can enrich the gaming experience and contribute to the atmosphere of game worlds.

Environmental Sound Effects

Environmental sound effects play a vital role in game development, contributing to the immersion and overall atmosphere of a game. This section explores the importance of sound in creating a believable environment, covering various types of sound effects, their implementation, and best practices for enhancing player experience.

Basic Usage

Sound effects can significantly enhance the player's experience by providing audio cues that complement visual elements. Basic usage involves

- **Ambiance**: Background sounds that create a sense of place, such as wind, water, and wildlife
- **Interaction Sounds**: Audio feedback for player actions, like footsteps, item pickups, and environmental interactions
- **Event Sounds**: Sounds triggered by specific events, such as explosions, weather changes, or dialogue

CHAPTER 4 ENVIRONMENTAL MECHANICS

Advanced Techniques

Advanced sound design techniques include

- **3D Audio**: Implementing spatial audio to give players a sense of directionality, making sounds feel as though they originate from specific locations in the game world
- **Dynamic Soundscapes**: Adjusting audio based on environmental changes or player actions, creating a responsive and immersive experience
- **Occlusion and Reverb**: Using algorithms to simulate how sound behaves in different environments, enhancing realism based on factors like distance and obstacles

Practical Applications

Environmental sound effects are crucial across various game genres, such as

- **Adventure Games**: Creating a rich soundscape that enhances exploration and storytelling
- **Horror Games**: Utilizing sound to build tension and create an unsettling atmosphere
- **Simulation Games**: Providing realistic environmental sounds to enhance the sense of realism

CHAPTER 4   ENVIRONMENTAL MECHANICS

Algorithm Overview

Sound design algorithms often include

- **Sound Prioritization**: Managing which sounds are played based on their importance and distance to the player
- **Dynamic Mixing**: Adjusting audio levels based on game state or player actions to ensure clarity and impact
- **Sound Layering**: Combining multiple sound sources to create a richer audio experience

Reviewing the Code

In this section, we will review a code template for implementing environmental sound effects, breaking down relevant functions and classes.

Listing 4-13 defines the `SoundManager` class, responsible for loading, playing, and managing sound effects. It includes methods for initialization, resource cleanup, volume adjustment, and sound playback.

- **SoundManager Class**: Manages loading and playing sound effects within the game
- **Constructor and Destructor**: Initializes and cleans up resources
- **LoadSound Method**: Loads sound files into memory and associates them with names for easy reference
- **PlaySound Method**: Plays the specified sound effect
- **SetVolume Method**: Adjusts the overall volume of the sound effects

CHAPTER 4   ENVIRONMENTAL MECHANICS

Listing 4-13. soundmanager.h

```
#pragma once

#include <map>
#include <string>
#include <SDL_mixer.h>

class SoundManager {
public:
    SoundManager();
    ~SoundManager();
    void LoadSound(const std::string& soundName,
    const std::string& filePath);
    void PlaySound(const std::string& soundName);
    void SetVolume(int volume);

private:
    std::map<std::string, Mix_Chunk*> sounds;
    int volume;
};
```

Listing 4-14 implements the SoundManager class, initializing the audio system, managing sound resources, handling playback, and adjusting volume levels.

- **Constructor**: Initializes the audio system with a specified format and settings

- **Destructor**: Cleans up loaded sound resources and closes the audio system

- **LoadSound Method**: Loads a sound file and stores it in a map for easy retrieval

CHAPTER 4   ENVIRONMENTAL MECHANICS

- **PlaySound Method**: Plays the sound associated with the given name on an available audio channel

- **SetVolume Method**: Adjusts the volume for all sounds based on the provided level

Listing 4-14. soundmanager.cpp

```cpp
#include "SoundManager.h"

SoundManager::SoundManager() : volume(128) {
    Mix_OpenAudio(22050, MIX_DEFAULT_FORMAT, 2, 4096);
}

SoundManager::~SoundManager() {
    for (auto& pair : sounds) {
        Mix_FreeChunk(pair.second);
    }
    Mix_CloseAudio();
}

void SoundManager::LoadSound(const std::string& soundName,
const std::string& filePath) {
    Mix_Chunk* sound = Mix_LoadWAV(filePath.c_str());
    if (sound != nullptr) {
        sounds[soundName] = sound;
    }
}

void SoundManager::PlaySound(const std::string& soundName) {
    if (sounds.find(soundName) != sounds.end()) {
        Mix_PlayChannel(-1, sounds[soundName], 0);
    }
}
```

```
void SoundManager::SetVolume(int volume) {
    this->volume = volume;
    Mix_Volume(-1, this->volume);
}
```

Explanation

In this section, we examined environmental sound effects and their critical role in enhancing the immersive experience of games. From basic ambiance to advanced techniques like 3D audio and dynamic soundscapes, we explored various methods developers use to create compelling audio environments.

In the next section, we will discuss dynamic skyboxes, focusing on how changing sky visuals can influence the atmosphere and mood of game worlds.

Dynamic Lighting Changes

Dynamic skyboxes are an essential element in game development, providing a visually stunning backdrop that enhances the atmosphere and immersion of a game world. This section explores the significance of skyboxes, techniques for creating dynamic environments, and how they can transform gameplay experiences.

Basic Usage

Skyboxes are used to represent the sky and distant scenery in a 3D environment. Basic usage involves

- **Static Skyboxes**: Simple, fixed images that serve as the background, providing a sense of depth and context

- **Dynamic Skyboxes**: Animated or procedurally generated backgrounds that change over time, simulating different weather conditions, times of day, or environmental effects

Advanced Techniques

Advanced techniques for implementing dynamic skyboxes include

- **Day-Night Cycles**: Transitioning between different skybox textures or shaders to simulate sunrise, midday, sunset, and night, often synchronized with lighting and atmospheric changes
- **Weather Effects**: Integrating dynamic elements like volumetric clouds, lightning, and rain that update in real time, altering the visual tone and mood of the skybox based on in-game conditions
- **Reflection and Refraction**: Using shaders to generate realistic reflections on surfaces like water or glass and applying refraction for light distortion, especially during atmospheric changes
- **Space Skyboxes**: Supporting fully 3D sky environments with stars, nebulae, planets, and deep-space lighting for sci-fi or space-themed levels, allowing for a seamless transition between atmospheric and space visuals

Practical Applications

Dynamic skyboxes are widely used in various game genres, including

- **Open-World Games**: Providing a seamless transition between different areas and times of day, enhancing exploration
- **Simulation Games**: Simulating real-world environments, including weather changes and celestial movements
- **Adventure and RPGs**: Creating immersive storytelling environments that adapt to narrative elements

Algorithm Overview

Key algorithms for dynamic skybox implementation include

- **Interpolation**: Smoothly transitioning between different skybox textures or colors to create a realistic time-of-day effect
- **Weather Simulation**: Randomizing weather patterns and effects based on gameplay, allowing for unique experiences each time the game is played
- **Sky Shader Management**: Adjusting shader parameters dynamically to match the current time of day and weather conditions

Reviewing the Code

In this section, we will review a code template for implementing dynamic skyboxes, focusing on relevant functions and classes.

CHAPTER 4　ENVIRONMENTAL MECHANICS

Listing 4-15 defines the Skybox class, managing the loading, rendering, and updating of the skybox with dynamic textures and scene integration.

- **Skybox Class**: Manages the loading, drawing, and updating of the skybox
- **Constructor**: Initializes the skybox with textures representing different sides
- **Draw Method**: Renders the skybox in the scene, using the current view and projection matrices
- **Update Method**: Updates the skybox's state based on the passage of time

Listing 4-15. skybox.h

```
#pragma once

#include <GL/glew.h>
#include <glm/glm.hpp>
#include <string>
#include <vector>

class Skybox {
public:
    Skybox(const std::vector<std::string>& faces);
    void Draw(const glm::mat4& view, const glm::mat4&
    projection);
    void Update(float deltaTime);

private:
    GLuint skyboxTexture;
    GLuint VAO, VBO;
    float timeOfDay;
};
```

CHAPTER 4 ENVIRONMENTAL MECHANICS

Listing 4-16 implements the Skybox class, handling texture loading, rendering setup, and dynamic updates based on the time of day.

- **Constructor**: Loads textures for the skybox from files and generates a cube map
- **Draw Method**: Sets up the rendering state and draws the skybox with appropriate shaders
- **Update Method**: Adjusts the time of day and implements changes to the skybox based on this value

Listing 4-16. skybox.cpp

```cpp
#include "Skybox.h"
#include <stb_image.h>

Skybox::Skybox(const std::vector<std::string>& faces) {
    // Load and generate the skybox texture
    glGenTextures(1, &skyboxTexture);
    glBindTexture(GL_TEXTURE_CUBE_MAP, skyboxTexture);

    for (GLuint i = 0; i < faces.size(); i++) {
        int width, height, nrChannels;
        unsigned char* data = stbi_load(faces[i].c_str(),
        &width, &height, &nrChannels, 0);
        if (data) {
            glTexImage2D(GL_TEXTURE_CUBE_MAP_POSITIVE_X + i, 0,
            GL_RGBA, width, height, 0, GL_RGBA, GL_UNSIGNED_
            BYTE, data);
            stbi_image_free(data);
        }
    }
```

```cpp
    glTexParameteri(GL_TEXTURE_CUBE_MAP, GL_TEXTURE_MIN_FILTER,
    GL_LINEAR);
    glTexParameteri(GL_TEXTURE_CUBE_MAP, GL_TEXTURE_MAG_FILTER,
    GL_LINEAR);
    glTexParameteri(GL_TEXTURE_CUBE_MAP, GL_TEXTURE_WRAP_S,
    GL_CLAMP_TO_EDGE);
    glTexParameteri(GL_TEXTURE_CUBE_MAP, GL_TEXTURE_WRAP_T,
    GL_CLAMP_TO_EDGE);
    glTexParameteri(GL_TEXTURE_CUBE_MAP, GL_TEXTURE_WRAP_R,
    GL_CLAMP_TO_EDGE);
}

void Skybox::Draw(const glm::mat4& view, const glm::mat4&
projection) {
    glDepthFunc(GL_LEQUAL);
    // Change depth function so depth values don't get
    overwritten
    // Render the skybox here using shaders
    // Set view and projection matrices
}

void Skybox::Update(float deltaTime) {
    timeOfDay += deltaTime;
    // Update skybox based on time of day
    // Implement logic for changing colors or textures
}
```

In this section, we explored dynamic skyboxes and their essential role in creating immersive game environments. We examined the transition from static backgrounds to dynamic systems that adapt to gameplay, enhancing realism and atmosphere. Techniques such as day-night cycles and weather effects were highlighted, along with the algorithms that support them.

CHAPTER 4 ENVIRONMENTAL MECHANICS

In the next section, we will discuss terrain texturing, focusing on methods to apply realistic textures to landscapes and environments within games.

Terrain Texturing

Terrain texturing is a critical component in game development, as it adds depth and realism to landscapes. This section delves into the techniques and methodologies used for effectively applying textures to terrain, enhancing the visual fidelity and immersive quality of game environments.

Basic Usage

The basic usage of terrain texturing involves

- **Base Textures**: Applying a primary texture that represents the main surface material of the terrain, such as grass, dirt, or rock
- **Layering Textures**: Using multiple textures to create a more complex surface appearance, simulating effects like worn paths or variations in vegetation
- **UV Mapping**: Mapping texture coordinates to terrain vertices to ensure textures align correctly on the surface

Advanced Techniques

Advanced techniques for terrain texturing include

- **Detail Textures**: Adding a secondary texture that enhances the details of the terrain, such as small rocks or dirt patches, which are blended with the base texture to increase realism

- **Triplanar Mapping**: A technique that projects textures onto surfaces from three different axes, useful for uneven terrain where UV mapping may create distortion
- **Texture Blending**: Implementing algorithms to blend multiple textures seamlessly, allowing for transitions between different surface types, such as grass to gravel

Practical Applications

Terrain texturing is used across various game genres, including

- **Open-World Games**: Creating expansive environments where players can explore diverse landscapes with realistic details
- **Simulation Games**: Accurately representing natural terrains to provide an authentic experience
- **First-Person Shooters**: Designing maps with varied surfaces that affect player movement and visibility

Algorithm Overview

Key algorithms for effective terrain texturing include

- **Height-Based Texture Blending**: Using heightmaps to determine where different textures should appear based on elevation
- **Slope-Based Texturing**: Applying textures based on the slope of the terrain, allowing for distinct materials on steep hills vs. flat areas
- **Procedural Generation**: Dynamically generating textures based on parameters such as noise functions, enabling diverse and unique terrain appearances

Reviewing the Code

In this section, we will review a code template for implementing terrain texturing, focusing on relevant functions and classes.

Listing 4-17 defines the `TerrainTexture` class, managing the loading and application of textures to terrain surfaces based on world position.

- **TerrainTexture Class**: Manages loading and applying textures to terrain surfaces
- **Constructor**: Initializes the terrain textures from provided file paths
- **ApplyTexture Method**: Applies the appropriate texture based on the given position in the world

Listing 4-17. TerrainTexture.h

```
#pragma once

#include <GL/glew.h>
#include <glm/glm.hpp>
#include <string>
#include <vector>

class TerrainTexture {
public:
    TerrainTexture(const std::vector<std::string>& textures);
    void ApplyTexture(const glm::vec3& position);
private:
    std::vector<GLuint> textureIDs;
    GLuint shaderProgram;
};
```

CHAPTER 4   ENVIRONMENTAL MECHANICS

Listing 4-18 implements the TerrainTexture class, handling texture loading, OpenGL configuration, and applying the appropriate texture based on terrain position.

- **Constructor**: Loads the specified textures into OpenGL and sets texture parameters for wrapping and filtering
- **ApplyTexture Method**: Implements logic to determine and apply the correct texture based on the position of the terrain

Listing 4-18. TerrainTexture.cpp

```
#include "TerrainTexture.h"
#include <stb_image.h>

TerrainTexture::TerrainTexture(const std::vector<std::string>& textures) {
    glGenTextures(textures.size(), textureIDs.data());
    for (size_t i = 0; i < textures.size(); i++) {
        int width, height, nrChannels;
        unsigned char* data = stbi_load(textures[i].c_str(),
        &width, &height, &nrChannels, 0);
        if (data) {
            glBindTexture(GL_TEXTURE_2D, textureIDs[i]);
            glTexImage2D(GL_TEXTURE_2D, 0, GL_RGBA, width,
            height, 0, GL_RGBA, GL_UNSIGNED_BYTE, data);
            glTexParameteri(GL_TEXTURE_2D, GL_TEXTURE_WRAP_S,
            GL_REPEAT);
            glTexParameteri(GL_TEXTURE_2D, GL_TEXTURE_WRAP_T,
            GL_REPEAT);
            glTexParameteri(GL_TEXTURE_2D, GL_TEXTURE_MIN_
            FILTER, GL_LINEAR_MIPMAP_LINEAR);
```

```
            glTexParameteri(GL_TEXTURE_2D,
            GL_TEXTURE_MAG_FILTER, GL_LINEAR);
            stbi_image_free(data);
        }
    }
}

void TerrainTexture::ApplyTexture(const glm::vec3& position) {
    // Determine which texture to apply based on position
    // Set shader uniforms and bind the correct texture
}
```

In this section, we explored terrain texturing and its vital role in enhancing the realism of game environments. We discussed techniques such as layering, detail textures, and advanced mapping methods that contribute to visually rich landscapes. Additionally, we reviewed practical applications across different genres and the underlying algorithms that facilitate effective texture application.

In the next section, we will discuss interactive foliage, focusing on how dynamic vegetation can enrich gameplay experiences and add realism to environments.

Interactive Foliage

Interactive foliage refers to vegetation that responds to the player's presence or other environmental factors, enhancing immersion and realism in game environments. From bending grass underfoot to leaves moving with the wind, interactive foliage can bring dynamic life to a scene, making it feel vibrant and engaging.

Basic Usage

The basic use of interactive foliage includes

- **Wind Simulations:** Adding subtle movements to foliage based on wind intensity, creating a lifelike setting
- **Player Interaction:** Implementing effects like bending grass, parting bushes, or scattering leaves when the player passes through foliage
- **Physics-Based Movement:** Using physics to simulate realistic foliage movement, such as leaves reacting to touch or branches swaying

Advanced Techniques

Advanced techniques for interactive foliage include

- **Shader-Based Effects:** Using shaders to control foliage movement in real time, allowing for efficient and complex animations
- **Procedural Animation:** Applying procedural techniques to generate foliage movement without manually animating each piece, making it resource-efficient
- **Collision Detection with Foliage:** Implementing precise collision detection for more accurate player interactions, especially for dense vegetation or larger plants

Practical Applications

Interactive foliage has diverse applications across game genres:

- **Adventure Games**: Creating immersive forest environments where plants respond to the player's actions
- **Survival Games**: Enhancing the realism of natural settings, which can impact stealth, tracking, or navigating dense terrain
- **Role-Playing Games (RPGs)**: Adding responsive foliage to amplify the connection with the world, creating a deeper exploration experience

Algorithm Overview

The algorithm behind interactive foliage usually involves

- **Wind Vector Calculations**: Using wind vector data to determine the direction and intensity of foliage movement
- **Bending and Parting Logic**: Calculating foliage deformation when the player or NPCs interact with it, often using a deformation shader
- **Physics Integration**: Incorporating physics simulations for large plants and trees, adding realistic movement in response to environmental factors

Reviewing the Code

Here's a code template that demonstrates how interactive foliage could be implemented with basic player interaction and wind effects.

Listing 4-19 defines the `InteractiveFoliage` class, managing foliage positions, updates based on player and environmental factors, and rendering transformations.

- **InteractiveFoliage Class**: Manages foliage positions, updates them based on player and environmental factors, and handles rendering

- **UpdateFoliage Method**: Takes player position and wind strength as input, adjusting foliage accordingly

- **RenderFoliage Method**: Responsible for rendering the foliage with any applied transformations

Listing 4-19. InteractiveFoliage.h

```
#pragma once

#include <GL/glew.h>
#include <glm/glm.hpp>
#include <vector>

class InteractiveFoliage {
public:
    InteractiveFoliage();
    void UpdateFoliage(const glm::vec3& playerPosition, float windStrength);
    void RenderFoliage();
```

CHAPTER 4 ENVIRONMENTAL MECHANICS

```
private:
    std::vector<glm::vec3> foliagePositions;
    GLuint foliageShader;
};
```

Listing 4-20 defines the `InteractiveFoliage` class, managing foliage positions, updates based on player and environmental factors, and rendering transformations.

- **Constructor**: Sets up the foliage shader and initializes foliage positions.

- **UpdateFoliage Method**: Checks the player's distance from each foliage element, bending foliage if the player is close. Wind effects are also applied based on a sine wave pattern to simulate oscillating movement.

- **RenderFoliage Method**: Renders each foliage instance at the updated positions, using the shader to apply any necessary transformations.

Listing 4-20. InteractiveFoliage.cpp

```
#include "InteractiveFoliage.h"
#include <glm/gtc/matrix_transform.hpp>

InteractiveFoliage::InteractiveFoliage() {
    // Load and compile foliage shader
    foliageShader = glCreateProgram();
    // Initialize foliage positions
}

void InteractiveFoliage::UpdateFoliage(const glm::vec3&
playerPosition, float windStrength) {
    for (auto& pos : foliagePositions) {
```

```
        float distance = glm::length(playerPosition - pos);
        if (distance < 1.0f) {
            // Bend foliage away from the player
            pos += glm::normalize(pos - playerPosition) * 0.1f;
        }
        // Apply wind effect
        pos.y += glm::sin(glfwGetTime() * windStrength)
        * 0.05f;
    }
}
void InteractiveFoliage::RenderFoliage() {
    glUseProgram(foliageShader);
    for (const auto& pos : foliagePositions) {
        // Render each foliage instance at the updated position
    }
}
```

In this section, we explored interactive foliage and its impact on making game environments more lifelike. By leveraging shaders, procedural animation, and collision detection, developers can create foliage that responds naturally to player interactions and environmental factors. This section provided a practical breakdown of foliage dynamics and the underlying algorithms for managing responsive vegetation.

Summary

As we conclude our exploration of environmental mechanics, we have examined the core systems that bring dynamic and immersive environments to life. From terrain generation and texturing to interactive foliage and dynamic weather, these mechanics enhance realism and player engagement. By integrating systems such as water simulation, skyboxes,

CHAPTER 4   ENVIRONMENTAL MECHANICS

and environmental interactions, we create a world that responds fluidly to both player actions and natural forces. These foundational elements ensure a more interactive and visually compelling game world, enriching the overall gameplay experience.

In Chapter 5, we'll shift focus to character mechanics, where we'll delve into core gameplay elements such as character movement, combat, stealth, health and stamina, and more. This next chapter will equip you with the tools and techniques needed to develop dynamic, interactive player experiences that elevate your game's immersive qualities.

CHAPTER 5

Character Mechanics

The way players control and interact with their characters is fundamental to creating an engaging gameplay experience. Character mechanics encompass everything from basic movement to complex abilities, giving players a sense of agency and connection to their virtual persona. Each mechanic, whether it's running, jumping, or engaging in combat, adds layers of depth and immersion to the game world, influencing how players interact with environments, overcome challenges, and engage in strategic play. This chapter introduces the techniques and systems that allow players to control their character's physical actions and abilities, enabling dynamic interactions with the game world.

At their core, character mechanics involve enabling the player to move, jump, and interact within the game environment. The foundational components include basic locomotion, such as walking, running, and crouching, as well as contextual actions like interacting with objects or initiating dialogue. These core mechanics serve as the building blocks that give players control over the character's movements and allow seamless interaction with the surrounding world.

In this chapter, we'll cover essential techniques like character movement, jumping mechanics, and basic interactions, providing you with a foundation to create responsive and intuitive player controls.

Advanced character mechanics go beyond simple movements, offering players enhanced abilities and deeper strategic options. Mechanics like swimming, climbing, and combat introduce complex interactions,

CHAPTER 5   CHARACTER MECHANICS

requiring developers to account for physics, animation blending, and environment-specific behaviors. Stealth mechanics, skill trees, and customization systems further expand gameplay options, allowing players to personalize their approach and progression. Mastering these advanced techniques enhances engagement, as players gain more ways to interact with and impact the game world.

In this chapter, we'll explore these intricate mechanics, discussing how they contribute to gameplay variety and replayability, from fluid climbing systems to robust combat mechanics and character customization.

This chapter will guide you through implementing a range of character mechanics, from basic movements to advanced abilities. You'll gain hands-on experience with core actions like walking and jumping and also dive into more complex systems like combat, stealth, and skill trees. By the end of this chapter, you'll understand how to create a versatile and responsive character capable of interacting with the game environment in multiple ways. These mechanics form the foundation of immersive gameplay, adding depth and engagement as players connect with their in-game personas.

Character Movement

Character movement is one of the most essential mechanics in any game, determining how the player navigates through the environment. At its core, movement involves basic actions such as walking, running, and sprinting, but can also be expanded to include more nuanced elements like strafing, acceleration, and deceleration. Effective character movement mechanics contribute to an immersive experience by making the controls feel responsive and natural, allowing players to feel in control and connected to their virtual surroundings.

Basic Usage of Character Movement

In its simplest form, character movement consists of basic directional inputs that move the character forward, backward, left, and right. This movement often involves implementing

- **Walk/Run/Sprint**: The character's movement speed varies depending on whether they are walking, running, or sprinting.
- **Acceleration/Deceleration**: These parameters create realistic changes in speed, such as when starting or stopping movement.
- **Gravity**: Ensures that characters adhere to the ground or fall when there's no ground beneath them.

In most engines, these mechanics are handled through character controllers, which manage how inputs translate into movement within the game world.

Advanced Techniques

More advanced movement mechanics add depth to gameplay and improve the realism of character interactions within the environment. These may include

- **Directional and Strafing Control**: Allows players to move in multiple directions simultaneously, enhancing control during combat or exploration
- **Slope Handling**: Enables the character to move realistically across slopes, sliding down steep surfaces or climbing gentle inclines

- **Obstacle Avoidance and Vaulting**: Automatically detects obstacles in the character's path and allows the character to vault over them or move around
- **Dynamic Movement Adjustments**: Adapts the character's speed based on terrain type, such as slowing down on sand or mud

By implementing these features, the game world becomes more interactive, and players gain greater freedom to explore and engage with their surroundings.

Practical Applications

Character movement mechanics are widely used across various game genres, and each genre may prioritize specific aspects of movement:

- **Shooter Games**: Focus on precise control and strafing for effective targeting and evasion
- **Platformers**: Require tight, responsive controls for accurate jumps and maneuvers
- **Open-World Games**: Emphasize smooth transitions between running, walking, and sprinting, allowing for seamless exploration

Algorithm Overview

To develop effective character movement mechanics, the following systems are often implemented:

1. **Input System**: Captures player input (keyboard or controller) and translates it into directional movement

2. **Character Controller**: Processes inputs and applies them to the character's position and orientation

3. **Physics Interactions**: Ensures that gravity, friction, and other physical properties affect the character's movement realistically

4. **Collision Detection**: Prevents the character from moving through objects, adjusting movement to navigate around obstacles

Reviewing the Code

Below is a basic implementation of a character movement system, focusing on capturing input and applying it to move the character in the game world.

Listing 5-1 defines the ACharacterMovementController class, which manages player movement and sprinting mechanics. Key components include WalkSpeed and SprintSpeed for movement control, MoveForward() and MoveRight() for directional input, and StartSprinting() and StopSprinting() to dynamically adjust movement speed.

- **ACharacterMovementController**: Manages the character's movement by tracking and responding to player input
- **WalkSpeed**: Determines the character's default walking speed
- **SprintSpeed**: Adjusts the character's speed when sprinting
- **MoveForward/MoveRight**: Functions that allow directional movement based on player input
- **StartSprinting/StopSprinting**: Adjust the character's speed based on whether the player is sprinting

CHAPTER 5   CHARACTER MECHANICS

Listing 5-1. CharacterMovementController.h

```cpp
#pragma once

#include "CoreMinimal.h"
#include "GameFramework/Character.h"
#include "CharacterMovementController.generated.h"

UCLASS()
class MYGAME_API ACharacterMovementController : public ACharacter
{
    GENERATED_BODY()

public:
    ACharacterMovementController();

protected:
    virtual void SetupPlayerInputComponent(class UInputComponent* PlayerInputComponent) override;

public:
    virtual void Tick(float DeltaTime) override;

    UPROPERTY(EditAnywhere, BlueprintReadWrite, Category = "Movement")
    float WalkSpeed;  // Character's walking speed

    UPROPERTY(EditAnywhere, BlueprintReadWrite, Category = "Movement")
    float SprintSpeed;  // Character's sprinting speed

    UFUNCTION(BlueprintCallable, Category = "Movement")
    void MoveForward(float Value);
```

CHAPTER 5   CHARACTER MECHANICS

```cpp
UFUNCTION(BlueprintCallable, Category = "Movement")
void MoveRight(float Value);

UFUNCTION(BlueprintCallable, Category = "Movement")
void StartSprinting();

UFUNCTION(BlueprintCallable, Category = "Movement")
void StopSprinting();
};
```

Listing 5-2 implements movement functionality, with MoveForward() and MoveRight() calculating directional movement based on controller rotation, while StartSprinting() and StopSprinting() dynamically adjust the character's speed.

- **MoveForward() and MoveRight()**: These functions calculate the forward and right directions based on the controller's rotation and apply movement in that direction.

- **StartSprinting() and StopSprinting()**: Adjust the character's speed by setting the maximum walk speed based on whether the player is sprinting.

To ensure this code works correctly, make sure you define the actions in your project settings:

- Open Edit ▶ Project Settings.

- Navigate to Input under the Engine section.

- Under Action Mappings, click the "+" icon to add a new action.

CHAPTER 5　CHARACTER MECHANICS

- Name the action, for example, "Sprint" (matching the code exactly).

- Assign a key (e.g., Left Shift) to trigger the sprint behavior.

Listing 5-2. CharacterMovementController.cpp

```
#include "CharacterMovementController.h"
#include "GameFramework/CharacterMovementComponent.h"
#include "Components/InputComponent.h"

ACharacterMovementController::ACharacterMovementController()
{
    PrimaryActorTick.bCanEverTick = true;
    WalkSpeed = 300.0f;
    SprintSpeed = 600.0f;
}
void ACharacterMovementController::SetupPlayerInputComponent(
UInputComponent* PlayerInputComponent)
{
    Super::SetupPlayerInputComponent(PlayerInputComponent);

    PlayerInputComponent->BindAxis("MoveForward", this,
    &ACharacterMovementController::MoveForward);
    PlayerInputComponent->BindAxis("MoveRight", this,
    &ACharacterMovementController::MoveRight);
    PlayerInputComponent->BindAction("Sprint", IE_Pressed,
    this, &ACharacterMovementController::StartSprinting);
    PlayerInputComponent->BindAction("Sprint", IE_Released,
    this, &ACharacterMovementController::StopSprinting);
}
```

CHAPTER 5   CHARACTER MECHANICS

```cpp
void ACharacterMovementController::Tick(float DeltaTime)
{
    Super::Tick(DeltaTime);
}

void ACharacterMovementController::MoveForward(float Value)
{
    if ((Controller != nullptr) && (Value != 0.0f))
    {
        const FVector Direction = FRotationMatrix(Controller->
        GetControlRotation()).GetUnitAxis(EAxis::X);
        AddMovementInput(Direction, Value);
    }
}

void ACharacterMovementController::MoveRight(float Value)
{
    if ((Controller != nullptr) && (Value != 0.0f))
    {
        const FVector Direction = FRotationMatrix(Controller->
        GetControlRotation()).GetUnitAxis(EAxis::Y);
        AddMovementInput(Direction, Value);
    }
}

void ACharacterMovementController::StartSprinting()
{
    GetCharacterMovement()->MaxWalkSpeed = SprintSpeed;
}

void ACharacterMovementController::StopSprinting()
{
    GetCharacterMovement()->MaxWalkSpeed = WalkSpeed;
}
```

In this section, you've learned the fundamentals of implementing character movement, from basic walking to sprinting. These mechanics are essential for building responsive and intuitive controls that help players navigate and explore game environments comfortably. In the next section, we'll dive into jumping mechanics, expanding upon character movement to introduce vertical navigation and environmental interaction.

Jumping Mechanics

Jumping mechanics add depth to gameplay by allowing players to navigate vertical obstacles, reach elevated areas, and avoid dangers on the ground. Jumping can vary widely in complexity—from simple, predefined jumps to dynamic, physics-based leaps that respond to player inputs. A basic jump might only change the player's vertical position briefly, while more advanced mechanics might involve stamina-based jumps, double jumps, wall jumps, and more.

Basic Usage

At its core, a jump is an upward movement initiated by the player, which is eventually counteracted by gravity. Typical components of a basic jump include

- **Vertical Velocity:** A force applied to propel the player upward
- **Gravity**: A downward force that pulls the player back to the ground
- **Ground Detection**: Checking if the player is on the ground to enable jumping

In a simple jumping system, the player presses a button to trigger an upward movement, with the game's physics system controlling the descent.

Advanced Techniques

Advanced jumping mechanics add complexity to gameplay and challenge players to master different jump types. Here are some examples:

- **Double Jump**: Allows the player to jump again while airborne, providing extra height or distance
- **Wall Jump**: Allows players to push off from walls to reach higher areas or change directions mid-air
- **Charged Jump**: A jump that gains height and distance based on how long the player holds down the jump button
- **Stamina-Based Jumps**: A system where jumps consume stamina, limiting consecutive jumps and adding a layer of strategy

Practical Applications

Jumping mechanics enhance player mobility in various game genres, including

- **Platformers**: Essential for traversing gaps, reaching new areas, and avoiding obstacles.
- **Adventure and Open-World Games**: Used to explore elevated terrain, scale structures, or interact with the environment.

CHAPTER 5   CHARACTER MECHANICS

- **Action and Fighting Games**: Jumping allows players to evade attacks, reach advantageous positions, or launch attacks from above.

Algorithm Overview

The jumping system typically involves several systems that interact to create the feeling of a natural jump. Here's a breakdown of the key components:

- **Input Handling**: Detects the jump command from the player
- **Ground Check System**: Determines if the player is on solid ground or mid-air
- **Physics System**: Applies forces to initiate the jump, handles gravity, and adjusts for mid-air controls
- **Collision Detection**: Detects landings and resets the ability to jump once the player touches the ground

Reviewing the Code

The following code provides a template for implementing a basic jump mechanic, covering essential elements such as vertical velocity, gravity, and ground detection.

Listing 5-3 defines the `APlayerCharacter` class, which includes jumping mechanics. Key components include `JumpHeight` for jump customization, `bIsGrounded` to track ground status, `PerformJump()` to trigger jumps, and `CheckGroundStatus()` to reset jump availability.

CHAPTER 5   CHARACTER MECHANICS

- **APlayerCharacter**: This class defines the character and includes jumping-related attributes.

- **JumpHeight**: Specifies the jump height, allowing customization for different characters or power-ups.

- **bIsGrounded**: Tracks whether the player is on the ground and able to jump.

- **PerformJump()**: A function that triggers a jump if the character is grounded.

- **CheckGroundStatus()**: A helper function to verify if the player is on solid ground, used to reset jump availability.

Listing 5-3. PlayerCharacter.h

```
#pragma once

#include "CoreMinimal.h"
#include "GameFramework/Character.h"
#include "PlayerCharacter.generated.h"

UCLASS()
class MYGAME_API APlayerCharacter : public ACharacter
{
    GENERATED_BODY()

public:
    APlayerCharacter();

protected:
    virtual void BeginPlay() override;
```

CHAPTER 5   CHARACTER MECHANICS

```
public:
    virtual void Tick(float DeltaTime) override;
    virtual void SetupPlayerInputComponent(class UInputCompo-
    nent* PlayerInputComponent) override;

    UPROPERTY(EditAnywhere, BlueprintReadWrite, Category = "Jump")
    float JumpHeight; // Controls how high the character jumps

    UFUNCTION(BlueprintCallable, Category = "Jump")
    void PerformJump();

private:
    void CheckGroundStatus();
};
```

Listing 5-4 implements jumping mechanics, with `Tick()` updating bIsGrounded, `PerformJump()` triggering jumps and setting bIsGrounded to false, and `CheckGroundStatus()` using `IsMovingOnGround()` to verify ground status and manage jump availability.

- **Tick()**: Continuously checks if the player is grounded, updating the bIsGrounded variable accordingly.

- **PerformJump()**: This method checks if the player is grounded and then initiates a jump by launching the character upward. Once the character jumps, bIsGrounded is set to false.

- **CheckGroundStatus()**: This function uses Unreal's IsMovingOnGround() method to verify the player's grounded status, enabling or disabling the jump accordingly.

CHAPTER 5 CHARACTER MECHANICS

Listing 5-4. PlayerCharacter.cpp

```cpp
#include "PlayerCharacter.h"
#include "GameFramework/CharacterMovementComponent.h"

APlayerCharacter::APlayerCharacter()
{
    PrimaryActorTick.bCanEverTick = true;
    JumpHeight = 600.0f;
    bIsGrounded = true;
}

void APlayerCharacter::BeginPlay()
{
    Super::BeginPlay();
}

void APlayerCharacter::Tick(float DeltaTime)
{
    Super::Tick(DeltaTime);

    // Check if the player is grounded
    CheckGroundStatus();
}

void APlayerCharacter::SetupPlayerInputComponent(UInputComponent* PlayerInputComponent)
{
    Super::SetupPlayerInputComponent(PlayerInputComponent);

    // Bind the jump action
    PlayerInputComponent->BindAction("Jump", IE_Pressed, this,
    &APlayerCharacter::PerformJump);
}
```

```cpp
void APlayerCharacter::PerformJump()
{
    if (!GetCharacterMovement()->IsFalling())
    {
        LaunchCharacter(FVector(0, 0, JumpHeight),
        false, true);
    }
}
void APlayerCharacter::CheckGroundStatus()
{
    // Simple ground check logic
    if (GetCharacterMovement()->IsMovingOnGround())
    {
        bIsGrounded = true;
    }
}
```

This section introduced the essentials of implementing jumping mechanics, from a basic jump to more advanced variations like double and wall jumps. We've covered key concepts like ground detection, input handling, and the application of physics to create responsive and immersive jumping actions. In the next section, we'll explore crouching and prone mechanics and the methods for creating them.

Crouching and Prone Mechanics

Crouching and prone mechanics allow players to change their stance, affecting their movement, visibility, and interaction with the environment. These mechanics are often essential in stealth and tactical games, where players need to stay hidden or navigate low obstacles. While crouching slightly lowers the player's stance, going prone takes it a step further by bringing the player almost fully to the ground, allowing for even greater concealment or stability at the cost of movement speed.

Key Differences Between Crouching and Prone

- **Crouching**: Reduces the player's height, making them less visible and allowing them to move under low obstacles. Crouching generally offers a moderate reduction in speed but allows for mobility.

- **Prone**: Places the player entirely on the ground, minimizing visibility to enemies and creating a stable firing stance. Prone often significantly reduces speed, limiting the player's movement to crawling.

Practical Applications

Crouching and prone mechanics are commonly used in a variety of genres for different purposes:

- **Stealth Games**: Enable players to stay hidden, avoid detection, and move silently

- **First-Person Shooters (FPS)**: Provide stability for shooting or reduce the player's visibility

- **Platformers and Puzzle Games**: Allow players to interact with or move under low obstacles

Basic Structure

The crouching and prone mechanics involve several core elements:

1. **Input Handling**: Detects player commands to crouch or go prone

2. **Movement Adjustment**: Adjusts the player's movement speed, collision size, and camera height

3. **Animation Triggers**: Transitions to the crouching or prone animation, if available

4. **Transition Constraints**: Conditions that restrict or prevent stance changes (e.g., from crouching to prone when in certain situations)

Crouching Code Implementation

Below is a template to implement basic crouching functionality in Unreal Engine. The code covers adjusting the player's stance, speed, and camera height when crouching.

Listing 5-5 implements crouching mechanics, with CrouchSpeed and StandSpeed defining movement speeds, bIsCrouching tracking the crouch state, and functions like StartCrouch(), EndCrouch(), and AdjustCrouchState() managing transitions and related adjustments.

- **CrouchSpeed** and **StandSpeed**: Define different movement speeds when crouching or standing

- **bIsCrouching**: A flag that indicates if the character is currently crouching

- **StartCrouch()** and **EndCrouch()**: Functions to initiate and stop crouching, adjusting speed and collision accordingly

- **AdjustCrouchState()**: A helper function to switch between crouching and standing states

Listing 5-5. PlayerCharacter.h

```
#pragma once

#include "CoreMinimal.h"
#include "GameFramework/Character.h"
#include "PlayerCharacter.generated.h"

UCLASS()
class MYGAME_API APlayerCharacter : public ACharacter
{
    GENERATED_BODY()

public:
    APlayerCharacter();

protected:
    virtual void BeginPlay() override;

public:
    virtual void Tick(float DeltaTime) override;
    virtual void SetupPlayerInputComponent
    (class UInputComponent* PlayerInputComponent) override;

    UPROPERTY(EditAnywhere, BlueprintReadWrite,
    Category = "Crouch")
    float CrouchSpeed; // Speed while crouching

    UPROPERTY(EditAnywhere, BlueprintReadWrite,
    Category = "Crouch")
    float StandSpeed; // Speed while standing
```

```cpp
UPROPERTY(EditAnywhere, BlueprintReadWrite,
Category = "Crouch")
bool bIsCrouching; // Tracks crouching state

UFUNCTION(BlueprintCallable, Category = "Crouch")
void StartCrouch();

UFUNCTION(BlueprintCallable, Category = "Crouch")
void EndCrouch();
private:
    void AdjustCrouchState(bool bCrouch);
};
```

Listing 5-6 implements crouch functionality, with StartCrouch() and EndCrouch() triggering crouch state transitions and AdjustCrouchState() managing movement speed, as well as adjusting collision size through Crouch() and UnCrouch().

- **StartCrouch()** and **EndCrouch()**: Called when the player presses and releases the crouch button. These functions call AdjustCrouchState() to manage crouching and standing transitions.

- **AdjustCrouchState()**: Handles the crouching state by changing the player's movement speed and calling Crouch() or UnCrouch() methods, which adjust the player's collision size.

Listing 5-6. PlayerCharacter.cpp

```cpp
#include "PlayerCharacter.h"
#include "GameFramework/CharacterMovementComponent.h"
```

CHAPTER 5   CHARACTER MECHANICS

```
APlayerCharacter::APlayerCharacter()
{
    PrimaryActorTick.bCanEverTick = true;
    CrouchSpeed = 300.0f;
    StandSpeed = 600.0f;
    bIsCrouching = false;
}

void APlayerCharacter::BeginPlay()
{
    Super::BeginPlay();
}

void APlayerCharacter::Tick(float DeltaTime)
{
    Super::Tick(DeltaTime);
}

void APlayerCharacter::SetupPlayerInputComponent(
UInputComponent* PlayerInputComponent)
{
    Super::SetupPlayerInputComponent(PlayerInputComponent);

    PlayerInputComponent->BindAction("Crouch", IE_Pressed,
    this, &APlayerCharacter::StartCrouch);
    PlayerInputComponent->BindAction("Crouch", IE_Released,
    this, &APlayerCharacter::EndCrouch);
}

void APlayerCharacter::StartCrouch()
{
    AdjustCrouchState(true);
}
```

```
void APlayerCharacter::EndCrouch()
{
    AdjustCrouchState(false);
}
void APlayerCharacter::AdjustCrouchState(bool bCrouch)
{
    if (bCrouch)
    {
        Crouch();
        GetCharacterMovement()->MaxWalkSpeed = CrouchSpeed;
        bIsCrouching = true;
    }
    else
    {
        UnCrouch();
        GetCharacterMovement()->MaxWalkSpeed = StandSpeed;
        bIsCrouching = false;
    }
}
```

Prone Mechanic Extension

Adding a prone mechanic involves similar principles but usually includes additional checks for entering or exiting the prone state.

PlayerCharacter Class Extensions

Listing 5-7 introduces a prone state, adding ProneSpeed to define movement speed while prone, bIsProne to track the character's prone status, and functions StartProne() and EndProne() to manage transitions between prone and standing states.

CHAPTER 5 CHARACTER MECHANICS

- **ProneSpeed** and **bIsProne**: Define the prone speed and state.

- **StartProne()** and **EndProne()**: Similar to the crouch functions, these methods change the character's speed and state when going prone. Additional collision adjustments and animations can be applied as necessary.

Listing 5-7. Playercharacter.h (Added for Prone Mechanic)

```
UPROPERTY(EditAnywhere, BlueprintReadWrite, Category = "Prone")
float ProneSpeed;

UPROPERTY(EditAnywhere, BlueprintReadWrite, Category = "Prone")
bool bIsProne;

UFUNCTION(BlueprintCallable, Category = "Prone")
void StartProne();

UFUNCTION(BlueprintCallable, Category = "Prone")
void EndProne();
```

Listing 5-8. Playercharacter.cpp (Updated for Crouch and Prone Together)

```
APlayerCharacter::APlayerCharacter()
{
    ProneSpeed = 150.0f; // Prone movement speed
    bIsProne = false;
}

void APlayerCharacter::SetupPlayerInputComponent(UInputComponent* PlayerInputComponent)
{
    Super::SetupPlayerInputComponent(PlayerInputComponent);
```

```
    PlayerInputComponent->BindAction("Prone", IE_Pressed, this,
    &APlayerCharacter::StartProne);
    PlayerInputComponent->BindAction("Prone", IE_Released,
    this, &APlayerCharacter::EndProne);
}

void APlayerCharacter::StartProne()
{
    if (!bIsCrouching && !bIsProne)  // Only go prone if not
    already crouching or prone
    {
        GetCharacterMovement()->MaxWalkSpeed = ProneSpeed;
        bIsProne = true;
        // Add prone animations, collision adjustments
        as needed
    }
}

void APlayerCharacter::EndProne()
{
    if (bIsProne)
    {
        GetCharacterMovement()->MaxWalkSpeed = StandSpeed;
        bIsProne = false;
        // Reset animations, collision for standing
    }
}
```

Crouching and prone mechanics enhance player movement by introducing stances that affect visibility, speed, and environmental interaction. By allowing players to move in a crouched or prone position, you can add layers of strategy, particularly useful in stealth and tactical gameplay. In the next section, we'll explore swimming mechanics, which will cover techniques for implementing underwater movement, buoyancy effects, and adapting controls for fluid motion.

Swimming Mechanics

Swimming mechanics introduce a unique dimension to gameplay by allowing players to navigate water environments, requiring adaptations in controls, physics, and animations. By enabling characters to swim, you can open up areas for exploration, hidden challenges, or even underwater combat. Implementing swimming effectively requires handling buoyancy, breath limits, and fluid motion that feels responsive and realistic.

Basic Implementation

At a fundamental level, swimming mechanics adjust a character's movement when in contact with water. Basic features often include

- **Modified Movement Speed**: Swimming speed is typically slower than walking or running on land.
- **Vertical and Horizontal Control**: Allows players to ascend or descend within water, with responsive directional control.
- **Breath Management**: Most games set a limit on how long a character can remain underwater, with a breath meter or timer indicating oxygen levels.

A straightforward approach to swimming mechanics involves detecting when a character enters water and toggling swimming mode, which changes the character's movement attributes and animations accordingly.

Advanced Techniques

Adding more depth to swimming mechanics involves a range of visual, auditory, and gameplay elements to make water interaction more immersive:

- **Buoyancy and Gravity**: Apply different gravity and buoyancy values underwater to simulate fluid resistance and natural floating effects. This makes the character's movements feel weightless and realistic.

- **Underwater Physics**: Alter jump and fall physics to slow down actions for a more fluid feel, as movements are generally more resistant in water.

- **Visibility Adjustments**: Reduced visibility underwater can create suspense or present challenges. Depth-based visibility reduction and water clarity effects can increase immersion.

- **Specialized Animations**: Integrate animations that allow for natural transitions between swimming strokes, surface treading, and underwater diving, enhancing the player experience.

- **Sound Effects and Filters**: Add sound effects and muffling to simulate underwater acoustics, giving a more isolated and atmospheric feeling.

These advanced methods contribute to a richer swimming experience, adding visual and physical layers that respond to player actions and environmental conditions.

Practical Applications

Swimming mechanics are utilized in various game genres:

- **Adventure and Exploration Games**: Games often feature underwater exploration sections, where swimming is essential to accessing hidden areas or solving puzzles.

- **Survival Games**: Swimming mechanics can introduce hazards, such as breath limits and underwater enemies, that add survival challenges.

- **Open-World Games**: Expansive games use swimming to enhance world traversal, allowing players to move between islands, investigate underwater treasures, or escape enemies through water.

Algorithm Overview

A basic algorithm for swimming mechanics involves the following steps:

1. **Water Detection**: Detect when the player enters a water volume and toggle swimming mode accordingly.

2. **Adjust Movement Physics**: Change movement attributes like gravity, drag, and speed to mimic underwater motion.

3. **Manage Breath Meter**: Track time underwater, decreasing the breath meter or oxygen level until the player resurfaces.

4. **Movement Control**: Enable full directional control and swimming animations for fluid motion, allowing the player to ascend, descend, and move in any direction.

5. **Exit Water**: When the player leaves water, restore standard movement attributes and reset the breath meter.

Reviewing the Code

Listing 5-9 implements the ASwimmingCharacter class, managing swimming mechanics with SwimSpeed for movement, MaxBreathTime for breath control, and functions like StartSwimming(), StopSwimming(), and UpdateBreath() to handle water entry, exit, and breath depletion.

- **ASwimmingCharacter**: Manages swimming actions and properties
- **SwimSpeed**: Adjusts player speed while in water
- **MaxBreathTime**: Sets the maximum time a character can stay submerged
- **StartSwimming()/StopSwimming()**: Trigger swimming mode on water entry and exit
- **UpdateBreath()**: Tracks and decreases breath over time while underwater

Listing 5-9. SwimmingCharacter.h

```
#pragma once

#include "CoreMinimal.h"
#include "GameFramework/Character.h"
#include "SwimmingCharacter.generated.h"
```

```cpp
UCLASS()
class MYGAME_API ASwimmingCharacter : public ACharacter
{
    GENERATED_BODY()

public:
    ASwimmingCharacter();

protected:
    virtual void BeginPlay() override;

public:
    virtual void Tick(float DeltaTime) override;

    UPROPERTY(EditAnywhere, BlueprintReadWrite, Category = "Swimming")
    float SwimSpeed;

    UPROPERTY(EditAnywhere, BlueprintReadWrite, Category = "Swimming")
    float MaxBreathTime;

    UFUNCTION(BlueprintCallable, Category = "Swimming")
    void StartSwimming();

    UFUNCTION(BlueprintCallable, Category = "Swimming")
    void StopSwimming();

private:
    float BreathRemaining;
    bool bIsSwimming;

    // Breath management

    void DecreaseBreath();

    FTimerHandle BreathTimerHandle;
};
```

CHAPTER 5 CHARACTER MECHANICS

Listing 5-10 implements swimming mechanics, with `Tick()` updating breath levels and movement speed, `StartSwimming()` and `StopSwimming()` toggling the swimming state, and `UpdateBreath()` managing breath depletion and triggering events upon full depletion.

- **Tick()**: Runs every frame, updating breath levels and adjusting movement speed if in swimming mode
- **StartSwimming()/StopSwimming()**: Enable or disable swimming, setting the appropriate movement mode
- **UpdateBreath()**: Continuously reduces remaining breath time while underwater, eventually triggering events if breath is fully depleted

Listing 5-10. SwimmingCharacter.cpp

```cpp
#include "SwimmingCharacter.h"
#include "GameFramework/CharacterMovementComponent.h"
#include "TimerManager.h"

ASwimmingCharacter::ASwimmingCharacter()
{
    SwimSpeed = 300.0f;
    MaxBreathTime = 15.0f;
    BreathRemaining = MaxBreathTime;
    bIsSwimming = false;
}

void ASwimmingCharacter::BeginPlay()
{
    Super::BeginPlay();
}
```

CHAPTER 5 CHARACTER MECHANICS

```cpp
void ASwimmingCharacter::Tick(float DeltaTime)
{
    Super::Tick(DeltaTime);

    if (bIsSwimming)
    {
        GetCharacterMovement()->MaxWalkSpeed = SwimSpeed;
    }
}

void ASwimmingCharacter::StartSwimming()
{
    bIsSwimming = true;
    GetCharacterMovement()->SetMovementMode(
    EMovementMode::MOVE_Flying);

    // Start breath timer
    GetWorldTimerManager().SetTimer(BreathTimerHandle, this,
    &ASwimmingCharacter::DecreaseBreath, 0.5f, true);
}

void ASwimmingCharacter::StopSwimming()
{
    bIsSwimming = false;
    GetCharacterMovement()->SetMovementMode(
    EMovementMode::MOVE_Walking);
    BreathRemaining = MaxBreathTime;

    // Stop breath timer
    GetWorldTimerManager().ClearTimer(BreathTimerHandle);
}
```

CHAPTER 5   CHARACTER MECHANICS

```cpp
void ASwimmingCharacter::DecreaseBreath()
{
    if (bIsSwimming && BreathRemaining > 0.0f)
    {
        BreathRemaining = FMath::Max(BreathRemaining - 1.0f, 0.0f);

        if (BreathRemaining <= 0.0f)
        {
            // Handle breath depletion logic here (e.g., apply damage)
        }
    }
}
```

This section has explored the essentials of implementing swimming mechanics, covering movement physics, breath management, and the impact of swimming on gameplay. Properly integrated swimming systems can add both exploratory opportunities and dynamic challenges for players. In the next section, we'll cover climbing systems, diving into the mechanics that allow players to scale walls, ladders, and other vertical obstacles for expanded world traversal.

Climbing Mechanics

Climbing mechanics allow players to traverse vertical surfaces like walls, ladders, and cliffs, expanding movement options and adding depth to gameplay. Integrating climbing mechanics effectively requires specialized animations, physics, and environmental detection. Climbing adds an exciting layer of exploration and strategy, as players use it to access otherwise unreachable areas or avoid obstacles.

Basic Implementation

At its core, a climbing system involves

- **Surface Detection**: Identifying climbable surfaces when the player comes in contact with walls or ledges
- **Movement Restriction**: Adjusting player movement to align with the surface, allowing only vertical or lateral movement while climbing
- **Climbing Animations**: Triggering animations that represent climbing actions, such as hand grips and foot placements

To create a basic climbing mechanic, detect when the player interacts with a climbable surface, switch to climbing mode, and adjust movement inputs to allow vertical and horizontal movement on that surface.

Advanced Techniques

Enhancing climbing mechanics can make the experience feel more immersive and fluid. Some advanced techniques include

- **Edge Detection and Handholds**: Implementing handhold detection for more realistic climbing, where the character reaches specific points on the surface
- **Ledge Grabbing**: Allowing the player to grab onto ledges and pull themselves up, even if initially out of reach, enabling more flexible traversal
- **Stamina System**: Adding a stamina meter to limit climbing duration or actions, creating a realistic challenge, especially in intense climbing scenarios

- **Dynamic Transitions**: Smooth transitions between climbing, jumping, and dropping down from walls or ledges, enhancing movement fluidity
- **Obstacle Interaction**: Allowing characters to avoid or maneuver around obstacles while climbing, providing players with a more challenging experience

Practical Applications

Climbing mechanics are widely used across various game genres, such as

- **Adventure Games**: Players climb to reach elevated viewpoints, find hidden items, or solve environmental puzzles.
- **Action Games**: Climbing enables players to escape danger, access high ground for tactical advantages, or perform ambushes.
- **Platformers**: Climbing adds layers to movement challenges, giving players options to scale walls and navigate multilayered environments.

Algorithm Overview

A basic climbing algorithm involves the following steps:

1. **Surface Detection**: Detect when the player character is in contact with a climbable surface.
2. **Activate Climbing Mode**: Switch movement input handling to allow vertical and horizontal movement along the surface.

CHAPTER 5 CHARACTER MECHANICS

3. **Execute Climbing Animation**: Start appropriate animations for climbing, based on surface orientation and player position.

4. **Handle Transitions**: Allow the player to jump or drop off from the climbing state when appropriate.

5. **Exit Climbing Mode**: When the player leaves the surface, switch back to standard movement mode.

Reviewing the Code

Listing 5-11 defines the AClimbingCharacter class, which manages climbing mechanics. Key properties include ClimbSpeed for controlling climbing movement, bCanClimb for detecting climbable surfaces, and StartClimbing()/StopClimbing() to activate or deactivate climbing based on player input and surface interaction.

- **AClimbingCharacter**: Manages climbing actions and properties
- **ClimbSpeed**: Adjusts the player's climbing speed on surfaces
- **bCanClimb**: Tracks if a surface is detected as climbable
- **StartClimbing()/StopClimbing()**: Methods for toggling climbing mode based on player input and surface detection

Listing 5-11. ClimbingCharacter.h

```
#pragma once

#include "CoreMinimal.h"
#include "GameFramework/Character.h"
#include "ClimbingCharacter.generated.h"
```

CHAPTER 5   CHARACTER MECHANICS

```cpp
UCLASS()
class MYGAME_API AClimbingCharacter : public ACharacter
{
    GENERATED_BODY()
public:
    AClimbingCharacter();

protected:
    virtual void BeginPlay() override;

public:
    virtual void Tick(float DeltaTime) override;

    UPROPERTY(EditAnywhere, BlueprintReadWrite, Category = "Climbing")
    float ClimbSpeed; // Sets climbing speed

    UPROPERTY(EditAnywhere, BlueprintReadWrite, Category = "Climbing")
    bool bCanClimb; // Detects if a surface is climbable

    UFUNCTION(BlueprintCallable, Category = "Climbing")
    void StartClimbing();

    UFUNCTION(BlueprintCallable, Category = "Climbing")
    void StopClimbing();

private:
    bool bIsClimbing; // Determines if the character is currently climbing
};
```

CHAPTER 5 CHARACTER MECHANICS

Listing 5-12 implements climbing behavior, with StartClimbing() and StopClimbing() toggling climbing mode based on surface detection. It utilizes MOVE_Flying to enable unrestricted movement, making it well suited for climbing mechanics.

- **StartClimbing()/StopClimbing()**: Toggle climbing mode based on whether a climbable surface is detected.

- **MOVE_Flying**: Using the flying movement mode allows unrestricted movement in all directions, making it ideal for climbing mechanics.

Listing 5-12. ClimbingCharacter.cpp

```cpp
#include "ClimbingCharacter.h"
#include "GameFramework/CharacterMovementComponent.h"

AClimbingCharacter::AClimbingCharacter()
{
    ClimbSpeed = 200.0f;
    bIsClimbing = false;
    bCanClimb = false;
}
void AClimbingCharacter::Tick(float DeltaTime)
{
    Super::Tick(DeltaTime);

    if (bIsClimbing)
    {
        GetCharacterMovement()->MaxWalkSpeed = ClimbSpeed;
        // Apply climbing movement controls here
    }
}
```

CHAPTER 5   CHARACTER MECHANICS

```cpp
void AClimbingCharacter::StartClimbing()
{
    if (bCanClimb)
    {
        bIsClimbing = true;
        GetCharacterMovement()->SetMovementMode(MOVE_Flying);

        // Optional: Zero out velocity to prevent unintended drifting
        GetCharacterMovement()->Velocity = FVector::ZeroVector;

        // Optionally limit movement input to vertical axis only
        // You can set a flag to ignore MoveRight/Forward in your input handlers
    }
}
void AClimbingCharacter::StopClimbing()
{
    bIsClimbing = false;
    GetCharacterMovement()->SetMovementMode(
    EMovementMode::MOVE_Walking);
}
```

Climbing mechanics add an engaging, vertical dimension to gameplay, allowing players to explore and interact with environments more dynamically. By combining basic and advanced climbing features, developers can create an immersive experience that enriches player interaction and exploration. In the next section, we'll cover stealth mechanics.

Stealth Mechanics

Stealth mechanics introduce an element of strategy by allowing players to avoid detection, sneak past enemies, and complete objectives undetected. This mechanic can create tension and suspense, as players navigate through levels using cover, shadows, and distractions to stay hidden. Implementing stealth effectively involves balancing visibility, sound, and AI detection to create an immersive experience.

Key Elements of Stealth Mechanics

Stealth mechanics require specific systems to manage player detection and reactions:

- **Visibility Detection**: Determines if the player is in an enemy's line of sight, often factoring in distance, lighting, and obstacles.

- **Sound Detection**: Detects player-generated noise, such as footsteps or interacting with objects, which can alert enemies nearby.

- **AI Awareness States**: Enemy AI typically operates in different awareness states, from "idle" to "alerted" or "investigating" when the player is detected.

- **Cover System**: Allows players to hide behind objects or blend into shadows to avoid detection.

- **Distraction Tools**: Items or abilities like throwing rocks, setting traps, or making sounds to lure enemies away.

Basic Implementation

For a basic stealth system, a few core elements are necessary:

1. **Line of Sight Checks**: Use raycasting to determine if the enemy has a direct line of sight to the player, factoring in obstacles.

2. **Sound Radius**: Implement a radius around the player that produces sound based on movement, with stealthy actions creating less noise.

3. **AI State Management**: Code AI states to switch between idle, searching, and alert depending on visibility and sound.

4. **Cover and Concealment**: Create objects or areas where the player can hide, reducing visibility and noise.

Advanced Techniques

To enhance stealth gameplay, consider these advanced features:

- **Dynamic Lighting and Shadows**: Adjust enemy detection based on light levels in the environment. Darkness makes players harder to detect, while light exposes them.

- **Noise Levels**: Assign noise values to different actions, like running vs. walking or jumping, impacting the radius at which enemies detect the player.

- **Disguise and Camouflage**: Allow players to use disguises or blend into surroundings, giving them a chance to hide in plain sight or mislead enemies.

- **Stealth Abilities**: Add skills like crouching, silent movement, or temporary invisibility for short durations, allowing players to avoid detection more easily.

- **Enemy Patrol Patterns**: Create predictable enemy patrols to encourage players to time their movements and find openings in enemy lines.

Practical Applications

Stealth mechanics can be applied across many game genres, such as

- **Stealth-Action Games**: Players focus on sneaking past enemies, avoiding combat whenever possible.

- **Horror Games**: Stealth mechanics are often essential for survival, as players evade monsters rather than fight.

- **Adventure Games**: Stealth elements encourage strategic navigation in open worlds, letting players bypass challenges or reach hidden areas.

Algorithm Overview

A simple stealth algorithm involves the following steps:

1. **Line of Sight Detection**: Check if an enemy has a clear view of the player using raycasting from the enemy's eyes to the player.

2. **Sound Detection**: Define a sound radius for the player based on movement and actions, with enemies detecting the player when within this radius.

3. **AI State Switching**: Move enemy AI between idle, alert, and search states based on whether the player is detected visually or by sound.

4. **Cover Detection**: Allow players to enter areas or behind objects that reduce their visibility and sound output.

5. **Player Action Response**: Program player actions to affect stealth levels, allowing them to evade detection by crouching, hiding, or using distractions.

Reviewing the Code

Listing 5-13 defines the AStealthCharacter class, managing stealth mechanics through properties like StealthSoundRadius and LineOfSightRange and functions such as CheckForEnemies(), EnterStealthMode(), and ExitStealthMode() to detect threats and toggle stealth state.

- **AStealthCharacter**: Defines the player character's properties and functions for stealth
- **StealthSoundRadius**: Sets the radius around the character where sound is detectable
- **LineOfSightRange**: Sets the detection range for enemies
- **CheckForEnemies()**: Scans for enemies within range and line of sight
- **EnterStealthMode()/ExitStealthMode()**: Methods for toggling stealth mode based on player actions

Listing 5-13. StealthCharacter.h

```cpp
#pragma once

#include "CoreMinimal.h"
#include "GameFramework/Character.h"
#include "StealthCharacter.generated.h"

UCLASS()
class MYGAME_API AStealthCharacter : public ACharacter
{
    GENERATED_BODY()

public:
    AStealthCharacter();

protected:
    virtual void BeginPlay() override;

public:
    virtual void Tick(float DeltaTime) override;

    UPROPERTY(EditAnywhere, BlueprintReadWrite,
    Category = "Stealth")
    float StealthSoundRadius; // Sets the radius for sound detection

    UPROPERTY(EditAnywhere, BlueprintReadWrite,
    Category = "Stealth")
    float LineOfSightRange; // Sets the range of enemy vision

    UFUNCTION(BlueprintCallable, Category = "Stealth")
    void CheckForEnemies();

    UFUNCTION(BlueprintCallable, Category = "Stealth")
    void EnterStealthMode();
```

CHAPTER 5 CHARACTER MECHANICS

```
    UFUNCTION(BlueprintCallable, Category = "Stealth")
    void ExitStealthMode();

private:
    bool bIsStealthy; // Determines if the character is in
    stealth mode
};
```

Listing 5-14 implements the AStealthCharacter functionality, with Tick() continuously monitoring enemy detection during stealth, CheckForEnemies() evaluating enemy proximity and line of sight, and EnterStealthMode()/ExitStealthMode() toggling stealth state by modifying visibility and sound output.

- **CheckForEnemies()**: Logic to assess if enemies are within line of sight and alert range
- **EnterStealthMode()/ExitStealthMode()**: Toggles the player's stealth mode, adjusting their visibility and sound output accordingly

Listing 5-14. StealthCharacter.cpp

```
#include "StealthCharacter.h"
#include "GameFramework/CharacterMovementComponent.h"
#include "Kismet/KismetSystemLibrary.h"

AStealthCharacter::AStealthCharacter()
{
    StealthSoundRadius = 300.0f;
    LineOfSightRange = 1000.0f;
    bIsStealthy = false;
}
```

```cpp
void AStealthCharacter::Tick(float DeltaTime)
{
    Super::Tick(DeltaTime);

    if (bIsStealthy)
    {
        CheckForEnemies();
    }
}

void AStealthCharacter::CheckForEnemies()
{
    // Implement logic to check for enemies within LineOfSightRange
    // and determine if the player is detected based on visibility and sound
}

void AStealthCharacter::EnterStealthMode()
{
    bIsStealthy = true;
    // Adjust movement or visibility attributes for stealth
}

void AStealthCharacter::ExitStealthMode()
{
    bIsStealthy = false;
    // Revert movement or visibility attributes to normal
}
```

Stealth mechanics add depth to gameplay, allowing players to choose a non-confrontational approach and strategize to avoid detection. By carefully balancing visibility, sound, and AI responses, developers can create tense and rewarding stealth experiences. In the next section, we will dive into **combat mechanics**, exploring systems and techniques for delivering responsive, exciting, and immersive combat experiences that keep players engaged in high-stakes action.

Combat Mechanics

Combat mechanics serve as one of the most pivotal systems in any action-oriented game. A well-designed combat system not only allows players to interact with enemies but also delivers a satisfying experience of skill-based progression, responsiveness, and tactical decision-making. Effective combat mechanics integrate elements such as timing, player control, damage calculations, and visual and sound feedback to create a dynamic experience that can range from fast-paced brawling to strategic, deliberate encounters.

Basic Combat Mechanics

At its core, a combat system should provide players with the means to execute basic attack, block, and dodge actions, allowing them to feel in control of their character and combat outcome. Here are the essentials:

- **Attack**: The player initiates an action to damage an enemy. Basic attacks can be mapped to different input buttons, each triggering a distinct animation and damage output.
- **Block/Parry**: Blocking reduces or nullifies incoming damage, while a parry requires precise timing, potentially leaving the enemy open to a counterattack.
- **Dodge**: Dodging allows the player to avoid enemy attacks by quickly moving out of harm's way. It is often associated with an invincibility window to ensure effective use.

These foundational mechanics can be combined to create a basic combat experience where players have a range of offensive and defensive options.

Advanced Combat Techniques

Once the basics are in place, advanced techniques can expand and deepen the combat experience. Some examples include

- **Combo Chains**: Allows players to link a series of attacks into fluid, continuous movements. Combos can reward players with increased damage, faster strikes, or even special moves at the end of the chain.

- **Stamina Management**: A stamina bar limits the player's ability to execute actions like attacks, blocks, or dodges. Managing stamina effectively becomes a tactical component, as running out leaves the player vulnerable.

- **Special Attacks and Abilities**: Beyond standard moves, players may access unique abilities or powerful attacks that consume special resources or have cooldowns. These can add variety and depth to combat strategy.

- **Hit Reactions and Knockbacks**: Both players and enemies should have visual and physical reactions to being hit. Knockbacks, stuns, or stagger states add realism and allow for creative combat flow.

Advanced combat mechanics provide a wider array of strategies and add depth to gameplay, catering to different playstyles and skill levels.

CHAPTER 5   CHARACTER MECHANICS

Practical Applications

Combat mechanics vary across genres and can serve different roles in gameplay:

- **Action RPGs**: These games often employ complex combo systems, skill trees, and special attacks, allowing players to choose combat styles and tactics based on character class and abilities.
- **Shooter Games**: For shooter games with melee elements, the combat system may be simplified but highly responsive, focusing on quick kill maneuvers or close-quarter attacks.
- **Fighting Games**: Fighting games often focus on combo timing, advanced blocking, and counter techniques, giving players a detailed system to master.
- **Stealth-Action Games**: Combat here may emphasize silent takedowns, quick escapes, and strategic engagement to avoid overwhelming odds.

Algorithm Overview

A combat system typically involves several key components working in harmony. Here's an outline of how such a system might function:

1. **Input Handling**: Captures player input to execute attacks, dodges, or defensive maneuvers
2. **Animation Control**: Triggers relevant animations for attacks, blocks, or dodges based on input and character state

CHAPTER 5   CHARACTER MECHANICS

3. **Hit Detection**: Determines whether the player's attack connects with an enemy and registers the hit

4. **Damage Calculation**: Calculates the damage output based on the player's attack power, enemy defense, and any critical hit multipliers

5. **Health Adjustment**: Updates health values for players or enemies based on successful hits, blocks, or healing actions

6. **Feedback and Effects**: Provides visual and auditory cues to indicate a successful hit, missed attack, or blocked damage

Reviewing the Code

Listing 5-15 defines the ACombatManager class, managing core combat mechanics such as attacking, blocking, and dodging. Key elements include AttackDamage for base damage, StaminaCost for action management, and functions like PerformAttack(), BlockAttack(), and Dodge() to handle player combat interactions.

- **ACombatManager**: Manages core combat functions like attacking, blocking, and dodging

- **AttackDamage**: Determines the base damage inflicted with each attack

- **StaminaCost**: Specifies the amount of stamina used per action, affecting player endurance

- **PerformAttack()**: Executes a standard attack, calculating hit registration and damage

CHAPTER 5 CHARACTER MECHANICS

- **BlockAttack()**: Enables blocking, reducing incoming damage
- **Dodge()**: Implements dodge functionality, allowing players to evade attacks momentarily

Listing 5-15. CombatManager.h

```cpp
#pragma once

#include "CoreMinimal.h"
#include "GameFramework/Actor.h"
#include "CombatManager.generated.h"

UCLASS()
class MYGAME_API ACombatManager : public AActor
{
    GENERATED_BODY()

public:
    ACombatManager();

protected:
    virtual void BeginPlay() override;

public:
    virtual void Tick(float DeltaTime) override;

    UPROPERTY(EditAnywhere, BlueprintReadWrite,
    Category = "Combat")
    float AttackDamage;   // Base damage dealt per attack

    UPROPERTY(EditAnywhere, BlueprintReadWrite,
    Category = "Combat")
    float StaminaCost;   // Stamina consumed per action
```

CHAPTER 5 CHARACTER MECHANICS

```
UFUNCTION(BlueprintCallable, Category = "Combat")
void PerformAttack();

UFUNCTION(BlueprintCallable, Category = "Combat")
void BlockAttack();

UFUNCTION(BlueprintCallable, Category = "Combat")
void Dodge();
};
```

Listing 5-16 represents a cpp file which implements core combat actions, with PerformAttack() checking conditions before applying damage and reducing stamina, BlockAttack() enabling damage reduction through blocking, and Dodge() allowing evasion while consuming half the stamina of a standard attack.

Listing 5-16. CombatManager.cpp

```
#include "CombatManager.h"

// Constructor
ACombatManager::ACombatManager()
{
    PrimaryActorTick.bCanEverTick = true;
    AttackDamage = 25.0f;
    StaminaCost = 10.0f;
}

// BeginPlay: Initializes Combat Settings
void ACombatManager::BeginPlay()
{
    Super::BeginPlay();
}
```

CHAPTER 5   CHARACTER MECHANICS

```cpp
// Tick: Updates per frame
void ACombatManager::Tick(float DeltaTime)
{
    Super::Tick(DeltaTime);
}

// PerformAttack: Executes attack and deals damage if successful
void ACombatManager::PerformAttack()
{
    if (CanAttack())
    {
        DealDamage(AttackDamage);
        ReduceStamina(StaminaCost);
        PlayAttackAnimation();
    }
}

// BlockAttack: Reduces damage while blocking
void ACombatManager::BlockAttack()
{
    if (CanBlock())
    {
        ActivateBlock();
        PlayBlockAnimation();
    }
}

// Dodge: Evades incoming attacks
void ACombatManager::Dodge()
{
    if (CanDodge())
```

CHAPTER 5   CHARACTER MECHANICS

```
    {
        Evade();
        ReduceStamina(StaminaCost / 2);
        PlayDodgeAnimation();
    }
}
```

This section has covered the fundamentals of creating combat mechanics in a game, focusing on delivering responsive and engaging interactions for players. Combat mechanics are crucial for crafting an immersive experience, making each encounter meaningful and allowing for diverse strategies.

To enhance the realism and impact of combat actions, developers can integrate motion warping—a powerful system that dynamically adjusts a character's position and rotation while playing animation montages. By using motion warping, actions like dodging, attacking, or executing finishing moves can be visually and physically synchronized with targets in the world, providing fluid, cinematic motion that feels responsive and intentional.

With a solid understanding of core combat mechanics and motion-driven enhancements, the next section will dive into health and stamina systems. These systems are essential for adding depth to gameplay, directly influencing player choices, pacing, and risk management during combat scenarios.

Health and Stamina System

Health and stamina systems are fundamental to maintaining balance and pacing in gameplay. While health determines a character's survivability, stamina introduces limits to physical actions, adding a strategic element that encourages players to manage resources wisely. Together, these systems create a framework for assessing risk, encouraging cautious gameplay, and adding layers of strategy to player decisions.

CHAPTER 5   CHARACTER MECHANICS

Basic Usage of Health and Stamina Systems

A straightforward health and stamina system serves as a baseline for any action or adventure game. In these systems

- **Health** acts as the player's "life bar." When health reaches zero, the character dies or loses the game.
- **Stamina** governs physical activities like sprinting, dodging, attacking, and other energy-intensive actions.

Basic systems typically involve

1. **Health Bar**: Visualizes the player's remaining health, often displayed as a bar or number.
2. **Stamina Bar**: Displays the player's stamina, which depletes with certain actions and gradually regenerates over time.
3. **Regeneration Mechanism**: Stamina typically regenerates quickly when not in use, while health regeneration, if enabled, is slower and may require items or skills.

These systems ensure a balance of actions, preventing players from overusing powerful moves and encouraging strategic play.

Advanced Techniques

Advanced health and stamina systems introduce unique features, such as

1. **Stamina-Based Attack Limits**: Certain moves or combos may cost more stamina, encouraging players to consider the stamina cost before using a powerful attack.

2. **Fatigue System**: Extended low stamina levels can reduce overall stamina regeneration or limit certain actions, like sprinting or jumping, until stamina recovers.

3. **Health Conditions**: Players may suffer temporary effects (like bleeding, poisoning, or armor reduction) based on health status, requiring medical items or skills to manage.

4. **Dynamic Health and Stamina Regeneration**: Factors like time of day, environmental hazards, or specific power-ups can influence regeneration rates.

5. **Environmental Influences**: Different environments may affect stamina consumption, such as higher stamina drain in cold areas or when climbing slopes.

These techniques add depth to the health and stamina systems, integrating them into the game's overall strategy and enhancing player immersion.

Practical Applications

Health and stamina systems are commonly used in

- **Survival Games**: Health and stamina management is crucial for survival, as activities like gathering, hunting, and combat are stamina-intensive.
- **Action RPGs**: Stamina systems limit combat and movement, encouraging strategic pacing and balanced use of attacks and dodges.

- **Simulation and Realism-Focused Games**: In games where realistic physical exertion is important, stamina simulates real-world fatigue.

Algorithm Overview

The following is a high-level overview of the core systems involved in managing health and stamina:

1. **Health Manager**: Tracks the player's current health level, handles damage input, and triggers player death if health reaches zero

2. **Stamina Manager**: Monitors the current stamina level, handles depletion and regeneration, and restricts specific actions when stamina is low

3. **Regeneration Logic**: Manages health and stamina recovery over time, with adjustable rates based on in-game factors or player status

4. **User Interface (UI)**: Displays the health and stamina status through bars, numbers, or icons, giving players real-time feedback

Reviewing the Code

Listing 5-17 manages player attributes with MaxHealth and CurrentHealth for health tracking, MaxStamina and CurrentStamina for stamina management, and StaminaRegenRate for recovery. Key functions include ApplyDamage() to reduce health, ConsumeStamina() to deduct stamina during actions, and RegenerateStamina() to restore stamina over time.

CHAPTER 5 CHARACTER MECHANICS

- **MaxHealth** and **CurrentHealth**: Store and track the player's health

- **MaxStamina** and **CurrentStamina**: Manage the player's stamina

- **StaminaRegenRate**: Controls the rate at which stamina regenerates

- **ApplyDamage()**: Decreases health based on the damage amount

- **ConsumeStamina()**: Reduces stamina based on the stamina cost of the action

- **RegenerateStamina()**: Increases stamina over time if not at max capacity

Listing 5-17. HealthStaminaManager.h

```
#pragma once

#include "CoreMinimal.h"
#include "GameFramework/Actor.h"
#include "HealthStaminaManager.generated.h"

UCLASS()
class MYGAME_API AHealthStaminaManager : public AActor
{
    GENERATED_BODY()

public:
    AHealthStaminaManager();

protected:
    virtual void BeginPlay() override;
```

CHAPTER 5 CHARACTER MECHANICS

```cpp
public:
    virtual void Tick(float DeltaTime) override;

    UPROPERTY(EditAnywhere, BlueprintReadWrite, Category = "Health")
    float MaxHealth;

    UPROPERTY(BlueprintReadOnly, Category = "Health")
    float CurrentHealth;

    UPROPERTY(EditAnywhere, BlueprintReadWrite, Category = "Stamina")
    float MaxStamina;

    UPROPERTY(BlueprintReadOnly, Category = "Stamina")
    float CurrentStamina;

    UPROPERTY(EditAnywhere, BlueprintReadWrite, Category = "Regeneration")
    float StaminaRegenRate;

    UFUNCTION(BlueprintCallable, Category = "Health")
    void ApplyDamage(float DamageAmount);

    UFUNCTION(BlueprintCallable, Category = "Stamina")
    void ConsumeStamina(float StaminaCost);
private:
    // Timer-based stamina regen
    FTimerHandle StaminaRecoverTimer;

    UFUNCTION()
    void StaminaRecovery(); // Called periodically by the timer
};
```

CHAPTER 5   CHARACTER MECHANICS

Listing 5-18 handles real-time updates to player stats, with Tick() calling RegenerateStamina() each frame, ApplyDamage() reducing health and checking for death, ConsumeStamina() deducting stamina based on actions, and RegenerateStamina() gradually restoring stamina when below maximum.

- **Tick()**: Calls **RegenerateStamina** each frame to restore stamina over time
- **ApplyDamage()**: Reduces health and checks if the player has died
- **ConsumeStamina()**: Reduces stamina based on action costs
- **RegenerateStamina()**: Gradually restores stamina if it's below the maximum

Listing 5-18. HealthStaminaManager.cpp

```
#include "HealthStaminaManager.h"
#include "TimerManager.h"

AHealthStaminaManager::AHealthStaminaManager()
{
    PrimaryActorTick.bCanEverTick = true;

    MaxHealth = 100.0f;
    CurrentHealth = MaxHealth;

    MaxStamina = 100.0f;
    CurrentStamina = MaxStamina;

    StaminaRegenRate = 5.0f;
}
```

CHAPTER 5   CHARACTER MECHANICS

```
void AHealthStaminaManager::BeginPlay()
{
    Super::BeginPlay();

    // Start timer to recover stamina every 0.5 seconds
    GetWorldTimerManager().SetTimer(StaminaRecoverTimer, this,
    &AHealthStaminaManager::StaminaRecovery, 0.5f, true);
}

void AHealthStaminaManager::Tick(float DeltaTime)
{
    Super::Tick(DeltaTime);

    // No stamina regen here anymore - handled by timer
}

void AHealthStaminaManager::ApplyDamage(float DamageAmount)
{
    CurrentHealth -= DamageAmount;
    if (CurrentHealth <= 0.0f)
    {
        CurrentHealth = 0.0f;
        // TODO: Trigger player death logic
    }
}

void AHealthStaminaManager::ConsumeStamina(float StaminaCost)
{
    if (CurrentStamina >= StaminaCost)
    {
        CurrentStamina -= StaminaCost;
    }
}
```

```
void AHealthStaminaManager::StaminaRecovery()
{
    if (CurrentStamina < MaxStamina)
    {
        CurrentStamina = FMath::Min(CurrentStamina +
        (StaminaRegenRate * 0.5f), MaxStamina);
    }
}
```

Health and stamina systems are essential for balancing action with endurance, offering players a resource they must carefully manage for survival and effective combat. This section has covered both basic and advanced mechanics, along with their practical applications across various game genres. You now have a foundation for implementing health and stamina systems that add depth to your gameplay. In the next section, we'll look at **skill trees and abilities**, exploring how these elements enhance character progression and customize playstyles.

Skill Trees and Abilities

Skill trees and abilities are core systems that enhance character progression in many role-playing and action games. They allow players to customize their playstyle by selecting from a range of powers, talents, or attributes. A well-designed skill tree system not only provides depth but also encourages replayability, as players experiment with different builds and approaches to challenges.

Basic Structure of Skill Trees

A basic skill tree consists of nodes connected by branches, where each node represents a specific ability, upgrade, or stat increase. These nodes are organized hierarchically, often with prerequisites that must be unlocked before certain skills can be accessed.

Core Elements of a Skill Tree

1. **Nodes**: Each node represents a specific skill or ability. These can range from simple passive boosts (e.g., increased health regeneration) to complex active abilities (e.g., a powerful attack).
2. **Branches**: Groups of connected nodes that lead to different pathways. A branch might represent a certain specialization, such as combat, magic, or crafting.
3. **Prerequisites**: Some skills or abilities can only be unlocked after the player has unlocked certain other abilities or reached a specific level.
4. **Unlocking and Progression**: Players typically gain experience points (XP) or other resources as they progress through the game. These points are spent to unlock or upgrade abilities within the skill tree.

Types of Abilities and Skills

Abilities in a skill tree can be broadly divided into **active** and **passive** abilities:

1. **Active Abilities**
   - These are abilities that require direct input from the player, such as using a special attack, casting a spell, or performing an evasive maneuver.
   - Examples include
     - **Magic Spells**: Fireball, ice shield, teleportation
     - **Combat Techniques**: Power strikes, combo moves, defensive stances
     - **Utility Skills**: Hacking, lockpicking, or crafting

2. **Passive Abilities**
   - These abilities offer ongoing benefits without direct input, improving overall stats, resistances, or enhancing certain actions automatically.
   - Examples include
     - **Health Regeneration**: Gradually restores health over time
     - **Damage Boost**: Increases damage dealt with specific weapons or abilities
     - **Speed Boost**: Increases movement speed or reduces stamina consumption

Advanced Skill Tree Techniques

Advanced skill tree systems can be made more dynamic by incorporating the following elements:

1. **Branching Paths**
   - Instead of a single linear progression, skill trees can offer multiple paths for players to take, with each path focusing on a different aspect of the character (e.g., offense, defense, stealth, or magic). This adds replayability and allows for more specialized builds.
2. **Multi-branch Specializations**
   - Some games feature hybrid skill trees, where players can choose to combine abilities from multiple skill categories. For instance, a character might be able to mix both magical and physical combat abilities, creating unique playstyles.

3. **Skill Synergy**
   - Some skills work better when combined with others. For example, a character who specializes in stealth might unlock a set of abilities that synergize with an offensive combo skill, allowing for more strategic combat approaches.

4. **Skill Tiers**
   - Higher-tier abilities often require players to fully upgrade lower-tier ones. This progressive unlocking ensures that powerful abilities remain balanced within the game's progression system.

5. **Character Traits and Affinities**
   - In addition to basic skills, some games incorporate traits, affinities, or personal qualities that affect how the character progresses in the skill tree. These might represent certain moral choices or personality traits that align with different abilities (e.g., a "warrior" trait boosting physical combat or a "sage" trait enhancing magical abilities).

Practical Applications

Skill trees and abilities are most used in

- **Role-Playing Games (RPGs)**: Allowing players to define their character's role, such as a tank, healer, or damage-dealer
- **Action and Adventure Games**: Enhancing combat and exploration by unlocking new abilities or techniques

- **Survival Games**: Offering skill upgrades that aid in gathering resources, combat, and survival
- **Strategy Games**: Allowing for tactical flexibility by unlocking various units, technologies, or abilities

Algorithm Overview

A typical skill tree system involves managing skill progression, unlocking abilities based on conditions, and providing feedback to the player. Here's an overview of how the algorithm functions:

1. **Experience and Leveling System**: Players earn experience points through various actions (e.g., combat, quests, exploration). These points are used to unlock skills in the tree.
2. **Skill Unlocking**: Abilities are unlocked when certain prerequisites are met (e.g., reaching a certain level or unlocking a lower-tier ability).
3. **Active Ability Activation**: Active skills are triggered based on player input, with cooldowns or resource management (e.g., stamina, mana).
4. **Passive Effects**: Passive abilities are always active once unlocked, affecting the player's stats or abilities continuously.

Reviewing the Code

Here's an example of how a simple skill tree and ability system can be implemented in Unreal Engine using C++.

CHAPTER 5　CHARACTER MECHANICS

Listing 5-19 manages the skill system with AvailableSkills for all unlockable abilities, UnlockedSkills for tracking acquired ones, and functions like UnlockSkill() to grant new skills and UseSkill() to activate them during gameplay.

- **AvailableSkills**: A list of all available skills that can be unlocked
- **UnlockedSkills**: A list of skills that the player has already unlocked
- **UnlockSkill()**: A function to unlock a given skill when the player has met the conditions
- **UseSkill()**: A function to activate a skill

Listing 5-19. SkillTreeManager.h

```
#pragma once

#include "CoreMinimal.h"
#include "GameFramework/Actor.h"
#include "SkillTreeManager.generated.h"

UCLASS()
class MYGAME_API ASkillTreeManager : public AActor
{
    GENERATED_BODY()

public:
    ASkillTreeManager();

protected:
    virtual void BeginPlay() override;

public:
    virtual void Tick(float DeltaTime) override;
```

CHAPTER 5　CHARACTER MECHANICS

```
    PROPERTY(EditAnywhere, BlueprintReadWrite,
    Category="SkillTree")
    TArray<class USkill*> AvailableSkills;

    UPROPERTY(BlueprintReadOnly, Category="SkillTree")
    TArray<class USkill*> UnlockedSkills;

    UFUNCTION(BlueprintCallable, Category="SkillTree")
    void UnlockSkill(class USkill* Skill);

    UFUNCTION(BlueprintCallable, Category="SkillTree")
    void UseSkill(class USkill* Skill);
};
```

Listing 5-20 implements skill system logic, with UnlockSkill() verifying and adding new skills to the unlocked list and UseSkill() executing the corresponding action if the skill has been unlocked.

- **UnlockSkill()**: Checks if the skill is already unlocked and adds it to the unlocked list if not
- **UseSkill()**: Executes the skill if it has been unlocked, allowing the player to perform actions associated with the skill

Listing 5-20. SkillTreeManager.cpp

```
#include "SkillTreeManager.h"
#include "Skill.h"

ASkillTreeManager::ASkillTreeManager()
{
    PrimaryActorTick.bCanEverTick = true;
}
```

CHAPTER 5　CHARACTER MECHANICS

```cpp
void ASkillTreeManager::BeginPlay()
{
    Super::BeginPlay();
}

void ASkillTreeManager::Tick(float DeltaTime)
{
    Super::Tick(DeltaTime);
}

void ASkillTreeManager::UnlockSkill(USkill* Skill)
{
    if (Skill && !UnlockedSkills.Contains(Skill))
    {
        UnlockedSkills.Add(Skill);
        // Trigger any additional actions, like UI updates
    }
}

void ASkillTreeManager::UseSkill(USkill* Skill)
{
    if (UnlockedSkills.Contains(Skill))
    {
        // Apply the skill's effect (e.g., cast a spell or
        boost stats)
    }
}
```

Skill trees and abilities are essential systems for character progression, offering players the freedom to customize and specialize their characters according to their preferred playstyle. By implementing skill trees and abilities effectively, you create an engaging and rewarding experience that keeps players invested in their characters' development.

Next, we will explore character customization, a key feature that allows players to personalize their avatars, tailoring their appearance, equipment, and even their abilities to match their unique preferences and gameplay style.

Character Customization

Character customization is one of the most engaging aspects of modern game design, allowing players to shape their in-game avatars according to their preferences. This feature provides the opportunity to adjust visual aspects such as appearance, clothing, and gear, as well as deeper modifications that influence gameplay, such as selecting specific abilities or equipment that complement the player's preferred playstyle.

Basic Usage

In its simplest form, character customization allows players to modify visual features, enabling them to alter aspects such as

- **Facial Features**: Adjusting facial structure, skin tone, eyes, hair color, and style
- **Body Type**: Customizing the body shape and size, sometimes with more detailed options like muscle definition or height
- **Clothing and Armor**: Equipping different outfits or armor pieces that may vary in aesthetics and functionality
- **Accessories**: Adding additional details such as tattoos, scars, glasses, or other adornments

These options are generally handled through a user-friendly interface, such as a character creation screen, where players can scroll through menus or use sliders to fine-tune their avatar's appearance. Some games also feature preset customization options, offering different character archetypes with a set of predefined features.

Advanced Customization

For deeper gameplay immersion, advanced character customization can extend beyond appearance and into aspects that directly affect gameplay mechanics:

- **Skill Selection:** Players may choose from a range of special abilities, determining how their character performs in combat, exploration, or problem-solving. These can include unique attacks, passive bonuses, or special actions like stealth or magic.

- **Attributes and Stats:** Players may have the option to invest points in various attributes such as strength, agility, intelligence, and more. This allows the character to become more specialized in certain areas of the game, influencing how they interact with the world.

- **Equipment and Loadouts:** Offering a wide array of weapons, tools, and armor gives players the flexibility to customize their combat style. Some games allow players to select specific gear that not only changes the character's appearance but also provides practical benefits such as enhanced defense or specialized attacks.

- **Dialogue and Behavior Choices**: Some RPGs and adventure games enable players to choose how their characters interact with NPCs, which can alter the storyline and how the game world responds to the player.

Practical Applications

Character customization is used in many genres, each applying it in unique ways:

- **Role-Playing Games (RPGs)**: In RPGs, character customization is often tied to both narrative and gameplay. It allows players to create a personal connection to the protagonist and make gameplay decisions that reflect their choices.

- **Survival Games**: In survival games, customization might be essential for developing a character's skill set or appearance based on the items they have gathered or the challenges they've faced.

- **First-Person and Third-Person Shooters**: In shooter games, customization often extends to weapon loadouts, giving players control over the types of weapons they use and how they are equipped for each mission or battle.

- **Fighting Games**: Customization in fighting games can influence both aesthetic features (such as skins or outfits) and combat abilities, allowing players to tailor their fighter to suit their strategy or style.

CHAPTER 5   CHARACTER MECHANICS

Algorithm Overview

To implement character customization, you must create a system that supports multiple layers of personalization. Here's an overview of the primary systems involved:

1. **Appearance System**: Manages all visual aspects of character customization, from facial features to clothing. This system works with a variety of assets (textures, meshes, animations) to reflect the changes the player makes.

2. **Stat/Attribute System**: Tracks the character's abilities and progress, allowing the player to increase their stats or unlock new abilities based on their choices.

3. **Equipment System**: Handles the player's inventory and equipped items, ensuring that any gear they select influences both the character's appearance and gameplay mechanics.

4. **Dialogue/Behavior System**: If applicable, this system manages how the player's choices influence dialogue options and interactions with NPCs, altering the narrative and gameplay accordingly.

Reviewing the Code

Listings 5-21 and 5-22 define the ACharacterCustomizationManager class, which handles character appearance and equipment customization. It includes CharacterMesh for skeletal mesh references, AvailableSkinTones for selectable visual options, and SelectedWeapon to track chosen equipment. Functions like ApplyAppearanceChanges() and ApplyWeaponSelection() apply these customizations based on player input.

Listing 5-21. CharacterCustomizationManager.h

```cpp
#pragma once

#include "CoreMinimal.h"
#include "GameFramework/Actor.h"
#include "CharacterCustomizationManager.generated.h"

UCLASS()
class MYGAME_API ACharacterCustomizationManager : public AActor
{
    GENERATED_BODY()

public:
    ACharacterCustomizationManager();

protected:
    virtual void BeginPlay() override;

public:
    virtual void Tick(float DeltaTime) override;

    UPROPERTY(EditAnywhere, BlueprintReadWrite, Category =
    "Appearance")
    class USkeletalMeshComponent* CharacterMesh;
    // Character's mesh

    UPROPERTY(EditAnywhere, BlueprintReadWrite, Category =
    "Appearance")
    TArray<class UMaterialInterface*> AvailableSkinTones;
    // Available skin tones for the character

    UPROPERTY(EditAnywhere, BlueprintReadWrite,
    Category = "Equipment")
    class AWeapon* SelectedWeapon;
    // Selected weapon by the player
```

CHAPTER 5   CHARACTER MECHANICS

```cpp
    UPROPERTY(EditAnywhere, BlueprintReadWrite,
    Category = "Stats")
    int32 Strength; // Strength stat for character

    UPROPERTY(EditAnywhere, BlueprintReadWrite,
    Category = "Stats")
    int32 Agility; // Agility stat for character

    UFUNCTION(BlueprintCallable, Category = "Customization")
    void ApplyAppearanceChanges(int32 SkinToneIndex);

    UFUNCTION(BlueprintCallable, Category = "Customization")
    void ApplyWeaponSelection(AWeapon* Weapon);
};
```

Listing 5-22. CharacterCustomizationManager.cpp

```cpp
#include "CharacterCustomizationManager.h"
#include "Components/SkeletalMeshComponent.h"
#include "Engine/World.h"
#include "Weapon.h"

// Constructor: Sets default values
ACharacterCustomizationManager::ACharacterCustomizationManager()
{
    PrimaryActorTick.bCanEverTick = true;
    Strength = 10;  // Default value
    Agility = 10;   // Default value
}

// BeginPlay: Called when the game starts
void ACharacterCustomizationManager::BeginPlay()
{
    Super::BeginPlay();
}
```

CHAPTER 5   CHARACTER MECHANICS

```cpp
// Tick: Called every frame
void ACharacterCustomizationManager::Tick(float DeltaTime)
{
    Super::Tick(DeltaTime);
}

// ApplyAppearanceChanges: Changes the skin tone based on the
player's selection void ACharacterCustomizationManager::
ApplyAppearanceChanges(int32 SkinToneIndex)
{
    if (AvailableSkinTones.IsValidIndex(SkinToneIndex))
    {
        CharacterMesh->SetMaterial(0, AvailableSkinTones[
        SkinToneIndex]);
    }
}

// ApplyWeaponSelection: Updates the selected weapon
void ACharacterCustomizationManager::ApplyWeaponSelection(
AWeapon* Weapon)
{
    SelectedWeapon = Weapon;
}
```

In this chapter, we have explored the critical elements of **character customization**, offering players the ability to personalize their in-game avatar's appearance, equipment, and abilities. This system enhances player immersion, allowing for a deeper connection with the character and offering a tailored gameplay experience. Whether it's visual adjustments, skill selection, or gear customization, character customization gives players the freedom to adapt the gameplay to their unique style.

CHAPTER 5   CHARACTER MECHANICS

Summary

With the foundational understanding of character customization in place, we now transition to combat mechanics. In the next chapter, we will explore the various aspects of combat, from basic melee and ranged combat to the complexities of boss fights, special moves, and combat AI. Understanding these mechanics is essential for creating engaging, dynamic combat systems that challenge players and keep them invested in the action.

CHAPTER 6

Combat Mechanics

Combat mechanics form the heart of many action-oriented games, where player skill and strategy directly influence the outcome of encounters. Combat mechanics are essential for creating an exciting, challenging, and rewarding gameplay experience. Whether players are engaging in intense hand-to-hand melee battles, using powerful ranged weapons, or casting devastating spells, combat systems play a crucial role in keeping players engaged and invested in the game world. In this chapter, we'll break down the various combat systems—from the basics of melee and ranged combat to more complex systems like magic, combo attacks, and AI behavior—that help shape dynamic and satisfying combat encounters.

At their core, combat mechanics involve the player interacting with enemies and the environment using a variety of attack types, defensive maneuvers, and strategic options. The basic components include melee attacks, ranged attacks, blocking, dodging, and the management of health and stamina during combat. These systems work together to create a combat loop where the player must balance offense and defense, positioning, and resource management.

In this chapter, we'll cover the foundational elements like basic melee and ranged combat, as well as defensive actions like blocking and dodging, to ensure your combat system feels responsive and intuitive. Understanding how these core systems function allows you to establish a strong combat foundation.

CHAPTER 6   COMBAT MECHANICS

As combat mechanics evolve, they grow in complexity to offer players a wider array of strategic options and depth. Advanced systems like magic and spellcasting introduce a layer of variety to combat, requiring players to manage magical resources and use elemental strategies. Meanwhile, more intricate combo systems enable players to chain together attacks, creating fluid and dynamic combat sequences that reward skillful timing and precision.

AI-controlled enemies also play a vital role in combat mechanics, with their behavior needing to reflect different tactics based on the situation. Hit detection and damage calculation become increasingly important as combat grows more complex, ensuring that attacks feel impactful and consistent.

Boss fights, in particular, require careful consideration of mechanics and AI behavior, offering players unique and challenging encounters that go beyond standard combat. These battles may introduce environmental challenges, specific attack patterns, or multiple phases, requiring players to adapt their strategy throughout the encounter.

In this chapter, we will explore these more advanced applications, delving into how systems like magic, combo chains, and boss fights enhance combat depth and provide a richer gameplay experience. You'll also learn how to create enemy AI that reacts intelligently to player actions, further refining the player's combat experience.

By the end of this chapter, you will have a comprehensive understanding of combat mechanics, equipped to implement a dynamic and engaging combat system that keeps players challenged and invested in every fight. Whether it's a simple brawl or a climactic boss battle, you'll be able to design combat systems that are as rewarding to master as they are to play.

Melee Combat

Melee combat is one of the most fundamental and engaging combat systems in many games, particularly in action and RPG genres. It involves direct physical combat between the player character and enemies using close-range weapons or unarmed attacks. The goal is to deliver a satisfying and dynamic combat experience where players must think strategically about timing, positioning, and attack choices to overcome foes. Whether the player is using a sword, a hammer, or their fists, melee combat mechanics provide a foundation for action-packed gameplay.

Basic Usage of Melee Combat

At the core of melee combat is the concept of close-range attacks that require the player to be in proximity to the enemy. The basic elements of melee combat include

- **Attack Types**: A variety of attack options like light, heavy, and charged strikes that differ in speed, power, and impact
- **Combo System**: A series of chained attacks that allow the player to perform complex moves and deliver higher damage
- **Blocking and Parrying**: Defensive actions that enable the player to deflect or absorb enemy attacks, reducing or avoiding damage
- **Stamina Management**: A system to limit the frequency of attacks and defensive actions, forcing players to manage their energy during combat

These core mechanics are typically controlled through simple inputs like buttons for light or heavy attacks and mechanics for defense, ensuring that players can control their character's actions fluidly while engaging in close combat.

Advanced Techniques

Advanced melee combat mechanics go beyond basic attack and defense to incorporate a wide range of abilities that add depth and strategy. Some of these techniques include

- **Combo Chains**: Combos allow players to chain multiple attacks together seamlessly, adding complexity to the combat system. Advanced combos can unlock special moves, dealing devastating damage.

- **Special Attacks**: Unique moves that the player can trigger under certain conditions, such as finishing moves, area-of-effect (AoE) attacks, or attacks that break enemy defense.

- **Counterattacks**: A system where players can wait for the perfect moment to strike back after an enemy attack, dealing extra damage and gaining an advantage.

- **Knockbacks and Staggering**: These mechanics provide physical feedback by affecting the enemy's position or movement. Successful hits might stagger an enemy or send them flying, creating opportunities for follow-up attacks.

By incorporating these advanced techniques, the player's mastery of melee combat becomes crucial to overcoming tougher enemies and winning battles.

Practical Applications

Melee combat mechanics are used across a wide range of games, from hack-and-slash action titles to tactical RPGs. Depending on the game's genre, melee combat might emphasize different aspects:

- **Hack-and-Slash Games**: Focus on fast-paced, fluid combat where players can perform continuous combos and manage multiple enemies at once
- **Action RPGs**: Emphasize strategy, with players needing to manage attack types, special abilities, and timing to overcome tougher opponents and bosses
- **Fighting Games**: Center around one-on-one combat, requiring precise input for each attack and counter, with a focus on skill and reflexes

Algorithm Overview

To develop effective melee combat mechanics, several systems are integrated:

1. **Input System**: Captures player input (usually through a button press or a combination of presses) and converts it into actions, such as light or heavy attacks
2. **Attack Animations**: Handles the character's movements during each attack, ensuring that the animation matches the action and provides feedback to the player

3. **Damage Calculation**: Determines how much damage an attack will deal, factoring in attack power, enemy defense, and whether the hit was critical or blocked

4. **Stamina/Resource Management**: Manages the player's stamina or other resources that govern how often they can perform actions, ensuring players cannot spam attacks without consequence

Reviewing the Code

Below is an implementation of a basic melee combat system, including basic attacks and a stamina management system.

Listing 6-1 defines a melee combat controller in the header file, managing core combat mechanics such as LightAttack(), HeavyAttack(), and Block(). Key properties include MaxStamina and StaminaRegenRate, while RegenerateStamina() handles stamina recovery over time.

- **MaxStamina**: The maximum stamina the player can have
- **StaminaRegenRate**: The rate at which stamina is regenerated after performing actions
- **LightAttack/HeavyAttack/Block:** Functions to execute specific combat actions
- **RegenerateStamina**: A function that gradually restores stamina over time

Listing 6-1. MeleeCombatController.h

```
#pragma once

#include "CoreMinimal.h"
#include "GameFramework/Character.h"
#include "InputAction.h"
#include "MeleeCombatController.generated.h"

UCLASS()
class MYGAME_API AMeleeCombatController : public ACharacter
{
    GENERATED_BODY()
public:
    AMeleeCombatController();

protected:
    virtual void SetupPlayerInputComponent(class
    UInputComponent* PlayerInputComponent) override;

public:
    virtual void Tick(float DeltaTime) override;

    UPROPERTY(EditAnywhere, BlueprintReadWrite, Category =
    "Combat")
    float MaxStamina;    // The maximum stamina available for
    the player

    UPROPERTY(EditAnywhere, BlueprintReadWrite, Category =
    "Combat")
    float StaminaRegenRate;    // The rate at which stamina
    regenerates

    UPROPERTY(VisibleAnywhere, BlueprintReadOnly, Category =
    "Combat")
```

```cpp
float CurrentStamina;  // The current stamina the player
has available

UFUNCTION(BlueprintCallable, Category = "Combat")
void LightAttack();

UFUNCTION(BlueprintCallable, Category = "Combat")
void HeavyAttack();

UFUNCTION(BlueprintCallable, Category = "Combat")
void Block();

UFUNCTION(BlueprintCallable, Category = "Combat")
void RegenerateStamina(float DeltaTime);

UPROPERTY(EditAnywhere, BlueprintReadOnly, Category = 
"Input")
class UInputAction* LightAttackAction;

UPROPERTY(EditAnywhere, BlueprintReadOnly, Category = 
"Input")
class UInputAction* HeavyAttackAction;

UPROPERTY(EditAnywhere, BlueprintReadOnly, Category = 
"Input")
class UInputAction* BlockAction;
};
```

Listing 6-2 implements stamina-based combat functionality, with LightAttack() and HeavyAttack() executing attacks while reducing stamina and RegenerateStamina() gradually restoring stamina when the player is not actively engaging in combat actions.

- **LightAttack() and HeavyAttack()**: These functions execute the respective attacks, reducing the player's stamina accordingly.

- **RegenerateStamina()**: This function regenerates the player's stamina over time when the player is not actively performing actions like attacking or blocking.

Listing 6-2. MeleeCombatController.cpp

```cpp
#include "MeleeCombatController.h"
#include "Components/InputComponent.h"
#include "EnhancedInputComponent.h"
#include "EnhancedInputSubsystems.h"

AMeleeCombatController::AMeleeCombatController()
{
    PrimaryActorTick.bCanEverTick = true;
    MaxStamina = 100.0f;
    StaminaRegenRate = 5.0f;
    CurrentStamina = MaxStamina;
}

void AMeleeCombatController::SetupPlayerInputComponent(
UInputComponent* PlayerInputComponent)
{
    Super::SetupPlayerInputComponent(PlayerInputComponent);

    if (UEnhancedInputComponent* EnhancedInput = Cast
    <UEnhancedInputComponent>(PlayerInputComponent))
    {
        EnhancedInput->BindAction(LightAttackAction,
        ETriggerEvent::Started, this, &AMeleeCombatController::
        LightAttack);
        EnhancedInput->BindAction(HeavyAttackAction,
        ETriggerEvent::Started, this, &AMeleeCombatController::
        HeavyAttack);
```

CHAPTER 6   COMBAT MECHANICS

```cpp
        EnhancedInput->BindAction(BlockAction, ETriggerEvent::
        Started, this, &AMeleeCombatController::Block);
    }
}
void AMeleeCombatController::Tick(float DeltaTime)
{
    Super::Tick(DeltaTime);

    // Regenerate stamina over time
    RegenerateStamina(DeltaTime);
}
void AMeleeCombatController::LightAttack()
{
    if (CurrentStamina >= 10.0f)
    {
        // Execute light attack logic here
        CurrentStamina -= 10.0f;   // Deduct stamina for
        light attack
    }
}
void AMeleeCombatController::HeavyAttack()
{
    if (CurrentStamina >= 20.0f)
    {
        // Execute heavy attack logic here
        CurrentStamina -= 20.0f;   // Deduct stamina for
        heavy attack
    }
}
```

```cpp
void AMeleeCombatController::Block()
{
    // Execute block logic here
}

void AMeleeCombatController::RegenerateStamina(float DeltaTime)
{
    if (CurrentStamina < MaxStamina)
    {
        CurrentStamina += StaminaRegenRate * DeltaTime;
        if (CurrentStamina > MaxStamina)
        {
            CurrentStamina = MaxStamina;
        }
    }
}
```

In this section, you've learned the fundamentals of melee combat mechanics, from basic attacks to stamina management. These mechanics are crucial in making combat engaging and strategic, where players must balance offensive and defensive actions to succeed. In the next section, we will explore ranged combat mechanics typically involving the use of weapons like guns, bows, crossbows, or magical projectiles.

Ranged Combat

Ranged combat is a core gameplay mechanic found in many action and strategy games, providing players with the ability to engage enemies from a distance. This mechanic typically involves the use of weapons like guns, bows, crossbows, or magical projectiles and often requires different strategies compared to melee combat. In ranged combat, the player must account for factors such as aiming, projectile speed, ammo management, and reload time, creating a dynamic combat experience. The use of ranged weapons can give players tactical advantages, such as attacking from cover, controlling the battlefield from a distance, or focusing on specific weak points of enemies.

Basic Usage

In its most basic form, ranged combat allows players to attack enemies from a distance, usually by aiming and firing a weapon. Key features of ranged combat mechanics include

- **Aiming and Shooting**: The player aims a weapon at the target and fires, typically requiring precise control of the crosshair or aiming reticle.

- **Projectile Speed and Trajectory**: Many ranged weapons feature projectiles that travel at varying speeds or follow specific trajectories, such as a curved path for arrows or gravity-affected bullets.

- **Ammo Management**: Ranged weapons often require ammunition, adding an element of resource management. Players must keep track of their available shots and reload when necessary.

- **Reloading**: To maintain a continuous assault, players may need to reload their weapons after firing a certain number of shots.

These mechanics work together to create a satisfying and strategic ranged combat system where players balance offensive actions with careful resource management and aiming precision.

Advanced Techniques

Advanced ranged combat mechanics can deepen gameplay and add complexity to how the player interacts with the environment and enemies. Some advanced techniques include

- **Cover System:** Allows players to take cover behind objects to shield themselves from enemy fire. Players can peek or blind fire from cover, encouraging tactical positioning.

- **Aimed Shots and Critical Hits:** Targeting specific body parts—such as the head or limbs—can reward precision with bonus damage, stagger effects, or dismemberment mechanics.

- **Weapon Customization:** Letting players attach scopes, silencers, extended magazines, or different ammo types introduces progression and personal combat style.

- **Environmental Interactions:** Wind, weather, gravity, or surface material can influence projectile trajectory or visibility, challenging players to adapt their aim and tactics.

- **Movement-Based Enhancements:** Incorporating **leaning, proning, sprinting, walking, crouching**, and **mantling** enables fluid traversal and stealthy or evasive combat behavior. These mechanics can impact accuracy, visibility, or detection, making movement itself a combat tool.

By adding these advanced features, developers can make ranged combat more engaging and strategic, providing players with more control and variety in how they approach combat situations.

CHAPTER 6   COMBAT MECHANICS

Practical Applications

Ranged combat mechanics are used across many game genres, each utilizing different aspects of this system depending on the game's focus:

- **First-Person Shooters (FPS)**: Precision aiming and rapid-fire actions are key components, with an emphasis on fast reactions and accuracy.

- **Third-Person Action Games**: Combines aiming and dodging mechanics with a focus on positioning and strategic attacks from a distance.

- **RPGs and Strategy Games**: Often features customizable or magical ranged attacks, with mechanics focusing on resource management, cooldowns, and tactical decision-making.

Algorithm Overview

To develop an effective ranged combat system, the following components are typically implemented:

1. **Input System**: Captures player input for aiming, firing, and reloading, ensuring smooth control over ranged actions

2. **Projectile System**: Calculates the trajectory and speed of projectiles, factoring in variables such as gravity, range, and velocity

3. **Weapon and Ammo Management**: Handles ammunition tracking, reloading, and switching between weapons

CHAPTER 6 COMBAT MECHANICS

4. **Hit Detection and Damage Calculation**: Ensures that projectiles hit their target and apply appropriate damage based on factors such as critical hits or damage multipliers

Reviewing the Code

Listing 6-3 defines key shooting mechanics, including FireRate to control firing speed, MaxAmmo and CurrentAmmo for ammo management, and functions FireWeapon() and ReloadWeapon() to handle shooting logic and reloading behavior.

- **FireRate**: Controls how quickly the player can fire the weapon
- **MaxAmmo** and **CurrentAmmo**: Manage the weapon's ammunition, allowing the player to reload when ammo runs out
- **FireWeapon()**: A function that triggers the shooting action, checking for available ammo and applying the necessary logic for firing
- **ReloadWeapon()**: Handles reloading when ammo is depleted, resetting the ammo count to its maximum

Listing 6-3. RangedCombatController.h

```
#pragma once

#include "CoreMinimal.h"
#include "GameFramework/Character.h"
#include "RangedCombatController.generated.h"
```

CHAPTER 6   COMBAT MECHANICS

```cpp
UCLASS()
class MYGAME_API ARangedCombatController : public ACharacter
{
    GENERATED_BODY()

public:
    ARangedCombatController();

protected:
    virtual void SetupPlayerInputComponent(class
    UInputComponent* PlayerInputComponent) override;
    virtual void BeginPlay() override;

public:
    virtual void Tick(float DeltaTime) override;

    UPROPERTY(EditAnywhere, BlueprintReadWrite, Category =
    "Combat")
    float FireRate;   // Rate of fire for ranged weapons

    UPROPERTY(EditAnywhere, BlueprintReadWrite, Category =
    "Combat")
    int32 MaxAmmo;   // Maximum ammo for the weapon

    UPROPERTY(VisibleAnywhere, BlueprintReadOnly, Category =
    "Combat")
    int32 CurrentAmmo;   // Current ammo available

    UPROPERTY(EditAnywhere, BlueprintReadWrite, Category =
    "Combat")
    float ReloadDuration;   // Time it takes to reload
    the weapon

    UFUNCTION(BlueprintCallable, Category = "Combat")
    void FireWeapon();
```

CHAPTER 6   COMBAT MECHANICS

```
    UFUNCTION(BlueprintCallable, Category = "Combat")
    void ReloadWeapon();

private:
    FTimerHandle ReloadTimerHandle;
    void FinishReload();

    bool bIsReloading;
};
```

Listing 6-4 implements core shooting functionality, with FireWeapon() checking for sufficient ammo before reducing the count and executing firing logic and ReloadWeapon() resetting the ammo to MaxAmmo, allowing the player to continue shooting.

- **FireWeapon()**: Checks if there is enough ammo to fire. If there is, it reduces the ammo count and handles the logic for firing the weapon.

- **ReloadWeapon()**: Reloads the weapon by resetting the ammo count to its maximum value, ensuring the player can continue firing.

Listing 6-4. RangedCombatController.cpp

```
#include "RangedCombatController.h"
#include "Components/InputComponent.h"
#include "TimerManager.h"

ARangedCombatController::ARangedCombatController()
{
    PrimaryActorTick.bCanEverTick = true;

    FireRate = 0.5f;
    MaxAmmo = 30;
    CurrentAmmo = MaxAmmo;
```

491

CHAPTER 6 COMBAT MECHANICS

```
    ReloadDuration = 2.0f;
    bIsReloading = false;
}

void ARangedCombatController::BeginPlay()
{
    Super::BeginPlay();
}

void ARangedCombatController::Tick(float DeltaTime)
{
    Super::Tick(DeltaTime);
}

void ARangedCombatController::SetupPlayerInputComponent(
UInputComponent* PlayerInputComponent)
{
    Super::SetupPlayerInputComponent(PlayerInputComponent);

    PlayerInputComponent->BindAction("Fire", IE_Pressed, this,
    &ARangedCombatController::FireWeapon);
    PlayerInputComponent->BindAction("Reload", IE_Pressed,
    this, &ARangedCombatController::ReloadWeapon);
}

void ARangedCombatController::FireWeapon()
{
    if (bIsReloading)
        return;

    if (CurrentAmmo > 0)
    {
        // Fire the weapon and subtract one from the ammo count
        CurrentAmmo--;
```

```
        // TODO: Add shooting logic (e.g., projectile spawn,
        sound, etc.)
    }
    else
    {
        // Ammo is depleted, trigger reload
        ReloadWeapon();
    }
}

void ARangedCombatController::ReloadWeapon()
{
    if (bIsReloading || CurrentAmmo == MaxAmmo)
        return;

    bIsReloading = true;

    // TODO: Play reload animation or sound here

    // Start reload timer
    GetWorldTimerManager().SetTimer(ReloadTimerHandle, this,
    &ARangedCombatController::FinishReload, ReloadDuration,
    false);
}

void ARangedCombatController::FinishReload()
{
    CurrentAmmo = MaxAmmo;
    bIsReloading = false;

    // TODO: Trigger reload complete feedback here (UI,
    sound, etc.)
}
```

In this section, you've explored the fundamentals of ranged combat, from basic aiming and shooting mechanics to more advanced techniques like cover systems and weapon customization. Implementing these features creates a dynamic and immersive combat experience, allowing players to engage in strategic and varied combat scenarios. In the next section, we'll delve into magic and spells, a layer of complexity to combat and exploration, offering players a variety of abilities that can enhance both offensive and defensive strategies.

Magic and Spells

Magic and spells are integral elements in many games, especially in fantasy genres. They introduce a layer of complexity to combat and exploration, offering players a variety of abilities that can enhance both offensive and defensive strategies. Magic systems typically feature a range of spells with different effects, such as elemental attacks, healing, buffing, and debuffing. Spells can be cast using various methods, such as incantations, gestures, or through the use of magical objects. The implementation of magic systems involves designing the rules for casting, cooldowns, resource management, and how these magical abilities interact with the game world.

Basic Magic System Mechanics

The basic mechanics of magic systems often revolve around the following key elements:

- **Casting Spells**: Players can cast spells by selecting them from their spellbook or hotbar and activating them. This usually involves a cooldown period to prevent overuse of powerful abilities.

- **Magic Resource Management**: Many games introduce a resource like mana or energy that is required to cast spells. Players must manage this resource, either by regenerating it or using items to restore it during gameplay.

- **Spell Effects**: Spells can have a wide range of effects, from simple damage-dealing attacks (fireball, lightning strike) to more complex abilities, such as healing, teleportation, or summoning creatures.

These fundamental mechanics lay the groundwork for a more intricate magic system that can be expanded with additional features like spell customization, elemental properties, and magical equipment.

Advanced Magic System Features

An advanced magic system can significantly enrich gameplay by offering deeper customization and strategy. Some advanced features might include

- **Elemental Magic**: Spells tied to specific elements, such as fire, ice, or lightning, each with distinct effects and synergies. For example, fire magic might deal damage over time, while ice spells slow down enemies.

- **Combo Spells**: The ability for players to combine different spells for more powerful effects. For instance, casting an ice spell followed by a lightning spell might freeze enemies and then electrocute them.

- **Spell Upgrades and Customization**: Some games allow players to improve their spells over time, either by gaining experience or through magical items. This could include increased damage, reduced mana cost, or new effects.

- **Magical Artifacts**: Objects such as wands, staffs, or rings that enhance spellcasting, providing benefits like increased mana regeneration or unique spell effects.

These advanced systems introduce more strategic depth, allowing players to experiment with different spell combinations and find the most effective tactics for each situation.

Practical Applications in Different Genres

Magic systems vary greatly depending on the genre of the game. Each genre might implement magic mechanics differently to suit its gameplay style:

- **RPGs**: Role-playing games often feature deep and customizable magic systems, where players can learn new spells, upgrade their abilities, and manage resources like mana. Spells are typically used for combat, healing, and exploration.

- **MMOs:** In multiplayer online games, magic plays a crucial role in both combat and social interactions. Players can specialize in different types of magic (damage-dealing, healing, or support spells), often contributing to team strategies.

- **Strategy Games**: Magic can be used as a tactical element in strategy games, with players using spells to manipulate the battlefield, enhance their units, or hinder their enemies.

- **Action/Adventure Games**: In these games, magic often serves as a means of enhancing combat or solving environmental puzzles, such as using wind magic to move obstacles or fire magic to burn through barriers.

CHAPTER 6   COMBAT MECHANICS

Algorithm Overview for Magic System

To develop an effective magic system, the following components are typically implemented:

1. **Spell Casting System**: Handles player input for casting spells, such as selecting the spell, casting the spell, and managing cooldowns

2. **Mana or Resource System**: Manages the amount of mana (or other resources) required to cast spells, including regeneration rates and the effects of using up all available resources

3. **Spell Effect System**: Defines the effects of spells, including damage, area of effect, debuffs, buffs, and environmental interactions

4. **Cooldown and Resource Recharge**: Implements cooldowns and resource recharge mechanisms, ensuring that players cannot spam powerful spells indefinitely

Reviewing the Code

Below is an example of a basic magic system implementation, focusing on casting spells, managing mana, and applying spell effects.

Listing 6-5 defines the core structure for a magic system, including MaxMana and CurrentMana for resource management, SpellList for available spells, and functions CastSpell() and RegenerateMana() to handle spellcasting logic and mana recovery.

- **MaxMana** and **CurrentMana**: Variables that manage the player's mana resources. The player can use spells as long as they have enough mana.

Chapter 6 Combat Mechanics

- **SpellList**: An array that stores the available spells that the player can cast.

- **CastSpell()**: Function that handles the logic for casting a selected spell, checking for available mana and applying the spell effect.

- **RegenerateMana()**: Function to regenerate mana over time or through certain in-game actions.

Listing 6-5. MagicSystemController.h

```
#pragma once

#include "CoreMinimal.h"
#include "GameFramework/Actor.h"
#include "MagicSystemController.generated.h"

UCLASS()
class MYGAME_API AMagicSystemController : public AActor
{
    GENERATED_BODY()
public:
    AMagicSystemController();

protected:
    virtual void BeginPlay() override;

public:
    virtual void Tick(float DeltaTime) override;

    UPROPERTY(EditAnywhere, BlueprintReadWrite, Category = "Magic")
    float MaxMana;  // Maximum mana for the player
```

```cpp
UPROPERTY(VisibleAnywhere, BlueprintReadOnly,
Category = "Magic")
float CurrentMana;   // Current mana available

UPROPERTY(EditAnywhere, BlueprintReadWrite,
Category = "Magic")
TArray<TSubclassOf<class ASpell>> SpellList;
// List of spells available for casting

UFUNCTION(BlueprintCallable, Category = "Magic")
void CastSpell(int32 SpellIndex);

UFUNCTION(BlueprintCallable, Category = "Magic")
void RegenerateMana(float Amount);
};
```

Listing 6-6 implements spellcasting functionality, with CastSpell() verifying sufficient mana before executing the spell's effect and RegenerateMana() gradually restoring mana over time or under specific conditions to support continued spell usage.

- **CastSpell()**: Handles the logic for casting a spell, checking if the player has enough mana, and applying the spell's effect
- **RegenerateMana()**: Restores mana over time or based on certain conditions, ensuring the player can continue to cast spells after replenishing their resources

Listing 6-6. MagicSystemController.cpp

```cpp
#include "MagicSystemController.h"
#include "Spell.h"
#include "Engine/World.h"
#include "GameFramework/Actor.h"
```

CHAPTER 6 COMBAT MECHANICS

```cpp
AMagicSystemController::AMagicSystemController()
{
    PrimaryActorTick.bCanEverTick = true;

    MaxMana = 100.0f;
    CurrentMana = MaxMana;
}

void AMagicSystemController::BeginPlay()
{
    Super::BeginPlay();
}

void AMagicSystemController::Tick(float DeltaTime)
{
    Super::Tick(DeltaTime);
}

void AMagicSystemController::CastSpell(int32 SpellIndex)
{
    if (CurrentMana <= 0 || !SpellList.IsValidIndex(SpellIndex))
        return;

    // Set spawn location/rotation (e.g., from player or
    controller location)
    FVector SpawnLocation = GetActorLocation() +
    GetActorForwardVector() * 100.f; // In front of player
    FRotator SpawnRotation = GetActorRotation();

    // Spawn the spell actor
    ASpell* SelectedSpell = GetWorld()->SpawnActor<ASpell>(
        SpellList[SpellIndex],
        SpawnLocation,
        SpawnRotation
    );
```

CHAPTER 6   COMBAT MECHANICS

```
    if (SelectedSpell)
    {
        // Cast the spell and subtract mana
        SelectedSpell->CastSpell();
        CurrentMana = FMath::Clamp(CurrentMana -
        SelectedSpell->GetManaCost(), 0.0f, MaxMana);
    }
}
void AMagicSystemController::RegenerateMana(float Amount)
{
    CurrentMana = FMath::Clamp(CurrentMana + Amount, 0.0f,
    MaxMana);
}
```

In this section, we've explored the basics of magic systems, from simple spellcasting and resource management to advanced features like elemental magic and spell customization. These systems not only enhance gameplay by offering diverse abilities but also encourage strategic thinking and resource management. The magic system's complexity can vary depending on the game's genre, but its core principles remain the same—offering players powerful tools to overcome challenges. In the next section, we'll dive into **combat AI**, focusing on how enemies react to the player's actions and how AI can challenge and adapt to the player's strategies.

Combat AI

Combat AI is a crucial component of many games, especially in action, RPG, and strategy genres, as it governs how enemies behave and react during combat. Effective combat AI ensures that enemies pose a challenge, adapt to the player's tactics, and provide a dynamic and engaging combat experience. Combat AI typically involves decision-making processes that allow enemies to choose actions based on the player's behavior, the environment, and their own abilities.

Core Components of Combat AI

The core components of a combat AI system can be broken down into several key areas:

- **Enemy Behavior States**: Combat AI often uses a finite state machine (FSM) or similar system to manage different states of an enemy, such as idle, patrol, attack, evade, or retreat. Each state has specific behaviors associated with it.

- **Pathfinding and Navigation**: Combat AI needs to navigate the environment to chase, dodge, or retreat from the player. Pathfinding algorithms, such as A* (A-star), help the AI move around obstacles and follow the player effectively.

- **Decision-Making**: AI must make decisions about which actions to take based on various factors, including the player's position, health, proximity to the enemy, and available resources. This often involves complex decision trees or behavior trees that evaluate different conditions and choose the best action.

- **Combat Tactics**: Enemies should adapt to the player's combat style, such as using different attacks based on the player's position, distance, or health. More advanced AI systems can even use tactics like flanking, grouping up with allies, or setting up ambushes.

Decision-Making in Combat AI

Effective combat AI requires a well-designed decision-making process. The simplest approach is a reactive model, where the AI performs specific actions in response to player actions. However, more advanced systems use a combination of the following:

- **Behavior Trees**: Behavior trees allow AI to execute complex sequences of actions based on different conditions. For example, an AI might first check if it has line of sight to the player. If true, it will evaluate whether the player is within attack range. If not, the AI might decide to close the distance before attempting an attack.

- **Finite State Machines (FSMs)**: FSMs are simpler but effective for combat AI. Enemies transition between different states (idle, alert, attacking) based on set conditions. For example, if an enemy's health drops below a certain threshold, it may switch to a "retreat" state.

- **Utility Systems**: A utility-based system assigns values to different actions, with the AI selecting the one with the highest value. This approach allows for more varied and unpredictable behaviors, as the AI weighs the benefits of different actions, such as attacking, retreating, or healing.

Pathfinding and Movement

Pathfinding is another critical component in combat AI. It ensures that enemies can move toward the player, avoid obstacles, and maintain tactical positioning during combat. The most common pathfinding algorithm is A*, which uses a grid-based approach to find the shortest path between two points while avoiding obstacles.

- **Chasing the Player**: AI should be able to intelligently chase the player, calculating the best path while avoiding obstacles and dynamically adjusting its route if the player changes position.

- **Evading**: In certain situations, enemies may need to retreat or move to a safer position. An AI can use pathfinding to find an optimal escape route when it is outmatched or low on health.

Combat AI and Adaptation

Advanced combat AI doesn't just react to player actions; it also adapts and learns. This can be achieved through systems such as

- **Adaptive AI**: Some games feature AI that learns from the player's actions, adjusting its tactics over time. For example, if the player frequently uses a particular spell or ability, the enemy AI might start to counteract it by using specific evasive maneuvers or protective spells.

- **Tactical AI**: Tactical AI is more concerned with how enemies interact with each other to create a challenging experience for the player. This can include flanking, calling for reinforcements, or coordinating attacks with multiple enemies to overwhelm the player.

Reviewing the Code

Below is an example of a basic combat AI system that uses finite state machines (FSMs) to handle different behaviors, such as idle, attacking, and evading. It also includes a basic pathfinding setup for chasing the player.

Listing 6-7 defines enemy AI behavior, including Health for tracking enemy vitality, bPlayerInRange to detect proximity to the player, and flags bCanAttack and bCanEvade to control combat decisions. The ChangeState() function manages transitions between AI behavior states.

- **Health**: Represents the enemy's health, which determines if it should retreat or attack
- **bPlayerInRange**: A boolean that checks if the player is within the enemy's attack range
- **bCanAttack** and **bCanEvade**: Flags that control whether the enemy is in a state to attack or evade based on its health or proximity to the player
- **ChangeState()**: Changes the AI's behavior state, such as switching from idle to attacking or evading

Listing 6-7. EnemyAIController.h

```
#pragma once

#include "CoreMinimal.h"
#include "GameFramework/Actor.h"
#include "EnemyAIController.generated.h"

UCLASS()
class MYGAME_API AEnemyAIController : public AActor
{
    GENERATED_BODY()

public:
    AEnemyAIController();

protected:
    virtual void BeginPlay() override;
```

```cpp
public:
    virtual void Tick(float DeltaTime) override;

    UPROPERTY(EditAnywhere, BlueprintReadWrite,
    Category = "AI")
    float Health;

    UPROPERTY(EditAnywhere, BlueprintReadWrite,
    Category = "AI")
    bool bPlayerInRange;

    UPROPERTY(EditAnywhere, BlueprintReadWrite,
    Category = "AI")
    bool bCanAttack;

    UPROPERTY(EditAnywhere, BlueprintReadWrite,
    Category = "AI")
    bool bCanEvade;

    UFUNCTION(BlueprintCallable, Category = "AI")
    void ChangeState(FString NewState);
private:
    FString CurrentState;
};
```

Listing 6-8 implements enemy AI decision-making based on player proximity and health status. Using a simple state system, the AI chooses to attack, evade, or remain idle. The ChangeState() method ensures smooth transitions between these behavior states.

- The AI checks for player proximity and health status to decide whether to attack, evade, or remain idle.

- It uses a simple state system to switch between behaviors. If the player is close, and the enemy's health is low, the AI will evade; otherwise, it will attack.

CHAPTER 6　COMBAT MECHANICS

- The **ChangeState()** method ensures that the AI switches states smoothly.

Listing 6-8. EnemyAIController.cpp

```
#include "EnemyAIController.h"
#include "Kismet/GameplayStatics.h"

AEnemyAIController::AEnemyAIController()
{
    PrimaryActorTick.bCanEverTick = true;
    Health = 100.0f;
    bPlayerInRange = false;
    bCanAttack = true;
    bCanEvade = true;
    CurrentState = "Idle";
}

void AEnemyAIController::BeginPlay()
{
    Super::BeginPlay();
}

void AEnemyAIController::Tick(float DeltaTime)
{
    Super::Tick(DeltaTime);

    // Check for player proximity
    AActor* Player = UGameplayStatics::GetPlayerCharacter(
    GetWorld(), 0);
    if (Player)
    {
        FVector PlayerLocation = Player->GetActorLocation();
        FVector EnemyLocation = GetActorLocation();
```

```cpp
        float Distance = FVector::Dist(PlayerLocation,
        EnemyLocation);

        if (Distance < 500.0f) // Player is within range
        {
            bPlayerInRange = true;
        }
        else
        {
            bPlayerInRange = false;
        }

        // Decision making based on health and proximity
        if (bPlayerInRange)
        {
            if (Health < 30.0f && bCanEvade)
            {
                ChangeState("Evading");
            }
            else if (bCanAttack)
            {
                ChangeState("Attacking");
            }
        }
        else
        {
            ChangeState("Idle");
        }
    }
}
```

CHAPTER 6 COMBAT MECHANICS

```
void AEnemyAIController::ChangeState(FString NewState)
{
    if (CurrentState != NewState)
    {
        CurrentState = NewState;

        if (CurrentState == "Attacking")
        {
            // Execute attacking behavior (e.g.,
            animation, damage)
        }
        else if (CurrentState == "Evading")
        {
            // Execute evading behavior (e.g., moving away
            from player)
        }
        else if (CurrentState == "Idle")
        {
            // Execute idle behavior (e.g., patrolling or
            standing still)
        }
    }
}
```

Alternative Approach Using Behavior Trees

Listings 6-9A and 6-10A implement a custom Behavior Tree task node that allows an AI character to move toward a target actor (typically the player). This task retrieves the target from the Blackboard and commands the AI to move to the specified location using `MoveToActor()`.

- The UBTTask_MoveToPlayer class inherits from UBT-TaskNode, making it compatible with Unreal's Behavior Tree system.

- The TargetActorKey property defines the Blackboard key used to fetch the target actor.

- The ExecuteTask() function retrieves the AI controller and Blackboard data, casts the target actor, and instructs the AI to move to it using Unreal's pathfinding.

- If no valid target is found or the controller is invalid, the task fails. Otherwise, it completes successfully.

Listing 6-9A. BTTask_MoveToPlayer.h

```cpp
#pragma once

#include "CoreMinimal.h"
#include "BehaviorTree/BTTaskNode.h"
#include "BTTask_MoveToPlayer.generated.h"

UCLASS()
class MYGAME_API UBTTask_MoveToPlayer : public UBTTaskNode
{
    GENERATED_BODY()

public:
    UBTTask_MoveToPlayer();

    virtual EBTNodeResult::Type ExecuteTask(UBehaviorTreeComponent& OwnerComp, uint8* NodeMemory) override;

protected:
    UPROPERTY(EditAnywhere, Category = "Blackboard")
    struct FBlackboardKeySelector TargetActorKey;
};
```

Listing 6-10A. BTTask_MoveToPlayer.cpp

```cpp
#include "BTTask_MoveToPlayer.h"
#include "AIController.h"
#include "BehaviorTree/BlackboardComponent.h"
#include "GameFramework/Actor.h"

UBTTask_MoveToPlayer::UBTTask_MoveToPlayer()
{
    NodeName = "Move To Player";
    bNotifyTick = false;

    TargetActorKey.AddObjectFilter(this, GET_MEMBER_
    NAME_CHECKED(UBTTask_MoveToPlayer, TargetActorKey),
    AActor::StaticClass());
}

EBTNodeResult::Type UBTTask_MoveToPlayer::ExecuteTask(
UBehaviorTreeComponent& OwnerComp, uint8* NodeMemory)
{
    AAIController* AICon = OwnerComp.GetAIOwner();
    if (!AICon)
    {
        return EBTNodeResult::Failed;
    }

    UBlackboardComponent* BlackboardComp = OwnerComp.Get
    BlackboardComponent();
    AActor* Target = Cast<AActor>(BlackboardComp->
    GetValueAsObject(TargetActorKey.SelectedKeyName));

    if (!Target)
    {
        return EBTNodeResult::Failed;
    }
```

```
    AICon->MoveToActor(Target, 5.0f);
    return EBTNodeResult::Succeeded;
}
```

Combat AI plays an essential role in enhancing gameplay by creating dynamic and challenging interactions between the player and enemies. By utilizing systems like finite state machines, behavior trees, and adaptive tactics, developers can craft AI that feels intelligent, responsive, and unpredictable. The next section will focus on hit detection and response, which directly influence how attacks are recognized and how the game reacts to those attacks.

Hit Detection and Response

Hit detection and response are critical aspects of combat systems in games, directly influencing how attacks are recognized and how the game reacts to those attacks. This process ensures that combat feels impactful and immersive, making players feel as though their actions are having a tangible effect on the world around them.

Understanding Hit Detection

Hit detection refers to the mechanics that determine whether an attack successfully hits an enemy or another character in the game. Depending on the game's design, this can be based on different systems, such as

- **Pixel-Perfect Detection**: Often used in 2D games, pixel-perfect hit detection involves checking if the pixels of a projectile, weapon, or character overlap with those of the target. It's highly accurate but can be computationally expensive.

- **Bounding Box or Sphere Collision**: This is a more common method in 3D games. The character or object is surrounded by a box or sphere, and collisions are detected based on the intersection of these volumes. It's computationally efficient but less accurate than pixel-perfect detection.

- **Raycasting**: Raycasting involves firing an invisible "ray" from the attacking entity toward the target to detect whether a collision occurs along the ray's path. This method is especially useful for ranged attacks or projectiles.

Raycasting Techniques in Unreal Engine

Unreal Engine provides several powerful trace functions for combat hit detection:

- **Line Trace** (LineTraceSingleByChannel): A straight-line ray from one point to another. Perfect for bullets, lasers, or precise melee strikes

  GetWorld()->LineTraceSingleByChannel(HitResult, Start, End, ECC_Visibility);

- **Sphere Trace** (SphereTraceSingleByChannel): Similar to Line Trace but with a radius, making it ideal for spells, AoE attacks, or detecting near misses

  GetWorld()->SweepSingleByChannel(HitResult, Start, End, FQuat::Identity, ECC_GameTraceChannel1, FCollisionShape::MakeSphere(Radius));

- **Capsule Trace** (`CapsuleTraceSingleByChannel`): A capsule-shaped trace—commonly used for detecting melee swings or character movement overlaps

  `GetWorld()->SweepSingleByChannel(HitResult, Start, End, FQuat::Identity, ECC_Pawn, FCollisionShape`

Implementing Hit Detection

The basic idea behind hit detection is to check if a weapon or attack intersects with an enemy's hitbox at the right time. When implementing hit detection, several key factors must be considered:

1. **Attack Animation**: The timing of the attack's hitbox activation (usually during the attack animation) is essential. For example, in a sword strike, the hitbox might only be active for a few frames, so proper timing must be ensured to register the hit.

2. **Player Position and Timing**: For melee attacks, hit detection can depend on where the player is standing relative to the enemy. For ranged combat, it often depends on projectile trajectories and impact points.

3. **Attack Range**: Determining the range at which an attack is considered to "hit" an enemy is also crucial. This can be affected by factors like character reach, weapon length, and attack type.

4. **Collision Layers**: In more complex games, different types of objects (characters, weapons, environmental objects) can exist on different collision layers. For example, certain attack types might only affect enemies or specific targets, and these layers need to be taken into account.

Hit Response and Feedback

Once an attack has successfully connected with an enemy, the game needs to provide immediate and satisfying feedback to the player. This feedback is what makes combat feel impactful and rewarding.

- **Visual Feedback**: Common responses include character animations, such as the enemy recoiling, flinching, or reacting to the hit. Flashing lights, blood splatters, or glowing effects can also visually indicate a successful hit.

- **Audio Feedback**: A satisfying sound effect, such as a sword clash, grunt, or explosion, can be a great way to enhance the sense of impact. Audio cues are also useful for players to understand the nature of the hit (whether it's a critical hit, regular strike, or blocked attack).

- **Damage Indicators**: Displaying damage numbers or health bars after each attack can offer immediate feedback to the player on how much damage was done.

- **Character Status Effects**: Hits can trigger status effects, like stunning the enemy, knocking them back, or applying debuffs (poison, burn, freeze, etc.), which can add further impact to the combat system.

Advanced Hit Detection: Parrying and Blocking

In more advanced combat systems, players may have the ability to parry or block attacks, which introduces an additional layer of complexity to hit detection.

- **Parrying**: A parry typically involves timing the defense action just right to deflect or counter an incoming attack. Hit detection for parrying often requires checking if the defensive action (e.g., blocking with a shield or sword) occurs at the exact moment an attack lands.

- **Blocking**: Blocking is another important mechanic in many combat games. When a player blocks an attack, the game checks whether the block is in the right position and whether the player's shield, armor, or other protective means are strong enough to absorb or deflect the hit.

Reviewing the Code

Listing 6-11 implements the attack logic, beginning with the calculation of attack direction and range. A raycast is fired from the character's location, and upon detecting a collision with an enemy, damage is applied accordingly.

- The attack function begins by calculating the direction and range of the attack.

- A raycast is fired from the character's location in the direction of the attack. It checks for collisions with other actors in the game world.

- If a collision is detected with an enemy, the system applies damage.

Listing 6-11. Update Character's Attack Function

```cpp
// In your Character's Attack Function
void AMyCharacter::PerformAttack()
{
    // Get the attack range and direction
    FVector AttackStart = GetActorLocation();
    FVector AttackEnd = AttackStart + (GetActorForwardVector()
    * AttackRange);

    // Perform a raycast to check for collision
    FHitResult HitResult;
    FCollisionQueryParams CollisionParams;
    CollisionParams.AddIgnoredActor(this);  // Ignore the
    character itself

    bool bHit = GetWorld()->LineTraceSingleByChannel(HitResult,
    AttackStart, AttackEnd, ECC_Visibility, CollisionParams);

    // If something is hit, process the hit
     if (bHit)
{
    AEnemy* HitEnemy = Cast<AEnemy>(HitResult.GetActor());
    if (HitEnemy)
    {
        // Create a generic damage event
        FDamageEvent DamageEvent;

        // Apply damage to the enemy properly
        HitEnemy->TakeDamage(DamageAmount, DamageEvent,
        GetInstigatorController(), this);
    }
}
}
```

CHAPTER 6   COMBAT MECHANICS

Hit detection and response play a vital role in ensuring that combat feels intuitive and impactful. By implementing solid hit detection systems and providing appropriate feedback to the player, developers can create satisfying combat experiences. The next section will delve into combo systems, exploring how combinations of attacks can be used to create more dynamic and fluid combat sequences.

Combo Systems

Combo systems are a fundamental component of many action-oriented games, providing players with a sense of progression and mastery over their character's abilities. These systems allow players to chain multiple attacks together in quick succession, often unlocking special moves, increased damage, or visually impressive animations. Combo systems help elevate combat by encouraging skillful play and offering more depth to the player's combat experience.

A combo system involves stringing together a series of different attacks, either by pressing specific sequences of buttons or executing a series of timed moves. This mechanic rewards players for executing a precise series of actions and offers various bonuses, including increased damage, the ability to perform special attacks, or unlocking combo finishers.

In many cases, combos require a set sequence of inputs or a rapid timing window to execute successfully. These systems are widely used in fighting games (e.g., *Street Fighter*, *Tekken*) and action RPGs (e.g., *Devil May Cry*, *Bayonetta*).

Key Elements of a Combo System

1. **Combo Input Sequences**: Players may need to input specific commands (like button presses or gestures) in a particular order and within a set time window to trigger a combo. This encourages rhythm and precision.

2. **Combo Timing and Flow**: Timing is essential in combo systems. A short, forgiving window for timing allows less-experienced players to pull off combos, while tighter windows provide more challenges for advanced players. The flow between attacks should feel smooth to ensure that the transitions between moves are seamless and satisfying.

3. **Combo Counters**: Combo systems often incorporate counters for attacking and defending. This introduces an additional layer of strategy, where the player must choose when to execute a combo or when to defend and evade incoming attacks. Some games feature "counter-combos" that allow players to break the opponent's combo by executing the right move at the right time.

4. **Extended Combos**: Some games allow players to extend their combos by performing additional attacks after the initial series. For example, a combo may open up a finishing move or special attack if the player successfully hits the enemy with a particular sequence. This encourages experimentation and creativity in attack patterns.

5. **Combo Variations**: Rather than following a single fixed combo, some games provide players with multiple variations of a combo, allowing for more freedom and adaptability. This might include changing the direction of attacks, using different types of strikes (e.g., light, heavy, special), or incorporating environmental elements into the combo.

Designing a Combo System

Designing an effective combo system involves several key factors:

- **Input Accessibility**: The combo system should be accessible to both casual players and experienced players. A good combo system often includes a "beginner" mode with easier-to-execute combos, alongside more difficult, advanced combos for those who want to master the game.

- **Skill Progression**: Players should feel a sense of progression as they learn new combos and increase their skill level. Early levels might introduce simple, easy-to-perform combos, with more complex and powerful combinations unlocked later in the game.

- **Visual and Audio Feedback**: Combos are made much more satisfying with visual and audio cues. For example, as each attack lands in a combo, a satisfying visual effect (such as sparks, glowing effects, or slow-motion moments) can make each move feel impactful. Additionally, sound effects like punches, slashes, and grunts add to the visceral feel of combo execution.

CHAPTER 6 COMBAT MECHANICS

- **Combo Breakers**: A combo breaker system allows enemies to escape or interrupt a combo if they time their actions correctly. This adds a layer of depth to the combat, forcing players to think strategically about their combo usage and when to stop attacking.

Reviewing the Code

Listing 6-12 implements a basic combo system for a combat game, using ComboSequence to track player input and TimeBetweenAttacks to define the allowable input window. The system triggers animations based on correct input order and resets the combo if the timing or sequence is broken.

- **ComboSequence** stores the sequence of attacks the player has input so far.
- **TimeBetweenAttacks** defines how much time a player has to press the next button to continue the combo.
- The system checks the input sequence and executes the corresponding animation if the correct move is made in the right order.
- If the player fails to input the correct sequence within the given time, the combo sequence resets.

Listing 6-12. Update Character's Attack Function

```
// Define an array to hold combo strings
TArray<FString> ComboSequence;
int32 ComboIndex = 0;
float TimeBetweenAttacks = 0.2f; // Time allowed to execute the next combo move
float LastAttackTime = 0.0f;
```

521

CHAPTER 6 COMBAT MECHANICS

```cpp
// Player input detection during combat
void AMyCharacter::HandleAttackInput()
{
    if (GetWorld()->GetTimeSeconds() - LastAttackTime <=
    TimeBetweenAttacks)
    {
        // Detect next attack in sequence
        ComboSequence.Add("Light Attack");

        // Check combo sequence
        if (ComboSequence[ComboIndex] == "Light Attack")
        {
            PerformComboMove(ComboIndex);
            ComboIndex++;
        }
    }
    else
    {
        // Reset combo
        ComboSequence.Empty();
        ComboIndex = 0;
    }

    LastAttackTime = GetWorld()->GetTimeSeconds();
}
// Perform combo move based on the index
void AMyCharacter::PerformComboMove(int32 Index)
{
    switch (Index)
    {
        case 0:
            // Execute Light Attack animation
```

```
            PlayAnimation(LightAttackAnim);
            break;
        case 1:
            // Execute Heavy Attack animation
            PlayAnimation(HeavyAttackAnim);
            break;
        case 2:
            // Execute Special Move
            PlayAnimation(SpecialMoveAnim);
            break;
        default:
            // End combo sequence
            ResetCombo();
            break;
    }
}

// Reset combo sequence after final move
void AMyCharacter::ResetCombo()
{
    ComboSequence.Empty();
    ComboIndex = 0;
}
```

Balancing Combo Systems

While combo systems are an engaging mechanic, it's important to balance them carefully within the context of the overall gameplay:

- **Difficulty Curve**: Combos should get progressively harder to perform, encouraging players to grow and improve without feeling overwhelmed early in the game. Offering combo challenges or combo achievements can help encourage mastery.

- **Combo Length**: Long combos that are difficult to execute may frustrate some players, while very short combos may feel too repetitive. Striking the right balance ensures that combos remain fun and rewarding.
- **Enemy and Boss Reactions**: Some enemies may be resistant or immune to certain types of combos. For example, larger enemies or bosses might break out of standard combo chains, requiring players to adapt their strategy.

A well-implemented combo system enhances gameplay by rewarding skillful execution and offering players opportunities for creativity and mastery. By creating meaningful combos that flow naturally with the combat mechanics, developers can add depth and excitement to the game's fighting experience. In the next section, we will explore special moves and finishing moves, two critical elements that elevate the stakes of combat with powerful, visually striking attacks.

Special Moves and Finishing Moves

Special moves and finishing moves are crucial elements in many action games, providing players with unique and powerful abilities that can turn the tide of battle. These moves often feature dramatic animations, and powerful effects, and serve as a reward for skilled gameplay. Special moves can differentiate a game's combat system from others, offering players the opportunity to unleash their character's full potential when used correctly. Similarly, finishing moves create a climactic end to a battle, allowing players to defeat enemies in spectacular and rewarding ways.

What Is Special Moves?

Special moves, often called "signature attacks" or "ultimate abilities," are powerful abilities that go beyond the standard combat mechanics. These moves usually consume a resource, such as stamina, magic, or an energy bar, and often require certain conditions to be met before they can be executed. Special moves are typically visually impressive, accompanied by dramatic effects and sometimes slow-motion moments, making them a satisfying aspect of combat.

Examples of special moves include energy blasts, powerful elemental attacks, devastating sword strikes, or complex combos that result in a high-damage move. These abilities allow players to break through enemy defenses, deal massive damage, or affect the environment in unique ways.

Key Characteristics of Special Moves

1. **Energy or Resource Management**: Special moves often require a resource to execute. This could be a health bar, a stamina bar, a magic meter, or some form of energy that is built up through combat. Managing this resource adds a layer of strategy, as players must decide when to use these powerful moves for maximum effect.

2. **Powerful Impact**: Special moves are designed to be impactful, often dealing significantly more damage than regular attacks. They can also have other effects, such as stunning enemies, breaking shields, or causing environmental destruction.

3. **Unlockable or Progressive**: Many games allow special moves to be unlocked or upgraded as players progress through the story or through leveling up. This progression gives players a sense of growth and rewards them for continued effort in mastering the game's combat system.

4. **Animation and Cinematics**: Special moves are often accompanied by dramatic animations or cinematics that emphasize the power and uniqueness of the move. This not only provides visual satisfaction but also makes the player feel as if they're performing something extraordinary.

What Is Finishing Move?

Finishing moves, sometimes called "fatalities" or "executions," are used to end combat encounters in a dramatic and visually spectacular manner. Typically, finishing moves are executed when an enemy is near death and may be triggered through specific conditions (such as the enemy being stunned, weakened, or in a vulnerable state). These moves often involve exaggerated animations that highlight the severity and impact of the attack.

Finishing moves serve both gameplay and narrative purposes. They are rewarding for the player, providing a satisfying end to difficult battles, and they help showcase the power of the character. They also elevate the emotional tone of the battle, especially if the move has been built up throughout the combat.

Key Characteristics of Finishing Moves

1. **High Damage and Impact**: Finishing moves usually deal massive damage and are often the final blow to defeat an enemy. They are typically designed to visually overwhelm the player and the opponent, creating a climactic and rewarding experience.

2. **Conditional Triggers**: In many games, finishing moves can only be triggered under certain conditions. For example, a character might need to be in a specific state (e.g., low health) or the player might need to complete a quick-time event (QTE) to execute the finishing move. These conditions create an exciting moment where players must react quickly to perform the finishing blow.

3. **Visual and Audio Impact**: The presentation of a finishing move is just as important as the gameplay mechanics behind it. Elaborate animations, special effects, and impactful sound design all contribute to making the finishing move a memorable moment. Players are often given a moment to savor the sequence, with slow-motion or cinematic effects to emphasize the importance of the move.

4. **Variety of Styles**: Finishing moves can come in many forms, such as brutal physical attacks, magical spells, or environmental interactions. Some games allow players to unlock different types of finishing moves for specific enemies or under different circumstances, adding to the replay value.

CHAPTER 6   COMBAT MECHANICS

Designing Special and Finishing Moves

When designing special and finishing moves, developers need to consider the following factors:

- **Balance**: Special and finishing moves should not dominate the gameplay but should feel like powerful tools that add depth to the combat system. Overpowered moves can make the game feel less challenging, while underpowered moves may be underwhelming for players.

- **Resource Management**: Implementing a resource system for special moves adds a strategic element, as players must manage when and how they use their abilities. Giving players the option to save resources for the most critical moments can enhance the excitement and tension during battles.

- **Visual Appeal**: The impact of these moves relies heavily on visual design. Special moves should feel exciting and unique, with animations that match the magnitude of the attack. Additionally, finishing moves need to be over-the-top and satisfying, creating a sense of accomplishment for the player.

- **Timing and Execution**: Special and finishing moves often require precise timing or specific actions to be performed successfully. For example, a player may need to press a sequence of buttons within a short window to unleash a finishing move. The key is ensuring that the execution feels rewarding without being too difficult or frustrating.

CHAPTER 6 COMBAT MECHANICS

Reviewing the Code

Let's look at how special and finishing moves might be implemented in a combat system.

Listing 6-13 defines the EnergyMeter class for managing player energy used in special moves, with ExecuteSpecialMove() checking energy levels and resetting the meter upon use. It also includes the CombatSystem class, which oversees combat flow and triggers finishing moves when enemies become vulnerable.

- **EnergyMeter** class manages the player's energy, which is used to execute special moves.

- **ExecuteSpecialMove** checks if the player has enough energy and performs the special move, resetting the energy bar after use.

- **CombatSystem** class handles combat progression and calls finishing moves when the enemy is vulnerable (e.g., low health).

Listing 6-13. Update Character's Attack Function

```
// Class representing a character's energy meter
class EnergyMeter {
public:
    float CurrentEnergy;
    float MaxEnergy;

    // Method to charge energy over time
    void ChargeEnergy(float amount) {
        CurrentEnergy = FMath::Clamp(CurrentEnergy + amount,
           0.0f, MaxEnergy);
    }
```

CHAPTER 6 COMBAT MECHANICS

```cpp
    // Method to check if special move can be executed
    bool CanExecuteSpecialMove() {
        return CurrentEnergy >= MaxEnergy;
    }

    // Execute Special Move
    void ExecuteSpecialMove() {
        if (CanExecuteSpecialMove()) {
            // Perform powerful special move animation
            PerformSpecialMoveAnimation();
            CurrentEnergy = 0.0f; // Reset energy after use
        }
    }
};

// Class representing the combat system
class CombatSystem {
public:
    EnergyMeter PlayerEnergy;

    // Method to handle combat progression
    void HandleCombatProgression() {
        if (PlayerEnergy.CanExecuteSpecialMove()) {
            PlayerEnergy.ExecuteSpecialMove();
            // Trigger finishing move if conditions met (e.g.,
            enemy low health)
            if (IsEnemyLowHealth()) {
                PerformFinishingMoveAnimation();
            }
        }
    }
```

```
    bool IsEnemyLowHealth() {
        // Check if enemy's health is low for finishing move
        return Enemy->Health <= 0.1f * Enemy->MaxHealth;
    }
};
```

Special and finishing moves play a vital role in enhancing the excitement and depth of a game's combat system. Special moves allow players to unleash devastating attacks, while finishing moves provide a satisfying, climactic conclusion to battle encounters. When designed thoughtfully, these moves create powerful moments of gameplay that add intensity and reward to the player's experience. In the next section, we will explore damage types and resistances, focusing on how different types of damage interact with enemies and how resistance systems can further shape the strategy of combat.

Damage Types and Resistances

In combat systems, damage types and resistances are essential mechanics that add depth, strategy, and complexity to the gameplay. By diversifying how damage can be dealt with and absorbed, developers can create more engaging and varied combat scenarios. These mechanics encourage players to consider factors such as enemy weaknesses, environmental conditions, and the nature of the attack itself when choosing their combat strategies. In this section, we will examine different types of damage, how they are applied, and how resistances play a role in mitigating or enhancing damage.

CHAPTER 6   COMBAT MECHANICS

What Are Damage Types?

Damage types refer to the different categories of harm that can be inflicted on a character or enemy. These types are often linked to specific abilities, weapons, or elemental forces within the game world. The damage type influences how much damage is dealt and whether any additional effects or status conditions are applied to the target. Common damage types include

1. **Physical Damage**: This is the most basic type of damage, typically dealt by weapons like swords, axes, or unarmed attacks. Physical damage can often be mitigated by armor, shields, or other protective equipment.

2. **Fire Damage**: Fire damage is usually caused by elemental attacks, such as fire-based spells or environmental hazards like lava. This type of damage often comes with a burn effect that deals additional damage over time.

3. **Ice Damage**: Ice damage typically slows or freezes enemies in addition to dealing direct damage. This can be useful for crowd control, as it prevents enemies from moving or attacking for a brief period.

4. **Electric Damage**: Electric attacks can stun enemies or cause chain reactions, affecting multiple targets. Electric damage often disables enemy defenses or abilities, making it ideal for breaking through shields.

5. **Poison Damage**: Poison damage causes health to deplete over time, often accompanied by debuffs such as reduced movement speed or attack power. This type of damage is often used by enemies to weaken players gradually.

6. **Magical or Arcane Damage**: Magical damage comes from various magical spells, abilities, or enchanted weapons. This can have a range of effects, from direct damage to status effects like confusion or weakening.

7. **Psychic Damage**: Psychic damage can disrupt the mental state of an enemy, leading to confusion, fear, or paralysis. This type of damage often requires special resistance and is typically used by enemies with mind-controlling abilities.

8. **True Damage**: True damage bypasses most resistances and protections, often representing the raw, unfiltered damage that cannot be reduced. This type of damage is typically reserved for powerful abilities or attacks from bosses or key characters.

Applying Damage Types in Combat

Damage types are often linked to different weapons, abilities, and elements within the game. For example, fire-based spells may deal fire damage, while swords and axes generally deal physical damage. Each damage type has its strengths and weaknesses against various enemies or enemy attributes. For instance:

- **Fire-based attacks** may be highly effective against enemies that are weak to fire but less effective against fire-resistant creatures.
- **Ice-based attacks** may freeze enemies in place, preventing them from attacking, while also dealing damage.

CHAPTER 6   COMBAT MECHANICS

- **Electric damage** can chain between multiple enemies, potentially striking several at once, making it ideal for crowd control situations.

By incorporating multiple damage types, developers allow players to choose the best type of damage for a given situation. Some games may even offer mixed damage types, such as a spell that combines both fire and electric damage, offering a diverse range of tactical choices.

What Are Resistances?

Resistances refer to a character or enemy's ability to reduce or negate the damage from specific types of attacks. Enemies may have resistance to one or more types of damage, making them less vulnerable to certain attacks. For instance, a dragon may be highly resistant to fire damage but weak to ice or electric attacks. Similarly, some characters may possess immunities or increased resistance against certain status effects like poison, burn, or stun.

Types of resistances include

1. **Armor**: Armor resistance is generally applied to physical damage and can reduce the amount of damage taken by wearing specific types of armor. Heavy armor may provide high physical resistance but lower mobility, whereas light armor might offer lower resistance but greater speed.

2. **Elemental Resistances**: These resistances are applied to elemental damage types, such as fire, ice, or electricity. An enemy that lives in a fiery environment might have high fire resistance, while creatures found in icy caverns might resist ice-based attacks.

3. **Magical Resistances**: Some characters or enemies may have resistance to magical or arcane damage, either through their natural abilities or the use of protective spells. This is particularly relevant in games where magic plays a major role.

4. **Poison Resistance**: Poison resistance reduces the effect of poison-based attacks. Characters with high poison resistance can endure the ongoing damage from poison for longer durations before being debilitated by it.

5. **Mental Resistances**: This type of resistance is often related to psychic or mind-affecting damage. Enemies with high mental resistance are less likely to be affected by fear, confusion, or paralysis caused by psychic attacks.

6. **Immunities**: Immunities go beyond resistances, offering complete protection against certain damage types. For example, an undead enemy might be immune to poison damage but take regular damage from physical or magical attacks. Immunities are often reserved for certain conditions or elite enemies.

Balancing Damage Types and Resistances

Properly balancing damage types and resistances is key to designing a challenging and dynamic combat system. Here are several considerations for balancing these mechanics:

1. **Enemy Diversity**: To keep combat engaging, developers should introduce enemies with varying resistances to different damage types. For example,

certain enemies might be vulnerable to fire but resistant to ice, encouraging players to use a variety of attacks to exploit weaknesses.

2. **Player Choice**: By designing systems where players can choose between weapons, spells, or abilities that apply different damage types, players are encouraged to strategize and experiment. Having a variety of damage types ensures that the combat system remains fresh and dynamic.

3. **Environmental Effects**: Environmental factors can also impact damage and resistances. For instance, a character fighting in a thunderstorm may find their electrical attacks stronger, or an area filled with fire may enhance fire-based attacks while weakening ice- or water-based abilities.

4. **Status Effects and Buffs**: Many games incorporate resistances that tie into status effects or buffs. For example, a character may gain poison resistance when they wear a specific armor set or gain fire resistance after consuming a special potion.

5. **Progression**: As the player progresses through the game, their resistance to specific damage types should also evolve. This could mean unlocking new armor sets that provide resistance to elemental damage or learning skills that increase the character's resistance to poison or magic-based attacks.

Reviewing the Code

Here's an example of how damage types and resistances might be implemented in a combat system. The attacker's function (player's or AI's) should call this on the target.

Listing 6-14 defines a DamageType enum to categorize various types of damage, such as physical, fire, and ice. The ApplyDamage() method applies damage to a character, taking into account armor and resistances, except in the case of true damage, which bypasses all defenses.

- **DamageType Enum**: Defines different damage types such as physical, fire, ice, etc.

- **ApplyDamage Method**: Applies damage to a character, factoring in their armor and resistances to different damage types. For true damage, no resistance is applied, as it bypasses all defenses.

Listing 6-14. Update Character's Attack Function

```
enum class DamageType {
    Physical,
    Fire,
    Ice,
    Electric,
    Poison,
    Magic,
    True
};
```

CHAPTER 6 COMBAT MECHANICS

```
class Character {
public:
    float Health;
    float Armor;
    float FireResistance;
    float IceResistance;
    float PoisonResistance;

    // Method to apply damage to character
    void ApplyDamage(float amount, DamageType damageType) {
        float finalDamage = amount;

        // Apply resistances based on damage type
        switch (damageType) {
            case DamageType::Physical:
                finalDamage -= Armor; // Armor reduces
                physical damage
                break;
            case DamageType::Fire:
                finalDamage *= (1.0f - FireResistance);
                // Fire resistance reduces fire damage
                break;
            case DamageType::Ice:
                finalDamage *= (1.0f - IceResistance);
                // Ice resistance reduces ice damage
                break;
            case DamageType::Poison:
                finalDamage *= (1.0f - PoisonResistance);
                // Poison resistance reduces poison damage
                break;
            case DamageType::Magic:
                // No specific resistance for magic in
                this example
```

```
            break;
        case DamageType::True:
            // True damage bypasses all resistances
            break;
        }

        // Reduce health by final damage
        Health -= finalDamage;
    }
};
```

Damage types and resistances are integral to creating a multifaceted and strategic combat system. By designing varied types of damage and resistances, developers can offer players a dynamic and challenging experience. Whether it's exploiting elemental weaknesses, utilizing status effects, or making use of special resistance-based strategies, these mechanics add layers of depth and excitement to the combat. In the next section, we will explore enemy spawning, focusing on how and when enemies are introduced into the game and how this impacts pacing and gameplay.

Enemy Spawning

Enemy spawning is a crucial mechanic in game design that dictates how and when enemies appear within the game world. It directly impacts the pacing, difficulty, and overall gameplay experience, ensuring that the player is continuously engaged. Whether it's through scripted encounters, random spawns, or dynamic systems that adapt to the player's actions, enemy spawning can provide a variety of challenges and opportunities for the player. In this section, we will explore the different methods of enemy spawning, the factors that influence it, and how it can be used to create a balanced and engaging combat experience.

CHAPTER 6   COMBAT MECHANICS

Types of Enemy Spawning

There are several ways enemies can spawn in a game. The most common methods include **scripted spawns, random spawns, wave-based spawns**, and **dynamic spawns**. Each type has its advantages and can be used in different situations to enhance gameplay:

1. **Scripted Spawning**: Scripted spawns are predetermined events where enemies appear at specific points in the game world. These encounters are often tied to the story or progression of the game and occur at key moments to drive the narrative forward. For example, an enemy may spawn after a player reaches a particular checkpoint or after completing a certain objective. This method is often used in boss fights, cutscene-triggered encounters, or where the game needs to guide the player through specific challenges.

   Example: A boss fight may be triggered when the player reaches the end of a dungeon, with enemies spawning to defend the boss.

2. **Random Spawning**: Random spawns occur without specific triggers and are generated unpredictably in the game world. This can add an element of surprise and tension, as the player never knows when or where enemies will appear. Random spawns are often used in open-world games or areas where the player is exploring, adding a layer of challenge as they move through the environment.

   Example: In an open-world RPG, enemies might appear randomly while the player is traveling between locations, requiring the player to stay alert.

3. **Wave-Based Spawning**: Wave-based spawning involves enemies appearing in waves, often with each subsequent wave being more difficult than the last. This system is commonly used in survival modes, tower defense games, or arenas where the player must defeat several waves of enemies before progressing. Wave-based spawns allow for controlled difficulty progression and can help pace the challenge of the game.

   Example: In a tower defense game, waves of enemies spawn periodically, and each wave becomes progressively stronger as the player's defenses are tested.

4. **Dynamic Spawning**: Dynamic spawning adapts to the player's actions and the current state of the game. This type of spawn system may use algorithms to determine the appropriate number and types of enemies based on factors like the player's health, level, location, and the current difficulty setting. Dynamic spawning is often used in games with adaptive difficulty systems, ensuring that the challenge always feels appropriate for the player's skill level.

   Example: In a dynamic difficulty adjustment system, if the player is struggling with combat, the game may spawn fewer enemies or provide easier types of enemies to balance the challenge. Conversely, if the player is performing exceptionally well, tougher enemies may spawn to keep the challenge high.

Factors Influencing Enemy Spawning

Several factors influence how and when enemies spawn in a game. These factors help developers tailor the experience to match the intended difficulty curve, provide variety, and keep the player engaged.

1. **Player Progression**: As the player progresses through the game, the types of enemies spawned may change to reflect their increased power and abilities. Early on, enemies might be weak and easily defeated, while later in the game, enemies may become more powerful and require more strategic thinking to defeat.

2. **Location and Environment**: The environment in which the player is located often dictates the types of enemies that spawn. For example, enemies in a jungle area may differ from those in a tundra or a dark cave. The game may also have spawn points tied to specific locations, such as entrances to dungeons, specific zones, or combat arenas.

3. **Difficulty Settings**: Many games feature difficulty settings that impact enemy spawning. On easier difficulty levels, fewer or weaker enemies may spawn, while higher difficulty levels may spawn more numerous or tougher enemies. Dynamic spawning can further refine this by adjusting the number and strength of enemies based on the player's current performance.

4. **Story and Events**: Enemy spawning is often used to support the game's narrative. As players reach significant plot points or complete objectives, enemies may spawn to challenge their progress. This can create tension or excitement, such as when a villain sends waves of enemies to stop the player or when a major story event triggers a spawn to change the game world dynamically.

5. **Time and Game Mechanics**: Time-based mechanics can also affect enemy spawning. Some games use a time system where enemies spawn after a certain amount of time has passed or based on the player's activities. For example, in a day-night cycle, stronger enemies may spawn at night, or in a stealth-based game, enemies might appear in response to certain sound triggers.

Balancing Enemy Spawns

One of the key challenges when implementing enemy spawning is ensuring that the spawns are well-balanced. Too many enemies at once can overwhelm the player, while too few can make the game feel monotonous. Effective balance can be achieved through careful consideration of the following:

1. **Spawn Frequency**: For optimization purposes, spawn frequency needs to be highly viewed upon, as enemies that are not relevant to the player (distance, view frustum, etc.) should not be spawned or, if spawned, should be handled accordingly to ensure good performance.

2. **Spawn Location**: The placement of enemy spawn points is also crucial. Spawning enemies in narrow corridors or areas with little room to maneuver can make encounters feel more intense, while spawning enemies in open areas gives players room to strategize and use their environment.

3. **Enemy Variety**: Introducing variety in the types of enemies that spawn helps keep the gameplay fresh. Mix up enemy types, abilities, and weaknesses to encourage players to adapt their strategies. For example, mixing high-damage, low-health enemies with slower, tankier ones forces players to balance offense and defense.

4. **Difficulty Scaling**: Spawning should scale with the player's level, progression, and skill. As players become more powerful, the enemies they face should also become more challenging, ensuring that the game remains engaging. Dynamic difficulty adjustment is one way to scale this appropriately.

Reviewing the Code

Listing 6-15 implements the AEnemySpawner class, responsible for spawning enemy characters in the game world at timed intervals. It tracks elapsed time, handles spawning logic, and uses a helper function to determine random spawn positions.

- **AEnemySpawner Class**: This class represents an actor in the world that spawns enemies. It has a SpawnInterval property that determines how often enemies spawn, an ElapsedTime to track time passed, and a TSubclassOf<AEnemy> property that holds the enemy blueprint or class to spawn.

- **SpawnEnemy()**: This method handles the logic of spawning an enemy at a random location. It uses the GetWorld()->SpawnActor<AEnemy>() method, which is specific to Unreal Engine to spawn actors in the world.
- **GetRandomSpawnLocation()**: This function generates a random spawn location around the spawner actor's current position.

Listing 6-15. EnemySpawner.h

```
#pragma once

#include "CoreMinimal.h"
#include "GameFramework/Actor.h"
#include "EnemySpawner.generated.h"

// Forward declaration of AEnemy class
class AEnemy;

UCLASS()
class YOURGAME_API AEnemySpawner : public AActor
{
    GENERATED_BODY()
public:
    // Sets default values for this actor's properties
    AEnemySpawner();

protected:
    // Called when the game starts or when spawned
    virtual void BeginPlay() override;
```

```cpp
public:
    // Called every frame
    virtual void Tick(float DeltaTime) override;

    // Time interval between enemy spawns
    UPROPERTY(EditAnywhere, BlueprintReadWrite, Category = 
    "Spawning")
    float SpawnInterval;

    // Timer to track time between spawns
    float ElapsedTime;

    // Reference to the Enemy class
    UPROPERTY(EditAnywhere, BlueprintReadWrite, Category = 
    "Spawning")
    TSubclassOf<AEnemy> EnemyClass;

    // Method to spawn an enemy at a random location
    void SpawnEnemy();
private:
    // Get a random spawn location within the bounds
    FVector GetRandomSpawnLocation();
};
```

Listing 6-16 highlights critical Unreal Engine constructs used in the enemy spawning system, including class references, spawning functions, and macro declarations necessary for UE4's reflection system.

Listing 6-16. EnemySpawner.cpp

```cpp
#include "EnemySpawner.h"
#include "Enemy.h"
#include "Engine/World.h"
```

```cpp
// Sets default values
AEnemySpawner::AEnemySpawner()
{
    PrimaryActorTick.bCanEverTick = true;
    SpawnInterval = 5.0f; // Default spawn interval
    of 5 seconds
    ElapsedTime = 0.0f;
}

// Called when the game starts or when spawned
void AEnemySpawner::BeginPlay()
{
    Super::BeginPlay();
}

// Called every frame
void AEnemySpawner::Tick(float DeltaTime)
{
    Super::Tick(DeltaTime);

    ElapsedTime += DeltaTime;

    // Check if it's time to spawn an enemy
    if (ElapsedTime >= SpawnInterval)
    {
        SpawnEnemy();
        ElapsedTime = 0.0f; // Reset the timer
    }
}

// Spawns an enemy at a random location
 void AEnemySpawner::SpawnEnemy()
{
    FVector SpawnLocation = GetRandomSpawnLocation();
```

```cpp
    FRotator SpawnRotation = FRotator::ZeroRotator;
    FVector SpawnScale = FVector(1.0f); // Default scale

    // Create transform and spawn parameters
    FTransform SpawnTransform(SpawnRotation, SpawnLocation,
    SpawnScale);
    FActorSpawnParameters SpawnParams;

    // Spawn the enemy actor in the world
    GetWorld()->SpawnActor<AEnemy>(EnemyClass, SpawnTransform,
    SpawnParams);
}

// Get a random location for spawning an enemy
FVector AEnemySpawner::GetRandomSpawnLocation()
{
    // For example, spawn within a certain range around the
    spawner's location
    FVector Origin = GetActorLocation();
    float XOffset = FMath::RandRange(-500.f, 500.f);
    float YOffset = FMath::RandRange(-500.f, 500.f);
    return FVector(Origin.X + XOffset, Origin.Y + YOffset,
    Origin.Z);
}
```

Enemy spawning plays a critical role in shaping the flow and difficulty of combat within a game. Whether through scripted events, random encounters, or adaptive systems, the way enemies appear influences player experience by creating challenges that keep the gameplay dynamic. Properly balancing spawn frequency, locations, and variety ensures that the game remains engaging without overwhelming the player. In the next section, we will discuss **boss fights**, which provides players with some of the most intense and memorable combat experiences in a game.

Boss Fights

Boss fights are often considered one of the most thrilling and challenging elements in video games. They serve as climactic moments that test the player's skills, often providing a sense of accomplishment and progression upon their defeat. A well-designed boss fight can leave a lasting impression, offering not only intense combat but also an emotionally charged or narrative-driven experience. In this section, we will explore the importance of boss fights, the various types of bosses, and how they are integrated into the gameplay to ensure they are both challenging and rewarding.

Types of Boss Fights

Boss fights can be categorized in various ways, depending on their structure, complexity, and role in the game. Below are some common types:

- **Scripted Boss Fights**: These boss fights are predetermined and often play a significant role in the game's narrative. They are designed to challenge the player at key moments in the story. These fights are usually more structured, with specific patterns or phases that the player must overcome to progress.

  Example: A player reaches a major plot point, and the boss fight is triggered, with specific mechanics tied to the narrative. Upon defeating the boss, the player moves to the next level or story chapter.

- **Endgame Boss Fights**: Typically found at the end of the game or at the conclusion of a major story arc, these boss fights are often the most challenging. They are designed to push the player to their limits, testing everything they've learned up until that point.

Example: A final boss in an RPG that requires the player to utilize all the skills, abilities, and strategies they have acquired throughout the game.

- **Survival Boss Fights**: These fights are usually part of survival modes or timed challenges where the player must hold off waves of enemies or survive against a particularly tough opponent for a limited time.

    Example: In a survival horror game, the player must survive a set amount of time against a relentless boss that cannot be easily defeated.

- **Multi-phase Boss Fights**: These bosses change their tactics or appearance in stages, often becoming more difficult as the fight progresses. This can keep the player on their toes, requiring adaptability and quick thinking.

    Example: A giant creature might start the fight by attacking from a distance with ranged weapons and then shift to a more aggressive, close-combat approach once its health drops below a certain threshold.

- **Environmental Boss Fights**: These boss fights incorporate the game world's environment into the battle mechanics. The player might need to use the environment to their advantage, whether it's through terrain manipulation or environmental hazards.

    Example: A giant, elemental boss that causes earthquakes or storms that affect the battlefield, requiring the player to react quickly to avoid environmental damage while battling the boss.

CHAPTER 6   COMBAT MECHANICS

Key Elements of an Engaging Boss Fight

Several factors come into play when designing an exciting and memorable boss fight. Here are the key elements that contribute to a great boss battle:

- **Challenge and Balance:** A boss fight should be tough, but not impossible. It should provide a sense of accomplishment when defeated but avoid becoming frustrating. The difficulty should scale with the player's skill and abilities, ensuring that each boss feels like a significant challenge without being overwhelming.

- **Unique Abilities and Patterns:** One of the hallmarks of a great boss fight is its unique attack patterns, phases, and abilities. A well-designed boss should have moves that are distinct from other enemies, requiring the player to learn and adapt to these patterns. This helps keep the player engaged and creates a sense of discovery.

- **Tension and Drama:** The best boss fights create a sense of tension. Whether through music, dramatic dialogue, or the sheer intensity of the encounter, the boss fight should feel like a pivotal moment in the game. This can be achieved through pacing, atmosphere, and well-timed narrative moments.

- **Environmental Interaction:** Many bosses are designed to interact with the environment in a way that the player can use to their advantage. This could include destructible objects, traps, or environmental hazards that can be manipulated to deal extra damage or weaken the boss. These mechanics add layers of strategy to the encounter.

- **Narrative Significance**: Boss fights are often tied to the narrative, representing the culmination of a character's journey or the resolution of a central conflict. This connection to the story can make the boss fight more impactful and give the player a deeper emotional investment in the outcome.

Reviewing the Code

Listing 6-17 introduces the `ABossFightManager` class, which handles the entire flow of a boss encounter—from spawning the boss to detecting its defeat and ending the fight.

- **ABossFightManager Class**: This class is responsible for managing the boss fight, including starting and ending the fight, as well as checking if the boss has been defeated.

- **TSubclassOf<ABossCharacter> BossCharacterClass**: A reference to the class of the boss that will be spawned at the start of the fight.

- **StartBossFight()**: A method to initiate the boss fight, usually triggered when the player enters a boss arena or reaches a certain point in the game.

- **EndBossFight()**: This method is called once the boss is defeated, ending the fight and possibly triggering a victory animation or rewards for the player.

- **CheckBossDefeat()**: A method to check if the boss's health has reached zero, indicating the defeat of the boss.

Listing 6-17. BossFightManager.h

```cpp
#pragma once

#include "CoreMinimal.h"
#include "GameFramework/Actor.h"
#include "BossFightManager.generated.h"

// Forward declaration of ABossCharacter
class ABossCharacter;

UCLASS()
class YOURGAME_API ABossFightManager : public AActor
{
    GENERATED_BODY()

public:
    ABossFightManager();

protected:
    virtual void BeginPlay() override;

public:
    virtual void Tick(float DeltaTime) override;

    // Reference to the boss character
    UPROPERTY(EditAnywhere, BlueprintReadWrite, Category = "Boss Fight")
    TSubclassOf<ABossCharacter> BossCharacterClass;

    // The current boss in the fight
    ABossCharacter* CurrentBoss;

    // Method to start the boss fight
    void StartBossFight();
```

CHAPTER 6 COMBAT MECHANICS

```cpp
    // Method to end the boss fight
    void EndBossFight();

private:
    // Check if the boss has been defeated
    void CheckBossDefeat();
};
```

Listing 6-18 continues with a closer look at the core functions that drive the boss fight progression within the `ABossFightManager` class:

- **StartBossFight()**: This method spawns the boss character at the designated location when the fight begins.

- **EndBossFight()**: This method is invoked once the boss is defeated, triggering any end-of-fight animations or actions, such as player rewards or story progression.

- **CheckBossDefeat()**: Continuously checks if the boss's health has reached zero, at which point the fight ends.

Listing 6-18. BossFightManager.cpp

```cpp
#include "BossFightManager.h"
#include "BossCharacter.h"
#include "Engine/World.h"

// Sets default values
ABossFightManager::ABossFightManager()
{
    PrimaryActorTick.bCanEverTick = true;
}
```

```cpp
// Called when the game starts or when spawned
void ABossFightManager::BeginPlay()
{
    Super::BeginPlay();
}

// Called every frame
void ABossFightManager::Tick(float DeltaTime)
{
    Super::Tick(DeltaTime);

    // Check if the boss has been defeated
    CheckBossDefeat();
}

// Start the boss fight by spawning the boss
 void ABossFightManager::StartBossFight()
{
    FVector SpawnLocation = GetActorLocation();
    FRotator SpawnRotation = FRotator::ZeroRotator;
    FVector SpawnScale = FVector(1.0f); // Default scale

    // Create transform and spawn parameters
    FTransform SpawnTransform(SpawnRotation, SpawnLocation,
    SpawnScale);
    FActorSpawnParameters SpawnParams;

    // Spawn the boss character in the world
    CurrentBoss = GetWorld()->SpawnActor<ABossCharacter>(
    BossCharacterClass, SpawnTransform, SpawnParams);
}
```

CHAPTER 6 COMBAT MECHANICS

```
// End the boss fight and provide rewards or progression
void ABossFightManager::EndBossFight()
{
    if (CurrentBoss)
    {
        // Trigger victory animation or rewards
        CurrentBoss->Destroy();
    }
}

// Check if the boss has been defeated
void ABossFightManager::CheckBossDefeat()
{
    if (CurrentBoss && CurrentBoss->GetHealth() <= 0)
    {
        EndBossFight();
    }
}
```

Boss fights serve as climactic moments that test the player's mastery of combat systems, enemy patterns, and strategic decision-making. Whether through unique AI behaviors, multiple combat phases, or rewarding animations, boss encounters elevate gameplay tension and narrative impact. Properly implemented, boss fights provide players with a sense of accomplishment and act as major milestones in game progression.

Summary

With a solid understanding of Combat Mechanics, we now move on to physics and dynamics, where we will explore the complex systems that govern motion, interactions, and forces in the virtual world. From rigid body dynamics to fluid simulation, these systems bring realism and immersion to games, enriching the player experience with lifelike movement and environmental interactions. We will dive into key topics such as rigid body dynamics, soft body dynamics, particle systems, and more, all of which contribute to creating dynamic and responsive game worlds.

CHAPTER 7

Physics and Dynamics

Physics and dynamics are fundamental components in creating realistic and immersive game worlds. Whether it's the way objects interact with each other, how characters move, or how environmental forces like wind and gravity influence gameplay, physics systems bring a sense of realism and depth to your game. This chapter will guide you through the essential elements of physics and dynamics, covering topics like rigid body dynamics, fluid simulations, and gravity manipulation, as well as more advanced concepts like destructible environments and force fields.

At its core, physics in games enhances immersion by ensuring that interactions in the world feel consistent and believable. By simulating the natural laws of motion and force, players are given a sense of control over the environment and its reactions. In this chapter, we'll break down the basics of physics simulations and dynamics and explore how to implement them in a game engine. From simple interactions like object collisions to more complex systems like rope physics and fluid dynamics, this chapter will cover everything you need to understand the dynamics that make your game world tick.

As physics systems grow in complexity, they can add more depth to your game's world by simulating dynamic and interactive elements. More advanced physics simulations can introduce things like soft body dynamics, vehicle physics, fluid simulations, and destructible environments, which significantly enhance gameplay and realism.

This section dives deeper into these advanced systems, showing how to implement complex behaviors and interactions like cloth simulation, destructible environments, and force fields. These systems provide more immersive and interactive environments where players can manipulate the world in exciting ways.

Practical Applications of Physics Systems

Physics systems are applied in various gameplay contexts to create interactive and immersive experiences. Whether it's designing realistic movements for characters and vehicles, simulating environmental forces like wind and water, or creating dynamic destruction, these systems play a crucial role in the player's experience.

In this section, we will explore how physics and dynamics can be integrated into different genres and gameplay scenarios. From realistic vehicle handling in a racing game to interactive environmental destruction in an action-adventure, the potential applications of physics systems are vast.

Key Applications

- **Puzzle Games**: Physics-based puzzles, where players must manipulate objects, solve problems, and navigate challenges using the laws of physics (e.g., games like *Portal* or *The Incredible Machine*)

- **Racing Games**: Simulating realistic car behavior, including suspension, friction, and collisions to create authentic racing experiences
- **Action/Adventure Games**: Incorporating environmental destruction, gravity manipulation, and vehicle physics to enhance gameplay and immersion
- **Sports Games**: Simulating player movements, ball dynamics, and collisions to recreate realistic sports scenarios (e.g., football, soccer, or tennis)
- **Platformers**: Using gravity and collision detection to ensure smooth and responsive character movement and interactions with objects

In this chapter, we will explore the essential physics and dynamics systems needed to bring your game world to life. We'll cover both basic and advanced topics, ensuring that you understand the core principles and have the tools to implement complex systems.

By the end of this chapter, you will have a solid understanding of how to implement and fine-tune physics and dynamics in your game. Whether you're creating a racing game with realistic vehicle physics or an action adventure with destructible environments, you'll be equipped with the knowledge to design interactive and immersive physics systems that enhance gameplay and create dynamic worlds.

Rigid Body Dynamics

Rigid body dynamics is a critical component in physics simulations used in video games to create realistic movement and interaction between objects. This concept refers to the behavior of solid objects that do not deform or change shape when forces are applied. Implementing rigid body dynamics in games helps create immersive environments, where objects behave in a way that matches players' expectations, such as bouncing, colliding, or reacting to applied forces. Whether it's a character throwing a barrel, a car crashing into a wall, or an object falling to the ground, rigid body dynamics ensure that the physics feels authentic and consistent.

Basic Usage of Rigid Body Dynamics

At the heart of rigid body dynamics are key principles like motion, forces, and collisions. In video games, this is typically handled by physics engines that simulate the movement of objects based on physical properties such as mass, velocity, and acceleration. The basic components of rigid body dynamics include

- **Collision Detection**: Identifying when and where two objects interact or collide.

- **Forces and Torques**: Applying forces (e.g., gravity, friction, or applied impulses) and rotational forces to change the motion of objects.

- **Momentum and Inertia**: Objects move according to Newton's laws of motion, with properties like mass and velocity affecting their behavior.

- **Rigid Body Constraints**: Managing limits on an object's movement, such as locking certain rotations or positions to create more complex interactions.

These core principles are integrated into physics engines that work with the game's environment, ensuring that objects behave realistically when impacted by forces.

CHAPTER 7 PHYSICS AND DYNAMICS

Advanced Techniques

As rigid body dynamics evolve, they introduce more complexity to ensure that objects behave believably in a dynamic game world. Advanced techniques include

- **Complex Collisions**: Advanced collision detection that accounts for varying shapes and sizes of objects, ensuring they respond appropriately when they intersect.

- **Soft Body Dynamics**: A hybrid between rigid and deformable body physics, allowing some objects to flex or bend under pressure.

- **Friction and Material Properties**: Modifying how objects interact with surfaces, including factors like surface friction, elasticity, or how objects might slide or stick.

- **Realistic Impulse Reactions**: When an object collides with another, calculate the force of the impact and apply realistic rebound or destruction behaviors.

By implementing these advanced features, objects in the game can react more realistically to player actions and environmental changes, increasing immersion and dynamic interaction in the game world.

Practical Applications

Rigid body dynamics are used extensively in a variety of games and genres, where physical interaction is important. Examples include

- **Platformers**: Objects that the player can move or interact with, such as barrels or crates, should respond realistically when pushed, thrown, or collided with.
- **Racing Games**: Vehicles interact with the terrain and obstacles, requiring physics to simulate proper handling, crashes, and reactions to forces.
- **Puzzle Games**: Objects that the player manipulates to solve puzzles, such as rotating blocks or tumbling objects, rely heavily on rigid body physics to function properly.
- **Action Games**: Explosions, destructible environments, or large-scale environmental interactions are all driven by physics engines that simulate rigid body dynamics.

Algorithm Overview

To implement rigid body dynamics effectively in a game, several systems and algorithms are required:

- **Physics Engine**: Handles all interactions between objects, including motion calculations, collision detection, and response to forces
- **Force Application System**: A method to apply forces to objects, simulating gravity, pushes, pulls, or impacts

CHAPTER 7 PHYSICS AND DYNAMICS

- **Collision Detection and Response System**: Checks when two objects intersect and how they should respond (bounce, slide, stop, etc.)
- **Time Step Management**: Handles how physics calculations are updated during each frame, ensuring smooth and stable simulations

Reviewing the Code

Listing 7-1 defines a basic rigid body controller with velocity, gravity, and mass properties. It includes utility functions for applying forces and simulating gravity. These properties form the foundation for custom physics behavior.

- **Velocity**: The current speed and direction of the object.
- **Gravity**: The force of gravity acting on the object.
- **Mass**: The mass of the object affects its response to forces.

Listing 7-1. RigidBodyController.h

```
#pragma once

#include "CoreMinimal.h"
#include "GameFramework/Actor.h"
#include "RigidBodyController.generated.h"

UCLASS()
class MYGAME_API ARigidBodyController : public AActor
{
    GENERATED_BODY()
```

```cpp
public:
    ARigidBodyController();

protected:
    virtual void BeginPlay() override;

public:
    virtual void Tick(float DeltaTime) override;

    // Mesh with physics
    UPROPERTY(VisibleAnywhere)
    UStaticMeshComponent* MeshComponent;

    // Apply custom external force
    UFUNCTION(BlueprintCallable, Category = "Physics")
    void ApplyForce(const FVector& Force);
};
```

Listing 7-2 implements the core physics logic of the rigid body controller by applying forces and simulating gravity over time. These functions directly influence the object's velocity and movement.

Listing 7-2. RigidBodyController.cpp

```cpp
#include "RigidBodyController.h"
#include "Components/StaticMeshComponent.h"

ARigidBodyController::ARigidBodyController()
{
    PrimaryActorTick.bCanEverTick = true;

    // Set up mesh and enable physics
    MeshComponent = CreateDefaultSubobject<UStaticMeshComponent>
    (TEXT("MeshComponent"));
    RootComponent = MeshComponent;
```

```
    MeshComponent->SetSimulatePhysics(true); // Physics will
    now handle gravity, velocity, mass, etc.
}
void ARigidBodyController::BeginPlay()
{
    Super::BeginPlay();
}
void ARigidBodyController::Tick(float DeltaTime)
{
    Super::Tick(DeltaTime);
    // No need to manually apply gravity here; it's automatic
}
void ARigidBodyController::ApplyForce(const FVector& Force)
{
    if (MeshComponent && MeshComponent->IsSimulatingPhysics())
    {
        MeshComponent->AddForce(Force);
    }
}
```

In this section, you've learned the basics of rigid body dynamics, including how forces, collisions, and physical properties like mass and velocity affect object behavior. These mechanics are crucial for creating realistic interactions in a game world. In the next section, we will explore more complex physical interactions like soft body dynamics and fluid simulations.

CHAPTER 7   PHYSICS AND DYNAMICS

Soft Body Dynamics

Soft body dynamics is a simulation method used in games and physics engines to replicate objects that can deform, stretch, compress, and bend. Unlike rigid bodies that maintain their shape, soft bodies are flexible and can change from under external forces. This makes them ideal for simulating materials such as rubber, cloth, and jelly-like substances, which are crucial in creating more realistic environments and interactions in games, especially in the fields of physics-based puzzles, action sequences, and even character animations. Soft body dynamics aim to simulate real-world materials in a way that adds depth and immersion to the gameplay.

Basic Usage of Soft Body Dynamics

In basic terms, soft body dynamics refers to objects that are not rigid and can deform or bend based on external forces like gravity, collision, or pressure. The key concepts of soft body dynamics include

- **Deformation**: The ability of the object to change shape when forces are applied
- **Elasticity**: The material's ability to return to its original shape after deformation
- **Collision Handling**: Managing how soft bodies interact with other objects or surfaces, where they can deform on impact
- **Damping**: Reducing the energy of deformation over time, helping the soft body return to its rest state

These elements make soft body dynamics crucial in simulating materials such as rubber balls, soft cloth, or deformable jelly surfaces, enhancing the realism of physical interactions.

Advanced Techniques

Advanced soft body dynamics techniques provide deeper interaction with these flexible materials, making them more realistic and useful in games. These include

- **Tension and Compression:** The ability to simulate stretching (tension) and squishing (compression) within a soft body, based on the material's properties.

- **Bending Resistance:** A property that resists bending forces and helps simulate stiff materials like leather or rubber.

- **Material Properties:** Adjusting factors like elasticity, friction, and density to simulate different types of soft materials accurately.

- **Simultaneous Deformation and Collision:** More advanced simulations allow soft bodies to deform while also interacting with rigid bodies in real time, such as a cloth hanging on a character's body or a rubber ball bouncing on the ground.

Practical Applications

Soft body dynamics are often used in games for various purposes:

- **Character Animation:** Soft body dynamics can be applied to parts of a character's body or clothing that need to behave more naturally, like cloth, hair, or the jiggling of certain body parts.

- **Environmental Interactions**: Simulating environmental elements like water, jelly-like surfaces, or soft, bendable objects that react dynamically to the player's movements.

- **Physics-Based Puzzles**: Soft body dynamics can be used in puzzle games to simulate deformable objects that players must manipulate to solve challenges, such as squishing or stretching objects to fit through spaces or solve a mechanism.

Algorithm Overview

The implementation of soft body dynamics typically involves solving complex differential equations to simulate the deformation, pressure, and tension of soft objects. The core systems involved are

- **Spring-Mass Model**: A common approach for simulating soft bodies where the object is represented by a network of springs and masses. Each mass represents a point in the soft body, and the springs represent the material's resistance to stretching or compression.

- **Finite Element Method (FEM)**: A more complex technique that divides the soft object into small elements, each of which can deform according to physical laws. This method is computationally more intensive but offers higher realism.

- **Particle-Based Methods**: These methods use particles that interact with each other, creating a more fluid-like dynamic, useful in simulating materials like water or soft fluids.

CHAPTER 7 PHYSICS AND DYNAMICS

Reviewing the Code

Listing 7-3 introduces the foundational components of a soft body simulation system. This implementation models deformable objects using spring forces and mass points, enabling realistic squish-and-stretch physics behavior.

- **SpringConstant**: This property defines the stiffness of the soft body. A higher value means less deformation when forces are applied, making the body more rigid.

- **Damping**: The damping factor reduces the force acting on the soft body over time, helping it return to its original shape more smoothly.

- **Masses**: The array stores the positions of the points that make up the soft body, essentially representing a mesh or grid of deformable points.

- **Velocities**: This array stores the velocity of each mass point, allowing us to update their positions over time based on forces acting upon them.

- **ApplyForce()**: This function applies an external force (such as gravity or player interaction) to a specified mass, affecting its velocity.

- **SimulateSoftBody()**: This function simulates the soft body dynamics by calculating forces between mass points (spring forces) and updating their positions accordingly.

Listing 7-3. SoftBodyController.h

```cpp
#pragma once

#include "CoreMinimal.h"
#include "GameFramework/Actor.h"
#include "SoftBodyController.generated.h"

UCLASS()
class MYGAME_API ASoftBodyController : public AActor
{
    GENERATED_BODY()

public:
    ASoftBodyController();

protected:
    virtual void BeginPlay() override;

public:
    virtual void Tick(float DeltaTime) override;

    UPROPERTY(EditAnywhere, BlueprintReadWrite, Category = "Soft Body")
    float SpringConstant; // How stiff the soft body is

    UPROPERTY(EditAnywhere, BlueprintReadWrite, Category = "Soft Body")
    float Damping; // Damping of the spring force

    UPROPERTY(EditAnywhere, BlueprintReadWrite, Category = "Soft Body")
    TArray<FVector> Masses; // The points representing the soft body
```

CHAPTER 7　PHYSICS AND DYNAMICS

```
UPROPERTY(EditAnywhere, BlueprintReadWrite, Category = 
"Soft Body")
TArray<FVector> Velocities; // The velocities of each mass

void ApplyForce(FVector Force, int32 MassIndex);
void SimulateSoftBody(float DeltaTime);
};
```

Listing 7-4 outlines the actual soft body simulation process as implemented in `SoftBodyController.cpp`. It details how forces, damping, and spring-based interactions work together to simulate realistic soft body deformation.

- **SpringConstant**: This value determines the stiffness of the springs connecting the masses. A higher spring constant leads to less deformation under force, making the body stiffer.

- **Damping**: The damping factor reduces the velocity of each mass point over time, simulating resistance such as friction or internal energy dissipation, making the system return to equilibrium.

- **Masses**: The array Masses contains the positions of each point (mass) in the soft body mesh. The positions are updated over time to reflect movement and deformation.

- **Velocities**: This array holds the velocity of each mass. The velocity is updated based on the forces applied and is used to update the positions of the masses.

- **ApplyForce()**: This function applies a force to a specific mass, updating its velocity accordingly. The force could come from external sources like player interactions or environmental forces.

CHAPTER 7 PHYSICS AND DYNAMICS

- **SimulateSoftBody()**: The main simulation function calculates the spring forces between adjacent masses and applies damping to reduce oscillations. It updates the positions and velocities of the masses based on the spring forces and damping.

Listing 7-4. SoftBodyController.cpp

```
#include "SoftBodyController.h"

ASoftBodyController::ASoftBodyController()
{
    PrimaryActorTick.bCanEverTick = true;

    SpringConstant = 1000.0f;
    Damping = 0.1f;
}

void ASoftBodyController::BeginPlay()
{
    Super::BeginPlay();

    // Initialize the soft body with masses and velocities
    // For simplicity, we start with a few points that will
    represent the soft body
    Masses.Add(FVector(0, 0, 0)); // First mass point
    Masses.Add(FVector(100, 0, 0)); // Second mass point
    Velocities.Add(FVector(0, 0, 0)); // Initial velocity
    Velocities.Add(FVector(0, 0, 0)); // Initial velocity for
                                        second mass
}

void ASoftBodyController::Tick(float DeltaTime)
{
```

CHAPTER 7   PHYSICS AND DYNAMICS

```
    Super::Tick(DeltaTime);

    SimulateSoftBody(DeltaTime); // Simulate the soft body
                                    dynamics each frame
}

void ASoftBodyController::ApplyForce(FVector Force, int32
MassIndex)
{
    // Apply the force to the specified mass point
    if (MassIndex >= 0 && MassIndex < Masses.Num())
    {
        Velocities[MassIndex] += Force;
    }
}

void ASoftBodyController::SimulateSoftBody(float DeltaTime)
{
    // Simple spring-mass simulation: Calculate forces and up-
    date positions
    for (int32 i = 0; i < Masses.Num(); ++i)
    {
        FVector Force = FVector(0, 0, 0);
        // Reset the force for this mass

        // Apply spring force based on neighboring mass points
        (for simplicity)
        if (i < Masses.Num() - 1) // Check if there's a
                                    neighbor mass
        {
            FVector Direction = Masses[i + 1] - Masses[i];
            float Distance = Direction.Size();
            Direction.Normalize();
```

575

```
            float SpringForce = SpringConstant * (Distance -
            100.0f); // Deformation from resting distance
            Force += Direction * SpringForce;
            // Apply force in the direction of the spring

            // Apply damping to the velocity
            Velocities[i] -= Velocities[i] * Damping;
        }

        // Update the mass position based on the force applied
        Masses[i] += Velocities[i] * DeltaTime;
        // Simple update: position += velocity * time
    }
}
```

Soft body dynamics allow for the creation of materials that deform and react to forces in a realistic manner. While the implementation here is simplified for understanding, it serves as the foundation for more complex systems involving soft materials. These mechanics can be used in many applications, from character animation to dynamic environmental interactions.

Particle Systems

Particle systems are a versatile technique used in games and simulations to create dynamic visual effects such as fire, smoke, explosions, rain, and magic spells. These effects are achieved by simulating a large number of small particles that move and change size, color, or shape over time. Particle systems allow for highly customizable effects and are essential for adding realism or stylized visuals to a game world. By controlling various parameters like emission rate, lifespan, velocity, and gravity, particle systems create visually stunning effects that enhance the player's experience.

CHAPTER 7   PHYSICS AND DYNAMICS

Basic Usage of Particle Systems

At the core of a particle system are the individual particles that represent points in space, often with the following properties:

- **Emission Rate**: The rate at which new particles are spawned
- **Lifetime**: How long each particle exists before it disappears
- **Velocity**: The speed and direction of particle movement
- **Gravity**: The influence of gravitational force on the particles
- **Color over Lifetime**: The ability for particles to change color as they age

These basic parameters are controlled in the system to create various types of effects, whether it's a fiery explosion, a gentle snowflake fall, or the swirls of a magical aura.

Advanced Techniques

Advanced particle systems can incorporate several additional techniques to further enhance visual effects:

- **Particle Attractors**: Forces that can pull particles toward a specific point, simulating magnetic fields, explosions, or gravitational effects.
- **Collision Detection**: Particles can interact with other objects in the environment (like hitting a wall or water surface) and change their behavior accordingly.

- **Sub-emitter Systems**: Particles can emit other particles, creating complex chains of effects, such as sparks or smoke trailing after an explosion.
- **Custom Shaders**: For more advanced effects, custom shaders can be applied to the particles, allowing for glowing, reflective, or other material-specific behaviors.

By integrating these advanced features, particle systems can evolve into powerful tools for creating intricate and realistic visual effects.

Practical Applications

Particle systems are widely used in games and simulations across various genres to enhance both realism and gameplay:

- **Action Games**: Explosions, gunfire, and magical effects are enhanced using particle systems to convey the power and impact of attacks.
- **Simulation Games**: Environmental effects like rain, fog, and wind can be simulated with particle systems, adding depth to the game world.
- **Role-Playing Games (RPGs)**: Magical spells, fireballs, and enchantments are commonly represented with particle effects to give them visual impact and uniqueness.

Algorithm Overview

Particle systems are built upon several key algorithms and data structures:

- **Particle Emitter**: The part of the system that spawns new particles and initializes their properties (velocity, size, color, etc.).

- **Particle Update Loop**: A loop that updates the state of each particle in every frame, adjusting position, velocity, size, and other properties based on the elapsed time.

- **Particle Renderer**: This component handles how the particles are drawn on the screen, often using efficient techniques like billboarding to always face the camera.

These systems work together to simulate and display complex effects in real time.

Reviewing the Code

Listing 7-5 presents the essential elements of a basic particle system, outlining how particles are created, updated, and removed over time. This system serves as a lightweight custom alternative to engine-level particle emitters.

- **MaxParticles**: Defines the maximum number of particles that can be spawned by this emitter.

- **ParticleLifetime**: Controls how long each particle will exist before disappearing.

- **ParticleVelocity**: Sets the velocity of newly spawned particles.

- **Particles and Lifetimes**: Arrays that store the positions and lifetimes of all active particles.

- **EmitParticle()**: A function to create new particles and initialize their positions and velocities.

- **UpdateParticles()**: Updates each particle's position based on its velocity and reduces its lifetime. If a particle's lifetime expires, it is removed from the system.

Listing 7-5. ParticleEmitter.h

```
#pragma once

#include "CoreMinimal.h"
#include "GameFramework/Actor.h"
#include "ParticleEmitter.generated.h"

UCLASS()
class MYGAME_API AParticleEmitter : public AActor
{
    GENERATED_BODY()

public:
    AParticleEmitter();

protected:
    virtual void BeginPlay() override;
    virtual void Tick(float DeltaTime) override;

public:
    UPROPERTY(EditAnywhere, BlueprintReadWrite, Category = 
    "Particle")int32 MaxParticles;

    UPROPERTY(EditAnywhere, BlueprintReadWrite, Category = 
    "Particle")float ParticleLifetime;
```

CHAPTER 7   PHYSICS AND DYNAMICS

```
UPROPERTY(EditAnywhere, BlueprintReadWrite, Category =
"Particle")
FVector ParticleVelocity;

TArray<FVector> Particles;
// Array to store the particle positions
TArray<float> Lifetimes;
// Array to store the lifetime of each particle

void EmitParticle();
void UpdateParticles(float DeltaTime);
};
```

Listing 7-6 breaks down the logic that drives particle emission and updates in each frame. It ensures that particles behave realistically by moving, aging, and being recycled within the system.

- **EmitParticle()**: In each frame, new particles are emitted if their lifetime is over. Particles are initialized at the emitter's location and given the default velocity and lifetime.

- **UpdateParticles()**: This function is responsible for updating each particle's position and lifetime. As the particle ages, its lifetime decreases. Once the lifetime reaches zero, the particle is reset, and the process starts over.

Listing 7-6. ParticleEmitter.cpp

```
#include "ParticleEmitter.h"

AParticleEmitter::AParticleEmitter()
{
```

CHAPTER 7 PHYSICS AND DYNAMICS

```cpp
    PrimaryActorTick.bCanEverTick = true;
    MaxParticles = 100;
    ParticleLifetime = 5.0f;
    ParticleVelocity = FVector(0.0f, 0.0f, 1.0f);
    // Particles will move upwards initially
}

void AParticleEmitter::BeginPlay()
{
    Super::BeginPlay();

    // Initialize the particle arrays
    Particles.SetNum(MaxParticles);
    Lifetimes.SetNum(MaxParticles);
}

void AParticleEmitter::Tick(float DeltaTime)
{
    Super::Tick(DeltaTime);

    // Emit new particles
    EmitParticle();

    // Update particle positions and lifetimes
    UpdateParticles(DeltaTime);
}

void AParticleEmitter::EmitParticle()
{
    for (int32 i = 0; i < MaxParticles; i++)
    {
        if (Lifetimes[i] <= 0.0f)
        {
```

CHAPTER 7   PHYSICS AND DYNAMICS

```
            Particles[i] = GetActorLocation();
            // Set new particle position at emitter
            Lifetimes[i] = ParticleLifetime;
            // Reset lifetime
        }
    }
}
void AParticleEmitter::UpdateParticles(float DeltaTime)
{
    for (int32 i = 0; i < MaxParticles; i++)
    {
        if (Lifetimes[i] > 0.0f)
        {
            Particles[i] += ParticleVelocity * DeltaTime;
            // Update particle position
            Lifetimes[i] -= DeltaTime;
            // Decrease particle lifetime
        }
    }
}
```

In this section, you've explored the fundamentals of particle systems, from basic emission to advanced effects like sub-emission and collision detection. Particle systems are integral to creating dynamic and immersive visual effects in games, adding atmosphere, and enhancing the gameplay experience.

CHAPTER 7   PHYSICS AND DYNAMICS

Cloth Simulation

Cloth simulation is a critical aspect of game physics that involves replicating how fabrics and flexible materials behave in real life. This system enables the dynamic interaction of objects, such as clothing, flags, curtains, or any soft material, with forces like wind, gravity, and collision with other objects. The goal of cloth simulation is to make these materials move naturally in response to the environment, providing a more immersive and realistic experience.

Basic Usage of Cloth Simulation

At its core, cloth simulation involves representing cloth as a mesh of interconnected vertices, with each vertex simulating the behavior of a point on the fabric. These vertices are influenced by forces like gravity and collisions, and their positions are updated each frame. Key components of cloth simulation include

- **Vertex Simulation**: Cloth is modeled as a grid of vertices. Each vertex is connected to its neighbors, forming a mesh that simulates fabric.

- **Forces Acting on Cloth**: Gravity, wind, and other environmental forces affect the movement and deformation of the cloth.

- **Collisions**: Cloth interacts with other objects in the environment. This can include characters, terrain, and other static or dynamic objects.

- **Stretching and Compression**: Cloth simulation accounts for both stretching and compressing forces, ensuring that fabric behaves realistically under tension or compression.

These components work together to create a realistic simulation of fabric and soft materials in a dynamic environment, allowing for natural movement and interaction.

Advanced Techniques

As the simulation becomes more complex, additional techniques are used to improve realism and performance:

- **Wind Simulation**: Cloth can be affected by wind forces that alter its movement, simulating how it billows in the wind or flutters in the breeze.

- **Self-Collision**: In more advanced simulations, the cloth can detect when parts of itself overlap or collide, adding realism when dealing with complex clothing or drapery.

- **Tearing**: In some cases, the cloth may tear under extreme forces, simulating damage or stress on the fabric.

- **Damping and Friction**: Damping refers to reducing the movement of the cloth over time, while friction helps simulate how cloth interacts with surfaces and objects it comes in contact with.

By incorporating these advanced techniques, cloth simulation systems can create fabrics that respond dynamically to the environment and interactions within the game world.

Practical Applications

Cloth simulation is used in a variety of contexts across different types of games:

- **Character Clothing**: Characters in action games or RPGs often wear flowing garments, such as capes, dresses, or armor, which require realistic cloth simulation to respond naturally to movements and environmental factors.

- **Environmental Elements**: Cloth simulation is commonly used for flags, banners, or tents interacting with the wind, creating a dynamic and visually interesting world.

- **Interactive Objects**: Objects like parachutes or sails may need to simulate cloth behavior in response to wind and movement, adding complexity to the gameplay.

Algorithm Overview

To implement an effective cloth simulation system, several core elements must be integrated:

- **Vertex Positioning**: Updating the position of each vertex based on forces like gravity, wind, and collisions.

- **Spring Constraints**: Cloth is modeled as a mesh of vertices connected by springs, with each spring maintaining a distance between two connected vertices.

CHAPTER 7 PHYSICS AND DYNAMICS

- **Collision Handling**: Detecting and resolving collisions between the cloth and other objects.

- **Time Step Integration**: Updating the simulation each frame by applying forces and updating the vertices' positions.

Reviewing the Code

Listing 7-7 defines a foundational cloth simulation system using a custom class that models vertex behavior and edge constraints. It lays the groundwork for simulating cloth-like motion in a dynamic game environment.

- **GravityStrength**: Defines how strongly gravity will affect the cloth's vertices

- **ClothVertices**: Stores the positions of each vertex in the cloth mesh

- **ClothEdges**: Stores the connections between vertices (edges) to simulate how cloth stretches and bends

- **UpdateCloth()**: A function to update the positions of the vertices based on forces applied to them, such as gravity or wind

Listing 7-7. ClothSimulation.h

```
#pragma once

#include "CoreMinimal.h"
#include "GameFramework/Actor.h"
#include "ClothSimulation.generated.h"

UCLASS()
class MYGAME_API AClothSimulation : public AActor
```

CHAPTER 7   PHYSICS AND DYNAMICS

```
{
    GENERATED_BODY()
public:
    AClothSimulation();
protected:
    virtual void BeginPlay() override;
public:
    virtual void Tick(float DeltaTime) override;

    UPROPERTY(EditAnywhere, BlueprintReadWrite,
    Category = "Cloth")float GravityStrength;
    // The strength of gravity affecting the cloth

    UPROPERTY(VisibleAnywhere, BlueprintReadOnly,
    Category = "Cloth")TArray<FVector> ClothVertices;
      // Array to store the positions of cloth vertices

    UPROPERTY(VisibleAnywhere, BlueprintReadOnly,
    Category = "Cloth")TArray<int32> ClothEdges;
    // The edges connecting vertices

    void UpdateCloth(float DeltaTime);
};
```

Listing 7-8 focuses on the UpdateCloth() function, which simulates gravity on the cloth mesh by adjusting vertex positions frame by frame. This basic implementation creates realistic sagging and motion.

- **UpdateCloth()**: This function updates the position of each vertex in the cloth mesh by applying gravity each frame.

CHAPTER 7 PHYSICS AND DYNAMICS

- **Gravity Force**: The gravity force is applied to each vertex, pulling it downward based on the defined GravityStrength.

Listing 7-8. ClothSimulation.cpp

```
#include "ClothSimulation.h"
#include "Engine/World.h"

AClothSimulation::AClothSimulation()
{
    PrimaryActorTick.bCanEverTick = true;
    GravityStrength = 9.8f;
}

void AClothSimulation::BeginPlay()
{
    Super::BeginPlay();
}

void AClothSimulation::Tick(float DeltaTime)
{
    Super::Tick(DeltaTime);

    // Update cloth simulation each frame
    UpdateCloth(DeltaTime);
}

void AClothSimulation::UpdateCloth(float DeltaTime)
{
    for (int32 i = 0; i < ClothVertices.Num(); i++)
    {
```

```
        // Apply gravity force to each vertex
        ClothVertices[i] += FVector(0, 0, -GravityStrength) *
        DeltaTime;

        // Add additional forces (wind, collision, etc.) here
    }
}
```

In this section, we've explored the fundamentals of cloth simulation, covering key elements such as vertex positioning, forces, and collision handling. We also introduced advanced techniques that can enhance the realism of cloth systems, including wind simulation and tearing. Finally, we demonstrated how to implement a basic cloth simulation system through code. The next section will dive into vehicle physics, exploring how vehicles interact with forces and terrain.

Vehicle Physics

Vehicle physics is a crucial aspect of many simulation, racing, and open-world games. It involves replicating the real-world behavior of vehicles, including acceleration, braking, steering, and handling while accounting for factors such as friction, gravity, and aerodynamics. Implementing realistic vehicle physics enhances player immersion and provides a more authentic driving experience.

Basic Usage of Vehicle Physics

At its core, vehicle physics is built upon the following principles and mechanics:

- **Suspension System**: Simulates the behavior of the vehicle's wheels and how they interact with the terrain, accounting for uneven surfaces and shocks

- **Traction and Tire Friction**: Models the interaction between the vehicle's tires and the ground, affecting grip, sliding, and cornering
- **Engine and Transmission**: Replicates the power output and gear systems, controlling how the vehicle accelerates and reaches its top speed
- **Steering Dynamics**: Handles how the vehicle responds to input for turning and cornering, often including systems for oversteering or understeering
- **Braking System**: Simulates braking mechanics, including anti-lock braking systems (ABS) for enhanced control during hard braking

These foundational elements make up the core of a realistic vehicle physics system, ensuring that the vehicle behaves in a believable manner under various driving conditions.

Advanced Techniques

To further enhance realism, advanced techniques can be incorporated:

- **Drift and Skid Mechanics**: Adds the ability for the vehicle to lose traction and perform controlled or uncontrolled slides
- **Aerodynamics**: Simulates air resistance, downforce, and lift, impacting high-speed stability and cornering
- **Weight Transfer**: Models how the vehicle's weight shifts during acceleration, braking, and turning, influencing grip and handling

- **Damage System**: Incorporates physical deformations and performance impacts when the vehicle collides with objects or other vehicles
- **Environmental Interactions**: Accounts for factors such as weather conditions, road surfaces, and obstacles, which influence vehicle performance

These techniques deepen the driving experience, making the vehicle physics system adaptable to diverse gameplay scenarios.

Practical Applications

Vehicle physics systems are widely used in various game genres, each with its own emphasis:

- **Racing Games**: Focuses on high-speed dynamics, cornering precision, and performance tuning for competitive driving
- **Simulation Games**: Prioritizes realistic vehicle behavior, including fuel consumption, wear and tear, and advanced driving mechanics
- **Open-World Games**: Balances realism with accessibility, ensuring vehicles are fun and easy to control while retaining some realistic physics

Algorithm Overview

The implementation of vehicle physics involves a combination of simulation techniques and algorithms:

CHAPTER 7   PHYSICS AND DYNAMICS

- **Force Calculation**: Determines forces acting on the vehicle, such as engine thrust, drag, and gravity

- **Wheel Colliders**: Simulates the interaction of wheels with the ground, including suspension and traction mechanics

- **Rigidbody Dynamics**: Utilizes physics engines to manage the vehicle's movement and rotation

- **Steering and Braking**: Implements control algorithms for smooth handling and effective braking responses

Reviewing the Code

Listing 7-9 introduces the essential components of a basic vehicle controller using Unreal Engine's WheeledVehiclePawn. This setup allows the vehicle to move, steer, and respond to player input through native vehicle physics.

- **AMyWheeledVehiclePawn**: Inherits from AWheeledVehiclePawn, giving access to Unreal's built-in vehicle simulation system

- **SetupPlayerInputComponent()**: Binds player inputs (keyboard/controller) to control throttle and steering

- **MoveForward()**: Function to accelerate or reverse the vehicle

- **TurnRight()**: Function to steer the vehicle left or right

CHAPTER 7   PHYSICS AND DYNAMICS

Listing 7-9. MyWheeledVehiclePawn.h

```
#pragma once

#include "CoreMinimal.h"
#include "WheeledVehiclePawn.h"
#include "MyWheeledVehiclePawn.generated.h"

UCLASS()
class MYGAME_API AMyWheeledVehiclePawn : public
AWheeledVehiclePawn
{
    GENERATED_BODY()

public:
    AMyWheeledVehiclePawn();

protected:
    virtual void SetupPlayerInputComponent(UInputComponent*
    PlayerInputComponent) override;

    void MoveForward(float Value);
    void TurnRight(float Value);
};
```

Listing 7-10 implements the logic that connects player input with the movement of the vehicle. This makes use of the native WheeledVehicle MovementComponent for throttle and steering control.

- **SetupPlayerInputComponent()**: Binds the `MoveForward` and `TurnRight` functions to the corresponding input axis mappings
- **MoveForward()**: Applies throttle input, controlling acceleration and braking

CHAPTER 7   PHYSICS AND DYNAMICS

- **TurnRight()**: Sends steering input to turn the vehicle left or right

- **GetVehicleMovementComponent()**: Accesses the built-in vehicle movement system, handling all physics interactions like wheel torque, suspension, and friction

Listing 7-10. MyWheeledVehiclePawn.cpp

```
#include "MyWheeledVehiclePawn.h"
#include "WheeledVehicleMovementComponent.h"

AMyWheeledVehiclePawn::AMyWheeledVehiclePawn()
{
    // Optional initialization
}
void AMyWheeledVehiclePawn::SetupPlayerInputComponent
(UInputComponent* PlayerInputComponent)
{
    Super::SetupPlayerInputComponent(PlayerInputComponent);

    PlayerInputComponent->BindAxis("MoveForward", this,
    &AMyWheeledVehiclePawn::MoveForward);
    PlayerInputComponent->BindAxis("TurnRight", this,
    &AMyWheeledVehiclePawn::TurnRight);
}
void AMyWheeledVehiclePawn::MoveForward(float Value)
{
    GetVehicleMovementComponent()->SetThrottleInput(Value);
}
```

CHAPTER 7   PHYSICS AND DYNAMICS

```
void AMyWheeledVehiclePawn::TurnRight(float Value)
{
    GetVehicleMovementComponent()->SetSteeringInput(Value);
}
```

Vehicle physics is essential for simulating realistic and engaging vehicle behavior in games. This subtopic provided an overview of basic mechanics, advanced techniques, and a code implementation for vehicle dynamics. Next, we will explore rope and chain physics, delving into how flexible objects can be realistically simulated.

Rope and Chain Physics

Rope and chain physics are commonly used in games to simulate flexible, interconnected objects like ropes, chains, cables, or vines. These systems are vital for creating dynamic and interactive environments, allowing players to swing, pull, or manipulate objects in realistic ways.

Importance of Rope and Chain Physics

Rope and chain physics enhance gameplay by

- **Adding Realism**: Simulating natural bending, swinging, and stretching behavior
- **Improving Interactivity**: Allowing players to interact with objects dynamically, such as climbing ropes or using chains to lift weights
- **Creating Puzzle Mechanics**: Using ropes or chains in puzzles that require tension, weight balancing, or movement

Core Components of Rope and Chain Physics

A realistic rope or chain physics system typically includes

- **Nodes and Links**: Representing the rope or chain as a series of connected particles or rigid bodies
- **Constraints**: Ensuring links maintain a consistent distance to simulate the rigidity of a rope or chain
- **Forces**: Applying gravity, tension, and external forces to create realistic movement
- **Collision Detection**: Preventing the rope or chain from passing through objects or itself

Reviewing the Code

Listing 7-11 introduces the header structure for a rope simulation system using custom physics. The rope is represented as a chain of nodes, each storing position and velocity to simulate real-time rope behavior.

- **FNode**: Represents each point (or link) in the rope with position and velocity
- **NumNodes**: Defines how many nodes make up the rope
- **NodeMass**: Controls how external forces (like gravity) affect each node
- **SpringStiffness**: Dictates how stiff or stretchy the rope feels

CHAPTER 7   PHYSICS AND DYNAMICS

- **RopeNodes**: Stores all the rope points as an array of FNode
- **SimulateRope()/ApplyForces()/EnforceConstraints()**: Custom physics logic that determines how the rope moves and responds to forces

Listing 7-11. RopePhysicsComponent.h

```cpp
#pragma once

#include "CoreMinimal.h"
#include "Components/ActorComponent.h"
#include "RopePhysicsComponent.generated.h"

USTRUCT(BlueprintType)
struct FNode
{
    GENERATED_BODY()

    UPROPERTY(EditAnywhere, BlueprintReadWrite, Category = "Rope")
    FVector Position;

    UPROPERTY(EditAnywhere, BlueprintReadWrite, Category = "Rope")
    FVector Velocity;
};

UCLASS(ClassGroup=(Custom), meta=(BlueprintSpawnableComponent))
class MYGAME_API URopePhysicsComponent : public UActorComponent
{
    GENERATED_BODY()
```

```cpp
public:
    URopePhysicsComponent();

protected:
    virtual void BeginPlay() override;
    virtual void TickComponent(float DeltaTime, ELevelTick TickType, FActorComponentTickFunction* ThisTickFunction) override;

public:
    UPROPERTY(EditAnywhere, BlueprintReadWrite, Category = "Rope")
    int32 NumNodes;

    UPROPERTY(EditAnywhere, BlueprintReadWrite, Category = "Rope")
    float NodeMass;

    UPROPERTY(EditAnywhere, BlueprintReadWrite, Category = "Rope")
    float SpringStiffness;

    UPROPERTY(EditAnywhere, BlueprintReadWrite, Category = "Rope")
    TArray<FNode> RopeNodes;

    void SimulateRope(float DeltaTime);
    void ApplyForces(float DeltaTime);
    void EnforceConstraints();
};
```

Listing 7-12 provides the runtime implementation for simulating a rope's physical behavior. Each frame applies gravity and enforces distance constraints between the rope's nodes.

CHAPTER 7 PHYSICS AND DYNAMICS

- **ApplyForces()**: Applies gravity to each rope node, updating velocity and position
- **EnforceConstraints()**: Ensures nodes stay connected like a rope, preventing overstretching

Listing 7-12. RopePhysicsComponent.cpp

```
#include "RopePhysicsComponent.h"

URopePhysicsComponent::URopePhysicsComponent()
{
    PrimaryComponentTick.bCanEverTick = true;
    NumNodes = 10;
    NodeMass = 1.0f;
    SpringStiffness = 100.0f;
}

void URopePhysicsComponent::BeginPlay()
{
    Super::BeginPlay();

    // Initialize rope nodes
    for (int32 i = 0; i < NumNodes; ++i)
    {
        FNode Node;
        Node.Position = GetOwner()->GetActorLocation() +
        FVector(0, 0, -i * 10.0f);
        Node.Velocity = FVector::ZeroVector;
        RopeNodes.Add(Node);
    }
}

void URopePhysicsComponent::TickComponent(float DeltaTime,
ELevelTick TickType, FActorComponentTickFunction*
ThisTickFunction)
```

```cpp
{
    Super::TickComponent(DeltaTime, TickType, ThisTick-
    Function);

    SimulateRope(DeltaTime);
}

void URopePhysicsComponent::SimulateRope(float DeltaTime)
{
    ApplyForces(DeltaTime);
    EnforceConstraints();
}

void URopePhysicsComponent::ApplyForces(float DeltaTime)
{
    for (FNode& Node : RopeNodes)
    {
        FVector Gravity = FVector(0, 0, -980.0f);
        // Gravity force
        Node.Velocity += (Gravity / NodeMass) * DeltaTime;
        Node.Position += Node.Velocity * DeltaTime;
    }
}

void URopePhysicsComponent::EnforceConstraints()
{
    for (int32 i = 1; i < RopeNodes.Num(); ++i)
    {
        FVector& CurrentPosition = RopeNodes[i].Position;
        FVector& PreviousPosition = RopeNodes[i - 1].Position;

        FVector Direction = (CurrentPosition -
        PreviousPosition).GetSafeNormal();
```

```
        float Distance = FVector::Dist(CurrentPosition,
        PreviousPosition);
        float Correction = (Distance - 10.0f) *
        SpringStiffness;

        FVector CorrectionVector = Direction * Correction;
        CurrentPosition -= CorrectionVector * 0.5f;
        PreviousPosition += CorrectionVector * 0.5f;
    }
}
```

Rope and chain physics add dynamic realism and interactivity to games. This subtopic introduced their core principles, practical applications, and a code example. Next, we will explore destructible environments, which focus on creating realistic breakable objects and environments.

Destructive Environments

Destructible environments bring a dynamic and immersive experience to games by allowing players to interact with and destroy objects in real time. This feature enhances realism and provides exciting gameplay mechanics, such as breaking walls, toppling structures, or shattering glass.

Importance of Destructible Environments

- **Enhanced Realism**: Adds depth and believability to the game world
- **Interactive Gameplay**: Encourages players to explore and manipulate their surroundings
- **Strategic Elements**: Introduces tactical gameplay, such as creating cover by destroying obstacles

CHAPTER 7   PHYSICS AND DYNAMICS

Core Components of Destructible Environments

Key elements of destructible environments include

- **Physics Integration**: Simulating realistic object breakage and debris behavior

- **Damage Thresholds**: Determining how much force or damage an object can take before breaking

- **Dynamic Fracturing**: Splitting objects into smaller fragments during destruction

- **Performance Optimization**: Ensuring smooth gameplay despite complex calculations for breaking objects

Reviewing the Code

Listing 7-13 outlines the core components of a destructible object system. This system allows game objects to respond to damage and break apart dynamically based on a damage threshold.

- **DamageThreshold**: Specifies the amount of damage needed to break the object

- **ApplyDamage()**: Handles incoming damage and checks if it exceeds the threshold

- **DestroyObject()**: Breaks the object into fragments upon exceeding the damage threshold

- **bIsDestroyed**: Tracks whether the object has already been destroyed

603

CHAPTER 7   PHYSICS AND DYNAMICS

Listing 7-13. DestructibleComponent.h

```
#pragma once

#include "CoreMinimal.h"
#include "Components/ActorComponent.h"
#include "DestructibleComponent.generated.h"

UCLASS(ClassGroup=(Custom), meta=(BlueprintSpawnableComponent))
class MYGAME_API UDestructibleComponent : public UActorComponent
{
    GENERATED_BODY()

public:
    UDestructibleComponent();

protected:
    virtual void BeginPlay() override;

public:
    UPROPERTY(EditAnywhere, BlueprintReadWrite, Category = "Destruction")
    float DamageThreshold;

    UFUNCTION(BlueprintCallable, Category = "Destruction")
    void ApplyDamage(float Damage, const FVector& HitLocation);

    UFUNCTION(BlueprintCallable, Category = "Destruction")
    void DestroyObject();

private:
    bool bIsDestroyed;
};
```

CHAPTER 7   PHYSICS AND DYNAMICS

Explanation

This header file introduces the following concepts.

Listing 7-14 describes the runtime behavior of a destructible object. It highlights how damage is evaluated and how destruction is triggered with corresponding feedback elements.

- **ApplyDamage()**: Determines if the object receives enough damage to break. If the damage exceeds the threshold, it triggers destruction.

- **DestroyObject()**: Spawns visual and sound effects, then removes the object from the game.

Listing 7-14. DestructibleComponent.cpp

```
#include "DestructibleComponent.h"
#include "Kismet/GameplayStatics.h"

UDestructibleComponent::UDestructibleComponent()
{
    PrimaryComponentTick.bCanEverTick = false;
    DamageThreshold = 50.0f;
    bIsDestroyed = false;
}

void UDestructibleComponent::BeginPlay()
{
    Super::BeginPlay();
}

void UDestructibleComponent::ApplyDamage(float Damage, const FVector& HitLocation)
{
```

```cpp
    if (bIsDestroyed)
        return;

    if (Damage >= DamageThreshold)
    {
        DestroyObject();
    }
}
void UDestructibleComponent::DestroyObject()
{
    if (bIsDestroyed)
        return;

    bIsDestroyed = true;

    // Simulate destruction (e.g., spawn debris, play sound
    effects)
    UGameplayStatics::SpawnEmitterAtLocation(GetWorld(),
    DestructionEffect, GetOwner()->GetActorLocation());
    GetOwner()->Destroy();
}
```

Optional: Using Chaos Destruction and Fracture

For developers who want more advanced and visually rich destruction effects, Unreal Engine offers a powerful Chaos Destruction system. This allows you to fracture meshes and simulate realistic physical destruction without manually coding damage thresholds or debris spawning.

CHAPTER 7 PHYSICS AND DYNAMICS

Setup Steps

1. **Enable Chaos Destruction Plugin**

   a. Go to `Edit` ➤ `Plugins`.

   b. Search for **Chaos Destruction** and enable it.

   c. Restart the editor.

2. **Fracture a Mesh**

   a. Select a static mesh in the content browser.

   b. Right-click ➤ **Create Chaos Destructible Mesh**.

   c. Open the new Chaos Destructible Mesh and apply **Fracture Tools** (e.g., Uniform or Cluster).

3. **Place in World and Activate Physics**

   a. Place the fractured mesh in the level.

   b. Make sure `Simulate Physics` and `Enable Chaos` are checked.

Listing 7-14A introduces Chaos Destruction using Unreal Engine's GeometryCollectionComponent. This code showcases how to apply real-time damage to destructible assets using Chaos physics. It enables advanced destruction behavior like fractures and impulse-based breakage.

- **AGeometryCollectionActor**: A Chaos-specific actor class that supports dynamic fracturing and destruction

- **GetGeometryCollectionComponent()**: Retrieves the component responsible for simulating Chaos physics and handling fracture logic

- **ApplyDamage()**: A method that applies directional force and damage at a specific location with a defined radius

CHAPTER 7 PHYSICS AND DYNAMICS

Listing 7-14A. TriggeringChaosDestruction.cpp

```cpp
#include "GeometryCollectionActor.h"
#include "GeometryCollectionComponent.h"

void AMyActor::ApplyDamageToGeometry()
{
    AGeometryCollectionActor* DestructibleActor =
    Cast<AGeometryCollectionActor>(TargetActor);
    if (DestructibleActor && DestructibleActor->
    GetGeometryCollectionComponent())
    {
        DestructibleActor->GetGeometryCollectionComponent()->
ApplyDamage(
            100.0f,                        // Damage amount
            HitLocation,                   // Location of impact
            FVector::UpVector * 500.0f,    // Impulse direction/
                                           strength
            1000.0f                        // Radius
        );
    }
}
```

Destructible environments add excitement and realism by allowing players to interact with and alter their surroundings dynamically. This subtopic demonstrated their core principles, practical applications, and code implementation. Next, we will explore fluid dynamics, focusing on simulating realistic liquids and other flowing substances.

Fluid Dynamics

Fluid dynamics in game development focuses on simulating the behavior of liquids and gases. This includes water, smoke, lava, and other flowing substances, providing a realistic and immersive environment. Fluid simulations can range from simple particle effects to advanced real-time fluid interactions.

Importance of Fluid Dynamics

- **Realism**: Adds depth to environments by mimicking natural fluid behaviors
- **Interactivity**: Allows players to interact with dynamic liquids or gases
- **Visual Appeal**: Enhances the visual aesthetics of games with flowing water, smoke trails, and explosions

Core Components of Fluid Dynamics

Key elements include

1. **Particle-Based Simulation**: Using particles to represent fluid elements
2. **Navier-Stokes Equations**: Calculations for fluid flow, including velocity and pressure
3. **Volume Rendering**: Rendering realistic fluid volumes, such as splashes and waves
4. **Performance Optimization**: Ensuring fluid simulations are computationally efficient for real-time applications

CHAPTER 7 PHYSICS AND DYNAMICS

Reviewing the Code

Listing 7-15 introduces a fluid simulation system using a particle-based approach. This header sets up configurable parameters and essential methods for managing fluid dynamics and rendering.

- **MaxParticles**: Specifies the maximum number of fluid particles allowed in the simulation, helping control performance and density.

- **ParticleRadius**: Determines the physical size of each particle, which affects how particles appear visually and interact spatially.

- **Viscosity**: Defines how much resistance the fluid has to flow. Higher values create thicker, slower-moving fluids, while lower values simulate more free-flowing behavior.

- **AddParticle()**: Adds a new fluid particle to the simulation, typically with an initial position and velocity.

- **UpdateParticles()**: Advances the simulation by updating each particle's velocity and position based on forces like gravity, interaction with neighbors, and viscosity.

- **RenderParticles()**: Handles the visual representation of fluid particles, typically using sprites, meshes, or shader-based rendering.

CHAPTER 7 PHYSICS AND DYNAMICS

Listing 7-15. FluidSimulator.h

```
#pragma once

#include "CoreMinimal.h"
#include "GameFramework/Actor.h"
#include "FluidSimulator.generated.h"

UCLASS()
class MYGAME_API AFluidSimulator : public AActor
{
    GENERATED_BODY()

public:
    AFluidSimulator();

protected:
    virtual void BeginPlay() override;
    virtual void Tick(float DeltaTime) override;

public:
    UPROPERTY(EditAnywhere, BlueprintReadWrite, Category =
    "Fluid")
    int32 MaxParticles;

    UPROPERTY(EditAnywhere, BlueprintReadWrite, Category =
    "Fluid")
    float ParticleRadius;

    UPROPERTY(EditAnywhere, BlueprintReadWrite, Category =
    "Fluid")
    float Viscosity;

    UFUNCTION(BlueprintCallable, Category = "Fluid")
    void AddParticle(const FVector& Position, const FVector&
    Velocity);
```

CHAPTER 7   PHYSICS AND DYNAMICS

```
private:
    TArray<FVector> ParticlePositions;
    TArray<FVector> ParticleVelocities;

    void UpdateParticles(float DeltaTime);
    void RenderParticles();
};
```

Listing 7-16 describes the core logic behind particle-based fluid simulation, focusing on how particles are introduced, updated, and rendered in the game environment.

- **AddParticle()**: Initializes new particles with specific positions and velocities. This function is typically called when fluid is emitted into the world or when a simulation begins.

- **UpdateParticles()**: Simulates the motion of fluid particles by updating their velocities and positions. It incorporates viscosity to simulate flow resistance and helps achieve more realistic behavior.

- **RenderParticles()**: Draws each fluid particle as a visible entity in the scene—often using basic geometry like spheres or through specialized shaders for smoother fluid visuals.

Listing 7-16. FluidSimulator.cpp

```
#include "FluidSimulator.h"

AFluidSimulator::AFluidSimulator()
{
    PrimaryActorTick.bCanEverTick = true;
    MaxParticles = 1000;
```

```cpp
    ParticleRadius = 10.0f;
    Viscosity = 0.1f;
}

void AFluidSimulator::BeginPlay()
{
    Super::BeginPlay();
}

void AFluidSimulator::Tick(float DeltaTime)
{
    Super::Tick(DeltaTime);
    UpdateParticles(DeltaTime);
    RenderParticles();
}

void AFluidSimulator::AddParticle(const FVector& Position,
const FVector& Velocity)
{
    if (ParticlePositions.Num() >= MaxParticles)
        return;

    ParticlePositions.Add(Position);
    ParticleVelocities.Add(Velocity);
}

void AFluidSimulator::UpdateParticles(float DeltaTime)
{
    for (int32 i = 0; i < ParticlePositions.Num(); i++)
    {
        FVector& Position = ParticlePositions[i];
        FVector& Velocity = ParticleVelocities[i];

        // Apply velocity
        Position += Velocity * DeltaTime;
```

```
        // Apply viscosity (dampening)
        Velocity *= 1.0f - Viscosity * DeltaTime;
    }
}
void AFluidSimulator::RenderParticles()
{
    for (const FVector& Position : ParticlePositions)
    {
        // Visualization logic (e.g., draw spheres at particle
        positions)
        DrawDebugSphere(GetWorld(), Position, ParticleRadius,
        12, FColor::Blue, false, -1.0f);
    }
}
```

Fluid dynamics bring life to environments by simulating realistic fluid behavior. This subtopic showcased their principles, uses, and a practical code example. Next, we will discuss gravity manipulation, exploring how altering gravity affects gameplay mechanics and environmental interactions.

Gravity Manipulation

Gravity manipulation in game development involves dynamically altering gravity to affect objects, characters, or environments. This mechanic can create innovative gameplay experiences by allowing players or objects to defy, reverse, or customize gravitational forces.

CHAPTER 7   PHYSICS AND DYNAMICS

Core Components of Gravity Manipulation

Key aspects include

- **Global Gravity Changes**: Altering the world's gravitational force

- **Object-Specific Gravity**: Customizing gravity for individual objects or characters

- **Directional Gravity**: Adjusting gravity to act in specific directions

- **Transition Effects**: Smoothly blending between gravity states to enhance realism

Reviewing the Code

Listing 7-17 outlines the structure of a customizable gravity system. This header file provides the core properties and functions needed to control gravity's behavior in non-standard directions and magnitudes.

- **GravityDirection**: Specifies the direction in which gravity acts

- **GravityStrength**: Defines the magnitude of gravitational force

- **SetGravity()**: Allows dynamic changes to the gravity direction and strength

- **ApplyGravity()**: Applies the customized gravity to game objects

Listing 7-17. GravityManipulator.h

```cpp
#pragma once

#include "CoreMinimal.h"
#include "GameFramework/Actor.h"
#include "GravityManipulator.generated.h"

UCLASS()
class MYGAME_API AGravityManipulator : public AActor
{
    GENERATED_BODY()

public:
    AGravityManipulator();

protected:
    virtual void BeginPlay() override;
    virtual void Tick(float DeltaTime) override;

public:
    UPROPERTY(EditAnywhere, BlueprintReadWrite, Category = "Gravity")
    FVector GravityDirection;

    UPROPERTY(EditAnywhere, BlueprintReadWrite, Category = "Gravity")
    float GravityStrength;

    UFUNCTION(BlueprintCallable, Category = "Gravity")
    void SetGravity(const FVector& NewDirection, float NewStrength);

private:
    void ApplyGravity();
};
```

CHAPTER 7   PHYSICS AND DYNAMICS

Listing 7-18 presents the implementation of a flexible gravity system, demonstrating how gravity can be redefined and applied dynamically to game objects.

- **SetGravity()**: Dynamically updates the GravityDirection and GravityStrength based on input values. This allows the environment to shift gravitational behavior during gameplay, enabling scenarios like rotating worlds or gravity puzzles.

- **ApplyGravity()**: Applies the gravity force to all relevant physics objects in the scene. It multiplies the normalized GravityDirection by GravityStrength and updates the velocity or force of each object accordingly.

- **GravityDirection**: This directional vector is a core element of the system and can be customized to simulate unconventional effects such as reversed gravity, lateral pulls, or zero-gravity zones.

Listing 7-18. GravityManipulator.cpp

```cpp
#include "GravityManipulator.h"
#include "GameFramework/Actor.h"

AGravityManipulator::AGravityManipulator()
{
    PrimaryActorTick.bCanEverTick = true;
    GravityDirection = FVector(0.0f, 0.0f, -1.0f);
    GravityStrength = 980.0f; // Default gravity strength
    in cm/s²
}
```

CHAPTER 7 PHYSICS AND DYNAMICS

```cpp
void AGravityManipulator::BeginPlay()
{
    Super::BeginPlay();
}

void AGravityManipulator::Tick(float DeltaTime)
{
    Super::Tick(DeltaTime);
    ApplyGravity();
}

void AGravityManipulator::SetGravity(const FVector& NewDirection, float NewStrength)
{
    GravityDirection = NewDirection.GetSafeNormal();
    // Normalize the direction vector
    GravityStrength = NewStrength;
}

void AGravityManipulator::ApplyGravity()
{
    for (TActorIterator<AActor> ActorItr(GetWorld()); ActorItr; ++ActorItr)
    {
        AActor* Actor = *ActorItr;

        if (Actor && Actor->GetRootComponent() &&
        Actor->GetRootComponent()->IsSimulatingPhysics())
        {
```

```
            FVector Force = GravityDirection * GravityStrength
            * Actor->GetRootComponent()->GetMass();
            Actor->GetRootComponent()->AddForce(Force);
        }
    }
}
```

Gravity manipulation opens new possibilities for unique gameplay mechanics and immersive experiences. This subtopic demonstrated its concepts and an implementation example. Next, we will explore force fields, covering their uses in gameplay and techniques for simulating them.

Force Fields

Force fields are used in game development to create invisible barriers, zones of influence, or protective shields that interact with objects and characters. They add dynamic gameplay elements by affecting movement, projectiles, or environmental effects.

Importance of Force Fields

- **Gameplay Interaction**: Force fields can repel, attract, or block objects, influencing gameplay strategies.
- **Realistic Physics**: Simulates magnetic, electric, or other force-based interactions.
- **Immersive Mechanics**: Enhances environments with energy shields, protective barriers, or hazard zones.

CHAPTER 7   PHYSICS AND DYNAMICS

Core Components of Force Fields

Key aspects of force fields include

- **Repulsion or Attraction**: Forces that push objects away or pull them toward the source
- **Activation Zones**: Areas where the force field's effects are active
- **Customizable Strength**: Adjustable parameters to control the intensity of the force
- **Interactive Effects**: Visual and auditory feedback to represent the force field's presence

Reviewing the Code

Listing 7-19 introduces the key components of a force field system, designed to interact with nearby objects using a customizable radius and force intensity.

- **ForceStrength**: Determines the intensity of the force applied to objects
- **FieldRadius**: Specifies the effective range of the force field
- **SetForceStrength()**: Adjusts the strength dynamically
- **SetFieldRadius()**: Modifies the field's effective radius

Listing 7-19. ForceField.h

```
#pragma once

#include "CoreMinimal.h"
#include "GameFramework/Actor.h"
#include "ForceField.generated.h"

UCLASS()
class MYGAME_API AForceField : public AActor
{
    GENERATED_BODY()

public:
    AForceField();

protected:
    virtual void BeginPlay() override;

public:
    virtual void Tick(float DeltaTime) override;

    UPROPERTY(EditAnywhere, BlueprintReadWrite, Category =
    "Force Field")
    float ForceStrength;

    UPROPERTY(EditAnywhere, BlueprintReadWrite, Category =
    "Force Field")
    float FieldRadius;

    UFUNCTION(BlueprintCallable, Category = "Force Field")
    void SetForceStrength(float NewStrength);

    UFUNCTION(BlueprintCallable, Category = "Force Field")
    void SetFieldRadius(float NewRadius);
```

```cpp
private:
    void ApplyForceToObjects();
};
```

Listing 7-20 details how the force field system is applied in real time, dynamically interacting with objects based on their position relative to the field's origin.

- **ApplyForceToObjects()**: Calculates and applies force based on distance and direction from the field's center
- **ForceStrength**: Scales the force's intensity
- **FieldRadius**: Ensures the effect only applies to objects within a specified range

Listing 7-20. ForceField.cpp

```cpp
#include "ForceField.h"
#include "GameFramework/Actor.h"

AForceField::AForceField()
{
    PrimaryActorTick.bCanEverTick = true;
    ForceStrength = 500.0f;
    FieldRadius = 300.0f;
}

void AForceField::BeginPlay()
{
    Super::BeginPlay();
}

void AForceField::Tick(float DeltaTime)
{
```

CHAPTER 7 PHYSICS AND DYNAMICS

```
    Super::Tick(DeltaTime);
    ApplyForceToObjects();
}

void AForceField::SetForceStrength(float NewStrength)
{
    ForceStrength = NewStrength;
}

void AForceField::SetFieldRadius(float NewRadius)
{
    FieldRadius = NewRadius;
}

void AForceField::ApplyForceToObjects()
{
    TArray<AActor*> OverlappingActors;
    GetOverlappingActors(OverlappingActors);

    for (AActor* Actor : OverlappingActors)
    {
        if (Actor->GetRootComponent() && Actor->
        GetRootComponent()->IsSimulatingPhysics())
        {
            FVector Direction = Actor->GetActorLocation() -
            GetActorLocation();
            float Distance = Direction.Size();

            if (Distance <= FieldRadius)
            {
                Direction.Normalize();
```

```
            FVector Force = Direction * ForceStrength *
            (1.0f - Distance / FieldRadius);
            Actor->GetRootComponent()->AddForce(Force);
        }
      }
    }
}
```

Force fields add dynamic interactivity and immersion by influencing objects and characters within their range. This subtopic demonstrated their concepts and an implementation example.

Summary

This chapter explored the systems that drive motion and interaction in a game world. Starting with rigid body dynamics, we learned how to simulate mass, gravity, and force. We then covered soft body dynamics, particle systems, cloth, vehicle, and rope physics, each adding layers of realism to gameplay. The chapter also introduced custom gravity and force fields, offering ways to create unique interactions and environmental effects. Together, these mechanics form the foundation for building dynamic, responsive, and immersive game environments.

Let's now move to another core aspect of game development which is audio and visual effects.

CHAPTER 8

Audio and Visual Effects

In game development, audio and visual effects play a vital role in enhancing the player's sensory experience, creating a more immersive and emotionally engaging environment. These elements not only amplify the atmosphere but also provide feedback, cues, and rewards, enriching the overall gameplay experience. From dynamic soundtracks to impactful visual effects, this chapter explores the tools and techniques that bring games to life.

At their core, audio and visual effects add context and depth to player actions and environmental interactions. Sound effects like footsteps, weapon sounds, or environmental ambiance make the game world feel alive. Similarly, visual cues such as screen shakes or particle effects emphasize key events, ensuring players remain engaged and informed throughout their journey.

Advanced systems use dynamic and context-sensitive techniques to elevate the experience. For example, dynamic music systems adjust the soundtrack based on player progress or tension levels, while advanced post-processing effects transform the game's visuals to evoke specific moods. Combined with synchronized animations, UI transitions, and environmental audio, these features create a seamless and captivating experience.

CHAPTER 8 AUDIO AND VISUAL EFFECTS

In this chapter, we will delve into the intricacies of audio and visual effects, exploring concepts like sound triggering on events, dynamic music systems, and visual feedback mechanisms. You'll learn how to implement these effects in your game through practical examples and detailed explanations. By the end of this chapter, you'll understand how to create immersive environments that captivate players through sound and visuals.

Sound Triggering on Events

In game development, sound plays an integral role in enhancing the player's experience by providing auditory feedback, amplifying the emotional impact, and guiding the player through the environment. Sound triggering on events refers to the automatic playback of specific sounds based on in-game occurrences, such as player actions, interactions with objects, or environmental changes.

Importance of Sound Triggering on Events

Let's talk about why we need this:

- **Gameplay Feedback**: Sound cues provide immediate feedback to the player, signaling actions like picking up items, defeating enemies, or interacting with objects.

- **Immersion**: Dynamic sound effects based on events help build a deeper sense of immersion, enhancing the emotional and sensory impact of the game world.

- **Storytelling**: Sound effects can also be used to convey critical narrative moments, such as the sound of footsteps when approaching an enemy or the sound of a door creaking open, adding suspense and drama.

CHAPTER 8 AUDIO AND VISUAL EFFECTS

Core Components of Sound Triggering

Key aspects of sound triggering include

- **Event Detection:** Identifying specific events in the game that should trigger a sound, such as player actions, environmental changes, or game state transitions

- **Sound Files:** Pre-recorded or generated sounds that correspond to the specific event

- **Audio Triggers:** Mechanisms that play sound effects when the event occurs, such as calls to the sound system or animation triggers

- **Volume and Pitch Control:** Adjusting the audio based on the situation, such as lowering the volume when the player is far from the event or increasing the pitch during intense moments

Reviewing the Code

Listing 8-1 outlines a basic sound trigger system. This setup allows a sound to be played when the player comes within a certain distance of an actor, offering localized audio feedback that enhances immersion.

- **TriggerSound:** The sound that will be triggered

- **TriggerDistance:** The distance at which the sound is played relative to the player's position

- **PlaySoundAtTrigger():** The function to play the sound when the conditions are met

- **CheckTriggerDistance():** The function that checks if the player is within the specified range to trigger the sound

CHAPTER 8 AUDIO AND VISUAL EFFECTS

Listing 8-1. SoundTrigger.h

```
#pragma once

#include "CoreMinimal.h"
#include "GameFramework/Actor.h"

class USoundBase;
class UBoxComponent;

#include "SoundTrigger.generated.h"

UCLASS()
class MYGAME_API ASoundTrigger : public AActor
{
    GENERATED_BODY()

public:
    ASoundTrigger();

protected:
    virtual void BeginPlay() override;

public:
    virtual void Tick(float DeltaTime) override;

    UPROPERTY(EditAnywhere, BlueprintReadWrite, Category = "Sound")
    USoundBase* TriggerSound;

    UPROPERTY(EditAnywhere, BlueprintReadWrite, Category = "Sound")
    float TriggerDistance;
```

CHAPTER 8   AUDIO AND VISUAL EFFECTS

```
    UFUNCTION(BlueprintCallable, Category = "Sound")
    void PlaySoundAtTrigger();

private:
    void CheckTriggerDistance();
};
```

Listing 8-2 presents the runtime implementation of a collision-based sound trigger system. It uses a UBoxComponent to detect when the player enters a defined volume and plays a sound accordingly.

- **PlaySoundAtTrigger()**: This function plays the designated sound at the actor's location using UGameplayStatics::PlaySoundAtLocation().

- **OnPlayerEnter()**: Event triggered when the player overlaps the box component, used to determine if the sound should be played.

- **TriggerZone**: A UBoxComponent that defines the area in which the sound can be triggered.

- **TriggerSound**: The sound asset that is played when the player enters the trigger volume.

Listing 8-2. SoundTrigger.cpp

```
#include "SoundTrigger.h"
#include "Components/BoxComponent.h"
#include "Kismet/GameplayStatics.h"
#include "Sound/SoundBase.h"
#include "GameFramework/Actor.h"
#include "GameFramework/Pawn.h"

ASoundTrigger::ASoundTrigger()
{
    PrimaryActorTick.bCanEverTick = false;
```

629

CHAPTER 8   AUDIO AND VISUAL EFFECTS

```
    // Create and set up box component
    TriggerZone = CreateDefaultSubobject<UBoxComponent>
    (TEXT("TriggerZone"));
    RootComponent = TriggerZone;
    TriggerZone->SetCollisionEnabled(ECollisionEnabled::
    QueryOnly);
    TriggerZone->SetCollisionObjectType(ECC_WorldDynamic);
    TriggerZone->SetCollisionResponseToAllChannels(ECR_Ignore);
    TriggerZone->SetCollisionResponseToChannel(ECC_Pawn,
    ECR_Overlap);
    TriggerZone->SetBoxExtent(FVector(200.0f));

    TriggerZone->OnComponentBeginOverlap.AddDynamic(this,
    &ASoundTrigger::OnPlayerEnter);
}
void ASoundTrigger::BeginPlay()
{
    Super::BeginPlay();
}
void ASoundTrigger::PlaySoundAtTrigger()
{
    if (TriggerSound)
    {
        UGameplayStatics::PlaySoundAtLocation(this,
        TriggerSound, GetActorLocation());
    }
}
void ASoundTrigger::OnPlayerEnter(UPrimitiveComponent*
OverlappedComp, AActor* OtherActor, UPrimitiveComponent*
OtherComp, int32 OtherBodyIndexm, bool bFromSweep, const
FHitResult& SweepResult)
```

```
{
    if (OtherActor && OtherActor == GetWorld()->
    GetFirstPlayerController()->GetPawn())
    {
        PlaySoundAtTrigger();
    }
}
```

Sound triggering on events enhances gameplay by providing auditory feedback and immersing players in the game world. This subtopic demonstrated the process of detecting events and playing sounds, showing how simple mechanics can be used to enrich the player experience. Now that we've covered sound, let's move on to dynamic music systems.

Dynamic Music Systems

Dynamic music systems are a critical component in modern game development, designed to adjust the game's soundtrack based on in-game events, player actions, or the state of the environment. Unlike static music, which plays a continuous track throughout a game, dynamic music responds to changes, creating a more immersive and emotionally engaging experience for the player.

Importance of Dynamic Music Systems

Let's talk about why we need this:

- **Emotion and Atmosphere**: Dynamic music can enhance the emotional impact of a scene, whether it's building suspense during a chase, creating tension in a battle, or evoking calmness during exploration.

- **Adaptation to Gameplay**: It responds to the player's actions or game state, such as transitioning from peaceful exploration music to intense battle music when an enemy is encountered.

- **Immersive Experience**: By adapting to gameplay, dynamic music reinforces the narrative and gameplay experience, making the world feel more alive and reactive.

Core Components of Dynamic Music Systems

Key aspects of dynamic music systems include

- **Music Layers**: Music is often composed of multiple layers or stems that can be mixed and matched to reflect different gameplay states.

- **Triggers and Transitions**: Events or conditions in the game that trigger changes in the music, such as entering a new area, defeating enemies, or completing objectives.

- **Music States**: Defined conditions under which the music changes, such as combat, exploration, or special moments in the story.

- **Blending and Fading**: Smooth transitions between music tracks to avoid abrupt changes that can disrupt the player's immersion.

CHAPTER 8   AUDIO AND VISUAL EFFECTS

Reviewing the Code

Listing 8-3 introduces the structure for a dynamic music manager. This system adjusts background music based on the player's current gameplay state, enhancing immersion through audio cues.

- **ExplorationMusic, CombatMusic, BossMusic**: Music tracks corresponding to different states in the game
- **ChangeMusicState()**: A function to change the current music state based on the player's progression
- **PlayMusic()**: A function that plays the appropriate music track based on the current state
- **CurrentMusicState**: A variable that holds the current music state (e.g., Exploration, Combat, Boss)

Listing 8-3. DynamicMusicManager.h

```
#pragma once

#include "CoreMinimal.h"
#include "GameFramework/Actor.h"
#include "DynamicMusicManager.generated.h"

UENUM(BlueprintType)
enum class ESoundtrackState : uint8
{
    Exploration UMETA(DisplayName = "Exploration"),
    Combat      UMETA(DisplayName = "Combat"),
    Boss        UMETA(DisplayName = "Boss")
};
```

CHAPTER 8 AUDIO AND VISUAL EFFECTS

```cpp
UCLASS()
class MYGAME_API ADynamicMusicManager : public AActor
{
    GENERATED_BODY()

public:
    ADynamicMusicManager();

protected:
    virtual void BeginPlay() override;

public:
    virtual void Tick(float DeltaTime) override;

    UPROPERTY(EditAnywhere, BlueprintReadWrite, Category = "Music")
    USoundBase* ExplorationMusic;

    UPROPERTY(EditAnywhere, BlueprintReadWrite, Category = "Music")
    USoundBase* CombatMusic;

    UPROPERTY(EditAnywhere, BlueprintReadWrite, Category = "Music")
    USoundBase* BossMusic;

    UFUNCTION(BlueprintCallable, Category = "Music")
    void ChangeMusicState(ESoundtrackState NewState);

private:
    void PlayMusic(USoundBase* NewMusic);

    ESoundtrackState CurrentMusicState;
};
```

CHAPTER 8 AUDIO AND VISUAL EFFECTS

Listing 8-4 describes the implementation of a dynamic music system that adapts the background music to match gameplay scenarios in real time.

- **PlayMusic()**: This function plays the specified music using the UGameplayStatics::PlaySound2D() function, ensuring that the music plays globally.

- **ChangeMusicState()**: This function changes the music based on the current game state, for example, switching to combat music if the player enters a battle.

- **CurrentMusicState**: Keeps track of the current music state, ensuring that the music only changes when necessary.

Listing 8-4. DynamicMusicManager.cpp

```cpp
#include "DynamicMusicManager.h"
#include "Kismet/GameplayStatics.h"

ADynamicMusicManager::ADynamicMusicManager()
{
    PrimaryActorTick.bCanEverTick = true;
    CurrentMusicState = ESoundtrackState::Exploration;
    // Default state
}

void ADynamicMusicManager::BeginPlay()
{
    Super::BeginPlay();
    PlayMusic(ExplorationMusic);
    // Start with exploration music
}
```

CHAPTER 8 AUDIO AND VISUAL EFFECTS

```
void ADynamicMusicManager::Tick(float DeltaTime)
{
    Super::Tick(DeltaTime);
    // Add logic here to detect game state changes and call
    ChangeMusicState()
}

void ADynamicMusicManager::ChangeMusicState(ESoundtrackState NewState)
{
    if (NewState != CurrentMusicState)
    {
        CurrentMusicState = NewState;

        switch (NewState)
        {
        case ESoundtrackState::Exploration:
            PlayMusic(ExplorationMusic);
            break;
        case ESoundtrackState::Combat:
            PlayMusic(CombatMusic);
            break;
        case ESoundtrackState::Boss:
            PlayMusic(BossMusic);
            break;
        default:
            break;
        }
    }
}

void ADynamicMusicManager::PlayMusic(USoundBase* NewMusic)
{
```

CHAPTER 8   AUDIO AND VISUAL EFFECTS

```
    if (NewMusic)
    {
        UGameplayStatics::PlaySound2D(this, NewMusic);
    }
}
```

Dynamic music systems help create a responsive and emotionally engaging experience for the player by adjusting the soundtrack to match the game's state. This subtopic covered the key concepts behind dynamic music systems, including triggers and transitions, with an implementation example. Now that we've discussed dynamic music, let's move on to visual feedback on actions.

Visual Feedback on Actions

Visual feedback is a crucial element in game design, providing players with immediate, intuitive responses to their actions. Whether it's highlighting an interactable object, showing damage effects, or indicating successful completion of a task, visual feedback enhances gameplay clarity and player engagement.

Importance of Visual Feedback on Actions

Let's talk about why we need this:

- **Clarity and Communication**: Clearly shows players the outcome of their actions, reducing confusion and enhancing understanding
- **Immersion and Realism**: Creates a more immersive experience by visually connecting player actions to the game world's responses
- **Player Engagement**: Encourages continued interaction by rewarding actions with satisfying visual cues

CHAPTER 8   AUDIO AND VISUAL EFFECTS

Core Components of Visual Feedback

Key aspects of visual feedback include

- **Highlighting**: Using glowing or color changes to indicate interactable objects or areas

- **Damage Effects**: Visual cues such as screen flashes, blood splatters, or character animations to show damage taken

- **Success Indicators**: Particle effects, animations, or sound cues to signal successful actions like completing a puzzle or defeating an enemy

- **Real-Time Updates**: Dynamic elements like health bars, ammo counters, or quest progress markers that update instantly in response to player actions

Reviewing the Code

Listing 8-5 introduces a visual feedback system for object interaction, using dynamic materials and visual cues to enhance player experience.

- **HighlightObject()**: A function to apply or remove a highlight effect on an object

- **ShowActionSuccess()**: A function to trigger a success visual effect, like a particle burst or glow

- **DynamicMaterial**: A dynamically created material instance for altering object appearance at runtime

CHAPTER 8 AUDIO AND VISUAL EFFECTS

Listing 8-5. VisualFeedbackComponent.h

```
#pragma once

#include "CoreMinimal.h"
#include "Components/ActorComponent.h"
#include "VisualFeedbackComponent.generated.h"

UCLASS(ClassGroup = (Custom), meta =
(BlueprintSpawnableComponent))
class MYGAME_API UVisualFeedbackComponent : public
UActorComponent
{
    GENERATED_BODY()

public:
    UVisualFeedbackComponent();

protected:
    virtual void BeginPlay() override;

public:
    UFUNCTION(BlueprintCallable, Category = "Visual Feedback")
    void HighlightObject(bool bIsHighlighted);

    UFUNCTION(BlueprintCallable, Category = "Visual Feedback")
    void ShowActionSuccess();

private:
    UMaterialInstanceDynamic* DynamicMaterial;
};
```

Listing 8-6 describes the runtime implementation of a visual feedback system for highlighting and success indicators using dynamic materials.

- **HighlightObject()**: Adjusts a material parameter (HighlightIntensity) to visually indicate if the object is interactable.

- **ShowActionSuccess()**: Changes a material parameter (GlowColor) to indicate successful interaction with a green glow.

- **DynamicMaterial**: Dynamically created material instance enables runtime adjustments without altering the original material.

- **Scalar Parameter Named HighlightIntensity**: Connect this to either emissive intensity or a lerp between two color states to create a glowing or highlighting effect.

- **Vector Parameter Named GlowColor**: This is typically used to control the emissive color of the material. Changing it to green (e.g., FLinearColor::Green) visually confirms a successful action.

Listing 8-6. VisualFeedbackComponent.cpp

```
#include "VisualFeedbackComponent.h"
#include "GameFramework/Actor.h"
#include "Components/PrimitiveComponent.h"
#include "Materials/MaterialInstanceDynamic.h"

UVisualFeedbackComponent::UVisualFeedbackComponent()
{
    PrimaryComponentTick.bCanEverTick = false;
}
```

```cpp
void UVisualFeedbackComponent::BeginPlay()
{
    Super::BeginPlay();

    UPrimitiveComponent* PrimitiveComponent =
    Cast<UPrimitiveComponent>(GetOwner()->GetRootComponent());
    if (PrimitiveComponent)
    {
        DynamicMaterial = PrimitiveComponent->
        CreateAndSetMaterialInstanceDynamic(0);
    }
}

void UVisualFeedbackComponent::HighlightObject
(bool bIsHighlighted)
{
    if (DynamicMaterial)
    {
        DynamicMaterial->SetScalarParameterValue
        ("HighlightIntensity", bIsHighlighted ? 1.0f : 0.0f);
    }
}

void UVisualFeedbackComponent::ShowActionSuccess()
{
    if (DynamicMaterial)
    {
        DynamicMaterial->SetVectorParameterValue("GlowColor",
        FLinearColor::Green);
    }
}
```

Visual feedback on actions enhances gameplay by providing players with clear, immediate responses to their actions, improving both engagement and understanding. This subtopic covered the core concepts of visual feedback and demonstrated its implementation with a code example. Next, we'll explore screen shakes and camera effects, another crucial aspect of creating immersive gameplay.

Screen Shakes and Camera Effects

Screen shakes and camera effects are powerful tools in game development, used to convey impact, intensity, or emotion. Whether it's an earthquake, an explosion, or a dramatic cutscene, these effects immerse players and enhance the cinematic quality of the game.

Importance of Screen Shakes and Camera Effects

Let's talk about why we need this:

- **Conveying Impact**: Simulates physical force, such as a heavy attack or explosion, adding weight to in-game actions
- **Enhancing Drama**: Creates tension, excitement, or urgency during key moments
- **Immersion**: Involves players by making them feel part of the action, as the effects resonate directly through the game's perspective

Core Components of Screen Shakes and Camera Effects

Key aspects include

- **Screen Shake**: Small or large camera vibrations to simulate explosions, impacts, or intense motion
- **FOV (Field of View) Adjustment**: Dynamically altering the camera's FOV to create a sense of speed or focus
- **Motion Blur**: Adds realism during fast movements or dramatic shifts in the scene
- **Post-Processing Overlays**: Effects like color grading, vignette, or desaturation to convey mood or simulate damage
- **Dynamic Camera Movement**: Smooth transitions, rotations, or panning for cinematic sequences

Reviewing the Code

Listing 8-7 introduces the key components of a screen shake component system. This setup is commonly used to enhance gameplay feedback during sprinting, jumping, landing, or taking damage.

- **Amplitude**: Defines the intensity of the shake
- **Frequency**: Controls how quickly the shake oscillates
- **Duration**: Specifies how long the screen shake lasts
- **StartShake()**: Initiates the screen shake effect

Listing 8-7. CameraShakeComponent.h

```cpp
#pragma once

#include "CoreMinimal.h"
#include "Components/ActorComponent.h"
#include "Camera/CameraShakeBase.h"
#include "CameraShakeComponent.generated.h"

UCLASS( ClassGroup=(Custom), meta=(BlueprintSpawnableComponent) )
class MYGAME_API UCameraShakeComponent : public UActorComponent
{
    GENERATED_BODY()

public:
    UCameraShakeComponent();

    UPROPERTY(EditAnywhere, BlueprintReadWrite, Category = "Shake")
    TSubclassOf<UCameraShakeBase> SprintShake;

    UPROPERTY(EditAnywhere, BlueprintReadWrite, Category = "Shake")
    TSubclassOf<UCameraShakeBase> LandingShake;

    UPROPERTY(EditAnywhere, BlueprintReadWrite, Category = "Shake")
    float ShakeScale;

    UFUNCTION(BlueprintCallable, Category = "Shake")
    void TriggerSprintShake();

    UFUNCTION(BlueprintCallable, Category = "Shake")
    void TriggerLandingShake();
};
```

CHAPTER 8 AUDIO AND VISUAL EFFECTS

Listing 8-8 presents the implementation of a screen shake system using Unreal Engine's camera manager. It demonstrates how to apply shake effects dynamically based on in-game actions.

- **StartShake()**: Initializes and applies the camera shake effect based on the defined parameters
- **Amplitude, Frequency, Duration**: Key properties controlling the intensity, speed, and length of the shake
- **PlayerCameraManager**: Manages the player's camera and applies the shake effect

Listing 8-8. CameraShakeComponent.cpp

```cpp
#include "CameraShakeComponent.h"
#include "GameFramework/PlayerController.h"
#include "Camera/PlayerCameraManager.h"
#include "Kismet/GameplayStatics.h"

UCameraShakeComponent::UCameraShakeComponent()
{
    PrimaryComponentTick.bCanEverTick = false;
    ShakeScale = 1.0f;
}

void UCameraShakeComponent::TriggerSprintShake()
{
    APlayerController* PC = UGameplayStatics::
    GetPlayerController(GetWorld(), 0);
    if (PC && SprintShake)
    {
        PC->PlayerCameraManager->StartCameraShake(SprintShake,
        ShakeScale);
    }
}
```

```cpp
void UCameraShakeComponent::TriggerLandingShake()
{
    APlayerController* PC = UGameplayStatics::GetPlayer
    Controller(GetWorld(), 0);
    if (PC && LandingShake)
    {
        PC->PlayerCameraManager->StartCameraShake(LandingShake,
        ShakeScale);
    }
}
```

Screen shakes and camera effects are essential for creating impactful and immersive experiences in games. They bridge the gap between the player and the action, amplifying the intensity of gameplay moments. This subtopic demonstrated their importance and implementation with a practical code example. Next, we will delve into post-processing effects, which further elevate the visual quality of a game.

Post-Processing Effects

Post-processing effects are visual enhancements applied after a frame is rendered to improve the aesthetics and mood of a game. These effects are crucial for creating immersive environments, cinematic visuals, and distinctive artistic styles.

Core Components of Post-Processing Effects

Key aspects include

- **Color Grading**: Adjusts the color palette to create a specific mood
- **Bloom**: Adds a glow to bright areas for a more vibrant look

CHAPTER 8 AUDIO AND VISUAL EFFECTS

- **Depth of Field**: Focuses on specific areas, blurring the background or foreground

- **Motion Blur**: Simulates realistic movement for dynamic objects or fast camera transitions

- **Vignette**: Darkens edges of the screen to focus attention on the center

- **Lens Flares**: Simulates light scattering from strong light sources

Reviewing the Code

Listing 8-9 introduces a basic post-processing controller used to dynamically adjust visual effects in the game. It provides runtime control over visual parameters such as bloom and color grading to enhance mood or gameplay clarity.

- **PostProcessComponent**: Handles post-processing effects

- **BloomIntensity**: Adjusts the glow around bright areas

- **ColorGrading**: Changes the color tones for atmospheric effects

- **UpdatePostProcessing()**: Dynamically modifies post-processing settings

Listing 8-9. PostProcessingManager.h

```
#pragma once

#include "CoreMinimal.h"
#include "GameFramework/Actor.h"
#include "PostProcessingManager.generated.h"
```

```cpp
UCLASS()
class MYGAME_API APostProcessingManager : public AActor
{
    GENERATED_BODY()
public:
    APostProcessingManager();

protected:
    virtual void BeginPlay() override;

public:
    UPROPERTY(EditAnywhere, BlueprintReadWrite, Category =
    "Post Processing")
    class UPostProcessComponent* PostProcessComponent;

    UPROPERTY(EditAnywhere, BlueprintReadWrite, Category =
    "Post Processing Settings")
    float BloomIntensity;

    UPROPERTY(EditAnywhere, BlueprintReadWrite, Category =
    "Post Processing Settings")
    FVector4 ColorGrading;

    UFUNCTION(BlueprintCallable, Category = "Post Processing")
    void UpdatePostProcessing(float NewBloomIntensity, FVector4
    NewColorGrading);
};
```

Listing 8-10 explains the implementation of a post-processing controller that enables dynamic visual adjustments during gameplay.

- **PostProcessComponent**: Configures and applies the post-processing effects
- **BloomIntensity**: Adjusts the brightness and glow effect dynamically

CHAPTER 8 AUDIO AND VISUAL EFFECTS

- **ColorGrading**: Alters the overall tone and color saturation of the scene
- **UpdatePostProcessing()**: Updates settings for bloom and color grading during runtime

Listing 8-10. PostProcessingManager.cpp

```
#include "PostProcessingManager.h"
#include "Components/PostProcessComponent.h"

APostProcessingManager::APostProcessingManager()
{
    PrimaryActorTick.bCanEverTick = true;
    PostProcessComponent = CreateDefaultSubobject<UPostProcess
    Component>(TEXT("PostProcessComponent"));
    RootComponent = PostProcessComponent;

    BloomIntensity = 1.0f;
    ColorGrading = FVector4(1.0f, 1.0f, 1.0f, 1.0f);
}

void APostProcessingManager::BeginPlay()
{
    Super::BeginPlay();
    UpdatePostProcessing(BloomIntensity, ColorGrading);
}

void APostProcessingManager::UpdatePostProcessing
(float NewBloomIntensity, FVector4 NewColorGrading)
{
    if (PostProcessComponent)
    {
        PostProcessComponent->
        Settings.bOverride_BloomIntensity = true;
```

```
        PostProcessComponent->Settings.BloomIntensity =
        NewBloomIntensity;

        PostProcessComponent->
        Settings.bOverride_ColorSaturation = true;
        PostProcessComponent->Settings.ColorSaturation
        = FVector(NewColorGrading.X, NewColorGrading.Y,
        NewColorGrading.Z);
    }
}
```

Post-processing effects enhance the visual fidelity and artistic expression of a game. By carefully combining these effects, developers can create visually stunning and emotionally engaging experiences. Next, we will explore UI animations, which play a key role in delivering dynamic and intuitive user interfaces.

UI Animations

UI animations are integral to creating a smooth and engaging user experience in games. These animations enhance the visual appeal, provide feedback to player actions, and make interactions more intuitive.

Importance of UI Animations

Let's talk about why we need this:

- **Improved Usability**: Helps players understand system states and actions through visual cues
- **Feedback Mechanism**: Reinforces player interactions with dynamic transitions and animations

- **Aesthetic Appeal**: Enhances the overall visual quality and polish of the game
- **Guidance**: Directs player attention to critical UI elements or game features

Core Components of UI Animations

Key aspects include

- **Button Animations**: Highlight buttons when hovered or clicked
- **Progress Bars**: Smoothly animate filling to indicate loading or progress
- **Notifications and Pop-Ups**: Slide-in, fade, or scale effects for alerts and messages
- **Menu Transitions**: Fluid transitions between menus for better navigation
- **HUD Animations**: Dynamic updates to heads-up display elements like health bars or score counters

Reviewing the Code

Listing 8-11 describes the structure of a UI animation controller that manages visual feedback using UMG animations. It provides functions to trigger animations for interactive elements like buttons and notifications, enhancing player engagement through dynamic UI responses:

CHAPTER 8　AUDIO AND VISUAL EFFECTS

- **PlayButtonHoverAnimation()**: Triggers an animation when a button is hovered
- **PlayNotificationAnimation()**: Plays an animation for displaying notifications
- **UWidgetAnimation**: A reference to animations created in UMG

Listing 8-11. UIAnimationWidget.h

```cpp
#pragma once

#include "CoreMinimal.h"
#include "Blueprint/UserWidget.h"
#include "UIAnimationWidget.generated.h"

UCLASS()
class MYGAME_API UUIAnimationWidget : public UUserWidget
{
    GENERATED_BODY()
public:
    UFUNCTION(BlueprintCallable, Category = "UI Animations")
    void PlayButtonHoverAnimation();

    UFUNCTION(BlueprintCallable, Category = "UI Animations")
    void PlayNotificationAnimation();

protected:
    UPROPERTY(meta = (BindWidgetAnim), Transient)
    UWidgetAnimation* ButtonHoverAnimation;

    UPROPERTY(meta = (BindWidgetAnim), Transient)
    UWidgetAnimation* NotificationAnimation;
};
```

CHAPTER 8 AUDIO AND VISUAL EFFECTS

Listing 8-12 presents the runtime implementation of the UI animation controller. It shows how user interface feedback is triggered using predefined UMG animations to improve interactivity and user experience.

- **PlayButtonHoverAnimation()**: Plays the hover animation when a button is interacted with
- **PlayNotificationAnimation()**: Displays notifications with an engaging animation
- **PlayAnimation()**: A built-in function to trigger animations defined in the UMG editor

Listing 8-12. UIAnimationWidget.cpp

```
#include "UIAnimationWidget.h"

void UUIAnimationWidget::PlayButtonHoverAnimation()
{
    if (ButtonHoverAnimation)
    {
        PlayAnimation(ButtonHoverAnimation);
    }
}

void UUIAnimationWidget::PlayNotificationAnimation()
{
    if (NotificationAnimation)
    {
        PlayAnimation(NotificationAnimation);
    }
}
```

UI animations provide an essential layer of interactivity and polish to a game, ensuring that the interface is both functional and visually pleasing. By leveraging animations effectively, developers can create intuitive and engaging user experiences. Next, we will discuss HUD design, focusing on creating clear and immersive heads-up displays for players.

HUD Design

Heads-up displays (HUDs) are a critical component of a game's user interface, providing players with essential information without disrupting their immersion. HUD design focuses on clarity, functionality, and aesthetics to ensure players can access information seamlessly during gameplay.

Importance of HUD Design

Let's talk about why we need this:

- **Real-Time Information**: Displays key stats like health, ammo, score, and objectives during gameplay
- **Player Immersion**: Integrates visually into the game world without being obtrusive
- **Guidance**: Helps players make informed decisions by showing contextual data
- **Customization**: Offers options for players to tailor the HUD to their preferences

CHAPTER 8 AUDIO AND VISUAL EFFECTS

Core Components of HUD Design

Key aspects include

- **Health and Status Bars**: Visual indicators for player or NPC health and states

- **Mini-Maps**: Displays locations, objectives, or enemy positions

- **Action Prompts**: Shows context-sensitive controls or actions

- **Score and Objectives**: Keeps players updated on goals or achievements

- **Timers and Cooldowns**: Indicates time-sensitive tasks or abilities

Reviewing the Code

Listing 8-13 introduces the core functions and properties of a custom HUD system. It manages the rendering of UI elements such as health bars and player scores, allowing visual feedback on gameplay status directly on screen.

- **DrawHealthBar()**: Renders a health bar on the HUD

- **DrawScore()**: Displays the player's score on screen

- **HealthBarPosition**: Specifies the position of the health bar

- **HealthBarSize**: Determines the dimensions of the health bar

- **HealthBarColor**: Sets the visual color for the health bar

CHAPTER 8   AUDIO AND VISUAL EFFECTS

Listing 8-13. GameHUD.h

```cpp
#pragma once

#include "CoreMinimal.h"
#include "GameFramework/HUD.h"
#include "GameHUD.generated.h"

UCLASS()
class MYGAME_API AGameHUD : public AHUD
{
    GENERATED_BODY()

public:
    virtual void DrawHUD() override;

protected:
    void DrawHealthBar(float HealthPercentage);
    void DrawScore(int32 PlayerScore);

private:
    UPROPERTY(EditAnywhere, Category = "HUD Settings")
    FVector2D HealthBarPosition;

    UPROPERTY(EditAnywhere, Category = "HUD Settings")
    FVector2D ScorePosition;

    UPROPERTY(EditAnywhere, Category = "HUD Settings")
    FVector2D HealthBarSize;

    UPROPERTY(EditAnywhere, Category = "HUD Settings")
    FLinearColor HealthBarColor;
};
```

Listing 8-14 describes the runtime behavior of a custom HUD system. It leverages Unreal Engine's built-in drawing functions to display key gameplay data, such as health and score, directly on the player's screen.

CHAPTER 8   AUDIO AND VISUAL EFFECTS

- **DrawHUD()**: The main function called every frame to render HUD elements

- **DrawHealthBar()**: Draws a health bar that adjusts based on the player's health percentage

- **DrawScore()**: Displays the player's score at a specified position

- **DrawRect() and DrawText()**: Unreal Engine functions for rendering shapes and text on the HUD

Listing 8-14. GameHUD.cpp

```
#include "GameHUD.h"
#include "Engine/Canvas.h"

void AGameHUD::DrawHUD()
{
    Super::DrawHUD();

    // Example: Draw health bar and score
    DrawHealthBar(0.75f); // 75% health
    DrawScore(1500); // Player score
}

void AGameHUD::DrawHealthBar(float HealthPercentage)
{
    FVector2D HealthBarEnd = HealthBarPosition + HealthBarSize
    * HealthPercentage;
    DrawRect(HealthBarColor, HealthBarPosition.X,
    HealthBarPosition.Y, HealthBarEnd.X - HealthBarPosition.X,
    HealthBarSize.Y);
}
```

```
void AGameHUD::DrawScore(int32 PlayerScore)
{
    FString ScoreText = FString::Printf(TEXT("Score: %d"),
    PlayerScore);
    DrawText(ScoreText, FLinearColor::White, ScorePosition.X,
    ScorePosition.Y);
}
```

A well-designed HUD enhances gameplay by providing crucial information in a visually appealing and non-intrusive way. By incorporating key elements such as health bars, scores, and prompts, developers can ensure that players remain informed and immersed. Next, we will explore dialogue sound effects, focusing on audio elements that bring conversations to life.

Dialogue Sound Effects

Dialogue sound effects are a crucial element in game audio design, bringing life and realism to character interactions. Whether through voice acting or synthesized audio, these effects enhance storytelling and player immersion.

Importance of Dialogue Sound Effects

Let's talk about why we need this:

- **Immersion**: Makes characters feel more lifelike and relatable
- **Storytelling**: Adds emotional depth to dialogue and narrative delivery

CHAPTER 8   AUDIO AND VISUAL EFFECTS

- **Player Engagement**: Captures player attention and emphasizes key story moments
- **Atmosphere**: Enhances the tone and setting through vocal cues

Core Components of Dialogue Sound Effects

Key aspects include

- **Voice Acting**: Professional or AI-generated voices for character dialogue
- **Lip-Syncing**: Synchronizing character animations with audio
- **Emotion Cues**: Using vocal tones and pitches to convey emotions
- **Spatial Audio**: Positioning dialogue based on the character's location relative to the player
- **Contextual Effects**: Adding effects like echo or distortion for specific environments (e.g., caves, radio communication)

Reviewing the Code

Listing 8-15 introduces a dialogue system header that allows triggering and managing audio-based character dialogues. It provides mechanisms to play voice lines, handle defaults, and respond when the audio finishes.

- **PlayDialogue()**: Plays the specified dialogue sound cue
- **DefaultDialogue**: A fallback dialogue sound if none is specified
- **HandleDialogueFinished()**: Called when the dialogue audio ends

CHAPTER 8   AUDIO AND VISUAL EFFECTS

Listing 8-15. DialogueManager.h

```cpp
#pragma once

#include "CoreMinimal.h"
#include "GameFramework/Actor.h"
#include "Sound/SoundCue.h"
#include "DialogueManager.generated.h"

UCLASS()
class MYGAME_API ADialogueManager : public AActor
{
    GENERATED_BODY()

public:
    ADialogueManager();

    UFUNCTION(BlueprintCallable, Category = "Dialogue")
    void PlayDialogue(USoundCue* DialogueCue);

protected:
    virtual void BeginPlay() override;

private:
    UPROPERTY(EditAnywhere, Category = "Dialogue")
    USoundCue* DefaultDialogue;

    UFUNCTION()
    void HandleDialogueFinished();
};
```

Listing 8-16 describes the runtime behavior of a dialogue system. It enables dynamic playback of dialogue audio and handles follow-up actions when the dialogue ends.

CHAPTER 8 AUDIO AND VISUAL EFFECTS

- **PlayDialogue()**: Plays a specified sound cue, defaulting to a fallback if none is provided
- **UGameplayStatics::PlaySound2D()**: Plays the sound for the player, ensuring it is audible regardless of position
- **HandleDialogueFinished()**: Logs or triggers events after the dialogue ends
- **FTimerHandle**: Ensures that the next action occurs after the dialogue finishes

Listing 8-16. DialogueManager.cpp

```cpp
#include "DialogueManager.h"
#include "Kismet/GameplayStatics.h"

ADialogueManager::ADialogueManager()
{
    PrimaryActorTick.bCanEverTick = false;
}

void ADialogueManager::BeginPlay()
{
    Super::BeginPlay();
}

void ADialogueManager::PlayDialogue(USoundCue* DialogueCue)
{
    if (!DialogueCue && DefaultDialogue)
    {
        DialogueCue = DefaultDialogue;
    }
```

```
    if (DialogueCue)
    {
        UGameplayStatics::PlaySound2D(this, DialogueCue);
        FTimerHandle TimerHandle;
        GetWorld()->GetTimerManager().SetTimer(TimerHandle,
        this, &ADialogueManager::HandleDialogueFinished,
        DialogueCue->GetDuration(), false);
    }
}
void ADialogueManager::HandleDialogueFinished()
{
    UE_LOG(LogTemp, Log, TEXT("Dialogue finished playing."));
}
```

Dialogue sound effects are indispensable for crafting memorable characters and immersive storytelling. By integrating sound cues, spatial audio, and emotional nuances, developers can create a more engaging and dynamic player experience. Next, we will explore environmental ambience, diving into the creation of atmospheric audio for game environments.

Environmental Ambience

Environmental ambience is the background audio that brings a game's world to life. It establishes the mood, enhances immersion, and provides auditory clues about the environment, making the game more dynamic and engaging.

Importance of Environmental Ambience

Let's talk about why we need this:

- **Atmosphere Creation**: Sets the tone of the game world (e.g., eerie silence for horror, bustling streets for urban settings)
- **Immersion**: Helps players feel present in the game world
- **Environmental Context**: Gives players audio cues about their surroundings (e.g., chirping birds in forests, howling winds in snowy regions)
- **Dynamic Feedback**: Reacts to in-game changes, such as weather or player location

Core Components of Environmental Ambience

Key aspects include

- **Ambient Loops**: Continuous audio tracks that play in the background, such as wind, rain, or crowd noise
- **Dynamic Triggers**: Sounds that activate based on player actions or environmental changes
- **Spatial Audio**: 3D positioning of sounds relative to the player
- **Weather Effects**: Audio representing rain, thunder, snow, or storms
- **Layered Soundscapes**: Combining multiple ambient sounds for richer environments

CHAPTER 8   AUDIO AND VISUAL EFFECTS

Advanced Audio Settings and Features

To enhance realism and responsiveness in sound design:

- **Sound Concurrency**: Controls how many instances of a sound can play simultaneously. Useful for preventing repetitive sounds from stacking unnaturally (e.g., multiple footstep sounds).

- **Sound Attenuation**: Defines how sound volume changes with distance and environmental occlusion. This helps simulate sound fading in hallways or being muffled by walls.

- **Reverb Settings**: Simulates how sound bounces in different environments (e.g., large halls vs. small rooms) using reverb zones.

- **Interior/Exterior Sound Zones**: Dynamically adjusts sound profiles based on whether the player is inside or outside.

These settings can be fine-tuned in Unreal Engine using Sound Attenuation Assets, Sound Mixes, and Audio Volumes, giving developers full control over how sound behaves in complex environments.

Reviewing the Code

Listing 8-17 introduces the key components of an ambient audio controller, enabling dynamic ambience playback in a game environment.

- **PlayAmbience()**: Starts playing a specified ambient sound

- **StopAmbience()**: Stops any currently playing ambience

CHAPTER 8   AUDIO AND VISUAL EFFECTS

- **DefaultAmbience**: A fallback ambient sound if none is specified
- **ActiveAudioComponent**: Manages the currently playing audio

Listing 8-17. EnvironmentalAmbienceManager.h

```
#pragma once

#include "CoreMinimal.h"
#include "GameFramework/Actor.h"
class USoundCue;
class UAudioComponent;
#include "EnvironmentalAmbienceManager.generated.h"

UCLASS()
class MYGAME_API AEnvironmentalAmbienceManager : public AActor
{
    GENERATED_BODY()
public:
    AEnvironmentalAmbienceManager();

    UFUNCTION(BlueprintCallable, Category = "Ambience")
    void PlayAmbience(USoundCue* AmbienceCue);

    UFUNCTION(BlueprintCallable, Category = "Ambience")
    void StopAmbience();

protected:
    virtual void BeginPlay() override;

private:
    UPROPERTY(EditAnywhere, Category = "Ambience")
    USoundCue* DefaultAmbience;
```

CHAPTER 8   AUDIO AND VISUAL EFFECTS

```
    UPROPERTY()
    UAudioComponent* ActiveAudioComponent;
};
```

Listing 8-18 describes the runtime behavior of an ambient audio controller. This implementation allows dynamic playback and control of ambient sounds during gameplay.

- **PlayAmbience()**: Plays a specified ambient sound using the audio component
- **StopAmbience()**: Stops any currently playing ambience, useful for transitioning between environments
- **DefaultAmbience**: Automatically plays a default ambient track when the game starts

Listing 8-18. EnvironmentalAmbienceManager.cpp

```
#include "EnvironmentalAmbienceManager.h"
#include "Components/AudioComponent.h"
#include "Sound/SoundCue.h"
#include "Kismet/GameplayStatics.h"

AEnvironmentalAmbienceManager::AEnvironmentalAmbienceManager()
{
    PrimaryActorTick.bCanEverTick = false;
    ActiveAudioComponent = CreateDefaultSubobject
    <UAudioComponent>(TEXT("ActiveAudioComponent"));
    ActiveAudioComponent->bAutoActivate = false;
}
void AEnvironmentalAmbienceManager::BeginPlay()
{
    Super::BeginPlay();
```

```cpp
    if (DefaultAmbience)
    {
        PlayAmbience(DefaultAmbience);
    }
}

void AEnvironmentalAmbienceManager::PlayAmbience(USoundCue* AmbienceCue)
{
    if (ActiveAudioComponent && AmbienceCue)
    {
        ActiveAudioComponent->SetSound(AmbienceCue);
        ActiveAudioComponent->Play();
    }
}

void AEnvironmentalAmbienceManager::StopAmbience()
{
    if (ActiveAudioComponent)
    {
        ActiveAudioComponent->Stop();
    }
}
```

Environmental ambience enhances immersion and sets the stage for the player's journey by providing auditory context. By layering and dynamically triggering sounds, developers can create captivating worlds that react to player actions and environmental changes. Up next, we will discuss particle effects on interactions, focusing on how visual particles can complement audio effects for a more holistic experience.

CHAPTER 8   AUDIO AND VISUAL EFFECTS

Particle Effects on Interactions

Particle effects are a powerful tool in game development used to visually represent events, interactions, and environmental phenomena. When paired with gameplay mechanics, they add an extra layer of feedback, helping players understand and feel connected to their actions in the game world.

Importance of Particle Effects on Interactions

Let's talk about why we need this:

- **Visual Feedback**: Helps players understand the results of their actions (e.g., a spark when hitting a metal object)
- **Aesthetic Appeal**: Enhances the visual richness of the game world
- **Environmental Storytelling**: Represents natural phenomena like rain, smoke, or fire
- **Immersive Interactions**: Makes interactions more engaging by visually depicting changes in the environment

Core Components of Particle Effects on Interactions

Key elements include

- **Trigger Conditions**: Defines when the particle effects should activate
- **Effect Variety**: Includes sparks, smoke, fire, explosions, and more

- **Lifetime and Dissipation**: Determines how long the particles stay visible before fading

- **Dynamic Behavior**: Allows particles to react to physics or interact with objects in the environment

- **Optimized Rendering**: Ensures smooth performance even with complex effects

Reviewing the Code

Listing 8-19 introduces the core structure for a particle effect controller. This setup allows visual effects to be spawned dynamically at runtime to enhance player feedback and immersion.

- **SpawnParticleEffect()**: A function used to spawn particle effects in the world at a specified location, typically for effects like explosions, impacts, or visual feedback

- **ParticleEffect**: A reference to a particle system asset that defines what visual effect will be played when the function is called

Listing 8-19. InteractionParticleManager.h

```
#pragma once

#include "CoreMinimal.h"
#include "GameFramework/Actor.h"
class UParticleSystem;
#include "InteractionParticleManager.generated.h"

UCLASS()
class MYGAME_API AInteractionParticleManager : public AActor
{
    GENERATED_BODY()
```

CHAPTER 8 AUDIO AND VISUAL EFFECTS

```
public:
    AInteractionParticleManager();

    UFUNCTION(BlueprintCallable, Category = "Particles")
    void SpawnParticleEffect(FVector Location, UParticleSystem*
    ParticleEffect);

protected:
    virtual void BeginPlay() override;
};
```

Listing 8-20 describes the runtime behavior of the particle effect system. It demonstrates how visual effects can be triggered dynamically during gameplay to enhance responsiveness and immersion.

- **SpawnParticleEffect()**: Uses UGameplayStatics:: SpawnEmitterAtLocation to spawn a particle system at the specified location

- **ParticleEffect**: Ensures the appropriate particle system is selected before spawning

Listing 8-20. InteractionParticleManager.cpp

```
#include "InteractionParticleManager.h"
#include "Particles/ParticleSystem.h"
#include "Kismet/GameplayStatics.h"

AInteractionParticleManager::AInteractionParticleManager()
{
    PrimaryActorTick.bCanEverTick = false;
}
```

```cpp
void AInteractionParticleManager::BeginPlay()
{
    Super::BeginPlay();
}

void AInteractionParticleManager::SpawnParticleEffect(FVector 
Location, UParticleSystem* ParticleEffect)
{
    if (ParticleEffect)
    {
        UGameplayStatics::SpawnEmitterAtLocation(GetWorld(), 
        ParticleEffect, Location);
    }
}
```

Usage Example

Imagine a player shoots a fireball at an enemy. When the fireball hits, you can call SpawnParticleEffect() to trigger a fiery explosion at the impact location, enhancing the visual feedback of the action.

Particle effects enrich player interactions by visually emphasizing the results of their actions. Whether it's a burst of energy, a cloud of dust, or sparks from a collision, particles add depth and excitement to gameplay.

Summary

In this chapter, we explored how audio and visual effects bring depth, feedback, and immersion to a game. From environmental ambience and dynamic music systems to UI animations and particle effects, each component plays a critical role in shaping the player's emotional and sensory experience. We covered implementations of sound triggers, music state transitions, dialogue systems, screen shake effects, post-processing, and HUD visuals all designed to enrich gameplay and responsiveness.

CHAPTER 8   AUDIO AND VISUAL EFFECTS

These systems not only support core gameplay mechanics but also elevate the overall polish of the game world. With a solid understanding of audiovisual feedback, we now move into AI and pathfinding, where we will focus on designing intelligent agents, enemy behavior, and navigation systems to create lifelike and challenging gameplay interactions.

CHAPTER 9

AI and Pathfinding

AI (artificial intelligence) and pathfinding are integral components of modern games, enabling non-player characters (NPCs) to navigate, react, and interact with the game world in intelligent and dynamic ways. From basic movement algorithms to complex decision-making processes, AI systems breathe life into games by creating challenging enemies, helpful companions, and engaging environments.

AI systems define how non-player characters (NPCs) behave, while pathfinding ensures they can navigate the environment efficiently. Together, they create dynamic challenges, enhance immersion by making NPCs act logically, and improve gameplay flow by allowing smooth movement through complex game worlds.

In this chapter, we will explore various aspects of AI and pathfinding to enhance your game's depth and realism. We begin by covering basic AI movement, focusing on how to set up simple NPC navigation. Then, we delve into advanced pathfinding, implementing algorithms to ensure efficient movement through complex environments. The chapter also addresses enemy patrols and combat behavior, providing strategies for designing engaging and dynamic enemy interactions. Additionally, we will explore companion and stealth AI, helping you create allies and adversaries for stealth-based gameplay. Lastly, we'll cover dynamic AI systems, including decision trees, state machines, and response mechanisms. By the end of the chapter, you will be equipped with the knowledge to design robust AI systems and pathfinding techniques to improve your game's overall experience.

CHAPTER 9   AI AND PATHFINDING

Basic AI Movement

Basic AI movement is essential for creating responsive and interactive NPCs in any game. It involves setting up simple navigation systems that allow characters to move autonomously within the game world. This foundational aspect of AI ensures that characters can perform tasks such as walking, running, or patrolling, without requiring constant player input.

Importance of Basic AI Movement

Let's explore why this is crucial:

- **Smooth Navigation**: Ensures NPCs can move fluidly around the environment, enhancing realism.
- **Autonomous Action**: Allows NPCs to carry out their tasks independently, contributing to dynamic gameplay.
- **Player Engagement**: Well-implemented movement systems create more immersive and interactive NPCs, making the world feel alive.
- **Foundation for Advanced AI**: Basic movement serves as the building block for more complex AI behaviors like combat or companion interactions.

Core Components of Basic AI Movement

Key elements include

- **Navigation Meshes (NavMesh)**: Defines walkable areas and helps the AI determine where it can go
- **Movement Speed and Direction**: Adjusts the speed and direction of the NPC's movement

CHAPTER 9 AI AND PATHFINDING

- **Pathfinding Algorithms**: Guides NPCs from one point to another while avoiding obstacles

- **Animation Blending**: Combines different animations (e.g., walking, running) for smooth transitions

Reviewing the Code

Listing 9-1 introduces the structure of a basic AI movement system. This header file defines the core elements needed to move an AI character toward a designated target location using a basic directional input approach.

- **TargetLocation**: Specifies the destination the AI character should move toward

- **MoveToTarget()**: A function that allows the AI to move to a new target location

- **UpdateMovement()**: A function responsible for handling the movement update each frame

Listing 9-1. AICharacterMovement.h

```
#pragma once

#include "CoreMinimal.h"
#include "GameFramework/Character.h"
#include "AICharacterMovement.generated.h"

UCLASS()
class MYGAME_API AAICharacterMovement : public ACharacter
{
    GENERATED_BODY()
```

CHAPTER 9   AI AND PATHFINDING

```
public:
    AAICharacterMovement();

protected:
    virtual void BeginPlay() override;

public:
    virtual void Tick(float DeltaTime) override;

    UPROPERTY(EditAnywhere, BlueprintReadWrite, Category = "AI
    Movement")
    FVector TargetLocation;

    UFUNCTION(BlueprintCallable, Category = "AI Movement")
    void MoveToTarget(FVector NewTarget);

private:
    void UpdateMovement();
};
```

Listing 9-2 implements the movement logic by applying input toward the target direction every frame.

- **MoveToTarget()**: Sets the new target location for the AI character to move toward

- **UpdateMovement()**: Continuously moves the AI toward the target location by normalizing the direction vector and using AddMovementInput() to apply movement

- **AddMovementInput()**: A built-in Unreal function used to apply directional input to characters

CHAPTER 9 AI AND PATHFINDING

Listing 9-2. AICharacterMovement.cpp

```cpp
#include "AICharacterMovement.h"
#include "NavigationSystem.h"
#include "AIController.h"

AAICharacterMovement::AAICharacterMovement()
{
    PrimaryActorTick.bCanEverTick = true;
}

void AAICharacterMovement::BeginPlay()
{
    Super::BeginPlay();
}

void AAICharacterMovement::Tick(float DeltaTime)
{
    Super::Tick(DeltaTime);
    UpdateMovement();
}

void AAICharacterMovement::MoveToTarget(FVector NewTarget)
{
    TargetLocation = NewTarget;
}

 void AAICharacterMovement::UpdateMovement()
{
    if (TargetLocation != FVector::ZeroVector)
    {
        AAIController* AIController = Cast<AAIController>
        (GetController());
        if (AIController)
```

CHAPTER 9   AI AND PATHFINDING

```
    {
        FAIMoveRequest MoveRequest;
        MoveRequest.SetGoalLocation(TargetLocation);
        MoveRequest.SetAcceptanceRadius(5.0f);
        // You can adjust the acceptance radius

        FNavPathSharedPtr NavPath;
        AIController->MoveTo(MoveRequest, &NavPath);
    }
  }
}
```

Usage Example

Imagine an NPC needs to walk toward a player in the game. You can call the MoveToTarget() function, passing in the player's location. The AI will then automatically adjust its movement to reach that point.

Basic AI movement is a fundamental aspect of game development that lays the groundwork for more complex AI systems. It ensures that NPCs can interact with the environment and perform basic tasks autonomously. This subtopic provided a foundational understanding of implementing AI movement, which can later be expanded upon with advanced behaviors like pathfinding and combat. Next, we will explore advanced pathfinding techniques to optimize NPC navigation.

Advanced Pathfinding

Advanced pathfinding is a crucial aspect of AI in games, allowing NPCs (non-playable characters) to navigate complex environments efficiently. It involves using sophisticated algorithms to determine the best route from one point to another while avoiding obstacles and adapting to dynamic

CHAPTER 9   AI AND PATHFINDING

changes in the environment. Pathfinding ensures that NPCs can find their way in large, open-world environments, tight corridors, or around moving obstacles, improving their realism and interactivity.

Importance of Advanced Pathfinding

Let's explore why this is vital:

- **Efficient Navigation**: Enables NPCs to find the shortest or most efficient path through complex environments

- **Dynamic Interaction**: Allows NPCs to respond in real time to environmental changes, such as moving obstacles or new hazards

- **Immersion**: Creates more believable AI by ensuring NPCs behave naturally as they navigate through the world

- **Optimized Performance**: Helps balance resource-intensive computations by using efficient algorithms that minimize processing time

Core Components of Advanced Pathfinding

Key elements include

- **Navigation Meshes (NavMesh)**: Precomputed data that defines the walkable areas in the environment, used by pathfinding algorithms

- **A* (A-Star) Algorithm**: A widely used pathfinding algorithm that finds the shortest path while avoiding obstacles and considering various factors like terrain costs

- **Dynamic Obstacle Avoidance**: Adjusts the path dynamically when new obstacles appear or if the environment changes
- **Path Smoothing**: Ensures that the AI's movement is natural, avoiding sharp turns or unrealistic behavior
- **Heuristic Functions**: Estimates the best path to take, improving the efficiency of the algorithm

Reviewing the Code

Listing 9-3 introduces the key components of a pathfinding system using the A* algorithm. These elements are fundamental for enabling intelligent navigation across complex environments.

Listing 9-3. AIPathfinding.h

```
#pragma once

#include "CoreMinimal.h"
#include "GameFramework/Actor.h"
#include "AIPathfinding.generated.h"

UCLASS()
class MYGAME_API AAIPathfinding : public AActor
{
    GENERATED_BODY()

public:
    AAIPathfinding();

protected:
    virtual void BeginPlay() override;
```

CHAPTER 9 AI AND PATHFINDING

```
public:
    virtual void Tick(float DeltaTime) override;

    UFUNCTION(BlueprintCallable, Category = "Pathfinding")
    void FindPath(FVector Start, FVector End);

private:
    TArray<FVector> CalculatePath(FVector Start, FVector End);
    float Heuristic(FVector A, FVector B);
    TArray<FVector> SmoothPath(TArray<FVector> Path);

    TArray<FVector> Path;
};
```

Listing 9-4 describes the implementation details of the A pathfinding algorithm and related functions. This setup allows AI to determine optimal movement paths in complex environments:

- **CalculatePath()**: Implements the A* algorithm. It maintains open and closed lists of nodes and their associated costs. It iteratively explores the least costly path, eventually finding the shortest route to the target.

- **Heuristic()**: Uses Euclidean distance as a heuristic to estimate the cost from a node to the target.

- **SmoothPath()**: A placeholder function that can be used to smooth the path by removing sharp turns or unnecessary waypoints.

Listing 9-4. AIPathfinding.cpp

```
#include "AIPathfinding.h"
#include "NavigationSystem.h"
#include "NavigationPath.h"
#include "AIController.h"
```

CHAPTER 9   AI AND PATHFINDING

```cpp
#include "Kismet/GameplayStatics.h"

AAIPathfinding::AAIPathfinding()
{
    PrimaryActorTick.bCanEverTick = true;
}

void AAIPathfinding::BeginPlay()
{
    Super::BeginPlay();
}

 void AAIPathfinding::Tick(float DeltaTime)
{
    Super::Tick(DeltaTime);

    // Only find a new path if necessary
    if (bShouldFindPath)
    {
        FVector Start = GetActorLocation();
        FVector End = TargetLocation;
        // Set dynamically somewhere else in the game
        FindPath(Start, End);
        bShouldFindPath = false; // Reset until next update
    }

    // Continue movement logic if you already have a path
    FollowPath(DeltaTime);
}

void AAIPathfinding::FindPath(FVector Start, FVector End)
{
    Path = CalculatePath(Start, End);
    Path = SmoothPath(Path);
}
```

```cpp
TArray<FVector> AAIPathfinding::CalculatePath(FVector Start,
FVector End)
{
    TArray<FVector> ResultPath;

    UNavigationSystemV1* NavSystem = FNavigationSystem::
    GetCurrent<UNavigationSystemV1>(GetWorld());
    if (NavSystem)
    {
        UNavigationPath* NavPath = NavSystem->
        FindPathToLocationSynchronously(GetWorld(), Start, End);

        if (NavPath && NavPath->IsValid())
        {
            ResultPath = NavPath->PathPoints;
            // Automatically calculated and smoothed path
        }
    }

    return ResultPath;
}

float AAIPathfinding::Heuristic(FVector A, FVector B)
{
    return FVector::Dist(A, B);
    // Euclidean distance as heuristic
}
```

```
TArray<FVector> AAIPathfinding::SmoothPath(TArray
<FVector> Path)
{
    // Implement a smoothing algorithm (e.g., removing
    unnecessary waypoints)
    // For simplicity, returning the path as is for now
    return Path;
}
```

Usage Example

Imagine you have an NPC that needs to navigate from its current position to a target destination. By calling FindPath(), the NPC will automatically calculate and follow the best path, avoiding obstacles and adapting to dynamic changes in the environment.

Advanced pathfinding is essential for creating AI that can navigate complex environments intelligently. By using algorithms like A*, NPCs can find efficient routes while avoiding obstacles and adapting to dynamic conditions. This subtopic covered the implementation of an advanced pathfinding system, which can be expanded with additional features such as dynamic obstacle avoidance or path smoothing. Next, we will explore enemy patrols and combat behaviors in more detail.

Enemy Patrols and Combat

Enemy patrols and combat behaviors are integral components of game AI, making the world feel more alive and dynamic. These systems allow enemies to move through the environment, engage in combat, and react to player actions, providing challenges and creating more engaging gameplay. Properly implemented patrols and combat behaviors can significantly enhance the realism of your game, making it feel more immersive and interactive.

CHAPTER 9 AI AND PATHFINDING

Importance of Enemy Patrols and Combat

Let's examine why this is essential:

- **Immersion**: Realistic enemy movements and combat behaviors contribute to a more believable game world.

- **Challenge**: Well-designed patrols and combat create dynamic challenges for the player, requiring them to plan and react.

- **Engagement**: A combination of patrols and combat can keep players engaged by offering opportunities for both strategic planning and action.

- **AI Variety**: Different types of patrols and combat behavior patterns make enemies feel unique, preventing repetitive gameplay.

Core Components of Enemy Patrols and Combat

Key elements of enemy patrols and combat include

- **Patrol Routes**: Defines the path enemies take as they move through the environment, with waypoints marking key locations

- **Line of Sight**: Determines whether an enemy can detect the player based on visibility, often tied to the enemy's field of view and obstacles in the environment

- **Combat States**: Defines the different phases of combat, such as idle, attacking, defending, and fleeing

- **Aggro System**: Tracks the enemy's awareness of the player and how aggressively they will respond

CHAPTER 9   AI AND PATHFINDING

- **Combat AI**: Determines how enemies engage in combat, such as when to attack, dodge, or use special abilities
- **Alertness/Detection**: Determines how quickly enemies detect the player or other stimuli (e.g., noise, visual cues)

Reviewing the Code

Listing 9-5 introduces the core components of an AI enemy behavior system utilizing Unreal's AI Perception system. This setup supports patrol behavior and combat engagement while enabling optimized player detection using built-in sensing. These elements form a robust and efficient framework for responsive enemy AI behavior.

- **StartPatrolling()**: Begins the patrolling behavior by initiating movement to the first patrol point
- **EngageCombat()**: Switches the enemy into combat mode when the player is detected
- **MoveToNextPatrolPoint()**: Uses the AI controller to move toward the next waypoint in the patrol route
- **OnTargetPerceived()**: Uses the AI Perception component to detect the player and trigger combat or resume patrol accordingly

Listing 9-5. EnemyAI.h

```
#pragma once

#include "CoreMinimal.h"
#include "GameFramework/Character.h"
```

```cpp
#include "Perception/AIPerceptionTypes.h"
#include "EnemyAI.generated.h"

class UAIPerceptionComponent;
class UAISenseConfig_Sight;

UCLASS()
class MYGAME_API AEnemyAI : public ACharacter
{
    GENERATED_BODY()

public:
    AEnemyAI();

protected:
    virtual void BeginPlay() override;

public:
    virtual void Tick(float DeltaTime) override;

    void StartPatrolling();
    void EngageCombat();

private:
    TArray<FVector> PatrolPoints;
    int32 CurrentPatrolIndex;
    bool bIsInCombat;

    void MoveToNextPatrolPoint();

    // Perception system
    UPROPERTY(VisibleAnywhere, BlueprintReadOnly, Category =
    "AI", meta = (AllowPrivateAccess = "true"))
    UAIPerceptionComponent* AIPerception;
```

CHAPTER 9 AI AND PATHFINDING

```
    UPROPERTY()
    UAISenseConfig_Sight* SightConfig;

    UFUNCTION()
    void OnTargetPerceived(AActor* Actor, FAIStimulus
    Stimulus);
};
```

Listing 9-6 presents the runtime implementation of a patrol-based enemy AI system that seamlessly transitions into combat when the player is perceived. By leveraging Unreal Engine's AI Perception system, this implementation ensures better performance, modularity, and scalability for larger games.

- **StartPatrolling()**: Initiates the enemy patrol cycle if waypoints are available.
- **MoveToNextPatrolPoint()**: Commands the AI controller to move toward the current patrol target and update the index for the next destination.
- **OnTargetPerceived()**: Replaces manual distance checks with event-based sensing to determine if the player is in view. If so, the AI enters combat; otherwise, it resumes patrol.
- **EngageCombat()**: Flags the AI as being in combat, allowing combat behavior to execute in subsequent frames.

Listing 9-6. EnemyAI.cpp

```
#include "EnemyAI.h"
#include "AIController.h"
#include "Kismet/GameplayStatics.h"
#include "Perception/AIPerceptionComponent.h"
```

```cpp
#include "Perception/AISenseConfig_Sight.h"
#include "Perception/AISense_Sight.h"

AEnemyAI::AEnemyAI()
{
    PrimaryActorTick.bCanEverTick = true;

    bIsInCombat = false;
    CurrentPatrolIndex = 0;

    AIPerception = CreateDefaultSubobject<UAIPerceptionComponent>
    (TEXT("AIPerception"));
    SightConfig = CreateDefaultSubobject<UAISenseConfig_Sight>
    (TEXT("SightConfig"));

    SightConfig->SightRadius = 800.0f;
    SightConfig->LoseSightRadius = 1000.0f;
    SightConfig->PeripheralVisionAngleDegrees = 90.0f;
    SightConfig->SetMaxAge(5.0f);
    SightConfig->DetectionByAffiliation.bDetectEnemies = true;
    SightConfig->DetectionByAffiliation.bDetectFriendlies
    = false;
    SightConfig->DetectionByAffiliation.bDetectNeutrals
    = false;

    AIPerception->ConfigureSense(*SightConfig);
    AIPerception->SetDominantSense(SightConfig->
    GetSenseImplementation());

    AIPerception->OnTargetPerceptionUpdated.AddDynamic(this,
    &AEnemyAI::OnTargetPerceived);
}
```

CHAPTER 9   AI AND PATHFINDING

```
void AEnemyAI::BeginPlay()
{
    Super::BeginPlay();

    PatrolPoints.Add(FVector(100, 100, 0));
    PatrolPoints.Add(FVector(300, 300, 0));
    PatrolPoints.Add(FVector(500, 100, 0));

    StartPatrolling();
}
void AEnemyAI::Tick(float DeltaTime)
{
    Super::Tick(DeltaTime);

    if (!bIsInCombat)
    {
        // Optional: continue patrol logic or monitor movement
    }

    if (bIsInCombat)
    {
        // Execute combat logic
    }
}
void AEnemyAI::StartPatrolling()
{
    if (PatrolPoints.Num() > 0)
    {
        MoveToNextPatrolPoint();
    }
}
```

CHAPTER 9   AI AND PATHFINDING

```cpp
void AEnemyAI::MoveToNextPatrolPoint()
{
    if (PatrolPoints.IsValidIndex(CurrentPatrolIndex))
    {
        FVector PatrolPoint = PatrolPoints[CurrentPatrolIndex];
        AAIController* AIController = Cast<AAIController>
        (GetController());

        if (AIController)
        {
            AIController->MoveToLocation(PatrolPoint);

            CurrentPatrolIndex = (CurrentPatrolIndex + 1) %
            PatrolPoints.Num();
        }
    }
}

void AEnemyAI::EngageCombat()
{
    bIsInCombat = true;

    // You can now trigger combat logic like animation or
    attack here
}

void AEnemyAI::OnTargetPerceived(AActor* Actor, FAIStimulus
Stimulus)
{
    if (Stimulus.WasSuccessfullySensed())
    {
        // Player detected
        EngageCombat();
    }
```

```
    else
    {
        // Player lost, resume patrol
        bIsInCombat = false;
        StartPatrolling();
    }
}
```

Usage Example

Imagine an enemy patrolling a set of waypoints. As the player gets closer, the enemy detects the player and enters combat mode. The enemy then switches to a combat behavior, such as attacking or defending, depending on the player's actions.

Enemy patrols and combat behaviors create engaging challenges for the player. They are vital for building an interactive world where enemies are not passive, but actively patrol, detect threats, and engage in combat. This subtopic covered a basic implementation of enemy patrols and combat, which can be expanded to include more complex behaviors like covering fire, different combat states, and special attacks. In the next section, we will look at companion AI systems and how they can interact with the player.

Companion and Stealth AI

Companion and stealth AI systems are essential components for crafting unique gameplay experiences. Companion AI involves creating allies who support the player through combat, puzzles, or exploration, while stealth AI focuses on adversaries who can be outsmarted through quiet and strategic player actions. These systems must be responsive, reliable, and engaging to enhance the player's connection with the game.

CHAPTER 9 AI AND PATHFINDING

Importance of Companion and Stealth AI

Let's see why these systems are important:

- **Player Support**: Companion AI assists in combat, healing, or solving puzzles, making the player feel less isolated.

- **Tactical Gameplay**: Stealth AI introduces opportunities for strategic planning and stealth mechanics, allowing players to bypass enemies.

- **Immersion**: Realistic behaviors for companions and enemies contribute to the game world's believability.

- **Dynamic Interactions**: Encourages players to use different strategies, whether cooperating with a companion or sneaking past an enemy.

Core Components of Companion and Stealth AI

Key features of these AI systems include

- **Pathfinding for Companions**: Ensures companions follow the player effectively, avoiding obstacles.

- **Combat Support**: Allows companions to assist in combat, such as attacking enemies or providing buffs.

- **Stealth Awareness**: Enables enemies to detect the player through visual or auditory cues.

- **Behavioral States**: For companions, these could be idle, assist, or defend. For stealth AI, states might include idle, alert, and searching.

CHAPTER 9 AI AND PATHFINDING

- **Contextual Actions**: Companions react to player commands or game events. Stealth enemies respond dynamically to sounds, distractions, or sudden movements.

Reviewing the Code

Listing 9-7 introduces the core components of companion AI behavior, utilizing Unreal Engine's AI controller to enable responsive and supportive actions such as following the player, engaging in combat, or remaining stationary when commanded.

- **FollowPlayer()**: Continuously makes the companion stay near the player, maintaining a strategic offset
- **AssistInCombat()**: Commands the companion to move toward a specified enemy target, setting up for an attack or combat support
- **StayInPlace()**: Instructs the companion to stop all movement immediately, useful for defensive or tactical scenarios
- **MoveToLocation()**: Internally used to direct the companion to a specific location using the AI controller's navigation functions

Listing 9-7. CompanionAI.h

```
#pragma once

#include "CoreMinimal.h"
#include "GameFramework/Character.h"
#include "NavigationSystem.h"
#include "CompanionAI.generated.h"
```

CHAPTER 9   AI AND PATHFINDING

```
UCLASS()
class MYGAME_API ACompanionAI : public ACharacter
{
    GENERATED_BODY()
public:
    ACompanionAI();
protected:
    virtual void BeginPlay() override;
public:
    virtual void Tick(float DeltaTime) override;

    void FollowPlayer();
    void AssistInCombat(AActor* EnemyTarget);
    void StayInPlace();
private:
    FVector TargetLocation;
    AActor* PlayerActor;
    AActor* CurrentEnemyTarget;

    void MoveToLocation(FVector Location);
};
```

Listing 9-8 presents the runtime implementation of the companion AI system, integrating navigation and behavior logic to dynamically assist the player. The companion uses the controller-based MoveToLocation functionality for natural navigation.

- **FollowPlayer()**: Updates the target location relative to the player with an offset and initiates movement to maintain a helpful position

Chapter 9   AI and Pathfinding

- **AssistInCombat()**: Directs the companion to move toward the enemy target's location and prepares for further combat logic
- **StayInPlace()**: Uses `StopMovement()` from the AI controller to freeze movement instantly
- **MoveToLocation()**: Leverages `MoveToLocation()` from `AAIController` for smooth and pathfinding-aware travel across the game world

Listing 9-8. CompanionAI.cpp

```cpp
#include "CompanionAI.h"
#include "GameFramework/PlayerController.h"
#include "Kismet/GameplayStatics.h"
#include "NavigationSystem.h"
#include "AIController.h"

ACompanionAI::ACompanionAI()
{
    PrimaryActorTick.bCanEverTick = true;
}

void ACompanionAI::BeginPlay()
{
    Super::BeginPlay();

    PlayerActor = UGameplayStatics::GetPlayerPawn
    (GetWorld(), 0);
}

void ACompanionAI::Tick(float DeltaTime)
{
    Super::Tick(DeltaTime);
```

```cpp
    if (PlayerActor)
    {
        FollowPlayer();
    }
}

void ACompanionAI::FollowPlayer()
{
    if (PlayerActor)
    {
        TargetLocation = PlayerActor->GetActorLocation() -
        FVector(200, 200, 0); // Avoid overlapping
        MoveToLocation(TargetLocation);
    }
}

void ACompanionAI::AssistInCombat(AActor* EnemyTarget)
{
    if (EnemyTarget)
    {
        CurrentEnemyTarget = EnemyTarget;
        MoveToLocation(EnemyTarget->GetActorLocation());

        // Optional: Add attack logic here
    }
}

void ACompanionAI::StayInPlace()
{
    AAIController* AIController = Cast<AAIController>(GetCont
    roller());
    if (AIController)
    {
```

```
        AIController->StopMovement();
    }
}

void ACompanionAI::MoveToLocation(FVector Location)
{
    AAIController* AIController = Cast<AAIController>
    (GetController());
    if (AIController)
    {
        AIController->MoveToLocation(Location);
    }
}
```

Listings 9-9 and 9-10 describe a performance-optimized stealth AI detection and response system that uses overlap-based player detection, directional movement toward the player's last known location, and recovery back to patrol behavior when the threat is no longer present. This system supports realistic enemy awareness and state transitions without relying on per-frame distance checks.

- **DetectionSphere**: A collision sphere that detects player proximity via overlap events instead of polling every frame
- **OnPlayerEnterRange()**: Triggered when the player enters the detection radius; stores the last known position and initiates a search
- **SearchForPlayer()**: Directs the enemy to move to the player's last seen location using Unreal's `AIController::MoveToLocation`
- **ReturnToPatrol()**: Resets the AI's alert state so the character can resume regular patrol behaviors

Listing 9-9. StealthEnemyAI.h

```
#pragma once

#include "CoreMinimal.h"
#include "GameFramework/Character.h"
#include "StealthEnemyAI.generated.h"

UCLASS()
class MYGAME_API AStealthEnemyAI : public ACharacter
{
    GENERATED_BODY()
public:
    AStealthEnemyAI();

protected:
    virtual void BeginPlay() override;

public:
    virtual void Tick(float DeltaTime) override;

    void DetectPlayer();
    void SearchForPlayer();
    void ReturnToPatrol();

private:
    bool bPlayerDetected;
    FVector LastKnownPlayerLocation;
};
```

CHAPTER 9   AI AND PATHFINDING

Listing 9-10. StealthEnemyAI.cpp

```cpp
#include "StealthEnemyAI.h"
#include "Kismet/GameplayStatics.h"

AStealthEnemyAI::AStealthEnemyAI()
{
    PrimaryActorTick.bCanEverTick = true;
    bPlayerDetected = false;
}
#include "StealthEnemyAI.h"
#include "Components/SphereComponent.h"
#include "Kismet/GameplayStatics.h"
#include "AIController.h"

AStealthEnemyAI::AStealthEnemyAI()
{
    PrimaryActorTick.bCanEverTick = false;

    bPlayerDetected = false;

    DetectionSphere = CreateDefaultSubobject<USphereComponent>(
    TEXT("DetectionSphere"));
    DetectionSphere->InitSphereRadius(300.0f);
    DetectionSphere->SetupAttachment(RootComponent);
    DetectionSphere->SetCollisionResponseToAllChannels
    (ECollisionResponse::ECR_Ignore);
    DetectionSphere->SetCollisionResponseToChannel(ECC_Pawn,
    ECR_Overlap);
}

void AStealthEnemyAI::BeginPlay()
{
    Super::BeginPlay();
```

CHAPTER 9 AI AND PATHFINDING

```cpp
    DetectionSphere->OnComponentBeginOverlap.AddDynamic(this,
    &AStealthEnemyAI::OnPlayerEnterRange);
}

void AStealthEnemyAI::OnPlayerEnterRange(UPrimitiveComponent*
OverlappedComp, AActor* OtherActor, UPrimitiveComponent*
OtherComp, int32 OtherBodyIndex, bool bFromSweep, const
FHitResult& SweepResult)
{
    if (!bPlayerDetected && OtherActor == UGameplayStatics::
    GetPlayerPawn(GetWorld(), 0))
    {
        bPlayerDetected = true;
        LastKnownPlayerLocation = OtherActor->
        GetActorLocation();
        SearchForPlayer();
    }
}

void AStealthEnemyAI::SearchForPlayer()
{
    if (bPlayerDetected)
    {
        AAIController* AIController = Cast<AAIController>
        (GetController());
        if (AIController)
        {
            AIController->MoveToLocation(LastKnownPlayer
            Location);
        }
    }
}
```

CHAPTER 9 AI AND PATHFINDING

```cpp
void AStealthEnemyAI::ReturnToPatrol()
{
    bPlayerDetected = false;
    // Add logic for returning to patrol path
}
void AStealthEnemyAI::BeginPlay()
{
    Super::BeginPlay();
}

void AStealthEnemyAI::Tick(float DeltaTime)
{
    Super::Tick(DeltaTime);

    if (!bPlayerDetected)
    {
        DetectPlayer();
    }
}

void AStealthEnemyAI::DetectPlayer()
{
    AActor* Player = UGameplayStatics::GetPlayerPawn(GetWorld(), 0);
    if (Player && FVector::Dist(GetActorLocation(), Player->GetActorLocation()) < 300.0f)
    {
        bPlayerDetected = true;
        LastKnownPlayerLocation = Player->GetActorLocation();
        SearchForPlayer();
    }
}
```

```cpp
void AStealthEnemyAI::SearchForPlayer()
{
    if (bPlayerDetected)
    {
        MoveToLocation(LastKnownPlayerLocation);
        // Add search logic like scanning the area
    }
}
void AStealthEnemyAI::ReturnToPatrol()
{
    bPlayerDetected = false;
    // Add logic to return to the patrol path
```

Companion and stealth AI systems create dynamic interactions and enrich the gameplay experience. With companions, players feel supported, while stealth AI provides tactical challenges. These systems add depth to the game world by encouraging player strategy and engagement. Next, we will dive into dynamic AI response mechanisms.

Dynamic AI Response

Dynamic AI response systems are designed to enable AI characters to react and adapt to the player's actions, creating a more immersive and challenging gameplay experience. These systems are integral to making the game world feel alive, with NPCs and enemies that don't just follow preset routines but adapt to changing circumstances, events, and player behaviors.

Importance of Dynamic AI Response

Why is dynamic AI response essential?

- **Immersion**: AI that responds to the player's actions makes the world feel reactive, as if the game is alive and aware.
- **Variety**: Adds variety and unpredictability to gameplay by making each encounter or interaction unique.
- **Challenge**: Increases the difficulty of the game by forcing the player to adapt to the ever-changing responses of AI characters.
- **Realism**: Creates a more believable and realistic game world where AI characters can react logically to stimuli.

Core Components of Dynamic AI Response

Key features for dynamic AI responses include

- **Perception Systems**: Sensory systems (sight, hearing, etc.) that enable AI to detect the player or other events.
- **Response to Player Actions**: AI that adjusts its behavior based on player choices, such as fleeing, attacking, or taking cover.
- **State Transitions**: AI can switch between different states (idle, combat, alert, etc.) depending on stimuli.
- **Environmental Interaction**: AI can respond to changes in the environment, such as explosions, gunfire, or changes in the player's position.
- **Emotion Simulation**: Some systems simulate emotional responses (fear, aggression, confusion) to make AI more unpredictable.

CHAPTER 9 AI AND PATHFINDING

Reviewing the Code

Listing 9-11 introduces a threat detection and response system for AI characters. This system enhances immersion by allowing AI to dynamically assess and react to the player or other perceived dangers.

- **DetectPlayer()**: Detects the player through a perception system
- **ReactToThreat()**: Changes AI behavior when a threat is detected, such as preparing for combat or fleeing
- **ReturnToNormalState()**: Resets the AI to its idle state if no threat is present

Listing 9-11. DynamicAIResponse.h

```
#pragma once

#include "CoreMinimal.h"
#include "GameFramework/Character.h"
#include "DynamicAIResponse.generated.h"

class USphereComponent;

UCLASS()
class MYGAME_API ADynamicAIResponse : public ACharacter
{
    GENERATED_BODY()

public:
    ADynamicAIResponse();

protected:
    virtual void BeginPlay() override;
```

```cpp
    // Detection overlap event
    UFUNCTION()
    void OnPlayerDetected(UPrimitiveComponent* OverlappedComp,
    AActor* OtherActor, UPrimitiveComponent* OtherComp,
    int32 OtherBodyIndex, bool bFromSweep, const FHitResult&
    SweepResult);
public:
    void ReactToThreat();
    void ReturnToNormalState();
private:
    UPROPERTY(VisibleAnywhere, Category = "Detection")
    USphereComponent* DetectionSphere;

    bool bPlayerDetected;
    bool bIsUnderThreat;
    FVector LastKnownPlayerLocation;
};
```

Listing 9-12 describes the runtime behavior of an AI system that responds dynamically to nearby threats. It highlights how detection and reaction mechanisms are managed at runtime.

- **DetectPlayer()**: The AI checks if the player is within a certain radius, triggering a state change.
- **ReactToThreat()**: If the player is within a close range, the AI switches to an aggressive state, preparing for combat.
- **ReturnToNormalState()**: If the player is no longer detected, the AI returns to its normal idle state.

CHAPTER 9   AI AND PATHFINDING

Listing 9-12. DynamicAIResponse.cpp

```
#include "DynamicAIResponse.h"
#include "Components/SphereComponent.h"
#include "Kismet/GameplayStatics.h"
#include "GameFramework/Actor.h"
#include "AIController.h"

ADynamicAIResponse::ADynamicAIResponse()
{
    PrimaryActorTick.bCanEverTick = false;

    DetectionSphere = CreateDefaultSubobject<USphereComponent>(
    TEXT("DetectionSphere"));
    DetectionSphere->InitSphereRadius(500.0f);
    DetectionSphere->SetupAttachment(RootComponent);

    DetectionSphere->OnComponentBeginOverlap.AddDynamic(this,
    &ADynamicAIResponse::OnPlayerEnterDetectionSphere);
    DetectionSphere->OnComponentEndOverlap.AddDynamic(this,
    &ADynamicAIResponse::OnPlayerExitDetectionSphere);

    bPlayerDetected = false;
    bIsUnderThreat = false;
}

void ADynamicAIResponse::BeginPlay()
{
    Super::BeginPlay();
}

void ADynamicAIResponse::OnPlayerEnterDetectionSphere
(UPrimitiveComponent* OverlappedComponent, AActor* OtherActor,
UPrimitiveComponent* OtherComp, int32 OtherBodyIndex,
bool bFromSweep, const FHitResult& SweepResult)
```

CHAPTER 9   AI AND PATHFINDING

```cpp
{
    if (OtherActor && OtherActor == UGameplayStatics::GetPlayer
    Pawn(GetWorld(), 0))
    {
        bPlayerDetected = true;
        LastKnownPlayerLocation = OtherActor->GetActorLocation();
        ReactToThreat();
    }
}

void ADynamicAIResponse::OnPlayerExitDetectionSphere
(UPrimitiveComponent* OverlappedComponent, AActor* OtherActor,
UPrimitiveComponent* OtherComp, int32 OtherBodyIndex)
{
    if (OtherActor && OtherActor == UGameplayStatics::GetPlayer
    Pawn(GetWorld(), 0))
    {
        ReturnToNormalState();
    }
}

void ADynamicAIResponse::ReactToThreat()
{
    if (bPlayerDetected)
    {
        AActor* Player = UGameplayStatics::GetPlayerPawn
        (GetWorld(), 0);
        if (Player && FVector::Dist(GetActorLocation(),
        Player->GetActorLocation()) < 200.0f)
        {
```

```
            bIsUnderThreat = true;
            // Switch to aggressive behavior (e.g., attack or
            take cover)
        }
    }
}
void ADynamicAIResponse::ReturnToNormalState()
{
    bPlayerDetected = false;
    bIsUnderThreat = false;
    // Reset to idle behavior
}
```

Dynamic AI response systems add a layer of depth to the gameplay, where the AI is not static but constantly adapts to the player's actions and environmental changes. This makes every encounter feel different and keeps the player on their toes, enhancing the immersion and challenge of the game. In the next section, we'll explore AI decision trees, a powerful tool for implementing more complex and reactive AI behaviors.

AI Decision Trees

AI decision trees are a popular technique for creating more structured, yet dynamic, decision-making systems for AI characters. By using a tree-like structure of decisions and actions, decision trees allow AI to evaluate conditions and choose appropriate actions based on the current game state, player interactions, or environmental changes.

CHAPTER 9   AI AND PATHFINDING

Importance of AI Decision Trees

Why should you use AI decision trees in your game?

- **Structured Decision-Making**: Decision trees offer a clear, hierarchical approach to decision-making, making it easier to manage complex behaviors.

- **Flexibility**: They can handle a variety of conditions and adapt to multiple scenarios, allowing for dynamic AI behavior.

- **Reusability**: Once a decision tree is created, it can be reused across different AI characters or game scenarios, saving time in development.

- **Scalability**: As game complexity increases, decision trees can grow in size, accommodating more complex and varied AI behaviors without losing performance.

Core Components of AI Decision Trees

Key elements of a decision tree include

- **Nodes**: Each node represents a decision or an action, such as "Is the player visible?" or "Move to cover."

- **Branches**: These are the possible outcomes or conditions that lead to the next node, such as "Yes" or "No."

- **Leaf Nodes**: These are the final actions taken by the AI based on the evaluated conditions, like attacking, patrolling, or fleeing.

- **Conditions**: The criteria or checks that determine which branch to follow, like distance to the player or the player's weapon.

CHAPTER 9 AI AND PATHFINDING

Reviewing the Code

Listing 9-13 introduces the decision-making components of an AI system that evaluates conditions and adapts behavior accordingly.

- **MakeDecision()**: This function checks the conditions and makes decisions based on the current game state.
- **bPlayerInSight**: A condition to check if the player is visible.
- **bPlayerTooClose**: A condition to check if the player is within a dangerous range.

Listing 9-13. AI_DecisionTree.h

```
#pragma once

#include "CoreMinimal.h"
#include "GameFramework/Character.h"
#include "AI_DecisionTree.generated.h"

UCLASS()
class MYGAME_API AAI_DecisionTree : public ACharacter
{
    GENERATED_BODY()

public:
    AAI_DecisionTree();

protected:
    virtual void BeginPlay() override;

public:
    virtual void Tick(float DeltaTime) override;

    void MakeDecision();
```

CHAPTER 9 AI AND PATHFINDING

```
private:
    bool bPlayerInSight;
    bool bPlayerTooClose;
};
```

Listing 9-14 outlines the logic for dynamic AI decision-making based on situational awareness.

- **MakeDecision()**: In this function, the AI checks the distance to the player and updates the conditions (bPlayerInSight and bPlayerTooClose).

- Based on these conditions, the AI decides whether to move to cover, engage in combat, or resume patrolling.

Listing 9-14. AI_DecisionTree.cpp

```
#include "AI_DecisionTree.h"
#include "Kismet/GameplayStatics.h"

AAI_DecisionTree::AAI_DecisionTree()
{
    PrimaryActorTick.bCanEverTick = true;
    bPlayerInSight = false;
    bPlayerTooClose = false;
}

void AAI_DecisionTree::BeginPlay()
{
    Super::BeginPlay();
}

void AAI_DecisionTree::Tick(float DeltaTime)
{
```

```cpp
    Super::Tick(DeltaTime);
    MakeDecision();
}

void AAI_DecisionTree::MakeDecision()
{
    AActor* Player = UGameplayStatics::GetPlayerPawn
    (GetWorld(), 0);
    if (!Player || !AIController || !AIController->GetBlackboard
    Component())
        return;

    FVector PlayerLocation = Player->GetActorLocation();
    FVector AICharacterLocation = GetActorLocation();
    float Distance = FVector::Dist(PlayerLocation,
    AICharacterLocation);

    UBlackboardComponent* Blackboard = AIController->
    GetBlackboardComponent();

    bool bInSight = Distance < 1000.0f;
    bool bTooClose = Distance < 200.0f;

    Blackboard->SetValueAsBool(TEXT("bPlayerInSight"),
    bInSight);
    Blackboard->SetValueAsBool(TEXT("bPlayerTooClose"),
    bTooClose);
    Blackboard->SetValueAsVector(TEXT("PlayerLocation"),
    PlayerLocation);
}
```

CHAPTER 9   AI AND PATHFINDING

Usage Example

Imagine a guard AI in a stealth game. If the player is spotted at a distance but isn't too close, the guard might move to a position for better sightlines. If the player gets too close, the guard will switch to a combat mode, ready to attack or defend. If no player is nearby, the guard will return to patrolling.

AI decision trees allow you to manage complex behaviors in a hierarchical, understandable way. By structuring decisions in a tree-like manner, you can create responsive, adaptive AI that can handle multiple conditions and actions. This approach not only enhances the realism of AI in your game but also simplifies the management of complex logic. In the next section, we'll dive into pathfinding optimization.

Pathfinding Optimization

Pathfinding is a critical aspect of AI, determining how characters navigate the game world to reach their goals. However, as game worlds become larger and more complex, pathfinding can become computationally expensive. Optimizing pathfinding ensures smoother gameplay performance, even in large, open environments with many AI agents.

Importance of Pathfinding Optimization

Why is pathfinding optimization essential?

- **Performance**: Large, open-world games with multiple AI agents can suffer from lag if pathfinding calculations are inefficient.

- **Scalability**: Optimized pathfinding systems can handle a higher number of agents without degrading game performance.

CHAPTER 9   AI AND PATHFINDING

- **Smooth Gameplay**: Efficient pathfinding ensures AI characters move fluidly through the environment, avoiding issues like getting stuck or taking overly long routes.

- **Realism**: Optimization techniques ensure that AI characters can navigate complex environments intelligently and without hiccups, enhancing player immersion.

Core Components of Pathfinding Optimization

Key components to focus on include

- **Pathfinding Algorithms**: Using optimized algorithms like A* or Dijkstra's algorithm, but with improvements to handle large datasets efficiently

- **Navigation Meshes (NavMesh)**: A precomputed representation of the walkable areas in the game world that allows for faster pathfinding computations

- **Reusing Paths**: Storing previously computed paths and reusing them when possible to reduce the need for repeated calculations

- **Hierarchical Pathfinding**: Breaking the world into smaller sections and using different pathfinding methods for different levels of detail, speeding up the process

- **Obstacle Avoidance**: Ensuring AI can dynamically avoid obstacles during movement without needing a full path recalculation

CHAPTER 9   AI AND PATHFINDING

Reviewing the Code

Listing 9-15 introduces an optimized AI navigation system using Unreal's built-in NavMesh support.

- **FindOptimizedPath()**: This function triggers pathfinding between the start and end locations, utilizing the precomputed NavMesh for fast pathfinding.
- **NavSystem**: An Unreal Engine navigation system that facilitates AI pathfinding and route calculations.

Listing 9-15. PathfindingOptimization.h

```
#pragma once

#include "CoreMinimal.h"
#include "GameFramework/Actor.h"
#include "NavigationSystem.h"
#include "PathfindingOptimization.generated.h"

UCLASS()
class MYGAME_API APathfindingOptimization : public AActor
{
    GENERATED_BODY()

public:
    APathfindingOptimization();

    UFUNCTION(BlueprintCallable, Category = "Pathfinding")
    void FindOptimizedPath(FVector StartLocation, FVector EndLocation);
```

CHAPTER 9 AI AND PATHFINDING

```
protected:
    virtual void BeginPlay() override;
private:
    UNavigationSystemV1* NavSystem;
};
```

Listing 9-16 demonstrates how to execute efficient AI pathfinding using Unreal Engine's NavMesh system.

- **NavSystem->FindPathToLocationSynchronously()**: This function calculates the optimized path from the start location to the end location using the NavMesh, avoiding obstacles and recalculating the path only if necessary.

- **AIController->MoveToLocation()**: Once the optimized path is found, the AI will begin to move toward the destination.

Listing 9-16. PathfindingOptimization.cpp

```cpp
#include "PathfindingOptimization.h"
#include "NavigationSystem.h"
#include "GameFramework/Actor.h"
#include "AIController.h"
#include "NavigationPath.h"

APathfindingOptimization::APathfindingOptimization()
{
    PrimaryActorTick.bCanEverTick = false;
}
```

CHAPTER 9   AI AND PATHFINDING

```cpp
void APathfindingOptimization::BeginPlay()
{
    Super::BeginPlay();
    NavSystem = UNavigationSystemV1::GetCurrent(GetWorld());
}

void APathfindingOptimization::FindOptimizedPath
(FVector StartLocation, FVector EndLocation)
{
    if (NavSystem)
    {
        FNavLocation StartNavLocation;
        FNavLocation EndNavLocation;

        if (NavSystem->ProjectPointToNavigation(StartLocation,
        StartNavLocation) &&
            NavSystem->ProjectPointToNavigation(EndLocation,
            EndNavLocation))
        {
            // Request the path from the navigation system
            UNavigationPath* Path = NavSystem->FindPathToLoc
            ationSynchronously(GetWorld(), StartNavLocation.
            Location, EndNavLocation.Location);

            if (Path && Path->IsValid())
            {
                // Move the AI along the path
                AAIController* AIController =
                Cast<AAIController>(GetController());
                if (AIController)
                {
```

```
            AIController->MoveToLocation
              (EndNavLocation.Location);
          }
        }
      }
    }
  }
}
```

Usage Example

Imagine an NPC in a large city. The NPC needs to find the quickest route to a target location, but there are many obstacles in the way. By utilizing a precomputed NavMesh and hierarchical pathfinding, the AI can efficiently navigate around buildings and streets, providing a seamless experience even in a complex urban environment.

Pathfinding optimization ensures that AI characters can navigate the game world smoothly without putting unnecessary strain on the system's performance. By using techniques like precomputed NavMeshes, hierarchical pathfinding, and caching paths, developers can handle more complex worlds and a larger number of AI agents while maintaining fluid gameplay. In the next section, we will explore AI state machines, which further help in managing the behavior of AI agents based on their current state.

AI State Machines

AI state machines are a fundamental concept in game AI development. They provide a structured way to manage the different behaviors of AI agents by defining distinct states that the agent can be in and the transitions between those states. By using state machines, AI characters can react to the game environment in an organized, predictable manner, making them feel more intelligent and responsive.

CHAPTER 9   AI AND PATHFINDING

Importance of AI State Machines

Why are AI state machines critical for game development?

- **Behavioral Clarity**: AI state machines allow you to clearly define an agent's behavior based on its current state (e.g., idle, attacking, patrolling).

- **Predictable Transitions**: They provide a mechanism for the AI to smoothly transition between different behaviors based on triggers, ensuring more lifelike actions.

- **Complexity Management**: By dividing behaviors into separate states, managing complex AI behaviors becomes more manageable and organized.

- **Flexible Decision-Making**: State machines enable an agent to make context-sensitive decisions (e.g., an NPC will switch from idle to combat mode when a player enters their line of sight).

Core Components of AI State Machines

AI state machines define structured behavior by managing what an AI character is doing at any given moment and under what conditions it should change. Key components include

- **States**: Represent specific behaviors such as *Patrolling*, *Attacking*, or *Fleeing*. Each state defines how the AI acts in that mode.

- **Transitions**: Conditions that trigger movement from one state to another. For example, an enemy might transition from *Patrolling* to *Attacking* upon detecting the player.

CHAPTER 9   AI AND PATHFINDING

- **State Handlers**: Logic blocks or functions that execute the behavior of the current state, such as movement, animations, or combat actions.

- **State Transitions**: Rules or checks that continuously evaluate whether the AI should move to another state (e.g., player escapes ➤ transition to *Searching*).

Suggestion: Try Unreal's State Trees

Unreal Engine 5 introduces State Trees, a powerful visual tool to author complex AI behaviors. They allow developers to

- Visually design state machines directly in the editor
- Assign conditions and actions to each state
- Integrate tightly with blackboards and gameplay logic

For developers looking to expand AI behaviors with more flexibility and editor support, State Trees offer a robust alternative to hand-coded state machines.

Reviewing the Code

Listing 9-17 introduces a simple state management system for AI behavior using string-based state identifiers.

- **ChangeState()**: This function allows the AI to change its state to a new state, which is identified by a string (e.g., "Patrolling," "Attacking").

- **CurrentState**: A variable that tracks the current state of the AI agent.

Listing 9-17. AIStateMachine.h

```cpp
#pragma once

#include "CoreMinimal.h"
#include "GameFramework/Actor.h"
#include "AIStateMachine.generated.h"

UCLASS()
class MYGAME_API AAIStateMachine : public AActor
{
    GENERATED_BODY()
public:
    AAIStateMachine();

    UFUNCTION(BlueprintCallable, Category = "AI State")
    void ChangeState(FString NewState);

protected:
    virtual void BeginPlay() override;

private:
    FString CurrentState;
};
```

Listing 9-18 demonstrates the runtime logic of an AI state management system using a simple string comparison to handle behavior transitions.

- **ChangeState()**: The ChangeState() function checks if the AI's current state differs from the new state and, if so, updates the current state. This can be expanded with more logic to handle visual effects, sound cues, or animations based on state changes.

- **CurrentState**: The state is logged to the console for debugging, but in a real-world scenario, this could trigger animations or behavioral changes for the AI.

Listing 9-18. AIStateMachine.cpp

```cpp
#include "AIStateMachine.h"

AAIStateMachine::AAIStateMachine()
{
    PrimaryActorTick.bCanEverTick = true;
    CurrentState = "Idle"; // Initial state
}

void AAIStateMachine::BeginPlay()
{
    Super::BeginPlay();
}

void AAIStateMachine::ChangeState(FString NewState)
{
    if (CurrentState != NewState)
    {
        CurrentState = NewState;
        // Add logic here to handle state transition effects
        (e.g., animations, behavior changes)
        UE_LOG(LogTemp, Warning, TEXT("State changed to: %s"),
            *CurrentState);
    }
}
```

CHAPTER 9   AI AND PATHFINDING

Usage Example

Imagine an enemy AI that moves through a level patrolling, but when it detects the player, it switches to an "Attack" state. This can be handled with state transitions, such as

- **Idle**: When the enemy is not doing anything, it remains in the "Idle" state.
- **Patrolling**: The enemy follows a set path or randomly moves around the environment.
- **Attacking**: When the player is detected, the enemy enters the "Attack" state and tries to engage the player.

AI state machines are a vital tool for managing the complex behaviors of AI agents. By breaking down behaviors into clear, manageable states and defining the transitions between them, developers can create AI systems that are both responsive and predictable. This structure improves gameplay by allowing NPCs to react to the environment in dynamic and realistic ways.

Summary

In this chapter, we explored how AI and pathfinding define the intelligence and movement of non-player characters within a game. From simple patrol systems to reactive enemy behavior and decision-making, these mechanics shape how NPCs interact with players and their environment. We implemented patrol logic, companion systems, player detection, and behavior switching—all contributing to lifelike, responsive agents. Pathfinding using NavMesh and algorithms like A* helped ensure efficient and intelligent navigation across complex terrain.

CHAPTER 9   AI AND PATHFINDING

These systems form the foundation of believable game worlds, where NPCs not only react logically but also support gameplay tension and strategy. With AI systems in place, we now move into networking and multiplayer, where we will explore how to synchronize game states, handle communication between players, and ensure smooth online gameplay.

CHAPTER 10

Networking and Multiplayer

In modern gaming, networking and multiplayer systems form the backbone of interactive experiences that connect players worldwide. This chapter delves into the complexities of developing multiplayer games, exploring how to synchronize game states, manage player interactions, and implement advanced systems for communication and matchmaking. Networking is not just about enabling connectivity but ensuring a seamless and engaging experience for players across diverse platforms and environments.

By understanding core networking principles, developers can create games that handle real-time interactions with precision and efficiency. This chapter focuses on techniques to manage lag, maintain server authority, and implement robust matchmaking and communication systems. Whether you're designing a cooperative game or a competitive multiplayer experience, mastering these networking fundamentals is essential.

Networking and multiplayer systems are essential for creating dynamic and engaging gaming experiences. They enable players to connect, compete, and cooperate in real time, bringing communities together across the globe. From casual matches with friends to large-scale competitive tournaments, networking is the foundation that drives social and interactive gameplay. Mastering multiplayer development allows creators to deliver seamless and immersive experiences, fostering connection and competition in the digital world.

CHAPTER 10 NETWORKING AND MULTIPLAYER

This chapter explores key aspects of multiplayer game development, including basic networking concepts, player synchronization, and real-time interactions. We'll dive into designing multiplayer game modes, building lobby systems, managing lag compensation, and implementing voice and text communication. By the end of this chapter, you'll have the knowledge to create secure, responsive, and immersive multiplayer experiences.

Basic Networking Concepts

Networking forms the backbone of multiplayer gaming by allowing devices to communicate and share data in real time. Understanding the basic concepts of networking is essential to building reliable and efficient multiplayer systems.

Importance of Basic Networking Concepts

Here's why mastering networking fundamentals is vital for game developers:

- **Seamless Communication**: Ensures consistent data flow between clients and servers
- **Reliable Gameplay**: Minimizes disruptions caused by connectivity issues
- **Scalable Systems**: Lays the foundation for handling a large number of players
- **Security**: Protects data and ensures fair gameplay

CHAPTER 10 NETWORKING AND MULTIPLAYER

Core Components of Basic Networking Concepts

Key aspects include

- **Client-Server Model**: The architecture where a server hosts the game world, and clients (players) connect to it

- **Peer-to-Peer (P2P) Networking**: A decentralized approach where each device communicates directly with others

- **Latency and Ping**: Measures the time taken for data to travel between devices

- **Packets**: Units of data sent between players and servers

- **Protocols**: Rules for data transfer, such as TCP (reliable) and UDP (fast)

Reviewing the code

Listing 10-1 introduces a basic networking manager class that serves as the foundation for handling multiplayer connections in Unreal Engine. This setup is essential for enabling player communication and synchronizing game state across the network.

- **EstablishConnection()**: A Blueprint-callable function used to initiate a network connection, such as joining a server or host

- **ANetworkingManager**: The class responsible for managing networking logic and events

CHAPTER 10   NETWORKING AND MULTIPLAYER

Listing 10-1. NetworkingManager.h

```
#pragma once

#include "CoreMinimal.h"
#include "GameFramework/Actor.h"
#include "NetworkingManager.generated.h"

UCLASS()
class MYGAME_API ANetworkingManager : public AActor
{
    GENERATED_BODY()
public:
    ANetworkingManager();

protected:
    virtual void BeginPlay() override;

public:
    virtual void Tick(float DeltaTime) override;

    UFUNCTION(BlueprintCallable, Category = "Networking")
    void EstablishConnection();
};
```

Listing 10-2 presents the runtime behavior of the networking manager, showing how it simulates establishing a connection and logs network activity. This setup lays the groundwork for more complex multiplayer functionality.

- **EstablishConnection()**: Outputs a log to the console simulating the initiation of a network connection. This function acts as a placeholder for future real networking logic.

- **UE_LOG()**: Used to print debugging information in the output log, indicating the networking process is active.

CHAPTER 10   NETWORKING AND MULTIPLAYER

Listing 10-2. NetworkingManager.cpp

```cpp
#include "NetworkingManager.h"

ANetworkingManager::ANetworkingManager()
{
    PrimaryActorTick.bCanEverTick = true;
}

void ANetworkingManager::BeginPlay()
{
    Super::BeginPlay();
}

void ANetworkingManager::Tick(float DeltaTime)
{
    Super::Tick(DeltaTime);
}

void ANetworkingManager::EstablishConnection()
{
    UE_LOG(LogTemp, Warning, TEXT("Establishing
    Connection..."));
    // Simulated connection logic
}
```

Usage Example

To create a functional multiplayer lobby, the EstablishConnection() function would be extended to include actual network setup logic, such as connecting to a remote server or initializing a P2P connection.

Understanding basic networking concepts is the first step in creating robust multiplayer games. Mastery of these fundamentals ensures smooth, secure, and scalable gameplay experiences. In the next section, we'll delve into player synchronization for seamless real-time interactions.

CHAPTER 10   NETWORKING AND MULTIPLAYER

Player Synchronization

Player synchronization ensures that all participants in a multiplayer game share the same view of the game world. By accurately replicating player positions, actions, and states across devices, it enables seamless interactions and a cohesive gaming experience.

Importance of Player Synchronization

Here's why synchronization is crucial in multiplayer games:

- **Consistency**: Maintains a shared game state across all players
- **Real-Time Interactions**: Allows for smooth movement and actions between players
- **Fair Gameplay**: Prevents desync issues that can lead to unfair advantages
- **Immersion**: Provides players with a believable and engaging multiplayer experience

Core Components of Player Synchronization

Key elements include

- **Position and Rotation Updates**: Ensures that player movements are consistent across all clients
- **State Replication**: Synchronizes player actions like shooting, jumping, or interacting with objects
- **Interpolation and Prediction**: Smooths out movement for clients experiencing lag

CHAPTER 10   NETWORKING AND MULTIPLAYER

- **Authority Management**: Determines whether the client or server has control over updates

- **Delta Time Adjustments**: Accounts for varying frame rates to ensure uniform gameplay

Reviewing the Code

Listing 10-3 presents the runtime behavior of a player synchronization component. This system ensures that a player's position and rotation are consistently updated across all connected clients using Unreal Engine's replication system.

- **UpdatePositionAndRotation()**: A custom function intended to update the player's position and rotation for network synchronization.

- **PlayerPosition**: Stores the current position of the player and is marked for replication to ensure network consistency.

- **PlayerRotation**: Stores the player's current orientation, also replicated across the network.

- **Replicated**: The UPROPERTY(Replicated) specifier ensures that variables are automatically synchronized from server to clients in multiplayer games. For character movement, Unreal Engine already provides a robust system via the CharacterMovementComponent, which handles replication and prediction out of the box.

Listing 10-3. PlayerSyncComponent.h

```cpp
#pragma once

#include "CoreMinimal.h"
#include "Components/ActorComponent.h"
#include "PlayerSyncComponent.generated.h"

UCLASS(ClassGroup=(Custom), meta=(BlueprintSpawnableComponent))
class MYGAME_API UPlayerSyncComponent : public UActorComponent
{
    GENERATED_BODY()

public:
    UPlayerSyncComponent();

protected:
    virtual void BeginPlay() override;

public:
    virtual void TickComponent(float DeltaTime, ELevelTick
    TickType, FActorComponentTickFunction* ThisTickFunction)
    override;

    UPROPERTY(Replicated, BlueprintReadWrite, Category =
    "Synchronization")
    FVector PlayerPosition;

    UPROPERTY(Replicated, BlueprintReadWrite, Category =
    "Synchronization")
    FRotator PlayerRotation;

    void UpdatePositionAndRotation();
};
```

CHAPTER 10   NETWORKING AND MULTIPLAYER

Listing 10-4 completes the implementation of the player synchronization system by handling replication and runtime updates. It ensures all connected clients receive accurate player position and rotation data in real time.

- **SetIsReplicatedByDefault(true)**: Called in the constructor to ensure the entire component is set up for replication across the network by default

- **GetLifetimeReplicatedProps()**: Overrides Unreal's replication function to explicitly mark PlayerPosition and PlayerRotation for network synchronization

- **UpdatePositionAndRotation()**: Updates both the position and rotation values, which can then be transmitted across the network for consistency between clients and the server

Listing 10-4. PlayerSyncComponent.cpp

```
#include "PlayerSyncComponent.h"
#include "Net/UnrealNetwork.h"

UPlayerSyncComponent::UPlayerSyncComponent()
{
    PrimaryComponentTick.bCanEverTick = true;
    SetIsReplicatedByDefault(true);
}

void UPlayerSyncComponent::BeginPlay()
{
    Super::BeginPlay();
}
```

```cpp
void UPlayerSyncComponent::TickComponent(float DeltaTime,
ELevelTick TickType, FActorComponentTickFunction*
ThisTickFunction)
{
    Super::TickComponent(DeltaTime, TickType,
    ThisTickFunction);

    if (GetOwnerRole() == ROLE_AutonomousProxy)
    {
        UpdatePositionAndRotation();
    }
}

void UPlayerSyncComponent::UpdatePositionAndRotation()
{
    PlayerPosition = GetOwner()->GetActorLocation();
    PlayerRotation = GetOwner()->GetActorRotation();
}

void UPlayerSyncComponent::GetLifetimeReplicatedProps(TArray
<FLifetimeProperty>& OutLifetimeProps) const
{
    Super::GetLifetimeReplicatedProps(OutLifetimeProps);
    DOREPLIFETIME(UPlayerSyncComponent, PlayerPosition);
    DOREPLIFETIME(UPlayerSyncComponent, PlayerRotation);
}
```

Usage Example

When a player moves, their position and rotation are updated locally and then replicated to other clients, ensuring all players see the same movements in real time.

Player synchronization is critical to providing a seamless multiplayer experience. By replicating player states and actions effectively, developers can eliminate desync issues and deliver smooth, real-time interactions. The next section focuses on networked player interactions, enhancing how players interact in a shared game world.

Networked Player Interactions

Networked player interactions are the backbone of multiplayer gameplay, enabling players to engage with each other and the game world in meaningful ways. From trading items to collaborative tasks and competitive actions, interactions must be designed to function smoothly across all connected devices.

Importance of Networked Player Interactions

Here's why these interactions are essential:

- **Collaboration and Competition**: Encourages teamwork and rivalries, central to multiplayer experiences
- **Immersion**: Deepens player engagement by creating shared, impactful interactions
- **Dynamic Gameplay**: Facilitates diverse mechanics like trading, combat, and cooperative puzzle-solving

CHAPTER 10   NETWORKING AND MULTIPLAYER

Core Components of Networked Player Interactions

Key elements include

- **Event Replication**: Ensures actions (e.g., picking up items) are visible to all players

- **Ownership Management**: Determines which player controls an object

- **Interaction Range**: Defines the proximity required for interaction to occur

- **Latency Handling**: Minimizes the impact of network lag during interactions

- **Conflict Resolution**: Manages simultaneous actions from multiple players (e.g., both attempting to pick up the same item)

Remote Procedure Calls (RPCs) and Network Proxies

Before diving into Listings 10-5 and 10-6, it's important to understand the concept of Remote Procedure Calls (RPCs) in Unreal Engine:

- **Server RPCs (UFUNCTION(Server, Reliable))**: These functions are executed on the server but can be called from the client. Used for authoritative actions like interactions or combat.

- **Multicast RPCs (UFUNCTION(NetMulticast, Reliable))**: Executed on the server and then broadcast to all clients. Ideal for synchronized visual/audio feedback.

CHAPTER 10 NETWORKING AND MULTIPLAYER

- **Validation Functions**: Ensure the integrity of RPC calls made by clients to prevent cheating.

- **Proxies**: Unreal Engine uses autonomous and simulated proxies to manage authority and replication. Autonomous proxies (usually the local player) can request actions. Simulated proxies (other clients) receive replicated updates.

Reviewing the Code

Listing 10-5 introduces a networked interaction component that uses Remote Procedure Calls (RPCs) to coordinate actions between server and clients.

- **Server_Interact()**: A server RPC that performs secure, authoritative interaction logic

- **Multicast_PlayInteractionEffect()**: Broadcasts visual/audio cues to all clients

- **Server Validation (WithValidation)**: Prevents invalid or malicious RPC calls from clients

Listing 10-5. PlayerInteractionComponent.h

```
#pragma once

#include "CoreMinimal.h"
#include "Components/ActorComponent.h"
#include "PlayerInteractionComponent.generated.h"

UCLASS(ClassGroup=(Custom), meta=(BlueprintSpawnableComponent))
class MYGAME_API UPlayerInteractionComponent : public UActorComponent
```

CHAPTER 10 NETWORKING AND MULTIPLAYER

```cpp
{
    GENERATED_BODY()
public:
    UPlayerInteractionComponent();
protected:
    virtual void BeginPlay() override;
public:
    UFUNCTION(Server, Reliable, WithValidation)
    void Server_Interact(AActor* TargetActor);

    UFUNCTION(NetMulticast, Reliable)
    void Multicast_PlayInteractionEffect(AActor* TargetActor);
};
UCLASS(ClassGroup=(Custom), meta=(BlueprintSpawnableComponent))
class MYGAME_API UPlayerInteractionComponent : public UActorComponent
{
    GENERATED_BODY()
public:
    UPlayerInteractionComponent();
protected:
    virtual void BeginPlay() override;
public:
    UFUNCTION(Server, Reliable, WithValidation)
    void Server_Interact(AActor* TargetActor);

    UFUNCTION(NetMulticast, Reliable)
    void Multicast_PlayInteractionEffect(AActor* TargetActor);
};
```

CHAPTER 10 NETWORKING AND MULTIPLAYER

Listing 10-6 finalizes the player interaction component by implementing the server-client communication flow required for reliable multiplayer interaction.

- **Server_Interact()**: Ensures only the server handles critical game logic like item pickup or door unlocking
- **Multicast_PlayInteractionEffect()**: Ensures all clients see or hear the same interaction outcome
- **Validation**: Guards against unauthorized or malformed input from the client side

Listing 10-6. PlayerInteractionComponent.cpp

```cpp
#include "PlayerInteractionComponent.h"
#include "Net/UnrealNetwork.h"

UPlayerInteractionComponent::UPlayerInteractionComponent()
{
    PrimaryComponentTick.bCanEverTick = false;
}

void UPlayerInteractionComponent::BeginPlay()
{
    Super::BeginPlay();
}

void UPlayerInteractionComponent::Server_Interact_Implementation(AActor* TargetActor)
{
    if (TargetActor)
    {
        // Perform interaction logic
        Multicast_PlayInteractionEffect(TargetActor);
    }
}
```

```cpp
bool UPlayerInteractionComponent::Server_Interact_
Validate(AActor* TargetActor)
{
    return true;
}

void UPlayerInteractionComponent::Multicast_
PlayInteractionEffect(AActor* TargetActor)
{
    if (TargetActor)
    {
        // Play visual or sound effect here
    }
}
```

Usage Example

When a player opens a chest in a multiplayer game

- The action is sent to the server using Server_Interact().
- The server validates the action and updates the game state.
- Feedback (e.g., a sound or animation) is broadcasted to all clients using Multicast_PlayInteractionEffect().

Networked player interactions form the foundation of meaningful multiplayer gameplay. By ensuring consistency, fairness, and responsiveness, these systems create a seamless and engaging experience. The next section will explore multiplayer game modes, diving into structuring diverse and exciting gameplay scenarios.

Multiplayer Game Modes

Multiplayer game modes define the structure of how players interact within the game, setting the rules, objectives, and dynamics for the experience. Whether it's team-based competition, cooperative gameplay, or free-for-all chaos, a well-designed game mode can enhance player engagement and replayability.

Importance of Multiplayer Game Modes

Multiplayer game modes are essential for shaping the player's experience, engagement, and satisfaction. Offering a variety of game modes helps developers cater to different playstyles, skill levels, and social preferences. For example, some players may enjoy fast-paced competitive gameplay, while others prefer cooperative objectives or casual exploration with friends. Diverse modes also increase replayability by providing fresh challenges and dynamics. Rotating through different objectives and formats keeps players invested over time and encourages them to return to the game regularly. Whether it's a strategic capture-the-flag session or a chaotic battle royale, each mode brings a unique rhythm and feel to the gameplay loop.

Common Types of Multiplayer Game Modes

There are several types of modes in multiplayer games, like

- **Team Deathmatch (TDM):** Players form teams and compete to achieve the highest number of kills.
- **Capture the Flag (CTF):** Teams attempt to capture and return the enemy's flag to their base.
- **Battle Royale:** Players fight to be the last one standing in a shrinking play area.

- **Cooperative Modes**: Players work together to achieve objectives or defeat AI enemies.

- **Objective-Based Modes**: Teams compete to complete specific tasks, such as holding control points.

Key Elements of Multiplayer Game Modes

The main elements of multiplayer game modes are

- **Objective Management**: Tracks goals, such as kill counts or captured flags

- **Player Team Assignment**: Dynamically balances teams for fair competition

- **Victory Conditions**: Defines when and how a match ends

- **Game Mode Rules**: Customizes settings like respawn times, round limits, and scoring

- **Event Synchronization**: Ensures that critical events (e.g., capturing a flag) are consistent across all clients

Reviewing the Code

Listing 10-7 introduces a basic multiplayer GameMode class that supports team assignment and server-authoritative match control. This class forms the backbone for managing competitive or cooperative multiplayer experiences, enabling structured team to play and match conclusion handling.

- **AssignTeams()**: A callable function that distributes players into two teams, helping balance the game dynamically as new players join or respawn

- **Server_EndMatch()**: A server-side reliable function used to end a match and determine which team won, allowing secure game state updates across the network
- **TeamOnePlayers/TeamTwoPlayers**: Internal arrays to store player controllers for each team, aiding in team-specific logic like scoring, spawning, or communication

Listing 10-7. MultiplayerGameMode.h

```
#pragma once

#include "CoreMinimal.h"
#include "GameFramework/GameModeBase.h"
#include "MultiplayerGameMode.generated.h"

UCLASS()
class MYGAME_API AMultiplayerGameMode : public AGameModeBase
{
    GENERATED_BODY()

public:
    AMultiplayerGameMode();

    UFUNCTION(BlueprintCallable, Category = "GameMode")
    void AssignTeams();

    UFUNCTION(Server, Reliable, WithValidation)
    void Server_EndMatch(bool bTeamOneWins);

protected:
    virtual void BeginPlay() override;

private:
    TArray<APlayerController*> TeamOnePlayers;
    TArray<APlayerController*> TeamTwoPlayers;
};
```

CHAPTER 10   NETWORKING AND MULTIPLAYER

Listing 10-8 finalizes the multiplayer game mode logic by implementing team assignments and match-ending functionality. This code defines the runtime behavior of your multiplayer match system and ensures proper synchronization across clients using server-authoritative methods.

- **BeginPlay()**: Automatically calls AssignTeams() at the start of the match to distribute players into teams.

- **AssignTeams()**: Iterates through all connected player controllers and alternates assignments between Team One and Team Two, ensuring balance.

- **Server_EndMatch()**: A server-side function that declares the match winner and logs the result. You can expand this to include UI updates, rewards, or match transitions.

- **Server_EndMatch_Validate()**: Provides basic validation to allow the server to accept the match-ending call.

Listing 10-8. MultiplayerGameMode.cpp

```cpp
#include "MultiplayerGameMode.h"
#include "GameFramework/PlayerController.h"
#include "Net/UnrealNetwork.h"

AMultiplayerGameMode::AMultiplayerGameMode()
{
    PrimaryActorTick.bCanEverTick = false;
}

void AMultiplayerGameMode::BeginPlay()
{
    Super::BeginPlay();
    AssignTeams();
}
```

```cpp
void AMultiplayerGameMode::AssignTeams()
{
    TArray<APlayerController*> AllPlayers;
    GetWorld()->GetPlayerControllerIterator().
    GetAll(AllPlayers);

    for (int32 i = 0; i < AllPlayers.Num(); ++i)
    {
        if (i % 2 == 0)
        {
            TeamOnePlayers.Add(AllPlayers[i]);
        }
        else
        {
            TeamTwoPlayers.Add(AllPlayers[i]);
        }
    }
}

void AMultiplayerGameMode::Server_EndMatch_Implementation
(bool bTeamOneWins)
{
    FString Winner = bTeamOneWins ? TEXT("Team One") :
    TEXT("Team Two");
    UE_LOG(LogTemp, Log, TEXT("%s wins the match!"), *Winner);
}

bool AMultiplayerGameMode::Server_EndMatch_Validate
(bool bTeamOneWins)
{
    return true;
}
```

CHAPTER 10 NETWORKING AND MULTIPLAYER

Usage Example

In a team deathmatch scenario

- Players are distributed evenly into Team One and Team Two using AssignTeams().
- As kills are recorded, the game mode tracks the score for each team.
- When one team reaches the target score, Server_EndMatch() announces the winner and ends the match.

Multiplayer game modes shape the player experience by defining the rules, objectives, and dynamics of the game. By offering diverse and well-crafted modes, developers can cater to a wide range of player preferences, ensuring lasting engagement. Next, we'll explore lobby systems, the gateway to seamless multiplayer gameplay.

Lobby Systems

Lobby systems serve as the entry point for multiplayer games, where players gather, prepare, and customize their experience before joining a match. A well-designed lobby ensures smooth matchmaking, team organization, and pre-game interactions.

Importance of Lobby Systems

Here's why a robust lobby system is essential:

- **Seamless Match Preparation**: Allows players to set preferences, such as game mode and team selection
- **Player Interaction**: Provides a space for socializing via chat or emotes

CHAPTER 10   NETWORKING AND MULTIPLAYER

- **Customizable Options**: Let players adjust loadouts, skins, or other settings
- **Readiness Check**: Ensures all players are prepared before the game starts

Key Features of a Lobby System

Key elements of the lobby system for any game:

- **Player List**: Displays all connected players
- **Team Assignment**: Organizes players into teams or groups
- **Game Settings**: Allow the host to configure match options
- **Ready System**: Tracks player readiness to start the game
- **Chat Functionality**: Facilitates communication between players
- **Match Countdown**: Starts the game when all players are ready or the host initiates

Reviewing the Code

Listing 10-9 introduces the core structure of a multiplayer lobby system. This setup manages player connections in a pre-game environment and prepares for match start logic via server-side validation.

- **AddPlayer()**: Adds a new player controller to the lobby's player list when they join
- **RemovePlayer()**: Removes a player controller from the list when they leave the lobby

CHAPTER 10 NETWORKING AND MULTIPLAYER

- **Server_StartMatch()**: Server-authoritative function to begin the match, ensuring conditions like player readiness are met
- **AllPlayersReady()**: A private helper function to check whether all players are ready before starting

Listing 10-9. LobbySystem.h

```
#pragma once

#include "CoreMinimal.h"
#include "GameFramework/GameModeBase.h"
#include "LobbySystem.generated.h"

UCLASS()
class MYGAME_API ALobbySystem : public AGameModeBase
{
    GENERATED_BODY()
public:
    ALobbySystem();

    UFUNCTION(BlueprintCallable, Category = "Lobby")
    void AddPlayer(APlayerController* NewPlayer);

    UFUNCTION(BlueprintCallable, Category = "Lobby")
    void RemovePlayer(APlayerController* ExitingPlayer);

    UFUNCTION(Server, Reliable, WithValidation)
    void Server_StartMatch();

protected:
    virtual void BeginPlay() override;
```

CHAPTER 10 NETWORKING AND MULTIPLAYER

```
private:
    TArray<APlayerController*> ConnectedPlayers;
    bool AllPlayersReady() const;
};
```

Listing 10-10 presents the runtime implementation of a multiplayer lobby system. It manages player entry and exit, checks readiness conditions, and allows the server to initiate the match when criteria are met.

- **AddPlayer()**: Adds a new player to the lobby and logs the current count
- **RemovePlayer()**: Removes a player from the list and updates the lobby state
- **AllPlayersReady()**: A placeholder function that determines if enough players are present to begin the match
- **Server_StartMatch()**: Executes on the server to validate conditions and start the match, logging success or failure
- **UE_LOG()**: Provides runtime feedback in the output log for debugging or monitoring lobby activity

Listing 10-10. LobbySystem.cpp

```
#include "LobbySystem.h"
#include "Net/UnrealNetwork.h"

ALobbySystem::ALobbySystem()
{
    PrimaryActorTick.bCanEverTick = false;
}
```

CHAPTER 10 NETWORKING AND MULTIPLAYER

```cpp
void ALobbySystem::BeginPlay()
{
    Super::BeginPlay();
}

void ALobbySystem::AddPlayer(APlayerController* NewPlayer)
{
    if (NewPlayer)
    {
        ConnectedPlayers.Add(NewPlayer);
        UE_LOG(LogTemp, Log, TEXT("Player added. 
        Total players: %d"), ConnectedPlayers.Num());
    }
}

void ALobbySystem::RemovePlayer(APlayerController* 
ExitingPlayer)
{
    if (ExitingPlayer)
    {
        ConnectedPlayers.Remove(ExitingPlayer);
        UE_LOG(LogTemp, Log, TEXT("Player removed. 
        Total players: %d"), ConnectedPlayers.Num());
    }
}

bool ALobbySystem::AllPlayersReady() const
{
    // Placeholder logic to check if all players are ready.
    return ConnectedPlayers.Num() >= 2;
}
```

CHAPTER 10 NETWORKING AND MULTIPLAYER

```cpp
void ALobbySystem::Server_StartMatch_Implementation()
{
    if (AllPlayersReady())
    {
        UE_LOG(LogTemp, Log, TEXT("All players ready. Starting
        match!"));
        // Logic to transition to the game level.
    }
    else
    {
        UE_LOG(LogTemp, Warning, TEXT("Not all players are
        ready."));
    }
}
bool ALobbySystem::Server_StartMatch_Validate()
{
    return true;
}
```

Usage Example

That's how we can use this code:

- Players connect to the lobby using AddPlayer().
- A readiness system checks if all players are prepared.
- When ready, the host triggers Server_StartMatch() to begin the game.

Lobby systems act as the organizational hub for multiplayer games, providing structure and a smooth transition into matches. By offering features like team assignment, chat, and readiness tracking, they enhance the multiplayer experience. Up next, we'll discuss networked AI and its role in multiplayer gameplay.

753

Networked AI

In multiplayer games, AI entities such as enemies, NPCs, or environmental elements need to behave consistently across all clients. Networked AI ensures that these elements are synchronized, responsive, and perform reliably in a multiplayer environment.

Importance of Networked AI

Networked AI is crucial because

- **Consistency**: Ensures all players see the same AI behavior regardless of their client
- **Fairness**: Maintains balance by preventing exploits or desynchronized states
- **Immersion**: Provides a cohesive game world where AI actions are predictable and reliable

Key Features of Networked AI

Key features of networked AI:

- **Server-Side Authority**: The server controls AI behavior, ensuring consistency across clients.
- **Replication**: AI state and actions are sent to all connected players.
- **Pathfinding and Decision-Making**: Server-based logic ensures unified AI responses.
- **Event Handling**: AI reacts to player actions or environmental changes in real time.

CHAPTER 10   NETWORKING AND MULTIPLAYER

Reviewing the Code

Listing 10-11 introduces the foundational structure for a networked AI manager. This class ensures that AI movement commands issued on the server are reflected on all clients through replication.

- **Server_MoveAI()**: Executes movement commands on the authoritative server to ensure consistency across the network
- **AIActorLocation**: A replicated variable that holds the current location of the AI actor, synchronized across clients
- **OnRep_AIActorLocation()**: A notification function triggered automatically on clients when AIActorLocation is updated, allowing client-side response to movement changes

Listing 10-11. NetworkedAIManager.h

```
#pragma once

#include "CoreMinimal.h"
#include "GameFramework/Actor.h"
#include "NetworkedAIManager.generated.h"

UCLASS()
class MYGAME_API ANetworkedAIManager : public AActor
{
    GENERATED_BODY()

public:
    ANetworkedAIManager();
```

```cpp
    UFUNCTION(Server, Reliable, WithValidation)
    void Server_MoveAI(FVector NewLocation);
protected:
    virtual void BeginPlay() override;
private:
    UPROPERTY(Replicated)
    FVector AIActorLocation;

    UFUNCTION()
    void OnRep_AIActorLocation();
};
```

Listing 10-12 presents the runtime implementation of a networked AI synchronization system. It ensures consistent AI positioning across all clients using Unreal Engine's replication framework.

- **Server_MoveAI()**: This server-side method receives movement instructions, updates the replicated AIActorLocation, and triggers position updates across the network.

- **OnRep_AIActorLocation()**: Automatically called on clients when AIActorLocation is modified, this method updates the actor's position in the world.

- **DOREPLIFETIME**: Registers AIActorLocation for replication so it stays synchronized across all clients.

- **SetActorLocation()**: Moves the AI actor to the new replicated position on clients.

Listing 10-12. NetworkedAIManager.cpp

```
#include "NetworkedAIManager.h"
#include "Net/UnrealNetwork.h"

ANetworkedAIManager::ANetworkedAIManager()
{
    PrimaryActorTick.bCanEverTick = false;
    bReplicates = true;
}

void ANetworkedAIManager::BeginPlay()
{
    Super::BeginPlay();
}

void ANetworkedAIManager::Server_MoveAI_Implementation
(FVector NewLocation)
{
    AIActorLocation = NewLocation;
    OnRep_AIActorLocation();
}

bool ANetworkedAIManager::Server_MoveAI_Validate
(FVector NewLocation)
{
    return true;
}
```

```cpp
void ANetworkedAIManager::OnRep_AIActorLocation()
{
    AAIController* AIController = Cast<AAIController>
    (GetController());
    if (AIController)
    {
        AIController->MoveToLocation(AIActorLocation, -1.0f,
        true, true, true, false, 0, true);
    }
}
void ANetworkedAIManager::GetLifetimeReplicatedProps(TArray
<FLifetimeProperty>& OutLifetimeProps) const
{
    Super::GetLifetimeReplicatedProps(OutLifetimeProps);
    DOREPLIFETIME(ANetworkedAIManager, AIActorLocation);
}
```

Networked AI is vital for creating a seamless multiplayer experience. By centralizing control on the server and replicating AI states to all clients, developers can ensure fairness, consistency, and immersion. Next, we'll delve into lag compensation, a critical feature for responsive multiplayer gameplay.

Lag Compensation

Lag compensation is a technique used in multiplayer games to mitigate the effects of latency, ensuring fair and consistent gameplay for all players, regardless of their connection speed. This is particularly important in competitive or fast-paced games where timing and precision are critical.

Importance of Lag Compensation

Lag compensation ensures

- **Fairness**: Players with higher latency are not at a disadvantage during interactions like shooting or hitting.

- **Accuracy**: Actions are registered correctly as if they occurred in real time.

- **Player Experience**: Minimizes frustration caused by delayed or missed actions due to lag.

Key Features of Lag Compensation

Key features of lag compensation in multiplayer games:

- **Rewind Mechanics**: The server simulates past game states to determine the outcome of player actions.

- **Hit Registration**: Ensures accurate recognition of hits or collisions regardless of latency.

- **Interpolation and Extrapolation**: Smooths out player and object movement across clients.

- **Server Authority**: The server verifies and resolves actions to maintain fairness.

Reviewing the Code

Listing 10-13 introduces the framework for a lag compensation system. It captures player snapshots and allows the server to validate hits based on historical game states, crucial for ensuring fairness in networked gameplay.

CHAPTER 10   NETWORKING AND MULTIPLAYER

- **Server_RegisterHit()**: Server-side function that receives a hit request from the client and verifies it using saved historical data
- **FPlayerSnapshot**: A lightweight structure storing player location, rotation, and the corresponding timestamp
- **PlayerSnapshots**: An array that maintains a history of player states for use during hit validation or state rewinding
- **SavePlayerSnapshot()**: Captures the player's current state at regular intervals
- **ValidateHit()**: Rewinds time to verify whether a reported hit was valid at the given timestamp

Listing 10-13. LagCompensationManager.h

```
#pragma once

#include "CoreMinimal.h"
#include "GameFramework/Actor.h"
#include "LagCompensationManager.generated.h"

UCLASS()
class MYGAME_API ALagCompensationManager : public AActor
{
    GENERATED_BODY()

public:
    ALagCompensationManager();

    UFUNCTION(Server, Reliable, WithValidation)
    void Server_RegisterHit(FVector HitLocation, float Timestamp);
```

CHAPTER 10   NETWORKING AND MULTIPLAYER

```
protected:
    virtual void BeginPlay() override;

private:
    struct FPlayerSnapshot
    {
        FVector Location;
        FRotator Rotation;
        float Timestamp;
    };

    TArray<FPlayerSnapshot> PlayerSnapshots;

    void SavePlayerSnapshot();
    bool ValidateHit(FVector HitLocation, float Timestamp);
};
```

Listing 10-14 completes the lag compensation system by recording player states and validating hits using historical data. This mechanism ensures reliable hit registration in multiplayer games with varying latencies.

- **SavePlayerSnapshot()**: Captures and stores the player's position, rotation, and current world time. It maintains only the latest 50 snapshots to optimize performance.

- **ValidateHit()**: Compares the reported hit location and timestamp against recent snapshots to determine if the hit is legitimate, using both time proximity and spatial distance.

- **Server_RegisterHit()**: Called remotely by clients to register a hit. It uses `ValidateHit()` to approve or reject the action and logs the result accordingly.

- **Server_RegisterHit_Validate()**: Performs basic validation of input data for security.

CHAPTER 10 NETWORKING AND MULTIPLAYER

Listing 10-14. LagCompensationManager.cpp

```cpp
#include "LagCompensationManager.h"
#include "GameFramework/PlayerController.h"

ALagCompensationManager::ALagCompensationManager()
{
    PrimaryActorTick.bCanEverTick = true;
}
void ALagCompensationManager::BeginPlay()
{
    Super::BeginPlay();
}

void ALagCompensationManager::SavePlayerSnapshot()
{
    FPlayerSnapshot Snapshot;
    Snapshot.Location = GetActorLocation();
    Snapshot.Rotation = GetActorRotation();
    Snapshot.Timestamp = GetWorld()->GetTimeSeconds();

    PlayerSnapshots.Add(Snapshot);

    // Remove old snapshots to optimize performance
    while (PlayerSnapshots.Num() > 50)
    {
        PlayerSnapshots.RemoveAt(0);
    }
}
bool ALagCompensationManager::ValidateHit(FVector HitLocation, float Timestamp)
{
    for (const FPlayerSnapshot& Snapshot : PlayerSnapshots)
```

```
    {
        if (FMath::Abs(Snapshot.Timestamp - Timestamp) < 0.05f)
        {
            if (FVector::Dist(Snapshot.Location, HitLocation)
            < 50.0f)
            {
                return true;
            }
        }
    }
    return false;
}

void ALagCompensationManager::Server_RegisterHit_
Implementation(FVector HitLocation, float Timestamp)
{
    if (ValidateHit(HitLocation, Timestamp))
    {
        UE_LOG(LogTemp, Log, TEXT("Hit validated!"));
    }
    else
    {
        UE_LOG(LogTemp, Warning, TEXT("Hit rejected due to lag
        mismatch."));
    }
}

bool ALagCompensationManager::Server_RegisterHit_
Validate(FVector HitLocation, float Timestamp)
{
    return true;
}
```

Lag compensation ensures multiplayer games remain fair and responsive, even under varying network conditions. By implementing techniques like state rewinding and server validation, developers can create a balanced and enjoyable experience for all players. Next, we'll explore server authority, a critical concept for maintaining control and integrity in multiplayer games.

Server Authority

Server authority refers to the practice of granting the game server the ultimate control over the game state in multiplayer games. This ensures that all decisions, validations, and updates are centralized, reducing the risks of cheating, desynchronization, and inconsistent game behavior.

Importance of Server Authority

Server authority is crucial for

- **Security**: Prevents cheating by validating all player actions on the server.
- **Consistency**: Ensures all players see the same game state, minimizing desynchronization issues.
- **Fair Play**: Resolves conflicts between client actions to maintain a balanced experience.
- **Reliable State Management**: The server serves as the definitive source of truth for the game world.

CHAPTER 10   NETWORKING AND MULTIPLAYER

Key Features of Server Authority

Key features of server authority:

- **Command Validation**: The server verifies all player inputs and actions before execution.

- **Centralized Game Logic**: Critical game mechanics, such as physics and combat, are handled on the server.

- **Conflict Resolution**: The server reconciles discrepancies between client data.

- **Cheat Prevention**: Clients have limited control, reducing vulnerabilities.

- **Synchronization**: The server continuously updates clients with the latest game state.

Reviewing the Code

Listing 10-15 introduces a server-authoritative movement system to ensure secure and accurate player movement in multiplayer games.

- **Server_MovePlayer()**: A server RPC (Remote Procedure Call) that accepts client movement input and applies it on the server. This prevents cheating or desync caused by unreliable client-side movement.

- **WithValidation**: Ensures that movement requests are verified before being accepted, enhancing security.

- **Reliable**: Guarantees that movement commands sent from the client will be received and executed by the server.

CHAPTER 10 NETWORKING AND MULTIPLAYER

Listing 10-15. ServerAuthoritativeMovement.h

```
#pragma once

#include "CoreMinimal.h"
#include "GameFramework/Actor.h"
#include "ServerAuthoritativeMovement.generated.h"

UCLASS()
class MYGAME_API AServerAuthoritativeMovement : public AActor
{
    GENERATED_BODY()

public:
    AServerAuthoritativeMovement();

    UFUNCTION(Server, Reliable, WithValidation)
    void Server_MovePlayer(FVector NewLocation);

protected:
    virtual void BeginPlay() override;
};
```

Listing 10-16 completes the implementation of server-authoritative movement, validating and applying position updates exclusively on the server.

- **Server_MovePlayer_Implementation()**: Executes movement logic on the server, ensuring only authoritative updates are applied. It sets the actor's location and logs the result.

- **HasAuthority()**: Confirms that the server is the one applying the move, preventing client-side manipulation.

- **Server_MovePlayer_Validate()**: A placeholder for future validation logic (e.g., distance checks or allowed movement areas) to prevent exploitative behavior.
- **UE_LOG()**: Provides real-time feedback for developers by logging the movement event.

Listing 10-16. ServerAuthoritativeMovement.cpp

```cpp
#include "ServerAuthoritativeMovement.h"

AServerAuthoritativeMovement::AServerAuthoritativeMovement()
{
    PrimaryActorTick.bCanEverTick = false;
}

void AServerAuthoritativeMovement::BeginPlay()
{
    Super::BeginPlay();
}

void AServerAuthoritativeMovement::Server_MovePlayer_
Implementation(FVector NewLocation)
{
    if (HasAuthority())
    {
        SetActorLocation(NewLocation);
        UE_LOG(LogTemp, Log, TEXT("Player moved to: %s"),
        *NewLocation.ToString());
    }
}
```

CHAPTER 10   NETWORKING AND MULTIPLAYER

```
bool AServerAuthoritativeMovement::Server_MovePlayer_
Validate(FVector NewLocation)
{
    // Add validation logic here, e.g., ensuring movement is
    within allowed bounds return true;
}
```

Server authority establishes a secure and consistent foundation for multiplayer games. By centralizing control, it reduces cheating risks and ensures a cohesive experience for all players. In the next section, we'll dive into matchmaking systems, exploring how to connect players effectively in multiplayer environments.

Matchmaking Systems

Matchmaking systems serve as the foundation of multiplayer experiences by grouping players into sessions that are balanced, fair, and enjoyable. While competitive games may require skill-based matchmaking that analyzes player statistics and performance data, many co-op or casual games prioritize smooth connectivity, quick queue times, and low latency.

These systems often consider factors such as player region, ping, game preferences, and current lobby availability to optimize the player experience.

Importance of Matchmaking Systems

Let's know why matchmaking systems are important:

- **Fair Competition**: Groups players of similar skill levels to ensure balanced gameplay
- **Reduced Latency**: Matches players based on geographic proximity to minimize lag

- **Enhanced Player Retention**: Improves the player experience by ensuring enjoyable matches

- **Efficient Game Setup**: Automates the process of finding suitable matches, saving players time

Core Features of Matchmaking Systems

There are some features on which we can do the matchmaking among players:

- **Skill-Based Matchmaking (SBMM)**: Uses player rankings or metrics to create balanced teams

- **Latency Optimization**: Considers server ping and geographic location for smooth gameplay

- **Custom Match Preferences**: Allows players to specify game modes or roles they prefer

- **Dynamic Queues**: Adjusts matchmaking parameters to reduce wait times during low activity

- **Cross-Platform Compatibility**: Enables matchmaking across different gaming platforms

Reviewing the Code

Listing 10-17 introduces a basic matchmaking manager for multiplayer games. It supports queueing players and starting matches when enough players are ready.

- **AddPlayerToQueue()**: Adds players to the matchmaking queue

- **StartMatchIfReady()**: Checks if the queue has enough players and initiates a match

CHAPTER 10 NETWORKING AND MULTIPLAYER

- **PlayerQueue**: A private array that holds queued player controllers
- **PlayersPerMatch**: Sets the required number of players needed to begin a match (default is 4)

Listing 10-17. MatchmakingManager.h

```
#pragma once

#include "CoreMinimal.h"
#include "GameFramework/Actor.h"
#include "MatchmakingManager.generated.h"

UCLASS()
class MYGAME_API AMatchmakingManager : public AActor
{
    GENERATED_BODY()
public:
    AMatchmakingManager();

    UFUNCTION(BlueprintCallable, Category = "Matchmaking")
    void AddPlayerToQueue(APlayerController* Player);

    UFUNCTION(BlueprintCallable, Category = "Matchmaking")
    void StartMatchIfReady();

protected:
    virtual void BeginPlay() override;

private:
    TArray<APlayerController*> PlayerQueue;
    int32 PlayersPerMatch = 4;
};
```

CHAPTER 10　NETWORKING AND MULTIPLAYER

Listing 10-18 provides the implementation of the matchmaking system, demonstrating how players are added to a queue and how matches are triggered when ready.

- **AddPlayerToQueue()**: Adds a player controller to the matchmaking queue and logs the current count. Automatically calls `StartMatchIfReady()` to check for match readiness

- **StartMatchIfReady()**: Verifies if the number of queued players meets the requirement and logs match initiation. Clears the queue after starting

- **UE_LOG()**: Used for debugging and confirming system behavior in the output log

Listing 10-18. MatchmakingManager.cpp

```
#include "MatchmakingManager.h"

AMatchmakingManager::AMatchmakingManager()
{
    PrimaryActorTick.bCanEverTick = false;
}

void AMatchmakingManager::BeginPlay()
{
    Super::BeginPlay();
}

void AMatchmakingManager::AddPlayerToQueue(APlayerController*
Player)
{
    if (Player)
    {
```

```
        PlayerQueue.Add(Player);
        UE_LOG(LogTemp, Log, TEXT("Player added to matchmaking
        queue. Total: %d"), PlayerQueue.Num());

        StartMatchIfReady();
    }
}

void AMatchmakingManager::StartMatchIfReady()
{
    if (PlayerQueue.Num() >= PlayersPerMatch)
    {
        UE_LOG(LogTemp, Log, TEXT("Match is ready to start!"));

        // Logic to group players into a match and start
        the game
        PlayerQueue.Empty();
    }
}
```

Usage Example

Example of how we can use the code in the game:

- Players join the matchmaking queue by calling AddPlayerToQueue().

- When the queue reaches the required number of players, StartMatchIfReady() is triggered.

- The system assigns players to a match and begins gameplay.

Matchmaking systems play a vital role in creating fair and engaging multiplayer experiences. By dynamically grouping players based on skill, location, and preferences, they enhance player satisfaction and retention. In the next section, we'll explore voice and text chat, which facilitate communication in multiplayer environments.

Voice and Text Chat

Voice and text chat systems are essential components of multiplayer games, enabling players to communicate and coordinate effectively. These systems enhance teamwork, foster social interactions, and provide a platform for building strong player communities.

Importance of Voice and Text Chat

Importance of voice and text chat in games:

- **Team Coordination**: Facilitates real-time communication for better collaboration
- **Enhanced Player Experience**: Promotes social interaction and community building
- **Game Immersion**: Adds a layer of realism and connectivity to the multiplayer experience
- **Accessibility**: Provides text-based alternatives for players who cannot or prefer not to use voice chat

CHAPTER 10   NETWORKING AND MULTIPLAYER

Core Features of Voice and Text Chat

Main features of voice and text chat system in games:

- **Voice Communication**: Supports live audio streams for seamless communication
- **Text Messaging**: Offers instant messaging channels for various game scenarios
- **Channel Management**: Includes team-specific, global, and private channels
- **Mute/Block Options**: Allows players to block unwanted communication or mute disruptive players
- **Cross-Platform Support**: Ensures compatibility across devices and platforms
- **Language Filters**: Filters offensive or inappropriate text messages

Options for Voice Chat

Voice chat systems in multiplayer games offer real-time communication, helping players coordinate and interact more effectively:

- **Built-In Subsystem Voice**: Uses Unreal's OnlineSubsystem (like Steam/EOS) for peer-to-peer voice communication
- **Vivox Plugin**: Provides cross-platform 3D positional voice, channel control, and mute/block features and is free for indie use
- **Custom WebRTC or Mumble Integration**: Enables custom proximity or radio chat setups with full backend control

CHAPTER 10 NETWORKING AND MULTIPLAYER

- **Console/Platform Voice Services**: Leverages Xbox/PlayStation native chat systems with auto-managed party and game communication

Reviewing the Code

Listing 10-19 provides the implementation of a basic text chat system in Unreal Engine, demonstrating how players can send messages globally or to their team only.

- **SendMessageToAll()**: Broadcasts a formatted chat message to all players in the game. Useful for global announcements or open communication
- **SendMessageToTeam()**: Sends a team-specific message, ensuring that only teammates see the communication
- **GEngine->AddOnScreenDebugMessage()**: Used to display messages on the player's screen for debugging or basic chat feedback

Listing 10-19. ChatManager.h

```
#pragma once

#include "CoreMinimal.h"
#include "GameFramework/Actor.h"
#include "ChatManager.generated.h"

UCLASS()
class MYGAME_API AChatManager : public AActor
{
    GENERATED_BODY()
```

CHAPTER 10   NETWORKING AND MULTIPLAYER

```
public:
    AChatManager();

    UFUNCTION(BlueprintCallable, Category = "Chat")
    void SendMessageToAll(const FString& Message,
    APlayerController* Sender);

    UFUNCTION(BlueprintCallable, Category = "Chat")
    void SendMessageToTeam(const FString& Message,
    APlayerController* Sender);

protected:
    virtual void BeginPlay() override;
};
```

Listing 10-20 provides the implementation of the chat manager system, showing how messages are formatted and displayed in the game for all players or specific teams.

- **SendMessageToAll()**: Formats the player's name and message, then broadcasts it to all players using AddOnScreenDebugMessage() for basic chat visibility
- **SendMessageToTeam()**: Creates a team-specific message prefix and shows it in a distinct color for teammates, simulating a private team chat
- **GEngine->AddOnScreenDebugMessage()**: Displays the message on screen for visual feedback, useful for prototypes or lightweight messaging systems

Listing 10-20. ChatManager.cpp

```
#include "ChatManager.h"
#include "GameFramework/PlayerState.h"

AChatManager::AChatManager()
{
```

```cpp
    PrimaryActorTick.bCanEverTick = false;
}

void AChatManager::BeginPlay()
{
    Super::BeginPlay();
}

void AChatManager::SendMessageToAll(const FString& Message,
APlayerController* Sender)
{
    if (Sender)
    {
        FString SenderName = Sender->PlayerState->
        GetPlayerName();
        FString FullMessage = FString::Printf(TEXT("%s: %s"),
        *SenderName, *Message);

        // Broadcast the message to all players
        GEngine->AddOnScreenDebugMessage(-1, 5.f, FColor::Green,
        FullMessage);
    }
}

void AChatManager::SendMessageToTeam(const FString& Message,
APlayerController* Sender)
{
    if (Sender)
    {
        FString SenderName = Sender->PlayerState-
        >GetPlayerName();
        FString FullMessage = FString::Printf(TEXT("%s (Team):
        %s"), *SenderName, *Message);
```

```
    // Logic to send message to team members only
    GEngine->AddOnScreenDebugMessage(-1, 5.f, FColor::Blue,
    FullMessage);
  }
}
```

Voice and text chat systems are fundamental for fostering communication and teamwork in multiplayer games. By implementing robust chat features, developers can create a more interactive and engaging gaming environment.

Summary

In this chapter, we explored the foundational systems that enable multiplayer gameplay in Unreal Engine. From establishing network connections and synchronizing player data to implementing server-authoritative logic, matchmaking, and chat systems, this chapter provided the core mechanics necessary to build scalable and responsive online experiences. In the next chapter, we will talk about advanced mechanics.

CHAPTER 11

Advanced Mechanics

As game development continues to evolve, incorporating advanced mechanics is essential for creating innovative and engaging experiences. This chapter delves into cutting-edge techniques and systems that push the boundaries of modern gaming.

In this chapter, we'll explore advanced mechanics that push the boundaries of modern game development. Topics include procedural generation techniques for creating dynamic and unique content, save and load systems for implementing robust and flexible game state management, and modding support to empower community-driven content creation. We'll delve into VR and AR mechanics to design immersive virtual and augmented realities and performance optimization strategies to ensure smooth gameplay across devices. The chapter also covers cross-platform development for building games that cater to diverse platforms, advanced scripting techniques to enhance game logic and functionality, and plugin and middleware integration to leverage third-party tools effectively. Finally, we'll explore future trends in game development, providing insights into what's next for the industry. By the end of this chapter, you'll be equipped to incorporate these advanced mechanics and keep your game competitive in the ever-evolving gaming landscape.

Advanced mechanics are the backbone of innovation in gaming. They allow developers to break conventional barriers, offering players more immersive, interactive, and versatile experiences. These mechanics enhance gameplay depth and provide developers with the tools to address evolving player expectations and industry trends.

CHAPTER 11   ADVANCED MECHANICS

Procedural Generation

Procedural generation is a technique used to create dynamic, unique, and often infinite game content algorithmically, rather than crafting everything manually. It enables developers to build immersive and unpredictable experiences, such as randomly generated levels, terrain, or even entire worlds. Unreal Engine, coupled with C++, provides powerful tools for implementing procedural generation effectively.

Importance of Procedural Generation in Games

Let's explore why procedural generation is a critical mechanic:

- **Replayability**: Generates unique game content, encouraging players to revisit the game multiple times
- **Development Efficiency**: Reduces the need for manual content creation, saving time and resources
- **Dynamic Environments**: Creates unpredictable gameplay experiences, enhancing immersion
- **Infinite Content**: Enables open-world and sandbox games to deliver vast, explorable areas

Core Components of Procedural Generation

Key elements of procedural generation include

- **Random Seed**: A numeric value that ensures consistency or variety in generated content
- **Noise Functions**: Used for smooth and natural variations, such as Perlin or Simplex noise

- **Algorithms**: Commonly used methods like cellular automata or fractals for terrain and level creation
- **Modular Assets**: Prefabricated pieces that are procedurally assembled to build complex structures

Reviewing the Code

Listing 11-1 introduces the header for a procedural terrain generation system. This setup enables dynamic world creation by leveraging Perlin noise and spawning modular terrain tiles based on calculated positions.

- **Width and Height**: Define the grid size of the terrain
- **TileSize**: Sets the spacing between each terrain tile
- **NoiseScale**: Controls the scale of Perlin noise for terrain height variation
- **GenerateTerrain()**: Handles the logic for looping through the grid and applying noise
- **SpawnTile()**: A helper function used to spawn individual tiles based on position+

Listing 11-1. ProceduralTerrainGenerator.h

```
#pragma once

#include "CoreMinimal.h"
#include "GameFramework/Actor.h"
#include "ProceduralTerrainGenerator.generated.h"

UCLASS()
class MYGAME_API AProceduralTerrainGenerator : public AActor
{
    GENERATED_BODY()
```

CHAPTER 11 ADVANCED MECHANICS

```cpp
public:
    AProceduralTerrainGenerator();

    UPROPERTY(EditAnywhere, BlueprintReadWrite, Category = 
    "Terrain")
    int32 Width;

    UPROPERTY(EditAnywhere, BlueprintReadWrite, Category = 
    "Terrain")
    int32 Height;

    UPROPERTY(EditAnywhere, BlueprintReadWrite, Category = 
    "Terrain")
    float TileSize;

    UPROPERTY(EditAnywhere, BlueprintReadWrite, Category = 
    "Terrain")
    float NoiseScale;
protected:
    virtual void BeginPlay() override;

    void GenerateTerrain();
private:
    void SpawnTile(FVector Location);
};
```

Listing 11-2 presents the implementation of the terrain generation logic. It demonstrates how to use Perlin noise in a 2D grid to create natural-looking elevation patterns.

- **GenerateTerrain()**: Iterates through the grid (Width × Height), calculates noise-based Z-values, and constructs world-space locations for each tile.

CHAPTER 11 ADVANCED MECHANICS

- **PerlinNoise2D()**: Returns a float value for terrain elevation, simulating hills or valleys.

- **SpawnTile()**: Logs tile locations; this function is intended to be extended for spawning mesh tiles, actors, or instanced components.

- **BeginPlay()**: Automatically triggers terrain generation when the level begins.

Listing 11-2. ProceduralTerrainGenerator.cpp

```cpp
#include "ProceduralTerrainGenerator.h"
#include "Kismet/KismetMathLibrary.h"

AProceduralTerrainGenerator::AProceduralTerrainGenerator()
{
    PrimaryActorTick.bCanEverTick = false;
    Width = 10;
    Height = 10;
    TileSize = 100.0f;
    NoiseScale = 10.0f;
}

void AProceduralTerrainGenerator::BeginPlay()
{
    Super::BeginPlay();
    GenerateTerrain();
}

void AProceduralTerrainGenerator::GenerateTerrain()
{
    for (int32 X = 0; X < Width; ++X)
    {
        for (int32 Y = 0; Y < Height; ++Y)
```

CHAPTER 11 ADVANCED MECHANICS

```
        {
            float NoiseValue = UKismetMathLibrary::PerlinNoise2
            D(FVector2D(X, Y) * NoiseScale);
            FVector Location = FVector(X * TileSize, Y *
            TileSize, NoiseValue * 100.0f);
            SpawnTile(Location);
        }
    }
}

void AProceduralTerrainGenerator::SpawnTile(FVector Location)
{
    // Replace with spawning logic for modular terrain pieces
    UE_LOG(LogTemp, Warning, TEXT("Tile spawned at: %s"),
    *Location.ToString());
}
```

Example Usage

In the game, you can use this generator to create a randomized landscape at runtime. You can control the terrain's size and complexity by adjusting properties such as Width, Height, TileSize, and NoiseScale in the editor.

Procedural generation empowers developers to create rich, varied game environments algorithmically reducing manual design time while increasing replay ability. From roguelike dungeons to vast open-world terrains, procedural techniques foster creativity by generating content that adapts to the player's actions or evolves across sessions.

Unreal Engine now includes a **Procedural Content Generation (PCG) plugin**, offering a powerful and extensible toolset for generating terrain, foliage, structures, and more. It integrates seamlessly with both Blueprint and C++, making it easier than ever to author runtime or editor-based procedural systems using graph-based logic.

The PCG plugin allows designers to work visually while still retaining full control over spawning rules, filtering logic, and data-driven instancing. Next, we'll explore how to build **save and load systems** to manage persistent game states, an essential feature for tracking player progress across sessions.

Save and Load Systems

In modern game development, providing players with the ability to save and load their progress is essential. This functionality ensures that players can continue their journey without losing progress, enhancing the user experience and engagement. Unreal Engine, combined with C++, offers robust tools to implement flexible and efficient save and load systems.

Importance of Save and Load Systems

Let's explore why the save and load system is important:

- **Player Progression**: Allows players to preserve their achievements and progress
- **User Experience**: Offers flexibility for players to pause and resume gameplay
- **Dynamic Worlds**: Enables saving complex game states, such as character stats, world states, and inventory systems

CHAPTER 11   ADVANCED MECHANICS

Core Components of Save and Load Systems

Key elements of the save and load system:

- **Save Game Class**: A specialized class for storing game data
- **Serialization**: Converts data into a storable format and back for game use
- **File Management**: Handles the creation, reading, and writing of saved files
- **Customizable Data**: Includes player stats, inventory, world state, and more

Reviewing the Code

Listing 11-3 introduces a custom save game class used for storing essential gameplay data such as player score and location. This structure is designed for seamless saving and loading of game state in Unreal Engine.

- **USaveGameManager**: Inherits from USaveGame, making it compatible with Unreal's save/load system
- **PlayerScore**: Saves the player's current score, useful for tracking progress or high scores
- **PlayerLocation**: Records the player's position in the world, allowing them to resume from the same spot
- **PlayerRotation**: Stores the direction the player was facing, enhancing immersion upon reload
- **BlueprintReadWrite**: Enables read and write access to these variables in Blueprint, making the save system accessible to designers without requiring C++ changes

Listing 11-3. SaveGameManager.h

```cpp
#pragma once

#include "CoreMinimal.h"
#include "GameFramework/SaveGame.h"
#include "SaveGameManager.generated.h"

UCLASS()
class MYGAME_API USaveGameManager : public USaveGame
{
    GENERATED_BODY()

public:
    USaveGameManager();

    UPROPERTY(BlueprintReadWrite, Category = "SaveData")
    int32 PlayerScore;

    UPROPERTY(BlueprintReadWrite, Category = "SaveData")
    FVector PlayerLocation;

    UPROPERTY(BlueprintReadWrite, Category = "SaveData")
    FRotator PlayerRotation;
};
```

Listing 11-4 provides a simple yet effective implementation of a save/load system in Unreal Engine using `UGameplayStatics`. This setup demonstrates how player progress and position can be preserved across game sessions.

- **CreateSaveGameObject()**: Instantiates a new save game object based on the `USaveGameManager` class.
- **PlayerScore, PlayerLocation, PlayerRotation**: These values are assigned to the save game instance to store the player's current state.

CHAPTER 11   ADVANCED MECHANICS

- **SaveGameToSlot()**: Saves the initialized data into a named slot ("PlayerSaveSlot") so it can be retrieved later.
- **LoadGameFromSlot()**: Loads saved game data from the same slot, casting it to USaveGameManager for access to saved properties.
- **UE_LOG()**: Outputs the loaded data to the console for verification, aiding in debugging and confirming that the state was restored correctly.

Listing 11-4. SaveGameHandler.cpp

```
#include "SaveGameManager.h"
#include "Kismet/GameplayStatics.h"

void SaveGameState()
{
    USaveGameManager* SaveGameInstance = Cast<USaveGameManager>
    (UGameplayStatics::CreateSaveGameObject(USaveGameManager::S
    taticClass()));

    SaveGameInstance->PlayerScore = 100; // Example value
    SaveGameInstance->PlayerLocation = FVector(200.0f, 300.0f,
    400.0f); // Example location
    SaveGameInstance->PlayerRotation = FRotator(0.0f, 45.0f,
    0.0f); // Example rotation

    UGameplayStatics::SaveGameToSlot(SaveGameInstance,
    TEXT("PlayerSaveSlot"), 0);
}
```

```cpp
void LoadGameState()
{
    USaveGameManager* LoadedGameInstance = Cast<USaveGameManager>
    (UGameplayStatics::LoadGameFromSlot(TEXT("PlayerSaveSlot"),
    0));

    if (LoadedGameInstance)
    {
        int32 PlayerScore = LoadedGameInstance->PlayerScore;
        FVector PlayerLocation = LoadedGameInstance->
        PlayerLocation;
        FRotator PlayerRotation = LoadedGameInstance->
        PlayerRotation;

        // Apply the loaded values (example)
        UE_LOG(LogTemp, Warning, TEXT("Score: %d, Location: %s,
        Rotation: %s"),
            PlayerScore,
            *PlayerLocation.ToString(),
            *PlayerRotation.ToString());
    }
}
```

Save and load systems ensure seamless player experiences, preserving progress and enhancing engagement. With Unreal Engine's USaveGame class and built-in utilities like UGameplayStatics::SaveGameToSlot and UGameplayStatics::LoadGameFromSlot, developers can implement efficient and flexible systems tailored to their game's needs.

CHAPTER 11   ADVANCED MECHANICS

Modding Support

Modding support enables players and third-party creators to extend a game's lifespan by introducing custom content, mechanics, and modifications. Supporting modding requires robust systems that allow users to modify assets, integrate custom logic, and safely deploy their creations without compromising the base game. Unreal Engine provides various tools to empower developers to create modding-friendly games.

Importance of Modding Support

Let's explore why modding support is important:

- **Community Engagement**: Encourages player creativity and fosters a loyal community
- **Longevity**: Extends the game's lifecycle with user-generated content
- **Replayability**: Adds new experiences for players, increasing game replayability
- **Revenue Opportunities**: Supports monetization models like paid mods or Downloadable Content (DLC) expansions

Core Components of Modding Support

Key elements of the modding support:

- **Modding Framework**: A system that allows the integration of external content
- **Asset Loading**: Mechanisms for dynamically loading custom models, textures, and other assets

- **Script Execution**: Support for custom logic through scripting languages or plugins

- **Sandbox Environment**: Prevents mods from affecting the core game files

Reviewing the Code

Listing 11-5 defines a foundational system for mod support by introducing a manager class that allows loading of external assets and mod packages at runtime. This setup is essential for supporting user-generated content and extending the game's lifespan.

- **Class Declaration**: `AModdingManager` inherits from `AActor` and serves as a centralized handler for all mod-related operations in the game.

- **LoadModFromPath(FString ModPath)**: Provides functionality to load mods dynamically from a given directory path. This could include entire content packs or script-based behaviors.

- **LoadAsset(FString AssetPath)**: Allows retrieval of individual assets from a specified path, enabling runtime access to textures, meshes, sound effects, and more.

Listing 11-5. ModdingManager.h

```
#pragma once

#include "CoreMinimal.h"
#include "GameFramework/Actor.h"
#include "ModdingManager.generated.h"
```

CHAPTER 11   ADVANCED MECHANICS

```
UCLASS()
class MYGAME_API AModdingManager : public AActor
{
    GENERATED_BODY()
public:
    AModdingManager();

    UFUNCTION(BlueprintCallable, Category = "Modding")
    void LoadModFromPath(FString ModPath);

    UFUNCTION(BlueprintCallable, Category = "Modding")
    UObject* LoadAsset(FString AssetPath);
};
```

Listing 11-6 finalizes the implementation of the modding system by enabling runtime file and asset loading through Unreal Engine's StreamableManager and path validation. This feature provides the foundation for dynamic user-generated content integration.

- **FPaths::FileExists()**: Checks whether the mod file exists at the provided file path, ensuring the engine doesn't try to load non-existent resources

- **UE_LOG()**: Logs successful or failed attempts to load a mod file or asset, assisting in debugging and development feedback

- **FStreamableManager::LoadSynchronous()**: Loads a referenced asset synchronously at runtime, enabling dynamic and flexible mod integration without needing to hardcode asset references

- **TSoftObjectPtr<UObject>**: A soft reference to the asset, ensuring that the engine can resolve it only when needed, helping reduce memory usage and load times

Listing 11-6. ModdingManager.cpp

```
#include "ModdingManager.h"
#include "Engine/StreamableManager.h"
#include "Engine/AssetManager.h"

AModdingManager::AModdingManager()
{
    PrimaryActorTick.bCanEverTick = false;
}

void AModdingManager::LoadModFromPath(FString ModPath)
{
    // Example: Load a plugin or script from the file system
    if (FPaths::FileExists(ModPath))
    {
        UE_LOG(LogTemp, Warning, TEXT("Mod Loaded from Path:
        %s"), *ModPath);
        // Custom logic for integrating mod data
    }
    else
    {
        UE_LOG(LogTemp, Error, TEXT("Mod path not found: %s"),
        *ModPath);
    }
}

UObject* AModdingManager::LoadAsset(FString AssetPath)
{
    FStreamableManager& StreamableManager = UAssetManager::GetS
    treamableManager();
    TSoftObjectPtr<UObject> AssetReference(AssetPath);
```

CHAPTER 11   ADVANCED MECHANICS

```
    UObject* LoadedAsset = StreamableManager.
    LoadSynchronous(AssetReference, false);
    if (LoadedAsset)
    {
        UE_LOG(LogTemp, Warning, TEXT("Asset Loaded: %s"),
        *AssetPath);
    }
    else
    {
        UE_LOG(LogTemp, Error, TEXT("Failed to Load
        Asset: %s"), *AssetPath);
    }

    return LoadedAsset;
}
```

Modding support creates a vibrant ecosystem where players contribute directly to the game's evolution. By enabling dynamic asset loading and external mod integration, Unreal Engine makes it possible to foster a strong modding community.

VR Mechanics

Virtual reality (VR) mechanics are essential for creating immersive experiences that transport players into virtual worlds. Developing for VR requires careful consideration of player interaction, motion control, and optimized performance to ensure a seamless experience. Unreal Engine provides comprehensive tools to build VR applications efficiently, including VR templates, motion tracking, and interaction systems.

Importance of VR Mechanics

Let's delve into why VR mechanics are critical:

- **Immersive Gameplay**: Enables players to feel physically present in the game world
- **Natural Interactions**: Facilitates intuitive interactions using motion controllers
- **Innovative Experiences**: Opens possibilities for unique gameplay scenarios like hand tracking and haptic feedback
- **Broad Market Appeal**: Attracts audiences seeking next-generation gaming experiences

Core Components of VR Mechanics

Key elements of VR mechanics include

- **Motion Controllers**: Track player hand movements and translate them into the game world
- **Head Tracking**: Follows the player's head orientation for immersive visuals
- **Interaction Systems**: Enable actions like grabbing objects or pushing buttons
- **Comfort Features**: Include teleportation and snap turning to minimize motion sickness
- **Performance Optimization**: Ensures stable frame rates for a comfortable VR experience

CHAPTER 11   ADVANCED MECHANICS

Reviewing the Code

Listing 11-7 introduces the foundational structure for handling VR object interaction in Unreal Engine, allowing players to grab and release objects using motion controllers.

- **Class Declaration**: AVRInteractionManager inherits from AActor and serves as the central component for managing object interaction in VR environments.

- **GrabObject()**: A callable function that initiates grabbing behavior, allowing the player to pick up nearby objects.

- **ReleaseObject()**: Handles the logic for letting go of a held object.

- **MotionController**: A pointer to the UMotionControllerComponent, which tracks the VR controller's spatial position and rotation.

- **GrabbedObject**: Holds a reference to the object currently in the player's grip, allowing the system to manage release and physics updates appropriately.

Listing 11-7. VRInteractionManager.h

```
#pragma once

#include "CoreMinimal.h"
#include "GameFramework/Actor.h"
#include "MotionControllerComponent.h"
#include "VRInteractionManager.generated.h"

UCLASS()
class MYGAME_API AVRInteractionManager : public AActor
```

CHAPTER 11   ADVANCED MECHANICS

```
{
    GENERATED_BODY()
public:
    AVRInteractionManager();

    UFUNCTION(BlueprintCallable, Category = "VR")
    void GrabObject();

    UFUNCTION(BlueprintCallable, Category = "VR")
    void ReleaseObject();

protected:
    virtual void BeginPlay() override;

private:
    UPROPERTY()
    UMotionControllerComponent* MotionController;

    UPROPERTY()
    AActor* GrabbedObject;
};
```

Listing 11-8 implements the runtime logic for VR object interaction. It enables players to grab and release objects within reach by performing a line trace from the motion controller and managing physics appropriately.

- **GrabObject()**: Performs a forward line trace from the controller. If an object is detected, it is attached to the controller using `AttachToComponent`, and its physics simulation is disabled for stable holding behavior.

- **ReleaseObject()**: Detaches the currently held object and re-enables physics to allow the object to behave naturally after being dropped.

CHAPTER 11   ADVANCED MECHANICS

- **LineTraceSingleByChannel**: Used to detect interactable objects in front of the VR controller.

- **AttachToComponent()**: Ensures the object moves with the motion controller, creating a realistic grabbing experience.

- **SetSimulatePhysics()**: Toggled on grab/release to switch between physics-based and controller-based object manipulation.

Listing 11-8. VRInteractionManager.cpp

```
#include "VRInteractionManager.h"
#include "GameFramework/Actor.h"
#include "Components/PrimitiveComponent.h"

AVRInteractionManager::AVRInteractionManager()
{
    PrimaryActorTick.bCanEverTick = true;

    MotionController = CreateDefaultSubobject
    <UMotionControllerComponent>(TEXT("MotionController"));
    RootComponent = MotionController;
}
void AVRInteractionManager::BeginPlay()
{
    Super::BeginPlay();
}

 void AVRInteractionManager::GrabObject()
{
    FVector Location = MotionController->Get
    ComponentLocation();
```

```cpp
    FHitResult Hit;

    FCollisionQueryParams Params;
    Params.AddIgnoredActor(this);

    if (GetWorld()->LineTraceSingleByChannel(Hit, Location,
    Location + MotionController->GetForwardVector() * 200.0f,
    ECC_Visibility, Params))
    {
        GrabbedObject = Hit.GetActor();

        if (GrabbedObject)
        {
            UPrimitiveComponent* Primitive = Cast<UPrimitive
            Component>(GrabbedObject->GetRootComponent());
            if (Primitive)
            {
                Primitive->SetSimulatePhysics(false);
                GrabbedObject->AttachToComponent
                (MotionController, FAttachmentTransformRules::
                SnapToTargetNotIncludingScale);
            }
        }
    }
}
void AVRInteractionManager::ReleaseObject()
{
    if (GrabbedObject)
    {
        GrabbedObject->DetachFromActor(FDetachment
        TransformRules::KeepWorldTransform);
        UPrimitiveComponent* Primitive = Cast<UPrimitive
        Component>(GrabbedObject->GetRootComponent());
```

```
        if (Primitive)
        {
            Primitive->SetSimulatePhysics(true);
        }
        GrabbedObject = nullptr;
    }
}
```

VR mechanics bring unprecedented levels of immersion and interactivity to games. By leveraging Unreal Engine's powerful tools, developers can create rich VR experiences that captivate players. The example above demonstrates how to implement basic VR interactions like grabbing and releasing objects, forming the foundation for more complex VR systems.

AR Mechanics

Augmented reality (AR) mechanics blend the digital and physical worlds by overlaying interactive virtual objects onto the real-world environment. Developing AR games involves integrating spatial tracking, real-world object recognition, and intuitive interaction models. Unreal Engine provides AR development support through its AR template and ARCore/ARKit integrations.

Importance of AR Mechanics

Let's see why AR mechanics are crucial in gaming:

- **Enhanced Realism**: Combines virtual elements with real-world surroundings for immersive gameplay
- **Broader Accessibility**: Leverages widely available AR-capable devices like smartphones and tablets

CHAPTER 11   ADVANCED MECHANICS

- **Unique Gameplay Opportunities**: Introduces mechanics like object recognition and spatial interactions

- **Cross-Industry Appeal**: Applies to gaming, education, training, and retail experiences

Core Components of AR Mechanics

Key elements of AR mechanics include

- **Camera and Sensor Integration**: Captures real-world visuals and sensor data

- **Spatial Tracking**: Detects and maps the environment for accurate object placement

- **Anchors and Planes**: Allows virtual objects to be positioned and interact with real-world surfaces

- **Interaction Models**: Enables player interaction with virtual elements via gestures or touch

- **Performance Optimization**: Ensures smooth AR rendering without latency

Reviewing the Code

Listing 11-9 introduces a foundational class for building augmented reality (AR) interactions in Unreal Engine. This class allows you to detect flat surfaces and spawn virtual objects in the real-world environment through AR.

CHAPTER 11   ADVANCED MECHANICS

- **Class Declaration**: AARInteractionManager is a custom AR manager responsible for surface detection and virtual content placement in AR mode.

- **SpawnARObject(FVector Location)**: Spawns an instance of the specified ARObjectClass at the given world location.

- **DetectARPlanes()**: Gathers all currently tracked AR planes in the environment using the AR system.

- **DetectedPlanes**: A container holding all the detected UARPlaneGeometry objects for further interaction or visualization.

- **ARObjectClass**: A Blueprint-exposed property that defines which actor to instantiate when placing objects in AR.

Listing 11-9. ARInteractionManager.h

```
#pragma once

#include "CoreMinimal.h"
#include "GameFramework/Actor.h"
#include "ARBlueprintLibrary.h"
#include "ARInteractionManager.generated.h"

UCLASS()
class MYGAME_API AARInteractionManager : public AActor
{
    GENERATED_BODY()
```

CHAPTER 11 ADVANCED MECHANICS

```cpp
public:
    AARInteractionManager();

    UFUNCTION(BlueprintCallable, Category = "AR")
    void SpawnARObject(FVector Location);

    UFUNCTION(BlueprintCallable, Category = "AR")
    void DetectARPlanes();

protected:
    virtual void BeginPlay() override;

private:
    UPROPERTY()
    TArray<UARPlaneGeometry*> DetectedPlanes;

    UPROPERTY(EditAnywhere, Category = "AR")
    TSubclassOf<AActor> ARObjectClass;
};
```

Listing 11-10 finalizes the functionality of the AR interaction system by implementing plane detection and virtual object spawning. This setup forms the basis of placing objects in real-world environments through AR.

- **StartARSession()**: Initiates the AR session using a default configuration, enabling the system to begin tracking surfaces and camera input.

- **SpawnARObject()**: Spawns a virtual actor at the specified world location using `ARObjectClass`. If no class is assigned, it logs an error.

- **GetAllTrackedPlanes()**: Fetches all planes currently recognized by the AR system, such as flat surfaces like tables or floors.

CHAPTER 11   ADVANCED MECHANICS

- **DetectedPlanes**: Filters out non-tracking planes and stores valid geometries for later use, such as placing AR content.
- **UE_LOG()**: Logs the success or failure of spawning objects and detecting planes for debugging purposes.

Listing 11-10. ARInteractionManager.cpp

```cpp
#include "ARInteractionManager.h"
#include "ARSessionConfig.h"
#include "Engine/World.h"

AARInteractionManager::AARInteractionManager()
{
    PrimaryActorTick.bCanEverTick = true;
}

void AARInteractionManager::BeginPlay()
{
    Super::BeginPlay();
    UARBlueprintLibrary::StartARSession(NewObject
    <UARSessionConfig>());
}

void AARInteractionManager::SpawnARObject(FVector Location)
{
    if (ARObjectClass)
    {
        GetWorld()->SpawnActor<AActor>(ARObjectClass, Location,
        FRotator::ZeroRotator);
        UE_LOG(LogTemp, Warning, TEXT("AR Object Spawned at
        Location: %s"), *Location.ToString());
    }
```

```
        else
        {
            UE_LOG(LogTemp, Error, TEXT("AR Object Class not
            set."));
        }
    }
}
void AARInteractionManager::DetectARPlanes()
{
    DetectedPlanes.Empty();
    TArray<UARPlaneGeometry*> AllPlanes = UARBlueprintLibrary::
    GetAllTrackedPlanes();

    for (UARPlaneGeometry* Plane : AllPlanes)
    {
        if (Plane->GetTrackingState() == EARTrackingState::
        Tracking)
        {
            DetectedPlanes.Add(Plane);
            UE_LOG(LogTemp, Warning, TEXT("AR Plane Detected:
            %s"), *Plane->GetName());
        }
    }
}
```

AR mechanics provide players with immersive and innovative gameplay that bridges the digital and physical worlds. Unreal Engine's AR tools simplify the development of features like object spawning and plane detection. The example demonstrates how to integrate essential AR functionalities into a game, paving the way for more complex augmented experience.

CHAPTER 11   ADVANCED MECHANICS

Performance Optimization

Performance optimization is crucial for delivering smooth gameplay experiences, especially in resource-intensive games. Effective optimization ensures that games run seamlessly across various platforms while maintaining visual quality and responsiveness. Unreal Engine offers powerful profiling and debugging tools to help developers identify and resolve performance bottlenecks.

Importance of Performance Optimization

Let's see why performance optimization is critical:

- **Smooth Gameplay**: Prevents frame rate drops and latency, ensuring an immersive experience
- **Cross-Platform Compatibility**: Adapts the game to different hardware capabilities
- **Player Retention**: Reduces frustration caused by lag or stuttering
- **Energy Efficiency**: Minimizes resource usage, improving battery life on portable devices

Core Components of Performance Optimization

Key areas for optimization:

- **Frame Rate Management**: Ensures a consistent frame rate by balancing CPU and GPU loads
- **Level Streaming**: Loads game assets dynamically to reduce memory usage

CHAPTER 11   ADVANCED MECHANICS

- **Asset Optimization**: Compresses textures, reduces polygon counts, and simplifies materials

- **Code Profiling**: Identifies performance bottlenecks in game logic

- **Rendering Optimization**: Implements techniques like LOD (Level of Detail) and culling

Reviewing the Code

Listing 11-11 introduces a dedicated optimization utility class that targets runtime performance improvements. This system helps ensure smoother gameplay by managing frame rate control and texture memory optimization.

- **Class Declaration**: `APerformanceOptimizer` is an `AActor` subclass designed to handle performance-related tasks at runtime.

- **EnableFramerateSmoothing()**: Blueprint-callable function that configures Unreal Engine's frame rate smoothing settings to maintain consistent frame pacing and reduce stuttering.

- **OptimizeTextureSettings()**: Allows dynamic adjustment of texture streaming and compression settings to balance quality and memory usage, especially useful for performance tuning on lower-end devices.

CHAPTER 11 ADVANCED MECHANICS

Listing 11-11. PerformanceOptimizer.h

```cpp
#pragma once

#include "CoreMinimal.h"
#include "GameFramework/Actor.h"
#include "PerformanceOptimizer.generated.h"

UCLASS()
class MYGAME_API APerformanceOptimizer : public AActor
{
    GENERATED_BODY()

public:
    APerformanceOptimizer();

    UFUNCTION(BlueprintCallable, Category = "Performance")
    void EnableFramerateSmoothing();

    UFUNCTION(BlueprintCallable, Category = "Performance")
    void OptimizeTextureSettings();

protected:
    virtual void BeginPlay() override;
};
```

Listing 11-12 presents the implementation of runtime performance optimization strategies within the `APerformanceOptimizer` class. These adjustments help fine-tune gameplay experience and reduce resource usage in real time.

- **BeginPlay()**: Automatically applies both frame rate smoothing and texture optimizations when the game starts

CHAPTER 11 ADVANCED MECHANICS

- **SetMaxFPS()**: Caps the game's frame rate to 60 FPS using GEngine->SetMaxFPS(60), helping to maintain smoother frame pacing and prevent overheating or power drain on certain hardware

- **MipGenSettings = TMGS_NoMipmaps**: Disables mipmaps for textures to reduce memory footprint, particularly useful on performance-constrained platforms

- **CompressionSettings = TC_Default**: Ensures textures use a standard, GPU-efficient compression format for optimal rendering

- **UpdateResource()**: Applies the changes made to each texture so the optimizations take effect at runtime

- **TObjectIterator<UTexture>**: Iterates through all loaded textures and applies optimization settings in a loop

Listing 11-12. PerformanceOptimizer.cpp

```
#include "PerformanceOptimizer.h"
#include "Engine/Engine.h"
#include "Engine/Texture.h"

APerformanceOptimizer::APerformanceOptimizer()
{
    PrimaryActorTick.bCanEverTick = false;
}
```

CHAPTER 11   ADVANCED MECHANICS

```cpp
void APerformanceOptimizer::BeginPlay()
{
    Super::BeginPlay();
    EnableFramerateSmoothing();
    OptimizeTextureSettings();
}

void APerformanceOptimizer::EnableFramerateSmoothing()
{
    if (GEngine)
    {
        GEngine->SetMaxFPS(60);
        UE_LOG(LogTemp, Warning, TEXT("Framerate Smoothing
        Enabled: Max FPS set to 60."));
    }
}

void APerformanceOptimizer::OptimizeTextureSettings()
{
    for (TObjectIterator<UTexture> It; It; ++It)
    {
        UTexture* Texture = *It;
        if (Texture)
        {
            Texture->MipGenSettings = TMGS_NoMipmaps;
            Texture->CompressionSettings = TC_Default;
            Texture->UpdateResource();
            UE_LOG(LogTemp, Warning, TEXT("Texture Optimized:
            %s"), *Texture->GetName());
        }
    }
}
```

Performance optimization ensures a smooth and enjoyable gaming experience, even on devices with limited resources. By leveraging Unreal Engine's built-in tools and applying techniques like frame rate smoothing and asset optimization, developers can create visually compelling games that run efficiently across a wide range of hardware.

During development, Unreal's Profiler can be used to analyze performance in real time. It provides critical statistics that help identify bottlenecks related to environments, materials, AI, characters, and more—enabling targeted optimizations and better resource management.

Cross-Platform Development

Cross-platform development allows games to reach a wider audience by running seamlessly on multiple platforms such as PC, consoles, and mobile devices. Unreal Engine simplifies this process with its versatile toolset and cross-platform support, enabling developers to build, test, and deploy games efficiently across diverse platforms without rewriting core functionality.

Importance of Cross-Platform Development

Why focus on cross-platform development?

- **Increased Reach**: Expands the player base by targeting multiple platforms

- **Development Efficiency**: Streamlines workflows with a unified codebase

- **Revenue Potential**: Maximizes earnings by tapping into different markets

- **Player Accessibility**: Ensures that players can access the game on their preferred devices

CHAPTER 11   ADVANCED MECHANICS

Core Components of Cross-Platform Development

Key aspects of cross-platform development:

- **Input Handling**: Adapts to different control schemes like keyboard, mouse, gamepad, and touch
- **Graphics Scalability**: Adjusts settings for varying hardware capabilities
- **Platform-Specific Features**: Integrates features like achievements, leaderboards, and cloud saves
- **Build Systems**: Supports creating platform-specific builds efficiently
- **Testing and Debugging**: Ensures consistent performance and functionality on all target platforms

Reviewing the Code

Listing 11-13 introduces the `ACrossPlatformManager` class, responsible for detecting the target platform and configuring appropriate input settings. This ensures consistent behavior and usability across devices such as PC, consoles, and mobile.

- **Class Declaration**: `ACrossPlatformManager` derives from `AActor` and acts as the central handler for platform-specific adaptations in the game.
- **DetectPlatform()**: Blueprint-callable function that checks the runtime platform (e.g., Windows, Android, iOS) and can be used to apply tailored logic or visual settings.

- **ConfigureInputSettings()**: Dynamically sets up control mappings (keyboard, touch, controller, etc.) based on the platform to ensure optimal input response and accessibility.

Listing 11-13. CrossPlatformManager.h

```
#pragma once

#include "CoreMinimal.h"
#include "GameFramework/Actor.h"
#include "CrossPlatformManager.generated.h"

UCLASS()
class MYGAME_API ACrossPlatformManager : public AActor
{
    GENERATED_BODY()

public:
    ACrossPlatformManager();

    UFUNCTION(BlueprintCallable, Category = "Cross-Platform")
    void DetectPlatform();

    UFUNCTION(BlueprintCallable, Category = "Cross-Platform")
    void ConfigureInputSettings();
};
```

Listing 11-14 completes the implementation of the ACrossPlatformManager, enabling runtime platform detection and dynamic input configuration. This provides developers with the tools to build responsive, accessible experiences across a variety of platforms.

CHAPTER 11　ADVANCED MECHANICS

- **UGameplayStatics::GetPlatformName()**: Retrieves the name of the current platform (e.g., Windows, Android, PS5), allowing platform-specific logic to be executed conditionally

- **Platform Logging**: Logs distinct messages based on the identified platform, helpful for debugging and ensuring conditional logic behaves correctly

- **AddAxisMapping()**: Dynamically maps input keys and gamepad controls (e.g., W key and gamepad stick) to a shared movement axis, ensuring input consistency across devices

- **SaveKeyMappings()**: Commits the updated input mappings to be used in-game, allowing for flexible runtime adjustments without editing the default configuration files

Listing 11-14. CrossPlatformManager.cpp

```
#include "CrossPlatformManager.h"
#include "Engine/Engine.h"
#include "GameFramework/InputSettings.h"

ACrossPlatformManager::ACrossPlatformManager()
{
    PrimaryActorTick.bCanEverTick = false;
}

 void ACrossPlatformManager::DetectPlatform()
{
#if PLATFORM_WINDOWS
    UE_LOG(LogTemp, Warning, TEXT("Running on Windows"));
#elif PLATFORM_ANDROID
```

CHAPTER 11 ADVANCED MECHANICS

```
    UE_LOG(LogTemp, Warning, TEXT("Running on Android"));
#elif PLATFORM_PS5
    UE_LOG(LogTemp, Warning, TEXT("Running on PlayStation 5"));
#else
    UE_LOG(LogTemp, Warning, TEXT("Running on an Unknown or
    Unsupported Platform"));
#endif
}

void ACrossPlatformManager::ConfigureInputSettings()
{
    UInputSettings* InputSettings = UInputSettings::
    GetInputSettings();
    if (InputSettings)
    {
        InputSettings->AddAxisMapping(FInputAxisKeyMapping
        ("MoveForward", EKeys::W, 1.0f));
        InputSettings->AddAxisMapping(FInputAxisKeyMapping
        ("MoveForward", EKeys::Gamepad_LeftStick_Up, 1.0f));
        InputSettings->SaveKeyMappings();
        UE_LOG(LogTemp, Warning, TEXT("Input settings
        configured for cross-platform use."));
    }
}
```

Cross-platform development is essential for modern game design, ensuring that games are accessible across a variety of platforms. Unreal Engine's tools and features simplify this process, allowing developers to detect platforms, adapt input settings, and implement platform-specific optimizations efficiently. This example demonstrates how to handle input across different platforms seamlessly.

CHAPTER 11 ADVANCED MECHANICS

Advanced Scripting Techniques

Advanced scripting techniques involve utilizing Unreal Engine's powerful scripting capabilities to build intricate game mechanics, systems, and features. By leveraging Unreal Engine's C++ framework alongside Blueprint scripting, developers can achieve an optimal balance of performance and flexibility, enabling the creation of highly customized gameplay experiences.

Importance of Advanced Scripting Techniques

Why are advanced scripting techniques crucial?

- **Customization**: Allows developers to implement unique features beyond default engine capabilities
- **Performance Optimization**: Provides control over resource-intensive tasks
- **Scalability**: Facilitates the creation of reusable and modular systems
- **Flexibility**: Combines the power of C++ with Blueprints for rapid prototyping and efficient development

Core Components of Advanced Scripting

Key elements of advanced scripting in Unreal Engine:

- **Custom Game Systems**: Developing tailored mechanics like combat systems or AI behaviors
- **Dynamic Memory Management**: Ensuring efficient use of system resources

CHAPTER 11   ADVANCED MECHANICS

- **Event-Driven Programming**: Creating responsive and interactive gameplay

- **Blueprint and C++ Integration**: Leveraging the strengths of both tools

Reviewing the Code

Listing 11-15 introduces a custom event system using delegates, enabling responsive and extensible damage handling in both C++ and Blueprints.

- **FOnDamageTaken Delegate**: Declares a dynamic multicast delegate that accepts a single float parameter (damage value). This delegate can be bound to multiple listeners at runtime, supporting event-driven design.

- **OnDamageTaken**: Marked as `BlueprintAssignable`, this allows the delegate to be bound and triggered from Blueprints, enabling designers to implement reactions like UI updates, sound effects, or animations without modifying C++ code.

- **ApplyDamage(float Damage)**: A Blueprint-callable function that broadcasts the OnDamageTaken delegate, signaling that damage has occurred. It forms the foundation of a modular damage system where multiple systems can react to damage independently.

Listing 11-15. AdvancedScriptingManager.h

```
#pragma once

#include "CoreMinimal.h"
#include "GameFramework/Actor.h"
#include "AdvancedScriptingManager.generated.h"
```

CHAPTER 11 ADVANCED MECHANICS

```cpp
DECLARE_DYNAMIC_MULTICAST_DELEGATE_OneParam(FOnDamageTaken,
float, DamageAmount);

UCLASS()
class MYGAME_API AAdvancedScriptingManager : public AActor
{
    GENERATED_BODY()
public:
    AAdvancedScriptingManager();

    UPROPERTY(BlueprintAssignable, Category = "Damage")
    FOnDamageTaken OnDamageTaken;

    UFUNCTION(BlueprintCallable, Category = "Damage")
    void ApplyDamage(float Damage);
};
```

Listing 11-16 completes the damage event system by implementing the logic that triggers custom scripted responses through delegates.

- **ApplyDamage()**: Validates the damage value and broadcasts the event if it's greater than zero. This check prevents unnecessary or incorrect event calls for invalid damage.

- **OnDamageTaken.Broadcast(Damage)**: Notifies all bound listeners (e.g., UI systems, audio cues, animation triggers) that damage has been received. This dynamic event system allows for clean separation between damage logic and how the game visually or mechanically reacts to it.

- **UE_LOG**: Provides runtime debugging information, confirming when and how much damage was applied.

Listing 11-16. AdvancedScriptingManager.cpp

```
#include "AdvancedScriptingManager.h"
#include "GameFramework/Actor.h"

AAdvancedScriptingManager::AAdvancedScriptingManager()
{
    PrimaryActorTick.bCanEverTick = false;
}

void AAdvancedScriptingManager::ApplyDamage(float Damage)
{
    if (Damage > 0)
    {
        UE_LOG(LogTemp, Warning, TEXT("Damage Applied: %f"),
        Damage);
        OnDamageTaken.Broadcast(Damage);
    }
    else
    {
        UE_LOG(LogTemp, Warning, TEXT("No damage to apply."));
    }
}
```

Using the System in Blueprints

Let's see how to use this:

1. Add the AdvancedScriptingManager actor to the level.

2. Create a Blueprint for the actor and bind the OnDamageTaken event to custom logic (e.g., updating health UI or triggering a particle effect).

CHAPTER 11   ADVANCED MECHANICS

Advanced scripting techniques empower developers to build unique and complex game systems that elevate the gameplay experience. By combining Unreal Engine's C++ capabilities with event-driven programming and Blueprint integration, you can create highly efficient and responsive mechanics. This example demonstrates a damage system that highlights the potential of these techniques.

Plugin and Middleware Integration

Integrating plugins and middleware into your Unreal Engine project allows developers to expand their game's functionality with third-party tools and solutions. Plugins offer prebuilt features, while middleware provides robust systems for tasks like physics simulation, audio processing, or online services. This integration reduces development time while enabling access to advanced technologies.

Importance of Plugin and Middleware Integration

Why is this integration crucial?

- **Time Efficiency**: Reduces the need for creating systems from scratch
- **Enhanced Functionality**: Leverages specialized tools for complex tasks
- **Cross-Disciplinary Support**: Integrates systems like physics, AI, or networking seamlessly
- **Industry Standards**: Adopts tried-and-tested tools, ensuring compatibility and scalability

Core Components of Plugin and Middleware Integration

Key elements involved in integrating plugins and middleware:

- **Plugin Installation**: Adding Unreal Engine plugins to enhance features

- **Middleware Integration**: Configuring external tools like Firelight Media's sound engine (FMOD) for audio or Havok for physics

- **Custom Plugin Development**: Creating tailored plugins for specific game needs

- **Performance Monitoring**: Ensuring smooth operation without performance degradation

Reviewing the Code

Listing 11-17 introduces the header structure for a basic custom plugin module, defining its interface and lifecycle hooks within Unreal Engine.

- **IModuleInterface**: The Unreal Engine interface that every plugin must implement. It provides standardized methods for initialization and cleanup.

- **StartupModule()**: This function is automatically called by the engine when the plugin is loaded. It's the ideal place to register custom components, initialize systems, or bind events.

- **ShutdownModule()**: Called when the plugin is unloaded. It ensures any allocated resources or registered elements are properly cleaned up to avoid memory leaks or dangling references.

Listing 11-17. MyCustomPlugin.h

```cpp
#pragma once

#include "CoreMinimal.h"
#include "Modules/ModuleManager.h"

class FMyCustomPluginModule : public IModuleInterface
{
public:
    virtual void StartupModule() override;
    virtual void ShutdownModule() override;
};
```

Listing 11-18 demonstrates how to implement a custom Unreal Engine plugin by defining its startup and shutdown behavior. This is essential for extending engine functionality with modular tools and features.

- **IMPLEMENT_MODULE**: Registers the module with Unreal Engine, defining the entry and exit points. It connects your plugin to the engine's module system.

- **StartupModule()**: Executes logic when the plugin is first loaded—ideal for setting up editor tools, registering components, or initializing data systems.

- **ShutdownModule()**: Handles cleanup when the plugin is unloaded, such as unregistering features or releasing resources.

- **UE_LOG()**: Outputs log messages for visibility into when the plugin is activated or deactivated, useful for debugging and tracking plugin behavior.

Listing 11-18. MyCustomPlugin.cpp

```cpp
#include "MyCustomPlugin.h"
#include "Modules/ModuleManager.h"
#include "Engine/Engine.h"

IMPLEMENT_MODULE(FMyCustomPluginModule, MyCustomPlugin)

void FMyCustomPluginModule::StartupModule()
{
    UE_LOG(LogTemp, Warning, TEXT("My Custom Plugin Loaded!"));
}

void FMyCustomPluginModule::ShutdownModule()
{
    UE_LOG(LogTemp, Warning, TEXT("My Custom Plugin Unloaded!"));
}
```

Example: Using Middleware (FMOD for Audio)

To integrate FMOD middleware for audio:

1. **Install FMOD Plugin**: Add the FMOD plugin to your Unreal Engine project via the Epic Games Launcher.

2. **Configure FMOD**: Link your FMOD Studio project and set up necessary settings in the editor.

3. **Integrate Audio Events**: Use Blueprints or C++ to trigger FMOD audio events in your game.

Plugin and middleware integration offers immense potential for expanding your game's capabilities. By leveraging Unreal Engine's plugin system or third-party middleware, you can enhance functionality, streamline workflows, and adopt industry-standard technologies for complex systems like audio, physics, and networking. This approach not only saves time but also ensures your game can compete in the modern gaming landscape.

Future Trends in Game Development

The game development industry is constantly evolving with advancements in technology, tools, and player expectations. Future trends offer a glimpse into where the industry is headed, enabling developers to prepare for the next generation of gaming experiences. Unreal Engine, with its state-of-the-art features, is already paving the way for many of these innovations.

Importance of Understanding Future Trends

Why keep an eye on future trends?

- **Staying Competitive**: Helps developers remain relevant in a rapidly changing industry
- **Innovating Player Experiences**: Incorporates cutting-edge technologies for immersive gameplay
- **Adapting to Market Demands**: Meets player expectations by adopting the latest trends
- **Long-Term Viability**: Future-proofs games to stay playable and appealing for years to come

CHAPTER 11   ADVANCED MECHANICS

Core Trends in Game Development

- **AI-Driven Game Design**: Using AI for procedural generation, adaptive gameplay, and intelligent NPCs
- **Metaverse and Social Gaming**: Expanding shared virtual spaces for collaborative and interactive experiences
- **Photorealistic Graphics**: Leveraging advanced rendering techniques like ray tracing and virtual texturing
- **Cloud Gaming**: Reducing hardware dependency through streaming services
- **Sustainability**: Building eco-friendly games with energy-efficient technologies
- **Neural Interfaces**: Experimenting with brain-computer interaction for controlling gameplay
- **Blockchain and NFTs**: Exploring decentralized economies and player-owned digital assets

Reviewing the Code

Listing 11-19 defines a custom AI controller that dynamically adjusts its behavior based on player actions or game conditions. This type of controller is useful for creating more reactive and intelligent AI characters in your game.

- **AAdaptiveAIController**: A custom subclass of AAIController that enables dynamic and context-sensitive decision-making for NPCs

CHAPTER 11 ADVANCED MECHANICS

- **AdjustBehaviorBasedOnPlayer()**: A private method responsible for modifying AI strategies, such as becoming more aggressive or defensive based on player performance or proximity

Listing 11-19. AIController.h

```
#pragma once

#include "CoreMinimal.h"
#include "AIController.h"
#include "AdaptiveAIController.generated.h"

UCLASS()
class MYGAME_API AAdaptiveAIController : public AAIController
{
    GENERATED_BODY()
public:
    virtual void Tick(float DeltaTime) override;
protected:
    virtual void BeginPlay() override;
private:
    void AdjustBehaviorBasedOnPlayer();
};
```

Listing 11-20 showcases the implementation of an adaptive AI controller that updates NPC behavior based on the player's distance, making enemy characters more responsive and dynamic during gameplay.

- **AdjustBehaviorBasedOnPlayer()**: Contains the core logic for decision-making. If the player is within 500 units, the AI switches to an aggressive behavior (e.g., attacking or chasing). If farther away, it continues patrolling or performs other passive behaviors.

CHAPTER 11　ADVANCED MECHANICS

- **FVector::Dist()**: Measures the distance between the AI-controlled pawn and the player, which is critical for proximity-based decision-making.
- **UE_LOG()**: Outputs key behavioral decisions to the log for debugging and observation during gameplay testing.

Listing 11-20. AIController.cpp

```
#include "AdaptiveAIController.h"
#include "GameFramework/Actor.h"

void AAdaptiveAIController::BeginPlay()
{
    Super::BeginPlay();
    UE_LOG(LogTemp, Warning, TEXT("Adaptive AI Initialized!"));
}

void AAdaptiveAIController::Tick(float DeltaTime)
{
    Super::Tick(DeltaTime);
    AdjustBehaviorBasedOnPlayer();
}

void AAdaptiveAIController::AdjustBehaviorBasedOnPlayer()
{
    // Example logic: Change NPC behavior based on
       player's actions
    AActor* Player = GetWorld()->GetFirstPlayerController()->GetPawn();
    if (Player)
    {
```

```
        FVector PlayerLocation = Player->GetActorLocation();
        FVector NPCLocation = GetPawn()->GetActorLocation();

        float Distance = FVector::Dist(PlayerLocation,
        NPCLocation);
        if (Distance < 500.0f)
        {
            UE_LOG(LogTemp, Warning, TEXT("Player is nearby!
            Switching to aggressive behavior."));
        }
        else
        {
            UE_LOG(LogTemp, Warning, TEXT("Player is far away!
            Patrolling."));
        }
    }
}
```

Future trends like AI-driven game design, photorealistic rendering, and cloud gaming are reshaping the gaming industry. By staying informed and leveraging Unreal Engine's capabilities, developers can prepare for these changes and create games that push the boundaries of technology and player engagement. Adopting these trends ensures a competitive edge in the dynamic and innovative world of game development.

Summary

This chapter explored a wide range of advanced gameplay systems that empower developers to create immersive, dynamic, and interactive experiences. From procedural content generation to cross-platform support and modding integration, this chapter provided hands-on code implementations and architectural strategies for taking your game to the next level.

CHAPTER 11   ADVANCED MECHANICS

In the next chapter, we'll analyze real-world case studies and development scenarios that bring together the mechanics you've learned so far. You'll explore how different systems integrate in a complete game loop, including matchmaking, boss battles, quest progression, multiplayer arenas, and more.

CHAPTER 12

Case Studies

This chapter delves into real-world applications of game mechanics by providing case studies from complete game projects. Each case study showcases the implementation of specific game mechanics in Unreal Engine, offering a detailed walk-through that combines theory and practice. By the end of this chapter, readers will have a comprehensive understanding of how these mechanics are brought to life in full-scale projects.

This chapter will explore the practical implementation of game mechanics through detailed case studies. We'll start by building a functional and immersive game level, focusing on layout design and gameplay flow. Next, we'll delve into creating a boss fight, showcasing the development of challenging encounters with custom AI and combat mechanics. Designing a multiplayer arena comes next, where we'll craft an environment suited for fast-paced, competitive gameplay. We will also cover the development of a quest system, highlighting the creation of dynamic objectives and progression mechanics. Lastly, we'll implement a dynamic weather system to enhance realism and immersion, demonstrating how environmental factors can elevate the gaming experience.

CHAPTER 12   CASE STUDIES

Implementing a Complete Level

Creating a complete game level involves designing an engaging environment, defining gameplay elements, and ensuring seamless player interactions. Unreal Engine provides a robust toolset for crafting immersive levels, including terrain tools, lighting systems, and scripting capabilities to bring the level to life.

Importance of a Complete Level

A well-designed level serves as the foundation for an engaging gameplay experience:

- **Player Engagement**: Keeps players invested through interactive environments and challenges
- **Narrative Delivery**: A medium to convey the game's story and objectives
- **Gameplay Flow**: Balances exploration, combat, and rewards to maintain player interest

Core Components of Level Design

Key aspects of implementing a complete level include

- **Environment Creation**: Sculpting terrain and placing assets to create a cohesive world
- **Gameplay Triggers**: Adding triggers for dynamic events like enemy spawns or cutscenes
- **Optimization**: Ensuring smooth performance through efficient asset usage and LODs

Reviewing the Code

Listing 12-1 introduces the declaration of a level management actor responsible for runtime asset handling and event trigger setup.

- **Class Declaration**: ALevelManager manages the assets and gameplay triggers for the level.
- **LoadLevelAssets()**: Loads required assets dynamically for better memory management.
- **SetGameplayTriggers()**: Sets up interactive gameplay elements like triggers and events.

Listing 12-1. LevelManager.h

```
#pragma once

#include "CoreMinimal.h"
#include "GameFramework/Actor.h"
#include "LevelManager.generated.h"

UCLASS()
class MYGAME_API ALevelManager : public AActor
{
    GENERATED_BODY()

public:
    ALevelManager();

    UFUNCTION(BlueprintCallable, Category = "Level")
    void LoadLevelAssets();

    UFUNCTION(BlueprintCallable, Category = "Level")
    void SetGameplayTriggers();
};
```

CHAPTER 12   CASE STUDIES

Listing 12-2 details the runtime implementation of the level manager, enabling real-time asset loading and trigger configuration.

- **PrimaryActorTick**: Ensures the manager updates as needed during gameplay
- **LoadLevelAssets()**: Demonstrates dynamic asset loading, crucial for optimizing larger levels
- **SetGameplayTriggers()**: Configures in-game events, enhancing interactivity and immersion

Listing 12-2. LevelManager.cpp

```cpp
#include "LevelManager.h"
#include "Engine/StreamableManager.h"
#include "Engine/AssetManager.h"

ALevelManager::ALevelManager()
{
    PrimaryActorTick.bCanEverTick = true;
}

void ALevelManager::LoadLevelAssets()
{
    UE_LOG(LogTemp, Warning, TEXT("Attempting to load assets asynchronously"));

    // Example: Asynchronously load a Static Mesh asset
    FStringAssetReference AssetRef(TEXT("/Game/Environment/Meshes/Tree.Tree")); // Change to your asset path

    FStreamableManager& Streamable = UAssetManager::GetStreamableManager();
```

```
    Streamable.RequestAsyncLoad(
        AssetRef,
        FStreamableDelegate::CreateUObject(this, &ALevelManager
        ::OnAssetLoaded)
    );
}
void ALevelManager::OnAssetLoaded()
{
    UE_LOG(LogTemp, Warning, TEXT("Asset loaded
successfully."));
    // You can now use the asset (e.g., spawn it into
the level)
}
void ALevelManager::SetGameplayTriggers()
{
    UE_LOG(LogTemp, Warning, TEXT("Gameplay Triggers Set"));
    // Logic for placing triggers and interactive elements
}
```

A complete level combines creative design and technical precision to give players a memorable experience. By leveraging Unreal Engine's tools and scripting features, developers can create polished and engaging game levels tailored to their vision.

Creating a Boss Fight

A boss fight is a significant event in many games, offering players a memorable challenge with unique mechanics. Designing an engaging boss fight involves not just creating a tough enemy but also crafting a compelling narrative, environment, and set of mechanics that make the encounter stand out. Unreal Engine provides a range of tools to build these complex encounters, from custom AI to unique combat systems.

CHAPTER 12   CASE STUDIES

Importance of Boss Fights

Boss fights are integral to a game's design and can significantly impact the player experience:

- **Challenge and Reward**: Provides players with a sense of accomplishment after defeating a tough adversary.

- **Narrative Moment**: Often acts as a pivotal moment in the story, revealing key plot points or advancing the narrative.

- **Game Pace**: This breaks up the regular gameplay loop, creating variation and excitement.

Core Components of a Boss Fight

Designing a compelling boss fight involves a combination of smart AI, dynamic environments, and escalating challenges that keep the player fully engaged. The following components contribute to creating a memorable and rewarding boss encounter:

- **AI Behavior**: Define how the boss reacts to the player through unique movement patterns, attack strategies, and defensive maneuvers. Consider varying behavior based on player proximity, timing, or specific events.

- **Multi-phase Mechanics**: Introduce multiple combat phases to increase tension. For example, the boss may enter a more aggressive phase at 50% health, gaining new attacks, faster speed, or a shift in strategy to surprise the player.

- **Environment Design**: Build a distinctive arena that complements the boss's abilities—tight spaces for close-combat bosses or vertical arenas for ranged, flying, or multi-target fights.

- **Combat Mechanics**: Include powerful attacks, dodge timings, vulnerabilities, or puzzle-based weaknesses that challenge the player to adapt.

- **Player Progression**: Tie the difficulty and complexity of the boss to the player's growth. Scale damage, resistance, or introduce skill checks that reflect the player's journey so far.

Reviewing the Code

Listing 12-3 introduces the core logic structure for managing a boss character's AI through a custom AI controller. This setup enables behaviors like detecting proximity to the player, attacking, and running logic per frame.

- **AIController**: Inherits from `AAIController`, allowing for autonomous behavior management of the boss character

- **PerformAttack()**: A function exposed to Blueprint to trigger the boss's attack logic

Listing 12-3. BossAIController.h

```
#pragma once

#include "CoreMinimal.h"
#include "AIController.h"
#include "BossAIController.generated.h"
```

CHAPTER 12 CASE STUDIES

```
UCLASS()
class MYGAME_API ABossAIController : public AAIController
{
    GENERATED_BODY()
public:
    ABossAIController();

    virtual void Tick(float DeltaTime) override;

    UFUNCTION(BlueprintCallable, Category = "Boss")
    void PerformAttack();

private:
    bool bIsInAttackRange;
};
```

Listing 12-4 describes the runtime logic of the boss AI controller, focusing on how the boss detects and chases the player and executes attacks based on proximity.

- **MoveToActor()**: Utilizes Unreal's navigation system to guide the boss toward the player during the encounter, maintaining pressure on the player.

- **PerformAttack()**: Executes a predefined attack routine, such as spawning a projectile, triggering an animation, or applying damage when in range.

- **bIsInAttackRange**: This boolean flag determines when the boss is close enough to initiate an attack and can be updated through collision or distance checks in future enhancements.

Listing 12-4. BossAIController.cpp

```cpp
#include "BossAIController.h"
#include "GameFramework/Actor.h"
#include "Kismet/GameplayStatics.h"

ABossAIController::ABossAIController()
{
    bIsInAttackRange = false;
}

void ABossAIController::Tick(float DeltaTime)
{
    Super::Tick(DeltaTime);

    // Example AI logic to chase the player
    AActor* PlayerActor = UGameplayStatics::GetPlayerPawn
    (GetWorld(), 0);
    if (PlayerActor)
    {
        MoveToActor(PlayerActor);
    }

    // Check if in attack range
    if (bIsInAttackRange)
    {
        PerformAttack();
    }
}
```

```cpp
void ABossAIController::PerformAttack()
{
    // Logic for performing an attack
    UE_LOG(LogTemp, Warning, TEXT("Boss is Attacking!"));
    // Custom attack logic, such as spawning a projectile or
        triggering an animation
}
```

Creating a Boss Fight Arena

In Unreal Engine, a boss fight isn't complete without an appropriate environment. This includes designing a large, interactive arena that complements the boss's abilities and the player's strategy.

Listing 12-5 introduces a utility actor class that handles the environmental setup of a boss arena. It allows developers to control visual and structural elements used during major gameplay events.

- **ArenaSetup**: A dedicated actor that manages the arena's layout and structure for the boss fight

- **SetArenaEnvironment()**: A Blueprint-callable method that activates the arena's visual and gameplay elements

- **ArenaWalls**: A configurable array of static mesh components representing arena boundaries and structures

Listing 12-5. ArenaSetup.h

```cpp
#pragma once

#include "CoreMinimal.h"
#include "GameFramework/Actor.h"
#include "ArenaSetup.generated.h"
```

```
UCLASS()
class MYGAME_API AArenaSetup : public AActor
{
    GENERATED_BODY()
public:
    AArenaSetup();

    UFUNCTION(BlueprintCallable, Category = "Arena")
    void SetArenaEnvironment();

private:
    UPROPERTY(EditAnywhere)
    TArray<UStaticMeshComponent*> ArenaWalls;
};
```

Listing 12-6 demonstrates the implementation of arena setup logic, showing how to dynamically activate structural components of the boss arena. This enhances immersion and ensures gameplay is framed within an intended combat space.

- **SetArenaEnvironment()**: Loops through the ArenaWalls array and makes each wall visible, simulating the activation of an enclosed battle arena
- **PrimaryActorTick = false**: Disables unnecessary ticking, as the setup is called explicitly when needed

Listing 12-6. ArenaSetup.cpp

```
#include "ArenaSetup.h"

AArenaSetup::AArenaSetup()
{
    PrimaryActorTick.bCanEverTick = false;
}
```

CHAPTER 12   CASE STUDIES

```cpp
void AArenaSetup::SetArenaEnvironment()
{
    // Setup arena walls and environment details
    for (UStaticMeshComponent* Wall : ArenaWalls)
    {
        Wall->SetVisibility(true);
    }
}
```

Creating a boss fight is a combination of storytelling, AI development, and environmental design. By using Unreal Engine's AI and gameplay tools, developers can build challenging and rewarding encounters that will be remembered by players. Crafting these encounters requires balancing difficulty, narrative, and environment, ensuring that the fight is not only difficult but also rewarding.

Multiplayer Arena

Designing a multiplayer arena is crucial for creating a competitive and enjoyable experience in online games. The arena must be well-balanced, strategically interesting, and optimized for performance to ensure fair and dynamic gameplay. Unreal Engine provides a wide range of tools to create multiplayer maps, including networking support, dynamic environmental elements, and performance optimization techniques to ensure smooth online play.

Importance of a Multiplayer Arena

Multiplayer arenas are vital to competitive gameplay and player retention. Let's explore why they are important:

- **Fairness**: A well-designed arena ensures that no player has an unfair advantage.
- **Competitive Balance**: Different strategies should be viable, providing variety in how matches are played.
- **Engagement**: The arena should be visually appealing and varied to maintain player interest in repeated playthroughs.
- **Replayability**: The design of the arena can keep players coming back, offering unique experiences every time.

Core Components of a Multiplayer Arena

Key components to consider when designing a multiplayer arena:

- **Arena Layout**: Creating different paths, obstacles, and opportunities for players to strategize
- **Spawn Points**: Strategic placement of player spawn points to avoid unfair advantages
- **Environmental Interactions**: Features like destructible objects, traps, or interactive elements that add depth
- **Balance and Flow**: Ensuring that no area is too advantageous or disadvantageous for any team or player
- **Performance Optimization**: Ensuring that the arena runs smoothly in multiplayer scenarios, even when there are many players

CHAPTER 12   CASE STUDIES

Reviewing the Code

Listing 12-7 outlines the structure of a multiplayer arena manager class, designed to control the setup and gameplay dynamics of a competitive or cooperative multiplayer environment.

- **SetupArena()**: Initializes key arena elements such as boundaries, props, and layout before gameplay starts
- **SpawnPlayers()**: Handles spawning all participating players at predetermined spawn points
- **PlacePowerUps()**: Spawns interactive items such as health packs or power-ups at specific or randomized locations
- **SpawnLocations/PowerUpLocations**: Arrays that store positions for player starts and item placement within the arena

Listing 12-7.   MultiplayerArena.h

```
#pragma once

#include "CoreMinimal.h"
#include "GameFramework/Actor.h"
#include "MultiplayerArena.generated.h"

UCLASS()
class MYGAME_API AMultiplayerArena : public AActor
{
    GENERATED_BODY()

public:
    AMultiplayerArena();
```

```cpp
    UFUNCTION(BlueprintCallable, Category = "Arena")
    void SetupArena();

    UFUNCTION(BlueprintCallable, Category = "Arena")
    void SpawnPlayers();

    UFUNCTION(BlueprintCallable, Category = "Arena")
    void PlacePowerUps();

private:
    TArray<FVector> SpawnLocations;
    TArray<FVector> PowerUpLocations;
};
```

Listing 12-8 describes the implementation of a multiplayer arena system, focusing on dynamic player spawning and power-up placement. This enhances gameplay diversity and fairness in competitive or cooperative matches.

- **SetupArena()**: Predefines player spawn points within the level, setting up the foundation for balanced starting positions.
- **SpawnPlayers()**: Iterates over spawn points and spawns player actors using the PlayerClass, logging each spawn event.
- **PlacePowerUps()**: Spawns power-ups using PowerUpClass at predetermined or strategic locations for gameplay variety.
- **GetWorld()->SpawnActor()**: Used to spawn actors dynamically during runtime, this function is crucial in multiplayer environments where entities like players, power-ups, or enemies may need to be instantiated based on in-game events or logic.

For static or semi-static elements like spawn points, power-ups, or environmental objects, consider placing them directly in the level via the Unreal Editor. This method reduces the runtime overhead and improves overall performance by avoiding unnecessary actor instantiation during gameplay.

Listing 12-8. MultiplayerArena.cpp

```cpp
#include "MultiplayerArena.h"
#include "GameFramework/Actor.h"
#include "Engine/World.h"
#include "Kismet/GameplayStatics.h"

AMultiplayerArena::AMultiplayerArena()
{
    PrimaryActorTick.bCanEverTick = true;
}

void AMultiplayerArena::SetupArena()
{
    // Define spawn locations for players
    SpawnLocations.Add(FVector(0, 0, 0));
    // Example spawn point
    SpawnLocations.Add(FVector(1000, 1000, 0));
    // Another spawn point
}

void AMultiplayerArena::SpawnPlayers()
{
    // Example of spawning two players at the defined
        spawn points
    for (int32 i = 0; i < SpawnLocations.Num(); i++)
```

```cpp
    {
        FVector SpawnLocation = SpawnLocations[i];
        AActor* PlayerCharacter = GetWorld()->SpawnActor
        <AActor>(PlayerClass, SpawnLocation,
        FRotator::ZeroRotator);

        if (PlayerCharacter)
        {
            UE_LOG(LogTemp, Warning, TEXT("Player Spawned at:
            %s"), *SpawnLocation.ToString());
        }
    }
}

void AMultiplayerArena::PlacePowerUps()
{
    // Place power-ups at predefined locations
    for (FVector PowerUpLocation : PowerUpLocations)
    {
        AActor* PowerUp = GetWorld()->SpawnActor<AActor>
        (PowerUpClass, PowerUpLocation, FRotator::ZeroRotator);

        if (PowerUp)
        {
            UE_LOG(LogTemp, Warning, TEXT("Power-Up Spawned at:
            %s"), *PowerUpLocation.ToString());
        }
    }
}
```

Designing a multiplayer arena requires attention to both gameplay balance and technical performance. Unreal Engine's networking capabilities allow developers to implement multiplayer functionality with synchronized environments, player spawning, and dynamic interactions.

CHAPTER 12   CASE STUDIES

By balancing arena layout, spawn locations, and gameplay mechanics, you can create an engaging and competitive environment that will keep players invested in the game. Additionally, optimizing the arena for performance ensures a smooth and enjoyable experience for all players.

Developing a Quest System

A quest system is a fundamental aspect of many games, providing players with objectives, rewards, and progression. It's a vital component for creating compelling narratives, encouraging exploration, and enhancing player engagement. Whether for single-player or multiplayer experiences, a robust quest system allows for dynamic storylines and gameplay experiences that evolve based on player choices and actions. Unreal Engine offers powerful tools for integrating quest systems, allowing you to manage tasks, objectives, and player interactions.

Importance of a Quest System

A well-designed quest system provides structure, immersion, and motivation for players. Here's why it's essential:

- **Player Motivation**: Gives players clear objectives and a sense of purpose within the game.
- **Narrative Depth**: Supports the storytelling process, allowing for branching narratives and personalized experiences.
- **Replayability**: Dynamic questlines that change based on player decisions add replay value to the game.
- **Player Engagement**: Keeps players immersed by offering new challenges and rewards as they progress through the game.

Core Components of a Quest System

Key elements to consider when designing a quest system:

- **Quest Objectives**: Specific goals that the player must accomplish to complete the quest.

- **Quest Stages**: Quests can have multiple stages or phases, such as "Start," "In Progress," and "Completed."

- **NPC Interaction**: NPCs (non-playable characters) often play a central role in giving and progressing quests.

- **Rewards**: Completing quests should provide meaningful rewards, like items, experience, or story progression.

- **Tracking and Logs**: A system to track quest progress and display it to the player, keeping them informed on what to do next.

Reviewing the Code

Listing 12-9 introduces a basic quest manager system for handling dynamic in-game objectives. It allows quests to be started, updated, and completed during gameplay, serving as a foundational tool for narrative and progression systems.

- **StartQuest()**: Begins a new quest by adding it to the ActiveQuests array and initializing its progress in the QuestProgress map

- **CompleteQuest()**: Finalizes a quest, allowing for rewards, storyline progression, or unlocking future quests

CHAPTER 12 CASE STUDIES

- **UpdateQuestProgress()**: Tracks the player's advancement on a specific quest, enabling condition checks for partial or full completion
- **QuestProgress**: A TMap storing integer progress values keyed by quest names
- **ActiveQuests**: An array holding the names of currently active quests

Listing 12-9. QuestManager.h

```
#pragma once

#include "CoreMinimal.h"
#include "GameFramework/Actor.h"
#include "QuestManager.generated.h"

UCLASS()
class MYGAME_API AQuestManager : public AActor
{
    GENERATED_BODY()
public:
    AQuestManager();

    UFUNCTION(BlueprintCallable, Category = "Quest")
    void StartQuest(FString QuestName);

    UFUNCTION(BlueprintCallable, Category = "Quest")
    void CompleteQuest(FString QuestName);

    UFUNCTION(BlueprintCallable, Category = "Quest")
    void UpdateQuestProgress(FString QuestName, int32 Progress);
```

CHAPTER 12 CASE STUDIES

```
private:
    TMap<FString, int32> QuestProgress;
    TArray<FString> ActiveQuests;
};
```

Listing 12-10 presents the runtime implementation of the quest system, managing quest initiation, progress tracking, and completion. This system is essential for structuring game objectives and guiding narrative progression through gameplay.

- **StartQuest()**: Adds a new quest to the ActiveQuests list and initializes its progress to 0 in the QuestProgress map. Prevents duplicate quest entries.

- **CompleteQuest()**: Removes the quest from active tracking, cleaning up associated data. This step can be expanded to trigger rewards, cinematics, or further game progression.

- **UpdateQuestProgress()**: Updates the player's progress toward completing a quest. Ideal for tracking collectibles, objectives, or milestones.

- **UE_LOG()**: Used to provide real-time feedback in the output log, helping with debugging or informing the player through notifications.

Listing 12-10. QuestManager.cpp

```
#include "QuestManager.h"
#include "Engine/World.h"
#include "GameFramework/Actor.h"

AQuestManager::AQuestManager()
{
    PrimaryActorTick.bCanEverTick = true;
}
```

```cpp
void AQuestManager::StartQuest(FString QuestName)
{
    if (!ActiveQuests.Contains(QuestName))
    {
        ActiveQuests.Add(QuestName);
        QuestProgress.Add(QuestName, 0);
        UE_LOG(LogTemp, Warning, TEXT("Quest Started: %s"),
        *QuestName);
    }
}

void AQuestManager::CompleteQuest(FString QuestName)
{
    if (ActiveQuests.Contains(QuestName))
    {
        ActiveQuests.Remove(QuestName);
        QuestProgress.Remove(QuestName);
        UE_LOG(LogTemp, Warning, TEXT("Quest Completed: %s"),
        *QuestName);
    }
}

void AQuestManager::UpdateQuestProgress(FString QuestName,
int32 Progress)
{
    if (QuestProgress.Contains(QuestName))
    {
        QuestProgress[QuestName] = Progress;
        UE_LOG(LogTemp, Warning, TEXT("Quest Progress Updated:
        %s - %d%%"), *QuestName, Progress);
    }
}
```

A well-designed quest system enhances player engagement, provides structure, and creates compelling gameplay experiences. By using Unreal Engine's powerful tools and C++ coding capabilities, developers can build dynamic and flexible quest systems that react to player choices and progress. With features like objective tracking, NPC interactions, and rewards, the quest system serves as a key component of the game's narrative and progression.

Building a Dynamic Weather System

A dynamic weather system enhances the realism and immersion of a game by simulating changing weather patterns such as rain, snow, fog, and clear skies. By incorporating dynamic weather, you can create more engaging and atmospheric environments that evolve, impacting gameplay, visuals, and player experiences. In Unreal Engine, implementing a dynamic weather system involves manipulating environmental variables like light, fog, skyboxes, and particle systems to simulate different weather conditions that affect the game world.

Importance of a Dynamic Weather System

A dynamic weather system adds depth and immersion to the game world, offering several benefits:

- **Immersion**: This creates a more believable world where players experience different conditions based on the time of day or in-game events.
- **Atmosphere**: Weather can drastically change the atmosphere of a game, setting the tone for different environments and situations.

CHAPTER 12   CASE STUDIES

- **Gameplay Impact**: Weather can influence gameplay mechanics, such as visibility in fog or slowed movement in the snow.
- **Replayability**: Randomized or dynamic weather conditions can make each playthrough feel unique.

Core Components of a Dynamic Weather System

Key elements to consider when designing a dynamic weather system:

- **Weather States**: Different weather conditions like sunny, rainy, foggy, or stormy, each with specific characteristics
- **Weather Transitions**: Smooth transitions between weather states, such as rain turning to snow or clear skies becoming overcast
- **Environmental Effects**: Changes in lighting, skyboxes, particle effects, and sound to reflect the current weather conditions
- **Gameplay Impact**: Weather systems that influence gameplay, such as fog affecting visibility or rain creating slippery surfaces

Reviewing the Code

Listing 12-11 introduces the core components of a dynamic weather system. This system enhances environmental immersion by managing real-time transitions between various weather conditions like rain, fog, or sunlight.

CHAPTER 12　CASE STUDIES

- **SetWeatherCondition()**: A Blueprint-callable function that allows the developer to set the current weather state dynamically at runtime, such as "Rain", "Sunny", or "Fog"

- **UpdateWeather()**: Gradually updates the game world's atmosphere over time based on the current and target weather conditions

- **CurrentWeather**: Stores the current weather condition as a string

- **WeatherTransitionTime**: Determines how long it takes to transition between different weather states

- **WeatherTransitionProgress**: Keeps track of how far the transition has progressed, enabling smooth visual changes

Listing 12-11. WeatherManager.h

```
#pragma once

#include "CoreMinimal.h"
#include "GameFramework/Actor.h"
#include "WeatherManager.generated.h"

UCLASS()
class MYGAME_API AWeatherManager : public AActor
{
    GENERATED_BODY()
public:
    AWeatherManager();
```

```cpp
    UFUNCTION(BlueprintCallable, Category = "Weather")
    void SetWeatherCondition(FString WeatherCondition);

    UFUNCTION(BlueprintCallable, Category = "Weather")
    void UpdateWeather(float DeltaTime);

private:
    FString CurrentWeather;
    float WeatherTransitionTime;
    float WeatherTransitionProgress;
};
```

Listing 12-12 presents the runtime implementation of the dynamic weather system, focusing on smooth transitions between environmental states. This setup enables developers to enhance immersion by dynamically modifying atmosphere, particle effects, and lighting over time.

- **SetWeatherCondition()**: This function assigns a new weather type (e.g., `"Rainy"`, `"Sunny"`) and resets the transition timer. It's designed to trigger a gradual change rather than an abrupt switch.

- **UpdateWeather()**: Called every frame, this function handles real-time interpolation toward the target weather state. Developers can insert logic here to alter fog density, lighting, or spawn weather-specific particle effects.

- **WeatherTransitionProgress**: Tracks how far along the system is in completing the transition to the new weather type.

- **WeatherTransitionTime**: Defines how long the transition should take, creating a natural fade between effects.

Listing 12-12. WeatherManager.cpp

```cpp
#include "WeatherManager.h"
#include "Engine/World.h"
#include "GameFramework/Actor.h"

AWeatherManager::AWeatherManager()
{
    PrimaryActorTick.bCanEverTick = true;
    WeatherTransitionTime = 5.0f;
    // Time to transition to the next weather condition
    (in seconds)
    WeatherTransitionProgress = 0.0f;
}

void AWeatherManager::SetWeatherCondition(FString
WeatherCondition)
{
    CurrentWeather = WeatherCondition;
    WeatherTransitionProgress = 0.0f;
    // Reset transition progress
    UE_LOG(LogTemp, Warning, TEXT("Weather set to: %s"),
    *WeatherCondition);
}

void AWeatherManager::UpdateWeather(float DeltaTime)
{
    if (WeatherTransitionProgress < WeatherTransitionTime)
    {
        WeatherTransitionProgress += DeltaTime;
        // Gradually update weather effects like light, fog,
        and particle systems here
```

```
            UE_LOG(LogTemp, Warning, TEXT("Transitioning
            weather: %f%%"), (WeatherTransitionProgress /
            WeatherTransitionTime) * 100);
    }
    else
    {
            // Apply the full weather effects for the current
                weather condition
        if (CurrentWeather == "Rainy")
        {
            // Example: Increase particle effects for rain
        }
        else if (CurrentWeather == "Sunny")
        {
            // Example: Clear sky, no rain
        }
            // Add more conditions for other weather types
    }
}
```

Implementing a dynamic weather system enhances the overall immersion and realism of the game world. By using Unreal Engine's powerful features and C++, developers can create weather conditions that influence gameplay and provide a more engaging experience. The key to a successful dynamic weather system is the smooth transition between different states and the integration of environmental effects like lighting, fog, and particle systems that reflect the current weather. This allows players to experience a dynamic world that feels alive and responsive to the game's changing conditions.

Summary

In this chapter, we explored practical implementations of complex game systems through detailed case studies. From designing immersive levels and crafting dynamic boss fights to building competitive multiplayer arenas, implementing quest systems, and simulating dynamic weather, each case demonstrates how Unreal Engine and C++ can be used to create engaging and polished gameplay experiences.

CHAPTER 13

Appendix

This serves as a valuable reference section for all the essential tools, troubleshooting tips, and resources that will assist you in your game development journey. It includes a cheat sheet for Unreal Engine to quickly look up commands and shortcuts, a list of common errors and fixes to save time when debugging, a curated collection of additional resources for further learning and exploration, and a glossary of terms to ensure you fully understand the technical jargon and concepts used throughout the book. This Appendix is designed to be a practical companion, offering support as you continue to refine your game development skills.

This Appendix provides a practical toolkit to assist you in your game development journey. It includes an "Unreal Engine Cheat Sheet" section, offering a quick reference for key commands, shortcuts, and Unreal Engine–specific tips to speed up your workflow. You'll also find a "Common Errors and Fixes" section, offering troubleshooting advice to help you resolve typical issues encountered in Unreal Engine and C++ development. The "Additional Resources" section provides links to external resources like forums, documentation, tutorials, and tools to support your continued learning. Finally, the "Glossary of Terms" section offers clear definitions of important terms and concepts in game development, ensuring you fully understand the language used throughout the book. By the end of this Appendix, you'll have a comprehensive set of resources to make your development process more efficient and easier to navigate.

CHAPTER 13 APPENDIX

Unreal Engine Cheat Sheet

This Section provides a quick reference to essential commands, shortcuts, and coding practices that are frequently used by developers working in Unreal Engine. Whether you're navigating the Editor, scripting in C++, or designing Blueprints, this cheat sheet will help you streamline your workflow and make your development process more efficient.

Editor Hotkeys

- Viewport Navigation
    - Movement (Standard): LMB/RMB + Drag
    - Movement (GameStyle): RMB + WASD
    - Zoom: Mouse Wheel
    - Geometry Editing: Shift + 5
- Viewport Transformation
    - Translate: W
    - Rotate: E
    - Scale: R
    - Toggle Transform Mode: Spacebar
    - Focus on Selection: F
- Level Editor
    - Hide Selected Object: H
    - Unhide All Hidden Objects: Ctrl + H
    - Clone Active Object: Alt + (Translate or Rotate)

CHAPTER 13   APPENDIX

- Editor FullScreen: Shift + F11
- Game View: G
- Camera Shortcuts
  - Perspective View: Alt + G
  - Front View: Alt + H
  - Side View: Alt + K
  - Top View: Alt + J
- Blueprint Editor
  - Align Nodes Horizontally: Q
  - Align Nodes Vertically: Ctrl + Shift + SAI ➤ (custom-defined, user-dependent)
- AI and Debugging
  - Toggle NavMesh Visibility: P
  - Toggle AI Debugger (in PIE): ' (apostrophe)
- Miscellaneous
  - Command Console: ~
  - Clear Selection: ESC
  - Live Code Recompile: Ctrl + Alt + F11

C++ Syntax for Unreal Engine

- UPROPERTY Specifiers
  - **BlueprintAssignable**: Exposes property for assigning in Blueprints. Example: AActor* MyActor;
  - **BlueprintCallable**: Exposes property for calling in Blueprints. Example: bool bIsRunning;

CHAPTER 13 APPENDIX

- **BlueprintReadOnly**: Property can be read in Blueprints but cannot be written to. Example: enum EPlayerType PlayerType;
- **BlueprintReadWrite**: Property can be both read and written to in Blueprints. Example: FVector MyLocation;

- UFUNCTION Specifiers
  - **BlueprintCallable**: Function can be called from Blueprints. Example: UFUNCTION(BlueprintCallable) void MyFunction();
  - **BlueprintPure**: Function does not modify the owning object and can be executed from Blueprints. Example: UFUNCTION(BlueprintPure) int32 GetHealth();
  - **BlueprintNativeEvent**: Function can be overridden by a Blueprint but has a native implementation. Example: UFUNCTION(BlueprintNativeEvent) void OnDamageTaken();

- Additional Specifiers
  - **BlueprintGetter**: Marks a getter function as BlueprintCallable and Pure. Used when paired with meta = (BlueprintGetter = "FunctionName"). Example: UFUNCTION(BlueprintGetter) int32 GetScore();
  - **BlueprintImplementableEvent**: Declares a function that is meant to be implemented in Blueprints only, no C++ definition required. Example: UFUNCTION(BlueprintImplementableEvent) void OnQuestComplete();

- Common Data Types

  - **AActor**: Represents an object in the world (e.g., ACharacter* MyCharacter;)

  - **Boolean**: Represents a true/false value (e.g., bool bIsAlive;)

  - **UObject**: Base class for most objects in Unreal Engine (e.g., UCameraComponent* MyCamera;)

Additional Tips

- Blueprint Usage

  - BlueprintCallable functions allow for direct calls from Blueprints, enabling dynamic interaction in your game's logic.

  - BlueprintPure functions return data without altering the game's state, making them ideal for queries like health, position, or inventory status.

- Editor Customization: Customize your editor layout using the hotkeys for Viewport Transformation and Camera Shortcuts to switch between different views and transform modes quickly. This increases efficiency while designing levels and assets.

- C++ Best Practices

  - Use UPROPERTY correctly to control how data is serialized, replicated, or exposed to Blueprints.

  - Always declare variables that will be used within the engine with UPROPERTY to ensure they can be properly saved and exposed for manipulation in the editor or Blueprint system.

CHAPTER 13   APPENDIX

This cheat sheet serves as a quick yet comprehensive guide to help you navigate Unreal Engine and write efficient code, ensuring you spend less time searching for commands and more time creating.

Common Errors and Fixes

While developing games in Unreal Engine using C++ or Blueprints, encountering errors is inevitable. However, most errors can be resolved quickly with the right knowledge. This section will help you identify some of the most common issues developers face and provide solutions for resolving them.

1. Compiler Errors in C++

- **Error: 'ClassName' is not a class or namespace name**
    - **Cause**: You may have forgotten to include the appropriate header file, or the class is declared incorrectly.
    - **Fix**: Ensure that you've included the necessary header file using #include "ClassName.h". Verify that the class name is spelled correctly.
- **Error: 'TypeName' has no member 'FunctionName'**
    - **Cause**: You are calling a function or accessing a property that doesn't exist or is not visible in the context.
    - **Fix**: Double-check the function or property's name and its accessibility modifiers (e.g., UPROPERTY, UFUNCTION). Make sure it's correctly declared and visible in the scope you're trying to access.

CHAPTER 13   APPENDIX

- **Error: Incompatible pointer types**
  - **Cause**: You're trying to assign a pointer of one type to another incompatible pointer.
  - **Fix**: Ensure type compatibility. If you're working with class pointers, use Cast<TypeName>() to safely cast the object type when needed.
- **Error: Linking error/unresolved external symbol**
  - **Cause**: A function, module, or plugin is declared but not defined or not linked properly.
  - **Fix**: Ensure the implementation exists in a `.cpp` file, and the appropriate module/plugin is listed in the `.Build.cs` file (e.g., `"OnlineSubsystem"`, `"AIModule"`). This often happens when using functions across modules without linking dependencies correctly.

2. Blueprint Compilation Issues

- **Error: "Error compiling script"**
  - **Cause**: A Blueprint node is incorrectly set up, or you are trying to reference an undefined variable or function.
  - **Fix**: Review the Blueprint for any broken nodes or undefined variables. Reconnect or recreate the nodes to ensure that the Blueprint is correctly set up.

CHAPTER 13   APPENDIX

- **Error: "Function not found"**
  - **Cause**: This error usually occurs when a Blueprint function is either deleted or renamed, but the calls to it are still present.
  - **Fix**: Search for references to the function in the Blueprint and either remove them or update the calls with the correct function name.

3. Runtime Errors

- **Error: Access Violation (Crash)**
  - **Cause**: Attempting to access a null pointer or dereferencing an uninitialized object.
  - **Fix**: Ensure that pointers are properly initialized and that null checks are done before accessing object members. Use IsValid() or ensure() to prevent null pointer access during runtime.
- **Error: Memory Allocation Failed**
  - **Cause**: The game runs out of memory due to excessive asset loading or inefficient memory management.
  - **Fix**: Optimize memory usage by reducing the size of assets or properly managing memory allocation using TArray, TMap, or TSet to free up space. Additionally, check for any memory leaks that might occur during runtime.

4. Network and Replication Issues

- **Error: Replicated property is not updating across the network**
  - **Cause**: The property is either not marked for replication or the server-client sync is not set up correctly.
  - **Fix**: Ensure the UPROPERTY has the Replicated flag set and that you call OnRep functions when necessary. You can also use Multicast functions to synchronize data between server and clients.

- **Error: Actor not spawning on clients**
  - **Cause**: The actor is being spawned only on the server but not replicated to clients.
  - **Fix**: Use SpawnActor with the bOnlyOwnerSee flag set to false, or call Multicast functions to ensure that the actor is spawned and visible on all clients.

5. Asset Loading and Path Issues

- **Error: Asset is missing or failed to load**
  - **Cause**: The asset path may be incorrect or the asset is not included in the build.
  - **Fix**: Verify the asset's location within the project's content directory and ensure that its path is correct. Additionally, check that the asset is properly included in the packaging settings.

- **Error: Asset not found in the content browser**
  - **Cause:** The asset may have been moved, renamed, or deleted without proper updating.
  - **Fix:** Right-click the content folder and select "Fix up redirectors" to resolve any asset path issues.

6. Miscellaneous Errors

- **Error: "Blueprint class is not compatible"**
  - **Cause:** A Blueprint class may be incompatible with the parent class you're trying to use.
  - **Fix:** Ensure that the Blueprint class is properly inherited from the correct parent class and that no conflicting base classes or interfaces are being used.
- **Error: "Invalid parameter or argument"**
  - **Cause:** Incorrect arguments passed into a function or node.
  - **Fix:** Check function signatures and ensure that the arguments match the expected types and formats.

By understanding these common errors and knowing how to fix them, you'll be better equipped to troubleshoot issues quickly during development. Don't forget to always check the logs and debugging tools within Unreal Engine to further diagnose any problems that arise.

Additional Resources

Unreal Engine development can be complex, especially when you're working with C++ and Blueprints, but there are plenty of resources available to help you on your journey. From official documentation to community-driven forums, these resources will provide the additional support and learning materials you need to succeed. Below is a list of recommended resources that can help you stay updated, deepen your understanding, and overcome development challenges.

1. Official Unreal Engine Documentation

The official Unreal Engine documentation is the best place to start. It provides comprehensive and up-to-date guides on everything from engine features to C++ programming and Blueprint scripting.

- **Unreal Engine Documentation**
    - Topics covered include C++ classes, asset management, Blueprints, multiplayer networking, UI creation, and more.

2. Unreal Engine Forums

The Unreal Engine forums are a great place to connect with other developers, ask questions, and share knowledge. Whether you're a beginner or an experienced developer, you'll find threads that can assist you with troubleshooting, learning new tips, and solving common problems.

- **Unreal Engine Forums**
    - Explore sections like "C++ Programming," "Blueprint Visual Scripting," and "Community Resources."

CHAPTER 13   APPENDIX

3. Unreal Engine YouTube Channel

The official YouTube channel of Unreal Engine is filled with video tutorials, developer interviews, livestreams, and event recordings. It's a perfect resource for visual learners who prefer watching over reading.

- Link: https://www.youtube.com/user/UnrealDevelopmentKit
  - Watch tutorials on game development, engine features, and techniques used by professionals.

4. UE4 AnswerHub

AnswerHub is an official Q&A platform where developers can post questions, get answers from the community, and find solutions to their problems. It's a good resource for those who prefer a more community-driven support system.

- **UE4 AnswerHub**
  - Browse through questions, or submit your own to get personalized help from Unreal Engine experts.

5. Online Learning Platforms

There are several online platforms where you can take courses related to Unreal Engine, C++, game development, and more. Some of the top platforms include

- **Udemy**
- **LinkedIn Learning**
- **Pluralsight**

These platforms provide structured, in-depth lessons, often taught by industry professionals. They are especially helpful if you prefer more formalized learning over reading documentation.

6. Unreal Slackers (Discord Community)

Unreal Slackers is a popular Discord server with over 40,000 members who discuss all things related to Unreal Engine. You can ask questions, get feedback, and collaborate with others who are also learning or developing with Unreal Engine.

- Link: https://unreal-slackers.org/
    - Join channels for C++ programming, Blueprints, design, art, and more.

7. GitHub Repositories and Sample Projects

GitHub is a goldmine for Unreal Engine developers looking to learn from real-world examples. Many developers and studios share open source projects, sample games, and code snippets on GitHub. These repositories can serve as inspiration or be directly utilized in your projects.

- Link: https://github.com/EpicGames
    - Access the Unreal Engine source code, as well as community-made plugins and sample games.

8. Community Tutorials and Blogs

Some countless community-created tutorials and blogs can help you with specific features of Unreal Engine. Many independent developers share detailed guides and step-by-step instructions on various topics.

CHAPTER 13   APPENDIX

- **Link**: Unreal Engine Blog
  - Learn new techniques and read about updates and feature releases directly from the developers of Unreal Engine.
- **Link**: Ray Wenderlich Unreal Engine Tutorials
  - Offers in-depth tutorials for Unreal Engine users, especially those working with C++.

9. Online Communities and Social Media

Staying connected with other Unreal Engine users and developers on social media can help you stay updated on new techniques, challenges, and industry trends. Follow these platforms:

- **Twitter**: Search hashtags like #UnrealEngine, #UE4, or #UE5 to find the latest discussions and updates.
- **Reddit**: The subreddit r/unrealengine (`https://www.reddit.com/r/unrealengine/`) is a good place for asking questions and sharing projects.
- **Stack Overflow**: For specific C++ or coding issues, search Stack Overflow with the tag unreal-engine4 to find relevant answers.

By utilizing these resources, you'll have a wide range of tools and communities to help you overcome obstacles, expand your knowledge, and stay up to date with the latest Unreal Engine features and best practices.

CHAPTER 13 APPENDIX

Glossary of Terms

In game development, especially when working with Unreal Engine and C++, understanding key terminology is crucial for effective communication and implementation. This glossary provides definitions of common terms and concepts used throughout this book to ensure clarity and enhance your understanding.

A

Actor
An object or entity in the game world; can be anything from a character to a prop or even a light source. Actors are the primary building blocks in Unreal Engine.

AI (Artificial Intelligence)
The simulation of human intelligence in games; typically involves NPCs (non-playable characters) that respond to player actions and environmental factors.

B

Blueprint
A visual scripting system in Unreal Engine that allows developers to create gameplay elements and logic without writing code. It is highly integrated with Unreal's C++ system.

BSP (Binary Space Partitioning)
A method for rendering complex 3D environments, primarily used for level design and optimization.

C

C++

A high-level programming language commonly used for game development, offering performance advantages and the ability to work closely with hardware.

Component

A modular unit within an Actor that defines a specific behavior or feature, such as a camera or collision detection system.

D

Delegate

A type of event or callback used in Unreal Engine to facilitate communication between objects. Delegates are often used for handling events asynchronously.

Dynamic Loading

The ability to load assets or levels into a game at runtime rather than at the start, reducing memory usage and improving load times.

E

Event

A piece of code or logic triggered by a certain condition or action, such as the player interacting with an object or an NPC initiating a conversation.

EditAnywhere

A property specifier in Unreal Engine that allows the property to be edited in the editor across both archetypes and instances.

F

FVector
A struct representing a 3D vector in Unreal Engine, typically used for positions, directions, or velocities in the game world.

Foliage
The collection of plants, trees, and other vegetation that make up the landscape of a game level.

G

Gameplay Mechanics
The core rules and systems that define the player's interaction with the game world, such as combat systems, health management, and quest progression.

GameMode
The ruleset and logic that dictate how the game functions, including win conditions, game flow, and player behavior.

H

HUD (Heads-Up Display)
The visual elements present important information to the player, such as health bars, ammo counts, and objectives.

HotKey
A keyboard shortcut that allows a user to quickly execute a command or function within the Unreal Engine editor.

CHAPTER 13　APPENDIX

I

Instance
An individual occurrence of an object or class in a game world. An instance represents a specific object that can have its own state and behavior.

Interface
A blueprint class that defines a contract of functions, which can be implemented by other classes or blueprints to create flexible systems.

J

JIT (Just-In-Time) Compilation
A method of compilation where code is compiled during runtime, allowing for optimizations based on real-time data.

K

Kismet
An earlier scripting system used in Unreal Engine for creating gameplay logic. It was eventually replaced by Blueprints.

L

Lerp (Linear Interpolation)
A method for smoothly transitioning between two values is often used for animations or moving objects between points.

Level Streaming
The process of loading and unloading levels dynamically during gameplay to optimize memory and performance.

M

Mesh
A 3D model composed of vertices and polygons is used to represent objects in the game world.

Multiplayer
A mode where multiple players can connect to the game simultaneously, typically over a network, and interact within the same game world.

N

NPC (Non-playable Character)
A character in the game that is not controlled by the player but is programmed to perform certain behaviors and actions.

NetCode
The programming logic and protocols that manage the communication between players in a multiplayer environment, ensuring synchronization and consistency.

O

Object-Oriented Programming (OOP)
A programming paradigm based on the concept of objects, which are instances of classes containing both data and methods.

Overload
In C++, overloading refers to defining multiple functions or operators with the same name but different parameters.

CHAPTER 13 APPENDIX

P

Pathfinding
The process of determining the optimal route for an AI or character to take between two points in the game world, typically using algorithms like A*.

Pixel Shader
A program that processes the individual pixels of a texture, applying visual effects like color adjustment, lighting, or blurring.

Q

Quaternions
A mathematical concept used in Unreal Engine for representing rotations in 3D space, offering advantages over Euler angles in terms of smoothness and avoiding gimbal lock.

R

Replication
The process of synchronizing data, such as position or state, between clients and the server in a multiplayer environment.

Rigid Body
An object in the game world that does not deform but reacts to forces like gravity, collisions, and friction.

S

Spline
A mathematical curve is used for creating smooth paths or animations in 3D space, such as roads or character movements.

Static Mesh
A type of mesh in Unreal Engine that does not animate but is used to represent objects in the world, such as buildings or rocks.

T

Texture Mapping
The process of applying a 2D image (texture) to a 3D model to give it color, detail, and realism.

Time Dilation
A technique in Unreal Engine to slow down or speed up the flow of time within the game, often used for special effects like bullet time.

U

UObject
The base class for all objects in Unreal Engine; provides fundamental features like memory management and object lifecycle handling.

V

Vector
A data structure that represents a point or direction in 2D or 3D space, typically used for positions, velocities, and forces.

Volumetric Lighting
Lighting effects that create a sense of depth and atmosphere by simulating light scattering through particles, fog, or smoke in the game world.

CHAPTER 13   APPENDIX

W

World Composition

A system in Unreal Engine for creating large open-world environments by streaming different sections of the world in and out during gameplay.

Workflow

The series of steps or processes followed during game development to move from one stage of production to the next.

Index

A

AActor, 865
AAdaptiveAIController, 825
AAdvancedNPCSystem class, 269
A* (A-star) algorithm, 679–681, 715
AARInteractionManager, 802
ABossFightManager class, 552
Acceleration, 401
ACharacterMovement
  Controller, 403
AClimbingCharacter, 433
ACollectibleItem constructor, 76
ACombatManager, 447
ACrossPlatformManager, 812, 813
Action games, 351, 359, 373, 410,
  432, 462, 496, 561, 564, 578
Action prompts, 655
Action RPGs, 446, 453, 479
ActivateQuest function, 288
ActivateRespawn
  Point function, 174
ActivateTrap function, 233, 234
Activating traps
  advanced techniques,
    228, 232–236
  algorithm, 228, 229
  code reviewing, 229–232
  conditions, 227
  practical applications, 228
  usage, 227
Activation zones, 620
Active abilities, 460
ActiveAudio
  Component, 665
ActiveQuests, 850
Actor, 875
ActorsInCutscene, 239
Adaptation, 504, 632
Adaptive AI, 504
ADayNightManager, 343
AddAxisMapping(), 814
AddDynamic function, 14
AddEvent function, 27
AddInteractiveObject
  function, 41, 43
AddItem function, 81, 277
AddItemToInventory(), 162
AddMovementInput(), 676
AddParticle(), 610, 612
AddPlayer(), 749, 751
AddPlayerToQueue(), 769, 771
AdjustBehaviorBased
  OnPlayer(), 826
AdjustCrouchState(), 417, 418
AdjustDifficulty function, 302

INDEX

AdjustObjectRotation function, 205
AdjustObjectScale function, 195
AdjustParticleEffects function, 214
AdjustPrices function, 325, 326
AdvancedDoor class, 223
AdvancedInventorySystem class, 280
AdvancedMiniGameSystem class, 301
AdvancedQuestSystem class, 290
Advanced scripting techniques
    Blueprint system, 820
    code reviewing, 817–819
    components, 816
    description, 816
    importance, 816
AdvancedTrap class, 232
Adventure games, 351, 359, 373, 378, 394, 409, 425, 432, 439, 462, 496, 561
ADynamicLightManager class, 360, 362
ADynamicPricing class, 325
ADynamicPuzzle class, 313
AEnemySpawner class, 544
Aerodynamics, 591
Aesthetic appeal, 651, 668
AGeometryCollectionActor, 607
Aggro system, 685
AHazardZone, 352
AHitDetection constructor, 67
AIActorLocation, 755
AI behavior, 836
AI-controlled enemies, 476
AIController, 837
AIController->MoveToLocation(), 717
AI-driven game design, 825
AInteractiveObject constructor, 33
Alertness/detection, 686
ALevelManager, 833
AllPlayersReady(), 750, 751
Ambient loops, 663
Ammo management, 486, 488
AModdingManager, 791
Amplitude, 643, 645
AMyWheeledVehiclePawn, 593
ANetworkingManager, 729
Animation blending, 675
Animation control, 446
AnswerHub, 872
Anti-lock braking systems (ABS), 591
AoEDamageComponent class, 117
AParticleCollision class, 210
APerformanceOptimizer, 807
APhysicalObject class, 46
APlayerCharacter, 411
APlayerCharacter constructor, 36
Appearance system, 470
ApplyAoEDamage function, 117
ApplyDamage(), 90, 455, 457, 537, 603, 605, 607, 818
ApplyDamage(float Damage), 817
ApplyDirectionalInfluence function, 133
ApplyDynamicPushback function, 142

INDEX

ApplyFluidDynamics, 375, 376
ApplyForces(), 49, 571, 573, 598, 600
ApplyForceToObjects(), 622
ApplyGravity(), 615, 617
ApplyItemEffect(), 78, 162
ApplyKnockback function, 128
ApplyNoise, 369
ApplyPhysicsForces function, 185
ApplyPushback function, 139
ApplyTexture method, 390, 391
ApplyWeatherEffect function, 59
ApplyWeatherSettings(), 335
APuzzleElement class, 306
APuzzleInteraction class, 310
Arcane damage, 533
Area-of-effect (AoE), 86
   advanced techniques, 115, 121, 123–125
   algorithm, 116
   attacks, 478
   code reviewing, 116–120
   multiple targets, 114
   practical applications, 115
   usage, 114
Arena layout, 843
ArenaSetup, 840
ArenaWalls, 840
Armor resistance, 534
ARObjectClass, 802
Artificial intelligence (AI), 875
   awareness states, 437
   code reviewing, 755–758
   companion and stealth, 692–703

   decision trees, 709–714
   definition, 673
   dynamic response, 703–709
   enemy patrols and combat, 684–692
   entities, 754
   features, 754
   importance, 754
   movement, 674–678
   NPC navigation, 673
   state machines, 719–724
   state management, 438
   state switching, 440
   variety, 685
Asset loading and path issues, 790, 869
Asset optimization, 807
AssignTeams(), 744, 746
AssistInCombat(), 694, 696
AStealthCharacter, 440
ASwimmingCharacter, 426
Atmosphere, 631, 659, 663, 853
ATradeableItem class, 319, 320
ATradingSystem class, 321
AttachToComponent(), 798
AttackDamage, 447
Attack types, 477
Attraction, 620
Audio cues, 377
Audio feedback, 515, 520
Audio triggers, 627
Augmented reality (AR) mechanics
   code reviewing, 801, 803–805
   components, 801

INDEX

Augmented reality (AR)
  mechanics (*cont.*)
    importance, 800, 801
    virtual objects, 800
Authority management, 733
AvailableSkills, 464
Avoidance, 715
AVRInteractionManager, 796
AWeatherManager class, 332

B

Base textures, 388
Basic AI movement
  code reviewing, 675, 676, 678
  components, 674
  example, 678
  importance, 674
  navigation systems, 674
  tasks, 674
Battle royale, 743
bCanAttack, 505
bCanClimb, 433
bCanEvade, 505
BeginPlay function, 5, 7, 8, 12, 18, 36, 46, 57, 67, 74, 110, 117, 139, 149, 152, 160, 170, 210, 229, 269, 306, 310, 315, 320, 326, 362, 746, 783, 808
Behavioral clarity, 720
Behavioral states, 693
Behavior trees, 503, 509–512
Binary space partitioning (BSP), 875

Biomes, 367
bIsActive, 23, 352
bIsArmed, 233, 234
bIsCrouching, 416
bIsDestroyed, 603
bIsGrounded, 411
bIsInAttackRange, 838
bIsInteractable, 34
bIsLocked, 220
bIsPlayerNearby, 260, 267
bIsProne, 421
bIsPuzzleSolved
  Boolean, 310, 314
Block(), 480
BlockAttack(), 448
Blockchain, 825
Blocking, 477, 516
Blocking movement
  advanced techniques, 3
  algorithm, 3, 4
  code reviewing, 4
  maze configuration, 5–8
  player collision configuration, 8, 10, 11
  practical applications, 3
  restrictions, 11–15
  spatial navigation, 2
  usage, 2
Blogs, 873
BloomIntensity, 647, 648
Blueprint, 875
  advanced scripting techniques, 820
  C++ integration, 817

INDEX

compilation issues, 867, 868
BlueprintAssignable, 863
BlueprintCallable, 863–865
BlueprintGetter, 864
BlueprintImplementableEvent, 864
BlueprintNativeEvent, 864
BlueprintPure, 864, 865
BlueprintReadOnly, 864
BlueprintReadWrite, 89, 786, 864
Boolean, 865
Boss arena, 840–842
Boss battles, 115, 127
Boss fight, 476
    components, 836, 837
    creating arena, 840–842
    definition, 549
    description, 835
    elements, 551, 552
    importance, 836
    types, 549, 550
BossMusic, 633
Box/sphere collision, 513
bPlayerInRange, 505
bPlayerInSight, 711
bPlayerTooClose, 711
Braking system, 591
Branches, 460, 710
BranchingChoices, 253, 255
BranchingDialogueSystem
    class, 253
Branching paths, 461
BranchQuest function, 291
Breath management, 423
BuildStructure function, 181

Build systems, 812
Built-in subsystem voice, 774
Buoyancy simulation, 373
Button animations, 651

C

C++, 876
    best practices, 865
    compiler errors, 866, 867
    integration, 817
    syntax
        data types, 865
        UFUNCTION
            specifiers, 864
        UPROPERTY specifiers, 863
CalculateDamage function, 90
CalculatePath(), 681
CameraActor, 239
Capsule trace, 514
Capture the flag (CTF), 743
Casting spells, 494
CastSpell(), 498, 499
CategorizedInventory map, 280
CategorizeItems function, 280, 282
Celestial body movement, 343
Celestial movement, 341
Centralized game logic, 765
ChainReactionComponent
    class, 152
ChangeMusicState(), 633, 635
ChangeState() function, 267, 270,
    505, 507, 721, 722
ChangeWeatherToFoggy(), 336

INDEX

ChangeWeatherToRainy(), 333, 336
ChangeWeatherToStormy(), 336
ChangeWeatherToSunny(),
    333, 336
Channel management, 774
Chaos destruction, 121
Chaos destruction system, 606–608
Character animation, 569
Character clothing, 586
Character customization
    advanced, 468, 469
    algorithm, 470
    code reviewing, 470–473
    features, 467
    in-game avatars, 467
    practical applications, 469
Character development, 238, 248
Character knockback
    advanced techniques, 126, 132,
        134, 135
    algorithm, 127
    code reviewing, 128–131
    environmental forces, 125
    melee attacks, 125
    practical applications, 126
    usage, 125, 126
Character movement
    advanced techniques, 401, 402
    algorithm, 402
    code reviewing, 403–406, 408
    definition, 400
    practical applications, 402
    usage, 401
Character pushback
    advanced techniques,
        137, 142–145
    algorithm, 138
    code reviewing, 139, 140, 142
    intentional/environmental
        interactions, 136
    practical applications, 137
    usage, 136
Character respawn
    advanced techniques,
        168, 173–177
    algorithm, 169
    code reviewing, 170–173
    description, 167
    practical applications, 168
    usage, 167
Character traits/affinities, 462
Charged jump, 409
Chat functionality, 749
Cheat prevention, 765
CheckBossDefeat(), 552, 554
CheckForEnemies(), 440, 442
CheckForInteractableObjects
    function, 37, 38
CheckGroundStatus(), 411, 412
CheckProximity function, 260, 263,
    267, 269
CheckPuzzleCondition function,
    310, 312
CheckTriggerDistance(), 627
Client-server model, 729
Climbing mechanics
    advanced techniques, 431, 432
    algorithm, 432

INDEX

code reviewing, 433–436
implementation, 431
integration, 430
practical applications, 432
ClimbSpeed, 433
ClothEdges, 587
Cloth simulation
   advanced techniques, 585
   algorithm, 586
   code reviewing, 587–590
   components, 584
   game physics, 584
   goal, 584
   practical applications, 586
ClothVertices, 587
Cloud gaming, 825
Code profiling, 807
Collaboration, 737
CollectibleItem class, 74
Collision detection, 4, 46, 65, 73,
      96, 104, 188, 190, 197, 200,
      207, 210, 258, 372, 393, 403,
      410, 562, 563, 565, 568, 569,
      577, 587, 597
Collision mechanics
   AoE, 114–125
   blocking, 2
   character knockback, 125–135
   character pushback, 136–145
   character respawn, 167–177
   damage calculation,
      86–94, 155–166
   environmental effects, 54–63
   functionality, 1

game interactivity, 1
   hit detection, 63–71
   interaction detection, 30–44
   item collection, 72–82
   object destruction, 146–155
   object detection, 85
   object rotation, 197–207
   object scaling, 187–197
   particle effects, 207–216
   physics reactions, 44–54
   platforming, 102–113
   projectile deflection, 94–102
   terrain deformation, 177–187
   triggering events, 15–30
   visual effects, 86
Collision resolution, 4
CollisionSphere, 74, 76
ColorGrading, 647, 649
Color over lifetime, 577
Combat AI, 686
   and adaptation, 504
   behavior tree, 509–512
   code reviewing, 504, 506–509
   components, 502
   decision-making, 502, 503
   pathfinding and movement,
      503, 504
Combat dynamics, 126
Combat mechanics, 189, 837
   action-oriented games, 444, 475
   advanced techniques, 445
   AI (*see* Combat AI)
   algorithm, 446, 447
   boss fights, 549–556

889

INDEX

Combat mechanics (*cont.*)
    code reviewing, 447–451
    complexity, 476
    components, 475
    damage types and
        resistances, 531–539
    enemy spawning, 539–548
    essentials, 444
    hit detection and
        response, 512–518
    magic and spells (*see* Magic
        systems)
    melee (*see* Melee combat)
    practical applications, 446
    ranged, 485–494
    special and finishing
        moves, 524–531
CombatMusic, 633
Combat states, 685
Combat support, 693
Combat systems, 115
Combo breaker system, 521
Combo chains, 445
ComboSequence, 521
Combo spells, 495
Combo systems, 477
    action-oriented games, 518
    balancing, 523, 524
    bonuses, 518
    code reviewing, 521–523
    counters, 519
    designing, 520, 521
    elements, 519, 520
    timing, 519

    variations, 520
Command validation, 765
Communication, 637
Community engagement, 790
Community tutorials, 873
Companion and stealth AI systems
    code reviewing, 694, 695, 697,
        698, 700–703
    components, 693, 694
    crafting gameplay
        experiences, 692
    importance, 693
Competition, 737
Competitive balance, 843
Competitive gameplay, 168
Compiler errors, 866, 867
Complete game level
    code reviewing, 833–835
    components, 832
    creation, 832
    importance, 832
CompleteMiniGame function, 298
CompleteQuest() function, 288,
    849, 851
ComplexInteractionSystem
    class, 40
Complexity management, 720
Component, 876
Compression, 569, 584
CompressionSettings = TC_
    Default, 809
Conditional collection, 73
ConfigureInputSettings(), 813
Conflict resolution, 738, 765

INDEX

Console/platform voice services, 775
Constraints, 597
Constructor, 20, 24, 28, 369, 374, 375, 379, 380, 385, 386, 390, 391, 396
ConsumeStamina(), 455, 457
Contextual actions, 694
Contextual effects, 659
Control schemes, 812
Cooldown, 497
Cooperative modes, 744
Counterattacks, 478
Cover detection, 440
Cover system, 437, 487
Crafting, 274
CreateDefaultSubobject, 6, 10, 14, 24, 34, 221, 230, 308
CreateSaveGameObject(), 787
Critical hits, 92
Cross-platform compatibility, 769, 774
Cross-platform development
   code reviewing, 812–815
   components, 812
   description, 811
   importance, 811
Crouching
   code implementation, 416–420
   definition, 415
   practical applications, 415
   structure, 416
CrouchSpeed, 416
CurrentAmmo, 489

CurrentDialogueIndex, 250
CurrentHealth, 455
CurrentMana, 497
CurrentMusicState, 633, 635
CurrentStamina, 455
CurrentState, 267, 721, 723
CurrentTime, 360
CurrentWeather, 855
CurrentWeatherState, 333
Custom collision channels, 70
Custom game systems, 816
Customization, 495, 654, 816
Custom match preferences, 769
Custom plugin development, 821
Custom shaders, 578
Custom WebRTC, 774
Cutscenes
   advanced techniques, 237, 243–247
   algorithm, 238
   cinematic techniques, 237
   class, 239
   code reviewing, 239–243
   execution, 238
   practical applications, 238
   scripted events, 237
   usage, 237

D

Damage calculation, 86
   advanced techniques, 87, 92, 94
   algorithm, 88
   code reviewing, 88, 90

INDEX

Damage calculation (*cont.*)
   description, 86
   implementation, 90, 92
   practical applications, 87
   usage, 87
Damage event
      implementation, 117
Damage over time (DoT), 115
DamagePerSecond, 352
Damage system, 351, 592
DamageThreshold, 603
DamageType enum, 537
Damage types
   balancing, 535, 536
   categorization, 532, 533
   code reviewing, 537–539
   definition, 532
   enemies/enemy attributes, 533, 534
Damping, 568, 571, 573, 585
Data customization, 786
DayLength, 360
Day-night cycle, 61, 357, 383
   advanced techniques, 341
   algorithm, 343
   code reviewing, 343–349
   practical applications, 342
   transitions, 340
   usage, 341
DeactivateRespawnPoint
      function, 174
Death penalties, 167
Debugging, 812
Deceleration, 401

Decision-making, 502, 503, 710, 720, 754
Decision trees
   code reviewing, 711–713
   components, 710
   definition, 709
   example, 714
   importance, 710
DefaultAmbience, 665, 666
DefaultDialogue, 659
Deformation, 568, 569
Delegate, 876
Delta time adjustments, 733
DestroyObject() function, 149, 603, 605
Destructible environments
   chaos and fracture, 606–608
   code reviewing, 603–606
   components, 603
   header file, 605
   importance, 602
   runtime behavior, 605
DestructibleObject class, 149
Destructor, 379, 380
Detail textures, 388
DetectARPlanes(), 802
DetectedPlanes, 802, 804
DetectionSphere, 698
DetectPlatform(), 812
DetectPlayer(), 705, 706
Dialogue/behavior system, 470
DialogueChoices, 243, 245, 250
Dialogues, 239, 249, 260, 267
Dialogue sound effects

INDEX

audio design, 658
    code reviewing, 659, 660, 662
    components, 659
    importance, 658
DialogueSystem class, 249
Dialogue systems
    advanced techniques, 248, 253, 255-257
    algorithm, 248, 249
    code reviewing, 249-251, 253
    linear, 247
    practical applications, 248
    usage, 247
Diamond-square algorithm, 368
DigTerrain function, 181
Dijkstra's algorithm, 715
Directional gravity, 615
DirectionalInfluenceComponent class, 133
Directional influence (DI), 132
DisableMovement(), 53
Discord community, 873
DisplayDialogue function, 250, 251
Dissipation, 669
Distraction tools, 437
Dodge(), 448
Door class, 220
DoorTrigger class, 11, 12
DOREPLIFETIME, 756
Double jump, 409
DrawHealthBar(), 655, 657
DrawHUD(), 657
Draw method, 385, 386
DrawRect(), 657
DrawScore(), 655, 657
DrawText(), 657
Drift and skid mechanics, 591
Dynamic AI response systems
    code reviewing, 705-709
    components, 704
    importance, 704
    player's actions, 703
Dynamic camera movement, 643
Dynamic events, 26-30
Dynamic fracturing, 603
Dynamic gameplay, 737
Dynamic lighting
    advanced techniques, 358
    algorithms, 359, 360
    code reviewing, 360, 362, 364-366
    practical applications, 359
    usage, 357
    visual fidelity, 357
DynamicLighting class, 61, 62
Dynamic loading, 876
DynamicMaterial, 638, 640
Dynamic memory management, 816
Dynamic mixing, 379
Dynamic music systems, 625
    code reviewing, 633-637
    components, 632
    importance, 631, 632
    soundtrack, 631
Dynamic obstacle avoidance, 680
DynamicPushbackComponent class, 142

INDEX

Dynamic puzzles, 304
Dynamic queues, 769
Dynamic shadowing, 358
Dynamic skyboxes
    advanced techniques, 383
    algorithms, 384
    code reviewing, 384, 386–388
    description, 382
    practical applications, 384
    usage, 382
Dynamic soundscapes, 378
Dynamic spawning, 157, 541
Dynamic transitions, 432
Dynamic weather systems, 342
    advanced techniques, 331
    algorithm, 332
    code reviewing,
        332–340, 854–858
    components, 854
    effects, 350
    implementation, 330
    importance, 853
    patterns, 853
    practical applications, 331
    usage, 330

E

Ecosystems, 367
EditAnywhere, 89, 876
Elasticity, 568
Electric damage, 532, 534
Elemental magic, 495
Elemental resistances, 534

Emission rate, 577
EmitParticle(), 580, 581
Emotional impact, 631
Emotion cues, 659
Emotion simulation, 704
EnableFramerateSmoothing(), 807
EndBossFight(), 552, 554
EndCrouch(), 416, 418
EndCutscene function, 240, 241
EndDialogue
    function, 250, 251
Endgame boss fights, 549
EndInteraction function, 260, 263,
    267, 270
EndProne(), 421
EndStun function, 128
Enemy patrols and combat
    behaviors
    code reviewing, 686,
        688–690, 692
    components, 685, 686
    example, 692
    game AI, 684
    importance, 685
Enemy spawning
    balancing, 543, 544
    code reviewing, 544–548
    definition, 539
    factors, 542, 543
    frequency, 543
    location, 544
    types, 540, 541
Energy dissipation, 573
EnergyMeter, 529

EnforceConstraints(), 598, 600
EngageCombat(), 686, 688
ENPCInteractionType, 260
ENPCState enum, 267
EnterStealthMode(), 440, 442
Environmental ambience
   audio settings and features, 664
   code reviewing, 664–667
   components, 663
   description, 662
   importance, 663
Environmental boss fights, 550
Environmental context, 663
Environmental effects
   advanced techniques, 55
   algorithm, 55, 56
   code reviewing, 56–58
   components, 61
   handling interactions, 60
   implementation, 62, 63
   natural phenomena, 54
   practical applications, 55
   predefined conditions, 59
   usage, 54
Environmental hazards, 115, 127, 138
   advanced techniques, 350, 351
   algorithm, 351
   code reviewing, 352, 354, 355, 357
   definition, 349
   practical applications, 351
   usage, 350
EnvironmentalInteraction Component class, 121
Environmental interactions, 105, 146, 357, 487, 570, 592, 704
Environmental mechanics
   complexity, 330
   day-night cycle, 340–349
   description, 329
   dynamic lighting, 357–366
   dynamic skyboxes, 382–388
   dynamic weather systems, 330–340
   hazards (*see* Environmental hazards)
   interactive foliage, 392–397
   sound effects, 377–382
   terrain generation, 366–372
   terrain texturing, 388–392
   water and fluid dynamics, 372–377
Environmental sound effects
   advanced techniques, 378
   algorithms, 379
   code reviewing, 379–381
   creation, 377
   immersive experience, 382
   practical applications, 378
   usage, 377
Environmental storytelling, 668
Environment creation, 832
Environment design, 837
Equipment system, 470
ErodeTerrain, 369
Erosion, 178

INDEX

Erosion simulation, 367
Errors
    asset loading and path issues, 869
    Blueprint compilation issues, 867, 868
    compiler, 866, 867
    miscellaneous, 870
    network and replication issues, 869
    runtime, 868
EstablishConnection(), 729–731
Event, 876
EventChain class, 26
Event detection, 627
Event-driven programming, 817
Event handling, 352, 754
Event replication, 738
EventSequence array, 27
Event sounds, 377
Event synchronization, 744
EventTimerHandle, 27
EWeatherState enum, 333
ExecuteEvent function, 27, 28
ExecuteInteraction function, 260, 263, 267, 269
ExecuteSpecialMove, 529
ExecuteTask(), 510
Executions, *see* Finishing moves
ExitStealthMode(), 440, 442
Exploration, 104
Exploration games, 425
ExplorationMusic, 633
Extrapolation, 759

F

Fatalities, *see* Finishing moves
Fatigue system, 453
FCharacterStats struct, 89
Feedback mechanism, 650
Field of view (FOV) adjustment, 643
FieldRadius, 620, 622
Fighting games, 410, 446, 469, 479
File management, 786
FindItem function, 275, 277
FindMiniGame function, 296, 298
FindOptimizedPath(), 716
FindPath(), 684
FindQuest function, 286, 288
Finishing moves
    characteristics, 527
    code reviewing, 529–531
    definition, 526
    designing, 528
    gameplay and narrative purposes, 526
Finite element method (FEM), 570
Finite state machines (FSMs), 502–504
FInventoryItem struct, 275
Fire damage, 532, 533
FireRate, 489
FireWeapon(), 489, 491
First-person shooters (FPS), 389, 415, 469, 488

INDEX

Fluid dynamics, 559
    code reviewing, 610, 612–614
    components, 609
    importance, 609
    liquids and gases, 609
Fluid simulation, 374
FMiniGame struct, 295
FNode, 597
Foliage, 877
FollowPlayer(), 694, 695
FOnDamageTaken Delegate, 817
Force application system, 564
Force fields
    code reviewing, 620, 622, 624
    components, 620
    importance, 619
Forces, 562, 597
ForceStrength, 620, 622
FPaths::FileExists(), 792
FPlayerSnapshot, 760
FQuest struct, 286
Frame rate management, 806
Frequency, 643, 645
Friction, 563, 573, 585
FStreamableManager
    ::LoadSynchronous(), 792
FTimerHandle, 661
Future trends, game development
    code reviewing, 825–828
    components, 825
    experiences, 824
    importance, 824
FVector, 877
FVector::Dist(), 827

G

GameMode, 877
Game mode diversity, 169
Game mode rules, 744
Gameplay effects, 188
Gameplay feedback, 626
Gameplay mechanics, 854, 877
Gameplay triggers, 832
Game settings, 749
GenerateTerrain(), 369, 781, 782
GenerateWaves, 374, 376
GEngine->AddOnScreen
    DebugMessage(), 775, 776
GetAllTrackedPlanes(), 803
GetDirectionalLight(), 336, 362
GetGeometryCollection
    Component(), 607
GetHeightmap, 369
GetLifetime
    ReplicatedProps(), 735
GetRandomSpawn
    Location(), 545
GetReflectionVector, 99
GetVehicleMovement
    Component(), 595
GetWorld()->SpawnActor(), 845
GitHub repositories, 873
Global gravity changes, 615
Global illumination, 358
GlowColor, 640
GrabbedObject, 796
GrabObject(), 796, 797
Graphics scalability, 812

897

INDEX

Gravity, 401, 408, 424, 565, 577
GravityDirection, 615, 617
Gravity force, 589
Gravity manipulation
    code reviewing, 615, 617–619
    components, 615
GravityStrength, 587, 615
Ground check system, 410

H

Hack-and-slash games, 479
HandleBranchingChoice function, 253, 255
HandleCombat function, 263
HandleDialogueFinished(), 659, 661
HandleDialogue function, 263
HandleInteraction function, 41
HandlePlayerChoice function, 243, 245, 250, 251
HandleQuest function, 263
HandleTrade function, 263
HasAuthority(), 766
HasKey function, 225
Heads-up displays (HUDs), 877
    animations, 651
    code reviewing, 655, 656, 658
    components, 655
    importance, 654
    user interface, 654
Head tracking, 795
Health and stamina systems
    advanced techniques, 452, 453

    algorithm, 454
    character's survivability, 451
    code reviewing, 454–459
    practical applications, 453
    usage, 452
HealthBarColor, 655
HealthBarPosition, 655
HealthBarSize, 655
HeavyAttack(), 480, 482
Height-based texture blending, 389
Heightmap generation algorithms, 368
Heuristic(), 680, 681
Hierarchical pathfinding, 715
HighlightIntensity, 640
HighlightObject(), 638, 640
Hit detection
    action-oriented games, 63
    advanced techniques, 64, 69–71
    algorithm, 64, 65
    code reviewing, 65, 516–518
    definition, 512
    features, 512
    implementation, 69, 514
    parrying and blocking, 515, 516
    practical applications, 64
    raycasting, 513
    response and feedback, 515
    setting up, 65–68
    usage, 63
HitDetection class, 65
Hit registration, 759
Horror games, 351, 359, 378, 439
Hotkeys, 862, 863, 877

INDEX

I

Ice damage, 532, 533
Immersion, 559, 626, 632, 637, 642, 654, 658, 663, 679, 685, 693, 704, 732, 737, 754, 853
Immunities, 535
IModuleInterface, 821
IMPLEMENT_MODULE, 822
Inertia, 562
Infinite content, 780
Instance, 878
Interact function, 260, 263, 267, 269
Interaction detection
    advanced techniques, 31
    algorithm, 32
    code reviewing, 32–35
    mechanism, 30
    player interactions, 36–40
    practical applications, 31
    response, 40, 41
    types, 42–44
    usage, 31
    use cases, 41
InteractionRadius, 260, 267
Interaction range, 738
Interaction systems, 795, 801
InteractionType::Activate, 42
InteractionType::PickUp, 42
InteractionType::Talk, 42
InteractiveCutscene class, 243
Interactive foliage
    advanced techniques, 393
    algorithm, 394
    code reviewing, 395–397
    environmental factors, 392
    practical applications, 394
    usage, 393
InteractiveFoliage class, 395
Interactive hazards, 351
InteractiveObject class, 22, 32
Interface, 878
Interior/exterior sound zones, 664
Interpolation, 384, 732, 759
Inventory array, 275
InventoryComponent class, 81
Inventory management, 158
InventoryManagement class, 162
Inventory Structure (FInventoryItem), 162
Inventory system, 72
    advanced techniques, 273, 279–283
    algorithm, 274
    code reviewing, 275, 277–279
    definition, 273
    items, 273
    practical applications, 274
    usage, 273
InventorySystem class, 275
Item collection
    advanced techniques, 72, 80, 82
    algorithm, 73
    code reviewing, 74, 76, 77
    implementation, 78–80
    practical applications, 73
    usage, 72
    weapons and power-ups, 72

INDEX

ItemName, 319
ItemValue, 319

J

JumpAction function, 105
JumpHeight, 411
Jumping mechanics
    advanced techniques, 409
    algorithm, 410
    code reviewing, 410–414
    complexity, 408
    components, 408
    practical applications, 409
Just-in-time (JIT) compilation, 878

K

Kismet, 878
KnockbackComponent class, 128
Knockbacks, 445, 478

L

Lag compensation
    code reviewing, 759–762, 764
    definition, 758
    features, 759
    importance, 759
Language filters, 774
Latency, 729, 738, 769
LaunchCharacter, 112, 128
Laws of physics, 560
Layering textures, 388

Leaf nodes, 710
Ledge grabbing, 431
Lerp (linear interpolation), 878
Level design, 103
Level streaming, 806, 878
LightAttack(), 480, 482
Lighting adjustments, 343
Lighting interpolation, 359
Light source management, 359
Line of sight, 438, 685
LineOfSightRange, 440
Line trace, 513
LineTraceSingleByChannel, 69, 798
Links, 597
Lip-synchronization, 659
LoadAsset(FString AssetPath), 791
LoadGameFromSlot(), 788
LoadLevelAssets(), 833, 834
LoadModFromPath(FString
    ModPath), 791
LoadSound method, 379, 380
Lobby systems
    code reviewing, 749, 751, 753
    example, 753
    features, 749
    importance, 748
    multiplayer games, 748
Longevity, 790
Long-term viability, 824

M

Magical artifacts, 496
Magical damage, 533

INDEX

Magical resistances, 535
Magic resource management, 495
Magic systems
    algorithm, 497
    code reviewing, 497–501
    effects, 494
    elements, 494, 495
    features, 495, 496
    implementation, 494
    practical applications, 496
MakeDecision(), 711, 712
Mana/resource system, 497
Marching cubes
        algorithm, 369
Market demands, 824
Masses, 565, 571, 573
Matchmaking systems
    code reviewing, 769–772
    description, 768
    example, 772, 773
    factors, 768
    features, 769
    importance, 768
Material properties, 563, 569
MaxAmmo, 489
MaxBreathTime, 426
MaxHealth, 455
MaxMana, 497
MaxParticles, 579, 610
MaxStamina, 455, 480
MazeWall class, 5
MazeWall property, 5
Melee combat
    action and RPG genres, 477
    advanced techniques, 478
    algorithm, 479, 480
    code reviewing, 480–485
    elements, 477
    goal, 477
    practical applications, 479
Mental resistances, 535
Menu transitions, 651
Mesh, 879
Metaverse, 825
Middleware integration, 821
MiniGameDifficulties map, 301
MiniGameRewards map, 301
Mini-games
    advanced techniques,
        294, 300–304
    algorithm, 294
    code reviewing, 295–300
    completion, 295
    description, 293
    initiation, 295
    practical applications, 294
    state management, 295
    usage, 293
MiniGames array, 296
MiniGameSystem class, 296
Mini-maps, 655
MipGenSettings = TMGS_
    NoMipmaps, 809
Miscellaneous errors, 870
Modding framework, 790
Modding support
    code reviewing, 791, 792, 794
    components, 790

Modding support (cont.)
  importance, 790
  robust systems, 790
Modular assets, 781
Momentum, 562
Motion blur, 643, 647
MotionController, 796
Motion controllers, 795
Motion warping, 451
MOVE_Flying, 435
MoveForward() function, 105, 403, 405, 593, 594
Movement-based enhancements, 487
Movement blocking, see Blocking movement
Movement control, 426
Movement restriction, 431
MoveRight() function, 105, 403, 405
MoveToActor(), 509, 838
MoveToLocation(), 694, 696
MoveToNextPatrolPoint(), 686, 688
MoveToTarget(), 675, 676
Multi-branch specializations, 461
Multicast_PlayInteractionEffect(), 739, 741, 742
Multicast RPCs, 738
Multilayered effects, 208
Multi-phase boss fights, 550
Multi-phase mechanics, 836
Multiplayer, 879
Multiplayer arena
  code reviewing, 844–846, 848
  components, 843
  creation, 842
  importance, 843
Multiplayer game modes
  code reviewing, 745, 747
  definition, 743
  elements, 744
  example, 748
  types, 743
Multiplayer integration, 157
Multiplayer online games (MMOs), 496
Multiplayer synchronization, 189, 199
Multiplayer systems
  game modes, 743–748
  lag compensation, 758–764
  lobby systems, 748–753
  matchmaking, 768–773
  server authority, 764–768
  voice and text chat, 773–778
Multiple lives systems, 168
Mumble integration, 774
Music layers, 632
Music states, 632
Mute/block options, 774

N

Natural disasters, 350
Navier-Stokes equations, 373, 609
Navigation meshes (NavMesh), 674, 679, 715
NavSystem, 716

NavSystem->FindPathToLocation
    Synchronously(), 717
NetCode, 879
Network and replication
    issues, 869
Networked player interactions
    code reviewing, 739-741
    components, 738
    description, 737
    example, 742
    importance, 737
    RPCs and proxies, 738, 739
Networking
    AI, 754-758
    code reviewing, 729, 730
    components, 729
    description, 727
    example, 731
    importance, 728
    player interactions, 737-742
    player synchronization, 732-737
    social and interactive
        gameplay, 727
Neural interfaces, 825
NFTs, 825
NightLength, 360
NodeMass, 597
Nodes, 460, 597, 710
Noise functions, 367, 780
NoiseScale, 781
Non-playable characters (NPCs),
    41, 849, 879
Non-player characters (NPCs), 284,
    673, 678

advanced techniques,
    258, 266-272
algorithm, 259
code reviewing, 259-266
interactions, 257
practical applications, 258
usage, 258
NotifyHit function, 50
NPCSystem class, 259
NumNodes, 597

O

Object destruction
    advanced techniques, 147, 152,
        154, 155
    algorithm, 148
    code reviewing, 149-152
    practical applications, 147
    triggers, 146
    usage, 146
Objective-based modes, 744
Objective management, 744
ObjectMesh, 22, 34, 47
Object-oriented programming
    (OOP), 879
Object pickup
    advanced techniques, 156,
        162, 164-166
    algorithm, 158
    code reviewing, 158-161
    description, 155
    practical applications, 157
    usage, 156

INDEX

Object rotation
  advanced techniques, 198, 199, 204–207
  algorithm, 200
  code reviewing, 201, 203, 204
  collision events, 197
  practical applications, 199, 200
  usage, 197, 198
Object scaling
  advanced techniques, 188, 194–197
  algorithm, 190, 191
  code reviewing, 191, 192, 194
  collision events, 187
  practical applications, 189
  usage, 188
Object-specific gravity, 615
OnComponentBeginOverlap, 20, 66, 222, 225, 231, 234
OnDamageTaken, 817
OnDamageTaken.Broadcast(Damage), 818
OnHit function, 97, 99, 100
OnInteract function, 33, 37, 38, 306, 308
Online communities, 874
Online learning platforms, 872
OnObjectCollision function, 191, 201, 211
OnOverlapBegin function, 12, 18, 67, 74, 76, 78, 220, 222, 229, 231
OnOverlapEnd function, 12, 18

OnPlayerEnter() function, 60, 352, 354, 629
OnPlayerEnterRange(), 698
OnPlayerExit(), 352, 354
OnPlayerInteraction function, 313, 315
OnPlayerPickup function, 160
OnRep_AIActorLocation(), 755, 756
OnTargetPerceived(), 686, 688
Opening doors
  advanced techniques, 218, 223, 225–227
  algorithm, 219
  code reviewing, 220–223
  practical applications, 219
  triggers, 218
  usage, 218
Open-world games, 331, 342, 368, 384, 389, 402, 409, 425, 592
OptimizeTextureSettings(), 807
Overloading, 879
Ownership management, 738

P

Packets, 729
Parrying, 477, 516
Particle attractors, 577
Particle-based methods, 570
Particle-based simulation, 609
Particle effect binding, 78
ParticleEffect function, 669, 670
Particle effects

INDEX

advanced techniques, 208, 213–216
algorithm, 209, 210
code reviewing, 210–213, 669, 670
components, 668
example, 671
gameplay immersion, 207
gameplay mechanics, 668
importance, 668
practical applications, 209
usage, 207, 208
Particle emission, 210
Particle emitter, 579
ParticleLifetime, 579
ParticleRadius, 610
Particle renderer, 579
Particle systems, 208, 373
    advanced techniques, 577, 578
    algorithms, 579
    code reviewing, 579–583
    dynamic visual effects, 576
    parameters, 576
    practical applications, 578
    usage, 577
Particle update loop, 579
ParticleVelocity, 579
Passive abilities, 461
Pathfinding, 754, 880
    algorithms, 675, 715
    code reviewing, 680–683
    companions, 693
    components, 679
    definition, 673

example, 684
hierarchical, 715
importance, 679
and movement, 503, 504
and navigation, 502
NPCs, 678
optimization
    code reviewing, 716–719
    components, 715
    example, 719
    gameplay performance, 714
    importance, 714, 715
Path smoothing, 680
Patrol routes, 685
Peer-to-peer (P2P) networking, 729
Penetrable surface check, 100
Perception systems, 704
Performance monitoring, 821
Performance optimization, 208, 210, 603, 609, 795, 801, 816, 843
    code reviewing, 807–809, 811
    components, 806
    importance, 806
    resource-intensive games, 806
PerformAttack(), 447, 837, 838
PerformJump(), 411, 412
PerformRaycast function, 69
Perlin noise, 368
PerlinNoise2D(), 783
Photorealistic graphics, 825
Physical damage, 532
Physics-based puzzles, 560, 570
PhysicsConstraint, 47

INDEX

Physics-driven collision responses, 85
Physics engine, 564
Physics integration, 603
Physics reactions
    advanced techniques, 45
    algorithm, 46
    applying forces, 49, 50
    code reviewing, 46–48
    components, 53, 54
    definition, 44
    handling collisions, 50–52
    practical applications, 45
    usage, 45
Physics simulations, 137, 179, 181, 189, 199, 394
Physics systems, 410
    applications, 560, 561
    complexity, 560
    genres and gameplay scenarios, 560
    realistic movements, 560
    simulations, 559
PickupItem class, 158, 160
Ping, 729
Pitch control, 627
Pixel-perfect collision detection, 64
Pixel-perfect detection, 512
Pixel shader, 880
PlacePowerUps(), 844, 845
Platformers, 402, 409, 415, 432, 561, 564
Platforming mechanics, 86
    advanced techniques, 103, 112, 113
    algorithm, 104, 105
    code reviewing, 105, 107–109
    genres, 102
    implementation, 110, 111
    practical applications, 103, 104
    usage, 102, 103
Platform logging, 814
Platform-specific features, 812
PlayAmbience(), 664, 666
PlayAnimation(), 653
PlayButtonHoverAnimation(), 652, 653
PlayDialogue() function, 240, 241, 659, 661
PlayerCameraManager, 645
PlayerCapsule, 9
PlayerCharacter class, 8, 36, 105, 420–423
Player-driven environments, 179
PlayerLocation, 786, 787
PlayerPosition, 733
Player progression, 837
PlayerQueue, 770
Player retention, 169
PlayerRotation, 733, 786, 787
PlayerScore, 786, 787
PlayerSnapshots, 760
PlayersPerMatch, 770
Player synchronization
    code reviewing, 733, 735, 736
    components, 732
    description, 732

INDEX

example, 736
importance, 732
Player team assignment, 744
PlayMusic(), 633, 635
PlayNotificationAnimation(), 652, 653
PlaySoundAtTrigger(), 627, 629
PlaySound method, 379, 381
Plugin and middleware integration
    code reviewing, 821–823
    components, 821
    FMOD audio, 823
    importance, 820
    prebuilt features, 820
Plugin installation, 821
Poison damage, 532
Poison resistance, 535
Positional strategy, 126
PostProcessComponent, 647, 648
Post-processing effects
    aesthetics, 646
    code reviewing, 647–650
    components, 646
    overlays, 643
PowerUpLocations, 844
Predictable transitions, 720
Prediction, 732
Prerequisites, 460
PrimaryActorTick, 834, 841
PrimaryActorTick.bCanEverTick, 34, 38
Procedural algorithms, 188, 198
Procedural animation, 393

Procedural content generation (PCG) plugin, 784
Procedural generation, 55, 369, 389
    code reviewing, 781–783, 785
    components, 780
    description, 780
    importance, 780
ProceduralRotation class, 205
ProceduralScaling class, 195
ProcessHit function, 69
Projectile class, 97
Projectile deflection, 86
    advanced techniques, 95, 100–102
    algorithm, 96
    code reviewing, 96, 98
    definition, 94
    logic implementation, 99, 100
    practical applications, 95
    usage, 95
Projectile system, 488
Prone mechanics
    definition, 415
    PlayerCharacter class extensions, 420–423
    practical applications, 415
    structure, 416
ProneSpeed, 421
Protocols, 729
Proxies, 738, 739
Proximity triggers, 258
Psychic damage, 533
PushbackComponent class, 139
Puzzle elements, 311

INDEX

PuzzleElements array, 310
Puzzle games, 415, 560, 564, 570
Puzzle interaction, 309–312
PuzzleMesh component, 306, 313
Puzzle-solving mechanics, 104, 157
    advanced techniques, 304
    algorithm, 305
    code reviewing, 305–309
    implementation, 313–316
    interaction, 309–312
    logical thinking, 304
    practical applications, 305
    usage, 304

Q

Quaternions, 880
Quest activation
    advanced techniques, 284, 290–293
    algorithm, 285
    code reviewing, 285, 287–289
    practical applications, 284, 285
    story-driven missions, 283
    usage, 284
QuestDependencies map, 290
QuestProgress, 850
Quests, 258, 260, 267
Quest system
    code reviewing, 849, 851, 853
    components, 849
    description, 848
    importance, 848

QuestSystem class, 286
Quick-time event (QTE), 527

R

Racing games, 373, 561, 564, 592
Radial force, 121
Random spawns, 540
Ranged combat
    advanced techniques, 487
    advantages, 486
    algorithm, 488
    code reviewing, 489–494
    factors, 485
    features, 486
    practical applications, 488
    weapons, 485
Raycasting, 64, 69, 513, 516
Ray tracing, 825
ReactToThreat(), 705, 706
Realism, 329, 454, 596, 602, 609, 637, 704, 715
Realistic impulse reactions, 563
Realistic shadows, 341
Real-time information, 654
Recovery time, 125
Reddit, 874
Reflection, 373, 383
Refraction, 373, 383
RegenerateMana(), 498, 499
RegenerateStamina(), 455, 457, 480, 483
Regeneration mechanism, 452
ReleaseObject(), 796, 797

INDEX

ReloadWeapon(), 489, 491
Remote procedure calls (RPCs), 738, 739
RemoveItemFromInventory(), 162
RemoveItem function, 277
RemovePlayer(), 749, 751
RenderFoliage method, 395, 396
Rendering optimization, 807
Render method, 374, 376
RenderParticles(), 610, 612
Replayability, 780, 790, 843, 848, 854
Replicated specifier, 733
Replication, 754, 880
Repulsion, 620
RequiredKey, 223, 225
ResetTrap function, 233, 234
Resistances, 569
    balancing, 535, 536
    code reviewing, 537–539
    definition, 534
    types, 534, 535
Resource-intensive games, 806
Resource management, 480, 528
Resource recharge, 497
RespawnManager class, 173, 174
Respawn mechanics, 168
RespawnPlayer function, 170
RespawnPoint class, 170
Respawn timers, 167, 169
Response system, 565
ReturnToNormalState(), 705, 706
ReturnToPatrol(), 698
Reusability, 710
Reusing paths, 715

Revenue opportunities, 790
Reverb settings, 664
Rewards, 284, 294
Reward systems, 157
Rewind mechanics, 759
Rigid body, 880
Rigid body dynamics
    advanced techniques, 563
    algorithms, 564, 565
    code reviewing, 565–567
    components, 562
    concept, 561
    constraints, 562
    implementation, 561
    practical applications, 564
Role-playing games (RPGs), 247, 273, 284, 293, 384, 394, 462, 469, 488, 496, 578
Rope and chain physics
    code reviewing, 597–600, 602
    components, 597
    definition, 596
    importance, 596
RopeNodes, 598
RotateObject function, 201
Rotation mechanism, 198
RotationObject class, 201
Runtime errors, 868

S

Sample projects, 873
Sandbox environment, 791

INDEX

Save and load systems
    code reviewing, 786–789
    components, 786
    importance, 785
Save game class, 786
SaveGameToSlot(), 788
SaveKeyMappings(), 814
SavePlayerSnapshot(), 760, 761
ScaleObject function, 191
Scaling mechanism, 188
ScalingObject class, 191
Screen shakes and camera effects
    code reviewing, 643, 645, 646
    components, 643
    description, 642
    importance, 642
Scripted boss fights, 549
Scripted spawns, 540
Script execution, 791
SearchForPlayer(), 698
Self-collision, 585
SendMessageToAll(), 775, 776, 778
SendMessageToTeam(), 775, 776, 778
Sensory systems, 704
Sequential puzzles, 304
Serialization, 786
Server-authoritative movement, 766
Server authority, 759
    code reviewing, 765, 766, 768
    definition, 764
    features, 765
    importance, 764

Server_EndMatch(), 745, 746
Server_EndMatch_Validate(), 746
Server_Interact(), 739, 741, 742
Server_MoveAI(), 755, 756
Server_MovePlayer(), 765
Server_MovePlayer_Implementation(), 766
Server_MovePlayer_Validate(), 767
Server_RegisterHit(), 760, 761
Server_RegisterHit_Validate(), 761
Server RPCs, 738
Server-side authority, 754
Server_StartMatch(), 750, 751
Server validation, 739
SetActorLocation(), 756
SetArenaEnvironment(), 840, 841
SetCollisionEnabled, 6, 10, 20, 48, 221, 230, 308
SetCollisionProfileName("Ragdoll"), 53
SetCollisionResponseToAllChannels, 7, 10, 222, 231, 308
SetDayLength, 360
SetFieldRadius(), 620
SetForceStrength(), 620
SetGameplayTriggers(), 833, 834
SetGravity(), 615, 617
SetIsReplicatedByDefault(true), 735
SetMaxFPS(), 809
SetMiniGameReward function, 302
SetNightLength, 360
SetQuestDependency function, 291

INDEX

SetRespawnPoint function, 174
SetSimulatePhysics, 48
SetSimulatePhysics(), 798
SetupArena(), 844, 845
SetupPlayerInput
    Component() function, 105, 593, 594
SetVolume method, 379, 381
SetWeatherCondition(), 855, 856
SetWeatherState(), 333, 335
Shader-based effects, 393
Shadow mapping, 359
Shadows, 358
Shooter games, 402, 446
ShowActionSuccess(), 638, 640
ShutdownModule(), 821, 822
Signature attacks,
    see Special moves
SimulateRope(), 598
SimulateSoftBody(), 571, 574
SimulateTerrainErosion
    function, 185
Simulation games, 331, 342, 359, 368, 373, 378, 384, 389, 578, 592
Skeletal hitboxes, 64
Skill-based matchmaking (SBMM), 769
Skill development, 104, 294
Skill progression, 520
Skill selection, 468
Skill synergy, 462
Skill tiers, 462
Skill trees
    advanced techniques, 461, 462
    algorithm, 463
    character progression, 459
    code reviewing, 463, 465, 466
    practical applications, 462, 463
    structure, 459, 460
    types
        active abilities, 460
        passive abilities, 461
Skybox class, 385
Skybox transitions, 343
Sky shader management, 384
Slope-based texturing, 389
SmoothPath(), 681
Social gaming, 825
Social media, 874
Soft body dynamics, 563
    advanced techniques, 569
    algorithm, 570
    code reviewing, 571–576
    practical applications, 569
    simulation method, 568
    usage, 568
SortInventory function, 280, 281
Sound attenuation, 664
Sound binding, 78
Sound concurrency, 664
Sound cues, 626
Sound detection, 437, 439
Sound files, 627
Sound layering, 379
SoundManager class, 379
Sound prioritization, 379
Sound radius, 438

911

Soundscapes, 663
Sound triggering
    code reviewing, 627, 629–631
    components, 627
    definition, 626
    importance, 626
Space skyboxes, 383
Spatial audio, 659, 663
Spatial tracking, 801
SpawnARObject(), 803
SpawnARObject(FVector Location), 802
SpawnEnemy(), 545
Spawn influence, 168
Spawning, 55
SpawnLocations, 844
SpawnParticleEffect(), 669–671
SpawnPlayers(), 844, 845
Spawn points, 843
Spawn protection, 169
SpawnTile(), 781, 783
Special moves, 525
    characteristics, 525, 526
    code reviewing, 529–531
    definition, 525
    designing, 528
    examples, 525
Spell casting system, 497
Spell effects, 495, 497
SpellList, 498
Spell upgrades, 495
Sphere trace, 513
Spline, 880
Sports games, 561

SpringConstant, 571, 573
Spring constraints, 586
Spring-mass model, 570
SpringStiffness, 597
SprintSpeed, 403
Stack overflow, 874
Staggering, 478
Stamina-based jumps, 409
StaminaCost, 447
Stamina management, 445, 477, 480
StaminaRegenRate, 455, 480
Stamina system, 431
StandSpeed, 416
StartARSession(), 803
StartBossFight(), 552, 554
StartClimbing(), 433, 435
StartCrouch(), 416, 418
StartCutscene function, 239, 241
StartDialogue function, 249, 251
StartEventChain function, 27
StartMatchIfReady(), 769, 771
StartMiniGame function, 298
StartPatrolling(), 686, 688
StartProne(), 421
StartQuest(), 849, 851
StartShake(), 643, 645
StartSprinting(), 403, 405
StartSwimming(), 426, 428
StartupModule(), 821, 822
Stat/attribute system, 470
State handlers, 721
State machines
    code reviewing, 721, 723

components, 720, 721
example, 724
game AI development, 719
importance, 720
trees, 721
State management, 24, 219
State replication, 732
States, 720
State transitions, 704, 721, 724
Static mesh, 881
Static music, 631
StayInPlace(), 694, 696
Stealth-action games, 439, 446
Stealth awareness, 693
Stealth-based gameplay, 673
Stealth games, 415
Stealth mechanics
    advanced techniques, 438, 439
    algorithm, 439
    code reviewing, 440, 442, 444
    definition, 437
    elements, 437
    implementation, 438
    practical applications, 439
StealthSoundRadius, 440
StopAmbience(), 664, 666
StopClimbing(), 433, 435
StopMovement(), 696
StopSprinting(), 403, 405
StopSwimming(), 426, 428
Storytelling, 148, 190, 200, 248, 258, 626, 658
Strategic planning, 169
Strategy games, 463, 488, 496

Stretching, 584
Stun duration, 127
Sub-emitter systems, 578
SunLight, 344
Surface detection, 431, 432
Surface interaction, 374
Survival boss fights, 550
Survival games, 331, 342, 351, 368, 394, 425, 453, 463, 469
Suspension system, 590
Sustainability, 825
Swimming mechanics
    advanced techniques, 424
    algorithm, 425, 426
    code reviewing, 426–430
    implementation, 423
    practical applications, 425
    water environments, 423
SwimSpeed, 426
Synchronization, 181, 765

T

Tactical AI, 504
Tactical gameplay, 115, 693
TakeDamage function, 149
TargetLocation, 675
Team assignment, 749
Team coordination, 773
Team deathmatch (TDM), 743
TeamOnePlayers/TeamTwoPlayers, 745
Teamwork, 137
Tearing, 585

INDEX

Tension, 569
Terrain deformation, 373
   advanced technique, 179, 184–187
   algorithm, 180
   code reviewing, 181–184
   description, 177
   persistent changes, 179
   practical applications, 180
   procedural changes, 179
   usage, 178
TerrainDeformer class, 181
Terrain generation
   advanced techniques, 367
   algorithms
      heightmap generation, 368
      procedural generation, 369
   code reviewing, 369, 370, 372
   practical applications, 368
   procedural generation techniques, 366
   usage, 367
TerrainPhysics class, 185
TerrainTexture class, 390
Terrain texturing
   advanced techniques, 388
   algorithms, 389
   code reviewing, 390–392
   description, 388
   practical applications, 389
   usage, 388
Testing, 812
Text messaging, 774
Texture mapping, 881

Third-person action games, 488
Third-person shooters, 469
3D audio, 378
Tick(), 5, 7, 8, 12, 18, 36, 47, 57, 67, 74, 110, 149, 160, 170, 211, 229, 269, 306, 310, 312, 315, 320, 354, 412, 428, 457
TickComponent function, 117, 139, 152
TileSize, 781
TimeBetweenAttacks, 521
Time dilation, 881
Time-limited hazards, 350
Time management system, 343
TimeOfDay, 344
Timer setup, 38
TimeSpeedMultiplier, 344
Time step integration, 587
Time step management, 565
Timing mechanism, 352
Tire friction, 591
TObjectIterator<UTexture>, 809
ToggleFog(), 336
ToggleRain(), 336
Torques, 562
TrackMiniGameProgress function, 298
TrackQuestProgress function, 288
Traction, 591
TradeableItems array, 325
TradeItem function, 321, 322
Trading systems
   advanced techniques, 317
   algorithm, 318

INDEX

code reviewing, 318–320
functions, 325
implementation, 321, 322, 324, 326, 327
practical applications, 318
usage, 317
Transaction management, 318
Transition effects, 615
Transitions, 340, 632, 720
TransitionToDay, 362
TransitionToNight, 362
TriggerBox, 18, 220, 229
TriggerChainReaction function, 152
TriggerDistance, 627
TriggerExplosion function, 121
Triggering animations, 431
Triggering events
  advanced techniques, 16
  algorithm, 17
  code reviewing, 17, 18, 20, 21
  dynamic events, 26–30
  interactive elements, 22–26
  practical applications, 16
  usage, 15
Triggers, 632
TriggerSound, 627, 629
TriggerVolume class, 18
TriggerZone, 629
Trigger zones, 351
Triplanar mapping, 389
True damage, 533
TSoftObjectPtr<UObject>, 792

TSubclassOf<ABossCharacter> BossCharacterClass, 552
TurnRight(), 593, 595
Twitter, 874

U

UComplexInteractionSystem constructor, 41, 43
UDynamicParticles class, 214
UE4 AnswerHub, 872
UE_LOG(), 730, 751, 767, 771, 788, 792, 804, 818, 822, 827, 851
UGameplayStatics, 787
UGameplayStatics::GetPlatformName(), 814
UGameplayStatics::PlaySound2D(), 661
UGameplayStatics::SpawnEmitterAtLocation, 211
UI animations
  code reviewing, 651, 653, 654
  components, 651
  importance, 650
  user experience, 650
Ultimate abilities,
  see Special moves
UnlockedSkills, 464
Unlocking, 460
UnlockSkill(), 464, 465
Unreal Engine Cheat Sheet
  C++ syntax, 863–865
  editor hotkeys, 862, 863
Unreal Engine documentation, 871

INDEX

Unreal Engine forums, 871
Unreal Engine YouTube channel, 872
Unreal's AI perception system, 686, 688
Unreal slackers, 873
UObject, 865, 881
UParticleSystemComponent, 56
UpdateBreath(), 426, 428
UpdateCloth(), 587, 588
UpdateCurrency function, 321, 323
UpdateDayNightCycle(), 344, 345
UpdateFoliage method, 395, 396
UpdateInventory function, 321, 323
UpdateItemPrice function, 325, 326
UpdateLighting() function, 61, 62, 346, 362
Update method, 374, 375, 385, 386
UpdateMovement(), 675, 676
UpdateParticles(), 580, 581, 610, 612
UpdatePositionAndRotation(), 733, 735
UpdatePostProcessing(), 647, 649
UpdateQuestProgress(), 850, 851
UpdateResource(), 809
UpdateSunPosition(), 346
UpdateWeather(), 855, 856
UpdateWeatherEffects(), 333, 335
USaveGameManager, 786
UseItem function, 277
User interface (UI), 318, 454
UseSkill(), 464, 465
USphereComponent, 66

Utility systems, 503
UV mapping, 388
UWidgetAnimation, 652

V

ValidateHit(), 760, 761
Validation, 741
Validation functions, 739
Vector, 881
Vehicle physics
    advanced techniques, 591, 592
    algorithms, 592
    code reviewing, 593, 595, 596
    factors, 590
    practical applications, 592
    principles and mechanics, 590, 591
Velocity, 99, 408, 565, 571, 573, 577
Vertex positioning, 586
Vertex simulation, 584
Victory conditions, 744
Virtual reality (VR) mechanics
    code reviewing, 796–800
    components, 795
    immersive experiences, 794
    importance, 795
Virtual texturing, 825
Viscosity, 610
Visibility detection, 437
Visual cues, 188, 198, 625, 638
Visual feedback, 515, 520, 668
    code reviewing, 638, 640–642
    components, 638

INDEX

game design, 637
importance, 637
Visualization, 208
Vivox plugin, 774
Voice acting, 659
Voice and text chat systems
    code reviewing, 775–778
    description, 773
    features, 774
    importance, 773
    options, 774, 775
Voice communication, 774
Volume control, 627
Volume rendering, 609
Volumetric lighting, 358, 881
Voronoi diagrams, 369

W, X, Y, Z

WalkSpeed, 403
Wall jump, 409
Wall-run detection system, 16
Water and fluid dynamics
    advanced techniques, 373
    algorithms, 374
    code reviewing, 374–377
    practical applications, 373
    principles, 372
    usage, 372
Water detection, 425
WaterSimulation class, 374
Water surfaces, 372
Wave-based spawning, 541
Wave generation, 374
Weapon customization, 487, 488
WeatherEffect class, 56
Weather effects, 383, 663
Weather simulation, 384
Weather state management, 332
WeatherTransitionProgress, 855, 856
Weather transitions, 331
WeatherTransitionTime, 855, 856
Weight transfer, 591
Wind simulations, 393, 585
Wind system, 331
Wind vector calculations, 394
WithValidation, 765
Workflow, 882
World composition, 882

GPSR Compliance

The European Union's (EU) General Product Safety Regulation (GPSR) is a set of rules that requires consumer products to be safe and our obligations to ensure this.

If you have any concerns about our products, you can contact us on

ProductSafety@springernature.com

In case Publisher is established outside the EU, the EU authorized representative is:

Springer Nature Customer Service Center GmbH
Europaplatz 3
69115 Heidelberg, Germany

www.ingramcontent.com/pod-product-compliance
Lightning Source LLC
LaVergne TN
LVHW010331260326
834688LV00036B/646